Comparative Political Systems

COMPARATIVE
POLITICAL SYSTEMS

Edited by

Louis J. Cantori

University of Maryland

John C. Bollens, Consulting Editor

HOLBROOK PRESS, INC.

BOSTON, MASSACHUSETTS

Library of Congress Catalog Card Number: 73–86345

Printed in the United States of America

IN MEMORIAM

Lance Corporal William R. Burnett, U.S.M.C.

Vietnam

January 11, 1967

Contents

Preface

This book has been conceived and brought forth in the major conviction that the study of comparative politics is important in scholarly, policy, and personal terms. In scholarly terms, we have had about a decade and a half of concerted scholarly activity, the richness of whose fruits is only suggested in the readings collected here. If there can be a single characterization of the nature of this richness it is in the tendency for the student of comparative politics to ask big questions; for example, the nature of an entire political system or the direction that a political system is taking in the process of political change. The entire discipline of political science has been energized and reoriented as the result of the cumulative impact of this activity.

The policy importance of the study of comparative politics is undeniable. The major evidence of this is the fact that for the past decade and a half, the federal government has provided the major financial support for international studies. In the late 1950's a national need for greater knowledge of foreign politics was recognized and thousands of students have since received financial support for their studies of the languages, cultures, and politics of much of the world. Although the effects of this accumulated expertise came too late to provide much of an informed contribution to the war in Vietnam because basic policy decisions were made in the early 1960's, one can be perhaps slightly sanguine in seeing them result in more informed foreign policy decisions in the future. At a slightly more down-to-earth level in terms of the present volume, there is also the policy level of informed citizenry—how the college student as an individual can come to have greater analytical and substantive insight into world events in order to better evaluate the decisions of political leaders.

If the scholarly and policy importance of the sub-field can be somewhat readily understood, and it is one of the tasks of the present volume to assist in this understanding, its importance in personal terms might seem less readily understood. This importance is related to the "big question" point just made. Asking big questions about the operation of a political system culturally dissimilar to one's own can have the sometimes disquieting effect of leading to different perceptions regarding one's own political system. That which was previously taken for granted as an operative assumption is suddenly more questionable. That which was once thought unique to one's own political system is seen to be more universal and thereby perhaps loses some of its preciousness. Efforts to raise these questions will be found in this volume, sometimes in the introductory essays which begin each chapter and sometimes in the readings themselves. In the questioning process one seems to be led by empirical means down the philosophical path of the

questions posed by the great tenth century Muslim Arab philosopher
Al-Farabi: "Who are you [as an individual and as a people], what are you
doing, and by what means and for what purpose are you doing it?"[1]

More concretely, the scholarly importance of the study of comparative
politics demands, first, definition—what is meant by comparative politics.
The shorter and easier definition to give is that the study of comparative
politics is ideally the study of all politics, one's own and foreign politics, in
terms of their similarities and differences. In reality, however, comparative
politics has tended to be the study of foreign as opposed to American
politics. Only in exceptional instances has this study been literally comparative; that is, involving two or more subjects of study. What does occur
in this respect, however, is that while it is true that a single subject is most
often studied, such study is often by means of conceptual frameworks and
frames of reference derived from other similar studies and therefore suggestive and conducive to further comparisons.

A more difficult definition is that undertaken in Chapter 1 where a
serious effort is made to trace both the development of the sub-field of
comparative politics in the past thirty-year period and to assess where it
stands today in terms of its themes and issues in the 1970's. A major
reason for this focus upon the integral nature of the development of the
comparative politics field is the conviction that political science as a whole
must gain a sense of its development in order to avoid lapses in research
direction (e.g., the national character studies of the 1930's and the political
cultural studies of today) and even lapses in focus (e.g., the debate regarding the nature of political sovereignty in the 1900's and what might be
argued, as it is in the introduction to Chapter 1, a recent reemergence of
the question). The zigzags of what are at best intellectual thrusts of research into neglected areas of investigation and at worst mere fads can
thereby have the built-in disciplinary corrective of an awareness of where
"innovation" fits in the context of disciplinary development.

The empirical emphasis of the present volume is evident in three focuses;
(1) empirical conceptualizations (Chapter 2, "Comparisons of Total Systems"); (2) political process (Chapter 3, "Political Socialization and Political Culture" and Chapter 8, "Political Change"), and (3) political structures
(Chapter 4, "Comparative Electoral Systems," Chapter 5, "Comparative
Interest Groups," Chapter 6, "Comparative Political Parties," and Chapter
7, "Comparative Bureaucracy").

A final comment is to note that no effort has been made to distinguish
between developing and developed political systems. Both types are represented in the readings notwithstanding the underlying assumption that the

1. Al-Farabi, *The Philosophy of Plato and Aristotle,* trans. with an introduction by
Muhsin Mahdi (New York: Free Press, 1962), p. 23.

study of comparative politics has reached such a point of sufficient self-confidence that we are now more prepared than was the case in the 1950's to speak of universal political processes. It is in this self-confident and assertive spirit bred both of past accomplishment and anticipated continued intellectual excitement that we now turn to the readings.

Acknowledgments

A publication endeavor inevitably involves more people than the fact of single editorship indicates. The platoon of persons to whom I am indebted for research assistance and typing includes Karin Gomez of U.C.L.A. and Tina Van Sickle, Janice Hawkins, and especially Helen Pasquale of the University of Maryland, Baltimore County. One's wife is always routinely mentioned in terms of acknowledgments—Joan Cantori's contributions to the present task have not been routine, however, and mere formal thanks are insufficient. Greg, Eric, and Nadia's contributions to the present volume are something about which I shall speak with them when they are older!

1

Past and Present Trends and Issues in Comparative Politics

Introduction

The study of comparative politics is as old as the separate study of politics itself. The classical and medieval study of politics was primarily concerned with politics in its philosophical rather than its empirical dimension, being chiefly concerned with the ultimate question of the nature of truth and, as part of this, the more political question of justice. Whatever empirical attention was devoted to the study of politics had as its objective the understanding of politics in order to arrive at a practical approximation of a just regime, given real and limited circumstances. There was a further design in the esoteric teachings of the political philosophers, namely the intent to discover the best regime under which philosophers could pursue what were likely to be unpopular inquiries.[1]

The study of politics is at least as old as Aristotle. The growth of modern political science, however, is largely a nineteenth and twentieth century phenomenon, with the modern study of politics tending to coincide with the greater empirical study of the subject as it began with Machiavelli. The central focus of modern political science until well into the present century has been the study of law and political philosophy mixed with elements of political economy and history. These historical influences (described by Neumann in this chapter) are indicative of what remains one of the outstanding qualities of political science—its eclectic character. This eclecticism is a tremendous strength in that borrowing from other disciplines and fields contributes to a sense of intellectual openness. On the other hand, this tendency also creates problems of focus expressed in the question "what is political?" This combination of disciplinary openness accompanied by disciplinary self-questioning creates positive intellectual tensions which contribute to the attractiveness of political science as a

1. For an elaboration on these points, see the volume by Strauss listed in the suggested readings at the end of this chapter.

1

subject of study. Comparative politics has had its own contributions to make, both in terms of interdisciplinary borrowing and of defining the nature of the central focus of the discipline.

With these disparate influences in the background, the different sub-fields of the discipline have waxed and waned in its nineteenth and twentieth century development. Until World War I, the main fields of political science were law and political philosophy. In the inter-war period, under the impetus of a concern with the League of Nations and other factors, the study of international relations developed to the point where many American universities had separate departments devoted to its study. Similarly, the study of American politics also blossomed as a separate field of study. During this same period, the study of comparative government also became established but this occurred largely free from the behavioral, theoretical, and methodological innovations that were developing in the field of American politics. The study of foreign governments remained legally and institutionally oriented, largely to the study of European politics.

One of the major academic consequences of World War II, especially as the cold war set in, was the tremendous increase in interest in foreign governments and the concrete expression of this interest in the birth of specialized studies devoted to the social, economic, historical, linguistic, geographical, and political understanding of various regions of the world. The growth of these studies gave a tremendous impetus to what came increasingly to be called the sub-field of comparative "politics" rather than "government." The new label of politics signifies the present inclusion of the behavioral features of this science, particularly in American politics and its effects on the study of foreign politics. This heralded a movement away from the study of constitutions and institutions toward an emphasis upon individual and collective behavior, action, systems, and function.[2]

There is little doubt that the study of comparative politics has been the most rapidly expanding field of study in political science in the past two decades and has very nearly become the most populous. Development of these fields such as American politics, international relations, and comparative politics has tended to reflect real policy and mood changes on the part of American society. We noted the association of the League of Nations with the growth of the study of international relations and the effect of World War II and the cold war upon comparative politics. Likewise, the exposure of national scandal, or muckraking, gave a tremendous impetus to the behavioral study of American politics.

Perhaps reflecting the afterthoughts of the Vietnam war and domestic political disturbances on campuses and in cities in the late 1960's, there has been a shift to the study of urban politics and policy outcomes. The cen-

2. See the article by Dahl listed in the suggested readings at the end of this chapter for a succinct account of the nature of these behavioral influences and their present integration into the discipline.

trality of comparative politics is likely to continue for the obvious reason of continued intellectual and policy interest in foreign areas. Some evidence of this can be seen in the fact that even in these new emphases of the discipline one finds attention to the theories of *comparative* urban studies and *comparative* foreign policy. In a real sense, and in a manner having an impact upon such other fields as public administration and public law, the discipline of political science has become heavily if not nearly totally comparative.

The foregoing exposition of the contextual background of the development of political science and comparative politics may have suggested something seamless, continuous, and perhaps therefore cumulative regarding disciplinary sub-field development. In fact, it can be argued that there has been little continuity and practically no cumulation in the development of the discipline. The only substantial evidence of the cumulative process is that post-World War II political science has seen a largely seminal marriage of behavioral approaches and comparative concerns. What is absent from what might be called the historical consciousness of the discipline is, for example, attention to the non-behavioral issues that beset the discipline in its earlier development. Perhaps the major one of these is the necessity only recently felt and presently ill-expressed regarding the need for increased concern with the normative, prescriptive, and goal orientation of politics. This is the significance of the expression "post-behavioral revolution" to describe the present state of the discipline.[3]

There was a major scholarly statement in 1968 which illustrates somewhat inadvertently the point regarding the desirability of a cumulative sense of disciplinary progress. In doing so it also has a major bearing on a number of issues in the present volume such as normative ethnocentric theorizing in the form of pluralistic assumptions and the general subject of holistic approaches in political science. In the process of making an original and influential critique and reformulation of the nature of political change, Huntington has in effect returned the political science discipline to a scholarly debate that exercised many of the political science luminaries of the early twentieth century—this debate was between the so-called monists and pluralists. We shall elaborate on the meaning of this debate in a moment, but first something further needs to be said regarding what it is that Huntington has had to say before attempting to locate his ideas in a broader intellectual context. Huntington's central concern with political order and stability was reflected in his title, *Political Order in Changing*

3. This is the significance of Easton's coining of the phrase "post-behavioral revolution" of contemporary political science. David Easton, "The New Revolution in Political Science," *American Political Science Review,* 63 (December 1969), 1051–1061. The phrase is meant to capture the sense of the discipline, that it must become more responsive to societal needs and in the process reconcile scientific ambitions into the normative intentions of theory and scholar alike.

Societies.[4] The book has had an important impact upon the study of comparative politics because of its suggestive treatment of a myriad of themes, perhaps the most important of which is its treatment of the possibilities of political decay as opposed to political development and the question of political order. Huntington deals with the latter major theme in describing the process of political institutionalization. He is concerned to put institutionalization and order, i.e., the creation of the state, before the question of the future democratic or non-democratic nature of the regime that will govern that state. This position tends to put him at odds with most contemporary political scientists who, to the extent they have thought of the problem in this fashion at all, would reverse the order and place concerns regarding the conditions or possibilities of the establishment of democracy first or at least make it an equal concern. This is exactly what they have been doing in their theories of political development and we shall take note of this in the final chapter of this book which is devoted to the subject of political change. For the present, we shall note that what concerns Huntington is the formation of the state taking precedence over regime-type and any other competing political grouping. In short he is concerned with the problem of sovereignty or ultimate political authority.

Sovereignty is a topic that was much debated in the early years of this century, yet we read little about this in contemporary political science literature. The reason why this great debate has been forgotten will perhaps become evident when the issues and the outcome of the debate are indicated. The question was, did ultimate political authority reside in a centralized state in order to guarantee political stability or did it reside with each individual who could determine for himself a personal meaning of political authority?[5] The former position is characterized in the debate as

---

4. Samuel Huntington, *Political Order in Changing Societies* (New Haven, Conn.: Yale University Press, 1968). The themes of institutionalization are dealt with in Huntington's articles on single parties (Chapter 4) and political change (Chapter 8) in this book.

This monist-pluralist distinction is one which has been debated in the specialized subject of community power studies. In this debate, C. Wright Mills, *The Power Elite* (New York: Oxford University Press, 1956) and Floyd Hunter, *Community Power Structure* (Chapel Hill, N.C.: University of North Carolina Press, 1953) have been arrayed as latter-day "monists" against, notably, Robert Dahl, *Who Governs* (New Haven, Conn.: Yale University Press, 1961) and Nelson Polsby, *Community Power and Political Theory* (New Haven, Conn.: Yale University Press, 1963). For a summary of the debate, see Andrew McFarland, *Power and Leadership in Pluralist Systems* (Stanford, Calif.: Stanford University Press, 1969), pp. 32–52.

Our discussion of this distinction which follows is in effect simultaneously an exploration of the wider implications of the issue in contemporary political science while at the same time indicating the historical dimensions of the controversy.

5. Kung Chang Hsiao, *Political Pluralism* (London: Kegan Paul, 1927).

monist, i.e., possessing a single sovereignty, and is as old as Plato and Socrates. Among its notable modern day exponents were Thomas Hobbes in the seventeenth century and John Austin and his doctrine of positive law in the nineteenth. But in a real sense, the point of view tended to be the "received" and "logical" one. It was received from the tradition of absolute rule accorded European rulers as they struggled with the Church over the issue of who was to rule supreme. While democracy may have been proclaimed widely in the nineteenth century, the mode of thinking was still to accord the state ultimate political authority. It was the mode of thinking which of course in turn influenced its logic. Thus, for example, as John Austin articulated the doctrine of positive law he concluded that a final legal authority *had* to exist and this final authority rested with the political sovereign.

Against this mode of thinking, there began to develop in the nineteenth century concerns with individual freedom and economic and social injustice, which were voiced by such disparate thinkers as Marx, Thoreau, and John Stuart Mill. The thinking of these individuals had at least one thing in common: they upheld the individual and class as superior to the state. By the end of the nineteenth century and the expansion of suffrage and the nascence of a widespread socialist movement in Britain and elsewhere, the stage was set for the final assault on the monist position by a group of scholars who came to adopt a pluralistic position. Harold J. Laski, Leon Duguit, and G. D. H. Cole became the major English, and in the case of Duguit, Continental spokesmen of this position. Influenced by the researches of the German scholar Gierke and the English scholar Figgis into the diffuse nature of sovereignty in medieval Europe, they came to contrast the division of sovereignty among church and state and monarch and feudal baron with the continuing impact of the perhaps fleeting experience of absolutist rule in the seventeenth and eighteenth century. Inspired by these researches and influenced by the egalitarian thought of their time, they asserted the primacy of the individual or social grouping over the state.

Under this attack and the cumulative social effect of the thinkers that had influenced them, the monist position began to be eclipsed with occasional telling flashes of monist retaliation.[6] The monists came to fight a rearguard action that found them by the mid-1930's completely overcome by the pluralist position.

The pluralist position had triumphed, perhaps inevitably, as liberal democracy became the dominant feature on the political landscape. The consequences of this pluralist triumph for political science are only just now beginning to be recognized. In England, Laski's and G. D. H. Cole's inveighing against social injustice and the advocacy of the pluralist position took

6. John Dickenson, "A Working Theory of Sovereignty," I and II, *Political Science Quarterly*, 42 and 43 (December 1927 and March 1928), 524–48 and 32–63, a two-part article.

place in the context of a developing socialist movement. In the United States, on the other hand, such a socialist movement did not develop and when Laski and Graham Wallas, a further pluralist exponent, taught in America, their teaching fell upon the fertile ground of an indigenous pluralist tradition. Among the contemporary American exponents of pluralism were such figures as John Dewey and, more importantly for political science, Arthur Bentley. It was the latter's *Group Basis of Politics* published first in 1908 that was to contribute to the most obvious evidence of the triumph of pluralism in American academia, the so-called group approach to politics. Again, as we shall note further when we deal with interest groups in Chapter 5, pluralism and the group approach found fertile confirmation in the muckraking era of exposés of the meat packing industry, Standard Oil, and the Anti-Saloon League. The abuses of special interest groups seem to have occasioned the response that the only thing wrong with them was that they were unregulated. The subsequent enactment of antitrust legislation was perhaps greeted with a certain satisfaction, for pluralistic political competition was considered to be intrinsically sound and required only the equalization of the groups involved to be a success. This is the view held even in 1952 in John K. Galbraith's *American Capitalism.*

The urban rebellions of the 1960's as well as Vietnam war policies served to bring forth what can be called a New Left normative criticism of pluralism. The basic tenet of this criticism is that the model of political competition present in the pluralist position is likely to leave permanently disadvantaged minorities such as blacks, chicanos, Indians, and the poor in general.[7]

What, it might be asked, does all this have to do with political science generally and especially our concern with comparative politics? The essential point is that not only can something specific in the group approach to politics be attributed to the pluralist triumph but also it can be argued that virtually all non-Marxist American political science formulations have succumbed in some degree to pluralism. Communications models, systems models, functional theory, and structural functional theory all bear major and minor traces of pluralist normative and cultural commitment. One consequence of this for the study of comparative politics is that all of these approaches are thus committed to some degree to ethnocentric conceptions of politics with attendant problems of application.[8]

7. William Connolly, ed. *The Bias of Pluralism* (New York: Atherton, 1969), and Peter Bachrach and Morton Baratz, "The Two Faces of Power," *American Political Science Review,* 56 (December 1962), 947–52, are examples of the scholarly recognition of the problem.

8. An additional specification of the manner in which an implicit commitment to pluralism creates conceptual difficulties is tied up with the domination of the social sciences as well as political science by the equilibrium model. This model views the coherency of the social or political system to be understood as consisting of contend-

More directly to the point of Huntington and his concern with the creation of the state, it can be seen that contemporary American political science has been conditioned not to see the state but rather to concern itself with individual and group behavior. This has been the case especially with students of American politics but it has had its effect upon students of comparative politics as well. For example, another name for the comparative politics enterprise in the 1960's might have been "nation-building." The nation that these scholars desired to see come into being was to varying degrees explicit or implicit in their conceptions but ultimately it was to be a democratic one. (This is a concern of Chapter 8 in the present volume.) More importantly for present purposes we should note that the focus was upon building the nation and not on the state.

One of the tenets of pluralism, as we have noted, is that it denigrates the state and its sovereignty. American society is not stateless, of course, but American political scientists have tended to act as if it were. Taking the state for granted in their own cultural context they chose to focus upon those pluralistic features of other societies that they value in their own. Huntington's concern with institutionalization is thus a call for American political science to return to putting the horse before the cart, namely letting us be concerned with state formation before nation formation.

In our attempt to respond to the foregoing injunction, we are cautioned by LaPalombara in his contribution to this chapter to beware of the overly general character of the whole systems approach that we have been commenting upon favorably. He takes the position that comparative politics after more than a decade of studies at the "macro", country level of analysis needs now to begin investigating more narrowly defined subjects. His point of view is a usefully corrective one and this suggestion as expressed in the form of renewed interest in the historical nature of political change is an important emphasis in comparative politics in the 1970's.

No matter the particular emphasis, however, we political scientists in our role as scientists, have an obligation to methodological clarity and to the selection of an appropriate method for the study of a selected problem. The selection by Lijphart presents succinctly the method uniquely claimed by comparative politics, that of the basic comparative method itself. Lijphart's position is that the comparative method has too often been implicit in comparative political research. He is concerned to explicate its essential elements in its identification as a basic method of scientific investigation. If

---

ing, or pluralist, forces whose ultimate product is the solidarity of the system. In addition to raising the question of whether this adequately describes reality, there is also the question of its status quo orientation in both conceptual and normative terms. If equilibrium is the outcome, how does one account for change? For a critical discussion of the equilibrium model see David Easton, *The Political System*, 2nd ed. (New York: Alfred Knopf, 1971), pp. 266–306. For a discussion of the pervasiveness of the concept, see Cynthia Eagle Russett, *The Concept of Equilibrium in American Social Thought* (New Haven, Conn.: Yale University Press, 1966).

Lijphart clarifies for us some of the major intellectual assumptions of our methodology, Deutsch is more concerned to present first the sheer large number of varieties of data (nine according to his estimation) that political science has to work with, including elite, voting, and census data. He then shows how this data can be utilized in statistical and computer terms; for example, in cross-national political studies. The conclusion of his essay is interesting for the intentions of this anthology because he relates data and techniques to some of the theoretical conceptualizations of the total system that we examine in Chapter 2.

Past Trends and Issues

Comparative Politics: A Half-Century Appraisal*

Sigmund Neumann

THE ORIGIN OF A DISCIPLINE

In the beginning was Comparison. Or in the words of our centenarian, Woodrow Wilson: "I believe that our own institutions can be understood and appreciated only by those who know somewhat familiarly other systems of government and the main facts of general institutional history. By the use of a thorough comparative and historical method, moreover, a general clarification of views may be obtained. . . Certainly it does not now have to be argued that the only thorough method of study in politics is the comparative and historical."[1] What has happened to comparative politics since

*This paper was presented at the American Political Science Association meeting, Washington, D.C., September, 1956. The author is indebted to the valuable comments of the panel discussants: Taylor Cole, Herman Finer, Charles B. Robson, Lucian W. Pye, K. N. Thompson, F. C. Englemann. The paper was also critically read by two elder statesmen of the profession, Francis W. Coker and Henry R. Spencer. Their thoughtful suggestions were gratefully incorporated as far as the set space of the essay permitted it.

1. Woodrow Wilson, The State. Elements of Historical and Practical Politics (Boston, 1889), pp. xxxv–xxxvi. The significance of the comparative and historical approach for the young discipline was previously pronounced by Munroe Smith in the programmatic opening statement to the first American journal in the field: "What then are the methods of the social sciences? All the various methods employed may be grouped

Reprinted from Journal of Politics, IX (August 1957), 369–390, by special permission of the publisher.

those very early days of our Association and especially since its official birth in 1903, when the society was founded as "an outgrowth of a movement looking toward a National Conference on Comparative Legislation"?[2]

The celebration of Woodrow Wilson's centennial is an appropriate time to take account of our discipline. This tentative appraisal is an attempt to gain some historical perspective for our study of comparative politics, which, to the delight of its lone-wolf old-timers, suddenly seems to have received a new impetus. Both this reawakened interest and the characteristic stages of the preceding development—with its ups and downs—are not accidental, but a vivid illustration of the unfolding of our discipline within its specific historical and social setting. By its very nature, political science is embedded in time and space. Part and parcel of the social sciences, it shares with them the grandeur and the misery of a critical field. The sciences of man and his decisions ("sciences of ethics" in the meaningful classical terminology) flourish, if they do not actually originate, in times of crisis. As long as society, the state, the world community seem to be in order, one is not concerned about them. It is at the breaking-points of history when man's values are questioned, his institutions shattered, his international bonds cut—it is in the challenge of revolutionary upheaval or in the defense of a threatened system that eminent social scientists come to the fore. This is also the hour of the "great simplifiers" against whose appearance the famed Swiss historian, Jacob Burckhardt, warned a hundred years ago. It is the age of the sage and the charlatan, a dangerous era, full of both promise and perils. We are living in such a time of crisis.

Politics, in theory as well as in practice, is faced with pressing issues and decisions. Against this background we must rethink our traditional tenets and reconsider our changing comparisons. Politics demands a renewed response from each generation. What brought the discipline into being in the United States at the turn of the century? What does it mean today?

---

under one term: *comparison*. The single fact means nothing to us; we accumulate facts that seem akin; we classify and reclassify them, discarding superficial and accidental similarities as we discover deeper substantial identities. We accumulate and compare facts from our own and from foreign countries; we accumulate facts from the immediate and more remote past, and compare them with each other and with present facts. Statistics, comparative legislation, history—these are means and modes of accumulating facts for comparison. . . . Of all these auxiliary sciences, the most important is *history*. All other methods of comparative study may be said to operate on a single plane—the plane of the present. History gives to the Social Sciences the third dimension, and thus indefinitely increases the range of comparison. But it does far more than this. To the application of the historical method we owe the discovery that social institutions persist and at the same time change from generation to generation and from century to century. . . ." See "The Domain of Political Science," *Political Science Quarterly*, I (1886), 3*ff*.

2. Jesse S. Reeves, "Perspectives in Political Science 1903–1928," *American Political Science Review*, XXIII (February 1929), 1–16.

Observing public opinion as a whole, we see that it has undergone, within this half-century, significant changes in the approach to the affairs of the state—from political alchemy to political morphology to comparative government proper. The mere collection (out of curiosity) of haphazard, exotic facts was the stage for the beginner in world affairs a generation ago. A more serious and systematic consideration of significant dates became exciting to a young nation discovering the wide world between the two World Wars. And now, in their aftermath, a purposeful comparison of alternatives in policy decisions—a comparison which is the prerequisite for the maturing of protagonists among the great powers—makes demands that the academic discipline grow and change its character entirely. Who among the teachers of comparative government has not observed this amazing transformation as reflected in changing student attitudes within recent decades?

As for the young discipline itself, the shifts were even more articulate and characteristically quite separate from the prevailing climate of unlimited possibilities in the United States—a sign, indeed, of the intelligentsia's alienation (so much talked about at present, though probably with much less justification than formerly). To be sure, political science started out as an esoteric enterprise of a small group of academicians in the midst of an America that did not question its own existence, its power of absorbing an ever-growing population, its promises of the wide open spaces, and its continental security, guaranteed by the mighty British navy in control of the seven seas. If any criticism arose at all, it was merely out of a concern for particulars, calling for limited amelioration: the proper assimilation of successive waves of immigration, the integration of racial minority groups, the coordination of social strata in the fast-growing giant cities. If there had been only these concerns, however, political science would never have been developed.[3]

Political science as a distinct discipline is confined largely to the present century. Originally the study of the state, if undertaken at all, was dealt with by historians, jurists and philosophers. Even in this short period of its independent existence, three definite stages of development may be recog-

3. The same holds true of our good neighbor, sociology. It is not accidental that for decades it eked out a modest existence as a preparatory course for social workers in a few American women's colleges, somewhat glamorized by crusading publicists and disappointed ministers turned reformers. Apart from the lone giants William Graham Sumner at Yale and Lester F. Ward at Brown and small groups of sociologists such as those around the University of Chicago who were very much under the influence of continental theorists, sociology as a systematic discipline did not develop before the radical crisis of the late twenties that called for a reconsideration of the whole society as a major concern. For the specific "native" elements and the succeeding stages of this "American Science," see Roscoe C. and Gisela J. Hinkle, *The Development of Modern Sociology* (New York, 1954); for an equally short, suggestive treatment of the relations of sociology to the other social sciences, see George Simpson, *Man in Society: Preface to Sociology and the Social Sciences* (New York, 1954).

nized in the whole field and, with some slight, though characteristic variations, to be sure, equally detected in the specific areas of our research—in theory and public law, in national government and public administration, in international affairs and comparative politics. One may characterize the prevailing intellectual climate of these three phases as idealistic, positivistic, and realistic.

THE STAGES OF COMPARATIVE POLITICS

Rationalist Idealism   What brought about the first school of political scientists was the deep dissatisfaction among some young academicians who measured the reality of their American community against the ideals of an imagined *polis* and found it wanting. They were not ashamed to be called idealists. It is easy for today's sophisticate to smile at the naiveté of their concepts and convictions, yet their complaints about the disease of "Congressional Government,"[4] of "Boss rule," and "the shame of the cities" were real, and so were their models of proper politics. Not that they all agreed on any specific governmental system as the best, but they all shared the deep conviction that such an ideal did exist and could be pragmatically realized in a step-by-step development.

Three fundamental assumptions apparently served as the basis of their conception of comparative politics: the belief in the assured spread of democratic institutions, the essential harmony of interests among peoples, and the basic rationality of men who, by discussion and the interplay of opposing ideas, ultimately, and almost automatically, would reach a common understanding.[5]

4. *Cf.* Woodrow Wilson, *Congressional Government* (1884). The fluctuating popularity of this American classic in itself reflects the shifts of power in the United States government between the congressional and executive branches. Written in the period of weak presidential leadership between Lincoln and Cleveland, its findings were seriously questioned by Wilson himself in his preface to the 15th printing (1900) and practically repudiated by his later *Constitutional Government in the United States* (1908), written in praise of presidential leadership. The volume, following upon the careers of Cleveland and Teddy Roosevelt, shows a preparation for Wilson's own historical role. However, subsequent weak presidential leadership has evidenced the recurring nature of the disease and illustrated the renewed timeliness of Wilson's original attack.

5. To mention but one among many "confessions" of original motivation, there is the statement of the founder of the first School of Political Science at Columbia University: "My memory traveled back to that terrifying hour in the winter of 1863 when alone, amid the horrors of nature and war, I first resolved to consecrate my life's work to substituting the reign of reason for the rule of force." John W. Burgess, *Reminiscenses of an American Scholar* (New York, 1934), p. 197. These crucial assumptions and consequential policies were spelled out most dramatically in the field of world politics. The difficulties in international affairs, according to this idealistic school, were primarily due to a lack of communication and proper procedure. Promotion of

Form rather than function, means of communication rather than content-analysis of dynamic forces, were the main concerns of the experts. In comparative politics this meant a primary emphasis on a descriptive study of national institutions, constitutional structures and administrative organizations. This concern reflected not only the natural desire to give the young discipline a definite and concrete framework before it could grapple with the more fluid forces of dispersive dynamics; but such modesty in aim and aspirations was also meant to reject the doubts and accusations of the established older social sciences concerning the "scientific reliability" of politics. It was its essentially political orientation, and therewith its "subjective" ties, which made it suspect in the eyes of the so-called "objective" disciplines. Indeed, the emancipation of political science was to some extent a not-altogether-voluntary declaration of independence; it could have meant expulsion from the temples of the university. And in order to prevent this threatening fate, the young political science desperately tried to keep out of "politics" and to stand so to speak "on neutral ground." Such a position was understandable for the fledgling, whose uneasy flights fluctuated between a childlike dependence on its mother disciplines—philosophy, history, economics and public law—and a fierce fight for emancipation from their tutelage.

The retreat to factual description and expert advice, no doubt, allowed political science to develop pioneering tasks which in a way anticipated certain characteristic contributions of the next phase in its academic process. Yet such deep-seated, defensive dispositions led, especially in later periods, to strange adaptations of a conceptual course which in turn led political science to neglect the essential assignments of its domain. These trying adjustments were aggravated by an additional factor in the American academic picture. Without elaborating here on the complexities of trans-Atlantic acculturation, it is well to remember that the young political science borrowed heavily from continental experiences, as did American universities on the whole. Practically all the founders of the profession had received significant graduate training, if not their higher degrees, in European universities. Germany especially was the academic Mecca of a whole generation of social scientists and through this experience it made a deep impact on the development of higher learning in the United States.[6] What is even more important to recall in this connection is the altogether different intellectual

---

international intercourse and of new methods of arbitration, therefore, was regarded as the primary aim in that era of conferences. The Permanent Court of Arbitration at The Hague and the League of Nations became the epitome of the age's attainments and the efficacy of these institutions became the criterion of crisis in the succeeding decades.

6. The only institute of political science that had a marked influence on the young American discipline apart from the German universities, was the *École Libre des Sciences Politiques* at Paris.

position of the German universities, and of the social sciences in particular, in the Bismarck era. While some of the great German masters—Gneist, Roscher, Schmoller, Treitschke—of those impressionable young Americans wielded considerable influence on the political and social-economic make-up of the new German Empire, their academic role was circumscribed within a limited framework.

The universities, which had once been centers of the fight for freedom, had now been transformed into guardians of training for leadership in important public offices, the judiciary, the bureaucracy, and the teaching profession. To be sure, in performing this crucial function, the academicians could allow themselves the privilege of "freedom of research," especially in the less dangerous fields of philosophy and the arts. Even a professor of economics was permitted to utter some radical thoughts, for the Second Empire was not a totalitarian dictatorship. It did allow for certain aberrations, if only as a safety valve, as long as they did not disturb the political order—and this Hegel's disciples certainly did not do. Enthusiastic academic admirers of the omnipotent state that they were (reassured by the victories of the Iron Chancellor), they glorified the bureaucracy as the unquestioning guarantor of transcendental order against the anarchy of free-floating Western democratic ideas. With the uncomfortable exceptions of a few great liberal non-conformists, such as Theodor Mommsen, they increasingly retreated to the mere recruitment of experts and a conscious separation from policy decisions. This political castration and unassuming ivory-tower isolation was the price they paid for the social prestige they undoubtedly commanded. No wonder that, during the Wilhelminic Empire, a concept of the social sciences developed which sought to rationalize this specific historical plight. It hit most tragically those academic teachers who were born leaders and who in other nations and under different circumstances might well have become the spokesmen of their people. The fateful development of Max Weber serves as a vivid illustration of this crucial estrangement.[7]

Transmitted to an altogether different American atmosphere, such cultural borrowing could easily lead to new tensions between continental systems of rigid abstractions and the concrete world of the pragmatically-minded United States. And, strangely, it was often the most abstract theory that made the deepest impression on the master-practitioners of daily life. No doubt, Hegel found disciples, and even Bismarck, admirers among this first generation of American social scientists, some of whom found it difficult to reconcile their admiration with the national fervor after the entry of

7. Only seen against this background can the implication of his "theory of science" be fully grasped and especially his much discussed and often misunderstood concept of *Wertfreiheit*. A literal transposition of his socially conditioned formula of a "science free from value judgments" into a completely different American landscape has no doubt led to a most questionable reading of his essential teachings.

the United States into World War I. It would not be difficult to show fundamental discrepancies between an inherent inclination toward pragmatic
progressive politics and a determined drive for scientific systematics, embraced by the very same people.

What held this pioneer generation together was an unshaken belief in a
rational progress which justified the scientific undertaking as a genuine
moral crusade and directed the march to man's freedom. In the search for
the proper scientific technique there was undoubtedly much to admire and
to adopt in the European universities, especially if their deep-seated societal
breaks and persistent presuppositions were obscured by an idealistic perspective. While the stimulus and strength of American political scientists
sprang from altogether different sources, a seeming symbiosis of rationalist
idealism could thus prevail through the first decades.

The coming of the First World War was the first deep disturbance, but it
remained an isolated phenomenon, especially as Wilson succeeded in per-
suading the nation that this was "the war to end all wars" and the war "to
make the world safe for democracy." The unfortunate turn of events was
interpreted as a seemingly necessary step leading up to popular government
and the League of Nations. It was not until a decade later (a natural time-
span to be sure for such a radical breakthrough) that the full impact of this
new age of world wars and revolutions was felt, and that a changing climate of opinion could be observed.

Material Positivism The second phase of American political science
research was closely related to the frustrating experiences of the long Armi-
stice between the Great Wars, for they gave rise to a growing disillusionment with the basic tenets of the idealistic school. Instead of the "assured"
spread of free institutions, aggressive dictatorships emerged; despite a
galaxy of conferences to promote international understanding, the system
of collective security collapsed vis-à-vis its first tests; and irrational, integral
nationalisms held the perspective of reasonable man and the harmony of
interests up to ridicule.

In natural reaction to the sweeping philosophic idealism of the first
group of scholars, a new generation turned its interest to the concrete and
detailed study of material forces. This positivistic school rejected the naive
utopianism of the earlier stage by accepting an equally naive cynicism.
Ideologies were presented as subjective sentiments, superfluous and misleading rationalizations of the simple reality of objective power. Obviously such
a violent reaction did a great injustice to the actual accomplishments of the
early pathfinders of political science. Yet is this not the usual consequence
of "scientific progress"? Or, to quote Goethe, "People throw themselves in
politics, as they do on the sick-bed, from one side to the other in the belief
that they can thus find a better position." In retrospect both periods played
their part in the unfolding of political science; and critical though a new

team of researchers must be of the position taken by that of its predecessors, one will have to register equally their major contributions to the discipline.

What were the approaches and aims, procedures and postulates of the second stage? First of all it was a sobering phase, suspicious of great panaceas, quick generalizations, broad comparisons and unrecognized deductions; in short, of all speculative theory. Consequently it turned toward detailed, concrete phenomena, toward inductive empiricism, toward measurable and verifiable data in order to make politics at last "scientific."

No doubt, this period of "objective" fact-finding, in its preoccupation with methodological problems, sharpened the tools of our perception and our critical source analysis by introducing and testing elaborate techniques of case studies, survey methods and statistical research. Thus it contributed immeasurably to an exacting delineation of the discipline. Moreover, the material enrichment of comparative-government research during these years of strenuous, painstaking collections gave the field for the first time a substantive foundation from which to operate a rationally controllable body politic and to advance the frontiers of our knowledge.[8] New areas of scholarly inquiry developed, and the machinery of functioning political systems was subjected to intensive analysis. The rise of public administration was probably the most conspicuous corollary to this trend. At times it almost seemed as if the enterprising expansion and proselyting zeal of students of public administration were preempting the whole field.[9] In truth, the data brought together consisted mostly of the mere raw material out of which politics is made, and it was not a particularly exciting collection at that. In fact, one might venture to say, with one of comparative government's keenest students, evaluating his own specialty after it had passed this trying period, that it was caught in a "tedious and stagnating routine."[10]

8. The monumental *Encyclopedia of the Social Sciences* (which made its first appearance in 1934) served as a symbol of such stock-taking and is the pride of the period.

9. The importance of public administration at the time could be measured by its predominance in the programming of the American Political Science Association meetings, not to mention the financing of research projects. Such a development might have been regarded as a concomitant to a general return of interest in domestic politics. Yet a careful check of predominant comparative government texts would have revealed an extraordinary, if not exorbitant, extension of administrative analysis in that field. Noteworthy in this connection is the rapid emancipation of public administration, this most empirical and easily static specialty, from its rough and ready beginnings and its turn toward more sophisticated, dynamic, and philosophical approaches—an indication of the vital forces, embodied even in the seemingly formal paraphernalia of politics, which could be tapped by ingenious research. For these "emerging trends" see the series of essays by George A. Graham, John M. Gaus, Charles S. Ascher and Wallace S. Sayre in the *Public Administration Review* (1950–51), X, 69–77, 161–168, 229–235; XI, 1–9.

10. Karl Löwenstein, "Report on the Research Panel on Comparative Government," *American Political Science Review*, XXXVIII (June 1944), 540–548.

The young collegians knew it, too. If they entered the study of politics at all, they turned to the entertaining and enthralling "international relations," which in some universities had moved out of the domain of political science altogether. The increasing artificial separation of world politics and comparative government was certainly detrimental to both—the one often degraded to pontifical pronouncements on the daily headlines for up-to-date faddists and young men in a hurry; the other a dump heap of dusty data—where a common approach, with systematic penetration and scholarly perspective, to the burning issues of the time would instead have been mutually beneficial.

That comparative government seemed for a while to be completely overshadowed among its academic companions by the more exacting public administration and, among the college crowd, by the more exciting international affairs was not the most serious shortcoming in this low ebb of its esteem.

The real problem and peril of this second period only becomes apparent if one probes into the underlying assumptions and expectations of its protagonists; because, proud declarations not withstanding, this phase had its *raison d'être,* too, and was by no means "free from value judgments." The prevailing philosophy—uncouth and inarticulate to be sure—was that of positivism and, like August Comte's system itself, it was open to "positivist" criticism, so adroitly administered by Vilfredo Pareto, the newly elevated scholarly saint of this very period. This master mind of man's irrationality (seeking out constant and determining "residues" underlying the shifty and "non-logical derivations" of human conduct) indeed appealed to a generation whose belief in progress and rational man had been shaken by the chaos of war and revolution.

This shocking experience, if it was not to lead to the cynic's complete resignation and utter despair (and the American mood was hardly inclined toward such philosophical pessimism), aroused the desire to seek the persistent powers and determining laws which make irresponsible and irascible man operate. In search of this "Open Sesame" of the rationale behind man's irrationalism, twentieth-century scientific inquiry has indeed pushed forward the frontiers of knowledge and has made its pioneers (Freud, Köhler and many others) welcome pathfinders to a new political science. Its novelty was due in no small part to the rich influx in methods and material from neighboring and even distant research disciplines. Yet the pertinent impact of such scientific expansion and crossfield fertilizations was to be felt only later and more fully in its third stage, when a more cautious and confident discipline would weigh, digest and assimilate the findings of other fields.

Such careful differentiation was certainly not the order of the day in the earlier stages of the explorers' enthusiasm when an uncritical identification with the natural sciences was often proclaimed. Behind such a confession one might even have detected an urge for a simple, overall formula. And in justice to that past phase, one might remember that it was part and parcel of a cultural crisis—a period which, having lost basic values, was in desperate search for stable concepts, indisputable tenets, absolute standards. Such new signposts the universities' new scientific absolutism was to establish. Whenever its restless youth could not find satisfactory answers, it looked for them outside the lecture halls (and not seldom found them within the university walls). This was the attraction of Marxism that it seemed to give a complete comprehension of past history, a scientific prediction of the inescapable future, and above all a marching order for lost man by giving him a new footing outside himself. For such security he was even ready to surrender his freedom. These were the deeper roots of modern totalitarianism and its fascinating appeal (leaving aside the perplexing question whether the revolution which had found a fatherland had much in common with original Marxism). Only a new image of man and his meaningful place in society could defeat such morbid self-destruction.

Most certainly such a new perspective was not presented by the academic school which won some ardent disciples in the thirties, namely *Geopolitik*. On the contrary, this importation from the continent was the true counterpart to Marxism, and indeed in Europe had widely served as a "Bourgeois Marxism." Now instead of economics it was space that became the absolute and exclusive yardstick. Its attractiveness resided above all in its simultaneous promise of stability and dynamic action, its scientific absoluteness and its presumed concreteness. Geopolitics merged the disturbing complexities of life into one single and seemingly objective factor. In the unending flood of continuous change, space seems to be the invariable, independent of man and events. Rootless man seeks a new hold outside himself. His loud call for action—speedy, glamorous, continuous—in the big world is a desperate move to make him forget the emptiness of his small inner life. The powerful dynamics of the modern world-conqueror is only an expression of man's desire to escape from his despair of real values and from himself. He is at war with the world, because he is not at peace with himself. Yet man cannot escape his responsibility as a man. Nor can a science of society and social order establish itself as a "natural science" without missing its challenge completely.

The very fact that space represented the one stable element, presumably independent of man's decision, by no means made it the most important element in world affairs. But the natural science of politics,[11] with its impressive principles of an everlasting mechanism of power balances, *seemed*

11. For an analysis of this case study of a natural science of politics, see Sigmund Neumann, "Fashions in Space," *Foreign Affairs*, XXI (January 1943), 276–288. In its tri-partite division of *Geopolitik* as a science, a political weapon, and a *Weltanschauung*, the article warns against the present danger of forgetting the valuable emphasis on political geography as an essential element of political concern. Such forgetfulness is the frequent by-product of the passing of fashions.

to provide a monistic, scientific answer to a world longing for order and stability. When *Geopolitik* became instead the weapon of the unscrupulous Third Reich and an instrument of its unlimited drive for world conquest, it revealed a materialism devoid of any moral evaluation or restraint. The Second World War spelled the end of this cynical power politics and opened the way for a more adequate and exacting approach to a study of the state and society.

Before examining that third stage, a more serious, more subtle and, indeed, more scientific attempt at raising politics to the unimpeachability of an objective science must be dealt with: namely, the impact of the behavioral sciences.[12] No doubt political science gained much material enrichment, a refinement of research techniques, and some sober reassessment of its earlier generalizations through this confrontation and exchange with the developing findings of neighboring fields. At times, the very self-assurance and boldness of an expansive psychology and sociology intimidated a defeatist political science and threatened it with utter submission. One might find historical explanations for such unwarranted retreat from hardly-won positions. Political science had just passed through a period of insecurity and crisis, if not one of self-effacement. Its basic tenets had been shattered by war and revolution and the ensuing "retreat from reason." Deflated dreams of world order plunged a nation of missionaries back into a more accustomed and sober isolationism. In such a modest frame, politics did not look attractive to the enterprising youngster, if he entered the academic halls at all, instead of "the world that mattered." And when this world was shattered, too, by the Great Depression, the pressing problems of the economic crisis preoccupied the "braintrusters," who now concentrated their intellectual efforts upon finding "cures" for this internal disease.

Obviously this crisis did not occur in isolation, but required a worldwide perspective for its proper solution. Yet by and large (with the utopians' recent debacle still in mind), the country answered the threatening irrational breakthrough with a proud, "It can't happen here." Or was it "whistling in the dark," and fear of the unknown, that held back a courageous facing of the crisis? The successive one-track answers to the challenge of modern totalitarianism illustrate the changing moods of the time—from curiosity reports on inside stories of "megalomanian one-man rule," to apologetic accommodations to a proud people's grievances, to the "shame of Versailles" and to appeasers' acceptance of the "bulwark against the Red Peril"—until the democracies were finally locked in battle with "the efficiency state of master organizers and propagandists."

12. A suggestive balance sheet of pros and cons engendered by the emergence of the behavioral sciences is presented in a thoughtful essay by David B. Truman, "The Impact on Political Science of the Revolution in the Behavioral Sciences," in *Research Frontiers in Politics and Government* (Washington, D.C., Brookings Lectures, 1955), pp. 202–231.

The war, to be sure, awakened political science to its full responsibilities. Yet the martial exigencies called for quick action, for efficient services, and for specific and measurable results. In this respect the "behavioral sciences" seemed to excel, coming forward with verifiable propositions of refined sample-survey methods and models. Undoubtedly, the ascendancy of psychology and sociology derived in large part from the remarkable contribution which these disciplines rendered during the war. It is equally undeniable that the spectacular field of public opinion measurement developed greatly in response to dictatorial mass manipulation, and even frequently accepted its underlying assumptions concerning human behavior. This proven wartime utility and the even greater promise of measurable social predictability raised the repute of the behavioral approach to a point where it soon became the preferred, in fact for many serious scholars, the exclusive method of social science research. Only by becoming a natural science (in the way some of its eager converts defined it) could the social sciences justify their existence and the money spent by foundations on social research.

Political science, indeed, has profited greatly from collaboration with the so-called behavioral sciences and their exacting research methods. Yet it is in their absolutist dictum that only those phenomena which are measurable and calculable are worth scientific inquiry, that their influence may imperil the whole discipline of political science. If our research should concentrate exclusively, or even primarily, on these clearly circumscribed areas (which are often only peripheral), then political science would miss the key issues which are the crucial concern and daily dignity of our discipline.

Fortunately, under the cover of this seemingly "scientific" predominance, a silent revolution has taken place which indicates that political science is entering upon a new plane. Only the first contours of its character and consequences can be drawn at this early stage of development. In a sense this third phase constitutes a natural step from both preceding stages to a higher plane, and, in the preservation and conciliation of their conflicting positions, it may possibly constitute an advance to a more promising synthesis.

Realism with Vision Politics raised onto this third level must be modest in its claims and steady in its cautious endeavors. It has no blueprints, no great panaceas, no comprehensive concepts to offer, but a continuous adjustment and even improvisation in the light of an ever-changing political scene. Above all, it is impressed by the complexity of politics, the rich texture of the raw material, and the dynamic forces that constitute its full power. In this down-to-earth realism it has taken seriously the warning of the second school against easy generalizations and untested assumptions. Yet at the same time it has recognized that a mere fact-finding spree may only lead into a no-man's land of mountains of meaningless material, if not directed beforehand by fundamental questions reflecting the researchers' aspirations. For this reason contemporary political scientists have gained a renewed respect for the searching theories and visions of the first generation of political scientists and, as so often is the case, have joined hands with their intellectual grandparents. Woodrow Wilson has been restored to a position commensurate with his contribution and crucial for our time.

What are the chief characteristics of this new phase in the study of politics? They are threefold: an emphasis on dynamic processes, coupled with a rediscovery of the discipline's forgotten responsibility for policy decisions; a desire for the integration of the social sciences, dictated by a prevailing multi-causal approach to an entangled, intricate reality; and, as a consequence of the radical transformations around us, a new summons to a theoretical reorientation of the whole field. The emergence of these three trends is particularly evident in the field of comparative politics.

Our concern has turned away from a merely formal, legalistic and constitutional approach to a consideration of political dynamics and the processes of decision-making. Only when reaching beyond a mere political morphology of legislative, executive and judicial forms to the consequential comprehension of the political forces at work—men and movements in governments and parliaments, in political parties and pressure groups, and society's prevailing value structure—can responsible citizens recognize the different nature, purpose and direction of the political powers in being and in conflict. We want to know where, when and how politics is made in the constantly changing political scene. Such a new emphasis indicates that the instituted agencies, policies and procedures must have undergone fundamental changes, too.

It is at such a turning point that comparison gains a new momentum and a deeper meaning. "To know thyself, compare thyself to others." The comparative approach is, above all, an invaluable aid to a people's self-recognition and its sense of responsibility. It is not accidental that the great civilizations, like that of the Renaissance, were developed at the crossroads of history and articulated by the meeting of contrasting systems. This encounter alone made an awakening Western Europe more fully aware of her own character and quality, apart from being naturally and fruitfully influenced by the impact of the strange new forces.

We are again living in such a period of opening frontiers, which will force us to recognize the values and concepts we live by and to test them anew against their challenge from abroad. It is in this crisis of our own society that comparative government becomes significant for the mature citizen. Beyond that, the intensive study of contrasting civilizations provides the necessary background for present-day policy decisions. While our planet is continuously shrinking, bringing the politics of far-distant areas into our compass, thoughtful students of public affairs have often been troubled by our limited "knowledge by experience." Its only substitute seems to be "knowledge by learning," which puts a great responsibility on our generation to make comparative government a live issue—comprehensive and contemporary.

In order to have such contemporary comprehension, comparative politics must widen its area of research far beyond its customary domain. The thoughtful treatise of Dankwart Rustow suggests in this respect a widening of our comparative perspective by a novel "focus on the non-Western world."[13] It rightly questions our whole conceptual framework, which is still narrowly drawn within the patterns of Western experience alone. The altogether different historical setting of political problems and processes among the world's new protagonists necessitates a much more careful comparison of our global complexities. Moreover, this historical shift of power centers is accompanied by a radical upheaval of which the independence movement of formerly colonial peoples is only *one* significant feature.

This is an age of revolutions. And it is the very coincidence and confluence of these diverse streams that dramatizes the dynamics of our time and makes it difficult to grasp the direction it is taking. The contemporaneity of the much heralded liberations from "imperialism" with democratic, national and social revolutions indeed creates a combination, which presents an altogether new phenomenon even if its component parts are still described with familiar labels. Nationalism in mid-twentieth-century Asia constitutes a different and infinitely more disturbing phenomenon than its simpler nineteenth-century European prototype.[14]

The outcome of these concomitant drives is hardly predictable, yet if one can take a hint from the pages of history, one may say that in the interwoven mixture of patterns and policies, it is the stronger revolution which sets the style and which may well direct the contending forces into the stream of the "coming world revolution." The professional strategists of this world revolution know this all too well and are ready to exploit the consequent confusion of the reluctant resisters. To master the revolution of our time, one must first of all fully understand the complexities and dynamics of present-day politics. For such a crucial comprehension political science must reach out to its sister disciplines. Fortunately, and not alto-

13. Dankwart A. Rustow, "The Comparison of Western and Non-Western Political Systems" (paper read at the American Political Science Association meeting, Washington, D.C., September 8, 1956); see also his *Politics and Westernization in the Near East* (Princeton, Center of International Studies, 1956), and the fundamental reports of the Social Science Research Council's Committee on Comparative Politics, "Comparative Politics of Non-Western Countries" and "A Suggested Research Strategy in Western European Government and Politics," *American Political Science Review*, XLIX (December 1955), 1022–1049.

14. For some cogent thoughts along these lines, see Hans Kohn, "A New Look at Nationalism," *Virginia Quarterly Review*, XXXII (Summer 1956), 321–332; and "Some Reflections on Colonialism," *The Review of Politics*, XVIII (July 1956), 259–268.

gether accidentally, another *rapprochement,* which constitutes the second outstanding feature of the silent revolution in our decade, can be observed within the social sciences.

If one were to look for the historic breakthrough of the imaginary departmental borderlines which had hitherto been rigidly patrolled against incorrigible interdepartmental snipers and intruders, one might find that the Second World War marked that moment. War emergencies, no doubt, served as a major impetus to persuade difficult people to work together. The Office of Strategic Services and other governmental agencies became graduate schools for interdepartmental training and comprehensive comparisons such as we never attained before or after. Equally, the mushrooming area-study programs, while they naturally constituted a somewhat premature synthesis, did pioneering work in interdisciplinary cooperation and policy formation, in evaluating research techniques and providing indispensable material stock-taking. Above all, people learned to talk to each other. Such experiences fostered respect for the neighboring fields, an increasing appreciation of their fruitful contributions, and a mounting desire for integration.

It is on the basis of this experience that political science can reassess its sister disciplines and call upon their services without the past trepidations of an immature contender striving for independence and constantly afraid of its former masters and oncoming competitors. The background materials of history and economics, anthropology and linguistics, psychology, psychiatry and sociology, to mention only the main auxiliaries, become a necessity for comparative studies, especially in a depth analysis of the lesser known areas. But the political scientist must also be aware of the fact that these supporting sciences, which emphasize altogether different aspects as their own central concerns, may not always offer the needed material, and that their findings may not always lend themselves to immediate incorporation in his own discipline. In short, he may find himself obliged to search for his own sources of information and his special slant of investigation.

The use of history, for instance, in the study of politics may demand a new perspective of a discipline, which, in its traditional presentation, has often tried to separate itself from policy-making decisions. In fact, the professionals may have forgotten altogether that the historian is "a prophet looking backwards," who, in reviewing past events and rewriting history for his own generation, makes past experience a meaningful part of the present-day challenge. Such novel application of traditional tools, in fact, can restore time-honored though forgotten principles, or open fresh avenues of neglected research. New fruitful concepts may thus evolve in the cross-fertilization of fields.[15]

15. Such fructifications may be seen in the writings of Gabriel Almond and his developing concept of "political culture"; *cf.* his "Comparative Politics Systems" in *The Journal of Politics,* XVIII (August 1956), 391–409. For a most recent statement

Having said all that about the necessity for a reintegration of the artificially separated social sciences in our time, one must quickly add that such a tremendous expansion is also some cause for alarm. A caveat is in order against easy generalizations and the transfer of research findings from alien domains, against the eclectics' semantic confusion and childlike play with big words and new tools. Such procedures may not only destroy the reputation of scholarship, but also the attempt at bridge-building between the disciplines.

One way of checking this threat is presented by a third trend current in this third phase of political science: the auspicious revival of theory. There is indeed a great need for a conceptual housecleaning, as the ideas we live by are desperately dusty, if not buried altogether in the attic of past remembrances.

Truly one could argue that a time-lag always exists between historical reality and its conceptualization, especially in a great period of transition when the political vocabulary has become quickly outmoded and hence full of misnomers. We are still living within an ideological framework of a hundred years ago and naturally cannot master our present-day political conflicts with such obsolete and often romantic stereotypes. This is a time when a meaningful historical comparison is called for. More than that, a theoretical clarification becomes an essential preliminary for the adoption of appropriate strategies in this revolutionary age. All fundamental concepts of politics, like nationalism and sovereignty, imperialism and colonization, socialism and statism, classes and parties, leaders and masses, must therefore be redefined in the light of a new reality. On this basis alone can theory become, as it should, a guide to political action, a compass through chaos.

Not only do concepts change through the ages—and indeed at an accelerated pace in this twentieth century—but also different historical types arise concurrently in our time. The loose application of the same term to

---

see his Social Science Research Council paper (in collaboration with Myron Weiner), "A Comparative Approach to the Study of Political Groups" (Princeton, Center of International Studies, 1956).

In similar fashion, the encouraging development (at last!) of political sociology, promises substantial correlations between sociology and political science. For a sampling see: Rudolf Heberle, *Social Movements. An Introduction to Political Sociology* (New York, 1951); Hans Speier, *Social Order and the Risks of War; Papers in Political Sociology* (New York, 1952); S. M. Lipset, James Coleman and Martin Troer, *Union Democracy: The Internal Politics of the International Typographical Union* (Glencoe, Ill., 1956); S. M. Lipset and Juan Linz, *The Social Basis of Political Diversity in Western Democracies* (manuscript, Center for Advanced Study in the Behavioral Sciences, Stanford, 1956); S. N. Eisenstadt, *From Generation to Generation: Age Groups and the Social Structure.* See also Barrington Moore, "Sociological Theory and Contemporary Politics," *American Journal of Sociology,* XI (September 1956), 107–115.

the most divergent phenomena and the lack of their clear theoretical differentiation has led to dangerous confusions. Revolutions, like military battles, national and international, have been lost through obsolete strategy. Conceptual clarification thus becomes the indispensable preliminary for politics appropriate to our times. What is needed above all is a new realistic reappraisal of theory's proper place in the social sciences. Neither the beginner's absolute, overall generalizations nor the complete abandonment of a systematic scheme, such as characterized the despairing second generation of political scientists, could be the answer. It is necessary that our political science concepts be spelled out in time and space, both in their specific historical situation and in their local representation. This puts natural restraints on our theorizing.

The question of a proper approach to a meaningful theory of politics poses a dilemma of an even more fundamental nature. The overwhelming data of our material would fall into a conceivable pattern only if seen through the controlled order of a conceptual framework, which in turn cannot be conceived save in full appreciation of the rich texture of reality. The task of attempting to systematize our knowledge, therefore, is confronted by almost overwhelming difficulties and can proceed only by a simultaneous attack on both theory and practice. Social concepts evolve by stages, remaining necessarily fragmentary and tentative and, at best, present merely a useful working hypothesis for a deeper penetration into an ever-changing reality. Hence a conceptualization of politics must be a constantly renewed effort.

One further complication for a pertinent thought-pattern of twentieth-century politics derives from its extraordinary extension. In this indivisible world, which has become global and total in war and peace, in democracies and dictatorships, comfortable frontiers between man's private existence and social commitments, between domestic and foreign affairs are blurred, if not meaningless altogether. This is an age of international civil war. Its international conflicts are decided by the civilian morale and social cohesion in the nations' hinterlands. The impact of domestic forces on world politics plays havoc with Ranke's hitherto unchallenged postulate of the primacy of foreign policy. On the other hand, national upheavals are deeply affected, if not largely directed, by social and ideological forces, reaching far beyond the domestic domain. And last but not least, the restlessness of modern man—in his deep anxieties, his shifting loyalties, his drives for security—is at the base of great politics, at home and abroad. It is this simultaneous attack on all sides which gives twentieth-century politics its three-dimensional involvement—personal, national, and international—and its confusing complexity.

The study of comparative politics necessarily reflects this complexity. Strategically situated at the crossroads of politics, comparative politics must reach out from its national bases into the area of international power politics and at the same time dig down into the personal plight of individuals. Only from such a triple springboard can political science hope to launch a meaningful comparative analysis that will be at the same time comprehensive, circumspect, and contemporary. For that it will need a dynamic discernment of its own, the concerted support of adjoining disciplines, and a fresh theoretical perspective of the social sciences as a whole. The deep dissatisfaction, so widely felt with the teaching and research efforts in our field during the last decade, has centered exactly on these vital points.[16]

It could justly be argued that the traditional scope and method of comparative studies have not really allowed for genuine comparison, that in their formalistic, country-by-country descriptions of isolated aspects of a single culture, students of comparative government have not scientifically tested their inherent democratic bias, have shied away from farther-reaching research hypotheses, have evaded crucial policy issues and thus have missed out on the very contributions which the comparative advance should render to a mature and responsible political science. Such vigorous criticism is indeed a healthy sign that the field is taking a fresh look at itself, and, by measuring its own shortcomings, giving itself a new start.

Even more important and encouraging is the sudden sprouting of numerous productive and stimulating studies in the field, precisely professing these new concerns for dynamic analyses, interdisciplinary correlation and conceptual differentiation.[17] At this new stage, the discipline demands from its field-workers first of all the opening of virgin territory in the "underdeveloped areas" of Asia, Africa, South America, and a fresh reappraisal of the

16. For a measured catalogue of this mounting criticism, see Roy C. Macridis, *The Study of Comparative Government* (New York, 1955).

17. To name only a few, the following works should rank high among recent American monographs: Gabriel A. Almond, *The American People and Foreign Policy* (New York, 1950), and *The Appeals of Communism* (Princeton, 1954); David Apter, *The Gold Coast in Transition* (Princeton, 1955); Raymond A. Bauer, Alex Inkeles and Clyde Kluckhohn, *How the Soviet System Works* (Cambridge, 1956); Frederick C. Barghoorn, *Soviet Russian Nationalism* (New York, 1956); B. R. Berelson, Paul F. Lazarsfeld, W. N. McPhee, *Voting* (Chicago, 1954); Bernard C. Cohen, *Peace Making in a Democracy. The Political Process and the Japanese Peace Settlement* (Princeton, 1956); Robert A. Dahl, *A Preface to Democratic Theory* (Chicago, 1956); Louis Edinger, *German Exile Politics* (Berkeley, 1956); Henry Ehrmann, *Employers' Associations in France* (New York, 1956); Mario Einaudi and François Goguel, *Christian Democracy in Italy and France* (Notre Dame, 1952); Rupert Emerson, *Representative Government in South East Asia* (Cambridge, 1955); Merle Fainsod, *How Russia is Ruled* (Cambridge, 1953); Barrington Moore, *Soviet Politics—The Dilemma of Power* (Cambridge, 1950), and *Terror and Progress—USSR* (Cambridge, 1954); James K. Pollock, H. L. Bretton, F. Grace and D. S. McHargue, *German Democracy at Work* (Ann Arbor, 1955); Lucian Pye, *Guerilla Communism in Malaya* (Princeton, 1956); Dankwart A. Rustow, *The Politics of Compromise. A Study of Parties and Cabinet Governments in Sweden* (Princeton, 1955); Robert A. Scalapino, *Democracy and the Party Movement in Pre-War Japan* (Berkeley, 1953); Klemens von Klemperer, *Germany's New Conservatism* (Princeton, 1957); and Nobutaka Ike, *Japanese Politics* (New York, 1957).

seemingly familiar landscapes of the Western World. Beyond such necessary groundwork in the by now well-established and defined areas, research
must reach out for fruitful inter-regional studies in comparison and contrast.
Such far-flung tasks—all too often beyond one man's capacity—necessitate
teamwork which coordinates and respects the findings of many without ham-
pering individual initiative and enterprise, evaluation and inquisitiveness.[18]

Above all, in such a pioneering phase comparative politics must be cautious in its conceptual framework. Concepts it needs, but they must be now
—more than ever—of a dynamic nature, allowing for the fluidity and
flexibility of ever-new experiences. There are concepts available which have
that quality. It is up to our ingenuity to seek them out. Our definitions of
political parties and interest groups, of leaders and followers, of crisis strata
and political generations should never petrify the political dynamics, but
should present them as what they are: concrete and concise, colorful and
consequential. Only such directives will lead to a meaningful confrontation,
because, though the comparative approach is as old as political science, the
proper use of comparison has hardly been undertaken.

18. For such a preliminary project of cooperation, see Sigmund Neumann (ed.),
Modern Political Parties: Approaches to Comparative Politics (Chicago, 1956).

Present Trends and Issues:
Contemporary Issues in the Theory of Comparative Politics

Macrotheories and Microapplications in Comparative Politics

A Widening Chasm—Joseph LaPalombara

INTRODUCTION

As more than one commentator has informed us of late, no branch of political science has been in more extreme ferment than comparative politics

*A modified version of this article appears under the title "Parsimony and
Empiricism in Comparative Politics: An Anti-Scholastic View," in Robert
T. Holt and John E. Turner, eds.* Methodology of Comparative Research.
*I am indebted to Yale University's Stimson Fund for a grant that made
initial work on this manuscript possible. [Robert T. Holt and John E.
Turner, eds.* Methodology of Comparative Research *(New York: Free
Press, 1970)]*

Reprinted from Comparative Politics, *1:1 (October 1968), 52–78, by special permission
of the author and the publisher.*

during the last fifteen years.[1] Beginning with a summer seminar at Northwestern University in 1953,[2] followed by the Macridis critique of 1954[3] and the creation of the SSRC Committee on Comparative Politics that same year, a massive theoretical and methodological stocktaking was set in motion. That activity is still very much under way, and, as in any ongoing fermenting process, it is risky to predict what the aged product will look like. Nevertheless, those who have contributed to or sampled the intellectual output of most recent vintage may be expected and permitted to comment on the "new comparative politics" and perhaps to suggest where and how the continuing fermentation process should be accelerated, modified, or halted. It is in this spirit that I offer this essay, fully aware that most vintners will continue to pursue formulas that they find most palatable and congenial, even when the outcome is little more than old wine in shiny new containers.

There are some who view the discipline's transformation as nothing short of revolutionary, although the exact date of the revolution's emergence is unclear.[4] For those who emphasize changes in the broad theoretical orientation of the discipline, such transformations can be traced to the 1920's and, indeed, all the way back to Arthur Fisher Bentley's long-neglected *The Process of Government*.[5] For others who see revolutionary thrust primarily in methodological concerns, the important advances are said to begin following World War II.[6] Whatever the method of dating, everyone is agreed

1. See, for example, Sigmund Neumann, "Comparative Politics: A Half-Century Appraisal," *Journal of Politics*, IX (August 1957), 369–390. In his presidential address to the APSA in September 1966, Gabriel Almond notes both many aspects of the general ferment in the discipline of political science and the catalytic role in it played by the "subdiscipline" of comparative politics. See Gabriel A. Almond, "Political Theory and Political Science," *American Political Science Review*, LX (December 1966), 869–879.

2. Roy C. Macridis et al. "Research in Comparative Government," *American Political Science Review*, XLVII (September 1953), 641–675.

3. Roy C. Macridis, *The Study of Comparative Government* (New York, 1955). I understand that Macridis is revising this much quoted little book, and it will be interesting to learn how many of his trenchant indictments of the discipline have been quashed or removed by "good" behavior in the intervening years.

4. Gabriel Almond, in his APSA presidential address, associates the revolution with Charles Merriam's *New Aspects of Politics* (Chicago, 1925) and with the extraordinary number of seminal political scientists who emerged from graduate training at the University of Chicago in the 1920's. That list includes Herbert Simon, David Truman, Harold Lasswell, V. O. Key, and Almond himself.

5. The volume was first published in 1908 and elicited from Charles Beard the comment that it contained little to interest the political scientist. It was reissued in 1949.

6. See, for example, William C. Mitchell, "The Shape of Political Theory To Come: From Political Sociology to Political Economy," *American Behavioral Scientist*, XI

about the salience of the subdiscipline of comparative politics in these transformations. Thus, Somit and Tanenhaus have found that the profession itself identified "comparative government" as the field in which the "most significant work is now being done."[7] And, more recently, Braibanti has produced detailed evidence to demonstrate how radical has been the shift of scholarly attention to the comparative field in the period 1948–1966.[8]

It is not my purpose here to establish whether these changes represent revolution or, if so, how successful revolution has been. I doubt, however, that we are now all "behavioralists," whatever that means,[9] and I am much

---

(November–December 1967), 8–20. Cf. Heinz Eulau, *The Behavioral Persuasion in Politics* (New York, 1963).

7. Albert Somit and Joseph Tanenhaus, *American Political Science: A Profile of a Discipline* (New York, 1964).

8. Ralph Braibanti, "Comparative Political Analytics Reconsidered," *Journal of Politics,* XXX (February 1968), 25–65. See Braibanti's first footnote (p. 25) for a good list of works representing the recent effervescence of comparative government and comparative politics.

I should emphasize here that not all of the ferment of recent years is in the comparative field narrowly conceived. Books from both earlier and more recent periods which would be included on anyone's list of groundbreaking works are H. D. Lasswell, *The Analysis of Political Behavior: An Empirical Approach* (New York, 1948); David Truman, *The Governmental Process* (New York, 1951); Herbert Simon, *Administrative Behavior: A Study in Decision Making Processes in Administrative Organizations,* 2nd ed. (New York, 1957); David Easton, *The Political System* (New York, 1953); Robert A. Dahl, *A Preface to Democratic Theory* (Chicago, 1956), and his *Modern Political Analysis* (1963); Glendon Schubert, *Quantitative Analysis of Judicial Behavior* (New York, 1959); Gabriel A. Almond and James S. Coleman eds. *The Politics of the Developing Areas* (Princeton, 1960); Karl W. Deutsch, *Nationalism and Social Communication* (New York, 1953); John C. Wahlke et al. *The Legislative System* (New York, 1962).

I should add that such a list must include Carl J. Friedrich's *Constitutional Government and Democracy,* 4th ed. (Waltham, Mass., 1968), both because of its enormous impact on the profession during the last three decades and to illustrate my point that less is "new" in political science theory and methods than we might be led to believe.

9. See, for example, E. M. Kirkpatrick, "The Political Behavior Approach," *PROD,* II (November 1958), 9–13, whose "behavioral umbrella" seems to me to include too many political scientists. Cf. Roland Young, ed. *Approaches to the Study of Political Science* (Evanston, 1959). Eulau's *The Behavioral Persuasion* is much more meaningfully restrictive (even if open to the objection of "narrowness") in delineating what the "behavioral revolution" means. Robert Dahl's summary analysis of the "behavioral movement" is well worth reading: "The Behavioral Approach in Political Science: Epitaph for a Monument to a Successful Protest," *American Political Science Review,* LV (December 1961), 763–772.

Sidney Verba, in "Some Dilemmas in Comparative Research," *World Politics,* XX (October 1967), 111–127, makes my points about "revolution" very laconically. He says, "There has been a revolution in comparative politics. But as with all revolutions,

more inclined to be rather specific in distinguishing between the effervescence of theory, on the one hand, and the development of new, more rigorous methods, on the other. The general position I shall take in this article is that whatever the vantage point from which one views the changes of recent years, they do not look like unmixed blessings for the profession. Furthermore, I shall maintain that this observation is particularly true in the field of "systems theory," "holistic theory," "general theory," or "grand theory," that is, in that body of literature that purports to provide a theoretical explanation of the entire polity, government, political system, and so on. I shall argue in conclusion that the best hope for the discipline's future growth lies in the application of rigorous methodologies to important problems conceptualized at the "middle range" and involving *partial* segments of the polity. It seems to me that this procedure would constitute one way of responding to the growing criticism of scientism in the profession—criticism that is voiced not only by normative and speculative political theorists but also by empirical political scientists and sociologists who take a dim view both of high-flown theoretical exercises and of so-called value-free theory and research.[10]

One form of response to criticisms of proliferating macrotheories is to argue that proliferation itself is a sign of health and vigor and that a wide and dizzying array of macrotheories is inevitable in a profession that has had to discard sterile, culture-bound general theories of a past era. Even where the general theories are essentially metaphorical (as almost all of them seem to me to be in political science),[11] it is insisted that all possible

---

it is difficult to date its beginning, to chart its course, and now, when the revolution has become established, difficult to say what has been accomplished" (p. 111). Later, in reflecting on "theories," he adds, "But frameworks, paradigms, and theories proliferate at too rapid a rate. In addition, the general theoretical works float well above reality, and they often are so abstract as to suggest no clear problem focus" (p. 112).

10. The antibehavioral views of Leo Strauss and his followers are contained in H. Storing, ed. *Essays on the Scientific Study of Politics* (New York, 1962). A typically European criticism is Bernard Crick's *The American Science of Politics* (Berkeley, 1959). In sociology, some of this protest is contained in Maurice Stein and Arthur Vidich, *Sociology on Trial* (Englewood Cliffs, 1963). See particularly the brilliant critical essay by Alvin Gouldner in this volume.

My observations about some of the consequences of these developments are contained in my "Decline of Ideology: A Dissent and an Interpretation," *American Political Science Review*, LX (March 1966), 5–18. See also James C. Charlesworth, ed. *The Limits of Behavioralism in Political Science* (Philadelphia, 1962).

11. By "metaphorical" here I mean simply (and, all too often, simplistically) viewing the political system and its processes in terms of fundamental theoretical formulations derived from mechanics, biology, cybernetics, neurology, and so on. The metaphorical tradition is deeply rooted in political science, as expressions such as "ship of state," "father of his country," and "sick society" will attest.

avenues of potential theoretical breakthrough must be kept open until we have a better empirical basis for deciding which macrotheories to accept, which to discard. Viewed from this sort of vantage point, most, perhaps all, efforts to capture and clarify the more elusive aspects of whole political systems appear courageous and praiseworthy.

A less generous reaction to much of the recent whole-systems theoretical output of the discipline is the observation that we have returned to the ancient art of scholasticism, armed to be sure with new terminology, but not any more successful than were the ancients in narrowing the gap between abstract formulations and theoretical realities. It strikes me as enormously telling that at precisely that moment in the profession's development when methodological tools will permit the rigorous comparative testing of hypotheses the distance between hypotheses and general theory should be widening and that the linkage between hypotheses and macrotheory is either terribly obscure or of such problematical logical construction that theory itself cannot be falsified.

Let me try to be clear here and acknowledge that a great many hypotheses about the polity can be *associated* with, say, the "pattern-variable" or "four-sector" formulations of Talcott Parsons, or the "demand-support-output" model of David Easton, or the "cybernetic" model of Karl Deutsch, or the "capability" model of Gabriel Almond. Most such hypotheses, however, do not necessarily *depend* on such models; many of them are either self-evidently true or cannot be falsified, and empirical findings concerning them do not readily lead to modifications of the general theories. Many of these formulations have perhaps helped to make American comparative politics less parochial, less focused on formal Western institutions, less morphologically descriptive, less unaware of the importance of variables that lie "outside" something called the political system or polity. But unless my reading of the current state of "general theory" in political science is grossly in error, we are not, I think, moving perceptively in the direction of what Thomas Kuhn intends in his use of the term "paradigm."[12] Nor will we do so until we reduce the proliferation of general theories, begin making a bit of progress toward that common scientific vocabulary A. F. Bentley called for over fifty years ago, and pay more attention than we have to the question of the nature of the evidence that would suggest that a particular macrotheory be modified or discarded. One step in that direction would involve greater attention to partial systems, to middle-range propositions concerning them, to genuinely comparative analysis of political institutions, processes, and behavior, and, it is hoped, to the gradual refinement of theory by inductive inference that might then provide the basis for a "new paradigm."

We are not likely to go this particular route if, like Lipset, we react to the concepts of Talcott Parsons by limiting our observations to the fact

---

12. *The Structure of Scientific Revolutions* (Chicago, 1965).

that they are "obviously subject to considerable refinements" and that "little work has been done on the problem of linking such concepts to empirical indicators."[13] Concept-refining very quickly degenerates into the scholastic game; empirical indicators require less distance than currently exists between theoretical concepts and what it is we can measure in the field, in the null-hypothesis sense of the research enterprise.

Nor is it my purpose to provide a complete critique of the whole-systems approach to theory and research in comparative politics, or indeed to suggest that such an approach should be abandoned. However, it does seem to me that much of what is questionable, and even distressing, about present theories in comparative politics can be traced to something called structural-functional analysis. Judging by the work of structure-functionalism's more visible and esteemed practitioners, it seems to me that the charge that the so-called theory amounts to little more than a New Scholasticism is well founded.[14] It is therefore necessary to say some things about structure-functionalism before proceeding to an examination of some alternative orientations to theory and research in the field.

FUNCTIONALISM AND CROSS-CULTURAL COMPARISON

We seem to be agreed that a comparative political science that is not cross-cultural as well as cross-national would fall short of supporting the emergence of what Almond once called a "probabilistic theory of politics." The logic underlying this view is well known: Cross-national studies, whether of whole or partial systems, tend to be culture-bound. Where cross-national studies focus on institutions such as legislatures, political parties, interest

13. Seymour Martin Lipset, *The First New Nation* (New York, 1963), p. 344.

14. Much of what I would score as the New Scholasticism emanates from the prolific pen of Talcott Parsons and is especially found in Parsons and Edward A. Shils, eds. *Toward a General Theory of Action* (Cambridge, Mass., 1951). The best overall criticism of Parsons' theories is contained in Max Black, ed. *The Social Theories of Talcott Parsons* (Englewood Cliffs, 1962). Black's essay is a brilliant critique, and his rendering of Parsons' central postulates in "plain English" is both amusing and sobering.

The difficulties created by Parsons (not all of them intended, to be sure) are evident in the work of Fred Riggs, such as his *Administration in Developing Countries: The Theory of Prismatic Society* (Boston, 1964) and in his "Agraria and Industria: Toward a Typology of Public Administration," in William J. Siffin, ed. *Toward the Comparative Study of Public Administration* (Bloomington, 1957). Other works that contain one or more of the characteristics and problems I am alluding to here would include (but are not limited to) the following: Edward Shils, *Political Development in the New States* (Gravenhage, 1962); Almond and Coleman, *Politics of the Developing Areas;* S. N. Eisenstadt, *The Political Systems of Empires* (New York, 1963); David E. Apter, *The Politics of Modernization* (Chicago, 1965); and a number of the edited volumes on political development sponsored by the SSRC Committee on Comparative Politics, including my own *Bureaucracy and Political Development* (Princeton, 1963).

groups, and the like, they may obscure the nature of politics in cultural settings where such institutions do not exist or, if they do exist, represent radically different meanings for the societies involved. Even where the phenomena subjected to comparative analysis seem not to be narrowly limited in time and space (e.g., decision-making, political socialization), failure to extend analysis across cultural boundaries is likely to result in misleading and inaccurate generalizations. In short, a probabilistic theory of politics can emerge only from a consideration of the full range of cultures and societies in which politics and political systems are found.

Although such statements seem obvious enough today, it is only in recent years that some political scientists were liberated from the logical trap of assuming that the political process involves a given set of behaviors occurring within a given institutional framework. We may thus assume that it is unlikely today that political scientists who happen on a primitive tribe will conclude that legislation is absent where there does not exist some concrete approximation of the House of Commons, that public administration is wanting where a *Conseil d'État* or a Weberian-type bureaucracy is not to be found, or, indeed, that political participation exists (or is meaningful) only when it includes "free" elections or widespread public involvement in associations or political organizations ranging from the P-TA to political party directorates.

We owe these recent insights in part to structure-functionalism. Regardless of what the individual political scientist may want to do (or not to do) with functionalism, he must acknowledge that it is from this "theory" that we learned to conceptualize the political system as a set of finite, interrelated functions essential to its existence and to see that the manner in which such functions are performed anywhere in space and time is not necessarily bound to a specific set of institutions (read "concrete structures"). We learned, too, that it is not merely a formal institution that may represent a "structure" of the political system but that other analytically interesting and important patterns, such as value systems, economic allocation, or attitudes toward innovation can also be viewed from a structure-functional vantage point.

Our debt to functionalism does not stop here. We are increasingly aware of the applicability to comparative politics of the maxim—long ago offered us by Malinowski—that an artifact of one culture transferred to another in form may represent a radically different meaning and relate to a quite different function in its new setting. Thus Morroe Berger found, somewhat to his surprise, that a Weberian-type bureaucratic superstructure in Egypt did not in fact produce for that society the kinds of human interactions and consequences for the political system imputed to bureaucracy in the West.[15] Similarly, Riggs has taken considerable pains to depict the survival in

15. *Bureaucracy and Society in Modern Egypt* (Princeton, 1957).

"modern" institutional settings of patterns of behavior deeply rooted in "traditional" cultures.[16]

Perhaps the best cataloguing of the kinds of lessons political scientists can learn from structure-functionalism is included in Gabriel Almond's widely cited introductory essay to *The Politics of the Developing Areas*.[17] A more recent and ambitious attempt is made by the British political scientist, H. V. Wiseman, whose concluding chapter is the best example I can cite of the impossible morass of jargon, fuzzy conceptualization, circularity of reasoning, truisms propounded as scientific wisdom, and appeal to more scholasticism which characterizes the work of functionalists.[18] That Wiseman is primarily involved not in making his own critique but in distilling others' arguments pro and con serves merely to emphasize this unfortunate state of affairs. A reading of Wiseman's well-intentioned exercise quickly reveals why some political scientists find the structure-functional approach or other sociological approaches to systematic analysis extremely suspect. Consider, as one typical example, the following alleged contributions to the comparative study of political systems which Wiseman uncritically accepts as having come from sociologists:

1. That the "nation" and the "state" are not necessarily the same thing.

2. That the concepts of *power* and *influence* are as important in comparative politics as are institutional foci.

3. That "in the sociological sense," a legitimate government is one that has the support of those who are subject to it.

4. That "legitimacy" is never the sole basis of a government's power.

5. That the "effective government" of a society is always government by a small minority of the population, or that "rule is always the rule of the few."

To be sure, Professor Wiseman is reporting the claims of others and is moved, regarding the first "sociological discovery" cited above, to suggest, "with respect," that such generalizations are not "peculiarly sociological."[19]

16. See, for example, Riggs, *Administration in Developing Countries*, Parts 2 and 3.

17. Pages 3–64, esp. pp. 9–25 on "The Common Properties of Political Systems."

18. *Political Systems: Some Sociological Approaches* (London, 1966), pp. 101–117, et passim.

19. Wiseman derives these generalizations from H. Johnson, *Sociology: A Systematic Introduction* (London, 1961). I find it almost impossible to believe that a British scholar, trained at Balliol College, would let such intellectual pretentiousness pass with only the mildest reproach.

My point would be that if structure-functionalism clearly led to the theoretical validation of even such insights or self-evident propositions, it would represent an important gain. But it seems to me apparent that such is not the case, that most of the telling criticisms of the structure-functional approach[20]—when it masquerades as a descriptive or dynamic theory—have not been satisfyingly rebutted. Wiseman himself succinctly reflects my reservations about it when he says about T. B. Bottomore's critique, "What is most valuable in the functionalist approach, [Bottomore] concludes, is the greater emphasis and clarity given to the simple idea that in every particular society the different social activities are interconnected. It is then a matter of empirical enquiry as to which are the various social activities and how they are related."[21]

I am suggesting that once we have learned the important lesson of structural alternatives for functional performance and the multifunctionality of similar structures, little remains of structure-functionalism that is useful to political science, and much remains that can be damaging to comparative research.

To return to the matter of cross-national and cross-cultural research, it seems to me obvious that the kinds of functionally "diffuse" or "fused" societies and political systems that are of great interest to anthropology are rapidly disappearing and that the nation-states *do* manifest an amazing amount of institutional similarity—they *do* have executives, legislatures, public administrative systems, courts, armies, political parties, interest groups, and many other *institutional* arrangements that we have come to associate with Western societies but that may in fact be simply the most probable way in which "concrete structural differentiation" occurs at certain stages of political development.[22] To be sure, the functional meaning or

20. One of the most rigorous attacks on structure-functionalism is Carl G. Hempel, "The Logic of Functional Analysis," in Llewellyn Gross, ed. *Symposium on Sociological Theory* (New York, 1959), pp. 271–307. The Hempel critique is of functionalism as a logical system, and as such it is not immediately relevant here. Nevertheless, I do not think that anyone has provided a satisfactory reply to Hempel. See, for example, D. M. Martindale, ed. *Functionalism in the Social Sciences,* Monograph 5, American Academy of Political and Social Science (Philadelphia, 1965).

21. P. 216.

22. Although I cannot develop this point here, I wish to stress it for consideration. Whether it is the result of cultural diffusion or of endogenous development, the range of concrete structural alternatives for managing politics and government is, it seems to me, not only finite but limited to many of the very institutions we have come to identify as culturally "natural" to the West. After more than a decade of talking with colleagues who are non-Western scholars, reading their published output, and traveling in a number of non-Western areas, I am no longer easily convinced of the "exotic" character of such political systems.

A good case in point would be the political party, which appears to be ubiquitous, even if one may concede a variation in function, as well as the designation of "polit-

consequences of such institutions are not the same in Africa as in Europe, in Asia as in North America. Indeed, meaning and consequences of similar institutional arrangements may vary quite markedly in culturally homogeneous areas, as well as over time within the same nation-state. This elementary fact is not a discovery of functionalism; it was clearly understood by Aristotle, Hobbes, Burke, Rousseau, de Tocqueville, and Bagehot, to name only a few whose writings appear to me to be particularly sensitive on this score and who were concerned with whole-systems analysis.

The proliferation or diffusion of structurally similar institutions over much of the globe also occurs at levels of government below the nation-state. It may be that some continents contain primitive local societies where politics is intermittent and where clearly political institutions are not easily discernible. Here functionalism may provide an important descriptive guide, as it might were we to research the local-level societies of Western antiquity. But villages the world over today appear to possess strikingly similar institutions such as chiefs, elders, and councils, and there is no reason for assuming that functionalism provides a better guide to the subtleties of the political process in such places than would, say, an approach that began with certain culture-bound assumptions about village government but then moved on sensitively to try to discern process variations in different settings. I shall return to this matter below when I try to indicate why we can fruitfully engage in either cross-national or cross-cultural comparative research within a conceptual and institutional framework that is perhaps parochially derived from a limited cultural area like the West.

I would record one final difficulty in the study of whole political systems which, while not necessarily inherent in such a focus, is very much apparent in contemporary political science. I refer to the tendency to see the political system, no matter how well or poorly bounded, within a broader social, physical, and economic environment and then to assume that the political system itself is the more or less fatalistic outcome of environmental or "ecological" factors. I believe it is primarily, although not exclusively, among those who are concerned with whole systems that politics and political systems take on the qualities of exclusively dependent variables, the product of a wide range of independent factors including industrialization, political socialization, the degree of pluralism in society, the political culture, the distribution of information and energy in society, communications patterns, social stratification, and even such things as the per capita number of telephones and radios, domestic and international flow of letters, telegrams, cables, or commerce manifested within any society.

---

ical party," for groups and organizations that would not meet a reasonable definition of the concept. On this point see the introductory and concluding chapters of Joseph LaPalombara and Myron Weiner, eds. *Political Parties and Political Development* (Princeton, 1966).

There is thus more than a little truth to Sartori's complaint that systems theorists, functionalists or otherwise, have taken politics out of political science and have obscured the critically important fact that political institutions and political leaders constitute independent factors that manage to shape not merely the environment and some of the "ecological" factors but the operation and development of the political system (or parts thereof) itself.[23] Recent developments suggest that there is belated recognition of this problem, as witness the growing frequency with which we now read of the necessity of dealing more intensively with research on the "output" side of political systems. For all societies, that output side will include legislation, administration, and adjudication—the stuff of government from time immemorial, which remains the same old wine no matter how many new bottles theory produces or how many new labels one puts on bottles, old or new. It is in part because this is so that I believe theoretical parsimony and manageable, reasonably rigorous empirical research in comparative politics require greater attention to "partial systems," or a "segmented approach" to theory and research. That this orientation to political science can never logically be the limit of our professional concerns will be apparent from my concluding statement in this article. But any brief for the emphasis on partial systems in comparative politics necessarily requires some specification of how we might proceed and what problems are inherent in the choices we make.

COMPARATIVE RESEARCH ON SEGMENTS OF POLITICAL SYSTEMS

A segmented or partial-system approach to comparative analysis may be institutionally or behaviorally focused, morphological or analytical in its intention and execution. Comparisons may involve a search for similarities or for differences among nation-states regarding those aspects of the political system that constitute the focus of attention. Or the comparative enterprise may involve a more dynamic focus, such as that of identifying the determinants over time of aspects of the political process and discernible changes that occur in it. Today, for example, there is widespread and still growing interest in something called "political development," which, however the term is defined, involves an attempt to test whether specific institutional, behavioral, and process modifications within the polity can be related associatively (or causally) to similar or differing but empirically identifiable factors.[24]

Such comparative research may or may not relate to theories concerning whole political systems. It may or may not be based on a carefully articu-

23. See Giovanni Sartori, *Parties and Party Systems* (forthcoming).

24. The literature on "political development" is too vast to cite. The interested reader should consult the bibliography in R. T. Holt and J. Turner, *The Political Basis of Economic Development* (New York, 1966), and the excellent bibliographical essay in C. E. Black, *The Dynamics of Modernization* (New York, 1966).

lated and integrated set of propositions to be tested in two or more settings. Good research would require an understanding and specification of precisely what it is that is being compared and to what end. Now the end of any given piece of comparative research may and does vary considerably. How are laws made or enforced? How do formal occupants of political roles acquire them? What range of political participation is open to what segments of a nation's population and on the basis of what criteria? In what proportion of the problem-solving activities of society are formal institutions of government involved and in what way? What kinds of political decisions are centrally made, geographically diffused, hierarchically stratified, formally restricted to government officials or more widely shared— and through what sorts of patterned arrangements? What kinds of people "govern" formally, informally?

Clearly, the number of such questions we might pose for any nation is quite large, perhaps unlimited. It is this understanding, together with the fact that we must choose among the questions about which data will be accumulated, that naturally leads many scholars to insist that choice be disciplined by theory and theory-related propositions. Differently put, the caveat would read that neither a general, miscellaneous collection of facts about a political system nor the restriction of fact-gathering activity to narrow-gauge problems that lend themselves to rigorous, laboratory-type experimental controls is acceptable procedure in comparative politics. Moreover, both structure-functionalism and political science's disillusionment with past emphasis on the collection of legalistic, formalistic data about governmental institutions extend this caveat to fact-gathering about the "obvious" political institutions of any society. The overshadowing question we must all respond to therefore is, So what? This question compels us to ask what light our findings will shed on the *dynamics* of a political system.

Ideally, responses to the "so what" query would relate data-gathering and subsequent analysis to general theories pertaining to whole systems. For reasons I have already touched upon, we are a long way from such a desirable relationship between empirical research and theoretical formulations. At a somewhat more modest level of expectations, research on aspects of two or more political systems should be organized around a set of theoretical propositions relating to the *segment* of the total system that constitutes the focus for empirical scrutiny. Here too, however, the danger of bogging down in "general theories" of organizational behavior, decision-making, conflict, institutional development, or change is very great, and it is just as likely that scholasticism will infect our discussions of partial systems as it is that it will (and has) infected our treatment of whole systems.[25]

25. The work of Simon and March on complex organizations, and an emergent "theory of the firm," are examples of whole-systems theories that are meant to apply to segments of the broader phenomena to which organizations (such as the specific organization called the "firm") relate. Equally influential in this development has been

The seemingly verbal but really efficacious solution to this dilemma is Merton's now classic discussion of theories of the middle range. As Merton's discussion is applied to either whole systems or partial systems, I take it to mean that empirical research in the social sciences should avoid a theoretical fishing expedition and pretentious, impossible attempts to "test," say, the propositions generated out of Parsons' four-sector description of society and its subsystems. More specifically, Merton seems to be saying that comparative research is likely to be trivial unless the propositions we are probing empirically give us some (perhaps intuitive) reason to suppose that our findings will make the creation of general theories less impressionistic or deductive than they now so obviously are.[26]

It seems to me that the discipline might best proceed by formulating the kinds of theoretical propositions I believe Merton has in mind and restricting these propositions for the moment to institutions and institutional processes that are clearly, directly, and intimately involved in the political process. Such choice, I believe, is not dictated merely by considerations of parsimony; it is dictated as well by a growing realization that we are, as I have already noted, oversupplied with general theory and much more poverty-ridden not only regarding systematic empirical research but also regarding the possession of the most rudimentary kind of information on which the success of the enterprise of a modern comparative politics must finally rest.

Let me take a moment to illustrate some of what I have in mind.

One of the great problems we confront in comparative politics today is that of the enormous imbalance in the amount of subsystemic or partial-systemic information available for the United States, on the one hand, and the rest of the world, on the other. We speak of the West as containing political systems emanating from a common philosophical-historical tradition, little realizing that many of the things we would want and wish to know about the political processes of Western societies are simply not yet available to us. Our generalizations thus remain gross observations, obscur-

---

the broad field of macroeconomics, whose growing impact on political science I shall comment on below. Each of these approaches encounters considerable difficulty when it is meant to facilitate comparative analysis across space and time. Nevertheless, it is manifestly the case that administrative, organizational, and economic theory offers better "paradigms" for political science than does anything thus far generated by sociology, the sister discipline that has attracted the greatest interdisciplinary attention from political scientists.

26. This point cannot be overstressed. Useful general or macrolevel theory in political science is likely to be made possible in the degree that the knowledge accumulated about important aspects of the political process is (1) precise, (2) rigorously comparative, and (3) generated on the basis of explicit hypotheses to be tested (i.e., negated). What will emerge from badly phrased research problems, imprecise concepts, obscurity of empirical indicators, inadequate attention to problems of comparisons across space and time, and incorrect inference are general theories reflecting all of these shortcomings, and more.

ing or ignoring the more subtle aspects of political systems that seem to emanate from a common historical-philosophical matrix. To be sure, we know more, say, about the politics of England than of Egypt, of France than of Vietnam, of Germany than of China. But anyone who attempts to muster information involving the simplest comparisons among Western nation-states quickly discerns that the gap remains great and is in no wise closed by general theoretical constructs that beg certain relationships and processes presumed to be typical of Western political systems. For non-Western nations the situation is immensely worse, and we should not obscure this important fact by pointing to dazzling arrays of aggregative statistical data available for well over a hundred countries.[27]

Because our knowledge regarding the political systems of non-Western societies was very limited indeed, and because literally dozens of such systems emerged as nation-states only following World War II, we badly needed and have greatly benefited from works dealing with whole systems in Africa and Asia. At their best, such works provide a needed general orientation to the kinds of phenomena of interest to the political scientist, as well as a great many generalizations that have enriched the kinds of questions we now raise for comparative treatment.[28]

Nevertheless, we must secure more, and more reliable, information about segments of these political systems before we can hope to push the enterprise of comparative politics much beyond its present essentially impressionistic stage. I find it instructive, for example, that political scientists are loath to make high-flown generalizations about the American political sys-

27. It must be noted that my objection here cannot be met by the pat response that we must do the best we can with the data we have or, more directly put, that some data are better than no data at all. It seems apparent, given many publications of recent years, that (1) "theories" and propositions about political systems are too often *governed* by aggregative data "out there" in the public domain; (2) comparative matrices or tables of aggregative information about nation-states are constructed on the basis of sources that, as it turns out, rarely publish "all the news that's fit to print"; (3) error in the reporting of much of this information is probably more often systematic than random and therefore a cause of great concern, not easily diminished by asking the question, "What would it look like if we assume, say, a 25 percent error one way or another?"; and (4) the use of highly sophisticated mathematical-statistical methodologies on such data almost inevitably leads the reader to believe that the findings are "real." On the radically uneven flow and availability of information about nation-states, see Wilbur Schramm, *Mass Media and National Development: The Role of Information in the Developing Countries* (Stanford, 1964), esp. Chs. 2–3. On the perfectly fantastic failure to diffuse even what reliable research information we may already possess, see Everett M. Rogers, *Diffusion of Innovations* (New York, 1962).

28. One important result of postwar political research in Africa, Asia, and Latin America is the recognition by many scholars of those areas that it is now necessary to return to Western political systems, both for testing propositions about contemporary political institutions and behavior and for reusing Western historical data to analyze in more systematic ways the evolution of Western political systems. In this regard, C. E. Black's *Dynamics of Modernization* is very instructive reading, indeed.

tem (the one about which we have the greatest amount of information) while they will at the slightest stimulus generalize about large-scale societies in Africa, Asia, and Latin America, concerning which our lack of historical and contemporary information is perhaps the most striking thing we can say.

Filling these gaps is obviously essential. Doing so requires, I believe, attention to segments of political systems, whether these segments be institutional or behavioral in nature, whether their choice does or does not clearly relate to the validation or illumination of general systemic theories.[29] The comparative study of legislatures, public administrative systems, or political parties will serve as examples.

The comparative study of legislatures might range from the most traditional kind of formalistic and legalistic description of national legislatures and the legislative process to the most controlled kind of experimentation in legislative behavior, if, as is almost never the case in political science, the research site could be stringently controlled and manipulated. What we have by way of research findings today runs an interesting gamut of approaches; except at the most primitive level of post-factum comparisons, almost none of what we have has emerged from comparative research designs. At best, we are learning more things about more legislatures which relate to common theoretical concerns with such other things as decision-making models, coalition behavior, conflict management, the role of parties and interest groups in legislative behavior, and the patterns of leadership and followership in such complex organizations.

I do not mean to sound excessively pessimistic here. Surveying literature, it is apparent that we have come far from earlier studies that naturally focused on legalistic analyses, in part because that was the easiest and also (lest we forget) an important way to begin. For many countries where roll-

---

29. I cannot overstress the problem of the information gap. In a field where I have done considerable fieldwork—interest-group organization and behavior—I can testify that the amount of even straight descriptive information about the so-called developed societies of the West is extremely limited. No one in Italy has yet produced a full-scale study of one or more interest groups; German scholars have published a few articles and a book or two; for France, the work of Jean Meynaud remains striking for its lack of intellectual company. Only in England have there been more than a few books in the field published, and these tend to treat interest groups morphologically and as pathological phenomena. Some items that the reader may want to consult for illustrative purposes in this field are Jean Meynaud, *Les Groupes de pression en France* (Paris, 1958); Joseph LaPalombara, *Interest Groups in Italian Politics* (Princeton, 1964); J. D. Stewart, *British Pressure Groups* (Oxford, 1958); Henry Ehrmann, *Organized Business in France* (Princeton, 1957); James M. Clark, *Teachers and Politics in France* (Syracuse, 1967); S. E. Finer, *Anonymous Empire: A Study of the Lobby in Great Britain* (London, 1959); Harry Eckstein, *Pressure Group Politics* (Stanford, 1960); Myron Weiner, *The Politics of Scarcity: Public Pressure and Political Response in India* (Chicago, 1960); Richard F. Hamilton, *Affluence and the French Worker in the Fourth Republic* (Princeton, 1967). Most of the scholars cited here are American. Compare these studies with the literature on American interest groups cited in Harmon Zeigler, *Interest Groups in American Society* (Englewood Cliffs, 1964).

call votes are recorded, we have studies analyzing such things as party cohesion, the relationship between issues and voting or coalition patterns, and constituency-legislator relationships. Access to committee proceedings now means greater attention to variations in behavior from one legislative setting to another. From countries where direct interviewing of lawmakers is possible, we begin to get interesting information about personality and behavior, about the legislator's role, his self-perception, his views of third persons and organizations, even some information emerging from the administration of TAT's and Rokeach Dogmatism Scales. We know more than we ever did about career patterns and recruitment to legislative positions, about the social, economic, and professional characteristics of lawmakers, and about how and why these characteristics have changed or remained stable over time.[30]

One can produce a similar roll call of interesting studies for such institutions as bureaucracy, political parties, and interest groups. In each of

30. For England and the United States there are many "traditional" works, some of them of the highest quality, on the national legislature. The works of Walter Bagehot, Lord Campion, A. V. Dicey, Herman Finer, and Sir Ivor Jennings come quickly to mind for England. Works by Herman Finer, Carl J. Friedrich, and others have also served the United States well, as have more recent studies by scholars such as Donald Matthews, Gordon Baker, Dwaine Marvick, and James D. Barber. But once we leave these two countries, we are confronted once more with an enormous information gap. Giovanni Sartori's *Il parlamento italiano* (Naples, 1963) is an important exception, as is G. P. Gooch's now classic *The French Parliamentary System* (New York, 1935). Duncan MacRae, Jr. *Parliamentary Parties and Society in France, 1946-1958* (New York, 1967), is a groundbreaking (even if somewhat defective) work.

Article-length studies on the French legislature have been published by P. Campbell, "The French Parliament," *Public Administration* (1953); M. Debré, "Trois characteristiques du système parlementaire," *Revue française de science politique* (March 1955); and by Mattei Dogan, whose prolific works are too numerous to cite but can be found in the *Revue française de science politique* (1953, 1957), the *Revue française de sociologie* (1961, 1965), and other journals. Lewis Edinger, "Continuity and Change in the Background of German Decision-Makers," *Western Political Quarterly*, XIV (March 1961), 17–36, and "Post-totalitarian Leadership: Elites in the German Federal Republic," *American Political Science Review*, LIV (March 1960), 58–82; Otto Kirchheimer, "The Composition of the German Bundestag, 1950," *Western Political Quarterly*, III (December 1950), 590–601; Gerhard Loewenberg, "Parliamentarism in West Germany: The Functioning of the Bundestag," *American Political Science Review*, LV (March 1961), 87–102; and a few others have treated Germany. Gerhard Loewenberg's *Parliament in the German Political System* (Ithaca, 1967) is a splendid example of the kind of information and analysis of partial political systems of which we are so desperately in need. But except for these and studies of a few other countries we have a dearth of data, and almost none of the work that exists was *designed* as comparative study. We need, therefore, at both the national and local levels of many countries the kind of sophisticated, rigorously ordered and executed comparative work represented by Wahlke et al. *The Lesgislative System*. This volume clearly indicates how much that is useful we can in fact derive from comparative studies of segments of political systems.

these institutional sectors there are enormous gaps; for other institutions such as the courts, the military, the police, and local governments, our information is fragmentary at best, almost never susceptible to reasonably systematic comparisons across more than a few societies. A recent effort to organize a seminar on comparative legislative and electoral organization and behavior led me first to restrict the countries encompassed to the United States, Britain, Germany, France, and Italy. Then, as most who read these words will appreciate, the available data for continental European countries were found to be extremely limited, produced in relatively recent years by a very small handful of scholars. To be sure, the situation is improving, as European scholars themselves begin to fill in the gaps and as greater collaborative efforts involve Europeans and Americans in jointly designed and executed comparative studies. However, we remain some distance from even a minimally acceptable comparative data base for the most developed countries of the world, and no handbooks of "soft" or "hard" aggregate data should be permitted to obscure this elemental fact unless their relevance to *political science* can be unequivocally demonstrated.

To summarize, those political scientists who claim that we are deluged with randomly chosen empirical studies have never attempted, as I see it, to assess the nature of all of the supposed information we have about the political systems and processes of the West. Regardless of the range of our linguistic skill and the resources of American libraries, it is frequently impossible to come by the most elemental information about the political institutions of other countries. If this is the case, it is obvious that we are often depending on impressions that may or may not be accurate. General theories that proceed on the assumption that we *do* know much about similar institutions and processes the world over can only compound the chaos and confusion we begin with.

Thus, one of the most pressing reasons for increasing research attention to segments of political systems is the basic information gap and our need for filling it before we can subject general theoretical formulations to empirical confrontation. But other persuasive reasons can be adduced. One of these is that we must greatly increase the number of persons in other countries who are engaged in comparative political research. As excellent as their individual studies may be, we cannot depend for our knowledge of Ghana or Nigeria, Burma or India, Argentina or Chile on the small number of American—or in some cases European or indigenous—scholars who have been concerned with the political systems of such countries. We are moving in the direction of combining collaborative research and training in the comparative study of social and political systems. Such collaboration should eventually result in increased numbers of Asians, Africans, and Latin Americans who contribute to our storehouse of knowledge. The diffusion of the social sciences—certainly of comparative political science—is better served if initial joint endeavors focus on systematic work on segments of political systems rather than on speculative theorizing about whole systems which would be, at best, supported by empirical impressions rather than by what would pass for acceptable evidence.[31]

Another reason for focusing on partial-system analyses is that such foci better lend themselves to the articulation and testing of middle-range propositions. For any of the institutions normally accepted as intimately involved in the governmental process, we can produce a large number of interesting and important propositions which, while not designed to validate general theory, would permit us to make more universally applicable generalizations when validated in a wide range of nation-states. I might add that such propositions need not be strictly tied to political institutions, but might relate instead to decision-making models, analytic functional categories, or formulations concerning the relationship of personality or other psychological variables to organizational or individual behavior.

A third possible rationale for a narrower, more limited research focus is that it might bring comparative politics somewhat closer to policy-related problems. Now, I am aware that the profession has not yet settled the question of the proper scope of political science and that more than ever before political scientists insist that the profession's scientific concern is with the *process* rather than the *content* of politics or political policies.[32] Although this is not the place to try to explore that kind of thorny issue in any detail, it is necessary to stress that I do not accept the notion that our concern is

31. For a detailed treatment of this problem, see my "Social Science in Developing Countries: A Problem in Acculturation," a paper presented at the 1965 Annual Meeting of the American Political Science Association, Washington, D.C. (mimeographed). This paper is available in Spanish as "La ciencia social en los paises en desarrollo: Problema de culturización," *Revista española de la opinión pública* (July–December 1967), pp. 9–43.

32. The most recent organized effort to reexplore what it is political scientists should do, and how, is James C. Charlesworth, ed. *A Design for Political Science: Scope, Objectives, and Methods,* Monograph 6, American Academy of Political and Social Science (Philadelphia, 1966). Regarding the specific matter of proper scope, Vernon Van Dyke, in his "The Optimum Scope of Political Science," ibid., pp. 1–17, makes a balanced case for greater attention to policy content. My colleague Frederick W. Watkins presents a telling case for emphasis on process, all the more striking in my view in that as a distinguished scholar of "political thought" Watkins might have been expected to emphasize the "content" side. See ibid., pp. 28–33, for Watkins' statement, as well as for the lively conference discussion that follows.

A much broader (our-house-has-many-mansions) view of the discipline's scope, particularly in the field of comparative politics of new nations, is offered by David E. Apter, "Comparative Government: Developing New Nations," in the special issue of the *Journal of Politics* entitled "American Political Science: Advance of the Discipline, 1948–1968." Apter's appraisal of many of the trends I am discussing here is both more generous than mine and, I think, more sanguine. [David Apter and Charles Andrain, "Comparative Government: Developing New Nations," *Journal of Politics*, XXX (May 1968), 372–416.]

exclusively process and that, therefore, only those theories and methods that give us better leverage on process are worthy of our attention. One reason for stressing the concern of the political scientist with content or policy is that to acknowledge the issue openly helps to guard against several related dangers. The first of these dangers is the assumption that political science—at least in its American configuration—now has the means of rising above "vulgar ideology" and qualifies for co-optation into the "scientific culture." A second danger would be that of "social engineering," which requires no further elaboration here. A third danger is that of indiscriminate fishing expeditions for data and what I would call the methodological escalation that accompanies such fishing. The political process, divorced from issues or problems of policy, has become such a huge umbrella concept (particularly in view of what various abstract theories now suggest are integral parts of that process) that I fear such a narrow focus would further the well established trend toward removing politics from political science. In short, I would urge that reasons such as these can lead us to make parsimonious decisions regarding what it is the political scientist studies.

An additional reason for explicit concern with policy is that those who are policymakers (as well as our students!) expect modern political science to be aware of—and, they hope, to have something professional to say about—the kinds of major problems that beset domestic and international societies. In voicing such expectations, it seems to me that policymakers are simply articulating what most of us implicitly understand, namely, that more than any other field of intellectual or scientific endeavor, the social sciences are *not* expected to be merely "pure" sciences. I find it both amusing and ironic therefore that those social scientists who speak with increasing authority to policymakers concerned with problems of nation-building or community development are the economists and sociologists, with only a sprinkling of political scientists—and even these few often turn out to be experts in an outmoded, formalistic "science" of public administration.

To be sure, experts in comparative politics are sometimes also consulted, often with mutually distressing results. The policymaker strongly needs the "translated" implications of theory and research, and the political scientist —product of an intellectual pecking order that enthrones abstract theory— wishes to stress the elegance of theory and typology, leaving it to the men of public affairs to make what they can of such things. It is in such confrontations, I suspect, that the astronomical distance between our theoretical preachments and our research behavior is most strikingly revealed, and this may in part account for our tendency to shun policy matters.

The field of public administration will nicely illustrate these last observations. We are now painfully aware that Max Weber's ideal-typical formulations about authority systems and the patterns of public administration that accompany them will not take up much beyond morphological description of empirical situations. We are equally aware that prescriptions about administrative organization that derive in part from Weberian notions of bureaucracy and in part from the norms of democratic Western politics will not take policymakers far in resolving problems of social, economic, and political development. One result of such understanding is that a number of political scientists interested in comparative administration have tried to devise new general theories of administration or to construct typologies of political systems around certain differentiating criteria that are administratively based. Viewed as attempts at integrating a previously narrow, mechanistic, culture-bound public administration into the somewhat broader and dynamic field of comparative politics, such efforts merit approbation. Judged by the measure of their contribution to a general theory of politics or indeed of administrative systems, such endeavors strike me as being of limited utility.[33]

Where they are not essentially restatements of Weber *cum* Talcott Parsons, they are nevertheless formulated at levels of abstraction that defy systematic comparative empirical application and, for this reason among others, are of little or no use to those confronting problems of policy or operational alternatives. What differences ideal-typical morphologies adduce are generally gross; more often than not, both the typologies devised and the "models" of administrative systems suggested are based not so much on rigorously accumulated historical or contemporary evidence but on illustrations that are themselves often impressionistic. Where attempts are made to draw operational axioms from such theorizing and model-building, they often result in curious justifications for whatever patterns of power and administration actually emerge in the so-called developing areas. Above all, the classification of nation-states by the presumed characteristics of their administrative systems and the related conditions (environmental or ecological) that surround them generally results in grouping in single categories precisely those nation-states *among* which we must make refined discrimi-

33. Pioneers in the effort to transform the field of public administration would certainly include Fritz Morstein-Marx, whose *The Administrative State* (Chicago, 1957) reveals a debt to Max Weber unmarred by complex abstractions and excessive neologisms, and Fred W. Riggs, whose voluminous contributions have been instructive, even when readers such as myself have found some of his concepts and formulations unnecessarily complex. Riggs, however, has also been the prime mover in the development of the Comparative Administration Group, whose "Occasional Papers" series now includes a number of theoretical contributions of a less than cosmic ambition which are certain to have a favorable impact on the comparative analysis of public administrative systems. The first batch of the better "Occasional Papers" appears in John D. Montgomery and William J. Siffin, eds. *Approaches to Development: Politics, Administration and Change* (New York, 1966). I have attempted to provide an assessment both of theoretical models in comparative administration and of theories of political development in my "Public Administration and Political Change: A Theoretical Overview," in Charles Press and Alan Arian, eds. *Empathy and Ideology* (Chicago, 1967).

nations before we can say anything meaningful of a probabilistic or pre-scriptive nature. In this sense, such efforts serve us no better than massive accumulations of aggregate statistical data about the world's nation-states. Such data, when subjected to high-powered, computerized analytical techniques, reveal that, say, Sweden, the United States, Britain, France, Germany, Norway, and Italy are in one group and the Sudan, Nepal, Afghanistan, and Tanzania are in another. The only striking difference I have thus far detected in these two approaches is that the former, more impressionistic approach is cheaper and probably more sophisticated.

Are we then to abandon both grand theorizing and the accumulation of empirical data about bureaucratic systems? Clearly this is not what I in-tend, and the sector of public administration, as a *segment* of any political system, is one of the areas in which our empirical research can be fruitfully guided both by very important public policy concerns and by theoretical propositions of the middle range. We know, for example, that economic development in almost all of the developing nations is likely to take place largely through public-sector intervention and that participation of govern-ment in such change-directed enterprises is also increasingly true of the so-called developed countries. Now, while there is a vast and growing litera-ture produced by economists on the subject of planning, political scientists have paid scant attention to this problem, except at the fringes of macro-analytic considerations. To be sure, as our theoretical outpourings shift from the "input" side (where the political system seems to be abjectly dependent on elements in the evironment) to the "output" side (where the institutions of government are recognized as having an independent impact on societal change), we begin to read about the "capacities" or "capabilities" of the political system to achieve certain ends in view, including economic change or growth. No doubt it is important to acknowledge that political institutions must confront a wide range of challenges, from the maintenance of order and the provision of social overhead capital to the provision of the kinds of material and human resources (and their integrated coordination) that planned economic growth requires. In this regard, a number of writers have served us well, although I think it once again striking that several of these are either economists or sociologists and that with rare exceptions political scientists have been late in moving in this direction.[34]

34. Gabriel Almond, whose earlier work profoundly influenced important shifts in theoretical and empirical focus in comparative politics, is one political scientist who has led the movement toward greater attention to the output side of the polity. See, for example, his "Political Systems and Political Change," *American Behavioral Sci-entist*, VI (June 1963), 3–10, an early formulation that emerged from discussion and a summer seminar held by the SSRC Committee on Comparative Politics; and his more recent "A Developmental Approach to Political Systems," *World Politics*, XVII (January 1965), 183–214. There are other political scientists who could be named here as well, and an interesting overview of their writings and the approaches to the com-

Much more needed, however, is greater attention by political scientists, whose analyses of a partial political system such as the bureaucracy either explicate the bureaucratic process of a range of nation-states in considerable detail or deal comparatively with public administrative systems in terms of their problem-solving capabilities. One important step in this direction is the series of studies of national planning now under way at the University of Syracuse, under the general editorial direction of Bertram M. Gross. These national studies involve political scientists almost exclusively; the specific intention of Professor Gross is to begin to fill the most serious gap in the planning literature, namely, the differences in the phenomena that are introduced by specific segments or aspects of the political system in different national settings.[35]

I have also recently suggested a comparative approach to the relationship of public administration to problems of development which would involve the construction of national profiles. Such profiles would require gathering data on the developmental and related goals of national policymakers, the total and kind of administrative resources available for goal attainment, the obstacles to the creation of whatever additional resources are needed for goal achievement, and the potentiality for overcoming such obstacles and of achieving a reasonable balance between goals and administrative capacity.[36] Although some of the data categories implicit in such profiling would have

---

parative study of public administration they represent is included in Ferrel Heady, *Public Administration: A Comparative Perspective* (Englewood Cliffs, 1966).

Nevertheless, it is significant that much of both the theoretical and the empirical leadership in public administration during that last fifteen or twenty years has been provided by the work of sociologists such as S. N. Eisenstadt, *The Political Systems of Empire* (London, 1963); Berger, *Bureaucracy and Society;* Robert K. Merton et al. *Reader in Bureaucracy* (Glencoe, 1952); Reinhard Bendix, *Nation-building and Citizenship* (New York, 1964); Philip Selznik, *TVA and the Grass Roots* (Berkeley, 1949); and Michel Crozier, *The Bureaucratic Phenomenon* (Chicago, 1964); and by the work of economists such as Joseph J. Spengler, in his jointly edited *Administrative and Economic Development in India* (Durham, N.C., 1963); A. H. Hanson, *Public Enterprise and Economic Development* (London, 1959); and Bert F. Hoselitz, "Levels of Economic Performance and Bureaucratic Structures," in Joseph LaPalombara, ed. *Bureaucracy and Political Development* (Princeton, 1963).

35. Volumes thus far published in the Gross series include: B. Akzin and Y. Dror, *Israel: High Pressure Planning* (1966); H. J. Arndt, *West Germany: Politics of Non-Planning* (1966); D. E. Ashford, *Morocco-Tunisia: Politics and Planning* (1965); F. G. Burke, *Tanganyika: Preplanning* (1965); J. Friedman, *Venezuela: From Doctrine to Dialogue* (1965); E. E. Hagen and S. F. T. White, *Great Britain: Quiet Revolution in Planning* (1966); J. LaPalombara, *Italy: The Politics of Planning* (1966); and R. J. Shafer, *Mexico: Mutual Adjustment Planning* (1966).

36. See Joseph LaPalombara, "Alternative Strategies for Developing Administrative Capabilities in Emerging Nations," *CAG Occasional Papers* (Bloomington, 1966).

to be treated somewhat impressionistically, other potentially available aggregative data are available to the persistent researcher. Such data would *not* be accumulated merely because they are (correctly or falsely) easily available. Rather, decisions as to where to put data-accumulating energies to work would rest very firmly on the articulation of empirically manageable hypotheses about the relationship of public administrative organization to behavior and development. I should add that, if the hypothetical statements involve concepts as broad as the "pattern variables" of Talcott Parsons, the empirical indicators that would permit scoring—or, I would hope, ranking—each country on each of these variables as they apply to any sector of society would have to be carefully and persuasively specified, if for no other reasons than that (1) the number of such indicators approaches infinity and (2) the same indicators can be scored (rightly!) on both sides of each dichotomy. We have pretty much exhausted scholastic exercises about how much achievement orientation, universalism, collectivity orientation, effective neutrality, and functional specificity is required, say, by economic modernity or a public administrative apparatus conducive to economic modernization. For those who would in fact try to validate aspects of Parsons' theories, profiling of the kind I have in mind might be one potentially workable first step. Even for such scholars, I contend, an empirical focus on a segment of a whole political system would offer greater hope of succeeding than would a research enterprise requiring attention to the whole system.

To repeat and to reemphasize, I remain skeptical about the whole-systems approach to comparative politics. My skepticism can perhaps best be summarized by two quotations from Heinz Eulau, whose capacity to deal imaginatively and creatively with partial-systems analysis is well known. About whole-systems approaches, Eulau remarks, with characteristic bluntness, "But I have yet to read—and that includes David Easton's new book—a systems analysis from which one can derive testable propositions about politics."[37] About the most perplexing empirical problem of gathered data about whole systems, he remarks, "How does one observe whole systems? Well, I would say that at the present time it is impossible to observe whole systems. I think that one can make statements about whole systems, large systems, but that one cannot observe them."[38]

I would add that partial-systems comparisons of the kind I have discussed above should over time reduce the magnitude of the observational problem. In such a future, typologies will be less abstract, much more induced by reflections about empirical information gathered from carefully designed research on segments of the larger political system. No one will deny the desirability of a probabilistic theory of politics. My claim is that the quan-

37. In Charlesworth, *Design for Political Science*, p. 202.

38. Ibid., p. 207.

tum leap to the whole-systemic level of theorizing has tended to degenerate into a neo-scholasticism from which escape itself is difficult, and when escape occurs at all, it involves return to partial-systems analysis anyway.

It may well be, however, that we are at the threshold of scholasticism disguised as mathematical models, where the explicit acknowledgement of the model builders is precisely that their central assumptions have no correspondence to reality and that, indeed, it is probably better than such correspondence *not* be a major consideration for an indeterminate period. Some who urge such a line of disciplinary development ask us to look to macroeconomics for guidance—and for impressive evidence for the proposition that striking scientific advances can emerge from oversimplifications, even deliberate distortions, of the conditions of the real world. Now and then, the very same scholars who once borrowed indiscriminately from sociological theory (only to discover that the emperor was if not naked then strikingly ill-clad) now propose to do essentially the same thing with the sister discipline of economics. The same fears about the inferior status of political science vis-à-vis sociology expressed twenty years ago are now voiced regarding economics. Thus William Mitchell, a close student of Talcott Parsons, warns us that political scientists run the risk of being swallowed up by those adept at cost-benefit analysis, welfare economics, optimal rationality in goal achievement, exchange models, and systems theory.[39] For Mitchell, the emerging paradigm will be that of the new political economy. Accommodating to it will mean that "theory will become increasingly logical, deductive and mathematical. In terms of its content, we will make increasing use of economic theory, games theory, decision theory, welfare economics and public finance. Models of political systems, analogous to types of economies and markets, will proliferate."[40]

Although it may be an easy, even a logical, step from general theories in sociology to the sort of brave new world the quotation above suggests, such a step is neither inevitable nor desirable if we bear in mind the relative stage of development in the field of economics at which the breakthroughs discussed by Mitchell occurred. I refer primarily to the solid empirical base economics had established, as opposed to the very problematical empirical base that is currently available in political science and to which I have repeatedly alluded above. As Sidney Verba has aptly phrased our current dilemma, "In the old days, graduate students may have gone into the field as barefoot empiricists. Today they go equipped with elaborate systems models. . . . The barefoot empiricists didn't know where they might step; the recent students have trouble getting their feet on the ground."[41]

Verba suggests the need for a "disciplined configurative approach" and

39. "Shape of Political Theory," pp. 18–19.

40. Ibid., p. 19.

41. "Some Dilemmas," p. 117.

appropriately cites recent work by Dahl and others as strikingly promising examples of what he has in mind.[42] Such work is indicative of what I mean by less-than-whole-systems approaches to theory and research in comparative politics. Where the theories, models, and methods of sister social science disciplines can be used unequivocally to further this kind of work, they should be borrowed and adapted without hesitation. It seems to me that herein lies the road map to a stronger political science.

PROBLEMS IN COMPARATIVE RESEARCH

It is easy enough to say that comparative research at a partial-systems level will contribute to an additive political science. But this approach, too, is not free of perplexing problems, some of which affect comparative politics in general, some of which are highlighted or intensified when they emerge in partial-systems analysis.

If something less than the whole system is to be analyzed, the first and most obvious problem to resolve is that of the most important unit of analysis. My reference here is not to the *empirical* unit of analysis; I assume that the individual, whether singly viewed or conceptualized in some group or associational context, is the commonly accepted empirical unit in the behavioral sciences. I am referring instead to the *theoretical* unit of analysis, on the assumption that attention must be accorded this matter if we are to avoid falling into the crudest kinds of bare-facts empiricism, which Verba describes.

The question of the appropriate theoretical unit should not be confused with the question of the independent or dependent variables in comparative research. Presumably, the determination of what theoretically causes, influences, or is associated with what and for what reasons comes at a later stage in the design of comparative research. Nor should we confuse "concrete-structural" or institutional units with what I intend here by theoretical. We may, for example, decide that we want to compare fruit, noncitrus fruit, or just apples, but for each of these choices it is necessary to indicate the focus (or foci) of central theoretical concern. Likewise for politics, we might choose to study legislatures, legislative committees, or individual legislators, but it is important to specify the single or combined set of theoretical concerns around which the comparative analysis will proceed. Such a procedure is required for several reasons, not the least important of which is that of anticipating the messiness caused by confusion as to the *level* of analysis at which research itself is directed.[43] So many of

42. Robert A. Dahl, ed. *Political Oppositions in Western Democracies* (New Haven, 1966). See particularly the important theoretical implications Dahl is able to draw from the country-focused chapters, Chs. 11, 12, and 13.

43. One of the most lucid discussions of Harold Lasswell's contributions to interlevel relationships and theories about them will be found in Heinz Eulau, "The Maddening Methods of Harold D. Lasswell," *Journal of Politics*, XXX (February 1968), 17ff.

our generalizations about the political process move with apparent randomness from the micro- to the macroanalytic levels that it is difficult to know if, for example, a study of legislative roles is designed to test psychological theories about individual or group behavior or sociological theories about the institution of the legislature itself. In short, we must be clear about occasions when we intend that the study, say, of individual legislators or of legislative committees is intended to reflect in a microcosmic context propositions we intend to apply to all legislatures, to all representative organizations, to all complex organizations, to the political system, or to society.

Clearly, the social sciences now provide a rich variety of theoretical units of analysis, from the broad actor-situation framework associated with Parsons to voting behavior, where the act of voting can be conceptualized as illuminating theories about social stratification, communications, personality, functionalism, decision-making, and so on. The most widely utilized theoretical unit in political science seems to me to be decision-making, and a vast range of the research output of the discipline can be subsumed under this rubric. Thus whether we ask who governs, or who gets what, or who has how much power and how it is exercised, or what variables seem to account for executive or judicial behavior, or what things are associated with distributions of popular votes, or how political elites respond to historical crises, we seem to be posing as the generalized (independent or dependent) variable the making of political—or politically relevant—decisions.[44]

To be sure, a great many political scientists are also interested in change, that most elusive of the dynamic phenomena with which the social sciences are concerned. In today's world, we want to know as never before what difference (e.g., in reaching the takeoff stage in economics or in assuring legislative stability) a single-party or multiparty system will make in Ghana or Brazil, Thailand or Turkey. The problem of how bureaucrats should be trained or the question of whether the upper reaches of a bureaucracy should be dominated by generalists or specialists, "guardians" or "technocrats" as some would put it, has never been more poignantly posed than by political leaders and their followers who *say* that they simultaneously wish to promote man's material well-being and his freedom and dignity. For those who view "political development" as the increasing ability of political leaders and institutions to bring about a greater congruence between the demands they confront and the policy output of government, it is clear that,

44. It is this fact, I believe, that leads many political scientists to conclude that rational-choice models, decision-making under conditions of uncertainty, and other formulations in economics are potentially of great utility in our own discipline. This is probably true to the degree that the theoretical unit of analysis remains something smaller than the political system. Indeed, it may be necessary to narrow the focus still further either geographically and culturally, or by constraining specifications for such concrete structures as legislatures, political parties, and bureaucracies, or both.

at one level of analysis, concern with both how in specific concrete situations decisions are made and what their consequences are is inevitable.

Decision-making of course provides a very broad analytical framework and thus does not in itself resolve all of the difficulties inherent in comparative analysis. Yet it seems to me that one of its striking advantages is that it directs our attention to the outputs of the political system and therefore to those aspects of the political process that involve formal governmental institutions. Functionalism, on the other hand, leads one to emphasize the input side of the equation and therefore tends to push research in the direction of such problems as the political socialization of children, which, while intrinsically interesting as an area of research, appears far removed from the political process. I might add that political socialization research, when it does not concentrate on subjects who are probable future political elites, begs an important question, for we have not yet succeeded in demonstrating persuasively the assumption that the values, beliefs, and attitudes about politics and political institutions held by the mass population make a difference.

To put this in terms of parsimony, I would prefer comparative research on decision-making in legislatures, bureaucracies, political parties—even in elections—to comparative studies of the political socialization of children, patterns of recruitment to governmental roles, or the system of communication found within society. It isn't that these latter concepts or analytical units are uninteresting or irrelevant; it is that their relationship to the output side of the governmental system remains extremely tenuous since we know very little in fact about what goes on in the "black box" that stands between inputs and outputs.

A decision-making focus for the political scientist should also involve, again for reasons of parsimony, a preference for obviously political institutional settings for research. Case studies of trade unions may perhaps illuminate the political process, but political parties should be preferred if they are accessible. If trade unions are placed under the empirical microscope, propositions about them should relate to some specific aspect of the political process and, more stringently, the making of political decisions. To put it simply, it is necessary to respond, in more than vague or seemingly logical or self-evident terms, regarding the relevance of research into nonpolitical institutions for the operation of political institutions themselves.

The selection of institutions or "concrete structures" as the focus for research leads to a second major problem, namely, that of the comparability of the units selected for analysis. At least the problem appears at first blush to be more complex than would be the case were we to limit our focus, say, to decision-making, influence and power, or communications and leadership in complex organizations. But, unless we are easily stampeded by what turn out to be scholastic objections by structure-functionalists, it is plain enough that whether we begin with concrete institutions or with an analytical concept such as decision-making, the problem of comparability is essentially the same.

Let me push ahead with this line of argument to identify what is really our concern.

It is possible that for some the central theoretical concern would be simply the process or structure of choice—of reaching decisions—in a wide range of simple or complex formal organizations. For such scholars, I believe, comparative research would require the most careful specification and control over certain characteristics or parameters of organizations before meaningful comparative analysis could proceed. Assuming a large enough sample of organizations, such scholars would want to control for such things as the number of decision-makers involved, the structure of their values and belief systems, the degree of hierarchy and the administrative differentiation of roles, the structure of internal communications, the patterns of authority and sanctions prevailing, the degree and kind of discretion or permissiveness in role performance, the relationship to the organizationally external environment, and so on. Organizational theorists are able to draw research samples for comparative analysis from a much wider universe than is available to the political scientist—assuming for the moment that the political scientist is interested in politics or, in the case at hand, in *political* decision-making.

This being the case, it seems apparent that the political scientist will by the empirical nature of things be less able to "control" for certain parametric conditions than will the person interested in organizational behavior. The comparative research that the latter does may greatly assist the political scientist in designing a research project and in interpreting his findings. We cannot ask of the political scientist, however, that he adhere to the same canons of maximizing the comparability of his research endeavors that would be justified for a scientist whose unit of analysis (in this case, decision-making) encompasses a much wider range of empirical research sites and units.

Essentially the same argument can be developed where, say, the theoretical unit of analysis is some aspect of functionalism and where the institutional focus for comparative research is the interest group or pressure group. As the work in the interest-group field attests, pains are taken to abstract from the infinite number of group settings in which the individual might be found something called a *political* interest group. We need not be concerned with whether John Dewey was correct in insisting that all human behavior is group-centered behavior or whether A. F. Bentley was right in declaring that if we fully comprehend the "group process" we will have comprehended everything about politics. But if the interest group is to be made the institutional focus for comparative political science, we must be concerned with the designation of criteria that will permit us to abstract from a potentially infinite number of groups those that are of particular interest to the political scientist and that meet the minimal definitional requirements for inclusion in a sample.

The comparative political scientist, then, must be guided in the first instance by the central concern of what is political or what is relevant to the political process. If this is so, then it is unlikely, except at the very abstract and empirically unmanageable level I have associated with whole-system analysis, to satisfy David Easton's thought that "ideally, the units [of analysis] would be repetitious, ubiquitous, and uniform, molecular rather than molar."[45] Where, as in systemic and functional analysis, the units seem to be ubiquitous and uniform, they are molar rather than molecular; where, as in group analysis and decision-making, they appear to be molecular, they are not uniform and probably not minutely repetitious. The dilemma of comparative politics is that we have available neither the particles of physics nor the prices of economics to subject to comparative analysis.

The problem of the comparability of the unit of analysis is also apparent when one chooses such a seemingly obvious structure as political parties as the focus for research. The political party appears to be a deceptively stable unit concerning which much comparative research can be generated. Yet, it is obvious that little attention has been paid to the question of what we are comparing when we look analytically at parties either across national or cultural boundaries or within a single nation-state. Voting studies in the United States, for all of their display of methodological rigor, have ignored this problem, as indeed they have ignored most questions of theoretical relevance until recently.[46] Nevertheless, those who purport to execute comparative research here must arrive at some workable and consistent definition of a political party if comparison is to involve oranges, apples, or lemons rather than a shifting combination of these, or fruit salad. Myron Weiner and I in a recent published symposium attempt to respond to this problem. It is perhaps indicative of the state of the discipline that a number of our colleagues are willing to accept as political parties any organization whose leaders or members call it such, without regard to questions of definition.[47] Such resolutions will not do. Whenever we elect a segmented or

45. "The Current Meaning of Behavioralism in Political Science," in Charlesworth, *Limits of Behavioralism*, p. 17.

46. The studies of Michigan's Survey Research Center have been notoriously rich in methodology and poor in theory. The last volume published by the group, however, represents a first and welcome step toward correcting this deficiency. See Angus Campbell, Philip Converse, Warren E. Miller, and Donald E. Stokes, *The American Voter* (New York, 1960).

47. See LaPalombara and Weiner, *Political Parties*, Ch. 1. Cf. the chapter by Rupert Emerson in the same volume.

partial-systemic approach to comparative politics the kinds of problems I have raised here must be confronted and reasonably resolved.

A third major problem—not confined to partial-systems analysis—involves the nature of evidence, or the kind of data we will or can gather to validate or invalidate propositions. This problem is much too vast to pretend to treat here in detail, but a number of observations will help to round out my discussion.

First, I believe it is essential to recognize that some of the hypothesis-validating data we will need may not be easily accessible or may not be available to us at all. This is true in part because of the areas of secrecy that surround many aspects of the governmental process. It is true as well because many nation-states look with increasing reservation, even hostility, on the overseas legions of American field researchers whom the golden era of social science seems to have spawned in this country.

If we can't get at the relevant or most immediately relevant facts, what then? Why, we may have to delay—even give up—some lines of research endeavor. We may also *cautiously* choose to do the best we can with what data we have. But this alternative means that we must be scrupulously and not self-deceivingly careful about the data-collecting choices we make and, above all, that we must not gather and store data simply because they are available. It may be, as some claim, that the availability of vast quantities of data, when processed by high-speed computers, will help us to generate new theories, but for the present I find that expectation very doubtful.[48]

Second, it is necessary to pay more than lip service to the observation that much of the empirical information extant is not really comparable and that equally much of the seemingly reliable aggregate statistical data are just simply poor, that is, unreliable and subject to errors whose nature is neither random nor known to us. Such data, far from illuminating the processes we wish to study comparatively, may actually be totally misleading.

Karl Deutsch, recognizing that the quality of data available to us may vary considerably, ingeniously suggests that computers and new techniques of data analysis may help us to overcome the limitations inherent, say, in survey data or aggregate statistical information. If this is so, he says, "truth may be thought of as a relationship between different streams of evidence. A statement is more likely to be true, the larger the number of different classes or kinds of evidence that confirm it."[49] This statement

48. On this point, see Karl W. Deutsch, "Recent Trends in Research Methods in Political Science," in Charlesworth, *Design for Political Science*, pp. 149–178 [reprinted below in the present chapter]. I do not share Deutsch's enthusiasm about future data collections, and I must confess that, until I am assured that some of the questions of comparability I have raised in this article have been more adequately resolved, Deutsch's surmise that by 1975 we may have fifty million IBM cards of "data" to draw upon is much more disquieting than it is reassuring. See ibid., pp. 152–157.

49. Ibid., p. 158.

seems reasonable enough, so long as our decisions about the kinds of data to collect are made on the basis of propositions to be tested comparatively, and so long as we do not deliberately include in our "stream of evidence" data we suspect or know to be highly unreliable.

Third, as we look to history for information that will help us to confirm or disconfirm propositions about political development, we must have a better sense than we now do about what specific institutions (such as parliaments, interest groups, or political parties) have meant over time in a single society. To say this merely to restate the central problem implicit in comparative history as opposed to loose historical chronology: On the basis of what reasonably applicable criteria can we periodize societies, the institutions they give rise to, and the impact in turn of such institutions on subsequent development? Among the many useful purposes this exercise will serve is that of permitting those of us who are interested in a *particular* kind of political development, namely, some variation of the democratic state, to identify with greater precision generalized or generalizable "stages" of democratic institutional development.[50]

CONCLUSION

Is emphasis on partial political systems or segments of them the only legitimate or fruitful enterprise for contemporary comparative politics? Clearly not, nor have I intended to make this claim. If we are as far as most of us suspect from a probabilistic theory of politics, any closure at this time regarding levels of analysis, sectors of the political system to be analyzed or methods to be utilized in the testing of theoretical formulations would be premature—childish in the fullest sense of that term.

My purpose rather has been twofold. First, it seems to me that we ought to be absolutely candid about what it is political scientists do. This requires above all that we not be deluded into thinking we have evolved empirical general theories when what we have are a number of impressionistic, somewhat abstract, deceptively empirical observations strung together by logical statements of varying elegance. Nor should we fail to note that while ideal-typical constructs need not respond to empirical reality on a one-to-one basis, they are not very useful if we understand the real world to involve an infinite mixture of characteristics that ideal-typical constructs artificially separate, with no provision of insights into possible or probable "mixes."

50. With sobering reservations about the difficulty of relating historical data to propositions about political change, I have attempted this exercise with regard to administrative change in England, France, and Germany over a period of several centuries. See my "Values and Ideologies in the Administrative Evolution of Some Western Constitutional Systems," in Ralph Braibanti, ed. *Political and Administrative Development* (Durham, N.C., 1968).

My second purpose has been to suggest a rationale for emphasis on partial systems in comparative politics. Because I assume such research may serve to correct certain deficiencies in whole-systems analysis and therefore open the way to better empirical theories of whole systems, I may be said to have come full circle. That is, I am sure that most political scientists cannot—in any case, should not—sidestep concern with the difference their discoveries make in our understanding of how whole political systems are evolved, maintained, and changed.

If I want to profile the conditions that impinge on the public administrative problem-solving capability of a sample of nation-states, my interest in doing so must surely reflect more than an abstracted scientific curiosity about the relationship between human, physical, and organizational resources and goal attainment. If some of my colleagues design a comparative project aimed at probing the relationship between a long list of social, personality, cultural, and related variables and what occurs in a national legislature, they are surely interested in something more than decision-making or power relationships in *that* kind of an organization. If another group of my colleagues seeks to understand the circumstances under which those who formally occupy religious or military roles begin to impinge directly on the policy output of political structures, they are interested in something more than the conditions that bring functionally specific institutions and role occupants into aspects of the political process where they presumably have no "logical" or "theoretically acceptable" place.

My point here is double-edged. First, I would agree with David Easton that, in considering the so-called behavioral revolution, we should distinguish very carefully between the impetus toward better methodology and the thrust toward better empirical theory. However we may resolve how to attack the problems of concern to the political scientist, we should understand that a second aspect of all of the ferment we are experiencing involves not merely method but a concern with theories about how political systems evolve and function and what influences them. But I would go beyond Easton to insist that for most political scientists there is great concern for the "good society" and for how we can devise the set of institutions and behaviors that will enhance its development and survival. While such normative concerns must be distinguished from the more scientific concerns of comparative political science, they should not be submerged to the point at which we delude ourselves in thinking that we are more like physicists or pathologists than we are. We are, I believe, the intellectual descendants of Aristotle, proud to share some of his major concerns and perhaps humbled by the understanding that we have not advanced our scientific understanding of political organization and behavior much beyond what he elucidated in the *Politics*.

The Comparative Method
and Methodological Developments

Comparative Politics and the Comparative Method*

Arend Lijphart

Among the several fields or subdisciplines into which the discipline of
political science is usually divided, comparative politics is the only one
that carries a methodological instead of a substantive label. The term "comparative politics" indicates the *how* but does not specify the *what* of the
analysis. The label is somewhat misleading because both explicit methodological concern and implicit methodological awareness among students of
comparative politics have generally not been very high.[1] Indeed, too many
students of the field have been what Giovanni Sartori calls "unconscious
thinkers"—unaware of and not guided by the logic and methods of empirical science, although perhaps well versed in quantitative research techniques. One reason for this unconscious thinking is undoubtedly that the
comparative method is such a basic, and basically simple, approach, that a
methodology of comparative political analysis does not really exist. As
Sartori points out, the other extreme—that of the "overconscious thinkers,"
whose "standards of method and theory are drawn from the physical

*This article is a revised version of a paper presented to the Round Table
Conference on Comparative Politics of the International Political Science
Association, held in Turin, Italy, September 10–14, 1969. I am very grate-
ful to David E. Apter, Donald T. Campbell, Robert A. Dahl, Giuseppe Di
Palma, Harry Eckstein, Lewis J. Edinger, Samuel E. Finer, Galen A. Irwin,
Jean Laponce, Juan J. Linz, Stefano Passigli, Austin Ranney, Stein Rokkan,
Dankwart A. Rustow, and Kurt Sontheimer for their comments and sug-
gestions on earlier drafts of the paper, which were very helpful in the
preparation of the revision.

1. The reverse applies to the relatively new field of "political behavior": its name
indicates a substantive field of inquiry, but especially the derivative "behaviorism"
has come to stand for a general approach or set of methods. See Robert A. Dahl,
"The Behavioral Approach in Political Science: Epitaph for a Monument to a Successful Protest," *American Political Science Review*, 55 (December 1961), pp. 763–
72.

Reprinted from American Political Science Review, *LXV (September 1971), 682–693,*
by special permission of the author and the publisher.

paradigmatic sciences"—is equally unsound.[2] The purpose of this paper is to contribute to "conscious thinking" in comparative politics by focusing on comparison as a method of political inquiry. The paper will attempt to analyze not only the inevitable weaknesses and limitations of the comparative method but also its great strengths and potentialities.

In the literature of comparative politics, a wide variety of meanings is attached to the terms "comparison" and "comparative method." The comparative method is defined here as one of the basic methods—the others being the experimental, statistical, and case study methods—of establishing general empirical propositions. It is, in the first place, definitely a *method*, not just "a convenient term vaguely symbolizing the focus of one's research interests."[3] Nor is it a special set of substantive concerns in the sense of Shmuel N. Eisenstadt's definition of the comparative approach in social research; he states that the term does not "properly designate a specific method . . . , but rather a special focus on cross-societal, institutional, or macrosocietal aspects of societies and social analysis."[4]

Second, the comparative method is here defined as *one* of the basic scientific methods, not *the* scientific method. It is, therefore, narrower in scope than what Harold D. Lasswell has in mind when he argues that "for anyone with a scientific approach to political phenomena the idea of an independent comparative method seems redundant," because the scientific approach is "unavoidably comparative."[5] Likewise, the definition used here differs from the very similar broad interpretation given by Gabriel A. Almond, who also equates the comparative with the scientific method: "It makes no sense to speak of a comparative politics in political science since if it is a science, it goes without saying that it is comparative in its approach."[6]

Third, the comparative method is here regarded as a *method of discovering empirical relationships among variables,* not as a method of measure-

2. Giovanni Sartori, "Concept Misformation in Comparative Politics," *American Political Science Review,* 64 (December 1970), p. 1033.

3. Arthur L. Kalleberg, "The Logic of Comparison: A Methodological Note on the Comparative Study of Political Systems," *World Politics,* 19 (October 1966), p. 72.

4. Shmuel N. Eisenstadt, "Social Institutions: Comparative Study," in David L. Sills, ed., *International Encyclopedia of the Social Sciences* (New York: Macmillan & Free Press, 1968), Vol. 14, p. 423. See also Eisenstadt, "Problems in the Comparative Analysis of Total Societies," *Transactions of the Sixth World Congress of Sociology* (Evian: International Sociological Association, 1966), Vol. 1, esp. p. 188.

5. Harold D. Lasswell, "The Future of the Comparative Method," *Comparative Politics,* 1 (October 1968), p. 3.

6. Gabriel A. Almond, "Political Theory and Political Science," *American Political Science Review,* 60 (December 1966), pp. 877–78. Almond also argues that comparative politics is a "movement" in political science rather than a subdiscipline. See his "Comparative Politics," in *International Encyclopedia of the Social Sciences,* Vol. 12, pp. 331–36.

ment. These two kinds of methods should be clearly distinguished. It is the latter that Kalleberg has in mind when he discusses the "logic of comparison." He defines the comparative method as "a form of measurement"; comparison means "nonmetrical ordering," or in other words, ordinal measurement.[7] Similarly, Sartori is thinking in terms of measurement on nominal, ordinal (or comparative), and cardinal scales when he describes the conscious thinker as "the man that realizes the limitations of not having a thermometer and still manages to say a great deal simply by saying hot and cold, warmer and cooler."[8] This important step of measuring variables is logically prior to the step of finding relationships among them. It is the second of these steps to which the term "comparative method" refers in this paper.

Finally, a clear distinction should be made between *method* and *technique*. The comparative method is a broad-gauge, general method, not a narrow, specialized technique. In this vein, Gunnar Heckscher cautiously refers to "the method (or at least the *procedure*) of comparison,"[9] and Walter Goldschmidt prefers the term comparative *approach*, because "it lacks the preciseness to call it a method."[10] The comparative method may also be thought of as a basic research *strategy,* in contrast with a mere tactical aid to research. This will become clear in the discussion that follows.

THE EXPERIMENTAL, STATISTICAL, AND COMPARATIVE METHODS

The nature of the comparative method can be understood best if it is compared and contrasted with the two other fundamental strategies of research; these will be referred to, following Neil J. Smelser's example, as the *experimental* and the *satistical* methods.[11] All three methods (as well as

7. Kalleberg, *op. cit.,* pp. 72–73; see also pp. 75–78.

8. Sartori, *op. cit.,* p. 1033. See also Paul F. Lazarsfeld and Allen H. Barton, "Qualitative Measurement in the Social Sciences: Classification, Typologies, and Indices," in Daniel Lerner and Harold D. Lasswell, eds., *The Policy Sciences: Recent Developments in Scope and Method* (Stanford: Stanford University Press, 1951), pp. 155–92.

9. Gunnar Heckscher, *The Study of Comparative Government and Politics* (London: Allen and Unwin, 1957), p. 68 (italics added).

10. Walter Goldschmidt, *Comparative Functionalism: An Essay in Anthropological Theory* (Berkeley: University of California Press, 1966), p. 4. Oscar Lewis argues that "there is no distinctive 'comparative method' in anthropology," and that he therefore prefers to discuss "comparisons in anthropology rather than the comparative method." See his "Comparisons in Cultural Anthropology" in William L. Thomas, Jr., ed., *Current Anthropology* (Chicago: University of Chicago Press, 1956), p. 259.

11. For the idea of discussing the comparative method in relation to these other basic methods, I am indebted to Neil J. Smelser's outstanding and most enlightening article

certain forms of the case study method[12]) aim at scientific explanation, which consists of two basic elements: (1) the establishment of general empirical relationships among two or more variables,[13] while (2) all other variables are controlled, that is, held constant. These two elements are inseparable: one cannot be sure that a relationship is a true one unless the influence of other variables is controlled. The *ceteris paribus* condition is vital to empirical generalizations.

The experimental method, in its simplest form, uses two equivalent groups, one of which (the experimental group) is exposed to a stimulus while the other (the control group) is not. The two groups are then compared, and any difference can be attributed to the stimulus. Thus one knows the relationship between two variables—with the important assurance that no other variables were involved, because in all respects but one the two groups were alike. Equivalence—that is, the condition that the *cetera* are indeed *paria*—can be achieved by a process of deliberate randomization. The experimental method is the most nearly ideal method for scientific explanation, but unfortunately it can only rarely be used in political science because of practical and ethical impediments.

An alternative to the experimental method is the statistical method. It entails the conceptual (mathematical) manipulation of empirically observed data—which cannot be manipulated situationally as in experimental design—in order to discover controlled relationships among variables. It handles the problem of control by means of *partial correlations*. For instance, when one wants to inquire into the relationship between political participation and level of education attained, one should control for the influence of age

---

"Notes on the Methodology of Comparative Analysis of Economic Activity," *Transactions of the Sixth World Congress of Sociology* (Evian: International Sociological Association, 1966), Vol. 2, pp. 101–17. For other general discussions of the comparative method, see Léo Moulin, "La Méthode comparative en Science Politique," *Revue Internationale d'Histoire Politique et Constitutionelle*, 7 (January–June, 1957), pp. 57–71; S. F. Nadel, *The Foundations of Social Anthropology* (London: Cohen and West, 1951), pp. 222–55; Maurice Duverger, *Méthodes des Sciences Sociales* (3rd ed., Paris: Presses Universitaires de France, 1964), pp. 375–99; John W. M. Whiting, "The Cross-Cultural Method," in Gardner Lindzey, ed., *Handbook of Social Psychology* (Reading, Mass.: Addison-Wesley, 1954), Vol. 1, pp. 523–31; Frank W. Moore, ed., *Readings in Cross-Cultural Methodology* (New Haven, Conn.: HRAF Press, 1961); Adam Przeworski and Henry Teune, *The Logic of Comparative Social Inquiry* (New York: Wiley-Interscience, 1970); and Robert T. Holt and John E. Turner, "The Methodology of Comparative Research," in Holt and Turner, eds., *The Methodology of Comparative Research* (New York: Free Press, 1970), pp. 1–20.

12. The case study method will be discussed below.

13. Eugene J. Meehan, *The Theory and Method of Political Analysis* (Homewood, Ill.: Dorsey Press, 1965). He expresses this idea in three short sentences: "Science seeks to establish relationships" (p. 35); "Science . . . is empirical" (p. 37); "Science is a generalizing activity" (p. 43).

because younger generations have received more education than older generations. This can be done by partialing—dividing the sample into a number of different age groups and looking at the correlations between participation and education within each separate age group. Paul F. Lazarsfeld states that this is such a basic research procedure that it "is applied almost automatically in empirical research. Whenever an investigator finds himself faced with the relationship between two variables, he immediately starts to 'cross-tabulate,' i.e., to consider the role of further variables."[14]

The statistical method can be regarded, therefore, as an approximation of the experimental method. As Ernest Nagel emphasizes, "every branch of inquiry aiming at reliable general laws concerning empirical subject matter must employ a procedure that, if it is not strictly controlled experimentation, has the essential logical functions of experiment in inquiry."[15] The statistical method does have these essential logical functions, but it is not as strong a method as experimentation because it cannot handle the problem of control as well. It cannot control for all other variables, merely for the other *key* variables that are known or suspected to exert influence. Strictly speaking, even the experimental method does not handle the problem of control perfectly, because the investigator can never be completely sure that his groups are actually alike in every respect.[16] But experimental design provides the closest approximation to this ideal. The statistical method, in turn, is an approximation—not the equivalent—of the experimental method. Conversely, one can also argue, as Lazarsfeld does, that the ex-

14. Paul F. Lazarsfeld, "Interpretation of Statistical Relations as a Research Operation," in Lazarsfeld and Morris Rosenberg, eds., *The Language of Social Research: A Reader in the Methodology of Social Research* (Glencoe, Ill.: Free Press, 1955), p. 115. However, control by means of partial correlations does not allow for the effects of measurement error or unique factor components; see Marilynn B. Brewer, William D. Crano and Donald T. Campbell, "Testing a Single-Factor Model as an Alternative to the Misuse of Partial Correlations in Hypothesis-Testing Research, *Sociometry*, 33 (March 1970), pp. 1–11. Moreover, partial correlations do not resolve the problem of the codiffusion of characteristics, known in anthropology as "Galton's problem"; see Raoul Naroll, "Two Solutions to Galton's Problem," *Philosophy of Science*, 28 (January 1961), pp. 15–39, and Przeworski and Teune, *op. cit.*, pp. 51–53.

15. Ernest Nagel, *The Structure of Science* (New York: Harcourt, Brace, and World, 1961), pp. 452f.

16. For instance, if the groups are made equivalent by means of deliberate randomization, the investigator knows that they are alike with a very high degree of probability, but not with absolute certainty. Moreover, as Hubert M. Blalock, Jr., states, so-called "forcing variables" cannot be controlled by randomization. See his *Causal Inferences in Nonexperimental Research* (Chapel Hill: University of North Carolina Press, 1964), pp. 23–26. In general, Blalock emphasizes "the underlying similarity between the logic of making causal inferences on the basis of experimental and nonexperimental designs" (p. 26).

perimental method constitutes a special form of the statistical method, but only if one adds that it is an especially potent form.[17]

The logic of the comparative method is, in accordance with the general standard expounded by Nagel, also the same as the logic of the experimental method. The comparative method resembles the statistical method in all respects except one. The crucial difference is that the number of cases it deals with is too small to permit systematic control by means of partial correlations. This problem occurs in statistical operations, too; especially when one wants to control simultaneously for many variables, one quickly "runs out of cases." The comparative method should be resorted to when the number of cases available for analysis is so small that cross-tabulating them further in order to establish credible controls is not feasible. There is, consequently, no clear dividing line between the statistical and comparative methods; the difference depends entirely on the number of cases.[18] It follows that in many research situations, with an intermediate number of cases, a combination of the statistical and comparative methods is appro-

17. Lazarsfeld, "Interpretation of Statistical Relations as a Research Operation," p. 119. Talcott Parsons makes a similar statement with regard to the comparative method: "Experiment is . . . nothing but the comparative method where the cases to be compared are produced to order and under controlled conditions." See his *The Structure of Social Action* (2nd ed., New York: Free Press, 1949), p. 743. Another advantage of the experimental method is that the time variable is controlled, which is especially important if one seeks to establish causal relationships. In statistical design, this control can be approximated by means of the panel method.

18. In order to highlight the special problems arising from the availability of only a small number of cases, the comparative method is discussed as a distinct method. Of course, it can be argued with equal justice that the comparative and statistical methods should be regarded as two aspects of a single method. Many authors use the term "comparative method" in the broad sense of the method of multivariate empirical, but nonexperimental, analysis, *i.e.*, including both the comparative and statistical methods as defined in this paper. This is how A. R. Radcliffe-Brown uses the term when he argues that "only the comparative method can give us general propositions." (Brown, "The Comparative Method in Social Anthropology," *Journal of the Royal Anthropological Institute of Great Britain and Ireland*, 81 [1951], p. 22.) Émile Durkheim also follows this usage when he declares that "comparative sociology is not a particular branch of sociology; it is sociology itself, in so far as it ceases to be purely descriptive and aspires to account for facts." (Durkheim, *The Rules of Sociological Method*, translated by Sarah A. Solovay and John H. Mueller, [8th ed., Glencoe, Ill.: Free Press, 1938], p. 139.) See also the statements by Lasswell and Almond cited above. Rodney Needham combines the two terms, and speaks of "large-scale statistical comparison," *i.e.*, the statistical method. (Needham, "Notes on Comparative Method and Prescriptive Alliance," *Bijdragen tot de Taal-, Land- en Volkenkunde*, 118 [1962], pp. 160–82.) On the other hand, E. E. Evans-Pritchard uses exactly the same terminology as used by Smelser and as adopted in this paper, when he makes a distinction between "small-scale comparative studies" and "large-scale statistical ones." See his *The Comparative Method in Social Anthropology* (London: Athlone Press, 1963), p. 22.

priate. Where the cases are national political systems, as they often are in the field of comparative politics, the number of cases is necessarily so restricted that the comparative method has to be used.

From the vantage point of the general aims and the alternative methods of scientific inquiry, one can consider the comparative method in proper perspective and answer such questions as the following, raised by Samuel H. Beer and by Harry Eckstein: Can comparison be regarded as "the social scientist's equivalent of the natural scientist's laboratory?"[19] and: "Is the comparative method in the social sciences . . . really an adequate substitute for experimentation in the natural sciences, as has sometimes been claimed?"[20] The answer is that the comparative method is not the equivalent of the experimental method but only a very imperfect substitute. A clear awareness of the limitations of the comparative method is necessary but need not be disabling, because, as we shall see, these weaknesses can be minimized. The "conscious thinker" in comparative politics should realize the limitations of the comparative method, but he should also recognize and take advantage of its possibilities.

THE COMPARATIVE METHOD: WEAKNESSES AND STRENGTHS

The principal problems facing the comparative method can be succinctly stated as: many variables, small number of cases. These two problems are closely interrelated. The former is common to virtually all social science research regardless of the particular method applied to it; the latter is peculiar to the comparative method and renders the problem of handling many variables more difficult to solve.

Before turning to a discussion of specific suggestions for minimizing these problems, two general comments are in order. First, if at all possible one should generally use the statistical (or perhaps even the experimental) method instead of the weaker comparative method. But often, given the inevitable scarcity of time, energy, and financial resources, the intensive comparative analysis of a few cases may be more promising than a more superficial statistical analysis of many cases. In such a situation, the most fruitful approach would be to regard the comparative analysis as the first stage of research, in which hypotheses are carefully formulated, and the statistical analysis as the second stage, in which these hypotheses are tested in as large a sample as possible.

In one type of comparative cross-national research, it is logically possible

19. Samuel H. Beer, "The Comparative Method and the Study of British Politics," *Comparative Politics*, 1 (October 1968), p. 19.

20. Harry Eckstein, "A Perspective on Comparative Politics, Past and Present," in Eckstein and David E. Apter, eds., *Comparative Politics: A Reader* (New York: Free Press of Glencoe, 1963), p. 3.

and may be advantageous to shift from the comparative to the statistical method. Stein Rokkan distinguishes two aims of cross-national analysis. One is the testing of *"macro* hypotheses" concerning the "interrelations of structural elements of total systems"; here the number of cases tends to be limited, and one has to rely on the comparative method. The other is *"micro* replications," designed "to test out in other national and cultural settings a proposition already validated in one setting."[21] Here, too, one can use the comparative method, but if the proposition in question focuses on individuals as units of analysis, one can also use the statistical method; as Merritt and Rokkan point out, instead of the "one-nation, one-case" approach, nationality can simply be treated as an additional variable on a par with other individual attributes such as occupation, age, sex, type of neighborhood, etc.[22] Terence K. Hopkins and Immanuel Wallerstein make a similar distinction between truly "cross-national studies" in which total systems are the units of analysis, and "multi-national but *cross-individual* research."[23]

The second general comment concerns a dangerous but tempting fallacy in the application of the comparative method: the fallacy of attaching too much significance to negative findings. The comparative method should not lapse into what Johan Galtung calls "the traditional quotation/illustration methodology, where cases are picked that are in accordance with the hypothesis—and hypotheses are rejected if one deviant case is found."[24] All cases should, of course, be selected systematically, and the scientific search should be aimed at probabilistic, not universal, generalizations. The erroneous tendency to reject a hypothesis on the basis of a single deviant case is rare when the statistical method is used to analyze a large sample, but in the comparative analysis of a small number of cases even a single deviant finding tends to loom large. One or two deviant cases obviously constitute a much less serious problem in a statistical analysis of very many cases than

21. Stein Rokkan, "Comparative Cross-National Research: The Context of Current Efforts," in Richard L. Merritt and Rokkan, eds., *Comparing Nations: The Use of Quantitative Data in Cross-National Research* (New Haven: Yale University Press, 1966), pp. 19–20. Rokkan specifically recommends the use of "paired comparisons" for this purpose; see his "Methods and Models in the Comparative Study of Nation-Building," in *Citizens, Elections, Parties: Approaches to the Comparative Study of the Processes of Development* (Oslo: Universitetsforlaget, 1970), p. 52.

22. Merritt and Rokkan, *op. cit.,* p. 193.

23. Terence K. Hopkins and Immanuel Wallerstein, "The Comparative Study of National Societies," *Social Science Information,* 6 (October 1967), pp. 27–33 (italics added). See also Przeworski and Teune, *op. cit.,* pp. 34–43.

24. He adds: "This is a very naive conception of social science propositions; if only perfect correlations should be permitted social science would not have come very far." Johan Galtung, *Theory and Methods of Social Research* (Oslo: Universitetsforlaget, 1967), p. 505. The functions of deviant case analysis will be discussed below.

in a comparative study of only a few—perhaps less than ten—cases. But it is nevertheless a mistake to reject a hypothesis "because one can think pretty quickly of a contrary case."[25] Deviant cases weaken a probabilistic hypothesis, but they can only invalidate it if they turn up in sufficient numbers to make the hypothesized relationship disappear altogether.[26]

After these introductory observations, let us turn to a discussion of specific ways and means of minimizing the "many variables, small N" problem of the comparative method. These may be divided into four categories:

(1) *Increase the number of cases as much as possible.* Even though in most situations it is impossible to augment the number of cases sufficiently to shift to the statistical method, any enlargement of the sample, however small, improves the chances of instituting at least some control.[27] Modern comparative politics has made great progress in this respect as a result of the efforts of the field's innovators to fashion universally applicable vocabularies of basic politically relevant concepts, notably the approaches based on Parsonian theory and Gabriel A. Almond's functional approach.[28] Such a restatement of variables in comparable terms makes many previously inaccessible cases available for comparative analysis. In addition to extending

25. W. J. M. Mackenzie, *Politics and Social Science* (Harmondsworth: Penguin Books, 1967), p. 52. I have been guilty of committing this fallacy myself. In my critique of Giovanni Sartori's proposition relating political instability to extreme multipartism (systems with six or more significant parties), one of my arguments consists of the deviance of a single historical case: the stable six-party system of the Netherlands during the interwar years. See Arend Lijphart, "Typologies of Democratic Systems," *Comparative Political Studies,* 1 (April 1968), pp. 32–35.

26. It is clearly incorrect, therefore, to argue that on logical grounds a probabilistic generalization can *never* be invalidated; cf. Guenter Lewy's statement: "To be sure, a finding of a very large number of . . . [deviant cases] would cast doubt upon the value of the proposition, but logically such evidence would not compel its withdrawal. The test of the hypothesis by way of a confrontation with empirical or historical data remains inconclusive." Lewy, "Historical Data in Comparative Political Analysis: A Note on Some Problems of Theory," *Comparative Politics,* 1 (October 1968), p. 109.

27. Furthermore, unless one investigates all available cases, one is faced with the problem of how representative one's limited sample is of the universe of cases.

28. On the necessity of establishing general concepts not tied to particular cultures, see Smelser, *op. cit.,* pp. 104–09; Nadel, *op. cit.,* pp. 237–38; Douglas Oliver and Walter B. Miller, "Suggestions for a More Systematic Method of Comparing Political Units," *American Anthropologist,* 57 (February 1955), pp. 118–21; and Nico Frijda and Gustav Jahoda, "On the Scope and Methods of Cross-Cultural Research," *International Journal of Psychology,* 1 (1966), pp. 114–16. For critiques of recent attempts at terminological innovation in comparative politics, see Sartori, "Concept Misformation in Comparative Politics"; Robert T. Holt and John M. Richardson, Jr., *The State of Theory in Comparative Politics* (Minneapolis: Center for Comparative Studies in Technological Development and Social Change, 1968); Robert E. Dowse, "A Functionalist's Logic," *World Politics,* 18 (July 1966), pp. 607–23; and Samuel E. Finer, "Almond's Concept of 'The Political System': A Textual Critique," *Government and Opposition,* 5 (Winter 1969–70), pp. 3–21.

the analysis geographically, one should also consider the possibilities of "longitudinal" (cross-historical) extension by including as many historical cases as possible.[29]

It was the promise of discovering universal laws through global and longitudinal comparisons that made Edward A. Freeman enthusiastically espouse the comparative method almost a century ago. In his *Comparative Politics,* published in 1873, he called the comparative method "the greatest intellectual achievement" of his time, and stated that it could lead to the formulation of "analogies . . . between the political institutions of times and countries most remote from one another." Comparative politics could thus discover "a world in which times and tongues and nations which before seemed parted poles asunder, now find each one its own place, its own relation to every other."[30] The field of comparative politics has not yet achieved —and may never achieve—the goals that Freeman set for it with such optimism. But his words can remind us of the frequent utility of extending comparative analyses both geographically and historically. (The value of this suggestion is somewhat diminished, of course, because of the serious lack of information concerning most political systems; for historical cases in particular this problem is often irremediable.)

(2) *Reduce the "property-space" of the analysis.* If the sample of cases cannot be increased, it may be possible to combine two or more variables that express an essentially similar underlying characteristic into a single variable. Thus the number of cells in the matrix representing the relationship is reduced, and the number of cases in each cell increased correspondingly. Factor analysis can often be a useful technique to achieve this objective. Such a reduction of what Lazarsfeld calls the "property-space" increases the possibilities of further cross-tabulation and control without increasing the sample itself.[31] It may also be advisable in certain instances to reduce the number of classes into which the variables are divided (for instance, by simplifying a set of several categories into a dichotomy), and thus to achieve the same objective of increasing the average number of cases per cell. The latter procedure, however, has the disadvantage of sacrificing a part of the information at the investigator's disposal, and should not be used lightly.

(3) *Focus the comparative analysis on "comparable" cases.* In this context, "comparable" means: similar in a large number of important charac-

29. Michael Haas, "Comparative Analysis," *Western Political Quarterly,* 15 (June 1962), p. 298n. See also Lewy, *op. cit.,* pp. 103–10.

30. Edward A. Freeman, *Comparative Politics* (London: Macmillan, 1873), pp. 1, 19, 302. See also Gideon Sjoberg's argument in favor of global comparative research: "The Comparative Method in the Social Sciences," *Philosophy of Science,* 22 (April 1955), pp. 106–17.

31. Lazarsfeld and Barton, *op. cit.,* pp. 172–75; Barton, "The Concept of Property-Space in Social Research," in Lazarsfeld and Rosenberg, *op. cit.,* pp. 45–50.

teristics (variables) which one wants to treat as constants, but dissimilar as far as those variables are concerned which one wants to relate to each other. If such comparable cases can be found, they offer particularly good opportunities for the application of the comparative method because they allow the establishment of relationships among a few variables while many other variables are controlled.[32] As Ralph Braibanti states, "the movement from hypothesis to theory is contingent upon analysis of the total range of political systems,"[33] but it is often more practical to accord priority to the focus on a limited number of comparable cases and the discovery of *partial* generalizations.

Whereas the first two ways of strengthening the comparative method were mainly concerned with the problem of "small N," this third approach focuses on the problem of "many variables." While the total number of variables cannot be reduced, by using comparable cases in which many variables are constant, one can reduce considerably the number of *operative* variables and study their relationships under controlled conditions without the problem of running out of cases. The focus on comparable cases differs from the first recommendation not only in its preoccupation with the problem of "many variables" rather than with "small N," but also in the fact that as a by-product of the search for comparable cases, the number of cases subject to analysis will usually be *decreased*. The two recommendations thus point in fundamentally different directions, although both are compatible with the second (and also the fourth) recommendation.

This form of the comparative method is what John Stuart Mill described as the "method of difference" and as the "method of concomitant variations." The method of difference consists of "comparing instances in which [a] phenomenon does occur, with instances in other respects similar in which it does not." The method of concomitant variations is a more sophisticated version of the method of difference: instead of observing merely the presence or absence of the operative variables, it observes and measures the quantitative variations of the operative variables and relates these to each other. As in the case of the method of difference, all other factors must be kept constant; in Mill's words, "that we may be warranted in inferring

32. Smelser, *op. cit.*, p. 113. Holt and Turner refer to this strategy as the process of "specification" (*op. cit.*, pp. 11–13). It is probably also what Eisenstadt has in mind when he mentions the possibility of constructing "special intensive comparisons of a quasi-experimental nature" (*op. cit.*, p. 424). See also Erwin K. Scheuch, "Society as Context in Cross-Cultural Comparison," *Social Science Information,* 6 (October 1967), esp. pp. 20–23; Mackenzie, *op. cit.*, p. 151; Fred Eggan, "Social Anthropology and the Method of Controlled Comparison," *American Anthropologist,* 56 (October 1954), pp. 743–63; and Erwin Ackerknecht, "On the Comparative Method in Anthropology," in Robert F. Spencer, ed., *Method and Perspective in Anthropology* (Minneapolis: University of Minnesota Press, 1954), pp. 117–25.

33. Ralph Braibanti, "Comparative Political Analytics Reconsidered," *Journal of Politics,* 30 (February 1968), p. 36.

causation from concomitance of variations, the concomitance itself must be proved by the Method of Difference."[34]

Mill's method of concomitant variations is often claimed to be the first systematic formulation of the modern comparative method.[35] It should be pointed out, however, that Mill himself thought that the methods of difference and of concomitant variations could not be applied in the social sciences because sufficiently similar cases could not be found. He stated that their application in political science was "completely out of the question" and branded any attempt to do so as a "gross misconception of the mode of investigation proper to political phenomena."[36] Durkheim agreed with Mill's negative judgment: "The absolute elimination of adventitious elements is an ideal which cannot really be attained; . . . one can never be even approximately certain that two societies agree or differ in all respects save one."[37] These objections are founded on a too exacting scientific standard—what Sartori calls "overconscious thinking." It is important to remember, however, that in looking for comparable cases, this standard should be approximated as closely as possible.

The area approach appears to lend itself quite well to this way of applying the comparative method because of the cluster of characteristics that areas tend to have in common and that can, therefore, be used as controls.[38] But opinions on the utility of the area approach differ sharply: Gunnar Heckscher states that "area studies are of the very essence of comparative government," and points out that "the number of variables, while frequently still very large, is at least reduced in the case of a happy choice of area."[39]

34. John Stuart Mill, *A System of Logic* (8th ed., London: Longmans, Green, Reader, and Dyer, 1872), Book III, chapter 8.

35. Nadel, *op. cit.*, pp. 222–23; Kenneth E. Bock, "The Comparative Method of Anthropology," *Comparative Studies in Society and History*, 8 (April 1966), p. 272.

36. Mill, *op. cit.*, Book VI, chapter 7; see also Book III, chapter 10.

37. Durkheim, *op. cit.*, pp. 129–30. But he hailed the method of concomitant variations, which he evidently interpreted to mean a combination of the statistical and comparative methods, as "the instrument par excellence of sociological research" (p. 132). See also François Bourricaud, "Science Politique et Sociologie: Réflexions d'un Sociologue," *Revue Française de Science Politique*, 8 (June 1958), pp. 251–63.

38. If the *area* approach is often preferable to research efforts with a global range in order to maximize comparability, the *era* approach may be preferable to longitudinal analysis for the same reason. Cf. the following statement by C. E. Black: "There is much greater value in comparing contemporary events and institutions than those that are widely separated in time. The comparison of societies or smaller groups that are concerned with reasonably similar problems is more likely to lead to satisfactory conclusions than comparisons between societies existing many centuries apart." Black, *The Dynamics of Modernization: A Study in Comparative History* (New York: Harper and Row, 1966), p. 39.

39. Heckscher, *op. cit.*, p. 88.

Roy C. Macridis and Richard Cox also argue that if areas are characterized by political as well as non-political uniformities, "the area concept will be of great value, since certain political processes will be compared between units within the area against a common background of similar trait configuration"; they cite Latin America as an example of an area offering the prospect of "fruitful intra-area comparison."[40] On the other hand, Dankwart A. Rustow declares in a recent article that area study is "almost obsolete," and he shows little faith in it as a setting for "manageable comparative study." He argues that "mere geographic proximity does not necessarily furnish the best basis of comparison," and furthermore that "comparability is a quality that is not inherent in any given set of objects; rather it is a quality imparted to them by the observer's perspective."[41] This is a compelling argument that should be carefully considered.

It is not true that areas reflect merely geographic proximity; they tend to be similar in many other basic respects. By means of an inductive process—a factor analysis of 54 social and cultural variables on 82 countries—Bruce M. Russett discovered socio-culturally similar groupings of countries, which correspond closely to areas or regions of the world as usually defined.[42] Comparability is indeed not inherent in any given area, but it is more likely within an area than in a randomly selected set of countries. It seems unwise, therefore, to give up the area approach in comparative politics. But two important provisos should be attached to this conclusion. First, the area approach can contribute to comparative politics if it is an aid to the comparative method, not if it becomes an end in itself. Otherwise, area study may indeed become "a form of imprisonment."[43] It is against

40. Roy C. Macridis and Richard Cox, "Research in Comparative Politics," *American Political Science Review*, 47 (September 1953), p. 654. See also John D. Martz, "The Place of Latin America in the Study of Comparative Politics," *Journal of Politics*, 28 (February 1966), pp. 57–80.

41. Dankwart A. Rustow, "Modernization and Comparative Politics: Prospects in Research and Theory," *Comparative Politics*, 1 (October 1968), pp. 45–47. Area study may also be criticized on the ground that, in the words of Dell G. Hitchner and Carol Levine, in *Comparative Government and Politics* (New York: Dodd, Mead, 1967): "Its very method of delimitation puts emphasis on what may be particular to a limited group of states, as opposed to the universal generalizations which fully comparative study must seek" (pp. 7–8). This argument has been answered above in terms of the need for partial generalizations as a first step. See also Braibanti, *op. cit.*, pp. 54–55.

42. Bruce M. Russett, "Delineating International Regions," in J. David Singer, ed., *Quantitative International Politics: Insights and Evidence* (New York: Free Press, 1968), pp. 317–52. See also Russett, *International Regions and the International System* (Chicago: Rand McNally, 1967).

43. George I. Blanksten, "Political Groups in Latin America," *American Political Science Review*, 53 (March 1959), p. 126. See also Sigmund Neumann, "The Comparative Study of Politics," *Comparative Studies in Society and History*, 1 (January 1959), pp. 107–10; and I. Schapera, "Some Comments on the Comparative Method in Social Anthropology," *American Anthropologist*, 55 (August 1953), pp. 353–61, esp. p. 360.

this danger that the thrust of Rustow's argument is directed. Second, the area approach should not be used indiscriminately, but only where it offers the possibility of establishing crucial controls. In this respect, some of the smaller areas may offer more advantages than the larger ones—Scandinavia, for example, which has barely been exploited in this manner, or the Anglo-American countries, which have received greater comparative attention (but which do not constitute an area in the literal sense).[44]

An alternative way of maximizing comparability is to analyze a single country diachronically. Such comparison of the same unit at different times generally offers a better solution to the control problem than comparison of two or more different but similar units (e.g., within the same area) at the same time, although the control can never be perfect; the same country is not really the same at different times. A good example of diachronic comparative analysis is Charles E. Frye's study of the empirical relationships among the party system, the interest group system, and political stability in Germany under the Weimar and Bonn Republics. Frye argues that "for the study of these relationships, Weimar and Bonn make a particularly good case [strictly speaking, *two* cases] because there are more constants and relatively fewer variables than in many cross-national studies. Yet the differences could hardly be sharper."[45]

Unless the national political system itself constitutes the unit of analysis, comparability can also be enhanced by focusing on intranation instead of internation comparisons. The reason is again the same: comparative intranation analysis can take advantage of the many similar national characteristics serving as controls.[46] Smelser illustrates the utility of this strategy with the example of a hypothetical research project on industrialization in Germany and Italy: "For many purposes it would be more fruitful to compare northern Italy with southern Italy, and the Ruhr with Bavaria, than it

44. See Seymour Martin Lipset, "The Value Patterns of Democracy: A Case Study in Comparative Analysis," *American Sociological Review,* 28 (August 1963), pp. 515–31; Robert R. Alford, *Party and Society: The Anglo-American Democracies* (Chicago: Rand McNally, 1963); Leslie Lipson, "Party Systems in the United Kingdom and the Older Commonwealth: Causes, Resemblances, and Variations," *Political Studies,* 7 (February 1959), pp. 12–31.

45. Charles E. Frye, "Parties and Pressure Groups in Weimar and Bonn," *World Politics,* 17 (July 1965), pp. 635–55. (The quotation is from page 637.) The postwar division of Germany also offers the opportunity of analyzing the effects of democratic versus totalitarian development against a similar cultural and historical background. See Ralf Dahrendorf, "The New Germanies: Restoration, Revolution, Reconstruction," *Encounter,* 22 (April 1964), pp. 50–58. See also Sylvia L. Thrupp, "Diachronic Methods in Comparative Politics," in Holt and Turner, eds., *The Methodology of Comparative Research,* pp. 343–58.

46. Heckscher, p. 69; Heinz Eulau, "Comparative Political Analysis: A Methodological Note," *Midwest Journal of Political Science,* 6 (November 1962), pp. 397–407. Rokkan, too, warns against the "whole-nation" bias of comparative research ("Methods and Models," p. 49).

would be to compare Germany as a whole with Italy as a whole. These two countries differ not only in level of industrialization, but also in cultural traditions, type of governmental structure, and so on." The advantage of intra-unit comparison is that inter-unit differences can be held constant. "Then, having located what appear to be operative factors in the intra-unit comparisons, it is possible to move to the inter-unit comparisons to see if the same differences hold in the large."[47]

As Juan J. Linz and Amando de Miguel point out, a particularly promising approach may be the combination of intranation and internation comparisons: "The comparison of those sectors of two societies that have a greater number of characteristics in common while differing on some crucial ones may be more fruitful than overall national comparisons."[48] An illustrative example of this approach in the political realm is suggested by Raoul Naroll: "If one wishes to test theories about the difference between the cabinet and the presidential systems of government . . . one is better advised to compare Manitoba and North Dakota than to compare Great Britain and the United States, since with respect to all other variables Manitoba and North Dakota are very much alike, while Great Britain and the United States have many other differences."[49]

(4) *Focus the comparative analysis on the "key" variables.* Finally, the problem of "many variables" may be alleviated not only by some of the specific approaches suggested above but also by a general commitment to theoretical parsimony. Comparative analysis must avoid the danger of being overwhelmed by large numbers of variables and, as a result, losing the possibility of discovering controlled relationships, and it must therefore judiciously restrict itself to the really key variables, omitting those of only marginal importance. The nature of the comparative method and its special limitations constitute a strong argument against what Lasswell and Braibanti call "configurative" or "contextual" analysis: "the identification and interpretation of factors in the whole social order which appear to affect whatever political functions and their institutional manifestations have been identified and listed for comparison" (Braibanti's definition).[50] Lasswell argues that the comparative method as usually applied has been insuffi-

47. Smelser, *op. cit.,* p. 115.

48. Juan J. Linz and Amando de Miguel, "Within-Nation Differences and Comparisons: The Eight Spains," in Merritt and Rokkan, *op. cit.,* p. 268.

49. Naroll, "Scientific Comparative Politics and International Relations," in R. Barry Farrell, ed., *Approaches to Comparative and International Politics* (Evanston, Ill.: Northwestern University Press, 1966), pp. 336–37.

50. Braibanti, *op. cit.,* p. 49. In this context, "configurative" analysis is not synonymous with the traditional single-country approach, as in Eckstein's definition of the term: "the analysis of particular political systems, treated either explicitly or implicitly as unique entities" ("A Perspective on Comparative Politics," p. 11).

ciently configurative, and calls for the exploration of more variables: the entire context—past, present, and future—"must be continually scanned."[51]

Scanning all variables is not the same as *including* all variables, of course, as long as one is on one's guard against an unrealistic and eventually self-defeating perfectionism. Comparative politics should avoid the trap into which the decision-making approach to the study of international politics fell, of specifying and calling for the analysis of an exhaustive list of all variables that have any possible influence on the decision-making process.[52] Parsimony suggests that Joseph LaPalombara's call for a "segmented approach," aiming at the formulation of middle-range propositions concerning partial systems makes a great deal of sense.[53] Similarly, Eckstein's urgent call for greater manageability of the field should be carefully heeded: "The most obvious need in the field at present is simplification—and simplification on a rather grand scale—for human intelligence and scientific method can scarcely cope with the large numbers of variables, the heaps of concepts, and the mountains of data that seem at present to be required, and indeed to exist, in the field."[54]

It is no accident that the most fruitful applications of the comparative method have been in anthropological research. In primitive societies, the number of variables is not as bewilderingly large as in more advanced societies. All relevant factors can therefore be more easily surveyed and analyzed. In this respect, anthropology can be said to provide "almost a laboratory for the quasi-experimental approach to social phenomena."[55] Political science lacks this advantage, but can approximate it by focusing attention on the key variables in comparative studies.

A final comment is in order about the relationship of comparative politics as a substantive field and comparison as a method. The two are clearly not coterminous. In comparative politics, other methods can often also be employed, and the comparative method is also applicable in other fields and disciplines. A particularly instructive example is James N. Rosenau's study of the relative influence of individual variables (personal policy beliefs and "personalizing tendencies") and role variables (party role and committee

51. Lasswell, *op. cit.*, p. 6.

52. See Richard C. Snyder, H. W. Bruck, and Burton Sapin, eds., *Foreign Policy Decision-Making* (New York: Free Press of Glencoe, 1962).

53. Joseph LaPalombara, "Macrotheories and Microapplications in Comparative Politics," *Comparative Politics,* 1 (October 1968), pp. 60–77. As an example he cites Robert A. Dahl, ed., *Political Oppositions in Western Democracies* (New Haven: Yale University Press, 1966), esp. chapters 11–13. See also LaPalombara, "Parismony and Empiricism in Comparative Politics: An Anti-Scholastic View," in Holt and Turner, eds., *The Methodology of Comparative Research,* pp. 123–49.

54. Eckstein, "A Perspective on Comparative Politics," p. 30.

55. Nadel, *op. cit.*, p. 228.

role) on the behavior of United States senators during two similar periods: the "Acheson era," 1949–1952, and the "Dulles era," 1953–1956. Rosenau argues that these two eras were characterized by a generally similar international environment and that the two secretaries of state conducted similar foreign policies and also resembled each other in personal qualities. He terms the method that he uses in his analysis the method of "quantitative historical comparison." One of its basic characteristics is the testing of hypotheses by comparing two eras (cases) that are "essentially comparable . . . in all respects except for the . . . variables being examined." The method is called "quantitative" because the variables are operationally defined in quantitative terms, and "historical" because the two cases compared are historical eras.[56] The method is, therefore, a special form of the comparative method. It illustrates one of very many ways in which an imaginative investigator can devise fruitful applications of the comparative method.[57]

The Comparative Method and the Case Study Method

The discussion of the comparative method is not complete without a consideration of the case study method. The statistical method can be applied to many cases, the comparative method to relatively few (but at least two) cases, and the case study method to one case. But the case study method can and should be closely connected with the comparative method (and sometimes also with the statistical method); certain types of case studies can even be considered implicit parts of the comparative method.

The great advantage of the case study is that by focusing on a single case, that case can be intensively examined even when the research resources at the investigator's disposal are relatively limited. The scientific status of the case study method is somewhat ambiguous, however, because science is a generalizing activity. A single case can constitute neither the basis for a valid generalization nor the ground for disproving an established generalization.

56. James N. Rosenau, "Private Preferences and Political Responsibilities: The Relative Potency of Individual and Role Variables in the Behavior of U.S. Senators," in Singer, ed., *Quantitative International Politics,* pp. 17–50, esp. p. 19. Rosenau adds that if "the findings are not so clear as to confirm or negate the hypotheses unmistakably, then of course the analyst moves on to a third comparable period" (p. 19). If such a third or even more periods can be found—which seems unlikely in the case of Rosenau's particular research problem—they should be included regardless of the outcome of the analysis of the first two eras (if the available resources permit it, of course).

57. See also the proposed use of "multiple comparison groups," as an approximation of the experimental method, by Barney G. Glazer and Anselm L. Strauss, "Discovery of Substantive Theory: A Basic Strategy Underlying Qualitative Research," *American Behavioral Scientist,* 8 (February 1965), pp. 5–12.

Indirectly, however, case studies can make an important contribution to the establishment of general propositions and thus to theory-building in political science. Six types of case studies may be distinguished. These are ideal types, and any particular study of a single case may fit more than one of the following categories:

1. Atheoretical case studies;
2. Interpretative case studies;
3. Hypothesis-generating case studies;
4. Theory-confirming case studies;
5. Theory-infirming case studies;
6. Deviant case studies.

Cases may be selected for analysis because of an interest in the case *per se* or because of an interest in theory-building. The first two types of cases belong to the former category. *Atheoretical case studies* are the traditional single-country or single-case analyses. They are entirely descriptive and move in a theoretical vacuum: they are neither guided by established or hypothesized generalizations nor motivated by a desire to formulate general hypotheses. Therefore, the direct theoretical value of these case studies is nil, but this does not mean that they are altogether useless. As LaPalombara emphasizes, the development of comparative politics is hampered by an appalling lack of information about almost all of the world's political systems.[58] Purely descriptive case studies do have great utility as basic data-gathering operations, and can thus contribute indirectly to theory-building. It can even be claimed that "the cumulative effect of such studies will lead to fruitful generalization," but only if it is recognized that this depends on a theoretically oriented secondary analysis of the data collected in atheoretical case studies.[59]

As indicated earlier, the atheoretical case study and the other types of case studies are ideal types. An actual instance of an atheoretical case study probably does not exist, because almost any analysis of a single case is guided by at least some vague theoretical notions and some anecdotal knowledge of other cases, and usually results in some vague hypotheses or conclusions that have a wider applicability. Such actual case studies fit the first type to a large extent, but they also fit one or more of the other types (particularly the third, fourth, and fifth types) at least to some extent.

Interpretative case studies resemble atheoretical case studies in one respect: they, too, are selected for analysis because of an interest in the case rather than an interest in the formulation of general theory. They differ,

58. LaPalombara, "Macrotheories and Microapplications," pp. 60–65.

59. See Michael Curtis, *Comparative Government and Politics: An Introductory Essay in Political Science* (New York: Harper and Row, 1968), p. 7. See also Macridis, *The Study of Comparative Government* (New York: Random House, 1955).

however, in that they make explicit use of established theoretical propositions. In these studies, a generalization is applied to a specific case with the aim of throwing light on the case rather than of improving the generalization in any way. Hence they are studies in "applied science." Since they do not aim to contribute to empirical generalizations, their value in terms of theory-building is nil. On the other hand, it is precisely the purpose of empirical theory to make such interpretative case studies possible.[60] Because of the still very limited degree of theoretical development in political science, such case studies are rare. One interesting example is Michael C. Hudson's imaginative and insightful case study of Lebanon in the light of existing development theories, in which he discovers a serious discrepancy between the country's socio-economic and political development.[61]

The remaining four types of case studies are all selected for the purpose of theory-building. *Hypothesis-generating case studies* start out with a more or less vague notion of possible hypotheses, and attempt to formulate definite hypotheses to be tested subsequently among a larger number of cases. Their objective is to develop theoretical generalizations in areas where no theory exists yet. Such case studies are of great theoretical value. They may be particularly valuable if the case selected for analysis provides what Naroll calls a sort of "crucial experiment" in which certain variables of interest happen to be present in a special way.[62]

Theory-confirming and theory-infirming case studies are analyses of single cases within the framework of established generalizations. Prior knowledge of the case is limited to a single variable or to none of the variables that the proposition relates. The case study is a test of the proposition, which may turn out to be confirmed or infirmed by it. If the case study is of the theory-confirming type, it strengthens the proposition in question. But, assuming that the proposition is solidly based on a large number of cases, the demonstration that one more case fits does not strengthen it a great deal. Likewise, theory-infirming case studies merely weaken the generalizations marginally. The theoretical value of both types of case studies is enhanced,

60. As Przeworski and Teune state: "The main role of a theory is to provide explanations of specific events. These explanations consist of inferring, with a high degree of probability, statements about particular events from general statements concerning classes of events" (p. 86).

61. Michael C. Hudson, "A Case of Political Underdevelopment," *Journal of Politics,* 29 (November 1967), pp. 821–37. See also Beer, "The Comparative Method and the Study of British Politics," pp. 19–36.

62. Naroll, "Scientific Comparative Politics and International Relations," p. 336. An example of such a case study is my analysis of the determinants of Dutch colonialism in West Irian. In most cases, both objective (especially economic) and subjective factors can be discerned, but the case of West Irian is unique because of the complete absence of objective Dutch interests in the colony. See Lijphart, *The Trauma of Decolonization: The Dutch and West New Guinea* (New Haven: Yale University Press, 1966).

however, if the cases are, or turn out to be, extreme on one of the variables: such studies can also be labeled "crucial experiments" or crucial tests of the propositions.

Deviant case analyses are studies of single cases that are known to deviate from established generalizations. They are selected in order to reveal why the cases are deviant—that is, to uncover relevant additional variables that were not considered previously, or to refine the (operational) definitions of some or all of the variables.[63] In this way, deviant case studies can have great theoretical value. They weaken the original proposition, but suggest a modified proposition that may be stronger. The validity of the proposition in its modified form must be established by further comparative analysis.[64]

Of the six types of case studies, the hypothesis-generating and the deviant case studies have the greatest value in terms of their contribution to theory. Each of these two types, however, has quite different functions in respect to theory-building: The hypothesis-generating case study serves to generate new hypotheses, while the deviant case study refines and sharpens existing hypotheses. The deviant case study—as well as the theory-confirming and theory-infirming case studies—are implicitly comparative analyses. They focus on a particular case which is singled out for analysis from a relatively large number of cases and which is analyzed within the theoretical and empirical context of this set of cases. The deviant case may be likened to the "experimental group" with the remainder of the cases constituting the "control group." Just as the analytical power of the comparative method increases the closer it approximates the statistical and experimental methods, so the analytical power of the case study method increases the more it approximates the comparative method in the form of deviant case analysis. Such case analysis requires, of course, that the position of the deviant case on the variables under consideration, and consequently also its position relative to the other cases, are clearly defined.

The different types of cases and their unequal potential contributions to

63. See Patricia L. Kendall and Katherine M. Wolf, "The Analysis of Deviant Cases in Communications Research," in Lazarsfeld and Frank Stanton, eds., *Communications Research: 1948–49* (New York: Harper, 1949), pp. 152–57; Sjoberg, *op. cit.*, pp. 114–15; and Lijphart, *The Politics of Accommodation: Pluralism and Democracy in the Netherlands* (Berkeley: University of California Press, 1968), chapter 10.

64. This process of refining generalizations through deviant case analysis is what Robert M. Marsh calls "specification." See his article "The Bearing of Comparative Analysis on Sociological Theory," *Social Forces*, 43 (December 1964), pp. 191–96. Specification should therefore definitely not be regarded as "the garbage bin" of comparative research; see Conrad Phillip Kottak, "Towards a Comparative Science of Society," *Comparative Studies in Society and History*, 12 (January 1970), p. 102. See also Milton M. Gordon, "Sociological Law and the Deviant Case," *Sociometry*, 10 (August 1947), pp. 250–58; and André J. F. Köbben, "The Logic of Cross-Cultural Analysis: Why Exceptions?" in Rokkan, ed., *Comparative Research Across Cultures and Nations* (Paris: Mouton, 1968), pp. 17–53.

theory-building should be kept in mind in selecting and analyzing a single case. Some of the shortcomings in Eckstein's otherwise insightful and thought-provoking case study of Norway may serve as instructive examples.[65] Eckstein argues that the Norwegian case deviates from David B. Truman's proposition concerning "overlapping memberships,"[66] because Norway is a stable democracy in spite of the country's deep and non-overlapping geographic, economic, and cultural cleavages. But he fails to place the case of Norway in relation to other cases. In fact, although he describes Norway's divisions as "astonishingly great, sharp, and persistent," he explicitly rules out any comparison with the cleavages in other countries. This exclusion seriously weakens the case study. Furthermore, instead of trying to refine Truman's proposition with the help of the deviant findings, Eckstein simply drops it. In terms of the sixfold typology of case studies discussed above, his analysis of the Norwegian case is only a theory-infirming one and is not made into a deviant case study.

From then on, the case study becomes a theory-confirming one. Eckstein finds that the Norwegian case strikingly bears out his own "congruence" theory, which states that governments tend to be stable if there is considerable resemblance (congruence) between governmental authority patterns and the authority patterns in society.[67] He demonstrates persuasively that both governmental and social patterns of authority are strongly democratic in Norway and thus highly congruent. The problem here is not that the Norwegian facts do not fit the theory, but that they fit the theory too perfectly. The perfect fit strengthens the theory marginally, but does not contribute to its refinement. The theory does not hold that complete congruence of authority patterns is required for stable democracy. In his original statement of the congruence theory, Eckstein himself points out the necessity of further work on the important questions of how much disparity can be tolerated and how degrees of congruence and disparity can be measured.[68] Because the Norwegian case turns out to be a perfect theory-

65. Eckstein, *Division and Cohesion in Democracy: A Study of Norway* (Princeton, N.J.: Princeton University Press, 1966), esp. pp. 60–77, 177–201. Part of the critique which follows is included in my review of this book in the *Journal of Modern History*, 41 (March 1969), pp. 83–87.

66. David B. Truman, *The Governmental Process: Political Interests and Public Opinion* (New York: Knopf, 1951).

67. In one respect, it is not altogether correct to call the Norwegian case study a theory-confirming study. Because the congruence theory has a rather narrow empirical basis, consisting chiefly of only two cases (Britain and Germany), it is a hypothesis rather than an established theory. The case study of Norway is, of course, not a hypothesis-generating study either. Perhaps it should be called a "hypothesis-strengthening" case study or, as Eckstein himself suggests, a "plausibility probe" (oral comment at the IPSA Round Table Conference in Turin, September 1969).

68. Eckstein, *A Theory of Stable Democracy*, Research Monograph No. 10 (Princeton, N.J.: Center of International Studies, 1961).

confirming one, it cannot be used to *refine* the theory in any of these respects. Therefore, Eckstein was unlucky in his selection of this case as far as the development of his congruence theory is concerned, and he fails to take full advantage of the case study method in analyzing the case in terms of Truman's theory of overlapping memberships.

* * *

The comparative method and the case study method have major drawbacks. But precisely because of the inevitable limitations of these methods, it is the challenging task of the investigator in the field of comparative politics to apply these methods in such a way as to minimize their weaknesses and to capitalize on their inherent strengths. Thus, they can be highly useful instruments in scientific political inquiry.

Recent Trends in Research Methods in Political Science
Karl W. Deutsch

In the field of political science, the last decade, and particularly the last five years, have been marked by a large increase in the resources for political research that have become available. There has been an increase in the range, diversity, and effectiveness of empirical methods of investigation; an increase in the amounts, variety, and accuracy of quantitative data; and an increase in the breadth, versatility, and power of the available mathematical and statistical methods of data analysis and interpretation. All these resources have been further enhanced by the greater availability of electronic computing equipment and of IBM-type equipment for tabulations.

Together, these various new resources have permitted a new kind of theory about politics. The classic theories of politics—from Plato and Machiavelli to Marx and Pareto—had involved at bottom deterministic models which stressed one or a very few variables as supposed "causes." Each of these theories then relegated most of the other conditions surrounding the outcome into a large and ill-defined residual category of other factors. These other factors were treated as too numerous and complex to be dealt with explicitly by the theory, but also as too important to be completely disregarded. Accordingly, they were left to be summed up more or less vaguely by the intuition or judgment of each analyst. In the theory of international politics, comparable simplifications were employed. Nation-states in a balance-of-power process were treated as single actors comparable to the planetary "point masses" and hard billiard-ball-like cor-

Reprinted from A Design for Political Science: Scope, Objectives and Methods, *ed. by J. C. Charlesworth (Philadelphia: American Academy of Political and Social Science, 1966), pp. 149–178, by special permission of the publisher.*

puscles of Newtonian astronomy and physics. The simplicity of the basic models of all such theories and the paucity of major variables explicitly dealt with was thus matched by the diffuse multiplicity of minor factors and the insightful unreliability of the resulting interpretations and predictions.

The new theoretical approaches to politics permitted to dissolve each of these hard oversimplified entities of "nations," "classes," or "leaders" into a much larger array of components and subsystems within it. At the same time, they replaced a very few deterministic "causes" or "forces" by a much larger number of relevant conditions or significant variables. All of these were held to interact in a probabilistic manner, which could be analyzed statistically, by such methods as correlation analysis, so as to permit the calculation of the average contribution of each such condition or variable to the distribution of outcomes.[1]

Causality was thus replaced by probability, and the search for single causes and for master keys to prediction or control gave way to multivariate analysis.[2]

This change in approach had occurred in the natural sciences and their applications before it came in the social sciences. About the time of World War II, the most probable trajectory of the shell from a heavy naval gun was computed at the Massachusetts Institute of Technology by computing procedures which took into account numerous conditions for each shot, including the elevation and aiming of the gun; the powder charge; wind strength and direction; the course, pitching, and rolling of the ship; and the rotation speed of the earth's surface at the particular latitude. Each of these conditions could be thought of in deterministic terms as a "cause," but the outcome of their interplay was viewed probabilistically. Some of these conditions obviously had greater influence on the distribution of outcomes— here the scatter of shots around the target—than had others, but each factor produced a sufficient improvement in the prediction so as to be worth taking into account.

In the social sciences, an analysis of this type might show that the strongest condition making for more isolationist behavior by the voters of a congressional district and by the congressman representing it was the

1. On the significance of this change, see Seymour Martin Lipset, *Political Man* (London: Mercury Books, 1963), pp. 72–75; on the significance of the shift to probabilistic models, see Karl W. Deutsch, *The Nerves of Government* (New York: Free Press, 1963); Harold and Margaret Sprout, *The Ecological Perspective on Human Affairs with Special Reference to International Politics* (Princeton, N.J.: Princeton University Press, 1965).

2. For extended discussions of techniques, see Paul F. Lazarsfeld and Morris Rosenberg (eds.), *The Language of Social Research* (New York: Free Press of Glencoe, 1955), esp. pp. 206–283. For a knowledgeable discussion of some of the difficulties of the older viewpoints, cf. Robert M. McIver, *Social Causation* (Boston-New York: Ginn, 1942).

habitual Republicanism of the constituency. A weaker but still significant factor might be the rural—as opposed to urban—character of the district. A possible third and fourth constituency characteristic favoring isolationist behavior might be the percentage of voters of German or Irish stock and the distance of the district from the sea, but these last two conditions turned out to matter very little, if at all. Each condition thus contributed something to the outcome—the frequency of isolationist behavior—but none determined all of it, and where several or all of these favorable conditions coincided, the frequency of this outcome was much higher.[3]

What has just been recounted is merely one example of what is now a standard technique of multivariate analysis in political research. Yet, as has been suggested, this is more than change in technique. It is a change in basic viewpoint, replacing single overriding "causes," simple "ideal types," and implicit and irretraceable "judgments" by increasingly explicit images of complex processes, with many quantitatively measurable variables, each making its measurable contribution to the probability distribution of outcomes.

This joint change in basic outlook and method, however, could not have occurred without a large increase in the pool of available specific techniques of research and analysis, the pool of available data, and the pool of skilled personnel in political science and in the social sciences, and a substantial increase in the budgets required for research. As in other fields in the natural and social sciences, ranging from biology and meteorology to psychology and economics, the capitalization ratio of political science has been increasing, that is, there has been a substantial rise in the amount of capital, equipment, resources, and clerical and technical support required to give full effectiveness to the average professional scholar or social scientist in this field. Even so, political science will continue to need the labor of lonely men, thinking and writing at their desks, just as physics will continue to need the work of individual thinkers of the kind of Albert Einstein. For a substantial proportion of political scientists, particularly of the younger generation, the age of the hand-loom weavers is ending, but in all age groups the need for individual discoverers, creators, and designers will remain.

THE CONTRIBUTION OF NEW DATA

New data are becoming available on a rapidly increasing scale, and the availability of data categories particularly relevant to political science could be increased further by special efforts. Nine broad kinds of such data have been developed in recent years by political scientists who have made them

3. Leroy N. Rieselbach, *The Roots of Isolationist Behavior: Congressional Voting and Presidential Leadership in Foreign Policy* (Indianapolis: Bobbs-Merrill, to be published in 1967); and "The Basis of Isolationist Behavior," *Public Opinion Quarterly,* 34 (Winter 1960), pp. 645–657. [Leroy N. Rieselbach, *The Roots of Isolationist Behavior: Congressional Voting and Presidential Leadership in Foreign Policy* (Indianapolis: Bobbs-Merrill, 1966).]

more available, more comparable and accurate, or more meaningful in the context of more advanced interpretation.

The first of these are elite data, including data on elite positions, incumbents, recruitment, and attitudes. The gathering and interpretation of such elite data has been developed in recent years, at the national and international level by Harold Lasswell and his associates, and at the level of community elites by a number of investigators ranging from Floyd Hunter to Robert A. Dahl.[4]

The second category includes data on mass opinion, gathered in over forty countries by sample surveys of the general Gallup- or Roper-poll type, many of which are now stored at the Roper Center of Opinion Research at Williamstown, Massachusetts. It also includes less voluminous but still extensive data developed to further refinement by the techniques of such organizations as the University of Michigan Survey, directed by Angus Campbell, Philip Converse, Warren Miller, and Donald Stokes, or in the survey of Negro voting and registration in the South by James W. Prothro and his associates at the University of North Carolina.[5] Related data on political attitudes at the mass opinion level have been developed through extended depth interviews of smaller samples of voters by Robert E. Lane,[6] and through repeated panel-interview methods by Paul F. Lazarsfeld and his associates.[7]

The third and fourth categories of data are formed by voting statistics, similar to those gathered for the United States by Richard M. Scammon, and by legislative voting data, such as those analyzed for the United States

4. Cf. Harold D. Lasswell, Daniel Lerner and C. E. Rothwell, *The Comparative Study of Elites* (Stanford, Calif.: Stanford University Press, 1952); H. D. Lasswell and Daniel Lerner, *World Revolutionary Elites* (Cambridge, Mass.: M.I.T. Press, 1965); Robert North, *Kuomintang and Chinese Communist Elites* (Stanford, Calif.: Stanford University Press, 1951); Suzanne Keller, *Beyond the Ruling Class: Strategic Elites in Modern Society* (New York: Random House, 1963); Donald Matthews, *The Background of Political Decision Makers* (New York: Doubleday-Random House, 1954), and *U.S. Senators and Their World* (Chapel Hill: University of North Carolina Press, 1960); Karl W. Deutsch and Lewis J. Edinger, *Germany Rejoins the Powers* (Stanford, Calif.: Stanford University Press, 1959).

5. Angus Campbell, Philip E. Converse, Warren E. Miller, and Donald E. Stokes, *The American Voter* (New York: John Wiley & Sons, 1960); Ralph L. Bisco, "Social Science Data Archives: A Review of Developments," *American Political Science Review*, 60: 1 (March 1966), pp. 93–109; and the special section "Data in Comparative Research," *International Social Science Journal*, 16:1 (1964).

6. Robert E. Lane, *Political Ideology: Why the American Common Man Believes What He Does* (New York: Free Press of Glencoe, 1962); see also *Political Life: Why People Get Involved in Politics* (Glencoe, Ill.: Free Press, 1959).

7. See the articles on "Panel Analysis," in Paul F. Lazarsfeld and Morris Rosenberg (eds.), *The Language of Social Research* (New York: Free Press of Glencoe, 1955, 1962), pp. 231–259.

Congress by David Truman.[8] The fifth category is data from content analysis, developed early for political science by such scholars as Harold Lasswell and Ithiel Pool, and more recently by Richard L. Merritt, and adapted to powerful semiautomatic computer methods by Philip Stone, Robert North, Zvi Namenwirth, and others.[9]

The sixth category consists of aggregative data, such as social, economic, or demographic statistics, census data, and the like, which are gathered by governments or private organizations for operational purposes of their own, but from which one can learn by suitable and critical analysis a great deal about the social structure and process of a country, and particularly about their rates of change in different periods and conditions. Such aggregative data have been gathered in the *United Nations Compendium of Social Statistics* (1963), the *Cross-Polity Survey* by Arthur S. Banks and Robert Textor, and the *World Handbook of Political and Social Indicators* by Bruce M. Russett and his associates.[10] Major issues arising in the use of such data are discussed critically in the volume *Comparing Nations,* edited by Richard Merritt and Stein Rokkan.[11]

Closely related to aggregative data are the historical data which form the seventh category. Many of these are aggregative data for earlier periods, permitting the construction of time series and their study for possible trends, cycles, or secular changes. A handbook of such historical trend data for recent decades is in preparation at the Yale Political Data Program. Other historical data consist in lists of historical events, such as the list of the number and duration of wars and the number of fatalities in each compiled by Lewis F. Richardson, Quincy Wright and J. David Singer or the lists of deaths from domestic political violence, in the 1950's compiled by Rudolph

8. David Truman, *The Congressional Party* (New York: John Wiley & Sons, 1959); Richard M. Scammon (ed.), *America at the Polls: A Handbook of Presidential Election Statistics* (Pittsburgh: University of Pittsburgh Press, 1965) and *America Votes,* Vol. 1 *et seq.* (New York: The Macmillan Company, 1966).

9. Philip J. Stone, Robert F. Bales, J. Zvi Namenwirth, and Daniel M. Ogilvie, "The General Inquirer: A Computer System for Content Analysis and Retrieval Based on the Sentence as a Unit of Information," *Behavioral Science,* 7 (1962), pp. 484–494; Dexter C. Dunphy, Philip J. Stone, and Marshall S. Smith, "The General Inquirer: Further Developments in a Computer System for Content Analysis of Verbal Data in the Social Sciences," *Behavioral Science,* 10 (October 1965), pp. 468–480.

10. Arthur S. Banks and Robert Textor, *A Cross-Polity Survey* (Cambridge, Mass.: M.I.T. Press, 1963); Bruce M. Russett, Hayward R. Alker, Jr., Karl W. Deutsch and Harold D. Lasswell, *World Handbook of Political and Social Indicators* (New Haven: Yale University Press, 1964).

11. Richard L. Merritt and Stein Rokkan (eds.), *Comparing Nations: The Use of Quantitative Data in Cross-National Research* (New Haven: Yale University Press, 1965); cf. also Raymond A. Bauer (ed.), *Social Indicators* (Cambridge, Mass.: M.I.T. Press, 1966).

Rummel and by Raymond Tanter.[12] The preparation of carefully checked, consolidated, and revised lists of such historical data, as in the lists by David Singer and his collaborators, greatly enhances their usefulness for political analysis.

An eighth source of data is the other social and behavioral sciences, which are yielding increasing amounts of knowledge about the conditions and effects of communication and communication overload; the formation of images, attitudes, and motivations; the behavior of small groups; the patterns of decision-making in organizations; the changes in social roles, mobility, and structure; the interplay of child-rearing patterns, personality, and culture; and, generally, a large array of data about human behavior, gathered from skillful observation or sometimes even from controlled experiment. The broad survey by Bernard Berelson and Gary A. Steiner, *Human Behavior,* contains much information significant for political science, and so do the studies on *Communication and Persuasion* initiated by Carl Hovland, Irving Janis, and H. A. Kelley and the studies on communication overload by James G. Miller and his associates.[13]

The ninth and last group of new data is in part derived from the preceding eight. It includes the new analytic, mathematical, and statistical routines and computer programs that are now being developed for use in political and social science, and it also includes the new secondary data, such as ratios, rank-order profiles, statistical distributions, correlations, and the like, which have been computed with the aid of these methods.[14] Such secondary data also include a series of processed or "cleaned-up" data, derived from raw data but categorized according to relevant discriminative variables, with gaps in the data filled in, and with known biases or errors adjusted so as to make the residual error as nearly random—or even normally distributed—as possible. Such "data-making" is itself an essential step in the conversion of raw data to analytic usefulness, and its results are usually worth storing and retrieving for later analyses.[15]

12. Rudolph Rummel, "Testing Some Possible Predictors of Conflict Behavior within and between Nations," Peace Research Society (International), *Papers,* Vol. 1, Philadelphia, 1964 (Chicago Conference, 1963), pp. 79–111; David Singer and Melvin Small, "The Composition and Status-Ordering of the International Systems: 1815–1940," *World Politics,* 18: 2 (January 1966), pp. 236–282.

13. Raymond Tanter, "Dimension of Conflict Behavior within Nations, 1955–1960: Turmoil and Internal War," Peace Research Society, *Papers,* Vol. 3, Philadelphia, 1965 (Chicago Conference, 1964), pp. 159–184; James G. Miller, in D. McKenzie Rioch & E. A. Weinstein (eds.), *Disorders of Communication,* Research Publications, Association for Research into Nervous and Mental Disorders, 1964, pp. 42, 87–100.

14. Cf. some of the points raised in K. W. Deutsch, "Theoretical Bases for Data Programs," in Merritt and Rokkan (eds.), *Comparing Nations, op. cit.,* pp. 27–55.

15. Cf. J. David Singer, "Data-Making in International Relations," *Behavioral Science,* 10: 1 (January 1965), pp. 68–80; see also Raoul Naroll, *Data Quality Control: A New Research Technique* (New York: Free Press, 1962).

It is difficult to estimate the total volume of existing political science data from these nine sources and the volume of new data that is being added each year, but a rough guess may be attempted.[16] The largest single source by now is probably the opinion polls from many countries. About ten million standard IBM cards, or their information-carrying equivalents on tape or film, may be in existence, with perhaps 0.5 million being added each year. The second largest source is voting statistics the world over, which may amount to about five million IBM cards or card equivalents, with another 0.5 million accruing annually. The third largest category is much smaller: present stocks of quantitative historical data, other than the relatively recent poll and voting data already included in categories one and two, amount to no more than 0.7 million, with perhaps as many as 0.4 million card-equivalents of new historical data becoming available each year. The remaining six categories of data are much smaller at present, amounting to perhaps no more than 0.5 million cards in existence, but growing fast enough to contribute the equivalent of 1.25 million new cards each year. A more detailed presentation, with a tentative projection to 1975 —with a stock of fifty million card-equivalents existing by that time, and a total annual growth rate of perhaps as much as five million—is presented in Table 1.

The cost of storing and processing these political science data for easy retrieval and secondary analysis, by means of an interconnected network of data repositories and centers for data processing and analysis might run to about one million dollars at the 1965 level of such data, rising to perhaps as much as an annual cost of five million dollars by 1975.

A more extended discussion of the data needs of political science will be published elsewhere.[17] Here it may be more useful to deal with the question: How are the data from all these various sources to be coordinated to best effect?

THE COORDINATION OF DATA FROM DIFFERENT SOURCES AND TECHNIQUES

The diversity itself of the new data and techniques of reproducible—and hence verifiable—empirical research is creating a major research method through the mutual confrontation of different data and research results. In dealing with a major political science problem, it is becoming increasingly possible to plan at one and the same time for several convergent research attacks. Has European integration—and particularly integration between

---

16. K. W. Deutsch, "The Information Needs of Political Science," International Federation for Documentation (FID), *Proceedings of the 1965 Congress on Documentation* (Washington, D.C.–London: Spartan Books–Macmillan and Company, 1966), pp. 199–203. The figures given here are from a revised version of this paper which will be published in due course.

17. *Ibid.,* p. 203.

TABLE 1—Expectable Information Requirements of Political Science
(in Million Cards or Equivalents)*

ACTIVITY	DATA STOCK			ANNUAL ADDITIONS	
	1965	1970	1975	1965	1975
1 Elite Data	0.1	1.0	3.0	0.2	0.4
2 Mass Opinion	10.0	12.5	13.0	0.5	1.0
3 Voting Statistics	5.0	7.5	10.0	0.5	0.5
4 Legislative Voting Data	0.05	0.2	0.8	0.05	0.05
5 Content Analysis	0.1	0.6	1.6	0.05	0.2
6 Aggregative Data	0.1	2.5	7.5	0.5	1.0
7 Other Social Sciences	0.15	0.4	0.9	0.05	0.1
8 Mathematical Routines & Secondary Data	—	2.5	7.5	0.5	1.0
9 Historical Data	0.7	2.1	4.1	0.4	0.8
Total	16.20	29.3	50.4	2.65	5.05

* All these figures merely illustrate orders of magnitude. Some of them may well be subject to an error margin of up to 50 per cent.

France and Germany—increased, decreased, or remained substantially at the same level from 1955 to 1965? To answer this question, a recent study sought evidence from aggregative data of the results of actual behavior in trade, travel, mail, and student exchanges, together with data from the content analysis of elite newspapers and a broader range of periodicals, results of a large number of mass opinion polls, and a special survey of French and German elite opinion, gathered through extended interviews.[18]

In a case study of this type, these diverse data are then confronted with one another, in their bearing on the problems under study; the results of these confrontations are then evaluated critically by the investigators in the light of their general historical and descriptive knowledge—so to speak, their "clinical" experience—of these particular problems and of problems related or similar to it; and these confrontations and evaluations then serve as the basis for the investigators' judgment.

More generally, this emphasis on the problem-oriented confrontation of several streams of evidence should help us to get away from the familiar controversies as to whether one kind of data, such as survey data, should be preferred to some other, such as aggregate statistics either in general or in dealing with some particular class or problems.[19] The truth may reside

18. See K. W. Deutsch, L. J. Edinger, R. C. Macridis, and R. L. Merritt, *France, Germany, and the Western Alliance* (New York: Scribner's, 1967); and K. W. Deutsch, *Arms Control and the Atlantic Alliance: Europe Faces Coming Policy Decisions* (New York: John Wiley & Sons, 1967).

19. For a useful discussion of some of the problems involved, see Ralph H. Retzlaff, "The Use of Aggregate Data in Comparative Political Analysis," *The Journal of Politics*, 27: 4 (November 1965), pp. 797–817, esp. pp. 798–799; Austin Ranney, "The

not so much in any one kind of data, or in the result of any one technique, even if these data and techniques are used not naïvely and unskillfully, but in the most highly skilled manner. Rather, truth may be thought of as a relationship between different streams of evidence. A statement is the more likely to be true, the larger the number of different classes or kinds of evidence that confirm it. Also, a statement contains the more truth the larger that part of the information contained in it which will have to be included in any successor statement to it, reformulated or revised, by which the original statement will have to be replaced in the light of new evidence. Improved methods for the multiple confrontation and correlation of diverse bodies of evidence bearing on the same problem deserve, therefore, a high priority in our attention.

In order to make progress in this area, it might be desirable to collect systematically the various relevant empirical-observational or experimental techniques, survey instruments, questionnaires, and questions that have been used in the social sciences and to record:

1. Which of these have been applied repeatedly, under what conditions, with what results, and with what indications as to their replicability?[20]

2. What is the correlation among the results of different survey instruments, questions, or experimental techniques bearing on the same substantive problem or class of problems? How do mass opinion data generally correlate with the results of content analysis of mass media, or of school textbooks, or of other supposedly "representative" sources?

3. To what extent can the results obtained from different techniques or data sources be interpreted as indicators of a common underlying structure or process? To what extent are such indicators then interchangeable? On what grounds and by what procedures should preferred indicators be selected, or joint indicators be constructed?

4. What is the correlation between different aspects of reality, each of which is associated with its own indicators, but each of which is also linked to other aspects of reality, in some manner and to some

Utility and Limitations of Aggregate Data in the Study of Electoral Behavior," in Austin Ranney (ed.), *Essays on the Behavioral Study of Politics* (Urbana: University of Illinois Press, 1962), pp. 91–102.

20. For a provisional list of about two hundred test instruments or questionnaires relevant to the relationship of personality to political behavior, see Leroy N. Rieselbach, "Personality and Political Attitudes: Available Questionnaire Measures" (Ann Arbor: Mental Health Research Institute, University of Michigan, 1964), multigraphed.

degree? What, for instance, is the correlation between overt or salient attitudes, expressed "off-the-cuff" in response to brief opinion-poll questions, and latent and more deep-seated attitudes, that are revealed only in prolonged depth interviews?[21] Or what is the correlation between expressed attitudes or intentions on the one hand, and actual behavior, on the other? Could these correlations between attitudes and behavior be improved by including explicit data on such major discussions of each attitude as its salience, intensity, and the respondent's involvement and his closure of mind, as suggested by Louis Guttman?[22]

5. What is the correlation between panel responses and the responses elicited from comparable fresh samples interviewed at the intervals in time?[23]

In recent years, however, questions of this kind about empirical data sources and data-gathering techniques have been exceeded in interest by another group of questions: those about better mathematical and statistical methods of analysis and about new sources of theories and models.

SOME NEW METHODS OF ANALYSIS

When we speak of "new methods" of mathematical and statistical analysis in political science research, we are rarely if ever referring to such methods invented by political scientists. Ordinarily and expectably, such methods are being developed by statisticians or mathematicians spontaneously or in response to some request from some field of natural or social science. What is new is usually only the application of this or that method to some problem in the field of political science followed by the increasing acceptance and application of this method or its results by other political scientists.

In this manner, the use of statistical distributions for the analysis of political and social phenomena was pioneered by George K. Zipf and developed further by Herbert Simon and by Hayward Alker, Jr. and by Bruce

21. Cf. some of the material reported in footnote 10, above; see also Russett, *et al.*, *World Handbook, op. cit.*, pp. 192–195; and David McClelland, *The Achieving Society* (Princeton, N.J.: Van Nostrand, 1961).

22. Louis Guttman, "The Principal Components of Scalable Attitudes," in Paul F. Lazarsfeld (ed.), *Mathematical Thinking in the Social Sciences* (Glencoe, Ill.: Free Press, 1954), pp. 216–257.

23. The correlation may vary with the length of time over which the panel is being interviewed. For a survey designed to compare over a decade the responses of a large panel with those of comparable fresh samples, see Chikio Hayashi *et al.*, *A Study of Japanese National Character* (Tokyo: Institute of Mathematical Statistics, 1961, in Japanese with English summaries of tables).

Russett and their associates. Zipf applied such distributions to the study of the relation of capital cities, nation-states, and empires. Herbert Simon applied it in a more advanced manner to the study of processes that give rise to new organizations, such as business firms, or possibly—at least in principle—new states or other political groupings.[24] Alker and Russett surveyed a number of statistical measures of inequality, which were applied to the unequal distribution of such politically relevant variables as income, land holdings, voting representation.[25] Russett and his associates also presented, in their *World Handbook,* international distribution profiles for seventy-five politically relevant variables so as to make them available for further analysis.[26] Work is underway to prepare similar profiles of the distribution of many of these variables within particular nations, such as over the fifty states—or sometimes even the three million counties—of the United States. This would make it possible to compare the international and intranational distribution patterns of important variables, and thus to learn something about the possible effects of a particular nation-state either as an equalizer among its constituent districts or regions, or else as a promoter or stabilizer of inequality; and such comparisons could then be used to test some of the existing theories—such as that of Gunnar Myrdal—on this subject.[27]

Distribution patterns of variables can be studied not only among states or territories, but also among organizations, firms, or social groups or classes. Even a preliminary survey suggests that Vilfredo Pareto's well-known generalization—that in the long run the inequality of income distribution over different countries and periods does not substantially change— is incorrect. In the mid-1950's, the gini index of inequality for income distribution before taxes ranged from 0.54 for Mexico to 0.35 for Australia; and it may have dropped for West Germany from 0.47 in 1950 to 0.32 in

24. Herbert A. Simon, *Models of Man* (New York: John Wiley & Sons, 1956); George K. Zipf, *National Unity and Disunity: The Nation as a Big Social Organism* (Bloomington, Ind.: Principia Press, 1944). For a criticism of Zipf's approach, see Karl W. Deutsch, "Communication Models in the Social Sciences," *Public Opinion Quarterly,* 16: 3 (Fall 1952), pp. 356–380; and for the whole field, see Hayward R. Alker, Jr., *Mathematics and Politics* (New York: The Macmillan Company, 1965); and "The Long Road to International Relations Theory: Problems of Statistical Non-Additivity," *World Politics,* 18: 4 (July 1966), pp. 623–655.

25. Hayward R. Alker, Jr., and Bruce M. Russett, "On Measuring Inequality," *Behavioral Science,* 9: 3 (July 1964), pp. 207–218; see also Bruce M. Russett, "Inequality and Instability: The Relation of Land Tenure to Politics," *World Politics,* 16: 3 (April 1964), pp. 442–454.

26. Bruce M. Russett, Hayward R. Alker, Jr., Karl W. Deutsch, and Harold D. Lasswell, *World Handbook, op. cit.*

27. Gunnar Myrdal, *Rich Lands and Poor* (New York: Harper, 1957); and *An International Economy* (New York: Harper, 1956).

1959. The differences in inequality over time, or between nations, are quite substantial. It seems plausible that to a significant though not unlimited extent they are subject to the processes of political allocation and decision.[28]

Even more interesting are time series, that is, distribution patterns of variables over time. Under appropriate conditions and with the help of suitable techniques, such time series can be used to interpolate data for missing dates written the period they cover, and they can be extrapolated back into the past or forward into the future. For many purposes of analysis it would be desirable to develop a standard notation for reporting time series. Such a notation should include the trend line of the series, that is, more technically put, the monotonic regression line best fitted to the data; and with this, it should also give the standard deviation, that is, the distance from the regression line within which 68 per cent of the actual cases or data can be found in the case of a normal distribution. If the trend line measures the central statistical tendency of the time series—for example, how fast it is rising or falling over time, and at what rate its change is accelerating or slowing down—the standard deviation measures the extent of the scatter or variance of the actual cases around this trend.

Knowledge of this variance is often a matter of both theoretical and practical importance. Impecunious gamblers are often ruined not by the steady but small trend of the house odds against them, but by the large transitory fluctuations in their losses which may soon wipe out their meager capital so that they cannot stay long enough in the game to recoup some or all of these losses in a later winning sequence. And what happens to the limited resources of gamblers can similarly happen to the limited following of politicians or parties, or to the limited troop reserves of armies locked in fluctuating battles or campaigns.

In addition to the secular trend of a time series, its other major compounds should be reported. A cyclical change may be superimposed upon the trend, somewhat as a business cycle has been superimposed upon the trend of American and European economic growth during much of the nineteenth and early twentieth century. There may even be more than one such cyclical movement, for a short-wave or short-term cyclical movement may modify further the combined result of the secular trend and of a long-term cycle or long-wave process.

Another component of the time series may be a stochastic process, that is, the interplay of a random factor at each relevant instant with the present position or state of the system, as determined by its past. Thus, a drunkard on a level field might take a random step of equal length in any direction, but at any time he could only move one step away from where he just had been. If the drunkard is walking on a slope, gravity will add a long-time bias to his progress. The probability distribution of any such "random

28. Russett, *et al., World Handbook, op. cit.,* pp. 243–247.

walk" and the probable fate of the drunkard—for instance, his likelihood of overstepping the brink of a nearby precipice—can be calculated by a mathematician from the relevant data. Conversely, a time series of data can be analyzed for the possibility of fitting to it a relatively simple mathematical random-walk model or similar stochastic model, and thus improving its simulation and prediction significantly beyond what a relatively simple combination of cycles and monotonic trends could accomplish.

If an analysis of this kind should suggest the presence of a random input element or factor in the process by which the time series was generated, it may be desirable to separate this random element further into two components. The first would be that part of the random input which could be matched readily by a relatively simple normal distribution, i.e., a Gaussian curve, or by some other well-known distribution, such as a Poisson or a Yule distribution, and which, therefore, would lend itself to easy computer simulation. If so, that part of the random process that could be readily simulated by any such well-known distribution would be described in these terms, and the residual amount of randomness reported separately—as irrelevant "noise" or as intriguing mystery, depending on the interests of the investigators.

In this manner, the analysis of any time series will lead us to search for one or several process models. In examining a time series—such as an increase in literacy, or in political participation, or in some indicator of political stability or instability—we ask what process could have produced such an outcome. We are apt to be led to a similar search when we ask what could be the result of the interplay of the time series in which we are interested with another time series with which it connected by some underlying political, social, or economic process. We are all familiar with crossover effects which occur if one variable or time series grows beyond some other variable by which it had been balanced. Thus, if the manpower losses of an army come to exceed its recruitment, it will start to dwindle; if the expenditures of a firm continue to exceed its earnings, it will become unprofitable and may go bankrupt; and if the number of persons angered or alienated by a government continues to grow faster than the number of persons attracted to its support, this government may be headed for political bankruptcy and eventual collapse, unless it can reverse its loss of domestic popularity or else bring in foreign support in adequate amounts.

Other thresholds or cross-over points may occur in relation to the proportions of people on one side or another of a single indicator. Thus, by 1950, urban Negroes for the first time had come to form the majority of the American Negro population, which, as late as 1940, had been in its majority rural. In some sense, this shift of balance within the American Negro community might well have alerted social scientists to the subsequent change in Negro political behavior, which occurred in the 1950–1960 decade. In all such cases, however, we are still dealing with some balance or interplay among two or more magnitudes or elements, which requires for its study some implied or explicit process model or mode of process analysis.

A very primitive method for keeping track of a larger number of different variables of states or political systems to be compared consists in specifying a configuration of variables relevant to our analysis for each case, and in specifying for each variable anywhere between two and ten different gross states or levels, separated by cut-off points suitably chosen for each variable. In this manner, it is possible to construct a simple configuration code, with each digit corresponding to a variable, and each numerical value of that particular digit corresponding to a state or level of that variable. Such a notation can then be used as a mnemonic device in constructing an inventory of interesting trends and patterns in comparative and international politics.[29] Even as primitive a technique as the use of configuration codes permits us to identify frequent configurations, and to single out for special study deviant cases and the particular dimensions and degrees in which each such case is deviant.

Another technique for identifying a deviant case has been developed by Michael Hudson, with the help of the rank-order profiles of some of the standard variables in Russett's *World Handbook*. In studying the case of Lebanon, Hudson noted the ten countries closest to it on the rank-order profiles of several indicators of social mobilization and economic development. He then repeated this procedure for such political indicators as the ratio of government expenditure to gross national product, and the ratio of votes cast to total adult population. He found that Lebanon ranked close to relatively advanced countries in its social and economic development, but close to far less well-developed countries in its indicated levels of government services and of political participation, and he related this contrast between Lebanon's society and its politics to the observed political instability of the country.[30]

A more extended method of analysis consists in computing correlations for each pair of a set of variables selected as salient for a given collection of countries, units, or cases. For the 75 variables in Russett's *World Handbook*, this procedure produced about 2,800 correlations. The computer was then programmed to print out all correlations with coefficients of correlation of 20 per cent or higher, with interesting results.[31] In another adaptation the computer was programmed to print all correlations, but to rank

29. K. W. Deutsch, "Toward an Inventory of Basic Trends and Patterns in Comparative and International Politics," *American Political Science Review,* 54 (March 1960), pp. 34–57. For some critical points, see Retzlaff, *op. cit.*

30. Michael Hudson, "A Case of Political Underdevelopment," *Journal of Politics* (pub. sched. Fall 1967). [Michael Hudson, "A Case of Political Underdevelopment," *Journal of Politics,* XXIX (November 1967), 821–837.]

31. Russett *et al., op. cit.,* pp. 261–292.

for each variable all other variables in descending order from the strongest positive to the strongest negative correlation with it. It was possible, therefore, to see whether some particular theory was confirmed not only by the strength of each correlation but also by its rank order among other theories. In this manner, some useful information could be extracted even from weak correlations in terms of their rank-order distribution.[32]

It is well known that a pair correlation often is not very informative, but the introduction of a third, discriminating variable may reveal a much stronger or much weaker relationship among the first two variables for some or all of the subgroups created by the introduction of the third.[33] This being so, it should be possible and worthwhile to develop computer programs for the rapid searching of large fields of pair correlations so as to identify for each pair correlation those third, discriminating variables the introduction of which would produce, in at least some of the new subgroups generated by the third variable, the greatest changes from the original correlation between the first two variables. Differently put, it might be desirable to find rapid computer search methods to find the most interesting "triplets" of variables and to compute and print out the relationships to which they give rise.

Other computer routines for searching large numbers of correlations among variables have already been used, such as the "pattern search technique" employed in the *Cross-Polity Survey* by Banks and Textor (which would further gain in usefulness if some of its coding procedures could be confirmed by additional research and retesting).[34]

Beyond the correlation techniques used thus far at all widely by political scientists, there are the broader possibilities of using methods of multiple-regression analysis, so as to compute and rank more accurately the contribution made to our prediction of the value of one variable by our knowledge of each of several other variables correlated with it. In addition to multiple-regression analysis, the method of factor analysis and the various techniques comprised within it all appear suited to the treatment of a wide range of problems in political science.

Factor analysis in essence replaces many variables by a few "factors" each of which is more or less highly correlated with a group of the original variables which are highly correlated among themselves, but have much less or no correlation with other groups of variables. In this way it is not necessary to compare, say, sixty countries in regard to, say, twenty indi-

32. Karl W. Deutsch, unpublished research, Yale University, 1965.

33. Cf. Paul F. Lazarsfeld, "Interpretation of Statistical Relations as a Research Operation," in Paul F. Lazarsfeld and Morris Rosenberg (eds.), *The Language of Social Research* (New York: Free Press of Glencoe, 1955, 1962), pp. 115–125; and Russett *et al., World Handbook, op. cit.*, pp. 323–340.

34. Arthur S. Banks and Robert Textor, *A Cross-Polity Survey*, footnote 10, above.

cators of economic and social development, such as per-capita income, steel production, newsprint consumption, literacy, industrial employment and the like, but it may suffice to compare these countries in terms of a single factor, "economic and social development," which is highly correlated with all the special indicators in this particular group. Factor analysis has been applied effectively to regional analysis, to voting patterns in the United Nations General Assembly, and to West European mass opinion data.[35] Eventually, it should be possible to use factor analysis, or else multiple-regression analysis, to find out whether the nationality of respondents—for example, French or German—has not a much stronger bearing on the distribution of political attitudes expressed than do such familiar conditions as age, income, socioeconomic status, occupation, religion, or socialist or nonsocialist party affiliation. Preliminary work at Yale suggests that this may be the case, and may lead in time to quantitative measurement of the relative influence of each of these conditions.[36]

A different but intellectually related set of techniques of analysis is based on estimating with what probability an observed distribution of outcomes would be produced by some random process, and then searching for special influences or determinants only to account for the observed deviations from the results expectable from random probability. Such probabilistic "null-models" have been applied to the analysis of the appearance in large bureaucracies, of small numbers of "wise men" who made a seeming sequence of correct policy choices, or foresighted adjustments to some changing party line. The null-model would then predict how many spurious "wise men" would be produced by random probability among a given number of bureaucrats making a given sequence of choices, and how many additional "wise men"—that is, makers of a correct sequence of choices—would have to appear in an organization of this size in order to justify the presumption of some genuinely high competence in making such choices.[37]

Other uses of the null-model technique combine it with the matrix analysis of transaction flows among a plurality of actors. Here, each row in one matrix represents the actual transactions initiated by one actor or else a subtotal of such rows for all transactions initiated by a group of actors,

35. Hayward Alker, Jr., and Bruce M. Russett, *World Politics in the General Assembly* (New Haven: Yale University Press, 1965); Bruce Russett, "Discovering Voting Groups in the United Nations," *American Political Science Review*, 60: 2 (June 1966), pp. 327–339; Donald A. Puchala, *European Political Integration: Progress and Prospects* (New Haven: Yale University Political Science Research Library, 1966), multigraphed.

36. K. W. Deutsch, work in progress, Yale University, 1965–1967; and "Integration and Arms Control in the European Political Environment: A Summary Report," *American Political Science Review*, 60: 2 (June 1966), pp. 354–365, esp. p. 364.

37. K. W. Deutsch and William Madow, "On the Appearance of Wisdom in Large Bureaucratic Organizations," *Behavioral Science*, 6 (1961), pp. 72–78.

while each column in the matrix represents the transactions terminating at one of the actors, or at a subtotal of such actors. The right-hand marginal column then contains the total of all transactions initiated by each actor, and the bottom row contains the total transactions terminating with each actor. The cells in the matrix then contain the actual transactions flowing from each actor to every other. A second matrix is then constructed from the same marginal columns and totals, but replacing the actual transaction figures in each cell with an expected figure computed from the marginal data with the help of a null model based on random probability. A third matrix then contains in each cell an index of relative deviation of the actual from the expected value for each pair of actors in each direction of the transaction flow between them.[38] The method has been applied to studies of integration in colonial empires and in regions of sovereign states; to a world matrix of exports in 1938 and 1954; to exports and trade integration patterns in the North Atlantic area between 1890 and 1963; and to the flow of mail, travelers, and university students among the six states of the European Common Market for the period 1925–1963; and it has been developed by Harrison White for application to the analysis of matrices of intergenerational social mobility, in which the fathers' social status or class forms the rows (or origins), and the sons' status or class forms the columns (or destinations).[39]

The more extended such methods and techniques become, the more they attempt to come to grips with the complexities of social processes, the more they drive their users to search for new sources of broader theories and models. Here the development of new methods leads back more to a strengthened interest in theory.

Some New Sources of Theories and Models

"New" theories, in the context of the recent developments in empirical research methods, are any theories that can be tested operationally, that is,

38. A technical description of the method is given in I. Richard Savage and K. W. Deutsch, "A Statistical Model of the Gross Analysis of Transaction Flows," *Econometrica*, 28 (July 1960), pp. 551–572; and a computer program has been published by H. R. Alker, Jr., in *Behavioral Science*, 7: 4 (October 1962), pp. 498–499. For suggested improvements in the method, see Leo A. Goodman, "Statistical Methods for the Preliminary Analysis of Transaction Flows," *Econometrica*, 31 (1963), pp. 197–208; and "A Short Computer Program for the Analysis of Transaction Flows," *Behavioral Science*, 9: 2 (April 1964), pp. 176–186.

39. Harrison C. White, "Cause and Effect in Social Mobility Tables," *Behavioral Science*, 8: 1 (January 1963), pp. 14–27; see also Karl W. Deutsch, "Toward an Inventory of Basic Trends and Patterns in Comparative and International Politics" (see footnote 29, above), pp. 34–57, esp. pp. 46–48; Hayward R. Alker, Jr., and Donald A. Puchala, "Trends in Economic Partnership in the North Atlantic Area," in J. David Singer (ed.), *Quantitative International Politics* (New York: Free Press, 1967).

by procedures and evidence that can be reproduced impersonally, regardless of the political or cultural preferences of the observer, and that can also be tested, at least indirectly, against "nature," that is, against some aspect of physical reality. The community of social scientists is then the community of persons who can agree upon a growing body of interpersonally verifiable methods and data, and who through this use of reproducible evidence remain connected with one another and with the larger world of nature.

The first source of new empirical theories, then, is many of the old nonempirical theories of the classic tradition of political science. *Implication analysis* can be used to examine each such theory for those of its implications that can be empirically tested. A classic example of this technique is ascribed to a nine-year-old boy, young Heinrich Schliemann, who reportedly remarked one day at the family breakfast table that if Homer's account of the eight-foot-thick stone walls of Troy was true, then these stone walls still were likely to be in existence, and that he, Heinrich Schliemann, some day would dig them up—something which subsequently he did. Similarly, if certain of Plato's theories in *The Republic* are true, there ought to be born a certain proportion of highly gifted children among the total population, and there ought to be a corresponding proportion of jobs or social roles of leaders of either the "philosopher" or "guardian" type in the society. If these quantitative implications of Plato's should be confirmed by empirical data about the actual statistical distribution of intellectual ability and of social leadership roles in all societies, or at least, in some particular society, then Plato's theory might, of course, still be found in error in other grounds; but if already these relatively simple empirical data should contradict it, then the theory certainly could not be accepted even provisionally without substantial modification. A systematic search could be made of major existing political theories—both classic and modern—to find implications that can be confirmed or disconfirmed by verifiable data.

A related technique might be the construction of a *propositional inventory,* which would gather and exhibit all or at least many of the relevant and verifiable propositions that could be found in some particular political theory or in several such theories. Harold Lasswell's and Abraham Kaplan's book, *Power and Society,* would lend itself admirably to this procedure.[40] Many of its propositions are already explicitly labeled in the text, so that they only need to be put side by side, and each of them confronted with a file of data and testing procedures relevant to its verification.

Attempts to verify a specific proposition or a broader theory usually lead to its restatement. Discriminating variables or critical conditions have been overlooked and must now be provided for. Distinctions and qualifications

---

40. H. D. Lasswell and A. Kaplan, *Power and Society* (New Haven: Yale University Press, 1950).

must be added, or even more drastic reformations may be necessitated or at least suggested. The explication and testing of old political propositions and theories thus leads to the formulation of new ones.

A similar procedure can be applied to propositions, theories, and methods of inquiry drawn more broadly from the social sciences. Sociology, psychology, anthropology, and economics all can be searched for patterns of thought and for specific propositions or theories that could be applied with suitable modifications to the study of politics. J. David Singer's recent collection from the behavioral sciences of materials directly relevant to the analysis of international politics is an important step in this direction.[41]

Another source of new theories and models for political research is found in *general systems theory*. Here attention is drawn to relations that may be similar at different systems levels: Why do many suburbs in metropolitan areas defend their "sovereignty" against mergers with, or encroachments by, either the central city or else some proposed metropolitan federation or authority? What similarities and what difference does this suburban struggle for quasi-independence show to the resistance of many sovereign nation-states against the pressures and attractions of their larger neighbors, or of proposed regional federations or projects for world government? When does integration prevail, and when does separatism, at the metropolitan and at the international levels, respectively? A recent joint study by experts in metropolitan planning and specialists in international relations has tried to make a beginning toward answering these questions.[42]

General systems theory, however, has broader implications for the development of political and social science theory. The use of common terms and concepts drawn from general systems theory has been studied by Oran Young, both for a group of political theorists and for a group of scholars drawn from a wider range of disciplines.[43] Some specific concepts and models widely used in general systems theory—such as cybernetic models and the feedback concept—are at the heart of some recent efforts by contemporary political theorists.[44]

41. J. David Singer, *Human Behavior and International Politics: Contributions from the Social-Psychological Sciences* (Chicago: Rand McNally, 1965).

42. Philip E. Jacob and James V. Toscano (eds.), *The Integration of Political Communities* (Philadelphia: Lippincott, 1964).

43. Oran R. Young, "A Survey of General Systems Theory," and "The Impact of General Systems Theory on Political Science," *General Systems*, Vol. 9 (1964), pp. 61–80 and 239–253; cf. also Klaus E. Knorr and Sidney A. Verba (eds.), *The International System: Theoretical Essays* (Princeton, N.J.: Princeton University Press, 1961); Charles A. McClelland, *Theory and the International System* (New York: The Macmillan Company, 1960).

44. David Easton, *A System Analysis of Politics* (New York: John Wiley & Sons, 1965); and *A Framework for Political Analysis* (Englewood Cliffs, N.J.: Prentice-Hall, 1965); K. W. Deutsch, *The Nerves of Government* (rev. ed.; New York: Free

Cybernetic models stress not only systems but also processes, particularly the processes of communication and control. In a broader sense, general systems theory is also a theory of processes, that is, of changes over time. James G. Miller has pointed out, however, that general systems theory does not neglect the research advantages that can be reaped from the study of structures, that is, of systems considered at a single instant or relatively brief period of time. Studying both structures and processes permits us to pay attention to the location in space of relatively persistent nodes of inter-action which are embodied in relatively stable, enduring, or recurrent arrangements in space, that are then available for many different processes of interaction and that can be located, and sometimes manipulated, by investigators.[45] Models of particular processes, with direct or potential relevance to politics, have been proposed in regard to political power systems by Morton Kaplan, to arms races by L. F. Richardson, to "peaceful coexistence" by G. F. Gause, and to games of strategy by John Von Neumann and Oskar Morgenstern, by Thomas C. Schelling, by Anatol Rapoport, and by others.[46]

A good deal of work also has been done on models of the process of

---

Press, 1966); John Burton, *International Relations: A General Theory* (Cambridge, Eng.: Cambridge University Press, 1965); cf. also Charles Dechert (ed.), *The Social Impact of Cybernetics* (South Bend, Ind.: University of Notre Dame Press, 1966).

45. James G. Miller, "Living Systems: Basic Concepts," *Behavioral Science,* 10: 3 (July 1965), pp. 193–237; and "Living Systems: Structure and Process," *ibid.,* 10: 4 (October 1965), pp. 337–379; and "Living Systems: Cross-Level Hypothesis," *ibid.,* pp. 381–411.

46. On process models, see Morton Kaplan, *System and Process in International Politics* (New York: John Wiley & Sons, 1957); and "The New Great Debate: Traditionalism vs. Science in International Relations," *World Politics,* 19: 1 (October 1966), pp. 1–20; L. F. Richardson, *Arms and Insecurity* (Pittsburgh and Chicago: Boxwood Press and Quadrangle Books, 1960); G. F. Gause, *The Struggle for Existence* (Baltimore: Williams and Wilkins, 1934); and "Verifications experimentales de la théorie mathématique de la lutte pour la vie," *Actualités Scientifiques et Industrielles* (Paris: Hermann, 1935). On game theory, see John Von Neumann and O. Morgenstern, *Theory of Games and Economic Behavior* (2nd ed.; Princeton, N.J.: Princeton University Press, 1947); Martin Shubik (ed.), *Game Theory and Related Approaches to Social Behavior* (New York: John Wiley & Sons, 1964); Thomas C. Schelling, *The Strategy of Conflict* (Cambridge, Mass.: Harvard University Press, 1960); and *Arms and Influence* (New Haven: Yale University Press, 1966); Anatol Rapoport, *Fights, Games and Debates* (Ann Arbor: University of Michigan Press, 1960); *Strategy and Conscience* (New York: Harper & Row, 1964); *Two-Person Game Theory: The Essential Ideas* (Ann Arbor: University of Michigan Press, 1966); and Anatol Rapoport and Albert Chammah, *Prisoners' Dilemma* (Ann Arbor: University of Michigan Press, 1966); Kenneth E. Boulding, *Conflict and Defense* (New York: Harper, 1962); Edward S. Quade, *Analysis for Military Decisions* (Chicago: Rand McNally, 1964); Martin Cyril McGuire, *Secrecy and the Arms Race* (Cambridge, Mass.: Harvard University Press, 1965); A. V. S. deReuck and Julie Knight (eds.), CIBA Foundation Symposium on *Conflict in Society* (London: Churchill, 1966).

learning, as derived from various theories of learning and tested against diverse experimental data.[47] Learning models—and perhaps particularly those making use of probability and of stochastic processes—in principle, should be applicable to various political problems involving behavior change or development over time. Applying such concepts and models of learning to the political behavior of individuals and groups, perhaps in combination with cybernetic models of self-steering, autonomy, memory, and goal-seeking and goal-changing feedback processes may well constitute a promising line of advance for political research and analysis in the future.

A particularly interesting class of such process models are the stochastic processes, the models of gambler's ruin and of random walk between barriers, mentioned earlier in this paper. Another version of stochastic-process analysis can be applied to several stages, states, or groups. This method involves the construction of *transition matrices* in which each state or group, at one time—such as Republican, Democrat, Independent, and nonvoters —is represented by a row, and the same state or group at a later time is represented by a column. Those individuals who did not change their state or group then remain in the cells on the main diagonal. Each of the other cells then contains those individuals that changed from the state indicated by the row to the state indicated by the column. Some transition probability for each cell can be assumed for each cell, or calculated from data for an early stage; and the probable future population of all cells can then be calculated for a number of steps ahead. This method has been applied by Lazarsfeld and Anderson to the opinion changes of voters in Erie County, Pennsylvania.[48]

47. Cf., for example, Ernest R. Hilgard (ed.), *Theories of Learning* (Chicago: University of Chicago Press, 1964); and Ernest R. Hilgard and G. H. Bower, *Theories of Learning* (2nd ed.; New York: Appleton-Century-Crofts [rev. ed.], 1956); Ernest R. Hilgard and D. G. Marquis, *Conditioning and Learning* (2nd ed.; New York: Appleton-Century-Crofts, 1960); Patrick Suppes and Richard C. Atkinson, *Markov Learning Models for Multiperson Interactions* (Stanford, Calif.: Stanford University Press, 1960); Merrill M. Flood, "Stochastic Learning Theory Applied to Choice Experiments with Rats, Dogs, and Men," *Behavioral Science*, 7: 3 (July 1962), pp. 289–314; Robert R. Bush and W. K. Estes (eds.), *Studies in Mathematical Learning Theory* (Stanford, Calif.: Stanford University Press, 1959); cf. also Bernard Berelson and Gary A. Steiner, *Human Behavior: An Inventory of Scientific Findings* (New York: Harcourt, Brace, and World, 1964), pp. 133–235; B. F. Skinner, *Walden Two* (New York: The Macmillan Company, 1948); Otto Klineberg, *The Human Dimension in International Relations* (New York: Holt, Rinehart, and Winston, 1964); and *Tensions Affecting International Understanding: A Survey of Research* (New York: Social Science Research Council, 1950).

48. T. W. Anderson, "Probability Models for Analyzing Time Changes in Attitudes," in Paul F. Lazarsfeld (ed.), *Mathematical Thinking in the Social Sciences* (New York and Glencoe, Ill.: Free Press, 1954), pp. 17–66; for the survey data used, see also Paul F. Lazarsfeld, Bernard Berelson, and Hazel Gaudet, *The People's Choice* (New York: Columbia University Press, 1948).

A similar method could be applied in principle also to the analysis of revolutions and guerrilla wars. These processes could then be analyzed by means of a transition matrix, which might show in five rows the initial strength of government troops, active government-supporters, passive or latent government-sympathizers, neutrals and indifferents, passive or latent opponents of the government, active opponents of the government, and actual guerrilla forces or revolutionary troops. The corresponding columns might then show the subsequent strength of each of these groups, say, a year later. The transition probabilities for each cell then might indicate how many active government-supporters had joined the government troops and how many had lapsed into passivity, or how many of the initially indifferent or neutral had shifted to the rebel side or even joined the guerrillas. A calculation might then show what the state of affairs in the country might be five years later, if these trends should continue. How much of a government or a rebel army would then still be in existence? The introduction of foreign troops on one or both sides of the conflict would complicate the matrix—as it would the conflict—but could be covered in the same kind of analysis.

To gain data for our various process models we resort to *longitudinal studies,* that is, to studies of time series of behavior changes in the past. Sometimes, however, we can also use data from *cross-sectional analysis,* comparing at one point in time several individuals, organizations, or cases at what we believe or surmise are different stages of one and the same sequence of development. Thus, the development of kittens into cats can be studied by photography or studying one kitten day after day as it grows up, or else by photographing or studying on one and the same day, side by side, many kittens of different ages, ranking them by size and other presumed indicators of maturity. If we are dealing with a process similar to the succession of stages of biological maturation, then the results of longitudinal and cross-sectional studies should be closely similar. Insofar as the results of these two kinds of studies differ, however, it seems likely that the biological analogy does not apply. In comparing highly developed and underdeveloped countries in the world today, we may find sharper and more extreme contrasts between these groups than we find in examining the rise of any one of today's advanced countries from its lower levels of, say, a century ago to its present level of affluence. To the extent that this is the case, we may wonder whether today's developing countries in Asia, Africa, and Latin America are of a different kind than were their counterparts in Europe one hundred years ago, or whether the difference among the countries is less important than the difference between the periods. If so, the comparison of longitudinal and cross-sectional studies would have furnished some evidence that the world had changed in some relevant aspects, and it could even indicate something about the extent and direction of the change.

As models become more rich and more realistic, they lend themselves more readily to *simulation*. One approach to such simulation of processes is mathematical. A statistical or mathematical model is constructed that corresponds to the most important characteristics of the real-life process to be simulated. Various changes and contingencies are then represented by numerical inputs into the model, and the changes produced by them in the state of the model and in its outputs to its environment are noted. These output changes can be thought of as responses of the model to the changes in its various inputs or parameters.

Where data are too scant, processes too complex, or models too simple, complete mathematical or statistical computer simulation may not be practical. In this case, it may be possible, however, to limit the formal model to a very few structural relationships connecting in specific ways several actors —such as political groups or rival countries—and then have each of these actors played by a person, who uses his own mind, memories, and preferences to make moves and decisions and to respond to moves by other actors. Even if the players are high school or college students, such games may lead to discoveries; if they are experienced diplomats, or military or political experts, the likelihood of obtaining relevant new information—or at least to discover relevant and hitherto neglected contingencies—should be correspondingly higher. Some intermediate techniques also have been developed between the pure simulation by computer and the "war-game" type of more or less dramatic representation by human actors. These employ computation for some parameters, variables, and trends over time, but let human actors make the remaining decisions within their context. A rich literature on simulation has sprung up, and the work of Hans Speier, Harold Guetzkow, Richard Brody, Lincoln Bloomfield, and others has become a significant part of political science.[49]

49. See Harold Guetzkow (ed.), *Simulation in Social Science: Readings* (Englewood Cliffs, N.J.: Prentice-Hall, 1962), and Harold Guetzkow, Chadwick F. Alger, Richard A. Brody, Robert C. North, and Richard C. Snyder, *Simulations in International Relations: Developments for Research and Teaching* (Englewood Cliffs, N.J.: Prentice-Hall, 1963). A concise but very useful statement is E. A. Robinson, "Simulation and Theory Construction," in his chapter "Recursive Decomposition of Stochastic Processes," in Herman O. A. Wold (ed.), *Econometric Model-Building* (Amsterdam: North Holland Publishing Company, 1964), pp. 147–151. See also the review article by Sidney Verba, "Simulation, Reality, and Theory in International Relations," *World Politics*, 16: 3 (April 1964), pp. 490–519; Ithiel de Sola Pool, Robert Abelson and Samuel Popkin, *Candidates, Issues, and Strategies: A Computer Simulation of the 1960 Presidential Election* (Cambridge, Mass.: M.I.T. Press, 1964); and Ithiel Pool and A. Kessler, "The Kaiser, the Tsar, and the Computers: Information-Processing in a Crisis," *American Behavioral Scientist*, 8 (1965), pp. 39–44. See also the important survey by Robert P. Abelson, "Simulation of Social Behavior" (mimeographed), as well as his forthcoming study on the politics of fluoridation and the forthcoming comparative study on simulation methods by Hayward R. Alker, Jr. See also Herbert H. Goldhamer and Hans Speier, "Some Observations on Political Gaming," *World Politics*, 12 (1959), pp. 71–83; Leonard P. Bloomfield and Norman Padelford, "Three

Simulation at best cannot be much better than our understanding of the processes which we imagine we are simulating. Anatol Rapoport has proposed a broad distinction among three kinds of social and political processes, and particularly of processes of conflict.[50] The first kind of processes are *fights*. Here the parties to the fight do not think or calculate effectively; they just react each to the other's behavior. One dog growls, and the other dog growls louder; the first dog's hackles rise, and the second snarls, until the escalation ends in a dogfight. A sovereign state increases its armament; its neighbor tries to keep ahead of it by some margin, but the first tries again to keep ahead, and the arms race may end in exhaustion or a war. Processes of this kind resemble blind processes of nature, and they can be simulated by pairs of differential equations in the case of two parties.

The second kind of processes are *games*. Here the parties make rational decisions in the pursuit of their interest. This is for each player the interest to win, and it does not change. The outcome of each player's move also depends on the move chosen by his opponent. Each player must try, therefore, to know or estimate the probability distribution of all possible outcomes, with the distribution of the corresponding possible payoffs to himself; and he must choose his own moves accordingly, so as to increase his gains and cut his risks. This behavior of rational players can be simulated in principle by the mathematics of game theory which were referred to earlier in this paper.[51]

The third type of processes Rapoport calls *debates*. Here the viewpoints, intentions, and interests of the parties themselves may change. They may become more or less hostile to each other; one actor may become converted to the viewpoint of another; or both may shift to a perception of some overriding common interest. A fair amount is known about such processes from studies of psychology and semantics—and presumably of religion—but there are no mathematical techniques available for simulating them.[52]

This shortcoming is not trivial. Much of politics, and generally of human conflict, involves a combination of all three kinds of process. The intellec-

---

Experiments in Political Gaming," *American Political Science Review*, 53 (1959), pp. 1105–1115; G. H. Orcutt, "Simulation of Economic Systems," *American Economic Review*, 50 (1960), pp. 893–907; Thomas C. Schelling, "An Experimental Game for the Study of Bargaining," *World Politics*, 14 (1961), pp. 47–68; Andrew M. Scott *et al.*, *Simulation and National Development* (New York: John Wiley & Sons, 1966); R. Brody, "Some Systemic Effects of the Spread of Nuclear Weapons: A Study through Simulation of a Multi-Nuclear Future," *Journal of Conflict Resolution*, 7: 4 (December 1963), pp. 664–753.

50. Anatol Rapoport, *Fights, Games and Debates*, *op. cit.*, pp. 1–12.

51. *Ibid.*, pp. 107–242; also *Two-person Game Theory: The Essential Idea* (footnote 46, above).

52. *Ibid.*, pp. 245–309.

tual *style* of game theory—though not its actual mathematics—pervades much of the work of modern writers on strategy, while the style of the theory of the escalating "fight" processes can be seen in various writings on escalation, regardless of whether this process is viewed with favor or alarm. Hardly anyone, however, discusses international politics in terms of a debate in which not only each actor's tactics may eventually change, but also his viewpoint and interests—and they may do so autonomously or in response to what occurred in the debate. As a result, the topics of the debate may shift, as well as the roles and mutual attitudes of the opponents or partners.

This process is ubiquitous in politics and generally in human affairs. It is of crucial importance in domestic politics, and perhaps no less in the long run for international relations. Yet its nature is not well understood. Even the literature on international communication often deals more with propaganda, manipulation, and persuasion—all processes in which the views and interests of at least one partner in the process are expected to remain unchanged. Studies of genuine change in political images and goals in response to experiences and to autonomous processes within acting countries or governments are still few and far between, although the volume on *International Behavior,* edited by Herbert Kelman, represents an attempt to move some way in this direction.[53]

Here again, the search for models, data, and techniques for simulation leads us back to the age-old search for insight. Scientific techniques can only help to solve a problem that has been perceived. Ordinarily, they cannot overcome obstacles that have not been recognized. A failure of nerve to face these problems, a failure of heart to reach out beyond the politics of competition and manipulation to the politics of growth and new social learning—such failures could not be wiped out by improvements in methodology.

With the willingness, however, to confront all relevant political problems —even those that may be difficult and painful, such as the rigidities and blind spots in our own thoughts and practices—political science can use the new methods to make real progress. We need a cumulative political science where knowledge will grow and clearly improve in scope, amount, and quality, as it has done in so many other fields of human knowledge. Such a cumulative knowledge of what can and what cannot be done in politics under specific conditions should open the way to more effective applications of political science in the service of freedom and peace, within

53. Herbert C. Kelman (ed.), *International Behavior: A Social-Psychological Analysis* (New York: Holt, Rinehart and Winston, 1965). For several significant recent analyses of both historical and contemporary cases of cultural and attitude change of whole societies, see Carl J. Friedrich (ed.), *Revolution: Nomos VIII,* Yearbook of the American Society for Political and Legal Philosophy (New York: Atherton Press, 1966).

countries and among them. Medicine and economics have come a long way in developing from "dismal sciences" to humanistic sciences. Political science may yet move in the same direction.

Further Suggested Readings

Almond, Gabriel, and Coleman, James, eds. *The Politics of The Developing Areas*. Princeton: Princeton University Press, 1960.

Barker, Sir Ernest, trans. and ed. *The Politics of Aristotle*. New York: Oxford University Press, 1946.

Bendix, Reinhard. *Max Weber, An Intellectual Portrait*. New York: Doubleday, 1962.

Dahl, Robert. "The Behavioral Approach in Political Science: Epitaph for a Monument to a Successful Protest," *American Political Science Review*, 55 (December 1961), 763–72.

Easton, David. *The Political System*. New York: Knopf, 1953.

Eckstein, Harry, and Apter, David A., eds. *Comparative Politics: A Reader*. New York: Free Press, 1963.

Friedrich, Carl Joachim. *Man and His Government*. New York: McGraw-Hill, 1963.

Heckscher, Gunnar. *The Study of Comparative Government and Politics*. London: Allen and Unwin, 1957.

Holt, Robert T., and Turner, John E., eds. *The Methodology of Comparative Research*. New York: Free Press, 1970.

Kalleberg, Arthur. "The Logic of Comparison: A Methodological Note on the Comparative Study of Political Systems," *World Politics,* 19 (October 1966), 69–82.

Kuhn, Thomas. *The Structure of Scientific Revolutions*. Chicago: University of Chicago Press, 1962.

Macridis, Roy C. *The Study of Comparative Government*. New York: Random House, 1955.

Merritt, Richard L., and Rokkan, Stein, eds. *Comparing Nations: The Use of Quantitative Data in Cross-National Research*. New Haven: Yale University Press, 1965.

Przeworski, Adam, and Teune, Henry. *The Logic of Comparative Social Inquiry*. New York: John Wiley & Sons, 1970.

Runciman, W.G. *Social Science and Political Theory*. Cambridge: Cambridge University Press, 1963.

Storing, Herbert, ed. *Essays on the Scientific Study of Politics*. New York: Holt, Rinehart and Winston, 1962.

Strauss, Leo. *What Is Political Philosophy?* New York: Free Press, 1959.

2

Comparisons of Total Systems

Introduction

An intellectually exciting feature of the study of comparative politics that tends to set it apart from the study of exclusively behaviorally influenced American politics on the one hand and much of behaviorally influenced social science on the other is the manner in which it addresses itself explicitly to the study of the total political system. As we noted in the preceding chapter, the emphasis upon quantification and scientifically rigorous procedures in what has been called the behavioral revolution in political science had in effect the defects of its virtues in its impact upon the study of politics. The emphasis upon precision had an inevitable narrowing effect upon both the scope of the questions asked and the phenomenon being studied. The fact that behavioralism was essentially an American phenomenon facilitated this narrowing process. American scholars studying specific aspects of American voting behavior, for example, could feel comfortable in focusing narrowly because as Americans they could, for the most part, take for granted wider variables as basic as allegiance to the system (political legitimacy) or the relationship of voting behavior to the overall operation of the American political system.

Students of comparative politics, by way of contrast, take as their fundamental point of departure, first, a consideration of the totality of the political system. Although the reasons for their doing this will be discussed in a moment when it will be seen that these reflect certain intellectual tendencies of our own time, it can be observed that perhaps quite inadvertently comparative politics has become the custodian of a renewed emphasis upon the grand tradition of what can be termed holistic political analysis; that is, the past tradition exemplified by Aristotle and other political philosophers in their attempts to characterize entire political systems in terms of both the normative ends and the social elements of the population which these systems are meant to serve. Once again we see the manner in which the normative and empirical come together. Hopefully the manner in which this occurs will be made more specific as our present discussion develops.

106

The central concern of the older tradition of the holistic approach to political science was defining the nature and the merits of the principles of political legitimacy, i.e., the basic values and ends of a political system to which individuals can give their support. Efforts at judging the respective merits of constitutionalism and authoritarianism, for example, as in our readings, are something that has been for the most part neglected in modern political science. Assertion in support of democracy and against autocracy takes the place of reasoned argument until students and scholars alike end up by assuming the virtues of democracy. This is one further way of stating the impact of the commitment to pluralism both in empirical and normative terms discussed in the introduction to the preceding chapter. The area of greater linkage of twentieth century political science to the classical holistic approach is in the effort to define the nature of political legitimacy, especially in terms of how support of political principles is achieved. Treatment of the nature of political legitimacy as the basis of classification and analysis of political regimes is reflected in our readings on constitutionalism and authoritarianism. Recognition of the fact that such support is necessary and some indication of the manner in which this support is gained can be seen in the remaining readings by Easton and Almond under the heading of empirical conceptualizations. This concern with the modes of engendering a commitment to the principles of political legitimacy of a regime is further reflected specifically in Chapter 3 under the title "Political Socialization and Political Culture" as well as in the concluding chapter on political change.

In addition to the foregoing, however, it is useful, in understanding what it is that a student of comparative politics does, to realize that to some extent an approach to the study of a total political system is perhaps inevitable and intrinsic to the study of "foreign" politics. In approaching such a foreign political system the first comprehension is an external one that puts a premium upon understanding that system's most salient features. The student of comparative politics is thus put in the position of seeing the forest whereas often the native to the system most often sees only the trees. It is exactly this difference in perspective that makes de Tocqueville, Bryce, and Brogan the most insightful analysts of American politics and society.[1] It might be presumptuous to assume that scholars of comparative politics in the 1950's and 1960's have approached the genius of these figures, but it is true that the so-called country studies common in comparative politics from the 1950's onward, i.e., single volumes dealing with the politics of the entirety of foreign states in an effort to analyze them and perhaps less frequently to theorize about them, are analogous in approach.

1. Alexis de Tocqueville, *Democracy in America* (New York: New American Library, 1960 [1835]). James Bryce, *The American Commonwealth* (New York: Capricorn, 1960 [1888]), 2 vols. D. W. Brogan, *Politics in America* (New York: Doubleday, 1960).

Aside from this genetic explanation, there is perhaps a second explanation that might be proffered regarding this holistic analytical tendency, and that is inasmuch as the decolonization process tended to be a dominant feature of the 1950's and 1960's scholars quite naturally tended to take their intellectual cues from the newly established political leaderships. The Nkrumahs, the Sukarnos, and Nehrus of these turbulent decades defined their major domestic concerns as being the political integration of their societies, and students of these societies began defining themselves intellectually as being interested in nation-building, the processes contributing to the creation of a single political system.

The foregoing has given us some idea of how comparative politics has come to address itself to the understanding of total political systems but the question now needs to be asked, how is this done? To pick up the themes of the present volume in terms of normative and empirical perspectives once again, the answer can be given in terms of exactly these categories—the conceptually normative and empirical.

Two dominant concerns have been present in the normative perspectives regarding the nature of the total political system: constitutionalism and authoritarianism. They have been defined in mutually exclusive terms as systems which attempt to put limits upon exercise of executive political power on the one hand, and on the other hand as systems which permit freer exercise of executive power. For the scholars involved, the strength of such an approach permits both the recognition of the salient normative features of systems, usually in terms of greater or lesser democracy, and categories for comparisons under constitutional or authoritarian rubrics.

Rustow's representative selection of constitutionalism ably summarizes the scholarship bearing on the understanding of how democracy is maintained and presents some original insights of his own as to how democracy evolves. In reference to authoritarianism, the concern on the part of most scholars is not to appear as advocates but implicitly at least as critics. This normative commitment as critics has been maintained while at the same time they have attempted to understand the phenomenon dispassionately. Largely because authoritarianism has been identified in the post-World War II period with the Soviet Union (though we often fail to consider Spain, Portugal, and other countries) there has been a tendency not to examine authoritarianism or, as it has been more commonly called in the past, totalitarianism, comparatively. It is an effort to correct this that Tucker makes in the selection included here. Partly due to his efforts, the subject of comparative communism has had great emphasis in recent years.

A different approach to the study of total systems is of more recent vintage than the preceding, more normative ones of constitutionalism and authoritarianism. The latter approaches are more consistent with and an outgrowth of both classical political science approaches and more recent nineteenth century institutional legalistic approaches, whereas the conceptual approach is more modern and contemporary in that while building at least implicitly upon the earlier tradition, it now turns itself to scientific classifications with a greater emphasis upon behavioral phenomena such as process (Easton) and function (Almond).

Easton has become synonymous with the concept of "political system," which a close reading of his selection will reveal to be a more technically specific concept than its casual usage in political science may have led you to believe so far. Systems theory is intellectually challenging in the potential it holds for being a unifying concept of all contemporary knowledge. Its direct intellectual ancestor is the field of cybernetics, which has had a great societal impact in the form of computer technology. In addition, however, the concepts of biological, nervous, engineering, and other systems give some sense of the common concerns underlying, for example, the publication *General Systems Yearbook*. In its political aspects Easton's formulations have affected the thinking of a whole generation of political scientists. One criticism of the general approach has been that it is difficult to operationalize, that is, to find concrete and specific referents to its theoretical components. Perhaps partly in reaction to this criticism, Easton has completed research of which his selection in Chapter 3 is an example wherein he examines political socialization as a dimension of the "support" aspect of the inputs of the political system.

As with the Easton selection, the one by Almond likewise puts forth an approach, that of structural-functionalism, which has been highly influential in contemporary political science. Beginning with the publication of *The Politics of the Developing Areas* in 1960, Almond's effort to analyze all political systems in terms of the universal input-output functions they perform has been adopted by numerous scholars as a conceptual framework. Much more could be said regarding the ideas of these major figures but perhaps these brief characterizations and a reading of their selections will give you some feeling of the intellectual breadth of comparative politics.

Normative Conceptualizations: Constitutionalism

Transitions to Democracy*

Toward a Dynamic Model—Dankwart A. Rustow

I

What conditions make democracy possible and what conditions make it thrive? Thinkers from Locke to de Tocqueville and A.D. Lindsay have given many answers. Democracy, we are told, is rooted in man's innate capacity for self-government or in the Christian ethical or the Teutonic legal tradition. Its birthplace was the field at Putney where Cromwell's angry young privates debated their officers, or the more sedate House at Westminster, or the rock at Plymouth, or the forest cantons above Lake Lucerne, or the fevered brain of Jean Jacques Rousseau. Its natural champions are sturdy yeomen, or industrious merchants, or a prosperous middle class. It must be combined with strong local government, with a two-party system, with a vigorous tradition of civil rights, or with a multitude of private associations.

Recent writings of American sociologists and political scientists favor three types of explanation. One of these, proposed by Seymour Martin Lipset, Philips Cutright, and others, connects stable democracy with certain economic and social background conditions, such as high per capita income, widespread literacy, and prevalent urban residence. A second type of explanation dwells on the need for certain beliefs or psychological attitudes among the citizens. A long line of authors from Walter Bagehot to Ernest Barker has stressed the need for consensus as the basis of democracy— either in the form of a common belief in certain fundamentals or of procedural consensus on the rules of the game, which Barker calls "the Agreement to Differ." Among civic attitudes required for the successful working of a democratic system, Daniel Lerner has proposed a capacity for empathy and a willingness to participate. To Gabriel Almond and Sidney

*This article was presented at the annual meeting of the American Political Science Association, New York City, September 1969. The author is grateful for financial support at various stages of his researches into democracy from the John Simon Guggenheim Foundation, the Ford Foundation, and the National Science Foundation. He jealously claims the full blame for his errors, foibles, and follies as revealed in this essay.

Reprinted from Comparative Politics, II: 3 (April 1970), 389–412, by special permission of the author and the publisher.

Verba, on the other hand, the ideal "civic culture" of a democracy suggests not only such participant but also other traditional or parochial attitudes.[1]

A third type of explanation looks at certain features of social and political structure. In contrast to the prevailing consensus theory, authors such as Carl J. Friedrich, E. E. Schattschneider, Bernard Crick, Ralf Dahrendorf, and Arend Lijphart have insisted that conflict and reconciliation are essential to democracy.[2] Starting with a similar assumption, David B. Truman has attributed the vitality of American institutions to the citizens' "multiple membership in potential groups"—a relationship which Lipset has called one of "crosscutting politically relevant associations."[3] Robert A. Dahl and Herbert McClosky, among others, have argued that democratic stability requires a commitment to democratic values or rules, not among the electorate at large but among the professional politicians—each of these presumably linked to the other through effective ties of political organization.[4] Harry Eckstein, finally, has proposed a rather subtle theory of "congruence": to make democracy stable, the structures of authority throughout society, such as family, church, business, and trade unions, must prove the more democratic the more directly they impinge on processes of government.[5]

Some of these hypotheses are compatible with each other, though they may also be held independently—for example, those about prosperity, literacy, and consensus. Others—such as those about consensus and conflict—are contradictory unless carefully restricted or reconciled. Precisely such a synthesis has been the import of a large body of writing. Dahl, for

1. Ernest Barker, *Reflections on Government* (Oxford, 1942), p. 63; Daniel Lerner et al., *The Passing of Traditional Society* (Glencoe, 1958), pp. 49ff., 60ff.; Gabriel Almond and Sidney Verba, *The Civic Culture* (Princeton, 1963).

2. Carl J. Friedrich, *The New Belief in the Common Man* (Boston, 1942); E. E. Schattschneider, *The Semi-Sovereign People* (New York, 1960); Bernard Crick, *In Defence of Politics,* rev. ed. (Penguin Books, 1964); Ralf Dahrendorf, *Class and Class Conflict in Industrial Society* (Stanford, 1959); Arend Lijphart, *The Politics of Accommodation* (Berkeley and Los Angeles, 1968).

3. David B. Truman, *The Governmental Process* (New York, 1951), p. 514; S. M. Lipset, *Political Man* (New York, 1960), pp. 88ff. Already A. Lawrence Lowell had spoken of the need for a party alignment where "the line of division is vertical," cutting across the horizontal division of classes. *Government and Parties in Continental Europe* (Boston, 1896), vol. 2, pp. 65ff.

4. Robert A. Dahl, *Who Governs?* (New Haven, 1961); Herbert McClosky, "Consensus and Ideology in American Politics," *American Political Science Review,* LVIII (June 1964); James W. Prothro and Charles M. Grigg, "Fundamental Principles of Democracy: Bases of Agreement and Disagreement," *Journal of Politics,* XXII (May 1960).

5. Harry Eckstein, *The Theory of Stable Democracy* (Princeton, 1961) and *Division and Cohesion in a Democracy* (Princeton, 1965).

instance, has proposed that in polyarchy (or "minorities rule," the closest real-life approximation to democracy) the policies of successive governments tend to fall within a broad range of majority consensus.[6] Indeed, after an intense preoccupation with consensus in the World War II years, it is now widely accepted that democracy is indeed a process of "accommodation" involving a combination of "division and cohesion" and of "conflict and consent"—to quote the key terms from a number of recent book titles.[7]

The scholarly debate thus continues, and answers diverge. Yet there are two notable points of agreement. Nearly all the authors ask the same sort of question and support their answers with the same sort of evidence. The question is not how a democratic system comes into existence. Rather it is how a democracy, assumed to be already in existence, can best preserve or enhance its health and stability. The evidence adduced generally consists of contemporary information, whether in the form of comparative statistics, interviews, surveys, or other types of data. This remains true even of authors who spend considerable time discussing the historical background of the phenomena that concern them—Almond and Verba of the civic culture, Eckstein of congruence among Norwegian social structures, and Dahl of the ruling minorities of New Haven and of oppositions in Western countries.[8] Their key propositions are couched in the present tense.

There may be a third feature of similarity underlying the current American literature of democracy. All scientific inquiry starts with the conscious or unconscious perception of a puzzle.[9] What has puzzled the more influential authors evidently has been the contrast between the relatively smooth functioning of democracy in the English-speaking and Scandinavian countries and the recurrent crises and final collapse of democracy in the French Third and Fourth Republics and in the Weimar Republic of Germany.

This curiosity is of course wholly legitimate. The growing literature and the increasingly subtle theorizing on the bases of democracy indicate how fruitful it has been. The initial curiosity leads logically enough to the functional, as opposed to the genetic, question. And that question, in turn, is most readily answered by an examination of contemporary data about functioning democracies—perhaps with badly functioning democracies and nondemocracies thrown in for contrast. The functional curiosity also comes naturally to scholars of a country that took its crucial steps toward democracy as far back as the days of Thomas Jefferson and Andrew Jackson. It accords, moreover, with some of the characteristic trends in American

6. Robert A. Dahl, *A Preface to Democratic Theory* (Chicago, 1956).

7. Lijphart; Eckstein; Dahl, *Pluralist Democracy in the United States: Conflict and Consent* (Chicago, 1967).

8. Almond and Verba; Eckstein; Dahl, *Who Governs?* and ed. *Political Oppositions in Western Democracies* (New Haven, 1966).

9. See Thomas Kuhn, *The Structure of Scientific Revolutions* (Chicago, 1962).

social science in the last generation or two—with the interest in systematic equilibria, in quantitative correlations, and in survey data engendered by the researcher's own questions. Above all, it accords with a deep-seated prejudice against causality. As Herbert A. Simon has strikingly put it, ". . . we are wary, in the social sciences, of asymmetrical relations. They remind us of pre-Humeian and pre-Newtonian notions of causality. By whip and sword we have been converted to the doctrine that there is no causation, only functional interrelation, and that functional relations are perfectly symmetrical. We may even have taken over, as a very persuasive analogy, the proposition 'for every action, there is an equal and opposite reaction.' "[10]

Students of developing regions, such as the Middle East, Southern Asia, tropical Africa, or Latin America, naturally enough have a somewhat different curiosity about democracy. The contrast that is likely to puzzle them is that between mature democracies, such as the United States, Britain, or Sweden today, and countries that are struggling on the verge of democracy, such as Ceylon, Lebanon, Turkey, Peru, or Venezuela. This will lead them to the genetic question of how a democracy comes into being in the first place.[11] The question is (or at least was, until the Russian invasion of Czechoslovakia in 1968) of almost equal interest in Eastern Europe. The genesis of democracy, thus, has not only considerable intrinsic interest for most of the world; it has greater pragmatic relevance than further panegyrics about the virtues of Anglo-American democracy or laments over the fatal illnesses of democracy in Weimar or in several of the French Republics.

In the following sections of this article I should like to examine some of the methodological problems involved in the shift from functional to genetic inquiry and then proceed to outline one possible model of the transition to democracy.

II

What changes in concept or method does the shift from functional to genetic inquiry imply? The simplest answer would be, "None at all." The temptation is to make the functional theories do double duty as genetic theories, to extend the perspective of Westminster and Washington versus Weimar and Paris to Ankara, Caracas, and Bucharest as well. If conditions such as consensus or prosperity will help to preserve a functioning democracy, it may be argued, surely they will be all the more needful to bring it into existence.

10. Herbert A. Simon, *Models of Man: Social and Rational* (New York, 1957), p. 65.

11. For a general discussion of the question of democracy in the context of recent modernizing countries, see Rustow, *A World of Nations: Problems of Political Modernization* (Washington, 1967), Ch. 7, which states some of the present argument in summary form.

Alas, the simple equation of function and genesis is a little too simple, and the argument a fortiori is, in fact, rather weak.[12] The equation certainly does not seem to hold for most other types of political regimes. Military dictatorships, for instance, typically originate in secret plotting and armed revolt but perpetuate themselves by massive publicity and by alliances with civilian supporters. Charismatic leaders, according to Max Weber, establish their claim to legitimacy by performing seeming miracles but preserve it through routinization. A hereditary monarchy rests most securely on the subjects' unquestioning acceptance of immemorial tradition; it evidently cannot be erected on such a principle. Communist regimes have been installed by revolutionary elites or through foreign conquest but consolidated through the growth of domestic mass parties and their bureaucracies. From physics and chemistry, too, the distinction between the energy required to initiate and to sustain a given reaction is familiar. These arguments from analogy of course are just as inconclusive as the supposedly a fortiori one. Still, they shift the burden of proof to those who assert that the circumstances which sustain a mature democracy also favor its birth.

The best known attempts to apply a single world-wide perspective to democracy, whether nascent or mature, are the statistical correlations compiled by Lipset and by Cutright.[13] But Lipset's article well illustrates the difficulty of applying the functional perspective to the genetic question. Strictly interpreted, his data bear only on function. His statistical findings all take the form of correlations at a given single point in time. In the 1950s his "stable democracies" generally had substantially higher per capita incomes and literacy rates than did his "unstable democracies," or his unstable and stable authoritarianisms. Now, correlation evidently is not the same as causation—it provides at best a clue to some sort of causal connection without indicating its direction. Lipset's data leave it entirely open, for example, whether affluent and literate citizens make the better democrats; whether democracies provide superior schools and a more bracing climate for economic growth; whether there is some sort of reciprocal connection so that a given increase in affluence or literacy and in democracy will produce a corresponding increment in the other; or whether there is some further set of factors, such as the industrial economy perhaps, that causes both democracy *and* affluence and literacy. A corresponding objection can be urged against the findings of Almond, Verba, and others that are based mainly on contemporary opinion or attitude surveys. Only further investigation could show whether such attitudes as "civic culture," an eagerness

12. ". . . a political form may persist under conditions normally adverse to the *emergence* of that form" (Lipset, p. 46).

13. Seymour Martin Lipset, "Some Social Requisites of Democracy: Economic Development and Political Legitimacy," *American Political Science Review,* LIII (March 1959); idem. *Political Man*; Philips Cutright, "National Political Development: Measurement and Analysis," *American Sociological Review,* XXVIII (April 1963).

to participate, a consensus on fundamentals, or an agreement on procedures are cause or effect of democracy, or both, or neither.

Lipset's title is true to his functional concern. He is careful to speak of "Some Social Requisites," not prerequisites, "of Democracy," and thus to acknowledge the difference between correlation and cause. But the subtlety has escaped many readers who unthinkingly translate "requisites" into "preconditions."[14] The text of the article, moreover, encourages the same substitution, for it repeatedly slips from the language of correlation into the language of causality. Significantly, on all those occasions economic and social conditions become the independent, and democracy the dependent, variable.

A genetic theory will have to be explicit about distinguishing correlate from cause. This does not commit us to any old-fashioned or simpleminded view of causality, whereby every effect has but one cause and every cause but one effect. It does not preclude the "probabilistic" view recently argued by Almond and, indeed, espoused by every social statistician since Emile Durkheim and before.[15] It does not rule out somewhat more sophisticated causal concepts such as Gunnar Myrdal's spiral, Karl W. Deutsch's quorum of prerequisites, Hayward R. Alker's nonlinear correlations, or the notion of a threshold which Deane Neubauer recently applied to Lipset's and Cutright's propositions.[16] Above all, a concern for causality is compatible with—indeed is indispensable to—a sceptical view that attributes human events to a mixture of law and chance. Such semideterminism is tantamount to an admission that the social scientist will never know enough to furnish a complete explanation, that he is at least as unlikely as the natural scientist to rival Laplace's Demon. Nor do scholars who would theorize about the genesis of democracy need to concur in all their epistemology and metaphysics. But to be geneticists at all they do have to inquire into causes. Only by such inquiry, I would add, can the social scientist accomplish his proper task of exploring the margins of human choice and of clarifying the consequences of the choices in that margin.[17]

It probably is no simple confusion between correlate and cause that

14. Rupert Emerson, *From Empire to Nation* (Cambridge, 1960), p. 278, paraphrases Lipset to this effect. M. Rejai, in his useful anthology and commentary, *Democracy: The Contemporary Theories* (New York, 1967), includes an excerpt from the article under the heading, "Socioeconomic Preconditions" (pp. 242–247).

15. Gabriel A. Almond and James S. Coleman, eds. *The Politics of the Developing Areas* (Princeton, 1960), Introduction.

16. Gunnar Myrdal, *An American Dilemma* (New York, 1944), Appendix; Hayward R. Alker, Jr., "The Long Road to International Relations Theory: Problems of Statistical Non-Additivity," *World Politics*, XVIII (July 1966); Deane Neubauer, "Some Conditions of Democracy," *American Political Science Review*, LXI (December 1967).

17. This statement of the function of the social scientist is taken from Rustow, *A World of Nations*, p. 17; the next two paragraphs paraphrase ibid., pp. 142ff.

leads Lipset's readers astray, and, on occasion, the author as well. Rather it seems to be a tacit assumption that social and economic conditions are somehow more basic, and that we must look for the significant relations in this deeper layer rather than in the "superstructure" of political epiphenomena. Our current emphasis in political science on economic and social factors is a most necessary corrective to the sterile legalism of an earlier generation. But, as Lipset (together with Bendix) has himself warned in another context, it can easily "explain away the very facts of political life."[18] We have been in danger of throwing away the political baby with the institutional bathwater.

Note that this widespread American economicism goes considerably beyond Marx and Engels, who saw the state as created by military conquest, economic regimes defined by their legal relations of property, and changes from one to the next brought about through political revolution. If they proclaimed themselves materialists or talked like economic determinists, it was mainly in protest against the wilder flights of Hegelian "idealism."

Any genetic theory of democracy would do well to assume a two-way flow of causality, or some form of circular interaction, between politics on the one hand and economic and social conditions on the other. Wherever social or economic background conditions enter the theory, it must seek to specify the mechanisms, presumably in part political, by which these penetrate to the democratic foreground. The political scientist, moreover, is entitled to his rights within the general division of labor and may wish to concentrate on some of the political factors without denying the significance of the social or economic ones. With Truman, Dahl, and others, I would tend to see the patterns of conflict and of recurrent or changing alignments as one of the central features of any political system. With Apter, I would consider choice as one of the central concerns of the political process.[19]

What goes for economics and sociology goes for psychology as well. Here, too, the relationship with politics is one of interaction and interdependence, so that political phenomena may have psychological consequences as well as vice versa. In explaining the origins of democracy we need not assume—as does much of the current survey research literature—that beliefs unilaterally influence actions. Rather, we may recognize with Leon Festinger and other social psychologists of the "cognitive dissonance" school that there are reciprocal influences between beliefs and actions.[20] Many of the current theories about democracy seem to imply that to promote democracy you must first foster democrats—perhaps by preachment, propaganda, education, or perhaps as an automatic by-product of growing

18. Reinhard Bendix and Seymour Martin Lipset, "Political Sociology," *Current Sociology*, VI, No. 2 (1957), 85.

19. David E. Apter, *The Politics of Modernization* (Chicago, 1965).

20. Leon Festinger, *A Theory of Cognitive Dissonance* (Stanford, 1957).

prosperity. Instead, we should allow for the possibility that circumstances may force, trick, lure, or cajole nondemocrats into democratic behavior and that their beliefs may adjust in due course by some process of rationalization or adaptation.

To seek causal explanations, as I insisted earlier, does not imply simplemindedness. Specifically, we need not assume that the transition to democracy is a worldwide uniform process, that it always involves the same social classes, the same types of political issues, or even the same methods of solution. On the contrary, it may be well to assume with Harry Eckstein that a wide variety of social conflicts and of political contents can be combined with democracy.[21] This is, of course, in line with the general recognition that democracy is a matter primarily of procedure rather than of substance. It also implies that, as among various countries that have made the transition, there may be many roads to democracy.

Nor does a model of transition need to maintain that democratic evolution is a steady process that is homogeneous over time. Such a notion of temporal continuity and presumably of linear correlation seems to lurk behind much of the literature of the Lipset-Cutright genre. Temporal discontinuity, on the contrary, is implicit in the basic distinction drawn earlier in this article between the functional and genetic questions. The same discontinuity may be carried into the genetic scheme itself. For instance, it may be useful to single out certain circumstances as background factors and to proceed step-by-step to other factors that may become crucial in the preparation, decision, and consolidation phases of the process.

Even in the same country and during the same phase of the process, political attitudes are not likely to be spread evenly through the population. Dahl, McClosky, and others have found that in mature democracies there are marked differences in the attitudes of professional politicians and of common citizens.[22] Nor can we take it for granted that the politicians will all share the same attitudes. Insofar as democracy is based on conflict, it may take two attitudes to make a quarrel. All these differences are likely, moreover, to be compounded during the formative period when part of the quarrel must *ex hypothesi* be between democrats and nondemocrats. Finally, a dynamic model of the transition must allow for the possibility that different groups—e.g., now the citizens and now the rulers, now the forces in favor of change and now those eager to preserve the past—may furnish the crucial impulse toward democracy.

III

The methodological argument I have been advancing may be condensed into a number of succinct propositions.

21. Eckstein, *Division and Cohesion*, pp. 183–85.

22. Dahl, *Who Governs?;* McClosky; Prothro and Grigg.

1. The factors that keep a democracy stable may not be the ones that brought it into existence: explanations of democracy must distinguish between function and genesis.

2. Correlation is not the same as causation: a genetic theory must concentrate on the latter.

3. Not all causal links run from social and economic to political factors.

4. Not all causal links run from beliefs and attitudes to actions.

5. The genesis of democracy need not be geographically uniform: there may be many roads to democracy.

6. The genesis of democracy need not be temporally uniform: different factors may become crucial during successive phases.

7. The genesis of democracy need not be socially uniform: even in the same place and time the attitudes that promote it may not be the same for politicians and for common citizens.

My refrain, like Sportin' Life's, has been, "It ain't necessarily so." Each proposition pleads for the lifting of some conventional restriction, for the dropping of some simplifying assumption made in the previous literature, for the introduction of complicating, diversifying factors. If the argument were to conclude on this sceptical note, it would set the researcher completely adrift and make the task of constructing a theory of democratic genesis well-nigh unmanageable.

Fortunately, the genetic perspective requires or makes possible a number of new restrictions that more than compensate for the loss of the seven others. We may continue the listing of summary propositions before elaborating this second part of the methodological argument.

8. Empirical data in support of a genetic theory must cover, for any given country, a time period from just before until just after the advent of democracy.

9. To examine the logic of transformation *within* political systems, we may leave aside countries where a major impetus came from abroad.

10. A model or ideal type of the transition may be derived from a close examination of two or three empirical cases and tested by application to the rest.

That diachronic data, covering more than a single point in time, are essential to any genetic theory should be obvious. Such a theory, moreover, must be based on cases where the process is substantially complete. Although control data on nondemocracies and on abortive and incipient cases may become important at a later stage of theorizing, it is more convenient to start out by studying a phenomenon where it actually has come into existence. The "advent" of democracy must not, of course, be understood as occurring in a single year. Since the emergence of new social groups and the formation of new habits are involved, one generation is probably the minimum period of transition. In countries that had no earlier models to emulate, the transition is likely to have come even more slowly. In Britain, for example, it may be argued that it began before 1640 and was not accomplished until 1918. For an initial set of hypotheses, however, it may be best to turn to countries where the process occurred relatively rapidly.

The study of democratic transitions will take the political scientist deeper into history than he has commonly been willing to go. This implies many changes in method—beginning with suitable substitutions for survey data and for interviews. Even reliable statistics are harder to come by early in any democratic experiment. The United States Constitution (Article 1, Section 2) reminds us that our decennial census was introduced at that very time so that we might begin to govern ourselves by an accurate count of noses.

Whatever the difficulties in the vastly increased use of historical data by social scientists, at least three arguments can be made in extenuation and encouragement. Man did not become a political animal in 1960 or in 1945, as much of our recent literature pretends to suppose. History, to paraphrase Georges Clemenceau, is far too important a topic to be left just to historians. And recently scholars in comparative politics have turned with increasing zest to historical themes. The list includes Almond, Leonard Binder, Dahl, Samuel P. Huntington, Lipset, Robert E. Ward, and Myron Weiner—not to speak of those like Friedrich and Deutsch to whom a political-historical perspective was natural to start with.[23]

The next restriction—the omission early in the inquiry of cases where

23. Almond, current study on nineteenth-century Britain; Leonard Binder, ed. *Politics in Lebanon* (New York, 1966); Dahl, see nn. 4, 7, and 8; Karl W. Deutsch, *Nationalism and Social Communication* (New York, 1953) and Deutsch et al., *Political Community and the North Atlantic Area* (Princeton, 1957); Carl J. Friedrich, *Constitutional Government and Democracy* (Boston, 1950); Samuel P. Huntington, "Political Modernization: America vs. Europe," *World Politics*, XVIII (April 1966); S. M. Lipset, *The First New Nation* (New York, 1963), and Lipset and Stein Rokkan, eds. *Party Systems and Voter Alignments* (New York, 1967); Robert E. Ward and D. A. Rustow, eds. *Political Modernization in Japan and Turkey* (Princeton, 1964); Myron Weiner, current study on nineteenth-century social history of the Balkans.

the major impulse to democratization came from the outside—is in accord with the conventional division of labor between the subfields of comparative politics and international relations. There are topics such as the theory of modernization where that division should be transcended from the start.[24] In tracing the origins of democracy, too, both perspectives may be applied at once, as witness the suggestive work of Louis Hartz, the masterly synthesis by Robert Palmer, and the current research by Robert Ward on Japanese-American interaction in the shaping of the 1947 constitution.[25] But for a first attempt at a general theory it may be preferable to stick to countries where the transition occurred mainly within a single system.

To speak of "major impulses from outside" or transitions "mainly within the system" acknowledges that foreign influences are almost always present. Throughout history, warfare has been a major democratizing force, because it has made necessary the marshalling of additional human resources.[26] Democratic ideas, moreover, have proved infectious whether in the days of Rousseau or of John F. Kennedy. And the violent overthrow of one oligarchy (e.g., France in 1830, Germany in 1918) has often frightened another into peaceful surrender (e.g., Britain in 1832, Sweden in 1918). From such ever-present international influences we may distinguish situations where people arriving from abroad took an active part in the internal political process of democratization. A theory of democratic origins, that is to say, should leave aside at the beginning those countries where military occupation played a major role (postwar Germany and Japan), where democratic institutions or attitudes were brought along by immigrants (Australia and New Zealand), or where in these and other ways immigration played a major role (Canada, the United States, and Israel).

The preference expressed earlier for relatively rapid instances of transition and the omission of immigrant countries amount to a very serious restriction, for they leave out of account, at this first stage of theorizing, all the English-speaking democracies. The reasons, however, seem cogent. Indeed, it may well be that American social scientists have added to their difficulties in understanding transitions to democracy by paying undue attention to Britain and the United States, which for the reasons just suggested prove to be among the hardest instances to analyze in genetic terms. The total of eight provisional exclusions still leaves (among extant democracies) about twenty-three cases on which to base a comparative analysis, thirteen of which are in Europe: Austria, Belgium, Ceylon, Chile, Colombia, Costa Rica, Denmark, Finland, France, Iceland, Ireland, India, Italy,

24. In this combination lies the strength of Cyril E. Black's *Dynamics of Modernization* (New York, 1966) compared to most of the other literature on the subject.

25. Louis Hartz et al., *The Founding of New Societies* (New York, 1964); R. R. Palmer, *The Age of the Democratic Revolution*, 2 vols. (Princeton, 1959–64).

26. See, e.g., Bertrand de Jouvenel, *On Power* (New York, 1948).

Lebanon, Luxembourg, Netherlands, Norway, Philippines, Sweden, Switzerland, Turkey, Uruguay, Venezuela.[27]

Among these twenty-odd democracies, the last methodological proposition urges an even narrower selection at this preliminary stage of theorizing. What is here involved is a choice between three research strategies: inclusion of all relevant cases, concentration on a single country, or some intermediate course.

Completeness is of course desirable, and all the more so where the "universe" consists of no more than twenty or thirty cases. But the more nearly complete the coverage the shallower it will have to be. The number of possible variables is so enormous (economic conditions, social cleavages, political alignments, psychological attitudes) that they could be handled only by means of the kind of simplifying assumptions that we rejected earlier on logical grounds. A test, no matter how complete, of a fallacious set of propositions would hardly yield convincing results.

The country monograph would avoid this danger. Nor does it deliberately have to be antitheoretical or "merely descriptive." Any country study nevertheless sacrifices the advantages of comparison, the social scientist's nearest substitute for a laboratory. No such study can tell us which strands in a tangle of empirical factors represent the development of democracy and which the national idiosyncrasies of Monographistan.

The middle course avoids the twin dangers of inconclusive scholasticism and of fact-grubbing. Instead, it can offer a more balanced and hence more fruitful blend of theory and empiricism. The many possible variables that can affect the origins of democracy and the even more complex relations among them can best be sorted out by looking at their total configuration in a limited number of cases—perhaps no more than two or three at the start. What will emerge from this exercise is a model, or as Weber used to call it, an "ideal type," of the transition from oligarchy to democracy. Being an ideal type, it deliberately highlights certain features of empirical reality and deliberately distorts, simplifies, or omits others. Like any such construct, it must be judged initially by its internal coherence and plausibility but ultimately by its fruitfulness in suggesting hypotheses applicable to a wide variety of other empirical cases.[28] It is at this further stage of testing that the demand for completeness comes once again into its own.

27. This list, together with the eight omissions noted (Australia, Canada, Germany, Israel, Japan, New Zealand, United Kingdom, United States), corresponds to the one I gave in *A World of Nations*, pp. 290ff., with the following exceptions: Greece has been omitted because democracy was superseded by a military coup in 1967; Mexico was omitted because, on second thought, I do not believe that it meets the criterion of a government based on "three or more consecutive, popular, and competitive elections"—the problems of course being the severe de facto restrictions on competition; Turkey and Venezuela have been added because they now have begun to meet the criterion.

28. For a recent, lucid restatement of the rationale for such models or ideal types, see T. B. Bottomore, *Elites and Societies* (New York, 1965), p. 32.

The model I should like to sketch in the next few pages is based in large part on my studies of Sweden, a Western country that made the transition to democracy in the period from 1890 to 1920, and of Turkey, a Westernizing country where that process began about 1945 and is still underway. The choice of these two is accidental—except in terms of an autobiographical account for which this is not the occasion. I am now in the early stages of a study that will seek to refine the same set of hypotheses in the light of materials from a slightly larger and less arbitrary selection of countries.

IV

A. Background Condition   The model starts with a single background condition—national unity. This implies nothing mysterious about *Blut und Boden* or daily pledges of allegiance, about personal identity in the psychoanalyst's sense, or about a grand political purpose pursued by the citizenry as a whole. It simply means that the vast majority of citizens in a democracy-to-be must have no doubt or mental reservations as to which political community they belong to. This excludes situations of latent secession, as in the late Habsburg and Ottoman Empires or in many African states today, and, conversely, situations of serious aspirations for merger as in many Arab states. Democracy is a system of rule by temporary majorities. In order that rulers and policies may freely change, the boundaries must endure, the composition of the citizenry be continuous. As Ivor Jennings phrased it tersely, "the people cannot decide until somebody decides who are the people."[29]

National unity is listed as a background condition in the sense that it must precede all the other phases of democratization but that otherwise its timing is irrelevant. It may have been achieved in prehistoric times, as in Japan or Sweden; or it may have preceded the other phases by centuries, as in France, or by decades, as in Turkey.

Nor does it matter by what means national unity has been established. The geographic situation may be such that no serious alternative has ever arisen—Japan once again being the best example. Or a sense of nationality may be the product of a sudden intensification of social communication in a new idiom developed for the purpose. On the other hand, it may be the legacy of some dynastic or administrative process of unification. The various hypotheses proposed by Deutsch clearly become relevant here.[30]

I have argued elsewhere that in an age of modernization men are unlikely to feel a preponderant sense of loyalty except to a political community large enough to achieve some considerable degree of modernity in its social

29. W. Ivor Jennings, *The Approach to Self-Government* (Cambridge, 1956), p. 56.

30. Deutsch, *Nationalism and Social Communication;* Deutsch et al., *Political Community and the North Atlantic Area.*

and economic life.[31] This sort of hypothesis must be examined as part of a theory of nationhood, not of one of democratic development. What matters in the present context is only the result.

I hesitate to call this result a consensus, for at least two reasons. First, national unity, as Deutsch argues, is the product less of shared attitudes and opinions than of responsiveness and complementarity. Second, "consensus" connotes consciously held opinion and deliberate agreement. The background condition, however, is best fulfilled when national unity is accepted unthinkingly, is silently taken for granted. Any vocal consensus about national unity, in fact, should make us wary. Most of the rhetoric of nationalism has poured from the lips of people who felt least secure in their sense of national identity—Germans and Italians in the past century and Arabs and Africans in the present, never Englishmen, Swedes, or Japanese.

To single out national unity as the sole background condition implies that no minimal level of economic development or social differentiation is necessary as a prerequisite to democracy. These social and economic factors enter the model only indirectly as one of several alternative bases for national unity or for entrenched conflict (see B below). Those social and economic indicators that authors are fond of citing as "background conditions" seem somewhat implausible at any rate. There are always nondemocracies that rank suspiciously high, such as Kuwait, Nazi Germany, Cuba, or Congo-Kinshasa. Conversely, the United States in 1820, France in 1870, and Sweden in 1890 would have been sure to fail one or another of the proposed tests of urbanization or per capita income—not to speak of newspaper copies in circulation, or doctors, movies, and telephones available to each one thousand inhabitants.

The model thus deliberately leaves open the possibility of democracies (properly so called) in premodern, prenationalist times and at low levels of economic development. To find a meaningful definition of democracy that would cover modern parliamentary systems along with medieval forest cantons, ancient city states (the ones where slavery and metics were absent), and some of the pre-Colombian Indians may prove difficult. It is not a task that forms part of the present project; still, I should not like to foreclose the attempt.

B. Preparatory Phase   I hypothesize that, against this single background condition, the dynamic process of democratization itself is set off by a prolonged and inconclusive political struggle. To give it those qualities, the protagonists must represent well-entrenched forces (typically social classes), and the issues must have profound meaning to them. Such a struggle is likely to begin as the result of the emergence of a new elite that arouses a

31. Rustow, *A World of Nations,* pp. 30ff. and *International Encyclopedia of the Social Sciences,* s.v. "Nation."

depressed and previously leaderless social group into concerted action. Yet the particular social composition of the contending forces, both leaders and followers, and the specific nature of the issues will vary widely from one country to the next and in the same country from period to period.

In Sweden at the turn of the century, it was a struggle first of farmers and then of an urban lower-middle and working class against a conservative alliance of bureaucrats, large landowners, and industrialists; and the issues were tariffs, taxation, military service, and suffrage. In Turkey in the last twenty years it has mainly been a contest of countryside versus city, more precisely of large and middling-size farmers (supported by most of the peasant electorate) against the heirs of the Kemalist bureaucratic-military establishment; the central issue has been industrialization versus agricultural development. In both these examples, economic factors have been of prime importance, yet the direction of causality has varied. In Sweden, it was a period of intense economic development that created new political tensions; at one crucial point, rising wages enabled the Stockholm workers to overcome the existing tax barrier for the franchise. In Turkey, conversely, the demand for rural development was the consequence, not the cause, of beginning democratization.[32]

There may be situations where economic factors have played a much lesser role. In India and in the Philippines the prolonged contest between nationalist forces and an imperial bureaucracy over the issue of self-government may have served the same preparatory function as did class conflict elsewhere. In Lebanon the continuing struggle is mainly between denominational groups and the stakes are mainly government offices. Although political struggles of this sort naturally have their economic dimensions, only a doctrinaire economic determinist would derive colonialism or religious divisions from solely economic causes.

James Bryce found in his classic comparative study that, "One road only has in the past led into democracy, viz., the wish to be rid of tangible evils."[33] Democracy was not the original or primary aim; it was sought as a means to some other end or it came as a fortuitous by-product of the struggle. But, since the tangible evils that befall human societies are legion,

---

32. For developments in Sweden see Rustow, *The Politics of Compromise: A Study of Parties and Cabinet Government in Sweden* (Princeton, 1955), Chs. 1–3, and Douglas A. Verney, *Parliamentary Reform in Sweden, 1866–1921* (Oxford, 1957). On Turkey see Ward and Rustow and the following essays by Rustow: "Politics and Islam in Turkey," in R. N. Frye, ed. *Islam and the West* (The Hague, 1957), pp. 69–107; "Turkey: The Tradition of Modernity," in Lucian W. Pye and Verba, eds. *Political Culture and Political Development* (Princeton, 1965), pp. 171–198; "The Development of Parties in Turkey," in Joseph LaPalombara and Myron Weiner, eds. *Political Parties and Political Development* (Princeton, 1966), pp. 107–133; and "Politics and Development Policy," in F. C. Shorter, ed. *Four Studies in the Economic Development of Turkey* (London, 1967), pp. 5–31.

33. James Bryce, *Modern Democracies* (London, 1921), vol. 2, p. 602.

Bryce's single road dissolves into many separate paths. No two existing democracies have gone through a struggle between the very same forces over the same issues and with the same institutional outcome. Hence, it seems unlikely that any future democracy will follow in the precise footsteps of any of its predecessors. As Albert Hirschman has warned in his discussion of economic development, the search for ever more numerous preconditions or prerequisites may end up by proving conclusively that development always will be impossible—and always has been.[34]

More positively, Hirschman and other economists have argued that a country can best launch into a phase of growth not by slavishly imitating the example of nations already industrialized, but rather by making the most of its particular natural and human resources and by fitting these accurately into the international division of labor.[35] Similarly, a country is likely to attain democracy not by copying the constitutional laws or parliamentary practices of some previous democracy, but rather by honestly facing up to its particular conflicts and by devising or adapting effective procedures for their accommodation.

The serious and prolonged nature of the struggle is likely to force the protagonists to rally around two banners. Hence polarization, rather than pluralism, is the hallmark of this preparatory phase. Yet there are limitations implicit in the requirement of national unity—which, of course, must not only preexist but also continue. If the division is on sharply regional lines, secession rather than democracy is likely to result. Even among contestants geographically interspersed there must be some sense of community or some even balance of forces that makes wholesale expulsion or genocide impossible. The Turks are beginning to develop a set of democratic practices among themselves, but fifty years ago they did not deal democratically with Armenians or Greeks. Crosscutting cleavages have their place in this preparatory phase as a possible means of strengthening or preserving that sense of community.

Dahl notes wistfully that "one perennial problem of opposition is that there is either too much or too little."[36] The first two elements of the model between them will ensure that there is the right amount. But struggle and national unity cannot simply be averaged out, since they cannot be measured along the same scale. Strong doses of both must be combined, just as it may be possible to combine sharp polarization with crosscutting cleavages. Furthermore, as Mary Parker Follett, Lewis A. Coser, and others

34. Albert O. Hirschman, *Journeys Toward Progress* (New York, 1963), pp. 6ff.

35. Ibid., and Hirschman, *The Strategy of Economic Development* (New Haven, 1958), and Hirschman, "Obstacles to Development: A Classification and a Quasi-Vanishing Act," *Economic Development and Cultural Change,* XIII (July 1965), 385–393.

36. Dahl et al., *Political Oppositions in Western Democracies,* p. 397.

have insisted, certain types of conflict in themselves constitute creative processes of integration.[37] What infant democracy requires is not a lukewarm struggle but a hot family feud.

This delicate combination implies, of course, that many things can go wrong during the preparatory phase. The fight may go on and on till the protagonists weary and the issues fade away without the emergence of any democratic solution along the way. Or one group may find a way of crushing the opponents after all. In these and other ways an apparent evolution toward democracy may be deflected, and at no time more easily than during the preparatory phase.

C. Decision Phase   Robert Dahl has written that "Legal party opposition . . . is a recent and unplanned invention."[38] This accords with Bryce's emphasis on the redress of specific grievances as democracy's vehicle and with the assumption here that the transition to democracy is a complex process stretching over many decades. But it does not rule out suffrage or freedom of opposition as conscious goals in the preparatory struggle. Nor does it suggest that a country ever becomes a democracy in a fit of absent-mindedness. On the contrary, what concludes the preparatory phase is a deliberate decision on the part of political leaders to accept the existence of diversity in unity and, to that end, to institutionalize some crucial aspect of democratic procedure. Such was the decision in 1907, which I have called the "Great Compromise" of Swedish politics, to adopt universal suffrage combined with proportional representation.[39] Instead of a single decision there may be several. In Britain, as is well-known, the principle of limited government was laid down in the compromise of 1688, cabinet government evolved in the eighteenth century, and suffrage reform was launched as late as 1832. Even in Sweden, the dramatic change of 1907 was followed by the further suffrage reform of 1918 which also confirmed the principle of cabinet government.

Whether democracy is purchased wholesale as in Sweden in 1907 or on the installment plan as in Britain, it is acquired by a process of conscious decision at least on the part of the top political leadership. Politicians are

37. Mary Parker Follett, *The New State* (New York, 1918), and *Creative Experience* (New York, 1924); Lewis A. Coser, *The Function of Social Conflict* (Glencoe, 1956), p. 121 and passim. A widespread contrary position has recently been restated by Edward Shils, who writes in reference to Lebanon: "Civility will not be strengthened by crisis. It can only grow slowly and in a calm atmosphere. The growth of civility is a necessary condition for Lebanon's development . . . into a genuinely democratic system" (in Binder et al., *Politics in Lebanon,* p. 10). I find it hard to think of situations where there have been any notable advances in either civility or democracy *except* as the result of crisis.

38. Dahl et al., *Political Oppositions in Western Democracies,* p. xi.

39. Rustow, *The Politics of Compromise,* p. 69.

specialists in power, and a fundamental power shift such as that from oligarchy to democracy will not escape their notice.

Decision means choice, and while the choice of democracy does not arise until the background and preparatory conditions are in hand, it is a genuine choice and does not flow automatically from those two conditions. The history of Lebanon illustrates the possibilities of benevolent autocracy or of foreign rule as alternative solutions to entrenched struggles within a political community.[40] And of course a decision in favor of democracy, or some crucial ingredient of it, may be proposed and rejected—thus leading to a continuation of the preparatory phase or to some sort of abortive outcome.

The decision in favor of democracy results from the interplay of a number of forces. Since precise terms must be negotiated and heavy risks with regard to the future taken, a small circle of leaders is likely to play a disproportionate role. Among the negotiating groups and their leaders may be the protagonists of the preparatory struggle. Other participants may include groups that split off from one or the other side or new arrivals on the political stage. In Sweden these new and intermediate groups played a crucial role. Conservatives and Radicals (led by industrialists on one side and intellectuals on the other) had sharpened and crystallized the issues throughout the 1890s. Then came a period of stalemate when discipline in all the recently formed parliamentary parties broke down—a sort of randomization process in which many compromises, combinations, and permutations were devised and explored. The formula that carried the day in 1907 included crucial contributions from a moderately conservative bishop and a moderately liberal farmer, neither of whom played a very prominent role in politics before or after this decision phase.

Just as there can be different types of sponsors and different contents of the decision, so the motives from which it is proposed and accepted will vary from case to case. The forces of conservatism may yield from fear that continued resistance may lose them even more ground in the end. (Such thoughts were on the minds of British Whigs in 1832 and of Swedish conservatives in 1907.) Or they may belatedly wish to live up to principles long proclaimed; such was the Turkish transition to a multipary system announced by President Inönü in 1945. The radicals may accept the compromise as a first installment, confident that time is on their side and that future installments are bound to follow. Both conservatives and radicals may feel exhausted from a long struggle or fearful of a civil war. This consideration is likely to loom large if they have been through such a war in recent memory. As Barrington Moore has aptly proposed, the English civil war was a crucial "contribution of early violence to later gradualism."[41] In short, democracy,

40. Binder, ed. *Politics in Lebanon.*

41. Barrington Moore, Jr., *Social Origins of Dictatorship and Democracy* (Boston, 1966), p. 3.

like any collective human action, is likely to stem from a large variety of mixed motives.

The decision phase may well be considered an act of deliberate, explicit consensus. But, once again, this somewhat nebulous term should be carefully considered and perhaps replaced with less ambiguous synonyms. First of all, as Bryce suggests, the democratic content of the decision may be incidental to other substantive issues. Second, insofar as it is a genuine compromise it will seem second-best to all major parties involved—it certainly will not represent any agreement on fundamentals. Third, even on procedures there are likely to be continuing differences of preference. Universal suffrage with proportional representation, the content of the Swedish compromise of 1907, was about equally distasteful to the conservatives (who would rather have continued the old plutocratic voting system) and to the liberals and socialists (who wanted majority rule undiluted by proportional representation). What matters at the decision stage is not what values the leaders hold dear in the abstract, but what concrete steps they are willing to take. Fourth, the agreement worked out by the leaders is far from universal. It must be transmitted to the professional politicians and to the citizenry at large. These are two aspects of the final, or habituation, phase of the model.

D. Habituation Phase   A distasteful decision, once made, is likely to seem more palatable as one is forced to live with it. Everyday experience can supply concrete illustrations of this probability for each of us. Festinger's theory of "cognitive dissonance" supplies a technical explanation and experimental support.[42] Democracy, moreover, is by definition a competitive process, and this competition gives an edge to those who can rationalize their commitment to it, and an even greater edge to those who sincerely believe in it. The transformation of the Swedish Conservative Party from 1918 to 1936 vividly illustrates the point. After two decades those leaders who had grudgingly put up with democracy or pragmatically accepted it retired or died and were replaced by others who sincerely believed in it. Similarly, in Turkey there is a remarkable change from the leadership of Ismet Inönü, who promoted democracy out of a sense of duty, and Adnan Menderes, who saw in it an unprecedented vehicle for his ambition, to younger leaders in each of their parties who understand democracy more fully and embrace it more wholeheartedly. In short, the very process of democracy institutes a double process of Darwinian selectivity in favor of convinced democrats: one among parties in general elections and the other among politicians vying for leadership within these parties.

But politics consists not only of competition for office. It is, above all, a process for resolving conflicts within human groups—whether these arise from the clash of interests or from uncertainty about the future. A new

42. Festinger, *A Theory of Cognitive Dissonance.*

political regime is a novel prescription for taking joint chances on the unknown. With its basic practice of multilateral debate, democracy in particular involves a process of trial and error, a joint learning experience. The first grand compromise that establishes democracy, if it proves at all viable, is in itself a proof of the efficacy of the principle of conciliation and accommodation. The first success, therefore, may encourage contending political forces and their leaders to submit other major questions to resolution by democratic procedures.

In Sweden, for instance, there had been a general political stalemate in the last third of the nineteenth century over the prime issues of the day—the taxation and conscription systems inherited from the sixteenth century. But in the two decades after 1918, when democracy was fully adopted by the Swedes, a whole host of thorny questions was wittingly or unwittingly resolved. The Social Democrats surrendered their earlier pacifism, anticlericalism, and republicanism, as well as the demand for nationalization of industry (although they found it hard to admit this last point). The conservatives, once staunchly nationalist, endorsed Swedish participation in international organizations. Above all, conservatives and liberals fully accepted government intervention in the economy and the social welfare state.

Of course, the spiral that in Sweden went upward to greater and greater successes for the democratic process may also go downward. A conspicuous failure to resolve some urgent political question will damage the prospects of democracy; if such a failure comes early in the habituation phase, it may prove fatal.

Surveying the evolution of political debate and conflict in the Western democracies over the last century, it is striking to observe the difference between social and economic issues, which democracies handled with comparative ease, and issues of community, which have proved far more troublesome.[43] With the advantage of a century's hindsight, it is easy to see that Marx's estimate was wrong at crucial points. In nationality he saw a cloak for bourgeois class interests. He denounced religion as the opiate of the masses. In economics, by contrast, he foresaw very real and increasingly bitter struggles that would end by bringing bourgeois democracy crashing down. But in fact democracy has proved most effective in resolving political questions where the major divisions have been social and economic, as in Britain, Australia, New Zealand, and the Scandinavian countries. It has been the fight among religious, national, and racial groups, instead, that has proved most tenacious and has caused recurrent bitterness, as in Belgium, Holland, Canada, and the United States.

The reasons are not hard to find. On the socioeconomic front Marxism itself became a sufficient force in Europe to serve to some extent as a self-

---

43. The contrast emerges implicitly from the country studies in Dahl, ed. *Political Oppositions in Western Democracies.*

disconfirming prophecy. But beyond this there is a fundamental difference in the nature of the issues. On matters of economic policy and social expenditures you can always split the difference. In an expanding economy, you can even have it both ways: the contest for higher wages, profits, consumer savings, and social welfare payments can be turned into a positive-sum game. But there is no middle position between Flemish and French as official languages, or between Calvinism, Catholicism, and secularism as principles of education. The best you can get here is an "inclusive compromise"[44]—a logrolling deal whereby some government offices speak French and some Flemish, or some children are taught according to Aquinas, some, Calvin, and some, Voltaire. Such a solution may partly depoliticize the question. Yet it also entrenches the differences instead of removing them, and accordingly it may convert political conflict into a form of trench warfare.

The difficulty that democracy finds in resolving issues of community emphasizes the importance of national unity as the background condition of the democratization process. The hardest struggles in a democracy are those against the birth defects of the political community.

The transition to democracy, it was suggested earlier, may require some common attitudes and some distinct attitudes on the part of the politician and of the common citizen. The distinction is already apparent during the decision phase when the leaders search for compromise while their followers wearily uphold the banners of the old struggle. It becomes even more readily apparent during the habituation phase, when three sorts of process are at work. First, both politicians and citizens learn from the successful resolution of some issues to place their faith in the new rules and to apply them to new issues. Their trust will grow more quickly if, in the early decades of the new regime, a wide variety of political tendencies can participate in the conduct of affairs, either by joining various coalitions or by taking turns as government and opposition. Second, as we just saw, experience with democratic techniques and competitive recruitment will confirm the politicians in their democratic practices and beliefs. Third, the population at large will become firmly fitted into the new structure by the forging of effective links of party organization that connect the politicians in the capital with the mass electorate throughout the country.

These party organizations may be a direct continuation of those that were active during the preparatory, or conflict, phase of democratization, and a suffrage extension at the time of the democratic "decision" may now have given them a free field. It is possible, on the other hand, that no parties with a broad popular base emerged during the conflict phase and that the suffrage extension was very limited. Even under such conditions of partial democratization of the political structure, a competitive dynamic that completes the process may have been set off. The parliamentary

44. Rustow, *Politics of Compromise*, p. 231.

parties will seek support from constituency organizations to insure a steady supply of members for their group in future parliaments. Now this and now that political group may see a chance to steal a march on its opponents by enlarging the electorate or by removing other obstacles to majority control. This, roughly, would seem to have been the nature of British developments between 1832 and 1918. Complete democratization, of course, is the only logical stopping point for such a dynamic.

v

The model here presented makes three broad assertions. First, it says that certain ingredients are indispensable to the genesis of democracy. For one thing, there must be a sense of national unity. For another, there must be entrenched and serious conflict. For a third, there must be a conscious adoption of democratic rules. And, finally, both politicians and electorate must be habituated to these rules.

Secondly, the model asserts that these ingredients must be assembled one at a time. Each task has its own logic and each has its natural protagonists—a network of administrators or a group of nationalist literati for the task of unification, a mass movement of the lower class, perhaps led by upper class dissidents, for the task of preparatory struggle, a small circle of political leaders skilled at negotiation and compromise for the formulation of democratic rules, and a variety of organization men and their organizations for the task of habituation. The model thus abandons the quest for "functional requisites" of democracy; for such a quest heaps all these tasks together and thus makes the total job of democratization quite unmanageable. The argument here is analogous to that which has been made by Hirschman and others against the theory of balanced economic growth. These economists do not deny that the transition from a primitive subsistence economy to a mature industrial society involves changes on all fronts—in working skills, in capital formation, in the distribution system, in consumption habits, in the monetary system, and so forth. But they insist that any country that attempted all these tasks at once would in practice find itself totally paralysed—that the stablest balance is that of stagnation. Hence the economic developer's problem, in their view, becomes one of finding backward and forward "linkages," that is, of devising a manageable sequence of tasks.

Thirdly, the model does suggest one such sequence from national unity as background, through struggle, compromise, and habituation, to democracy. The cogency of this sequence is brought home by a deviant development in Turkey in the years after 1945. The Turkish commitment to democracy was made in the absence of prior overt conflict between major social groups or their leading elites. In 1950 there was the first change of government as the result of a new electoral majority, but in the next decade there was a drift back into authoritarian practices on the part of this newly elected party, and in 1960–1961 the democratic experiment was interrupted by a military coup. These developments are not unconnected: Turkey paid the price in 1960 for having received its first democratic regime as a free gift from the hands of a dictator. But after 1961 there was a further evolution in the more appropriate sequence. The crisis of 1960–1961 had made social and political conflict far more acceptable, and a full range of social and economic issues was debated for the first time. The conflict that shaped up was between the military on one side and the spokesmen of the agrarian majority on the other—and the compromise between these two allowed the resumption of the democratic experiment on a more secure basis by 1965.

In the interests of parsimony, the basic ingredients of the model have been kept to four, and the social circumstances or psychological motivations that may furnish each of them have been left wide open. Specifically, the model rejects what are sometimes proposed as preconditions of democracy, e.g., high levels of economic and social development or a prior consensus either on fundamentals or on the rules. Economic growth may be one of the circumstances that produces the tensions essential to the preparatory or conflict phase—but there are other circumstances that might also serve. Mass education and social welfare services are more likely to be the result of democratization.

Consensus on fundamentals is an implausible precondition. A people who were not in conflict about some rather fundamental matters would have little need to devise democracy's elaborate rules for conflict resolution. And the acceptance of those rules is logically a part of the transition process rather than its prerequisite. The present model transfers various aspects of consensus from the quiescent state of preconditions to that of active elements in the process. I here follow the lead of Bernard Crick, who has strikingly written:

> . . . It is often thought that for this 'master science' [i.e., democratic politics] to function, there must already be in existence some shared idea of a 'common good,' some 'consensus' or *consensus juris*. But this common good is itself the process of practical reconciliation of the interests of the various . . . aggregates, or groups which compose a state; it is not some external and intangible spiritual adhesive. . . . Diverse groups hold together, firstly, because they have a common interest in sheer survival, and, secondly, because they practise politics—not because they agree about 'fundamentals,' or some such concept too vague, too personal, or too divine ever to do the job of politics for it. The moral consensus of a free state is not something mysteriously prior to or above politics: it is the activity (the civilizing activity) of politics itself.[45]

The basis of democracy is not maximum consensus. It is the tenuous middle ground between imposed uniformity (such as would lead to some

45. Crick, *In Defence of Politics*, p. 24.

sort of tyranny) and implacable hostility (of a kind that would disrupt the community in civil war or secession). In the process of genesis of democracy, an element of what might be termed consensus enters at three points at least. There must be a prior sense of community, preferably a sense of community quietly taken for granted that is above mere opinion and mere agreement. There must be a conscious adoption of democratic rules, but they must not be so much believed in as applied, first perhaps from necessity and gradually from habit. The very operation of these rules will enlarge the area of consensus step-by-step as democracy moves down its crowded agenda.

But new issues will always emerge and new conflicts threaten the newly won agreements. The characteristic procedures of democracy include campaign oratory, the election of candidates, parliamentary divisions, votes of confidence and of censure—a host of devices, in short, for expressing conflict and thereby resolving it. The essence of democracy is the habit of dissension and conciliation over ever-changing issues and amidst ever-changing alignments. Totalitarian rulers must enforce unanimity on fundamentals and on procedures before they can get down to other business. By contrast, democracy is that form of government that derives its just powers from the dissent of up to one half of the governed.

Authoritarianism

On the Comparative Study of Communism*

Robert C. Tucker

For good historical reasons, scholarship on communism grew up within Russian area studies. As communism came to power in more countries after the Second World War, the expanded study of it proceeded, to a large extent, in similar established branches of scholarship, most notably East European studies and sinology. But now Communist studies seem to be outgrowing area studies, to be transcending their very perspective.

This article was prepared for a conference on the status and prospects of comparative Communist studies, held in New York in May 1966 by the American Council of Learned Societies with the assistance of the Carnegie Corporation of New York. In revising it for publication, I have taken account of a number of points raised in the discussion. I have also benefited from comments on the original paper by Professor Glenn D. Paige.

Reprinted from World Politics, *Vol. XIX, no. 2 (copyright © 1967 by Princeton University Press): pp. 242–257. Reprinted by permission of the Princeton University Press.*

It becomes increasingly clear that communism, despite its Russian origin, is not inherently a local phenomenon but a form of society or civilization that can spread and take root in virtually every part of the globe when circumstances are propitious. It likewise becomes more and more clear that it is the contemporary social sciences rather than area studies in the traditional sense that provide most of the promising concepts and methods for the study of Communist societies. These two basic facts point to the comparative study of communism as the most hopeful direction for scholarship in Communist studies to take in coming years. My aim in what follows is to amplify this thesis and to formulate some of the problems that arise in reorienting research toward "comparative communism."

First, a word on where we now stand. In a survey of the history of Russian studies in this country published in 1959, Philip Mosely observed: "An important task which has hardly been tackled at all is the comparative study of Communist systems. . . ."[1] Since then, however, the comparative study of communism has ceased to be a mere gleam in scholarship's eye. The new trend has been born and is showing vigorous signs of early growth.

Historians like Theodore von Laue,[2] Cyril Black,[3] and Robert Daniels[4] have examined the Russian and other Communist revolutions in comparative perspective rather than as strictly national events. In *Peasant Nationalism and Communist Power,*[5] Chalmers Johnson, a political scientist, has investigated the important role of nationalism in communism's rise to power not alone in China but likewise in Yugoslavia, which he treats as a comparable case in the category of "independent Communist states." Economists have begun to contribute to a comparative study of communism by constructing general models of "Soviet-type economies" and their characteristic institutions, such as central planning.[6] Increasing interest in the comparative study of Communist legal institutions is reflected in John Hazard's "Unity and Diversity in Socialist Law."[7] And the comparative study of Communist politics has been progressing quite rapidly in the 1960's.

1. H. H. Fisher, ed., *American Research on Russia* (Bloomington 1959), 18.

2. *Why Lenin? Why Stalin?* (Philadelphia and New York 1964).

3. *The Dynamics of Modernization* (New York 1966).

4. "The Chinese Revolution in Russian Perspective," *World Politics,* XIII (January 1961), 210–30.

5. (Stanford 1962).

6. See, for example, David Granick's "An Organizational Model of Soviet Industrial Planning," *Journal of Political Economy,* LXVII (April 1959), 109–30; Gregory Grossman's "Notes for a Theory of the Command Economy," *Soviet Studies* (October 1963); and John Montias' "Planning with Material Balances in Soviet-Type Economies," *American Economic Review,* XLIX (December 1959), 963–85.

7. *Law and Contemporary Problems,* XXX (Spring 1965), 270–90.

In *The Soviet Bloc,* for example, Zbigniew Brzezinski explored divergent institutional and policy patterns as well as the interrelations of Communist states.[8] Richard Burks contributed in an important way to comparative communism with *The Dynamics of Communism in Eastern Europe.*[9] In *Communist Strategies in Asia,* edited by A. Doak Barnett, a collaborating group of scholars looked at Asian Communist movements in relation to two major Communist models—the Soviet and Chinese.[10] A subsequent collaborative volume, *The Communist Revolution in Asia,* edited by Robert Scalapino, continued the comparative analysis of Asian Communist movements.[11] Still more recently, Gordon Skilling has produced, in *The Governments of Communist East Europe,* a systematic comparative politics of communism in Eastern Europe.[12] Meanwhile, at the Tahoe conference of June 1965 on "Soviet and Chinese Communism: Similarities and Differences," held under the auspices of the American Council of Learned Societies, an attempt was made to set going a scholarly dialogue between specialists in these two principal fields of area studies relating to communism.[13]

We are speaking, then, not of a hypothetical future possibility but of a developing intellectual movement and an already emergent new kind of scholarly inquiry in Communist studies. What I wish to contend is that the prerequisites now exist for a rapid and fruitful *expansion* of this kind of inquiry. First, we face the fact that communism itself has proliferated—not only geographically but likewise politically, economically, culturally, and even ideologically. The processes of differentiation that have been going on for a long time inside the Communist world have now reached a point where we must speak of communism in the plural, recognizing that we are no longer dealing with a single, simply identifiable entity even though there continue to be broad uniformities and continuities that give different Communist systems a common character. But to recognize the existence of diverse *communisms* is implicitly to adopt the perspective of comparative communism in scholarly work.

If data growing out of Communist diversity are one prerequisite for expanded comparative study of communism, the accumulation of area studies is another. Without a solid base of country studies to build upon, comparative analysis of communism may hang inconsequentially in the rarefied

8. (Cambridge, Mass., 1960; rev. ed. New York 1961).

9. (Princeton 1961).

10. (New York 1963).

11. (Englewood Cliffs 1965).

12. (New York 1966).

13. Donald Treadgold, "The Two Communist Giants Compared: A Report of the Conference on Soviet and Chinese Communism," *ACLS Newsletter,* XVI (November 1965), 1–4.

atmosphere of theoretical speculation. But we may have such a base today, or something approximating it. Especially in Soviet area studies there has grown up a very extensive scholarly literature on the history of institutions, economics, politics, law, culture, society, and ideology. Being younger, the scholarship on communism in Eastern Europe, China, and elsewhere in Asia, and on Communist movements in other places, is less extensive, and some specialists in these areas are understandably concerned to enlarge it as their first-priority task. Whether our present base in area studies is sufficient to support a full takeoff into comparative communism is therefore uncertain. But even if one takes the optimistic view that it is, much more area work will undoubtedly be needed as comparative communism progresses.

And as this implies, there is no real opposition, or should not be, between area studies and comparativism despite natural differences in outlook between those whose interests run in the one direction and those who gravitate toward the other. Area studies naturally point toward comparative analysis, and the latter in turn presupposes and makes use of the former. Far from depressing area studies, therefore, the swift future growth of comparative communism may well have a highly stimulating effect upon them by suggesting fresh lines of useful area research and enriching its analytic content. We may, in fact, see something of a convergence, with differing emphasis as the chief surviving distinction between an area scholarship that is characteristically hospitable to comparative inquiry and comparative studies that are solidly anchored in area knowledge.

A third and final prerequisite for rapid advance in the new direction is subjective. Here, as in other departments of life, prospects for extensive change are usually dependent upon a spreading sense of the need for change, a serious dissatisfaction with the existing state of affairs. Signs of such dissatisfaction among social scientists specializing in Communist studies have been multiplying in the recent past. There is a feeling among some scholars that area studies as such, unguided by the generalizing impulse that always lurks in the comparative approach, are in a blind alley. The gap between challenge and response in Communist studies appears to many to be not only great but also disturbingly constant. Two or three representative recent statements may serve to convey the mood. A specialist in Soviet politics complains that "political scientists in the West have failed, by and large, to apply the rich store of concepts developed for the comparative study of political systems to the communist world."[14] A China specialist, observing that much of the work done so far on Chinese communism has been in the

14. Alfred Meyer, "The Nature of Communist Systems," a paper prepared for presentation at the Midwest Political Science Conference, Chicago (April 1966), mimeographed. For a much earlier criticism of the same kind and a plea for comparativism, see H. Gordon Skilling, "Soviet and Communist Politics: A Comparative Approach," *Journal of Politics*, XXII (May 1960), 300–313.

nature of intelligence-collecting rather than social science research, comments on "the conceptual underdevelopment of our subdiscipline."[15] And noting that "the anecdotal exposition of Soviet organizational behavior eventually palls," an economist writes: "Too often our discussion of the Soviet economy goes along the lines, 'this is the way they go about it' and 'this is what happens,' which eventually evokes the retort, 'so what?' "[16] I take these various statements to be indicative of a spreading movement of thought that is critical of the traditional area approach in Communist studies and is in search of a new focus for scholarly inquiry in this field. The existence of this movement seems to reinforce the belief that the time is ripe for development of the subdiscipline along comparative lines.

Levels of Comparative Study

But what, broadly speaking, will it mean to develop along comparative lines? What, in other words, is "comparative communism" as a focus for scholarly inquiry?

It is probably best to let the answers to such questions emerge from much more accumulated experience in comparative scholarship. At the present stage of creative groping and experimentation, concentration on the methodology of comparative communism may be premature and unwise. Above all, it seems undesirable to lay down some particular approach as the one to be followed. The fact is that there are several different ways of pursuing the comparative study of communism, and the best hope for progress may lie in the encouragement of scholars to go in any and all of these directions. The watchword should be methodological pluralism.

Perhaps we might usefully distinguish different *levels* in the comparative study of Communist society. At the simplest level, comparative communism is simply area studies artfully juxtaposed. This might be called "aggregative comparison." A good example would be the above-mentioned volume *Communist Strategies in Asia*, which juxtaposed studies of different Communist movements by area specialists and did so in such a way as to bring out, comparatively, the several relationships of these movements to the two competing Communist great-power "models." Comparative communism at this level is a relatively simple kind of cooperative enterprise. It enables the area specialist to go on doing pretty much what he has been doing, but brings out a larger pattern. On the other hand, comparative com-

15. Chalmers Johnson, "The Role of Social Science in China Scholarship," *World Politics*, XVII (January 1965), 256–57.

16. Robert W. Campbell, "On the Theory of Economic Administration," in Henry Rosovsky, ed., *Industrialization in Two Systems: Essays in Honor of Alexander Gerschenkron* (New York 1966).

munism on this plane is low in analytic content and makes only a minimal contribution toward overcoming the limitations of the area approach.

A second level of comparative inquiry may be termed "empirical comparison." Daniels' article "The Chinese Revolution in Russian Perspective," comparing the developmental pattern of Communist China with that of Soviet Russia since 1917, is an illustration. Empirical comparison in this case was directed to two Communist societies in their total policy configuration. It could, alternatively, be directed to particular institutions, policies, ideological doctrines, or economic processes. And comparisons of this type may be made not only across space, between communism in two or more areas, but also over time, e.g., as between Stalinist and post-Stalinist communism within the USSR. Such empirical comparison of Communist societies and their institutions offers a very rich field for cooperative efforts in which area specialists would pool their linguistic skills. For example, a systematic study by cooperating specialists of the treatment of a particularly important theme by the press of three different Communist regimes over a period of time could yield results of much greater value than three isolated studies conducted on a noncomparative basis.

It is at the next level that comparative communism shows its theoretical bent. This is "generalizing comparison," in which the object is not just to compare societies or aspects of them but to build on such empirical comparisons a structure of generalizations concerning the characteristic tendencies of communism as a form of society, economy, polity, ideology, or cultural system. Such generalizations may, of course, refer to variations as well as to uniformities in the Communist pattern. Alternatively and less ambitiously, the aim may be to generalize about communism as it exists in a particular geopolitical setting, such as Asia or Eastern Europe. Thus in his general introduction to *The Communist Revolution in Asia,* Scalapino has offered a series of generalizations, based on comparative study, concerning Asian communism. Both Burks and Skilling move from empirical comparisons to generalizations about communism as such and about East European communism in particular. And as Skilling's work brings out very well, comparative communism at this level tends to carve up the subject matter along topical or functional lines. Data concerning the several East European Communist states were ordered comparatively in terms of such topics as constitutional structures, political leadership, the decision-making process, interests and their representation, force and legality, and so on.

Generalizing comparison leads naturally to a still higher level of comparative inquiry at which the work takes the form of model-building and the study of Communist societies in relation to the theoretical models. To generalize about Communist systems on the basis of comparative data is to move toward the formulation of an ideal-type concept or theoretical model of a Communist society, economy, political system, and so on. Such

models, moreover, can be either static or dynamic, i.e., they can endow
the Communist system with constant characteristics or, alternatively, with
a certain built-in developmental pattern. And here is where the comparative perspective becomes enormously significant. It signifies the recognition
on the theoretical plane of the need for a multiple model of communism.
There is presumably a unity-pattern in communism which makes it possible to formulate certain generalizations about all Communist systems and
in this sense to construct a uniform ideal type. But within this context communism may be plural in the sense that there are diverse possible patterns
of communism, e.g., orthodox Leninist-Stalinist communism, Maoist military communism, reform communism, and so on. If so, we must incorporate
into the agenda of comparative communism the task of working out a typology of communisms and then applying it to the study of existing Communist systems.

Since, moreover, Communist systems have arisen at different times and
at any given time are therefore likely to be at different stages of their internal development, variations over space may be closely linked with
typical variations over time. To a greater or lesser extent, that is, the differences between one Communist system and another may reflect systematic
changes that communism tends to undergo from one stage of its development to another. Some of the differences between Maoist Chinese communism and post-Stalin Soviet communism may, for example, lend themselves
to analysis in such terms. It follows that in the quest for a multiple model
of communism, comparativists may well address themselves to the task of
constructing a dynamic or developmental analysis of the Communist system. Instead of endowing communism with a set of stable characteristics,
in other words, we must strive to conceptualize it as a system with a built-in
life cycle, a sequence of typical stages of development. So far we have no
more than the bare beginnings of such a developmental analysis, partly
because the use of the "totalitarian model" has militated against that way
of thinking about communism.

SYSTEMS AND MOVEMENTS

If we take the proclaimed adherence of the ruling party and regime to
"Marxism-Leninism" as a decisive criterion of being Communist, there are
presently in existence fourteen Communist systems. So far in the discussion,
we have been speaking of these systems as the subject matter of comparative communism. But what of the nonruling Communist parties, which
now exist, legally or illegally, in nearly eighty different countries and have
an aggregate membership of about four million, of which Indonesia accounted (at least until recently) for nearly a half?

Such works as Franz Borkenau's prewar history of the Comintern, *World*

Communism,[17] attest that Communist movements as such have long been an object of scholarly inquiry. Much of the earlier research in this field was concerned with Communist movements in their relation to Soviet foreign policy or as parts of a Moscow-directed international Communist movement. But more recent studies, of which Lucian Pye's *Guerrilla Communism in Malaya* is a pioneering example,[18] show a shift of scholarly interest to indigenous factors in the emergence and development of Communist movements. This approach seems destined to persist in the present era of polycentric communism. The question is whether such study of Communist movements not in power should be considered an integral part of comparative communism. In my view, it should.

Although an individual scholar may properly confine himself to the study of communism in power, study of these movements that have not come to power can scarcely be excluded from the subject matter of comparative communism. If we view Communist regimes as being in some sense "movement-regimes," then the movement itself, and the party as its core and organizing nucleus, is the embryo of communism as a political and social system, and the usefulness of studying phenomena in the embryonic stage has often been established. To this it should be added that for various reasons the movement may be more accessible to study before coming to power than afterwards. Further, the comparative study of communism will always be directed in part to the problem of how communism comes to power, and data for its solution are found in movements that have not come to power as well as in those that have. Indeed, it may be scientifically as well as practically important to improve our understanding of why it is that certain Communist movements have failed to achieve power or to grow strong. Such understanding may point to critical variables in the successful cases.

Comparative study of nonruling Communist parties may be useful likewise as an independent form of research. It could throw light on the question of what happens to Communist movements when they exist for a long time *without* attaining power, or what characteristics nonruling Communist parties tend to take on in various political cultures precisely as a consequence of their nonruling status. One such project in the comparative politics of nonruling Communist parties has recently been initiated by Jan Triska and his associates in the Stanford Studies of the Communist System.[19]

17. (New York 1938).

18. (Princeton 1956).

19. "The Non-Ruling Communist Parties: National or Cross-National? Prospectus for a Symposium," Stanford Studies of the Communist System (June 1965), mimeographed.

CROSS-SYSTEM COMPARISON

An objection advanced against the proposal to develop the comparative study of communism is that the result may be to divert attention from the task of comparing Communist systems and their institutions with their non-Communist counterparts. To some the latter seems the most pressing item on the agenda of scholarship in Communist studies.

Efforts at such cross-system comparison are of course no novelty; they preceded comparative study of communism itself. Beginning in the later 1930's the Soviet Communist system in its Stalinist form was coupled with German national socialism and Italian fascism under the broad heading of "totalitarianism," and the latter concept greatly influenced the postwar development of Soviet studies in this country. It has lately come under criticism, however, owing to post-Stalin Soviet changes, the growth of Communist diversity, multiplying evidence that Communist systems are not the internal monoliths that this concept suggested, and so on. The comparative uses of the notion of totalitarianism have been questioned on the ground that it makes no provision for significant likenesses between, for example, Communist systems and some nationalist single-party systems in the new nations, and that it tends to obscure significant differences between communism and fascism on the one hand and between different Communist systems on the other. To meet such theoretical difficulties, some would incorporate diversity into the concept of totalitarianism by distinguishing different forms of the phenomenon, ranging from terrorist to voluntarist.[20] Others would redefine the base concept for a comparative theory of modern authoritarian systems in terms of "mobilization systems" and the like. According to one such scheme, the novel form of authoritarian system in the twentieth century is the revolutionary mass-movement regime under single-party auspices ("movement-regime"), which exists in Communist, Fascist, and nationalist varieties that share certain basic characteristics while differing significantly.[21]

An important characteristic shared by most Communist and some nationalist single-party systems is the commitment of the authorities to the goals of internal development and modernization of backward societies. This commitment raises the question of the relation between Communist studies and the study of the "developing countries." The past decade has

20. See Zbigniew Brzezinski, "The Nature of the Soviet System," *Slavic Review*, XX (October 1961), 351–68.

21. Robert C. Tucker, "Towards a Comparative Politics of Movement-Regimes," *American Political Science Review*, LV (June 1961), 281–89. On "mobilization systems" see David Apter, *The Politics of Modernization* (Chicago 1965). For a review of the recent criticisms of the concept of totalitarianism, see Skilling's "Interest Groups and Communist Politics," *World Politics*, XVIII (April 1966), 435–51.

seen a veritable burgeoning of research and theorizing on economic and political development and the processes of modernization. But there has been relatively little theoretical contact between this new scholarly front and Communist studies. The general theory of modernization has not had a great deal to say on communism as a mode (or modes) of modernization. In *The Stages of Economic Growth*,[22] for example, W. W. Rostow was willing at most to allow that communism is a "disease" of modernization, a pathological form of the process. And theorists of the politics of developing areas have concentrated all but exclusive attention upon the non-Communist new nations of Asia and Africa.[23] A potential field for cross-system comparison thus appears to have been relatively neglected. Communist studies and the comparative study of modernization remain to be brought fully into relation with one another. This is not to suggest that the former should be incorporated into the latter, but simply that Communist countries should be included for certain social science purposes in the category of "developing countries" and that Communist forms of modernization belong within the purview of the comparative study of modernization. Modernization theory has a significant place in Communist studies, and vice versa.

Reference has been made to conceptual bridges for comparative study of Communist and nationalist single-party systems. Now something further should be said about comparative study and the communism-nationalism dichotomy. Especially in an era of Communist polycentrism, this old dichotomy breaks down. Since "communism" and "nationalism" can no longer be viewed, if indeed it was ever proper to do so, as mutually exclusive sociopolitical forces, they should not be treated as mutually exclusive conceptual categories. Not only have Communist movements in various places sought to capitalize upon nationalist emotion in their drives for power and in policies followed after coming to power; communism and nationalism have in various ways undergone a fusion process in the course of Communist political development. As a result, nationalism has reappeared in Communist forms, ranging from great-power chauvinism to "national communism" as a tendency in certain small Communist countries. This has a bearing not only upon the comparative study of Communist societies, but also upon cross-system comparison between "Communist" and "nationalist" states. What may linguistically loom as a chasm in kind may be a rather subtle difference in reality.

22. (Cambridge 1960).

23. See, for example, Gabriel A. Almond and James S. Coleman, eds., *The Politics of the Developing Areas* (Princeton 1960). The concept of totalitarianism may have been an inhibition upon comparative treatment of non-Communist and Communist "developing areas." Thus in an earlier fourfold classification of political systems, Almond characterized the developing countries under the heading of "pre-industrial political systems" while placing communism in the classification "totalitarian political systems." See his "Comparative Political Systems," *Journal of Politics*, XVIII (August 1956), 391–409.

The publication in 1964 of the study by Brzezinski and Samuel P. Huntington, *Political Power: USA/USSR*, has done much to open up still a further sphere of fruitful cross-system comparison. The authors collaborated in a systematic comparative study of the Soviet and American political systems in terms of political beliefs, the individual, leadership, and policy-making. It was supplemented with a series of case studies comparing, for example, the paths to power of Kennedy and Khrushchev, the dismissals of MacArthur and Zhukov, and the behavior of the two systems in the Cuban and Hungarian crises. Even its critics have recognized this book as a breakthrough. Although its tendency is to stress the depth of differences between the two systems, by the very fact that it finds them empirically comparable it departs from the old habit of thinking of American and Soviet society as totally contrasting examples of the polar opposites "democracy" and "totalitarianism." By breaking down the absolutism of that dichotomy, the study has given impetus to cross-system comparison of a difficult but important new kind.

Empirical comparison of the United States and the Soviet Union raises deeper theoretical problems of comparison of the types of society or civilization that they represent. Brzezinski and Huntington address themselves, in particular, to the question of "convergence." Are Soviet and American societies, as two expressions of advanced industrial civilization, evolving along converging lines? Does industrialism wear away differences and foster a gradual rapprochement of advanced industrial civilizations? In his wartime book, *Russia and the United States*,[24] the Russian-born American sociologist Pitirim Sorokin argued that Russian and American societies were converging. Other American and West European thinkers have likewise argued the affirmative case. Still others, including Inkeles and Brzezinski and Huntington, have criticized their position.[25] Soviet scholars have in the recent past vigorously joined the debate, championing the anticonvergence position and contending that there is no uniform type of advanced industrial society.[26] Here, then, is a challenging field of inquiry in cross-system comparison between Communist and non-Communist society. As a stimulus to further discussion and research, might it be desirable to orga-

---

24. (New York 1944).

25. Sorokin reaffirmed his wartime position in a later article, "Mutual Convergence of the United States and the U.S.S.R." *International Journal of Comparative Sociology*, I (September 1960), 143–76. For a critique of his position, see Alex Inkeles, "Russia and the United States: A Problem in Comparative Sociology," in P. J. Allen, ed., *Pitirim Sorokin in Review* (Durham, N. Car., 1963). Skilling has given a useful review of the literature of the convergence debate in "Soviet and American Politics: The Dialectic of Opposites," *Canadian Journal of Economics and Politics*, XXXI (May 1965), 278–80.

26. See, for example, G. Khromushin, "Antisovetskaia 'sushchnost' teorii 'rastushchego skhodstva'" [The Anti-Soviet Essence of the Theory of "Convergence"], *Kommunist*, No. 11 (1965), 99–107.

nize in the near future an international scholarly conference on the convergence problem, to be attended by scholars from all relevant disciplines and from Communist as well as non-Communist countries?

Cross-system comparison includes not only the comparative study of systems in their totality but also comparison of particular kinds of institutions or social processes. Some examples might be the comparative study of Communist and non-Communist political parties or of the processes of urbanization as found in the two types of society. A further interesting vista for such microcomparative work is suggested by a remark made in conversation some years ago by Mikhail Pervukhin, a former member of the Politburo of the Soviet Communist party: "You call it General Electric; we call it the Ministry of the Communications Equipment Industry." As this very remark suggests, however, in undertaking such comparative study it is essential to bear in mind the anthropological principle that different institutions may serve similar functions and similar institutions different functions. For example, it might be both more appropriate and more fruitful to compare a non-Communist political party with a faction of a Communist party rather than with the Communist party as such. Again, a comparative study of the legislative process in Communist and non-Communist societies might do well to take the party central committee rather than the formal state legislature as the institutional setting of the legislative process in the Communist state.

The question was raised at the opening of this section whether cross-system comparison should take precedence over comparative communism. A formal way of resolving it would be to define the scope of the comparative study of communism more comprehensively, so as to embrace cross-system comparison too. The two kinds of study do seem to reinforce each other and to be natural accompaniments of one another. But even if we opt for the more comprehensive view, the question of priorities in theory and research still remains. Where should the principal emphasis be placed at the present stage? This may be one of those questions which each scholar must decide for himself and which different individuals will validly decide in different ways. If, however, we are in the process of creating a multiple model of communism, then it may be that major new progress in cross-system comparison waits upon the emergence, through comparative inquiry, of this more sophisticated theory of Communist society.

THE ROLE OF THE HUMANITIES

As an approach, comparative communism grows out of the interests, concepts, and methodologies of the contemporary social sciences. It expresses the analytic and generalizing impulse felt by students of Communist society working in the various social sciences. But may not the humanities too have a part to play in the comparative study of communism? Considering the peculiarly vital position that literature, the theater, and the rest of the arts have in Communist society, the comparative study of Communist culture would seem to be a field in which scholars in the humanities, along with social scientists, have potentially very significant contributions to make.

Literary scholarship and criticism have established themselves as principal avenues of understanding of the trends in Communist society. Suffice it to say that the essay *On Socialist Realism* by Tertz-Sinyavsky uses literary criticism as the medium for what is probably the most sensitive portrayal yet given of communism as a civilization.[27] This suggests that a comparative literature of Communist revolution may represent one fruitful direction for scholarship in the humanities to take in coming years. It is, of course, to be neither expected nor desired that scholars working in such fields as Slavic studies and sinology should abdicate their traditional interests. But those who do find it challenging to approach the literature of Communist society comparatively may achieve results of wide scholarly interest. It may be, moreover, that scholars in Slavic studies are especially well qualified to pursue such study because of the fact that they normally master more than one of the Slavic languages.

May not philosophy too have a very significant role in the comparative study of communism? We hardly need remind ourselves that communism, as an ideological civilization, places enormous emphasis upon philosophy. Furthermore, the diversification to which reference has been made earlier in this article finds manifestation too in Communist ideology and philosophy. Despite official claims that Marxism-Leninism is one and indivisible, the Communist world is nowadays the scene of controversy and competition between different Communist ideologies and philosophies. Philosophical scholars share with political scientists and sociologists an interest in these developments. Powerfully assisted by the relatively recent rediscovery of the early Marx and the emergence of an "alienation debate" inside Communist societies, the proliferation of Communist Marxisms is an event of profound significance and provides a field of comparative study in which philosophical scholars have much to contribute.

Mention should be made, finally, of the comparative study of education and science in Communist society. There has been a great growth of interest in these subjects during the past decade, and substantial studies have appeared. But so far very little of this work has been comparative in scope and approach. It may turn out, however, that comparative methods have fruitful potential application in the study of both science and education in Communist society. The comparative study of Communist educational systems, in particular, may be one of the roads to a better comprehension of the place of education in Communist society, its developmental trends, and its special problems.

27. Abram Tertz, *On Socialist Realism* (New York 1960).

THE TEACHING OF COMPARATIVE COMMUNISM

The interest in comparative communism as a focus of research and theory has undoubtedly arisen in part out of teaching experience at the college level. Teachers of Soviet politics, for example, have found themselves reaching out for comparisons between the Soviet and other Communist systems and for generalizations about their similarities and differences. Such experience fosters awareness of the need for, and possibility of, a comparative politics of communism. On the other hand, the development of theory and research along comparative lines may in turn have implications for the curriculum and for the methods of teaching courses about Communist society.

Comparative communism already has a certain place in the college curriculum in the social sciences. Some social science departments, for example, have organized courses, at the undergraduate or graduate level, along comparative lines. Thus a course may be offered in Soviet-*type* economies rather than simply in Soviet economics, and some universities already offer graduate seminars in comparative Communist political systems. The question is whether this trend toward comparativism should be carried further and, if so, along what lines. It might be held, for example, that undergraduate first courses in this or that aspect of Communist society should best confine themselves to a single important society, such as the Soviet or the Chinese, and that the comparative approach should be introduced, if at all, at the more advanced level. On the other hand, some (including the writer) have found that undergraduates in first courses react quite positively to the introduction of moderate doses of comparative material and comparative analysis and, indeed, that their interest is more quickly engaged and more easily sustained when a course offers the increased intellectual challenge that comparativism brings. To this it might be added that courses of comparative orientation may be especially appropriate to the needs of the majority of undergraduate students with no relevant language skills and no particular interest in specialized area training.

Similar considerations may apply at the graduate level. For the minority of graduate students who intend to specialize in one or another branch of Communist studies in the social sciences, the need for area training will remain. But what of those who do not? By transcending an area approach, it may be possible for graduate departments to make Communist studies a more integral and widely chosen part of their curriculum. To the extent that they do so, knowledge about Communist society will become less a special possession of a limited group of academic people and more a general mark of literacy about a world that is now one-third Communist and may remain so. The atmosphere of the occult that still hangs over Communist studies may be dispelled.

Do the prospects for the growth of comparative communism mean that the imposing structure of Russian, Chinese, and other relevant area programs that now exist in our universities should be dismantled or significantly reduced in size? No such implication would seem to be present. The dependence of comparative Communist studies upon a solid base of area scholarship, and hence upon the language skills and expertise that area training provides, has already been emphasized here. To dismantle the area programs would undercut future progress in the comparative study of communism. On the other hand, it may be that comparative courses have a greater place in area programs than that so far accorded them. For example, major academic centers that have area programs in both Russian and Chinese studies may well find that a comparative course or seminar offers one relatively effective way of bringing both faculty and students in the two programs into greater intellectual contact and giving each group an education in what is going on in the other's field. Such courses could on occasion be a bridge between area programs in adjacent universities. It might also be fruitful to use cross-system comparison as a way of bringing, for example, a Soviet area studies program and a program in American civilization into at least temporary systematic interrelation. Finally, experience shows that area training programs have a potentially much more important place in the undergraduate curriculum than that so far generally accorded them.

In conclusion, it may be useful to ponder the implications of comparative communism for the teaching of courses in communism at the high-school level. Such courses have mushroomed in the United States in the past decade and in many places have taken on from the beginning an aspect of ideological indoctrination in anticommunism. The unity and singleness of purpose of something sometimes called simply "international communism" is an underlying preconception in those cases. To the extent that the high-school courses follow this line of thought, the education that they give in communism is nowadays an education in unreality. On the other hand, for various reasons a comparative approach can rarely be introduced at this level. The result is an educational dilemma of large and troubling proportions. But college and university teachers can do something to assuage it by providing corrective education in comparative communism.

Empirical Conceptualizations

An Approach to the Analysis of Political Systems*

David Easton

I. SOME ATTRIBUTES OF POLITICAL SYSTEMS

In an earlier work I have argued for the need to develop general, empirically oriented theory as the most economical way in the long run to understand political life. Here I propose to indicate a point of view that, at the least, might serve as a springboard for discussion of alternative approaches and, at most, as a small step in the direction of a general political theory. I wish to stress that what I have to say is a mere orientation to the problem of theory; outside of economics and perhaps psychology, it would be presumptuous to call very much in social science "theory," in the strict sense of the term.

Furthermore, I shall offer only a Gestalt of my point of view, so that it will be possible to evaluate, in the light of the whole, those parts that I do stress. In doing this, I know I run the definite risk that the meaning and implications of this point of view may be only superficially communicated; but it is a risk I shall have to undertake since I do not know how to avoid it sensibly.

The study of politics is concerned with understanding how authoritative decisions are made and executed for a society. We can try to understand political life by viewing each of its aspects piecemeal. We can examine the operation of such institutions as political parties, interest groups, government, and voting; we can study the nature and consequences of such political practices as manipulation, propaganda, and violence; we can seek to reveal the structure within which these practices occur. By combining the results we can obtain a rough picture of what happens in any self-contained political unit.

In combining these results, however, there is already implicit the notion that each part of the larger political canvas does not stand alone but is re-

* In modified form, the substance of this article was presented to a meeting of the New England Political Science Association in May 1956 and to a special conference of the International Political Science Association held in Switzerland in September 1956.

Reprinted from World Politics, Vol. IX, no. 3 (copyright © 1957 by Princeton University Press): pp. 383–400. Reprinted by permission of Princeton University Press.

lated to each other part; or, to put it positively, that the operation of no one part can be fully understood without reference to the way in which the whole itself operates. I have suggested in my book, *The Political System,*[1] that it is valuable to adopt this implicit assumption as an articulate premise for research and to view political life as a system of interrelated activities. These activities derive their relatedness or systemic ties from the fact that they all more or less influence the way in which authoritative decisions are formulated and executed for a society.

Once we begin to speak of political life as a system of activity, certain consequences follow for the way in which we can undertake to analyze the working of a system. The very idea of a system suggests that we can separate political life from the rest of social activity, at least for analytical purposes, and examine it as though for the moment it were a self-contained entity surrounded by, but clearly distinguishable from, the environment or setting in which it operates. In much the same way, astronomers consider the solar system a complex of events isolated for certain purposes from the rest of the universe.

Furthermore, if we hold the system of political actions as a unit before our mind's eye, as it were, we can see that what keeps the system going are inputs of various kinds. These inputs are converted by the processes of the system into outputs and these, in turn, have consequences both for the system and for the environment in which the system exists. The formula here is very simple but, as I hope to show, also very illuminating: inputs—political system or processes—outputs. These relationships are shown diagrammatically in Figure I. This diagram represents a very primitive "model" —to dignify it with a fashionable name—for approaching the study of political life.

Political systems have certain properties because they are systems.[2] To present an overall view of the whole approach, let me identify the major attributes, say a little about each, and then treat one of these properties at somewhat greater length, even though still inadequately.

(1) Properties of identification. To distinguish a political system from other social systems, we must be able to identify it by describing its fundamental units and establishing the boundaries that demarcate it from units outside the system.

(a) Units of a political system. The units are the elements of which we say a system is composed. In the case of a political system, they are politi-

---

1. New York, 1953.

2. My conceptions relating to system theory have been enriched through my participation in the Staff Theory Seminar of the Mental Health Research Institute at the University of Michigan. There has been such thorough mingling of ideas in this Seminar that rather than try to trace paternity, I shall simply indicate my obligation to the collective efforts of the Seminar.

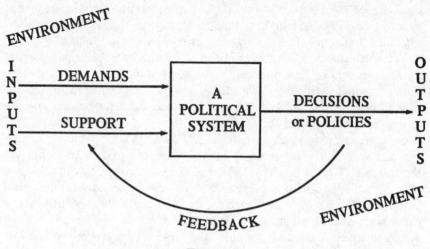

FIGURE I

cal actions. Normally it is useful to look at these as they structure themselves in political roles and political groups.

(b) Boundaries. Some of the most significant questions with regard to the operation of political systems can be answered only if we bear in mind the obvious fact that a system does not exist in a vacuum. It is always immersed in a specific setting or environment. The way in which a system works will be in part a function of its response to the total social, biological, and physical environment.

The special problem with which we are confronted is how to distinguish systematically between a political system and its setting. Does it even make sense to say that a political system has a boundary dividing it from its setting? If so, how are we to identify the line of demarcation?

Without pausing to argue the matter, I would suggest that it is useful to conceive of a political system as having a boundary in the same sense as a physical system. The boundary of a political system is defined by all those actions more or less directly related to the making of binding decisions for a society; every social action that does not partake of this characteristic will be excluded from the system and thereby will automatically be viewed as an external variable in the environment.

(2) Inputs and outputs. Presumably, if we select political systems for special study, we do so because we believe that they have characteristically important consequences for society, namely, authoritative decisions. These consequences I shall call the outputs. If we judged that political systems did not have important outputs for society, we would probably not be interested in them.

Unless a system is approaching a state of entropy—and we can assume that this is not true of most political systems—it must have continuing inputs to keep it going. Without inputs the system can do no work; without outputs we cannot identify the work done by the system. The specific research tasks in this connection would be to identify the inputs and the forces that shape and change them, to trace the processes through which they are transformed into outputs, to describe the general conditions under which such processes can be maintained, and to establish the relationship between outputs and succeeding inputs of the system.

From this point of view, much light can be shed on the working of a political system if we take into account the fact that much of what happens within a system has its birth in the efforts of the members of the system to cope with the changing environment. We can appreciate this point if we consider a familiar biological system such as the human organism. It is subject to constant stress from its surroundings to which it must adapt in one way or another if it is not to be completely destroyed. In part, of course, the way in which the body works represents responses to needs that are generated by the very organization of its anatomy and functions; but in large part, in order to understand both the structure and the working of the body, we must also be very sensitive to the inputs from the environment.

In the same way, the behavior of every political system is to some degree imposed upon it by the kind of system it is, that is, by its own structure and internal needs. But its behavior also reflects the strains occasioned by the specific setting within which the system operates. It may be argued that most of the significant changes within a political system have their origin in shifts among the external variables. Since I shall be devoting the bulk of this article to examining some of the problems related to the exchange between political systems and their environments, I shall move on to a rapid description of other properties of political systems.

(3) Differentiation within a system. As we shall see in a moment, from the environment come both energy to activate a system and information with regard to which the system uses this energy. In this way a system is able to do work. It has some sort of output that is different from the input that enters from the environment. We can take it as a useful hypothesis that if a political system is to perform some work for anything but a limited interval of time, a minimal amount of differentiation in its structure must occur. In fact, empirically it is impossible to find a significant political system in which the same units all perform the same activities at the same time. The members of a system engage in at least some minimal division of labor that provides a structure within which action takes place.

(4) Integration of a system. This fact of differentiation opens up a major area of inquiry with regard to political systems. Structural differentiation sets in motion forces that are potentially disintegrative in their results for the system. If two or more units are performing different kinds of activity at the same time, how are these activities to be brought into the minimal

degree of articulation necessary if the members of the system are not to end up in utter disorganization with regard to the production of the outputs of interest to us? We can hypothesize that if a structured system is to maintain itself, it must provide mechanisms whereby its members are integrated or induced to cooperate in some minimal degree so that they can make authoritative decisions.

II. Inputs: Demands

Now that I have mentioned some major attributes of political systems that I suggest require special attention if we are to develop a generalized approach, I want to consider in greater detail the way in which an examination of inputs and outputs will shed some light on the working of these systems.

Among inputs of a political system there are two basic kinds: demands and support. These inputs give a political system its dynamic character. They furnish it both with the raw material or information that the system is called upon to process and with the energy to keep it going.

The reason why a political system emerges in a society at all—that is, why men engage in political activity—is that demands are being made by persons or groups in the society that cannot all be fully satisfied. In all societies one fact dominates political life: scarcity prevails with regard to most valued things. Some of the claims for these relatively scarce things never find their way into the political system but are satisfied through the private negotiations of or settlements by the persons involved. Demands for prestige may find satisfaction through the status relations of society; claims for wealth are met in part through the economic system; aspirations for power find expression in educational, fraternal, labor, and similar private organizations. Only where wants require some special organized effort on the part of society to settle them authoritatively may we say that they have become inputs of the political system.

Systematic research would require us to address ourselves to several key questions with regard to these demands.

(1) How do demands arise and assume their particular character in a society? In answer to this question, we can point out that demands have their birth in two sectors of experience: either in the environment of a system or within the system itself. We shall call these the external and internal demands, respectively.

Let us look at the external demands first. I find it useful to see the environment not as an undifferentiated mass of events but rather as systems clearly distinguishable from one another and from the political system. In the environment we have such systems as the ecology, economy, culture, personality, social structure, and demography. Each of these constitutes a major set of variables in the setting that helps to shape the kind of demands entering a political system. For purposes of illustrating what I mean, I shall say a few words about culture.

The members of every society act within the framework of an on-going culture that shapes their general goals, specific objectives, and the procedures that the members feel ought to be used. Every culture derives part of its unique quality from the fact that it emphasizes one or more special aspects of behavior and this strategic emphasis serves to differentiate it from other cultures with respect to the demands that it generates. As far as the mass of the people is concerned, some cultures, such as our own, are weighted heavily on the side of economic wants, success, privacy, leisure activity, and rational efficiency. Others, such as that of the Fox Indians, strive toward the maintenance of harmony, even if in the process the goals of efficiency and rationality may be sacrificed. Still others, such as the Kachins of highland Burma, stress the pursuit of power and prestige. The culture embodies the standards of value in a society and thereby marks out areas of potential conflict, if the valued things are in short supply relative to demand. The typical demands that will find their way into the political process will concern the matters in conflict that are labeled important by the culture. For this reason we cannot hope to understand the nature of the demands presenting themselves for political settlement unless we are ready to explore systematically and intensively their connection with the culture. And what I have said about culture applies, with suitable modifications, to other parts of the setting of a political system.

But not all demands originate or have their major locus in the environment. Important types stem from situations occurring within a political system itself. Typically, in every on-going system, demands may emerge for alterations in the political relationships of the members themselves, as the result of dissatisfaction stemming from these relationships. For example, in a political system based upon representation, in which equal representation is an important political norm, demands may arise for equalizing representation between urban and rural voting districts. Similarly, demands for changes in the process of recruitment of formal political leaders, for modifications of the way in which constitutions are amended, and the like may all be internally inspired demands.

I find it useful and necessary to distinguish these from external demands because they are, strictly speaking, not inputs of the system but something that we can call "withinputs," if we can tolerate a cumbersome neologism, and because their consequences for the character of a political system are more direct than in the case of external demands. Furthermore, if we were not aware of this difference in classes of demands, we might search in vain for an explanation of the emergence of a given set of internal demands if we turned only to the environment.

(2) How are demands transformed into issues? What determines whether a demand becomes a matter for serious political discussion or remains some-

thing to be resolved privately among the members of society? The occurrence of a demand, whether internal or external, does not thereby automatically convert it into a political *issue*. Many demands die at birth or linger on with the support of an insignificant fraction of the society and are never raised to the level of possible political decision. Others become issues, an issue being a demand that the members of a political system are prepared to deal with as a significant item for discussion through the recognized channels in the system.

The distinction between demands and issues raises a number of questions about which we need data if we are to understand the processes through which claims typically become transformed into issues. For example, we would need to know something about the relationship between a demand and the location of its initiators or supporters in the power structures of the society, the importance of secrecy as compared with publicity in presenting demands, the matter of timing of demands, the possession of political skills or know-how, access to channels of communication, the attitudes and states of mind of possible publics, and the images held by the initiators of demands with regard to the way in which things get done in the particular political system. Answers to matters such as these would possibly yield a conversion index reflecting the probability of a set of demands being converted into live political issues.

If we assume that political science is primarily concerned with the way in which authoritative decisions are made for a society, demands require special attention as a major type of input of political systems. I have suggested that demands influence the behavior of a system in a number of ways. They constitute a significant part of the material upon which the system operates. They are also one of the sources of change in political systems, since as the environment fluctuates it generates new types of demand-inputs for the system. Accordingly, without this attention to the origin and determinants of demands we would be at a loss to be able to treat rigorously not only the operation of a system at a moment of time but also its change over a specified interval. Both the statics and historical dynamics of a political system depend upon a detailed understanding of demands, particularly of the impact of the setting on them.

III. INPUTS: SUPPORT

Inputs of demands alone are not enough to keep a political system operating. They are only the raw material out of which finished products called decisions are manufactured. Energy in the form of actions or orientations promoting and resisting a political system, the demands arising in it, and the decisions issuing from it must also be put into the system to keep it running. This input I shall call support.[3] Without support, demands could not be satisfied or conflicts in goals composed. If demands are to be acted upon, the members of a system undertaking to pilot the demands through to their transformation into binding decisions and those who seek to influence the relevant processes in any way must be able to count on support from others in the system. Just how much support, from how many and which members of a political system, are separate and important questions that I shall touch on shortly.

What do we mean by support? We can say that A supports B either when A acts on behalf of or when he orients himself favorably toward B's goals, interests, and actions. Supportive behavior may thus be of two kinds. It may consist of actions promoting he goals, interests, and actions of another person. We may vot for a political candidate, or defend a decision by the highest court of the land. In these cases, support manifests itself through overt action.

On the other hand, supportive behavior may involve not external observable acts, but those internal forms of behavior we call orientations or states of mind. As I use the phrase, a supportive state of mind is a deep-seated set of attitudes or predispositions, or a readiness to act on behalf of some other person. It exists when we say that a man is loyal to his party, attached to democracy, or infused with patriotism. What such phrases as these have in common is the fact that they refer to a state of feelings on the part of a person. No overt action is involved at this level of description, although the implication is that the individual will pursue a course of action consistent with his attitudes. Where the anticipated action does not flow from our perception of the state of mind, we assume that we have not penetrated deeply enough into the true feelings of the person but have merely skimmed off his surface attitudes.

Supportive states of mind are vital inputs for the operation and maintenance of a political system. For example, it is often said that the struggle in the international sphere concerns mastery over men's minds. To a certain extent this is true. If the members of a political system are deeply attached to a system or its ideals, the likelihood of their participating in either domestic or foreign politics in such a way as to undermine the system is reduced by a large factor. Presumably, even in the face of considerable provocation, ingrained supportive feelings of loyalty may be expected to prevail.

We shall need to identify the typical mechanisms through which sup-

3. The concept support has been used by Talcott Parsons in an unpublished paper entitled "Reflections on the Two-Party System." I am pleased to note that in this article Professor Parsons also seems to be moving in the direction of input-output analysis of political problems, although the extent to which he uses other aspects of system theory is not clear to me.

portive attitudes are inculcated and continuously reinforced within a political system. But our prior task is to specify and examine the political objects in relation to which support is extended.

(1) THE DOMAIN OF SUPPORT

Support is fed into the political system in relation to three objects: the community, the regime, and the government. There must be convergence of attitude and opinion as well as some willingness to act with regard to each of these objects. Let us examine each in turn.

(a) The political community. No political system can continue to operate unless its members are willing to support the existence of a group that seeks to settle differences or promote decisions through peaceful action in common The point is so obvious—being dealt with usually under the heading of the growth of national unity—that it may well be overlooked; and yet it is a premise upon which the continuation of any political system depends. To refer to this phenomenon we can speak of the political community. At this level of support we are not concerned with whether a government exists or whether there is loyalty to a constitutional order. For the moment we only ask whether the members of the group that we are examining are sufficiently oriented toward each other to want to contribute their collective energies toward pacific settlement of their varying demands.

The American Civil War is a concrete illustration of the cessation of input of support for the political community. The war itself was definitive evidence that the members of the American political system could no longer contribute to the existence of a state of affairs in which peaceful solution of conflicting demands was the rule. Matters had come to the point where it was no longer a question of whether the South would support one or another alternative government, or whether it could envision its demands being satisfied through the normal constitutional procedures. The issue turned on whether there was sufficient mutual identification among the members of the system for them to be able to work together as a political community. Thus in any political system, to the extent that there is an in-group or we-group feeling and to the extent that the members of the system identify one another as part of this unit and exclude others according to some commonly accepted criteria, such as territoriality, kinship, or citizenship, we shall say that they are putting in support for the political community.

(b) The regime. Support for a second major part of a political system helps to support the energy to keep the system running. This aspect of the system I shall call the regime. It consists of all those arrangements that regulate the way in which the demands put into the system are settled and the way in which decisions are put into effect. They are the so-called rules of the game, in the light of which actions by members of the system are legitimated and accepted by the bulk of the members as authoritative. Unless there is a minimum convergence of attitudes in support of these fundamental rules—the constitutional principles, as we call them in Western society—there would be insufficient harmony in the actions of the members of a system to meet the problems generated by their support of a political community. The fact of trying to settle demands in common means that there must be known principles governing the way in which resolutions of differences of claims are to take place.

(c) The government. If a political system is going to be able to handle the conflicting demands put into it, not only must the members of the system be prepared to support the settlement of these conflicts in common and possess some consensus with regard to the rules governing the mode of settlement; they must also be ready to support a government as it undertakes the concrete tasks involved in negotiating such settlements. When we come to the outputs of a system, we shall see the rewards that are available to a government for mobilizing support. At this point, I just wish to draw attention to this need on the part of a government for support if it is going to be able to make decisions with regard to demands. Of course, a government may elicit support in many ways: through persuasion, consent, or manipulation. It may also impose unsupported settlements of demands through threats of force. But it is a familiar axiom of political science that a government based upon force alone is not long for this world; it must buttress its position by inducing a favorable state of mind in its subjects through fair or foul means.

The fact that support directed to a political system can be broken down conceptually into three elements—support for the community, regime, and government—does not mean, of course, that in the concrete case support for each of these three objects is independent. In fact we might and normally do find all three kinds of support very closely intertwined, so that the presence of one is a function of the presence of one or both of the other types.

For example, withdrawal of support from the government of Louis XVI in effect also meant that members of the French monarchical system were challenging at least the regime; as it turned out in the ensuing revolution and civil war, there was even doubt whether the members of the system would continue to support a unified political community. In this case, what was initially opposition to the ruling sovereign—that is, to the government—quickly turned out to signify a lack of sufficient support for the regime and ultimately, to some extent, for the political community. But this is not always so and fortunately, from the point of view of social order, it is not typically the case. We are accustomed to calling for a change of government without thereby suggesting dissatisfaction with the regime or community. And at times, although this is less frequently true, the community shows sufficient intention to continue as a cooperating group to be able to accept a challenge to the regime. From 1832 to the 1880's England underwent a serious modification in its regime, introducing the basic elements of a system of popular democracy, without serious diminution of input of support at the community level. It is always a matter for empirical enquiry to discover the degree to which support at any one level is dependent upon support at the others.

This very brief discussion of support points up one major fact. If a system is to absorb a variety of demands and negotiate some sort of settlement among them, it is not enough for the members of the system to support only their own demands and the particular government that will undertake to promote these demands. For the demands to be processed into outputs it is equally essential that the members of the system stand ready to support the existence of a political community and some stable rules of common action that we call the regime.

(2) QUANTITY AND SCOPE OF SUPPORT

How much support needs to be put into a system and how many of its members need to contribute such support if the system is to be able to do the job of converting demands to decisions? No ready answer can be offered. The actual situation in each case would determine the amount and scope required. We can, however, visualize a number of situations that will be helpful in directing our attention to possible generalizations.

Under certain circumstances very few members need to support a system at any level. The members might be dull and apathetic, indifferent to the general operations of the system, its progress or decisions. In a loosely connected system such as India has had, this might well be the state of mind of by far the largest segment of the membership. Either in fact they have not been affected by national decisions or they have not perceived that they were so affected. They may have little sense of identification with the present regime and government and yet, with regard to the input of demands, the system may be able to act on the basis of the support offered by the known 3 per cent of the Western-oriented politicians and intellectuals who are politically active. In other words, we can have a small minority putting in quantitatively sufficient supportive energy to keep the system going. However, we can venture the hypothesis that where members of a system are putting in numerous demands, there is a strong probability that they will actively offer support or hostility at one of the three levels of the system, depending upon the degree to which these demands are being met through appropriate decisions.

Alternatively, we may find that all the members of a system are putting in support, but the amount may be so low as to place one or all aspects of the system in jeopardy. Modern France is perhaps a classic illustration. The input of support at the level of the political community is probably adequate for the maintenance of France as a national political unit. But for a variety of historical and contemporary reasons, there is considerable doubt as to whether the members of the French political system are putting in anything but a low order of support to the regime or any particular government. This low amount of support, even though spread over a relatively large segment of the population, leaves the French political system on somewhat less secure foundations than is the case with India. There support is less widespread but more active—that is, quantitatively greater—on the part of a minority. As this illustration indicates, the amount of support is not necessarily proportional to its scope.

It may seem from the above discussion as though the members of a political system either put in support or withhold it—that is, demonstrate hostility or apathy. In fact, members may and normally do simultaneously engage in supportive and hostile behavior. What we must be interested in is the net balance of support.

IV. Mechanisms of Support

To this point I have suggested that no political system can yield the important outputs we call authoritative decisions unless, in addition to demands, support finds its way into the system. I have discussed the possible object to which support may be directed, and some problems with regard to the domain, quantity, and scope of support. We are now ready to turn to the main question raised by our attention to support as a crucial input: how do systems typically manage to maintain a steady flow of support? Without it a system will not absorb sufficient energy from its members to be able to convert demands to decisions.

In theory, there might be an infinite variety of means through which members could be induced to support a system; in practice, certain well-established classes of mechanisms are used. Research in this area needs to be directed to exploring the precise way in which a particular system utilizes these mechanisms and to refining our understanding of the way in which they contribute to the making of authoritative policy.

A society generates support for a political system in two ways: through outputs that meet the demands of the members of society; and through the processes of politicization. Let us look at outputs first.

(1) Outputs as a Mechanism of Support

An output of a political system, it will be recalled, is a political decision or policy. One of the major ways of strengthening the ties of the members to their system is through providing decisions that tend to satisfy the day-to-day demands of these members. Fundamentally this is the truth that lies in the aphorism that one can fool some of the people some of the time but not all of them all of the time. Without some minimal satisfaction of demands, the ardor of all but the most fanatical patriot is sure to cool. The outputs, consisting of political decisions, constitute a body of specific inducements for the members of a system to support that system.

Inducements of this kind may be positive or negative. Where negative, they threaten the members of the system with various kinds of sanctions ranging from a small monetary fine to physical detention, ostracism, or loss of life, as in our own system with regard to the case of legally defined treason. In every system support stems in part from fear of sanctions or compulsion; in autocratic systems the proportion of coerced support is at a maximum. For want of space I shall confine myself to those cases where positive incentives loom largest.

Since the specific outputs of a system are policy decisions, it is upon the government that the final responsibility falls for matching or balancing outputs of decisions against input of demand. But it is clear that to obtain the support of the members of a system through positive incentives, a government need not meet all the demands of even its most influential and ardent supporters. Most governments, or groups such as political parties that seek to control governments, succeed in building up a reserve of support. This reserve will carry the government along even though it offends its followers, so long as over the extended short run these followers perceive the particular government as one that is in general favorable to their interests. One form that this reserve support takes in Western society is that of party loyalty, since the party is the typical instrument in a mass industrialized society for mobilizing and maintaining support for a government. However, continuous lack of specific rewards through policy decisions ultimately leads to the danger that even the deepest party loyalty may be shaken.

For example, labor has continued to support the Democratic Party even though much of the legislation promoted by members of that party has not served to meet labor's demands. In some measures, large sections of labor may continue to vote and campaign vigorously on behalf of the Democratic Party because they have no realistic alternative other than to support this party; but in addition the Democrats have built up in recent years, especially during the Roosevelt era, a considerable body of goodwill. It would take repeated neglect of labor's demands on the part of the Democratic Party to undermine the strong urban working-class support directed toward it and the government that the party dominates from time to time.

Thus a system need not meet *all the demands* of its members so long as it has stored up a reserve of support over the years. Nor need it satisfy even *some of the demands* of all its members. Just whose demands a system must seek to meet, how much of their demands, at what time, and under what conditions are questions for special research. We can say in advance that at least the demands of the most influential members require satisfaction. But this tells us little unless we know how to discover the influentials in a political system and how new sets of members rise to positions of influence.[4]

The critical significance of the decisions of governments for the support of the other two aspects of a system—namely, the political community and the regime—is clear from what I have said above. Not all withdrawal of support from a government has consequences for the success or failure of a regime or community. But persistent inability of a government to produce satisfactory outputs for the members of a system may well lead to demands for changing of the regime or for dissolution of the political community. It is for this reason that the input-output balance is a vital mechanism in the life of a political system.

(2) POLITICIZATION AS A MECHANISM OF SUPPORT

It would be wrong to consider that the level of support available to a system is a function exclusively of the outputs in the form of either sanctions or rewards. If we did so conclude, we could scarcely account for the maintenance of numerous political systems in which satisfaction of demands has been manifestly low, in which public coercion is limited, and yet which have endured for epochs. Alternately, it might be difficult to explain how political systems could endure and yet manage to flout or thwart urgent demands, failing thereby to render sufficient *quid pro quo* for the input of support. The fact is that whatever reserve of support has been accumulated through past decisions is increased and reinforced by a complicated method for steadily manufacturing support through what I shall call the process of politicization. It is an awkward term, but nevertheless an appropriately descriptive one.

As each person grows up in a society, through a network of rewards and punishments the other members of society communicate to and instill in him the various institutionalized goals and norms of that society. This is well known in social research as the process of socialization. Through its operation a person learns to play his various social roles. Part of these goals and norms relate to what the society considers desirable in political life. The ways in which these political patterns are learned by the members of society constitute what I call the process of politicization. Through it a person learns to play his political roles, which include the absorption of the proper political attitudes.

Let us examine a little more closely something of what happens during the process of politicization. As members of a society mature, they must absorb the various orientations toward political matters that one is expected to have in that society. If the expectations of the members of society with

4. See C. W. Mills, *The Power Elite*, New York, 1956.

regard to the way each should behave in specific political situations diverged beyond a certain range, it would be impossible to get common action with regard to the making of binding decisions. It is essential for the viability of an orderly political system that the members of the system have some common basic expectations with regard to the standards that are to be used in making political evaluations, to the way people will feel about various political matters, and to the way members of the system will perceive and interpret political phenomena.

The mechanism through which this learning takes place is of considerable significance in understanding how a political system generates and accumulates a strong reserve of support. Although we cannot pursue the details, we can mention a few of the relevant dimensions. In the first place, of course, the learning or politicization process does not stop at any particular period for the individual; it starts with the child and, in the light of our knowledge of learning, may have its deepest impact through the teen age. The study of the political experiences of and the influences operating on the child and the adolescent emerges as an important and neglected area of research.[5]

In the second place, the actual process of politicization at its most general level brings into operation a complex network of rewards and punishments. For adopting the correct political attitudes and performing the right political acts, for conforming to the generally accepted interpretations of political goals, and for undertaking the institutionalized obligations of a member of the given system, we are variously rewarded or punished. For conforming we are made to feel worthy, wanted, and respected and often obtain material advantages such as wealth, influence, improved opportunities. For deviating beyond the permissible range, we are made to feel unworthy, rejected, dishonored, and often suffer material losses.

This does not mean that the pattern of rewards and punishments is by any means always effective; if it were, we would never have changed from the Stone Age. A measure of non-conformity may at certain stages in the life history of a political system itself become a respected norm. Even where this is not the case, the most seductive rewards and the severest punishments will never succeed in preventing some of the members of a system from pursuing what they consider to be their inextinguishable interests and from seeking, with varying degrees of success, to change the goals and norms of the system. This is one of the important sources of political change closely associated with changes in the inputs of demands that are

5. I am happy to say that, since I wrote this statement, the neglect has begun to be remedied. My colleagues at the University of Chicago, Robert Hess of the Committee of Human Development and Peter Rossi of the Department of Sociology, and I have undertaken a questionnaire-interview study of the development of the political attitudes, opinions, and images held by children and adolescents. This research is an attempt to develop some useful generalizations about major aspects of the processes of politicization in the American political system and to formulate a design that, for comparative purposes, could be applied in other political systems as well.

due to a changing environment. But we cannot pursue this crucial matter of the nature of political change, as it would lead us off in a new direction.

In the third place, the means used for communicating the goals and norms to others tend to be repetitive in all societies. The various political myths, doctrines, and philosophies transmit to each generation a particular interpretation of the goals and norms. The decisive links in this chain of transmission are parents, siblings, peers, teachers, organizations, and social leaders, as well as physical symbols such as flags or totems, ceremonies, and rituals freighted with political meaning.

These processes through which attachments to a political system become built into the maturing member of a society I have lumped together under the rubric of politicization. They illustrate the way in which members of a system learn what is expected of them in political life and how they ought to do what is expected of them. In this way they acquire knowledge about their political roles and a desire to perform them. In stable systems the support that accrues through these means adds to the reservoir of support being accumulated on a day-to-day basis through the outputs of decisions.[6] The support obtained through politicization tends to be relatively—although, as we have seen, not wholly—independent of the vagaries of day-to-day outputs.

When the basic political attachments become deeply rooted or institutionalized, we say that the system has become accepted as legitimate. Politicization therefore effectively sums up the way in which legitimacy is created and transmitted in a political system. And it is an empirical observation that in those instances where political systems have survived the longest, support has been nourished by an ingrained belief in the legitimacy of the relevant governments and regimes.

What I am suggesting here is that support resting on a sense of the legitimacy of a government and regime provides a necessary reserve if the system is to weather those frequent storms when the more obvious outputs of the system seem to impose greater hardships than rewards. Answers to questions concerning the formation, maintenance, transmission, and change of standards of legitimacy will contribute generously to an understanding of the way in which support is sufficiently institutionalized so that a system may regularly and without excessive expenditure of effort transform inputs of demand into outputs of decisions.

That there is a need for general theory in the study of political life is apparent. The only question is how best to proceed. There is no one royal road that can be said to be either the correct one or the best. It is only a matter of what appears at the given level of available knowledge to be the most useful. At this stage it appears that system theory, with its sensitivity

---

6. In primitive systems, politicization, not outputs of decisions, is normally the chief mechanism.

to the input-output exchange between a system and its setting offers a fruitful approach. It is an economical way of organizing presently disconnected political data and promises interesting dividends.

A Developmental Approach to Political Systems
Gabriel A. Almond

During the past decade two tendencies have come to dominate the field of comparative politics. One of these is the concern for theoretical explication and methodological rigor, and the second is the emphasis on field studies of the "emerging," "new," and "non-Western" nations. The theoretical tendency has largely taken the form of applications of "systems" theory to the study of politics, and the chief criticism of this approach has been that it is a static theory, not suitable for the analysis and explanation of political change.

The great output of empirical studies of contemporary politics in the new and emerging nations and the relative decline in the volume of European political studies have similarly been criticized. Here the argument is that the relative neglect of Western political studies, and particularly of their historical dimension, handicaps us in our efforts to work out the developmental theories and approaches which we need for our research on the new and emerging nations.

Both of these criticisms have great cogency. Systems theory does have a static, "equilibrium" bias; and the stress on the politics of the new and emerging nations gives us an inadequate sampling of man's experience with social and political change. The only answer to this criticism is that this seems to be the way sciences develop—not by orderly, systematic progression, but in a dialectical process involving overemphases and neglects. If we are to come to grips more effectively with political change, we shall have to redress this imbalance, adapt systems theory in a developmental direction, and utilize historical knowledge of Western political development (but not only Western history) in elaborating theories of political systems and political change.

This article represents a move in this direction, an effort on the part of one political systems theorist to define what political development consists of and to take into account the variables which affect it.[1]

1. Whatever merit this contribution to the theory of political change may have is due to a long series of polemics which began with my paper, "Comparative Political Systems" (*Journal of Politics*, XVI [August 1956], 391–409), and became somewhat more lively after the appearance of my introductory essay in Almond and Coleman,

Reprinted from World Politics, *Vol. XVII, no. 2 (copyright © 1965 by Princeton University Press): pp. 183–214. Reprinted by permission of Princeton University Press.*

I. System and Function

The term "system" has become increasingly common in the titles of texts and monographs in the field of comparative politics. Older texts tended to use such terms as "governments" or "foreign powers." Something more is involved here than mere style in nomenclature. The use of the concept of system reflects the penetration into political theory of the anthropological and sociological theory of functionalism. The chief social theorists whose names are associated with functionalism are the anthropologists Malinowski and Radcliffe-Brown and the sociologists Parsons, Merton, and Marion Levy.[2] Though they differ substantially in their concepts of system and function, what these men have been saying is that our capacity for explanation and prediction in the social sciences is enhanced when we think of social structures and institutions as performing *functions* in *systems*.

The point being made here is both simple and important. A circulatory system in an organism makes little sense by itself. When we view it as serving a purpose or set of purposes for the functioning of the organism as a whole, we can begin to comprehend its significance. Similarly, political parties or administrative agencies mean little by themselves. Their significance becomes clear when we see them as interacting with other institutions to produce public policies and enforcements of public policies in the domestic or international environments.

Functional-system theory as formulated by such writers as Talcott Parsons and Marion Levy implies three conditions: functional requisites, interdependence, and equilibrium. A particular system, whether it be an organism, a machine, or a family, has to behave in particular ways, perform a set of tasks, in order to "be" the particular organism, machine, or family.

---

eds., *The Politics of the Developing Areas* (Princeton 1960). An early and partial version of some of the ideas contained here appeared in Almond, "Political Systems and Political Change," *American Behavioral Scientist*, VI (June 1963), 3–10. The polemics were in part with myself, in part with graduate students in seminars, in part with reviewers, and in most substantial part with my friends and colleagues of the Committee on Comparative Politics. These ideas were partly formulated during two summer workshops which the Committee held, one in 1962 and the second in 1963. Sidney Verba spent several weeks during both of these summers discussing "input-output" and "capabilities" theory with me. I am deeply in his debt for these formulations.

2. Bronislaw Malinowski, *Magic, Science, and Religion* (Anchor Books: Garden City, N.Y., 1954); A. R. Radcliffe-Brown, *Structure and Function in Primitive Society* (Glencoe 1957); Talcott Parsons, *Essays in Sociological Theory Pure and Applied* (Glencoe 1949); Parsons, *The Social System* (Glencoe 1951); Talcott Parsons and Edward Shils, eds., *Toward a General Theory of Action* (Cambridge, Mass., 1951); R. K. Merton, *Social Theory and Social Structure* (Glencoe 1957); Marion Levy, Jr., *The Structure of Society* (Princeton 1952).

Levy calls these requirements "functional requisites," and lists nine activities as essential to the existence of any society. To illustrate, Levy includes among these requisites adaptation to the natural environment, differentiation of and recruitment to social roles, the maintenance of a common body of knowledge and beliefs, the socialization of the young, and the control of disruptive behavior.[3] Parsons speaks of four "imperatives of any system of action," including adaptation, goal gratification, integration, and latent pattern maintenance and tension management.[4] These and other writers also make the point that, for a system to continue in operation, these functions must be performed in certain ways. When a function is performed in such a way as to maintain the equilibrium of the system, the performance of the function by the agency or structure is referred to as "functional" (or *eufunctional*, in Marion Levy's formulation). When the performance upsets the equilibrium, then it is referred to as "dysfunctional." We shall come back to this concept of functionality-dysfunctionality at a later point.

We need to elaborate a little on the other two assumptions of systems theory—*interdependence* and *equilibrium*. By the interdependence of the parts of a system, we mean that when the properties of one component in a system change, all the others, and the system as a whole, are affected. Thus if the rings of an automobile erode, we speak of the car as "burning oil"; the functioning of other systems deteriorates; and the power of the car declines. Or, in the growth of organisms there are points, for example, when some change in the endocrine system affects the overall pattern of growth, the functioning of all the parts, and the general behavior of the organism. In political systems, the emergence of mass parties or mass media of communication changes the performance of all the other structures of the political system, and affects the general capabilities of the system in its domestic and foreign environments. In other words, when one variable in a system changes in magnitude or in quality, the others are subjected to strains and are transformed, and the system changes its pattern of performance; or the dysfunctional component is disciplined by regulatory mechanisms, and the equilibrium of the system is reestablished. Parsons and Shils argue that social systems tend toward equilibrium;[5] i.e., families, economics, churches, politics tend to preserve their character through time, or to change slowly. Hence the analytical scheme which they propose for generalized use in the social sciences is this concept of system, implying the interdependent interaction of structures performing functions in such a way as to maintain the social system in equilibrium.

Even in this starkly simple form, the generic system model has value for the study of politics. The concept of function pushes us into realism and

3. Levy, *Structure of Society,* 149ff.

4. Talcott Parsons, *Economy and Society* (Glencoe 1956), 16ff.

5. Parsons and Shils, eds., *Toward a General Theory of Action,* 107ff.

away from normative or ideological definitions. To answer functional questions we have to observe what a particular social system actually is and does. The concepts of functionality and dysfunctionality sensitize us to the factors making for social stability and social change, and enable us to perceive them in an orderly and thorough way. The concept of interdependence forces us to examine the performance of any structure or institution systemically; i.e., in all of its ramifications and interdependences. We can no longer be contented with describing a single institution or looking at bilateral interactions. Our research must assume interdependence and interaction among all components.

II. Critique of Functional Theory

The introduction of functionalism into the social sciences has stirred up a good deal of controversy and polemic.[6] Among the critics of functional theory, the logician Hempel has raised questions about the scientific status of functionalism, arguing that its exponents fail to provide operational criteria of function and dysfunction, and of the kind of interaction among variables which maintain a system in equilibrium. Gouldner's principal criticism is that the concept of system and function has come from biology and mechanics, and that there has been a tendency to attribute the properties of organismic and mechanical systems to social systems. He points out that interdependence and equilibrium may be of a radically different character in social systems. The autonomy of the components of social systems —i.e., the extent to which they may vary without significantly affecting other variables and the system as a whole—may be far greater than in mechanical and organismic systems.

Gouldner also argues that there is a static tendency in systems theory, a tendency to stress the functionality of institutions and the equilibrium of social systems. The distinction as formulated in anthropological and sociological theory tends to be dichotomous; i.e., structures perform either functionally or dysfunctionally. He argues that they should be viewed as continua, since without specification and measurement it is impossible to say what kind and degree of performance by given structures and institutions produce what kind of social equilibrium. Here Gouldner and Hempel would agree that what we need is a model of interaction of components in which the relations among variables and their consequences for system performance are left open to empirical investigation.

A further valuable criticism is Gouldner's argument that there is a tendency to treat each component in a social system as having a value equal

6. See *inter alia* Carl G. Hempel, "The Logic of Functional Analysis," and Alvin W. Gouldner, "Reciprocity and Autonomy in Functional Theory," in Llewellyn Gross, ed., *Symposium in Sociological Theory* (New York 1959), 241ff.

to each of the others. Actually the significance and autonomy of the various parts of social systems may be quite unequal. Thus one may argue that the bureaucracy in differentiated political systems is in some sense the central structure of these systems, and that all other structures are significant by virtue of the way in which they affect the performance of the bureaucracy. Here again we need system models more appropriate for social and political phenomena.

Finally Gouldner argues that such a social system theorist as Parsons does not give sufficient stress to the special character of the interaction of social systems with their environments. He may attribute too great an impermeability to the boundaries of social systems. Thus political systems are quite porous, so to speak. The exchanges and movements which take place between political systems and their societies or their international environments, particularly in the modern world, are quite massive. It is impossible to account for either equilibrium or change in political systems without observing the volume and kind of their interactions with their social and international environments.

The main burden of these criticisms is that social system theory is still too much under the influence of biological and mechanical analogies, and that it fails to specify operational indices for such concepts as functionality, interdependence, and equilibrium. The criticisms have merit, but they should not obscure the importance of the original insights of the social system theorists. What we are engaged in here is simply an elaboration and adaptation of their work.

Before we drop the generic system concept and turn to the special characteristics of political systems, we need to deal with one or two other terms. Intrinsic to the concept of system is the notion of boundary and of exchanges or actions across boundaries. A system starts somewhere and stops somewhere. In dealing with an organism or a machine, it is relatively easy to locate the boundary and specify the interactions between it and its environment. The gas goes into the tank; the motor converts it into revolutions of the crankshaft and the driving wheels; and the car moves on the highway. In dealing with social systems, of which political systems are a class, the problem of boundary is not that easy. We may speak of what separates a social system from its environment as a boundary, but what we mean by this is not at all clear. Social systems are not made up of individuals but of roles; i.e., a family consists of the roles of mother and father, husband and wife, sibling and sibling, and the like. The family is only one set of interacting roles for a group of individuals who also may have extra-familial roles, and hence be involved in other social systems. In the same sense, a political system consists of the roles of nationals, subjects, voters, interacting—as the case may be—with legislators, bureaucrats, judges, and the like. The same individuals who perform roles in the political system perform roles in other social systems, such as the economy, religious community, family, and voluntary associations. As individuals expose themselves to political communication, vote, demonstrate, they shift from nonpolitical to political roles. One might say that on election day as citizens leave their farms, plants, and offices to go to the polling places, they are crossing the boundary from the economy to the polity. It is crossing the boundary in both an objective and a subjective sense. In the objective sense, a man leaves his assembly line, where he is performing a role in a manufacturing process, to enter the polling booth, where he is performing a role in a political process. In a psychological sense, some shift of norms, values, expectations, and cognitions takes place as well.

The concept of boundary as we apply it to social and political systems is, of course, an analogy. What we really mean by this analogy can be specified only if we examine empirically the actual exchanges which take place between one system and another. Thus, when we speak of the interaction of personalities and the political system, we are thinking of the impulses, attitudes, and values entering into the performance of political roles by the individuals who make up the political system. At some point in this interactive process, properties which we associate with personality, such as hostility and rigidity, get converted into attitudes toward or choices of particular foreign or defense policies or candidates for public office. In other words, there are boundaries here between general affective and value tendencies, and political attitudes and choices.

There is a boundary between the polity and the economy. For example, an inflation may reduce the real income of certain groups in the population. When these changes in the economic situations of particular groups get converted into demands for public policy or changes in political personnel, there is an interaction between the economy and the polity. What really happens in the empirical sense is that certain psychic states resulting from changes in the economic capabilities of groups are converted into demands on the political system, demands on trade union or other pressure group leaders that they lobby for particular actions by the legislative or executive agencies, and the like. Somewhere along the line here a boundary is passed from one system to another, from the economic system to the political system.

That we are using an analogy when we speak of the boundaries of political systems, and a misleadingly simple analogy at that, becomes clear when we consider the variety of phenomena we include under it. We use it in a simple physical sense, as when we speak of the boundaries of nations or of subnational political jurisdictions. We use it in a behavioral sense, as when we refer to the interactions of voters and candidates, governmental officials and citizens, as these are separated from the interactions of these same individuals in their roles as workers and employers, parishioners and clergy. We use it in a psychological sense, as when we refer to attitudes toward politics, politicians, public officials, and public policies, as these are differentiated from the other contents of the psyches of the members of a polity. Whenever we use the term we need to be clear just which one, or which combination, of these phenomena we have in mind.

Another way of thinking about the interaction of political systems with their environments is to divide the process into three phases, as is usually done in systems theory—input, conversion, output. The inputs and outputs which involve the political system with other social systems are transactions between the system and its environment; the conversion processes are internal to the political system. When we talk about the sources of inputs and how they enter the political system, and how outputs leave the political system and affect other social systems, we shall in effect be talking about the boundaries of the political system.

III. THREE TYPES OF FUNCTIONS

One further thought before we leave this generic concept of system and turn to political systems, properly speaking. We have talked about the functions of systems and how they give the system its identity. Actually, we need to think of systems as functioning at different *levels*. One level of functioning involves the unit as a whole in its environment. An animal moves, while plants do not. Some machines process data; others produce power. An economy produces and distributes physical goods and services. Families produce children and socialize them into adult roles and disciplines. Religious systems regulate the relations of their members with authorities and norms to which supernatural qualities are attributed. What we focus on at this level is the behavior of the system as a unit in its relations with other social systems and the environment.

The second kind of functioning is internal to the system. Here we refer to "conversion processes," such as the digestion of food, the elimination of waste, the circulation of the blood, the transmission of impulses through the nervous system. The conversion processes or functions are the ways particular systems transform inputs into outputs. Obviously the two levels of behavior are related. In order for an animal to be able to move, hunt, dig, and the like, energy must be created in the organism and the use of the energy controlled and directed. The level and kind of performance of the system in its environment are tied up with a particular kind of structural-functional performance inside the system.

In talking about politics, we shall speak of the performance of the political system in its environment as the political system's "capabilities." What happens inside the political system we shall refer to as "conversion functions." To illustrate, we shall speak here of the "responsive capability" of political systems, meaning by the term the openness of the political system to demands coming from various groups in the society, or from the international political system. This capacity to respond is associated with the performance inside the political system of such functions as communication, interest articulation, aggregation, and rule-making.

Finally, we shall speak of "system-maintenance and adaptation functions." For an automobile to perform efficiently on the road, parts must be lubricated, repaired, replaced. New parts may perform stiffly; they must be "broken in." In a political system the incumbents of the various roles (diplomats, military officers, tax officials, and the like) must be recruited to these roles and learn how to perform them. New roles are created and new personnel "broken in." These functions (in machines, maintenance and replacement of parts; in politics, *recruitment* and *socialization)* do not directly enter into the conversion processes of the system; they affect the internal efficiency and operations of the system, and hence condition its performance.

When we compare classes of political systems with each other, or individual political systems with each other, we need to make these comparisons in terms of *capabilities, conversion functions,* and *system-maintenance and adaptation functions,* and the interrelations among these three kinds of functions. And when we talk about political development, it will also be in terms of the interrelations of these three kinds of political functions. A change in capability will be associated with changes in the performance of the conversion functions, and these changes in turn will be related to changes in political socialization and recruitment.

While the individual categories that we use may, on empirical test, turn out to be inappropriate, this threefold classification of functions is important for political analysis, and we believe it will hold up under testing and examination.[7] The theory of the political system will consist of the discovery of the relations among these different levels of functioning—capabilities, conversion functions, and system-maintenance and adaptation functions— and of the interrelations of the functions at each level. The theory of political change deals with those transactions between the political system and its environment that affect changes in general system performance, or capabilities that in turn are associated with changes in the performance of the system-adaptation functions and the conversion functions.

7. This approach to functional requisites analysis is related to earlier work but differs in its explicit differentiation of these three classes of function. For other applications of functional theory to the study of political systems, see in particular David Apter, *The Gold Coast in Transition* (Princeton 1955), 325ff.; Apter, "A Comparative Method for the Study of Politics," *American Journal of Sociology,* LXIV (November 1958), 221–37; and Apter's contribution to Harry Eckstein and David Apter, eds., *Comparative Politics* (New York 1963), 723ff.; also William C. Mitchell, *The American Polity* (New York 1962), 7ff.

IV. THE POLITICAL SYSTEM: INPUTS AND OUTPUTS

This discussion of the concept of system has been useful, but we shall be open to the criticism of being carried away by an analogy if we fail to bring these analytical tools into the world of politics. What is the political system? What gives it its special identity? Much has been written on this subject, and it is difficult to get agreement among political theorists on the precise language of their definitions. Common to most of these definitions is the association of the political system with the use of legitimate physical coercion in societies. Easton speaks of *authoritative allocation of values,* Lasswell and Kaplan of *severe deprivations,* Dahl of *power, rule, and authority.*[8] Common to all of these definitions is their association of politics with legitimate heavy sanctions.[9] We have suggested elsewhere that "Legitimate force is the thread that runs through the inputs and outputs of the political system, giving it its special quality and salience and its coherence as a system. The inputs into the political system are all in some way related to claims for the employment of legitimate physical compulsion, whether these are demands for war or for recreational facilities. The outputs of the political system are also all in some way related to legitimate physical compulsion, however remote the relationship may be. Thus public recreational facilities are usually supported by taxation, and any violation of the regulations governing their use is a legal offense. . . ."[10] When we speak of the political system, we include all of the interactions—inputs as well as outputs—which affect the use or threat of use of physical coercion. "We mean to include not just the structures based on law, like parliaments, executives, bureaucracies, and courts, or just the associational or formally organized units, like parties, interest groups, and media of communication, but *all of the structures in their political aspects,* including undifferentiated structures like kinship and lineage, status and caste groups, as well as anomic phenomena like riots, street demonstrations, and the like."[11]

This is not the same thing as saying that political system is solely concerned with force, violence, or compulsion, but only that its relation to coercion is its distinctive quality. Political elites may be concerned with peace, social welfare, individual freedom and self-realization, but their

8. David Easton, *The Political System* (New York 1953), 130ff.; Harold Lasswell and Abraham Kaplan, *Power and Society* (New Haven 1950), 176; Robert Dahl, *Modern Political Analysis* (Englewood Cliffs, N.J., 1963), 5ff.

9. See Max Weber, "Politics as a Vocation," in Hans Gerth and C. Wright Mills, eds., *From Max Weber* (New York 1946), 78.

10. Almond and Coleman, eds., *Politics of the Developing Areas,* 7.

11. *Ibid.,* 8.

concern with these values as politicians is somehow related to compulsory actions such as taxation, law-making and law enforcement, foreign and defense policy. The political system is not the only system that makes rules and enforces them, but its rules and enforcements go "all the way" in compelling obedience or performance.

David Easton, who was the first political scientist to write about politics in explicit "system" terms, distinguishes two classes of inputs into the political system—*demands* and *supports*.[12] Demand inputs may be sub-classified in a variety of ways. We suggest that they may be classified under four headings: (1) demands for goods and services, such as wage and hour laws, educational opportunities, recreational facilities, roads and transportation; (2) demands for the regulation of behavior, such as provision of public safety, control over markets and labor relations, rules pertaining to marriage and the family; (3) demands for participation in the political system, for the right to vote, hold office, petition governmental bodies and officials, organize political associations, and the like; and (4) symbolic inputs, such as demands for the display of the majesty and power of the political system in periods of threat or on ceremonial occasions, or demands for the affirmation of norms, or the communication of policy intent from political elites.

Support inputs may be classified under four headings: (1) material supports, such as the payment of taxes or other levies, and the provision of services, such as labor contributions or military service; (2) obedience to laws and regulations; (3) participation, such as voting, joining organizations, and communicating about politics; and (4) manifestation of deference to public authority, symbols, and ceremonials.

On the output side, we may speak of four classes of transactions initiated by the political system that tend to match up with the supports we have listed above and may or may not be responsive to demands, depending on the kind of political system that is involved. These are: (1) extractions, which may take the form of tribute, booty, taxes, or personal services; (2) regulations of behavior, which may take a variety of forms and affect some subset of the whole gamut of human behavior and relations; (3) allocations or distributions of goods and services, opportunities, honors, statuses, and the like; and (4) symbolic outputs, including affirmations of values, displays of political symbols, statements of policies and intents.

When we speak of a stable political system, what we usually have in mind is a particular pattern of flow into and out of the political system, a particular kind of input-output flow. In the political system, properly speaking, the inputs of demands and supports are *converted* into extractive, regulative, distributive, and symbolic outputs. The demands can be handled

12. "An Approach to the Analysis of Political Systems," *World Politics,* IX (April 1957), 383–400.

by the political system; the strains which they impose are bearable without any basic change in structure or culture. The outputs are responsive to the demands in expected or legitimate ways; and the supports are responsive to the outputs again in expected or legitimate ways. When these conditions obtain, the political system may be said to be in a state of equilibrium both internally (in the performance of conversion functions by political structures) and in its relations with its environments.

One last point should be made about the flow of inputs and outputs. This is the question of the source of the inputs. We do not wish to leave the impression that inputs necessarily come only from the society of which the political system is a part, and that the political system must be viewed only in "conversion" terms. It is typical of political systems that inputs are generated internally by political elites—kings, presidents, ministers, legislators, and judges. Similarly, inputs may come from the international system in the form of demands and supports from foreign political systems. The flow of inputs and outputs includes transactions between the political system and the components of its domestic and foreign environments, and inputs may come from any one of these three sources—the domestic society, the political elites, and the international environment.

Something should be said about the relations between demands and supports. Generally speaking, demands stemming from inside or outside of the political system affect the policies or goals of the system, whether they be responsive, distributive, regulative, or the like, while supports of goods and services, obedience, deference, and the like provide the resources available to the political system which enable it to extract, regulate, and distribute—in other words, to carry out these goals.

V. The Conversion Functions

This brings us to the events which occur in the political system, properly speaking, or to what we have called the conversion functions. In every political system there is a set of political structures which initiates or processes inputs, and converts them into outputs. The demands entering the political system are articulated, aggregated, or combined; converted into policies, rules, regulations; applied, enforced, adjudicated. These kinds of conversion events occur in all political systems; they are incidental to any political process, no matter how simple or undifferentiated it may be. But the kinds of structures, institutions, or roles which perform these functions, and the way they perform them, vary from the intermittent political structure of a primitive band hardly distinguishable from the family, religious, and economic system, to the highly differentiated political systems of modern societies, with their complex interactions between domestic social and international systems, and the internal interaction of electorates, interest groups, political parties, media of communication, parliaments, bureaucracies, and courts. This conceptual language in regard to the political system enables us to discriminate effectively among these systems, to talk intelligently about their performance and prospects.

This list of political conversion functions is not derived from generic system theory, or from concepts in use in sociological theory. Whatever virtue this classification of functions has results from the fact that it is derived from the observation of political systems. In other words, we are not forcing our data into categories that fit system concepts formulated in other disciplines, but developing concepts which can help us codify and classify political events.

The problem of developing categories to compare the conversion processes in different kinds of political systems is not unlike the problem of comparative anatomy and physiology. Surely the anatomical structure of a unicellular organism differs radically from that of a vertebrate, but something like the functions which in the vertebrate are performed by a specialized nervous system, a gastrointestinal tract, a circulatory system, are performed in the amoeba by intermittent adaptations of its single cell. Hence we may say that the amoeba performs the same physiological functions as does the vertebrate. In addition we use the functional concepts which we derive from the study of more advanced biological forms to compare them with the less differentiated forms. Indeed, it is only by using the categories of physiological functioning derived from the analysis of differentiated organisms that we can compare them with the more simple ones.

In the same sense, if we look at complex political systems, we can observe specialized structures performing distinctive tasks. We observe electorates, media of communication, pressure groups, parties, parliaments, bureaucracies, and courts. By observing these structures and their interactions we can explicate what distinctive jobs are being done in the process of converting political inputs into outputs. And we can use these functional categories to compare complex political systems with one another, and these with the less differentiated ones.

We suggest a sixfold classification of political conversion functions: (1) the articulation of interests or demands, (2) the aggregation or combination of interests into policy proposals, (3) the conversion of policy proposals into authoritative rules, (4) the application of general rules to particular cases, (5) the adjudication of rules in individual cases, and (6) the transmission of information about these events within the political system from structure to structure and between the political system and its social and international environments.

VI. THE CAPABILITIES OF POLITICAL SYSTEMS

More than four decades ago when Max Weber delivered his lecture on "Politics as a Calling," he discouraged us from thinking of politics in terms of performance. He told us: ". . . The state cannot be defined in terms of its ends. There is scarcely any task that some political association has not taken in hand, and there is no task that has always been exclusive and peculiar to political associations. . . . Ultimately, we can define the modern state only in terms of the specific means peculiar to it . . . namely, the use of physical force."[13] Contemporary empirical political theory tends to follow Weber in its stress on power and process, the "who" and the "how" of politics. It emphasizes two questions: (1) Who makes decisions? (2) How are decisions made?[14] The performance of political systems tends to be inferred from structure and process or evaluated according to moral and ideological norms. When we introduce the concept of capabilities, their development and transformation, we explicitly add two more questions to the "who?" and the "how?" The first of these is what impact does the political system have, what does it do, in its domestic and international environments? And the second question is, what impact does the society and the international environment have on the political system?

Parsons comes closer to meeting the needs of the contemporary political theorist when he speaks of the function of the polity as that of the ". . . mobilization of societal resources and their commitment for the attainment of collective goals, for the formation and implementation of 'public policy.' "[15] Francis Sutton similarly emphasizes the importance of the functions of political systems in their social and international environments, stressing integration for the internal environment and representation for the international.[16] The development of the concept of the capabilities of political systems represents a pursuit of these leads, but we have had to go farther in specifying types of relationships between the political system and its environments, for "goal attainment," "integration," and "representation" must be broken down into their components, and these elements treated as continua, if we are to be able to code the performance of political systems in the environment in a discriminating way.

The concept of capabilities, then, is a way of characterizing the performance of the political system and of changes in performance, and of comparing political systems according to their performance. Our particular classification of capabilities is a coding scheme, derived from a kind of informal pre-testing operation. We have to try it out to determine whether it helps us discriminate among political systems, or handle political development in a meaningful way.

13. Gerth and Mills, eds., *From Max Weber*, 77.

14. See, for example, Harold D. Lasswell, *Politics: Who Gets What, When and How* (Glencoe 1959); Dahl, *Modern Political Analysis*.

15. Talcott Parsons, *Structure and Process in Modern Societies* (Glencoe 1960), 181.

16. "Social Theory and Comparative Politics," in Eckstein and Apter, eds., *Comparative Politics*, 77.

We suggest five categories of capability derived from our classification of inputs and outputs proposed at an earlier point. These are: (1) extractive, (2) regulative, (3) distributive, (4) symbolic, and (5) responsive. These five categories of capability may be viewed as functional requisites; that is, any political system—simple or complex—must in some measure extract resources from, regulate behavior in, distribute values in, respond to demands from, and communicate with other systems in its environments. There are surely other ways of categorizing the functional requisites of political systems at the system-environment level;[17] but this particular classification is presented as a useful starting point. It is the product of an informal coding of historical and contemporary political systems. A rigorous test of their usefulness can be made only by formal and explicit employment of these categories in coding historical and contemporary data.

But to say that these are functional requisites of any political system is only the beginning, since we are not interested in defining the minimal political system. We are concerned with characterizing real political systems both historical and contemporary, comparing them with one another at the system-environment level, dividing them into meaningful classes, and discovering their developmental properties.

For these purposes, we need to treat capabilities as performance magnitudes, either actual performance or potential performance. We stress that capability refers to performance and has to be separated from the institutions and agencies involved in the performance. To relate the institutions and structures to performance is one of the central problems of political analysis, and we ought not to confuse rates of performance with the means or instruments of performance.

Perhaps capabilities may be best thought of as ranges of particular kinds of performance. An examination of a particular system may show variation in its rate of resource extraction over time. In war situations, the rate may be high; in normal periods, the rate may be substantially lower. But the problem of ascertaining the range of capability is more complex than examining rates of performance in normal and crisis situations. We may need to specify the extractive *potential* of a political system. What rate of extraction is this system capable of and under what conditions? This is only partly inferable from past record of performance. To get at this aspect of the range of capability we need to look at the support aspects of capabilities.

It is also necessary to distinguish between capabilities and elite policies and goals. Elite policies and goals may and usually do involve more than one capability. For example, a policy of economic development will require increases in resource extraction, and regulation, perhaps holding the line on

17. See, for example, David Apter, "A Comparative Method for the Study of Politics," in *ibid.*, 82ff.

distribution, and coping with demand inputs by increasing the symbolic capability. From this point of view capabilities may be viewed as ends intermediate to the policy goals of the elites. Since policies are made up of different doses of the different classes of outputs, capabilities analysis is essential to rigorous comparative policy analysis. It may enable us to distinguish sharply and operationally among different kinds of economic development, welfare, and other kinds of public policies.

It may also be in order to point to the implications of capabilities analysis for normative political theory. The inclusion of the performance or capabilities aspect of political systems may help bridge the gap which has been developing between the scientific and normative study of political systems. Questions regarding the "proper ends" of the state need to be grounded on empirical evidence of the different ways different kinds of political systems interact with individuals and groups in their domestic societies, and with political and social systems in the international environment. Empirical studies of the *performance* of political systems, of the *what* of politics (in addition to the *who* and *how*), should enable us to grapple operationally with what we mean when we speak of good and evil, just and unjust, political systems.

We may turn now to definitions of the five categories of capability. By the *extractive* capability, we mean measures of the range of performance of the political system in drawing material and human resources from the domestic and international environment. We separate this capability out because there have been political systems like the Mongol Empire, the warlords in China, guerrilla chieftains in Mexico, which have had little more than an extractive capability. Thus it makes sense to treat it separately, since it is to be found in all political systems, and is the distinguishing mark of a particular class of political systems. The extractive capability may be estimated quantitatively as a proportion of the national product; and its variations may be estimated quantitatively over time.

The *regulative* capability refers to the flow of control over behavior and of individual and group relations stemming from the political system. It is even more difficult to express it in quantitative terms than is the extractive capability, though aspects of it are measurable, and in a general way its magnitude, its pattern, and changes in its magnitude and pattern can be estimated. Here we have to concern ourselves with the objects of regulation, the frequency and intensity of regulation, and the limits of tolerance of regulation. While formulating indices to measure changes in this capability is a complex problem, the utility of this concept as an approach to political classification and development is evident. With these two capability concepts we can distinguish between primarily extractive political systems such as those referred to above, and extractive-regulative ones such as the historic bureaucratic political systems described by Eisenstadt in his recent book.[18] Furthermore, we can chart the developmental process from the one to the other, as regulative outputs cease being primarily unintended consequences of or instrumental to extraction and acquire goals of their own, such as some conception of social justice, order, economic advantage, or religious conformity.

The *distributive* capability refers to the allocation of goods, services, honors, statuses, and opportunities of various kinds from the political system to individuals and groups in the society. It is the flow of activity of the political system as dispenser of values or as redistributor of values among individuals and groups. Some aspects of this capability are more readily measurable than others. The structure of taxation may be viewed in its distributive aspects. The magnitude of welfare and educational programs can be expressed quantitatively, as proportions, and in terms of the social strata affected. Thus, while the general impact of public policy on social stratification is difficult to express quantitatively, there are aspects of it which are measurable, and the total pattern may be characterized for comparative and developmental purposes.

What we have said about political capabilities suggests a logic of capability analysis. An extractive capability implies some regulation and distribution, though these consequences may be unintended. A regulative capability implies an extractive capability, if only to gain the resources essential to regulation; and it is difficult to conceive of a regulative capability which would not in some way affect the distribution of values and opportunities. They are not only logically related. They suggest an order of development. Thus political systems which are primarily extractive in character would appear to be the simplest ones of all. They do not require the degree of role differentiation and specialized orientations that extractive-regulative systems or extractive-regulative-distributive ones do. Regulative systems cannot develop without extractive capabilities; thus the development of the one implies the development of the other. Increasing the extractive capability implies an increase in the regulative capability, as when, for example, political systems move from intermittent collection of tribute or raids to some form of regularized taxation. Similarly, a distributive system implies an extractive capability, and obviously can reach a higher distributive level if it is associated with a regulative capability as well.

At an earlier point we spoke of *symbolic* inputs, referring to demands for symbolic behavior on the part of political elites—displays of the majesty and power of the state in periods of threat or on ceremonial occasions, affirmations of norms, or communication of policy intent from political elites. We referred to symbolic supports, meaning such behavior as showing respect for, pride in, or enthusiasm for political elites, physical symbols

18. S. N. Eisenstadt, *The Political Systems of Empires* (Glencoe 1963).

of the state such as flags and monuments, and political ceremonials. And we spoke of symbolic outputs, including affirmations of values by elites, displays of physical symbols, displays of incumbents of sacred or honored offices, or statements of policies and intents. Thus we need to deal with the *symbolic capability* of political systems and treat its relations to the other forms of capability. Surely we do not mean by symbolic capability simply the quantitative flow of symbolic events into and out of the political system. If capability is a profile of rates of performance—e.g., rates of extraction, regulation, and distribution—then symbolic capability is a rate of *effective symbol flow,* from the political system into the society and the international environment. The displays of flags, troops, and ships, the conduct of ceremonies on the occasion of anniversaries, or on the birth, marriage, coronation, and death of princes, kings, presidents, and the like, the construction of monuments, visits by royalty or high officials, are symbolic outputs either in response to demands or independently initiated by elites. The effectiveness of symbolic outputs of this kind is difficult to measure, but political elites (and journalists and scholars) often attempt to do so by counting crowds and audiences, recording the decibels and duration of applause, examining reports on the demeanor of audiences, or conducting surveys of attitudes. Similarly, affirmations of values by elites may be effective or ineffective. They may create or mobilize reserves of support, as did Churchill's speeches during World War II. Statements of policies may facilitate other kinds of system capability, increasing the rate of acquiescence in extraction, obedience to regulation, acceptance of distribution, and reducing the input of demands.

Symbolic output is not the same thing as symbolic capability. The output of symbols may cease to be edifying, menacing, stirring, credible, or even observed, listened to, or read. Royalty or high officials may be spat upon, pelted with rotten vegetables, statues thrown down from high places, pamphlets cast aside, television and radio sets turned off. Or, as in the case of new nations, the symbolism may have little if any resonance. Symbolic messages may be transmitted but not received. The symbols of local authority may be the only ones granted legitimacy, while the central symbolic output may have little, if any, meaning or effect.

While extractive, regulative, distributive, and symbolic capabilities are ways of describing the pattern of *outputs* of the political system into the internal and external environments, the *responsive* capability is a relationship between *inputs,* coming from the society or the international political system, and *outputs.* The responsive capability is an estimate of the degree to which outgoing activity is the consequence of demands arising in the environments of the political system. Again, the usefulness of this concept is suggested by the fact that it implies operational measures, i.e., a given quantity of responses to demands over the total of the demands. We are not minimizing the difficulties in translating this concept of responsiveness into specific measurable relationships. Obviously, in reality we shall have to settle for approximations, for measurement of aspects of the relationship between inputs and outputs.

The reader must forgive the crudeness of this provisional formulation of the concept of political capability. It is the logical next step from treating the political system in terms of interaction with its foreign and domestic environments, in input-conversion-output terms. The capabilities of a political system are a particular patterning of input and output, particular performance profiles of political systems. We are more interested in demonstrating the importance of this level of analysis than in making claims for the effectiveness of this particular schema, more concerned with focusing and directing theoretical speculation and research than in presenting what would be a prematurely formalized theory. The truth of the matter is that we shall only arrive at a good capabilities theory through historical and contemporary studies in which we test out these and other coding schemes.

Tentatively we suggest that we may use the same capabilities scheme for the international interaction of political systems. Just as a political system may have an extractive capability in regard to its own society, so also may it have an extractive capability in regard to the international environment. Thus it may draw spoils, booty of war, and tribute from the international environment, or it may conduct or protect trade and investment, receive subsidies or loans. In the same sense a political system may have an international regulative capability, as in the conquest and the assimilation of other territories and peoples, or in limiting the freedom of other political systems in their political, religious, or military arrangements, or through participation in international organizations which affect the conduct of nations. An international distributive capability may be expressed in tariff arrangements, the granting of subsidies, subventions, loans, and technical aid. The international symbolic capability is a set of measures of the impact of symbol output on political systems in the international environment. Revolutionary symbol output may have great impact on the performance and development of other political systems, and increase the impact of other capabilities in the international environment. Symbol output into the international environment in the form of appeals to common culture and tradition may similarly affect the performance and development of other political systems, and initiate feedbacks which benefit the initiating political system. Statements by political elites of foreign policies and intents may have important effects on the other capabilities of the initiating political system, as well as on the capabilities of other political systems. An international responsive or accommodative capability may be expressed as a relation between its extractive, regulative, and distributive capabilities, and demands from the international environment.

Again this concept of capabilities enables us to handle the relations between internal and international capabilities more systematically than has been the case in the past, just as it enables us to handle the relations among capabilities. Thus a political system which has developed only an internal extractive capability is unlikely to develop other forms of capability in the international environment. Only when a political system develops the institutions and orientations necessary for societal regulation is it likely to pursue regulative goals in the international environment. Similarly, a political system which has not developed an internal distributive capability is unlikely to pursue distributive goals in the international environment. Finally, a political system which has a high internal responsive capability will manifest a different kind of international responsiveness than a system in which internal responsiveness is less well developed. What we suggest here is that there are relations between domestic and international capabilities. But beyond this we can only say that the interrelation among domestic and international capabilities is a matter for deductive and empirical method used together, rather than for simple reliance on logical inference.

Thus the aims of research on political systems must be: (1) to discover and compare capabilities profiles summarizing the flows of inputs and outputs between these political systems and their domestic and international environments; (2) to discover and compare the structures and processes which convert these inputs into outputs; and (3) to discover and compare the recruitment and socialization processes which maintain these systems in equilibrium or enable them to adapt to environmental or self-initiated changes.

We have also to speak of the capabilities of other social systems. Just as the political system has a particular level and range of performance which we can summarize in terms of a capabilities profile, so also do other social systems in the society of which the political system is a part, and the international political system of which it is a member, have capabilities. Such social systems as the economy, the religious community, or family, kinship, and tribal structures also extract resources from the environment, regulate behavior, distribute values, display and transmit symbols, and respond to demands. Similarly, political systems in the international environment have capabilities, and the international political system may have some extractive, regulative, distributive, symbolic, and responsive capability. The flow of inputs into political systems, the kinds of problems they confront, and the pressure on them to develop capabilities will vary with the performance patterns or the capabilities of these other social systems. The distributive capability of an economy will affect the rate and intensity of demands for distribution, regulation, and the like entering into the political system. The need for developing the regulative capability of a political system will vary with the regulative capability of other social systems, including the international political system. When we think of the factors affecting the capabilities of a particular political system, we must see this problem in the context of interacting social systems, of which the political system is only one.

VII. THE SUPPORT ASPECTS OF CAPABILITY

Thus far we have stressed the performance aspect of capability, the rates which may be computed from the volume of particular kinds of output over time. We have already suggested that the range of capability can only partly be inferred from these performance rates, since political systems may operate at "less than capacity," or they may be drawing on reserves which in time will be exhausted. To get at this aspect of capability we need to deal with the question of supports. If we undertook the task of estimating the extractive capability of a political system, we would look for measures of the quantity or value of the money receipts, goods, and services drawn from the society in proportion to the total product of the society. But there are two aspects of political extraction which such a measure of the extractive capability would leave out. The first of these is the relation between the quantities "levied" by the political system, and the quantities delivered. How much tax evasion is there? How much evasion of military service, desertion? Is a day's work given for a day's pay? Do troops stand under fire? We speak of French and Italian *incivisme,* meaning by that a tendency toward nonperformance, evasion, unresponsiveness, desertion. In other words, we need some way of estimating social performance in response to the outputs of the political system. Does the population pay its taxes, obey the laws, accept the reallocation of values, opportunities, and wealth stemming from the political system, respond to symbolic displays and appeals?

Related to this support performance is the idea of "support potential." The tax receipts of a political system, the proportion of taxes paid to taxes levied, will not tell us what the tax potential of a political system is. In the same sense, measures of the output of obedience to regulations will not tell us what the obedience potential of a political system is.

The support aspect of capability has to be measured, therefore, in terms of the resources delivered in relation to the resources levied, the obedience accorded in proportion to the obedience required, the allocations accepted in relation to the allocations imposed, the responsiveness of the population to symbolic outputs in relation to that which is expected. And in addition to these support performance measures, we need to know what rate of extraction, regulation, distribution, and symbol receptivity a society might accept, under varying conditions, from its political system without fundamental structural change in the relations between the political system and the society.

This may appear to be a needless conceptual complication, but we are constantly making judgments of this kind about political systems, estimating loyalty, morale, and commitment in relation to the performance and stability of political systems. What we are suggesting is that the support aspect of capability may be measured in two ways, by estimates of support performance—in other words, of behavior—and by probing the political culture in order to ascertain what the support possibilities are, the depth of the loyalty, the intensity of the commitment, the availability of support for various purposes, and the like. These constitute a kind of political system "reserve," and we need to know something about this reserve in comparing political systems, or in speculating about developmental prospects.

One further point must be made about the support aspect of capability, and particularly about its system reserve aspect. It is a general reserve up to a point. It may be drawn upon in the form of support for the extractive, regulative, distributive, or symbolic outputs of the political system. Political loyalty and commitment, for example, may be drawn upon for support of a higher rate of taxation, a greater extent of regulation, a greater degree of social distribution, a more aggressive international capability. But there may be, and usually are, rigidities in the exchangeability of support for one kind of activity as against another. There may be greater potential support available for extractive measures than for distributive ones, or greater potential support for distributive measures than for regulative ones. And these potential supports will vary in different strata of the population, and under different circumstances. The system reserve component of capability is an aspect of political culture, the "support propensities" which are distributed among the various strata of the population, and the various roles of the political system. We have to estimate the content of this reserve, its magnitude, and its mobility, if we are going to be able to explain and predict political performance.

VIII. Dysfunctional Inputs

What we have presented so far is more than a classification of variables and less than a theory of political systems. It is more than a taxonomy, since it suggests interrelations among capabilities, and between capabilities, the structure and culture of the political system, and the performance of the system maintenance and adaptation functions. These relations, derived at least in part deductively, may be formulated as hypotheses for empirical testing against historical data. It is less than a theory, since prior to systematic study it is an open question whether these particular categories of capability and of conversion and maintenance functions will help us to discriminate the variables we need to know about in order to construct a good theory.

They may be viewed as a proposed first step toward constructing a theory of the political system and of the development of political systems. For example, our analysis of capabilities is suggestive of a theory of political growth, obviously not in any simple or unilinear sense. It is clear from the logic of capabilities analysis that there can be no extractive capability without some regulative capability, no regulative capability without a particular kind and level of extractive capability, no distributive capability without both a regulative and extractive capability, and that these output capabilities will be greatly affected by the development of a responsive capability. In addition, support of political system performance will be affected by the magnitude, content, and interrelations of the other capabilities, and in particular by symbol capability, and in turn will affect them. Finally, the particular pattern of domestic capabilities will significantly limit and affect, and be limited and affected by, the pattern of international capability.

In addition, capabilities theory enables us to relate the performance of the political system in its domestic and international environments to its internal characteristics. We mean that any level or pattern of system-environment performance rests on a set of structural and cultural conditions. An extractive capability, no matter how simple it may be, rests on some structural specialization and role orientations. A regulative capability requires some military, policing, and bureaucratic structure, and "command-obedience" expectations and orientations. A distributive capability requires further specialization of structure (a welfare bureaucracy, an educational system) and the development of distributive, welfare, and egalitarian orientations within the political system. A symbolic capability rests on some political liturgy and iconography, revered and respected offices and officeholders, and the development of attitudes of reverence and respect for these political rites and ceremonials, political roles, political persons. A responsive capability rests on the development of a specialized infrastructure and a political culture of participation, and the adaptation of the rest of the political system to their emergence. Finally, changes in the level and pattern of system performance require system adaptation in the form of role differentiation, changing recruitment patterns, and new forms and contents of political socialization.

What we have presented is less than a theory in still another sense. An analysis of the capabilities of a political system will enable us to characterize the kind of development a political system has attained, but it does not tell us what factors affect political change or development, what produces change in capabilities.

Changes in capability are the consequence of the interaction of *certain kinds* of inputs with the political system. Consider, for a moment, a political system in equilibrium. There are flows of demands and supports from various groupings in the society; flows of demands and supports from the international political system; and inputs from the political elites (within the political system iself). There are flows of output—extractions, regulations, allocations, communications—from the political system into the society and the international political system. Within the political system the demand and support inputs are converted into extractions, regulations, allocations, communications. When all these flows have a particular range of content and level of magnitude, such that the existing structure and culture of the political system can cope with them, we may speak of the political system as being in equilibrium. But suppose there is a change in the content of magnitude of any one or combination of these input flows.

Suppose there is a depression and the unemployed in a political system demand jobs and food from the government, or a war breaks out and a neighboring power threatens its territory. Or suppose a new dynasty in a political system wants to engage in large-scale construction of temples, palaces, and tombs. Or suppose a political elite embarks on a radical departure in taxation; or requires religious conformity of its entire population and suppresses other religions; or embarks on a large-scale program of welfare. Any one of these input flows may be innovative, dysfunctional—i.e., they may require significant changes in the magnitude and kind of performance of the political system. These dysfunctional input flows are what "cause" changes in the capabilities of political systems, in the conversion patterns and structures of the political system, and in the performance of the socialization and recruitment functions. What we need to know is how these dysfunctional flows affect political development, what kinds of dysfunctional flows affect what kinds of capability patterns.

To cope with this question operationally we need to lay out the dimensions in which the flow of inputs may vary. We suggest that they may vary (1) quantitatively, (2) in their substance or content, (3) in their intensity, (4) in their source, and (5) in the *number of kinds* of dysfunctional inputs affecting the political system at a given point in time. We also need to keep in mind, in considering the significance of these flows for political development, the reactions of elites to dysfunctional inputs from the domestic and international environments, and the capabilities of systems other than the one we are examining—other social systems in the same society and the international political system—as they affect or are affected by the processes of the political system. We will take these questions up separately.

First, the quantitative dimension. Dysfunctional inputs may be incremental. Thus demands for participation may begin in the middle classes, spread among the urban working classes, and then to the rural workers. In other countries, demands for participation may be for universal suffrage all at once. For lack of better terms, we may speak of this quantitative variable as a continuum with one extreme labeled "incremental" and the other "high magnitude." The quantity of dysfunctional inputs are of importance for political development because this will affect the scale of the cultural and structural adaptations which the political system is called upon to make. An incremental increase in demands for participation may require only a small adjustment in attitude and a limited set of structural adaptations; while a high magnitude increase may require a fundamental cultural reorientation and the establishment of a complex political infrastructure.

Second, dysfunctional inputs pertain to particular subject matter areas, such as the regulation of land-tenure, or of market relations, enfranchisement or eligibility for public office, religious practices, and family relations. The substance or content of the innovative flow will also significantly affect the pattern of political development, for a political system may be able, for example, to tolerate welfare innovations more readily than regulatory or participatory ones. In other words, the dysfunctionality of a particular kind of input will vary with the existing culture and structure of the political system.

Third, dysfunctional inputs may vary in their intensity. Demands by new strata of the population for the right to vote may take the form of orderly petitions or of violent demonstrations. Low-intensity demands will confront the political system with a different problem of adaptation than high-intensity demands. Low-intensity demands may produce no system adaptation, while high-intensity demands may result either in a change in the responsive capability of the political system in the form of enfranchisement of a new stratum of the population, or a change in the regulative capability in the form of a substantial increase in police forces and repressive action.

Fourth, dysfunctional inputs may vary according to their source. It will make a great deal of difference for the adaptation of the political system if the innovative flow comes from the international political system, from the political elite, or from the domestic society. And in the case of the last it will make a great deal of difference as to which stratum or subsystem of the domestic society is the source of the flow of demands. A political system which has been exposed to large-scale wars over a long period of time will develop a very different capability profile, and political structure and culture, than one which has been relatively protected from threats to its security. Innovation stemming from the political elites may be more immediately translated into changes in political capability than innovations stemming from either the domestic society or the international political system. And dysfunctional demands from the upper classes may involve less of a structural and cultural change in the political system than those emanating from less advantaged strata of the population.

Fifth, it will make a great deal of difference whether the political system is simultaneously confronted by demands for more than one kind of innovation. For example, a political system may be confronted by the threat of war at the same time that it is confronted by a rise in demands for political participation or welfare. It may have to choose among dysfunctional demands, responding to some and suppressing others. The political culture and structure of political systems will be fundamentally affected by such "simultaneous" or cumulative revolutions, just as those which have had the advantage of being able to meet crises one by one will show the marks of such historical experience.

We may also view political development from the vantage point of dysfunctional outputs. Whatever the source of the innovative outputs may be—the domestic society, the political system, the international political system—they may initiate a process of social change which affects inputs into the political system, or which produces capabilities in other social systems that affect the flow of demands and supports into the political system. But the relation of dysfunctional outputs to political development are indirect, through "input feedbacks." Thus the development of a welfare capability may produce changes in social structure and attitudes which will increase the support inputs of some elements of the society and the demand inputs of others. A shift from an aggressive to an accommodative foreign policy may increase the resources available for the development of a welfare capability, and result in innovative welfare inputs by the political elites.

In talking about dysfunctional inputs, we have stressed changes in the quantity, content, intensity, and incidence of different kinds of *demands*. But dysfunctionality can result from fluctuations in the flow of *supports* as well—losses of morale, failures of recruitment campaigns, declines in tax yields, widespread disobedience to regulations. Needless to say, fluctuations in support will be affected by the kinds of demands made by political elites on the society, as well as by the responsiveness of elites to demands stemming from the society.

The extent to which the political system is loaded by dysfunctional flows will vary with the capabilities of other social systems in the domestic society and international system. An economy may develop new capabilities—new systems of production and distribution—and as a consequence the loading of the political system with distributive demands may be significantly reduced, thereby affecting political development. Or a religious system may develop regulative capabilities that reduce the flow of innovative demands on the political system. Or the international political system may develop a regulative or distributive capability that reduces the pressure on the political system. A case in point would be the international military or technical assistance units of the United Nations that reduce the pressure for the development of extractive and regulative capabilities in some of the new nations. Thus the existence of, or the development of, capabilities in other social systems may affect the rate of flow of dysfunctional inputs, keeping the flow at the incremental and low-intensity level, and perhaps help avoid some of the disruptive consequences of multi-issue dysfunctional pressures.

We must never lose sight of innovation and change outside the political system in trying to account for a particular pattern of political development. But one variable which we must treat in greater detail is the reaction pattern of political elites, the behavior of important role incumbents in the political system as they are exposed to dysfunctional demands or supports. Perhaps the term "reaction" is incorrect, for it may lead us to overlook the originative and creative activities of political elites. Political elites both originate innovative flows and respond to innovative flows which originate elsewhere. When political elites are themselves the source of innovation, when they develop new goals and new capabilities in the pursuit of these goals, then we must examine these changes in capability and follow through the consequences of such developments for the society and the international system, and from these environments back into the political system again.

When political elites are "reacting" to dysfunctional inputs, then we must examine the relation between these reactions and the loading of the political system. The reaction pattern of political elites will often determine whether a flow of innovative demands changes from a low magnitude to a high magnitude, from a low intensity to a high intensity, from a simple to a multi-issue flow, from a single source to many sources. This interaction between dysfunctional pressures and elite reaction is on the same level of importance as is the response patterns of other social systems from the point of view of the development of political system capabilities.

A political elite confronted by dysfunctional flows of demands and supports has available to it three possible modes of reaction or some combination of these reactions. It may react adaptively. For example, if there is a demand for the suffrage among strata in the population, it may yield to these demands and accept the changes in culture, structure, and performance that this requires. An adaptive reaction is an acquiescence to demands in terms of those demands. Thus demands for innovation in welfare programs are met by such innovation, although even such adaptive behavior usually will require some creativity on the part of the elites. The content of a welfare program has to be specifically elaborated, staff recruited and trained, and modes of enforcement devised, tested, perfected.

A second possible mode of elite reaction may be described as rejective. The rejection of demands may take the form of elite indifference ("Let them eat cake"), explicit refusal to accept demands for innovation, or repression of the demands. The mode of rejection will, of course, affect the development of capabilities. Indifference may result in an accumulation of demands, in increases in their number, intensity, and the groups involved in the demands. The rise in pressure for innovation may reach the point where the elite must react either adaptively or repressively. Either reaction will affect the capabilities, culture, and structure of the political system but in different ways. For example, adaptation may result in the swelling of the welfare capability; repression may result in a swelling of the regulative capability.

The third mode of elite response is substitutive. Demands for "bread" may be met with an increased output of "circuses." Demands for the suffrage may be met by a tender of symbolic affirmations of national glory, an aggressive foreign policy, or by welfare measures. The history of elite reactions to dysfunctional demands—particularly for welfare and political participation—is full of examples of substitutive responses of this and other kinds. The ways in which substitutive elite behavior affects the development of the political system are rather complex. The substitutive reaction may "absorb" the dysfunctional demands, as in the case of Germany in the period after the establishment of the Second Reich, when the middle classes tended to "forget" their liberal impulses in their satisfaction with national unity and glory. Or the substitutive reaction may postpone the rendezvous with the innovative demands. Or it may do some of both. In addition, the substitutive reaction may in itself involve a change in capability—e.g., an expansion of international capability with all that this might entail in the development of bureaucracy, in the relative power of military and civil elites, and in political culture.

IX. System Adaptation, Recruitment, and Socialization

New roles and new attitudes are the essence of system change. New capabilities or levels of capability, new political institutions and processes, call for new elites, changes in elite training and indoctrination, and changes in expectation, commitment, values, and beliefs among the various strata of the population. The socialization and recruitment processes of a political system have a special relation to political change. We need to consider the different ways in which these system adaptation functions can become involved in the process of political change.

One common way in which recruitment and socialization patterns affect political development is through changes occurring in other social systems. Consider, for example, the process of industrialization. The spread of industrial technology and associated phenomena such as urbanization and the spread of mass communication tend to mobilize (in Karl Deutsch's terms) new strata of the population, recruit them into new economic and social roles and attitudes. These changes in activity and attitude may spill over into political orientations and stimulate new demands for participation and welfare. New elites (middle- or working-class demagogues and organizers) may be recruited and constitute the source of demands for structural change in the political system. Adults recruited into the industrial economy will be resocialized; children raised in urban-industrial families will be socialized differently from children in rural-agricultural families. This illustrates a sequence in which industrialization affects general socialization, role differentiation, and recruitment, which affects political socialization and recruitment, which in turn builds up innovative pressure on the political system.

Changes in the religious system may have similar consequences. The Protestant Reformation and the rise of individual sects, such as Methodism, changed the content and form of socialization and recruitment in England.

New religious elites—clerical and lay—were recruited and came to constitute a stratum from which political elites were drawn. In the case of Methodism, the early British trade union and labor leaders were in many cases recruited from the Methodist subculture; just as the "radical" middle-class elites of the first part of the nineteenth century were recruited in part from the earlier nonconformist sects.

A second way in which recruitment and socialization may affect political change is through actions originating with the political elites themselves. Thus a political elite may directly manipulate the socialization and recruitment processes. This is dramatically illustrated in the policies of totalitarian countries, where the whole social infrastructure of family, community, church, and school is infiltrated, and where the party sets up an organizational system to indoctrinate and recruit among the younger generations. Resocialization of adults through party and party-controlled organizations and control of the mass media is also a totalitarian tactic. While this pattern is more deliberately manipulative in totalitarian countries, it is common in many others. The introduction of civic training in the schools is a common practice in democratic countries; and in clerico-authoritarian countries the church and its schools are self-consciously used as a device for political socialization.

A third pattern is one in which elite reaction to innovative pressures may affect socialization and recruitment in an indirect way. An adaptive reaction by political elites to demands for participation and welfare will not only produce immediate changes in political culture, structure, and capabilities. It may also have the longer-run consequences of affecting family and community socialization processes, producing young adults committed to the political system, providing it with support in the form of goods, services, and loyalty. Passive or alienated adults may be resocialized by adaptive and responsive behavior among the political elites, changing from alienated to allegiant orientations. Rejective reactions among political elites may have the contrary effect, transforming allegiant to alienative orientations and affecting the flow of support into, and the support potential of, the political system.

The consequences for political socialization and recruitment of aggressive foreign policies and frequent warfare should also be stressed. If successful, an aggressive foreign policy may increase support and introduce a nationalist-militarist content into family, community, and school socialization. If unsuccessful or excessively costly, it may produce a withdrawal of support and alienative tendencies in a population. French and German political history is instructive in these connections. The radicalization and alienative tendencies of French political culture during the life of the Third and Fourth Republics have often been attributed in part to the humiliating defeats and costly victories of the Franco-Prussian War and World Wars I and II. The rapid growth of the French Communist Party has been attributed in part to the strong pacifist currents set in motion by the enormous casualties of World War I. The fall of the Fourth Republic was triggered off by army officers who had experienced military defeat and the collapse of the French colonial empire.

The failure of efforts to democratize Germany has been attributed to the bureaucratization and militarization of Prussian and German society in the course of their aggressive expansion in recent centuries. The German educational system and family life were shaped in this military-authoritarian society and tended to produce obedient subjects lacking in "civil courage." The National Socialist elites recruited heavily among the "irregulars" of World War I, the men who could not adjust to peaceful routines after years of battlefield life.

The sequence here involves a particular pattern of foreign policy which produces a feedback of socialization and recruitment consequences, which in turn affects the flow of demands and supports into the political system. In our efforts to relate political development to dysfunctional interaction among political systems and their social and international environments, we need particularly to illuminate the recruitment and socialization processes as they reflect social change and stimulate political change, as they are the direct instruments of political change, or as they become the instruments of political change through a particular pattern of public policy.

What we have been suggesting here is that the performance of a political system (e.g., its "immobilism" or "mobilism"), its conversion characteristics (e.g., the congruence or incongruence of its structures, the cohesion or fragmentation of its culture), the operations of its recruitment and socialization processes, are explainable in terms of a particular history of interaction between the political system and its social and international environments.

We are not simply making the obvious point that we can learn much about political development from the study of history. What we are proposing is an approach to political development in terms of systematic comparative history. This has to be done with a common coding scheme, a set of categories, and hypotheses about their interrelations. The adaptation of political systems theory proposed here may serve as a starting point. We need to meet both prongs of the critique of recent tendencies in comparative politics at the same time—by formulating a conception of the political system which is developmental, and by testing and elaborating this conception against the richness of knowledge of man's historical experience with politics.

Further Suggested Readings

Almond, Gabriel A., and Powell, G. Bingham, Jr. *Comparative Politics: A Developmental Approach.* Boston: Little, Brown & Co., 1966.

Blondel, Jean. *An Introduction to Comparative Government.* New York: Praeger Publishers, 1970.

Bluhm, William T. *Theories of the Political System.* Englewood Cliffs, N.J.: Prentice-Hall, Inc., 1965.

Brzezinski, Z. "Totalitarianism and Rationality." *American Political Science Review,* 50 (September 1956), 751–63.

Dahl, Robert A., ed. *Political Oppositions in Western Democracies.* New Haven: Yale University Press, 1966.

Easton, David. *A Framework for Political Analysis.* Englewood Cliffs, N.J.: Prentice-Hall, 1965.

————. *A Systems Analysis of Political Life.* New York: John Wiley, 1965.

Eckstein, Harry. *A Theory of Stable Democracy.* Princeton: Research Monograph, 1961.

————. *Division and Cohesion in Democracy.* Princeton: Princeton University Press, 1966.

Eisenstadt, S.N. *The Political Systems of Empires.* New York: Free Press, 1963.

————. "Primitive Political Systems: A Preliminary Comparative Analysis." *American Anthropologist,* 61 (April 1955), 200–20.

Emerson, Rupert. *From Empire to Nation.* Cambridge: Harvard University Press, 1960.

Herz, J.H. "The Problem of Successorship in Dictatorial Regimes: A Study in Comparative Law and Institutions." *Journal of Politics,* 14 (February 1952), 19–40.

Mair, Lucy. *Primitive Government.* London: Penguin Books, 1966.

Mecham, J. Lloyd. "Latin American Constitutions: Nominal and Real." *Journal of Politics,* 21 (2) (May 1959), 258–75.

Merritt, Richard L. *Systematic Approaches to Comparative Politics.* Chicago: Rand McNally & Co., 1970.

Moore, Barrington, Jr. *The Social Origins of Dictatorship and Democracy.* Boston: Beacon Press, 1966.

Neumann, F.L. "Approaches to the Study of Political Power." *Political Science Quarterly,* 65 (June 1950), 161–80.

Parsons, Talcott. "The Political Aspect of Social Structure and Process." In *Varieties of Political Theory,* edited by David Easton. Englewood Cliffs, N.J.: Prentice-Hall, 1966.

Scarrow, Howard A. *Comparative Political Analysis.* New York: Harper & Row, 1969.

Tocqueville, Alexis de. *The Old Regime and the French Revolution.* New York: Doubleday & Co., 1955.

3

Political Socialization and Political Culture

Introduction

The importance of the study of political socialization and culture might appear obvious. Even intuitively we are prepared to concede that both the socialization process by which youth acquire political knowledge, habits of thought and behavior, and the set of political cultural symbols that map the ideological belief system of the individual must be important. To deny this is to fly in the face of common sense that tells us that it is overly simplistic to confine ourselves only to the analysis of the most overt political features of society and to exclude, for example, childhood encounters with things political and generalizations about typical modes of political behavior by Americans, English or Germans according to the dictates of "national character."

Admittedly, it could be conceded, these things represent only the context or environment of political behavior. Yet such contexts or environments must be dealt with if we are to make complete statements of political behavior. While studies of national character date to the 1930's and 1940's, concern with political socialization and culture has arisen only since then in the field of political science. Thus, what was stated at the outset as an obvious importance is something that the political science discipline has concerned itself with only relatively recently.

The selections included here are among the most comprehensive and cogent in communicating what the study of political socialization and culture is all about. A main concern in these selections and this area of scholarship in general is to make it something more than a residual category in the effort to explain political behavior. Are political socialization and culture concepts that we resort to in order to rectify the gaps in our explanations, after we have finished with the study of interest groups, political parties, electoral systems, and so forth, in order to understand political behavior? Are they, in short, categories that we resort to when all else fails?

Or are they categories that have independent explanatory power? Verba, in the selection reprinted here, alerts us to this question; Easton addresses it head on. He is insistent upon constructing a separate theory of political socialization in order to demonstrate the relationship of political socialization variables to political behavior.

Before proceeding much further in our discussion we should make clearer what it is that we are speaking of when referring to political socialization and culture. Political culture represents the collective perceptions of individuals as they attempt to understand the political institutions, processes, and formal beliefs of the political system within which they are located. In short, in terms of the discussion of political legitimacy in the introduction to Chapter 2, political culture is a concept used to characterize the political principles underlying a political system. The emphasis in this definition is upon the phrase "collective perceptions." In this connection, an effort must be made to understand how "objective" political objects are understood subjectively by the population within the political system. What is meant by this might be understood in the following distinction drawn from American society. To the white middle class child, the policeman is usually characterized as a friendly, warm, protective figure. To the ghetto inhabitant, on the other hand, the policeman is "the man," a symbol of the repressiveness and abuses of a bigoted white majority in its efforts to control and exploit a black minority. In these different political cultural perceptions there is an inherent tension—a tension evident at a routine level in a conversation with one of these policemen as he recounts his different experiences in white middle class communities and in ghetto areas. The tension is evident at a less than routine level when the ghetto perceptions become transformed into urban rebellions such as those of Newark, Detroit, and Watts. In comparative political nation-building terms the problem is how to alter these differing perceptions in order to neutralize the policeman as an authority figure and help to contribute to harmonizing the relations of the white and black communities in America.

The foregoing analogy is a useful one for considering the meaning of political socialization as well. Political socialization is the process by which political cultural perceptions and attitudes are acquired. Thus, in terms of the ghetto child, simple efforts of promoting good relations with policemen can only be cosmetic in character. What is necessary is a transformation of both the nature of white society and the communication of these changes to the ghetto child in his formative experiences. "Communication of changes" is what is involved in the study of political socialization. The attempt to understand this communication process, especially as it occurs within a family or school, is the subject matter of the study of political socialization. These institutions as well as others are thus the means by which the political principles of legitimacy of a regime are inculcated in the individual.

Lest you be misled by these remarks into thinking that the study of political socialization is rather narrow in focus, consider the following ten "problem dimensions" of political socialization that one scholar has identified in the scholarly literature on the subject:

1. System relevance of political socialization
2. Varieties of content of political socialization
3. Political socialization across the life-cycle
4. Political socialization across generations
5. Cross-cultural aspects of political socialization
6. Sub-group and sub-cultural variations
7. The political learning process
8. The agents and agencies of political socialization
9. The extent and relative effects of political socialization upon different individuals
10. Specialized—especially elite—political socialization[1]

As students of comparative politics defined narrowly in terms of the study of foreign politics, we are concerned with all of these problem dimensions; as students of genuinely *comparative* politics we are especially concerned with cross-cultural aspects of political socialization and the remaining nine dimensions in comparative terms. Our ultimate concern as political scientists is with the overall operation of the political system, that is, with political socialization in its systemic aspects. It is this ultimate or most general question that Easton addresses when he deals with the distinction between system maintenance and system persistence, and argues in the process that to view political socialization simply in terms of the manner in which an older generation creates its own nearly identical replacement is to take a normatively conservative stand. He contends that what is necessary instead is a separate theory of political socialization so that the question of to what extent a new generation introduces change can be considered adequately. He calls this openness to the possibility of change system persistence rather than system maintenance.

In concluding this brief discussion of the subject of political socialization and culture it might be useful to note that these analytical headlines deal with politics at the level of individual, albeit aggregate, behavior. The remainder of this volume is largely concerned with the operation of political structures and institutions; in the final chapter the summary question is asked of the relevance of the preceding chapters to the problem of political change.

1. Jack Dennis, "The Major Problems of Political Socialization Research," *Midwest Journal of Political Science*, 12 (February 1968), 88.

Political Socialization

The Theoretical Relevance of Political Socialization

David Easton

What kinds of special interest might students of politics have in socialization? Political socialization I shall define restrictively as those developmental processes through which persons acquire political orientations and patterns of behaviour.

Clearly, as political scientists we are not particularly concerned with personality formation in and of itself, as are psychologists, or in exploring the way in which developmental patterns contribute to a theory of social structure in general or to the perpetuation and change of a culture, as are sociologists and anthropologists respectively. Major questions such as these in the area of general socialization are not beyond the bounds of our interests but they do not constitute the central focus of political science. They fall within our purview only when it can be shown that knowledge of this kind will somehow help us to understand some specifically political problems better.

But how are we to test the relevance of studies in socialization for political research? To do so, we need some guidance in the form of a theory or conceptual structure that will serve to identify the major variables on which research needs to be initiated. In this paper I propose to analyse and evaluate those theoretical criteria of relevance visible or latent in research about political socialization.

TYPES OF THEORIES OF SOCIALIZATION

Theory about socialization might take one of three forms, even though no one form is completely independent of the other. First, it might be a *general theory of socialization*. Presumably this would be designed to describe and explain at the most general level the way in which socialization occurs, regardless of subject area. Although such a theory may still lie on a very distant horizon, students of political science could use it to good advantage. Concentration of this type of theory, however, would distract them from their central concerns, the explanation of political phenomena.

Second, we might focus on a *theory of political socialization*. From this perspective our objective would be to attempt to understand the way in which socialization occurs in the political sphere. The nature of the subject matter and the salience level of politics in a society might give rise to special

Reprinted from Canadian Journal of Political Science, *1 (June 1968), 125–146, by special permission of the author and the publisher.*

socializing processes in this area different from socialization, say, of sex roles, economic behaviour, or religious patterns. Thus there is little question that the family plays a vital part in transmitting various aspects of the general culture in a society and in preparing a child for the kinds of general occupational or sex roles he may be called upon to play. But in the area of politics, some important differences seem to occur. Only certain kinds of orientations may be the subject of family socialization; others may depend more on agencies outside the family.[1] Childhood may be the period for learning basic orientations, and adolescence and young adulthood for attitudes on issues and specific candidates for office. We can conceive that in time a specific theory of socialization in the political sphere—a theory of political socialization—may emerge. This, when combined with theories of socialization about culture in general, personality, social structure, and the like, will be a source from which a more general theory of socialization might ultimately be constructed. A theory of political socialization has still to be contemplated in political science.

But there is a third kind of theory from which the most general guidance about the relevance of research in socialization might be obtained. This is a *political theory of political socialization*. Its objective would be to demonstrate the relevance of socializing phenomena for the operations of political systems. Logically it is prior to the other two kinds of theory just discussed. Unless we have some idea about why it is important or significant to study socialization processes in the first place, there would be little reason even to begin to talk about socialization in relation to political life. We must therefore begin by inquiring into the part that socialization plays in the workings of systems. At the theoretical level this means that we need to explore the position that we can attribute to socializing processes in a general theory seeking to understand the operation of any and all kinds of political systems.

It is on a political theory of socialization that I shall focus in this paper. But what I have to say will have implications for both other types of theory.

ALTERNATIVE CRITERIA OF RELEVANCE

To explain the relevance of socialization for political research we can find at least four kinds of alternatives in the literature. These consist of a non-theoretical option and three possible political theories of political socialization—allocative theory, system-maintenance or stability analysis, and systems (or systems-persistence) theory. The non- theoretical posture suggests

1. M. K. Jennings and R. G. Niemi, "Family Structure and the Transmission of Political Values," *American Political Science Review,* 62 (1968), 169–84. Compare with R. A. LeVine, "The Role of the Family in Authority Systems," *Behavioral Science,* 5 (1960), 291–96, where the role of family in a segmentary political system appears to be more significant.

only that we charge directly into unguided exploration of this new terrain, political socialization, a strategy not to be belittled when an area has hitherto been infrequently traversed. Among the three theoretical options, however, the first draws our interest to topics of socialization that fall within the sphere of what we may call political allocations. These topics would seem to be most relevant to a possible but as yet unformulated allocative theory. The second theoretical alternative draws us along in the train of presuppositions closely associated in the past with disciplines other than political science. This alternative would lead us to interpret political socialization as a means for helping us to understand integration and system-maintenance in the political sphere. The final theoretical option which I shall only foreshadow in this paper represents my own positive suggestion, at the most general level of analysis, for relating political socialization to the functioning of political systems.

To be able to follow out here the full implications of the non-theoretical and the first two theoretical options requires a very generous rule of interpretation. In the slender writings on socialization, these alternatives appear largely as latent premises and tendencies uncrystallized into deliberate or systematic formulations. Yet if we wish to evaluate the theoretical implications of past research and to appreciate the pressure it exerts for some viable theoretical alternative, we cannot avoid making the most of these options by attributing to them a coherence they have yet to obtain.

THE NON-THEORETICAL OPTION

Unfortunately the major unstated dilemma still confronting students of political socialization lies not in the selection among competing theories but in the decision to work with or without some explicit theoretical design. The easiest way out of this dilemma is to offer no pretence of operating within a definable theoretical context. Every political orientation has antecedents of some sort; hence there is no limit to the subjects that may be adopted for research in the area of socialization. We might plunge into a discussion of any subject that appears intuitively interesting, especially if we can link it up with later adult behaviour that has already drawn the continuing attention of students of politics. In this event there need be little theoretical guidance except for the assumptions that those topics of interest for the study of adults may be equally relevant for children and that childhood learning may point forward to adult behaviour.

If we were to take the research at its face value, without probing for latent theoretical perspectives, we might conclude that what has just been said indeed describes the character of the little empirical research in existence. Hyman's inventory of research in political socialization reveals that relevant research tends to do little more than to trace back to adolescence or, infrequently, to childhood, attitudes and knowledge already found useful in one way or another for understanding adult behaviour.[2] For the research worker this has seemed sufficient justification in itself. Similarly Remmers and Radler have found it cogent to test pre-adults for their attitudes towards a broad range of topical issues related to American democratic practices and to daily political concerns, much as one would survey the opinions and attitudes of adults.[3] The premise would appear to be that, since adolescents will soon be adults, it is helpful to try to get what may be a preview of the issue orientations of the upcoming adult generation. The selection of topics of inquiry—such as attitudes towards war, the atom bomb, civil liberties, medical care, and the economic role of government— seem to hinge on what the investigator feels most people would consider interesting and significant topics of the day. In most other studies, even in recent years, it is clear that the main topics of inquiry about political socialization have derived from or have been dependent upon research about adults.[4] Hence we find an intuitive concern in the studies on socialization for matters already made popular in the literature on voting behaviour, such as party identification, political interest, political information, and issue orientations or ideology.

A non-theoretical approach such as this might have some justification in the earliest stages of inquiry, when research workers are still trying to get their initial bearings in a subject matter. But if theoretically unfocused research were to continue unabated beyond this initial phase, it could readily lead to an enormous waste of resources. We would have little means except intuition for testing, either in advance or at the conclusion of the research, whether the results were worth the effort. The results themselves would accumulate into a consistent and scientifically useful body of knowledge only by chance.

ALLOCATIVE THEORY FOR DEMOCRATIC SYSTEMS

A more fruitful and at the same time more generous rule of theoretical analysis would dictate that, where no theoretical context has been explicated, the one that best fits the data might appropriately be imputed. If we were to abide by this rule, we might propose an alternative interpretation to the one just suggested, by way of accounting for the content of current

2. Herbert Hyman, *Political Socialization* (New York, 1959).

3. H. H. Remmers and D. H. Radler, *The American Teenager* (Indianapolis, 1957).

4. J. H. Patrick, "Political Socialization of American Youth: A Review of Research with Implications for Secondary School Social Studies," High School Curriculum Center in Government (Bloomington, Ind., 1967), mimeo; R. E. Dawson, "Political Socialization" in J. A. Robinson, ed., *Political Science Annual* (Indianapolis, 1966), 1–84; and an inventory by J. Dennis, *A Survey and Bibliography of Contemporary Research on Political Learning and Socialization*, Occasional Paper #8 (University of Wisconsin, Center for Cognitive Learning, 1967).

research. In this alternative, the subject-matter focus would represent a kind of interest that is consistent with what we may describe as a possible theory of political allocations in a democracy.[5]

A theory of political allocations would stand as a partial theory about system behaviour in contrast, say, to a more general systems theory. An allocative theory for a democratic system would attempt to provide a conceptual structure for understanding how values (valued things) are allocated among members of a democracy. Some efforts in this direction have already appeared in the form of an implicit equilibrium or explicit group theory of politics as they were developed between the two world wars,[6] and an allocative orientation suffuses the central frame of numerous theories about power and about decision-making.[7]

It is not that at the present stage of theoretical development in political science these efforts represent any pervasive, conscious striving towards a partial theory of political allocations. This would be ascribing a kind of awareness about theoretical needs and directions that is extremely difficult to achieve throughout any discipline and is only in process of developing in political science. But even in the existing theoretical literature we can already begin to see the dim outline of a partial theory of political allocation in democracies. However unsystematically the ideas may be presented, we have more than a vague idea of the major variables, and their important relationships, through which policies are made and implemented in democratic systems. The scrutiny of any up-to-date introductory text about politics will amply testify to this.

Indeed most research about the American political system, for example, is likely to be cast in allocative terms and to be consistent with one or another theoretical interpretation of the way in which values are transformed into policies. Voting research, for instance, characteristically gains its relevance from the understanding it provides about the way in which the public influences policy and policy-makers and about the means through which this is achieved. Research about legislative behaviour reveals the part that legislators play in the policy-making (allocative) process and unearths the determinants of this behaviour, as in party alignments, practices affecting recruitment to legislative office, conceptions of legislative roles, or sources of power vis-à-vis other branches of government. Similarly most

5. For this notion see D. Easton, *A Systems Analysis of Political Life* (New York, 1965), p. 31; D. Easton, "Political Science," *New International Encyclopaedia of the Social Sciences* (New York, 1968).

6. For the equilibrium approach see D. Easton, *The Political System* (New York, 1953), chap. xi; "Limits of the Equilibrium Model in Social Research," *Behavioral Science*, 1 (1956), 96–104; and *A Framework for Political Analysis* (Englewood Cliffs, NJ, 1965).

7. See, for example, A. Downs, *An Economic Theory of Democracy* (New York, 1957).

other institutional or behavioural research about American politics can be shown to be consistent with and contributory to an underlying concept of politics as a process through which valued things are allocated.

A great deal of the research on socialization that we have referred to before can now be reinterpreted as being relevant to a possible allocative theory. For example, Hyman organized his inventory about research on socialization so as to bring out its contribution to our understanding of the roots of such adult behaviour as political participation (party preferences and identification and political interest) and of ideological predispositions defined along a right-left axis.[8] In dealing with these matters Hyman was inadvertently also focusing on two major sets of determinants of the allocative processes in a democratic system. Others have similarly even if unwittingly enriched our understanding of this theoretical area in their explorations of the impact of pre-adult experiences on such matters as perceptions of political offices and recruitment to them,[9] the acquisition of information about political affairs, and the development of orientations to issues, candidates, and parties as a source of political preferences.[10]

Whereas previously we offered a less generous interpretation of topics like these, considering them merely as a follow-up or, more literally, a follow-back on adult research, we can now view them in a new light—as a way of attacking another major determinant of the allocative process. They seek to isolate and analyse the impact of early experiences and learning on future participation in the struggle over the making and implementing of public policies, that is, on the overall allocative process. In this light, pre-adult socialization would constitute an important set of variables the influence of which would have to be included in any rounded theory of political allocations.

Whatever the promise of these inarticulate premises in the study of political socialization, however, the fact is that no allocative theory has as yet been developed with sufficient coherence to provide explicit guidance for research about adult behaviour, even in gross terms. It is not surprising therefore that students of political socialization should find few serious constraints on the range of topics that they might select. Typically they have

8. In his *Political Socialization.*

9. J. Wahlke *et al., The Legislative System* (New York, 1962), especially chap. 4; K. Prewitt, "Political Socialization and Leadership Selection," *Annals of the American Academy of Political and Social Science,* 361 (1965), 96–111; K. Prewitt *et al.,* "Political Socialization and Political Roles," *Public Opinion Quarterly,* 30 (1966–67), 569–81; A. Kornberg and N. Thomas, "The Political Socialization of National Legislative Elites in the United States and Canada," *Journal of Politics,* 27 (1965), 761–74.

10. See F. Greenstein, *Children and Politics* (New Haven, 1965); Jennings and Niemi, "Family Structure"; Remmers and Radler, *The American Teenager*; L. A. Froman and J. K. Skipper, "An Approach to the Learning of Party Identification," *Public Opinion Quarterly,* 27 (1963), 473–80.

not even considered it necessary to search for an overall theoretical justification. But even if they had, they would not have needed to do more, to warrant their research on children, than to refer back to the ongoing research about adults. They could place the full onus, for establishing theoretical relevance, on students of adult behaviour because presumably inquiry in the area of socialization need merely follow up problems already set in the adult field. Yet if adult research itself lacks an explicit theoretical context, this shortcoming cannot help but work its way back to infect the whole area of pre-adult socialization as well. Thus to the extent that research in socialization could enable us to understand how time-determinants influence the way a system manages to allocate valued things, the current absence of any sustained and self-conscious theoretical inquiry at the adult level reduces the probability of any explicit theoretical contributions about earlier phases of the life-cycle.

Here the interest in socialization from an allocative perspective joins the non-theoretical option. Neither of these two approaches offers a theoretical justification for turning to socialization. Both options simply adopt the assumption that the task of the student of socialization is to explore the roots of existing adult behaviour and attitudes and to estimate the impact of this early learning on the future adult.

It is conceivable, however, that we need to go well beyond these two alternatives if we wish to begin to understand the overall place of socialization in political systems. For one thing, what these approaches tend to ignore is that socialization may be as significant for political change as it is for current behaviour. This we would fail to appreciate if we literally confined ourselves only to an effort to trace back the roots of present adult orientations. We shall return to this point later. Furthermore, socialization may have consequences for political systems of a broader and more profound sort than is implied merely in its identification as a newly discovered determinant of present adult orientations. It is to the merit of the third option—system-maintenance—to which we now turn that, whatever its other shortcomings, it does strive to draw attention to the broader implications of socialization for the operation of political systems.

A SYSTEM-MAINTENANCE THEORY OF SOCIALIZATION

Although allocative interests represent the mode of analysis most apparent in research about political socialization, interwoven in this approach we can discover the early beginnings of a more general theory, which we might call system-maintenance theory. Most research, with a few notable exceptions,[11] unobtrusively assumes that in one way or another the outcome of

11. Such as Greenstein, *Children and Politics*, esp. 158–9; L. W. Pye, *Politics, Personality and Nation Building* (New Haven, 1962); A. Inkeles, "Social Change and Social Character: The Role of Parental Mediation," *Journal of Social Issues*, 11

socializing processes is to assure the continuity of a political system in relatively unchanged form. Not that change is ignored, as we shall find, but it becomes a residual rather than a central or expected product of socialization. Allocative analysis is also shot through with assumptions such as these. For the most part the way in which a maturing generation participates in current political processes turns out to be replicative of the adult generation. In this view it would appear that the task and outcome of socialization is to contribute to the stability or maintenance of a political system.

As sparse as theorizing about socialization is in political science, this nterpretation has already taken more than a slight, if as yet an unheralded, old. If it were to become the dominant mode of analysis, it would ultimately and unfortunately distort our understanding of the multiple and divergent consequences that socialization may have for different kinds of systems and in varying circumstances. It would bias research towards investigating those conditions favouring the perpetuation of stability or the *status quo.*

THE MEANING OF STABILITY OR SYSTEM-MAINTENANCE

Stability is a highly ambiguous term in the social sciences.[12] It conveys two different kinds of meanings and both may be implied simultaneously in research on socialization. Frequently it is used to describe a system that incorporates whatever the writer considers to be the political virtues. In a broad usage such as this, to say a system is stable is somehow to impute to it the capacity to solve its problems pacifically and with some modicum of equity. It leads us to speak of systems as unstable when what we mean is that they are prone to violence, to sharp reversals of policies and regime, and to unpredictability of behaviour. In this sense stability tends to be an evaluative criterion varying somewhat with the predilection of the user.

But the term may also occur in a narrower, technical sense. It may refer simply to the constancy of a state of affairs over a period of time. Rigorously speaking, a system which characteristically employed violence and fluctuated wildly in its behaviour could be said to be constantly in a state of violent flux. It would be stable with respect to this quality if in the face of any change in its environment there was a tendency for the system to return to its unpredictable behaviour. In this technical meaning, very much in the tradition of its use in economics and the natural sciences, stability need not imply peace, order, or any other substantive state. It describes only the tendency of the given state of the system to continue over time.

At the very least the idea of system-maintenance embodies the notion of

---

(1955), 12–23; and F. A. Pinner, "Student Trade-Unionism in France, Belgium and Holland: Anticipatory Socialization and Role-Seeking," *Sociology of Education*, 37 (1964), 177–99.

12. See my "Limits of the Equilibrium Model in Social Research."

stability in this second or technical sense. A system maintains itself when it remains constant from one generation to the next. Although we would eliminate much confusion if we could confine stability to this phenomenon, unfortunately we shall see that in the social sciences outside of economics the idea also bears inescapable overtones of cohesion, consensus, peace, and harmony, states of affairs that are at times associated, however improperly, with the absence of forces pushing towards change. Given the prevalence of the broad usage in political science, it would be artificial and probably ineffectual to try to restrict the idea to its narrower, technical meaning. In our discussion we shall none the less seek to distinguish clearly each of these two meanings.

STABILITY AND PREVALENT DEFINITIONS OF SOCIALIZATION

Political science is not alone in attributing stabilizing consequences to the overall processes of socialization. In fact we might suspect that it has borrowed this assumption from elsewhere in the social sciences. Political science has only recently come to express an interest in socialization and has therefore had to lean on the other disciplines to inform itself initially of the major general issues. In doing so, it is understandable that political science might unsuspectingly absorb system-maintaining assumptions already prevalent in these other social sciences.

If we now look at some typical descriptions of what others from neighbouring disciplines have meant by socialization, we quickly see that the evidence does seem to bear this out. The hazards of this kind of theoretical perspective are so serious for future political research that evidence of its stabilizing imputations needs to be adduced. To that end I set forth here a number of definitions and descriptions drawn from several disciplinary contexts, aside from political science, and then compare them with a few from political science.

> [Socialization covers] the whole process by which an individual born with behavioral potentialities of enormously wide range, is confined within a much narrower range—the range of what is customary and acceptable for him according to the standards of the group.[13]

> Socialization consists of those patterns of action . . . which inculcate in individuals the skills . . . motives, and attitudes necessary for the performance of present and anticipated roles.[14]

13. I. L. Child, "Socialization," in G. Lindzey, ed., *Handbook of Social Psychology* (Cambridge, Mass., 1954), 655.

14. D. F. Aberle, "Culture and Socialization," in F. L. K. Hsu, ed., *Psychological Anthropology: Approaches to Culture and Personality* (Homewood, Ill., 1961), pp. 381–99, 387.

[Socialization describes] the acquisition of dispositions toward behavior that is positively valued by a group, and the elimination of dispositions towards behavior that is disvalued.[15]

[Socialization is a process] by which persons acquire knowledge, skills, and dispositions that make them more or less able members of their societies.[16]

[Socialization is a process] in which the child gradually comes to approximate the prevailing attitudes of the adults in his culture.[17]

These descriptions could be continued indefinitely so thoroughly have they become a part of the established literature. Various euphemisms take the place of the notion of stability but they add up to the same result. Acceptability according to "the standards of the group," becoming "an able member of their societies," or "approximating the prevailing attitudes of adults in his culture" are all formulations that reflect the conviction that more or less successful adaptation to existing social patterns, that is, a system-maintaining outcome, is a dominant element in the theoretical structure with which socialization is to be approached.

It is understandable that under the pressure from the widespread acceptance of these assumptions in the other disciplines, many of those who have come to apply themselves to parallel problems in politics should easily fit into the same system-maintaining mould.

The importance of such a formulation [of politics as learned behaviour] to understanding the stability of political systems is self-evident—*humans must learn their political behavior early and well and persist in it.* Otherwise there would be no regularity—perhaps even chaos.[18]

Political socialization is the process of induction into the political culture.[19]

Political socialization refers to the learning process by which the political norms and behaviors acceptable to an ongoing political system are transmitted from generation to generation.[20]

15. R. A. LeVine, "Political Socialization and Culture Image," in C. Geertz, ed., *Old Societies and New States* (New York, 1963), 280.

16. O. Brim, Jr., and S. Wheeler, *Socialization after Childhood* (New York, 1966).

17. M. Wolfenstein and G. Kliman, eds., *Children and the Death of a President* (Garden City, NY, 1965), xxi.

18. Hyman, *Political Stabilization*, 17, italics in original.

19. G. Almond, "Introduction: A Functional Approach to Comparative Politics," in G. Almond and J. S. Coleman, eds., *The Politics of Developing Areas* (Princeton, 1960), 27.

20. R. Sigel, "Assumptions about the Learning of Political Values," *Annals of the American Academy of Political and Social Science*, 361 (1965), 1.

> . . . the processes through which values, cognitions, and symbols are learned and "internalized", through which operative social norms regarding politics are implanted, political roles institutionalized and political consensus created, either effectively or ineffectively.[21]

These quotations leave little doubt that, regardless of disciplinary affiliation or perspectives, students of socialization typically tend to apprehend the process as one that helps to adapt the behaviour of the maturing generation to the existing patterns among adults in society. Whatever the term used in the literature, and they are numerous—inculcation, adequate socialization, customary and acceptable behaviour, able member, approximation of prevailing attitudes, effective learning, adaptation, maintenance, consensus, induction of a culture—and however ambiguous each may be, they all share one implication. They suggest that somehow an adult generation is able to mould a rising generation into something like its own adult image. Theoretically, this kind of conceptualization clearly implies that the outcome of socialization is to provide for the continuity of existing forms and actions, that is, to assure the stability, both in the sense of consensus or order (as against chaos) and of constancy of the system over time.

THE SYSTEM-MAINTAINING BIAS OF FUNCTIONAL ANALYSIS

Functional analysis as we find it in other social sciences and as in recent years it has haltingly been creeping into political research, particularly in the comparative field, similarly carries enquiry about socialization in a system-maintaining, stability-emphasizing direction. Functionalism assumes that social mechanisms can best be described in terms of their functions. The function of socialization becomes one of assuring the stability of a political system.

Political science has imported a functional approach from adjacent disciplines. Although the fact of being borrowed bears no relationship to its shortcomings as a mode of analysis,[22] its origins elsewhere suggest that we might look there to alert ourselves to some of the problems associated with its use.

Functionalism, as it appears in anthropology and sociology, stands on two fundamental tenets. It holds that no society can maintain itself or remain stable without meeting certain postulated invariant functional requirements. Derivative from this is the further principle that variable structures and processes in a society serve to fulfill these constant functions. As they

21. H. Eckstein, "A Perspective on Comparative Politics, Past and Present," in H. Eckstein and D. Apter, eds., *Comparative Politics* (New York, 1963), 26.

22. See D. Easton, ed., *Varieties of Political Theory* (Englewood Cliffs, NJ, 1966), chap. 1, in which the point is made that innovative theory in a discipline frequently results from the migration of ideas from other disciplines.

appear in functional analysis, system-maintenance and stability are usually interchangeable terms. They both imply not only constancy but subtly suggest peace and order as concomitants of the self-maintenance of a system over time.[23]

From this theoretical perspective, socialization stands as one of the basic functions necessary for system-maintenance or stability. Every society must provide for the fulfillment of such functions as the production of goods and services, the biological replacement of its members, the creation of a sense of common purpose, and the like. Although every scholar is free to specify his own list of functions, all agree that various roles need to be filled if the identified functions are to be met. Somehow the members of the system must acquire sufficient motivation, skill, knowledge, and values to induce and enable them to undertake the role activity necessary to serve the postulated social functions. Otherwise, as the existing role occupants died or retired, a society would find it lacked the personnel to meet its functional prerequisites.

The specific function of socialization, in this view, is to assure the continuity of those structures through which the other functional requirements are met. Each generation must learn what is expected of it if the postulated prerequisites of society are to be fulfilled. If socialization were to fail, no society could maintain itself; disorganization, even chaos, might ensue.

This is clearly brought out in the following typical description of socialization from the field of sociology.

> By the term *socialization* is meant the inculcation of the structure of action of a society on [*sic*] an individual (or group). Socialization in this sense is a matter of degree. An individual is *adequately socialized* if he has been inculcated with a sufficient portion of the structures of action of his society to permit the effective performance of his roles in the society. There is *adequate socialization* in a society if there is a sufficient number of adequately socialized individuals for the structural requisites of a society to operate.[24]

The function of socialization in the political sphere has been cast in a similar mould by those who lean towards a functional approach.[25] Con-

23. We cannot undertake here a thorough and rounded analysis of other shortcomings of functional theory, as applied to political science. Fortunately this is not essential in any event. The journals are filled with numerous, distinguished critiques. For one definitive evaluation of the inherent weaknesses of functional perspectives as a unique mode of analysis and its unavoidability as a simple, expected premise of all scientific research, see K. Davis, "The Myth of Functional Analysis as a Special Method in Sociology and Anthropology," *American Sociological Review*, 24 (1959), 757–73.

24. M. J. Levy, *The Structure of Society* (Princeton, 1952), 187.

25. In *Comparative Politics: A Developmental Approach* (Boston, 1966) G. A. Almond and G. B. Powell, Jr., explicitly adopt functionalism for political analysis. But

sistent with this approach, the language of research is couched in terms that assess the contribution of socialization to system-maintenance or stability. To the extent that socialization does serve this end, the members of the society may be said to be "effectively," "satisfactorily," or "adequately" socialized, depending upon the degree to which they have learned what is deemed necessary to adapt to the prevailing culture or to fulfill the existing roles. Elliptically, the literature speaks of a person as becoming or failing to become "socialized," meaning thereby that he has been adequately socialized or not. Socialization loses its neutral character as a term referring to a process that may have positive, negative, or indifferent consequences for society and typically carries a positive connotation for the fulfillment of the postulated functions.

In effect, the functional study of socialization represents an effort to understand the way in which persons learn to fit into a pre-existing pattern of roles or culture as though the structure and culture were out there somewhere just waiting to be reproduced on some *tabula rasa* of the child. In this sense socialization is essentially a process whereby one generation inculcates its patterns of behaviour and attitudes in the next. It may be from adult to child or from adult to adult as in the recruitment of adults to political office. Through this kind of replication of a system, stability in the sense of continuity of the system is implied and indeed is often made explicit, as we have just seen.

SOCIALIZATION AND MODES OF STABILITY

It is clear therefore that from a strictly functional point of view we would have to assume that socialization has certain functions or specifiable tasks to perform in society and in a political system. But in political science and, indeed, in the social sciences as a whole, there is no overwhelming commitment to a functional approach. The more prevalent assumptions do not embrace any postulated purposes of socialization in a system. Most students of politics go no further than to indicate that socialization has some possible consequences or outcomes for the system. But the point we need to make is that, as we have noted, regardless of whether socialization is interpreted as a postulated function or merely in the light of its observed conse-

---

even though they do employ the notion of "functions" extensively it would seem to be used so broadly as to lose most of whatever special systematic analytic significance it might have had. Indeed functionalism gradually seems to be overpowered by the categories of systems analysis (inputs-outputs) with which it becomes oddly intertwined. Functionalism seems to recede to the theoretically unobtrusive position it must normally hold in all scientific social research (see Davis, "The Myth of Functional Analysis"). Hence in their book Almond and Powell are able to employ socialization in a way that permits them to transcend the system-maintaining limitations hitherto implicit in a pristine functional analysis (see pp. 29–30, 121, 163).

quences, most research does unobtrusively incline towards the conclusion that it leads towards the maintenance of a system, to stability.

But we have also observed that the idea of stability is used ambiguously in a dual sense to mean both a substantive state associated with peace and harmony as well as a formal condition of constancy regardless of the substantive state. If we are able to appreciate fully the hazards of fixing on system-maintenance (in either sense) either as a presumed purpose or as an outcome of socialization, we need to probe much more deeply into how socialization is assumed to lead to stability.

We shall see that socialization is interpreted as contributing to system-maintenance in two fundamentally different ways: vertically (across the generations) and horizontally (within the generations). Not that we find these two terms in the literature as a way of distinguishing the differences they imply. But there is little doubt about the validity of our using them to describe the directions in which discussions of socialization do move. Furthermore there are two variants of the way in which horizontal stability seems to be attainable; through intra-generational group homogeneity and through subjective congruence in orientations and behaviour within the individual himself. We now need to examine what we refer to by the terms vertical and horizontal stability.

VERTICAL (INTER-GENERATIONAL) STABILITY

Normally, in speaking of stability as a function or an outcome of socialization, we have in mind continuity or constancy across the generations. Functional analysis postulates that if a system is to maintain itself, the existing generation must replicate itself in the maturing one, as we have observed. This is the vertical or inter-generational dimension of stability. We need not pursue this aspect of the socializing function further; it is very familiar in the literature, as the quotations have shown.

HORIZONTAL (INTRA-GENERATIONAL) STABILITY

But stability is also frequently linked to conditions that prevail within a single generation. When looking at a dominant generation in a political system we may speak about the similarity of views and behaviour, or at least about their compatibility, which contributes to internal harmony for the group. Here the subject is intra- rather than inter-generational. From this view, to say that a system is stable attributes its source to the presence of consensus, the absence of deep internal cleavages and conflicts within the dominant generations. There is little that threatens to upset the existing balance of forces or political accommodations. Here stability depends on the lack of horizontal discontinuities, strains, or incompatibilities rather than cross-generational ones.

In this context stability has the dual meaning previously noted. On the one hand, it describes a substantive state of affairs. The members have become mutually adjusted and are able to solve their problems in some specific way. On the other hand, it also implies that the members are able to maintain this condition over time. Stability therefore goes further than merely to suggest replication of generations; it depicts a relatively harmonious and continuing condition within one generation.

In this interpretation, the function (or consequences) of socialization would seem to be to work towards this congruence in outlook and behaviour within a generation, that is, to bring about *collective homogeneity*. System-stability would falter if socialization did not help to confine a generation within some minimal range of diversity. Strains and conflict might prevail. Since diversity and intra-generational discontinuities, so-called, are more likely to occur where there are ethnic, regional, economic, occupational, linguistic, and religious differences, socialization is presumed to act so as to bring about some congruence along these lines even within the generations, not only between them.

In one way or another most studies of political socialization seek to uncover the extent to which different categories of a population socialize their members differently over the generations. A major task of the study of socialization is to ascertain the extent to which discontinuities across subcategories of the members in a system can be discovered and explained. The interest in this subject rests on the latent premise that where different ethnic groups, social classes, regional groups, or even school systems, for example, implant contrasting political concepts and patterns of behaviour in children, the rising generation may be that much more likely to develop diverse and possibly conflicting political points of view. If the socialization process raises children who upon reaching adulthood have among themselves conflicting aspirations, conceptions of the rules of the game, attitudes towards compliance, and feelings about authority, it is assumed that this will probably build social and political cleavages into a system. Instability would result.

To put the matter in a positive way, stability would seem to require some congruence in what the varying components of a maturing generation learns. The implication is that there is some range of variability in political orientations and behaviour within a generation; beyond this range lie conflict and stress. A person is often said to be "well or satisfactorily socialized" or just "socialized" if he fits into the overall pattern in a harmonious way; "poorly or inadequately socialized" or just "not socialized" if he deviates beyond some unspecified range. So many studies of socialization take this theoretical premise for granted that no special reference to the literature is required. It suffuses most research.

It is clear, for example, that this approach to the contribution of socialization to system-stability has a particularly close affinity to the melting-pot assumptions with which most research on one major source of diversity, ethnicity, is conducted in the United States. From the beginning of multi-ethnic immigration, Americans have hoped that somehow over the generations ethnic and linguistic differences would slowly disappear. Educational practice and social policy have been strongly coloured by this expectation. Most social pressures have automatically moved in the same direction. Indeed immigrants to the United States have arrived psychologically prepared to blend into the dominant Anglo-Saxon cultural and linguistic environment. The failure to do so, the lingering ethnic differences and intractable resistance to assimilation by some ethnic minorities, needs to be accounted for on other grounds.[26]

The disappearance of diversity into this melting-pot was not sought for its own sake. It accompanied the conviction that social and political stability would otherwise be impossible. We shall return to the implications of this operating assumption in a moment. But here it is enough to establish that frequently research has treated socialization as a mechanism for promoting stability because it is seen as carrying out the process of harmonizing the political and other predispositions within any generation.

But the stability associated with system-maintenance at times has implied something other than intra-generational homogeneity. Strains within a generation, it is thought, may arise from the failure of the individual himself to achieve some minimal inner consistency in his own orientations and patterns of behaviour. System stability may therefore be associated with *subjective homogeneity or consistency,* in the individual himself.

For example, it might be argued that a democratic system would scarcely be likely to survive if children were brought up under highly authoritarian conditions in the family, school, job, and voluntary associations and then were expected to behave in a democratic manner in the political arena. Conversely if children grew up with a high degree of involvement and responsibility for their own affairs and a significant voice, appropriate with age, in decisions affecting them in family, school, and so forth, we might question whether an authoritarian political regime could operate without strain as the children attained their political maturity.

With assumptions such as these about a possible source of instability, we might be inclined to interpret socialization as an important device for bridging these discontinuities and for ameliorating or erasing these longitudinal diversities in the life-cycle of the individual. One might expect the system to display a "strain towards congruence"[27] in order to alleviate subjective discontinuities in experience.

26. See N. Glaser and D. P. Moynihan, *Beyond the Melting Pot* (Cambridge, Mass., 1963).

27. G. A. Almond and S. Verba, *The Civic Culture* (Princeton, 1963), 372. The authors also speak of the "strain toward homogeneity" among the various roles an individual plays (327).

This second variant of horizontal socialization, subjective consistency or homogeneity, therefore emphasizes the effect of discontinuities in the learning of the same individual and requires some exemplification. A good illustration is to be found in the five-nation study by Almond and Verba. There the authors address themselves to the question as to whether experiences in the non-political sphere such as the family, school, and job are consonant with those in the political sphere.[28] The problem centres on the extent to which discontinuities in the socialization of members in a system may produce conflicting attitudes and expectations within the individual that would ultimately contribute to political instabilities. As they put it themselves, they are searching for

> hypotheses about the kinds of personality tendencies and socialization practices that are likely to produce *congruent political cultures and stable polities*. Thus in the case of the civic culture, we may say that a pattern of socialization which enables the individual to *manage the inevitable dissonances* among his diffuse primary, his obedient output [compliance], and activist input roles supports a democratic polity. We can then look at socialization patterns and personality tendencies and ask just which of these qualities are crucial, to what extent they must be present, and what kinds of experience are most likely to produce this capacity for *dissonant political role management*.[29]

On the acknowledged uncertain basis of retrospective evidence[30] they find that, depending upon the specific political system and the generation in question, family and school experiences may lean towards the non-participatory side in contrast with the participatory behaviour expected in the adult political sphere in democratic systems. The implication is that normally we could expect this "dissonance," as they term it, to contribute to conflicting expectations among the affected members—lack of homogeneity in subjective experiences—and therefore to some instability in the political arena.

The authors argue that inner "dissonance" and any ensuing political instability is avoided for two reasons. In part it is because early life experiences may fail to carry over fully to adult behaviour.[31] But in part it may

28. *Ibid.*, 327.

29. *Ibid.*, 34–5, italics added.

30. The suspicion of unreliability has since been strongly reinforced by an as yet unpublished piece of research by R. G. Niemi, Department of Political Science, Rochester University.

31. "Family experiences do play a role in the formation of political attitudes, but the role may not be central; the gap between the family and the polity may be so wide that other social experiences, especially in social situation closer in time and in structure to the political system, may play a larger role." Almond and Verba, *The Civic Culture*, 373.

also be due to the low salience of politics in some systems and the related capacity of the members to handle their internal inconsistencies without strain. In reply to their own query about "whether these inconsistencies cause [the expected] instability in the civic culture,"[32] the authors argue that inconsistency "creates no undue strain within the citizen; for politics, as much of our data suggest and as the data from many other studies confirm, is not the uppermost problem in his [the citizen's] mind."[33] Thus by reversing Freud and undervaluing childhood experiences in the political sphere and by relying on low political salience to reduce inner tensions, the authors are able to explain away intra-generational subjective disharmony, a kind that might otherwise have been disastrous, presumably for the stability of a democratic regime.

In the five-nation study the authors in fact had been adducing evidence that seemed to lend weight to somewhat earlier speculations by Eckstein. The latter had addressed himself to the basic issues raised during the 1920s by the Freudian social scientists in Germany about the relationship of attitudes bred in the authoritarian family to the failure of the democratic Weimar constitution to strike deep roots.[34] Eckstein had reconsidered this question by theorizing about the impact of attitudes and practices with regard to authority learned in the family, school, and occupational groups, on the behaviour of persons towards political authority. Expanding on the Freudian theme about the significance of primary learning, he hypothesized that a "government will tend to be stable if its authority pattern is congruent with the other authority patterns of the society of which it is part."[35] But for him this does not necessarily imply that stability requires the congruence of experiences in all organizations or social institutions, particularly the primary ones. Some heterogeneity is possible but only on condition that those structures in which divergent authority patterns may be learned—as in the family, church, or schools—are not too close to governmental institutions themselves. In this the theory visibly departs from Freudian presuppositions. It is social distance from the governmental structure that seems to be the decisive factor in enabling a system to tolerate variations in learned responses to patterns of authority.

Thus Eckstein speculates that "government will be stable, (1) if social authority patterns are identical with the government patterns, or (2) if they constitute a graduated pattern in a proper segmentation of society, or (3) if a high degree of resemblance exists in patterns adjacent to government [such as parties, civil service] and one finds throughout the more distant segments

32. *Ibid.*, 482.

33. *Ibid.*

34. See the extensive writings of T. W. Adorno, M. Herkheimer, and E. Fromm.

35. H. Eckstein, *Division and Cohesion in Democracy* (Princeton, 1966), 234.

[such as families, schools] a marked departure from functionally appropriate patterns for the sake of initiating the governmental pattern or extensive imitation of the governmental pattern in ritual practice."[36] This theory requires the author to modify the intuitive meaning of congruence and to redefine it to suggest that "social authority patterns [will be considered] congruent, either if they are very similar, or if similarity to the governmental pattern increases significantly as one approaches the governmental segment itself."[37] In the face of diversity, distance breeds content.[38] The "further" a structure is from government the less likely are contradictory authority patterns to impose strains on the individual as he participates in the political sphere.

Regardless of the validity of this theory, its significance for us at the moment is not that early socialization here, as in the five-nation study, turns out to have little meaning for later political behaviour. Nor does it matter that in neither of these studies do the authors conclude that instability in the political system can be traced to inner consistency or conflict associated with early socialization. What does matter is that in the elaboration of their ideas about congruence, these studies do turn to political stability as a means for establishing the theoretical relevance of their speculations. Each considers that but for the presence of certain structural arrangements—the "distance" of early political socialization from the political sphere—the members of a political system might find themselves under conditions of subjective strain. This in turn would make it difficult to sustain a stable democratic order. For the authors the key to an understanding of socialization is its consequences, either positive or negative; for the stability of the system.

As we have observed, the literature is not particularly clear about this distinction between vertical and horizontal stability and about the two ways (collective homogeneity and subjective consistency) in which horizontal stability might be impaired. Nonetheless, there is little doubt that these are the theoretical modes dominant in the study of socialization. We have a substantive theory with strong functional overtones if we have anything at all. Socialization, it is implied, may produce generations in a political system each of which looks much like the preceding one. Socialization may also contribute to harmonious political behaviour within a given generation and may thereby help to reduce internal cleavages. If it fails to do so, the continued stability of a system requires some other kind of explanation. What is clear from all this is that the major focus of research about socialization

36. *Ibid.*, 240–1.

37. *Ibid.*, 239.

38. For a further study of the impact of subjective heterogeneity see J. Stoetzel, *Without the Chrysanthemum and the Sword* (New York, 1955). See also S. Verba, "The Comparative Study of Socialization," a paper prepared for delivery at the annual meeting of the American Political Science Association, Chicago, 1964.

is on stability and its conditions. This is also the reason why we have looked at these alternative, if latent, conceptualizations as closely as we have. They reveal that the study of socialization has steadily pushed forward in one direction, towards clarifying its place in the production of political stability or system-maintenance.

THE LIMITATIONS OF STABILITY AS A THEORETICAL CONTEXT

The major drawback of a theoretical perspective that emphasizes system-maintenance is that research inspired by a concern for stability, whether in the form of vertical continuity or horizontal integration, must overlook a whole range of consequences that socialization has for political diversity, conflict, and change.

Not that change has been completely ignored in present research, or that instability has been denied. By the nature of the case, especially in politics, this would be highly unlikely, if not impossible. Discontinuities, both vertical and horizontal, in the transmission of existing political patterns are too apparent to be neglected entirely. But the current theoretical premises do convey the impression that the primary task is to explain something other than change—how systems come to reproduce themselves over time and to sustain themselves in an integrated, relatively homogeneous state at any moment of time. This perspective directs our attention to the effectiveness with which socialization processes draw people together towards the creation of a melting pot or a politically harmonious population.

For much of current research on socialization, whether and how diversity itself may be perpetuated or how change may occur, do not appear to be significant or central questions. It is as though system-maintenance and stability are the norms from which all else, such as basic change or diversity and cleavage, are deviations. Theoretically they enter as exceptions to the rule rather than, if not the rule, at least as central to research. Yet in an age in which most children in the world are growing up in a culture alien to their parents and one in which change may be the rule and stability the exception, a theory of socialization that is not broad enough to encompass both change and continuity as equally imperative phenomena immediately reveals its inherent weaknesses.

If we conduct research with the assumption that socialization serves to reinforce stability of systems, we are forced to address ourselves to a limited even though significant order of problems. We would wish to know, for example, how new members learn the existing adult political roles. We would assume that what the new members acquire is supposed to prepare them to step into roles that are already waiting for them. In this way a political structure manages to maintain itself even though the personnel changes from generation to generation. We would attribute importance to socialization because it prepares a person in anticipation for roles the prescriptions for which would seem to be known in advance. We are easily led to conclude that to the extent to which a person learns how he is to behave politically, he has been "adequately" socialized. To the extent that he is unable "to take his place" in the system, socialization has "failed." Similarly where, say, a child learns differential patterns in different sectors of his experiences, or where varying classes of children are trained differently, the system fails, through "improper" socialization, to bring about the degree of homogeneity presumed to be necessary for stability. Other mechanisms need to be activated to achieve this result.

If we adopt broader theoretical horizons, however, we can begin to appreciate that system-maintenance theory with its inclinations for an understanding of the conditions of stability in both senses of the term is far too limiting to reveal the major consequences of political socialization. It elevates one possible major resultant to the exclusive and dominant position.

Socialization is neither inherently conservatizing nor is it for that matter fundamentally destabilizing. It can contribute to disorder just as it does to peace and harmony, depending on the specific circumstances. A useful theory would recognize that the consequences of socialization will depend upon the prior state of the political system (whether it is stable or already in a condition of change), what it is that one generation is transmitting to another one (replicative or otherwise), and what the persons being socialized independently learn from their experiences. Once we accept the fact that an interpretation of the consequences of socialization must be kept wide enough open to incorporate both stability and change as possible central outcomes, the kinds of questions we ask and the way we analyse data will differ significantly from those that adopt stability as a primary focus. In particular, childhood socialization assumes a new character and discontinuities within a group or individual will be differently interpreted.

REPLICATION AS AN OUTCOME

For example, a major difficulty with the replicative thesis of a system-maintenance perspective is that socialization does not always succeed in recapitulating one generation in the text. It does not always assure stability in the sense of continuity or constancy.

In the first place, the older generation itself may not be interested in perpetuating its patterns in its children. Adults may be only too well aware of the emergence of a new world. In the hope of preparing their children to take advantage of the benefits so made available and to avoid the deprivations that they might otherwise incur, the adults may deliberately train their children for the acceptance of new political goals, norms, and structures. Inkeles discovered this to be true for a small sample of the pre-revolutionary generation in the Soviet Union. In spite of their opposition to the new Soviet order, they were not prepared to subject their children to the hazards of opposition. They consciously sought to avoid replicating their own generation.[39] Indeed if they had reproduced their political behaviour in their children, this would undoubtedly have increased the probability of political instability. It would have perpetuated rather than ameliorated the post-revolutionary conflicts.

In the second place, replication may also fail to occur because experiences of the rising generation may lead them to reject what their elders seek to instil in them. Where children are socialized "poorly," according to system-maintenance standards, a different theoretical context enables us to interpret this not as a flaw in the outcome but as providing an opportunity for change. It may be that, in spite of what their parents and other significant adults would have them learn, as children mature their own experiences teach them to prefer new ways of handling things politically when they move into the politically more active stages of the life-cycle. They may end up by defining new roles for themselves and searching out new modes of political expression.

From a system-maintenance posture, the student protest movement of the sixties in Europe and the United States, for example, may be interpreted as a disequilibrating force resulting from "inadequacies" in socialization. This would seem to be an implicit inference from judgments such as the following that are so prevalent in the literature on socialization. "Unfortunately for the best adjustment of the adolescent, cultural change has been so rapid that his parents have grown up in a different world, and thus are ill-equipped to teach him how to behave and adjust in the here and now."[40] In this vein we might be inclined to attribute the "inadequacies" in socializing practices to such factors as the excessive permissiveness of parents who are themselves unable to set firm standards. Alternatively we might see in the "deviations" of young people from past adult political norms something that we might call the "cat's paw" effect, a situation where successful middle-class parents are subconsciously working out their own stifled liberal sentiments through their children.[41]

Research into problems such as these is suggested if we assume that socialization is supposed to replicate previous outlooks with perhaps tolerable variations. We need to account for its breakdown. But if we broaden our theoretical horizons, we may discover also that the protesting students are purposively in search of new roles. The total impact of their experiences with several wars, aimless affluence, and dangerous and difficult political forces in an atomic age may be leading them, not with the inadvertent inadequacy or connivance of their parents but in opposition to them, to seek a way of defining new purposes and inventing new kinds of struc-

39. Inkeles, "Social Change and Social Character," 22.

40. R. G. Kuhlen, *The Psychology of Adolescent Development* (New York, 1952).

41. R. Flacks, "The Liberated Generation: An Exploration of the Roots of Student Protest," *Journal of Social Issues*, 23 (1967), 52–75.

tures to implement them.[42] For research purposes the investigator is not called upon to approve or disapprove of these student activities. But as social scientists we must be prepared to enlarge the scope of our analytic tools so that we see widespread movements—such as the new student left— not only as deviations, for explainable reasons, from a norm called stability, but as an outcome of socializing experiences that may lead towards innovation and change. Novelty in political behaviour and orientations is as "legitimate" or expected an outcome of socialization as is conformity.

REPLICATION OF INSTABILITY

As we have said, the trouble with replicative theory is that socialization may not replicate. But even if it does, it need not always replicate stability. Here we now interpret stability to mean not constancy alone but peace and order as well. If a system is in process of change and if socialization tends to reproduce the patterns of the preceding generation, it would be the changing state of affairs that would be continued in the rising generations. Many of the political systems in the modern world exist under conditions of instability. Developing nations have been and may well continue in this state for long periods of time. Instability seems to be a better description of the political norm in this age than stability.[43] Under these circumstances it would be surprising if the new generations coming to political power necessarily learned patterns of behaviour and political outlooks that contributed more to stability than to its contradictory.

Thus to cast research about socialization in system-maintenance or stability terms is to interpret change pejoratively, as though it were a product of error or moral failure. In fact it may prove to be a way of life for many societies in certain historical epochs such as the present. As has been pointed out, "so few individuals may now hope to grow up under conditions of sociocultural [and we may add, political] stability that we may regard this situation as almost unusual, and its products as in a sense 'deviants'."[44] For long historical intervals political socialization might conceivably contribute more to instability than to peace and order.

THE MELTING POT AND THE MOSAIC AS OUTCOMES

The emphasis on group congruence or integration as a major expected function or consequence of socialization similarly draws unnecessarily rigid boundaries around political research. In assuming that socialization somehow tends to level differences, this emphasis unobtrusively commits the research worker to the idea that stability requires the elimination of differences. Assimilation, the melting pot, becomes a precondition of stability.

42. Pinner, "Student Trade-Unionism."

43. A. Zolberg, *Creating Political Order: The Party-States of West Africa* (Chicago, 1966).

44. Inkeles, "Social Change and Social Character," 12, paraphrasing Margaret Mead.

If, however, we were to adopt an entirely different posture and assume that what counts, even for the stability of social and political systems, is not the presence or absence of diversity but the way in which it is managed or organized,[45] we could immediately appreciate the fact that socialization may well replicate diversity as well as cleavages and a political system could continue even in some stable state. The responsibility for attaining and maintaining stability or integration might then be shifted back to some other mechanisms. This approach might lead us to substitute a conception of society that sees it as a mosaic of ethnic groups living in cooperative diversity, instead of an image that depends on the assimilative tendencies of the melting pot.[46] But the latent commitment to cultural homogenization is so deeply ingrained in American thinking, both lay and scholarly, that it is extraordinarily difficult to accept the assertion that enduring non-assimilative patterns are consistent with an orderly political life.

Yet it is no longer a moot point as to whether members of a political system need to share all or most political orientations and cultural assumptions in order to be able to support a common regime. Indeed, unless we accept the plausibility of a mosaic hypothesis, it would be difficult to understand how multi-ethnic political systems, as found, say, in Belgium, Switzerland, and Canada—based as they are on a plurality of languages, religions, and cultures—could possibly have continued. Current ethnic discontents and instability in some of these systems may not necessarily indicate that they have failed to manage their differences but only that their mode of management is undergoing some fundamental revisions. Change even if accompanied by turmoil is itself a process of adaptation to new circumstances. In developing systems where ethnic diversity has seemed to put major barriers in the way of creating a viable political system *de novo,* we may have evidence not of the failure of the mosaic pattern but of the time and ingenuity necessary to discover adequate mechanisms of accommodation. But regardless of the specific impact of diversity on the operations of a political system, it is clear that socialization may be as important for its capacity to retain variability of wide dimensions as for its creation of pressures towards homogenization of a people.

The tendency in the United States to interpret homogeneity as a condition of stability is perhaps linked with the almost instinctive dominance of the melting pot concept of society, for well-known reasons.[47] The levelling of linguistic and religio-cultural differences has hitherto been accepted almost without question as a preferred state of affairs. A theoretical premise about socialization built on this preconception would naturally tend to equate assimilation and stability. But if the major impulse for research in the field of socialization had come from scholars immersed in multi-ethnic societies,

45. A. F. C. Wallace, *Culture and Personality* (New York, 1961).

46. See John Porter, *The Vertical Mosaic* (Toronto, 1965).

47. See Glaser and Moynihan, *Beyond the Melting Pot.*

some political systems might have been more congenially interpreted as continuing mosaics of ethnic groups living under conditions of acceptable accommodations of interests. At the very least, with both melting pot and mosaic patterns as possible polar alternatives, and with many combinations in between, a political theory about socialization needs to be sufficiently broad to embrace them all.

CONCLUSION

Thinking about political socialization is now too well advanced to be able to fall back on the non-theoretical option as a meaningful alternative. Allocative interests do little but follow up on adult behaviour and continue to leave us at theoretically loose ends. System-maintenance theory at least has the merit of adumbrating a possible political theory of political socialization. Whatever its shortcomings, it does seek to assign relevance of socialization for the operation of a political system as a whole.

But system-maintenance analysis imposes excessively severe limits on the kinds of problems central for research about socialization. Our examination of these drawbacks does, however, help to reinforce further the utility of my conceptualization of socialization at the outset in a neutral way, as the acquisition of political orientations and behaviour, without regard to its consequences or presumed functions for the system as a whole. Were we to continue to define socialization so as to posit some pre-existing structure for participation in which the individual is being trained, it would be necessary to make some instrumental judgments about the adequacy of his learning for taking up his roles in society. This is the conserving, and therefore the conservative, bias of system-maintenance as a theoretical viewpoint.

However, if we start in a neutral vein and accept an interpretation of socialization as just those processes through which an individual learns about interaction with others, it may be that, even though his behaviour is inappropriate for conforming with the standards of existing generations, or for bringing about political consensus, for his own generation the individual's learning may reflect a search for new patterns of behaviour. What may be "inadequate" socialization for maintaining existing political structures may be highly "appropriate" for bringing into being new structures based upon new ideals and new kinds of political accommodations among the members of the system.

We are not concerned, in an explanatory science, with the appropriateness of the socialized behaviour. We simply seek to trace out the consequences for the existing system of whatever results from the socializing experiences of the members of the system. It would be hazardous to assume either indirectly or unwittingly that any given political structure is to be preserved intact. Rather, we need a more comprehensive conception of the theoretical relevance of socialization for the political system, one in which change is not interpreted as a failure of the system to reproduce itself but in which change is viewed in positive terms. Change needs to be as integral to the conceptualization as stability is today.

A revision of the approach along these lines in political science calls for a wholesale reconsideration of the way we interpret the theoretical tasks of research into socialization. We require a context that will encourage us to explore how it is that members of a system acquire their political orientations and behaviour regardless of whether they conform to adult standards, run into conflict with the existing political structure, or just move laterally in a neutral direction. What is of significance for the adoption of a political theory of political socialization is the impact that the socializing processes have on the political system, and the theory must leave us free of any preconceptions about the consequences it should have, or the functions it ought to fulfill. Elsewhere I shall argue that it is helpful to turn to system analysis (or persistence theory) for this kind of uncommitted interpretation of political socialization.[48]

48. See a forthcoming book by D. Easton and J. Dennis, *Children in the Political System: Roots of Political Legitimacy* (McGraw-Hill). [David Easton and Jack Dennis, *Children in the Political System: Roots of Political Legitimacy* (New York: McGraw-Hill, 1969).]

Political Culture

Comparative Political Culture*

Sidney Verba

This century has seen rapid changes in both the real world of politics and the study of politics. In the political world new nations appear suddenly at

*Note: This paper draws on some discussions by a group assembled at the Center for Advanced Study in the Behavioral Sciences by the Social Science Research Council's Committee on Comparative Politics during the summer of 1962. I am grateful to the members of the group: Gabriel Almond, Frederick Barghoorn, Leonard Binder, James Coleman, Alex Inkeles, Joseph LaPalombara, Daniel Lerner, Lucian Pye, Dankwart Rustow, Robert Scott, and Robert Ward. I am also grateful to Harry Eckstein for suggestions as to how to approach political culture. The author is grateful to the Center of International Studies of Princeton University and to the Center for Advanced Study in the Behavioral Sciences for providing the opportunity to prepare this paper.

From Political Culture and Political Development, ed. by Lucian W. Pye and Sidney Verba (copyright © 1965 by Princeton University Press), No. 5, Studies in Political Development, pp. 512–526. Reprinted by permission of Princeton University Press.

every turn and old ones change or disappear as fast. The new and changing nations face problems that challenge the imaginations of statesmen and the capacities of institutions. The needs and aspirations are many, and the tools available to meet them are barely adequate. And in the study of politics one can sense a parallel. New approaches, new methods, new theories proliferate on all sides, in many cases inspired by the rapid changes in the political world. The new politics—politics in new areas, politics of a new type—appear to require a new political science to understand them. And just as the demands of a changing political world strain the tools of the statesman, so do the intellectual problems of comprehension of these changes strain the tools of the scholar.

But though the world of politics and political science are both in periods of rapid change, in both there is continuity with the past. The problems of the new states are in some sense problems other states have faced in the past: how to create a stable political system; how to make such a system effective in meeting demands placed upon it; how to adapt to changing environments or to internal changes within a society. The problems may come faster and with more urgency, but they are not completely new ones. Nor, on the other hand, have they ceased to be problems in the older nations. They have been the abiding concern of the students of politics—both the "new" political scientists dealing with the new states and the older students and philosophers of politics. Why do some states survive and others fail? How do nations change? From what kind of polity to what other kind? What crucial tasks face the statesman, and how should he be trained to meet them? How is democracy established, and what makes it survive? And what are the role and obligations of the ordinary citizen? Though the way in which the contemporary political scientist may attempt to answer these questions differs from the approach of earlier students of politics, the substantive concerns are abiding ones.

I. THE POLITICAL CULTURE APPROACH

. . . . The political culture of a society consists of the system of empirical beliefs, expressive symbols, and values which defines the situation in which political action takes place.[1] It provides the subjective orientation to poli-

1. The term "political culture" is beginning to find currency in the political science literature. The first use of the term in roughly the way it is used in this volume (at least that I am aware of) is in Gabriel Almond, "Comparative Political Systems," *Journal of Politics,* Vol. 18, 1956. Another early use of the term is in Samuel Beer and Adam Ulam, eds. *Patterns of Government,* New York, Random House, 1958.

The use of the word "culture" is perhaps a bit unfortunate in this context. Surely few other words in the social sciences have a greater variety of uses. It is used here because it has some currency in the literature, and any substitute word would just introduce more confusion. Furthermore, as used in this essay, the term refers to a rather general

tics. The political culture is of course but one aspect of politics. If one wanted a full picture of the process of politics in a nation one would have to consider many other aspects as well. We have focused on the cultural aspect for several reasons. For one thing, though political systems represent complex intertwinings of political culture with other aspects of the political system both formal and informal, it is difficult with the tools currently at hand to deal with the totality of political systems all at once. One is almost forced to look at one aspect or another. Second, we believe that the political culture of a society is a highly significant aspect of the political system.

There are many other aspects of the political system that could have been selected for close analysis. For a long time students of politics dealt with formal political institutions. If one wanted to explain why a political system survived or failed, why it was successful or unsuccessful, one looked at its constitution. How were laws passed? Was the system a presidential or a parliamentary one? Was there an independent judiciary? Of particular interest to those studying democratic systems were the structures of electoral systems. Did a nation have a single-member district electoral system or some form of proportional representation? Political scientists have since turned to other questions as well, particularly questions about what has been called the "infrastructure" of politics—those institutions not directly within the government that play a major role in political decisions. In particular political parties and interest groups have come under close scrutiny. Our interest in this volume was to look beyond the structures of politics to the beliefs that affect the ways in which people act within these political institutions.

This concentration upon political culture should not be taken to imply that other aspects of the political system are not important for the functioning of that system. They are both important and intimately related to the political culture. The political culture of a nation, for instance, derives from, among other things, the experiences that individuals have with the political process. One way to learn about political beliefs is to observe the ways in which political structures operate. These beliefs affect and are affected by the way in which the structures operate and there is a close circle of relationships between culture and structure. The justification for separating out the cultural aspect for attention is that it may facilitate the analysis of these relationships.

The study of political culture is not new. It would be both presumptuous and historically inaccurate to argue that the essays contained in this book or the works of other political scientists concerned with what we have called political culture deal with aspects of the political system that have previously been ignored. Writers on politics, particularly those who have tried to

---

approach to politics and some imprecision in its definition is probably not too crucial. This point will be discussed further below.

explain why the political system of a nation operated the way it did, have been aware of and commented upon the belief systems of the members of the nations about which they have written. Surely the works of Montesquieu, de Tocqueville, and Bagehot represent contributions to the study of political culture, and one finds concern with such problems at least as far back as the Greeks. Nor is the interest in political culture a subject that we can claim to rediscover for contemporary political science. Many recent students of politics have focused upon the factors we consider to be important aspects of political culture.

These disclaimers about the political culture approach are needed because of an unfortunate tendency in the social sciences to oversell new concepts and to assume that the mere labeling of an old phenomenon with a new term represents a breakthrough in our understanding. The term "political culture" refers—as the essays in this book clearly suggest—to a very general phenomenon which can be approached from many points of view. The concept of political culture serves to focus our attention on an aspect of political life, and such a focus of attention is useful. The concept makes it easier for us to separate the cultural aspect of politics from other aspects (as well as the political culture from other forms of culture) and to subject it to more detailed and systematic analysis. The process of separating out the cultural aspects of politics puts us in a position to see more clearly the place they have within the political system. The term "political culture" ties our study of political beliefs to sociological and anthropological works on culture and focuses our attention on basic values, cognitions, and emotional commitments. It also focuses our attention on a subject that has been of major concern to the students of culture—the process by which such values, cognitions, and emotional commitments are learned. The study of political culture leads invariably to the study of political socialization, to the learning experiences by which a political culture is passed on from generation to generation and to the situations under which political cultures change. The study of political culture may also lead to a new perspective on the political history of a nation (discussed more fully below) by which one focuses on the ways in which basic political beliefs are affected by the memories of political events.

To focus one's attention on a significant aspect of political life is useful, but it is only the beginning of the analysis and explanation of political phenomena. What really is important is not that one deals with political culture, but how one deals with it and how it is used to further our understanding of politics. To say that political culture is important is not very informative; to say what aspects of political culture are determinants of what phenomena—what the significant political beliefs are, and how they are related to other aspects of politics—may be very important. . . .

But before turning to the specific dimensions of political culture that appear to be of most use in understanding problems of political change, we shall consider the question of why this particular focus is important. What exactly is it that we focus upon when we use the term "political culture"? Political culture does not refer to the formal or informal structures of political interaction: to governments, political parties, pressure groups, or cliques. Nor does it refer to the pattern of interaction among political actors—who speaks to whom, who influences whom, who votes for whom. As we use the term "political culture" it refers to the system of beliefs about patterns of political interaction and political institutions. It refers not to what is happening in the world of politics, but what people believe about those happenings. And these beliefs can be of several kinds: they can be empirical beliefs about what the actual state of political life is; they can be beliefs as to the goals or values that ought to be pursued in political life, and these beliefs may have an important expressive or emotional dimension.[2]

Political culture forms an important link between the events of politics and the behavior of individuals in reaction to those events; for, although the political behavior of individuals and groups is of course affected by acts of government officials, wars, election campaigns, and the like, it is even more affected by the meanings that are assigned those events by observers. This is to say no more than that people respond to what they perceive of politics and how they interpret what they see.[3] From the cultural point of view, for instance, we would look at political history not so much as a series of objective events but as a series of events that may be interpreted quite differently by different people and whose effects on future events depend upon this interpretation. The term "meaning" and "interpretation," it should be stressed, are relational terms. They do not refer to what exists in the mind of the individual or to what happens in the outside world, but to the interaction between the two. And in this interaction it would be wrong to assume that either the previously held beliefs or the external events necessarily are dominant. An event will be interpreted in terms of previously

2. The term "belief" is one that can cause almost as much trouble as "culture." It is used in this essay to refer not only to the cognitive aspects of thought—which will be referred to as "empirical beliefs"—but to the evaluative and expressive aspects as well. The specific thoughts that people have about politics involve no clear differentiation into their cognitive, evaluative, and expressive components, but usually involve a combination of all three. Furthermore, I use the term "belief" rather than "attitude" or "opinion" because I am interested in patterns of thought more deeply rooted and more general than the latter two terms imply.

3. Though politics is often defined in terms of its relationship to violence and coercion (the state defined as the possessor of the monopoly of legitimate coercion, for instance), it is interesting how little of political importance involves the direct application of violence. One can of course affect a person's political behavior through the direct use of violence or coercion, in which case the beliefs about or interpretations of the violent act by the victim may be irrelevant. But violence plays a larger political role as a threat. Or, if violence is actually applied, what is of political relevance is more often the effect of the violent act on those who learn of it. And the two latter uses of violence involve interpretations and beliefs.

held beliefs; but preconceptions can only go so far in affecting interpretation. (How far, indeed, may be a very important question and a very important source of differentiation among political cultures.)

Of course basic patterns of political belief affect not merely how individuals respond to external events. Since these basic belief systems consist of existential beliefs, general values that set the goals of behavior, norms that regulate the means used to achieve goals, as well as emotional attachments, these belief systems also affect when and in what ways individuals become involved in political life. Looked at this way, it can be seen that political culture represents a system of control vis-à-vis the system of political interactions.[4] Political culture regulates who talks to whom and who influences whom. It also regulates what is said in political contacts and the effects of these contacts. It regulates the ways in which formal institutions operate as well. A new constitution, for instance, will be perceived and evaluated in terms of the political culture of a people. When put into practice in one society it may look quite different from the same constitution instituted in another nation with another political culture. Similarly, political ideologies are affected by the cultural environment into which they are introduced. History is full of examples of constitutions that did not "take" as the constitution writers had hoped because their application was mediated through a particular political culture, and history is full of examples of the ways in which political ideologies have been adapted to fit the pre-existing culture of the nation into which they were introduced.

POLITICAL BELIEFS

Political culture is very broadly defined in this essay. The term refers to all politically relevant orientations whether of a cognitive, evaluative, or expressive sort. It refers to the orientations of all the members of a political system; and it refers to orientations to all aspects of politics. This broad and rather loose definition is useful for this essay, one purpose of which is to direct attention to a general area of concern. And it is useful so long as political culture in the general sense is not used as an explanatory term in propositions about political systems. If political culture is so generally defined, it is of little use to say that the political culture of nation X explains why it has political structures of the form Y. Rather one must specify what aspects of political culture—what beliefs about what subjects—are the important elements for explaining the operation of political systems. In a later section of this essay I suggest some dimensions of political culture that seem particularly relevant for explanatory purposes, dimensions which will emphasize political beliefs of the most general sort. Thus the political-

---

4. On the role of cultural systems as controllers of social systems see Talcott Parsons, "General Introduction" in Parsons *et al.*, *Theories of Society*, New York, The Free Press of Glencoe, 1961, Vol. I, p. 35.

culture focus of this paper differs from that of many of the attitude studies that deal with rather specific political attitudes such as partisan affiliation, attitudes on international issues, and beliefs on specific issues of domestic policy. In contrast, in this paper I shall try to specify some of the more general aspects of political beliefs that seem particularly relevant for comparisons among nations that may differ radically in the specificities of their political situation. This is not to argue that specific political attitudes are not important; indeed they are much more reliable guides to political action than beliefs about politics in general. But the more general beliefs are important in giving overall direction to political tendencies and in providing grounds for the justification of the attitudes on more specific political topics.

Thus the empirical beliefs we are interested in in this approach to political culture are the fundamental beliefs about the nature of political systems and about the nature of *other* political actors. In particular it is quite important to discover what political beliefs are—to borrow a term from Milton Rokeach—primitive beliefs. Primitive political beliefs are those so implicit and generally taken for granted that each individual holds them and believes all other individuals hold them. They are the fundamental and usually unstated assumptions or postulates about politics. In this sense they are unchallengeable since no opportunity exists to call them into question.[5] It may be, for instance, that one of the major characteristics of the transitional political cultures within developing nations and one of the major sources of their instability is the fact that there are few such unchallenged primitive political beliefs.

Similarly, in terms of the evaluative mode of orientation, we shall be concerned with the most general level of values—the guiding principles that

5. See Milton Rokeach, *The Open and the Closed Mind,* New York, Basic Books, 1960, pp. 40–42. I am using the concept of primitive beliefs in connection with political beliefs somewhat differently from the way Rokeach uses the term but in a way that is not, I believe, inconsistent with his meaning. By primitive beliefs he refers to such basic beliefs as that in one's own identity and in the nature of physical reality. These are so taken for granted that one assumes all others agree with one. Therefore the question is never opened. The primitive political beliefs I refer to are not quite as primitive as the ones Rokeach cites, for the political beliefs held in one society are not necessarily shared by those in other political systems. Or indeed the assumptions of one sub-group of a society may not be shared by the other members of that society. (It is perhaps only when one has a sub-group of society whose fundamental assumptions about politics differ from the assumptions predominant in that society that one can properly talk of a political "sub-culture.") Thus, political beliefs may be primitive and unquestioned only for the group within which the individual lives. He may, for instance, be aware that there are other patterns of political belief but not consider them as relevant. And of course the political beliefs of the ordinary man are not structured according to the logic of comparative political analysis. The fact that the universality of the belief would be called into question if he considered political systems other than his own may offer no challenge to the depth of his belief in them. Furthermore one basic political belief—that in one's political identity—is the sort Rokeach has in mind and, as we shall see, one of the most crucial of political beliefs.

set the general goals of a political system—rather than with the preferences for specific kinds of policies. And in terms of expressive commitment we shall try to deal with the fundamental symbols of political integration and with fundamental patterns of loyalty rather than with the specific satisfactions and dissatisfactions concerning politics. The selection of such a set of political orientations involves the risk that they may be so general as to be of little use in explaining behavior. But in the perspective of cross-national comparisons of political cultures this is not so, for one can find rather sharp differences among different political cultures in terms of these most general beliefs, a fact that makes them a useful explanatory tool.

Fundamental political beliefs are, furthermore, particularly relevant to the study of change. They play a major role in guiding the ways in which institutions develop and change. To a large extent these beliefs may represent stabilizing elements in a system; they may motivate the actors in a political system to resist change in the name of traditional beliefs or they may lead to fundamental modifications of innovative institutions so that they fit the traditional culture. The essays in this volume are replete with examples of the ways in which traditional belief systems have served to control and modify patterns of change. But though fundamental political beliefs may be closely connected with the maintenance of existing patterns of politics, this is not necessarily the case. In a number of ways the cultural patterns in a society may generate change. Not all political cultures are well integrated and consistent. There may be many sources of strain within such cultures: sets of beliefs that are incompatible with other beliefs, sets of beliefs held by one segment of society and not another, or unmanageable incongruities between belief and reality. Under such circumstances the culture may accelerate change as part of a search for a new and more integrative set of beliefs. Furthermore it is possible for a culture to incorporate change as part of its fundamental belief system. One of the hallmarks of modernity within the realm of culture may be the acceptance and indeed the positive value of continuing change and innovation—to put it somewhat paradoxically—the institutionalization of innovation. And lastly, it must be pointed out that the fundamental general beliefs we have been talking about are themselves not immutable. The basic political values of a group may not be easily changed, yet under certain types of pressure and over time they can change rather drastically.[6] The essays on political cultures in this volume illustrate that point. The political cultures in the nations studied impinge upon attempted changes in patterns of political interaction —in many cases to impede these changes, in some cases to facilitate them. But the political cultures in these nations are themselves in flux.

The changeability of basic political beliefs is indeed a crucial question to

6. On the stability but changeability of basic values see Florence R. Kluckhohn and Fred R. Strodtbeck, *Variations in Value Orientation*, Evanston, Row, Peterson, 1961, pp. 9–10.

the elites of the developing nations. It is customary to think that cultural dimensions are unchanging factors that form the setting within which politics is carried on; that culture conditions politics, but not vice versa. Certainly this was the main argument of much of the national character literature. But the situation is sharply different today. Basic beliefs have now become the object of direct concern and attempted manipulation by the political elites in many nations. This is especially true in the new nations, but it may also be true in more established nations when a political elite is trying to found a new type of political system. Thus in Germany as well as in Egypt or India basic political beliefs have become the object of direct governmental concern.[7] With a great deal of sophistication and with a great deal of self-consciousness, elites in those countries have taken upon themselves the task of remaking the basic belief systems in their nations as part of their overall task of nation building. Basic political attitudes have of course always been in part the objects of conscious manipulation—as when adults teach children what are considered to be the basic virtues—but the new cultural policies involve attempts to create new patterns of beliefs, not merely to transmit established patterns to new generations. And these attempts are being made at a time when technological changes in the realm of communications and symbol manipulation may make such policies particularly effective. In any case, the student of political culture would be wise to accept the fact that what seem today to be fundamental sets of political beliefs may be quickly cast aside.

Before dealing with the more specific dimensions of belief which seem particularly important for the uderstanding of political change, two more general points about political culture must be considered. One has to do with the relationship between political culture and the general cultural system of a society, and the other, with the problem of the distribution of political beliefs and the extent to which political culture refers to political meanings shared by the members of a political system.

CULTURE AND POLITICAL CULTURE

The distinction between political culture and the more general cultural system of a society is an analytical one. Political culture is an integral aspect of more general culture, the set of political beliefs an individual holds, being of course part of the totality of beliefs he holds. Furthermore the basic belief and value patterns of a culture—those general values that have no reference to specific political objects—usually play a major role in

7. References in this essay to cultural patterns of the nations covered in this book are, unless otherwise specified, to the respective essays in this volume. See also on this point McKim Marriott, "Cultural Policies in the New States," in Clifford Geertz, ed. *Old Societies and New States; The Quest for Modernity in Asia and Africa,* New York, The Free Press of Glencoe, 1963, pp. 27–56.

the structuring of political culture. Such basic belief dimensions as the view of man's relation to nature, as time perspective, as the view of human nature and of the proper way to orient toward one's fellow man, as well as orientation toward activity and activism in general would be clearly inter-dependent with specifically political attitudes.[8] In a culture in which men's orientation toward nature is essentially one of fatalism and resignation their orientation toward government is likely to be much the same. Political cultures in which the activities of the government are considered in the same class with such natural calamities as earthquakes and storms—to be suffered but outside of the individual's control—are by no means rare, and one would assume that such an attitude would be closely related to a fatalistic attitude toward man's role in relation to nature. The beliefs described in southern Italy and prerevolutionary Mexico are examples of that orienta-tion, and suggest that such a combination of fatalism toward nature and toward government may be general in peasant societies. On the other hand, if the basic cultural orientation toward the environment is one of mastery over nature rather than passivity, this too would have an effect on political orientations. It might take place in two ways. Insofar as the cultural system committed a society to attempt to master and manipulate its physical envi-ronment, it is likely that the government will be expected to be an active agent in the process. Furthermore individuals might generalize to politics from their other beliefs. A belief in one's personal ineffectiveness might be generalized to a belief in one's inability to master the political environment, as Scott suggests is the case in Mexico. Similarly one's view of human nature probably has a close connection with one's view of political actors. In Italy and Ethiopia a deeply felt sense of distrust in people in general is reflected in a striking sense of distrust within the realm of politics. Conversely, the individual who believes that man is by nature trustworthy and cooperative is more likely to trust political leaders as well as political opponents, and more likely to be willing to cooperate with them.[9]

The focus on the relationship between basic belief structure and political beliefs is of great use in determining what political attitudes are important to consider in describing a political culture. Too often, as Robert Lane has pointed out forcefully,[10] students of politics have asked questions about

8. This set of basic values is taken from Kluckhohn and Strodtbeck, *op. cit.,* pp. 11–20.

9. That individuals who are high in "faith in people" are more likely to trust political leaders and think that they act for the people's benefit is supported by the work of Morris Rosenberg, "Misanthropy and Political Ideology," *American Sociological Re-view,* Vol. 21, 1956, pp. 690–695. A cross-cultural study which illustrates the same connection between general attitudes toward other people and political attitudes is Gabriel A. Almond and Sidney Verba, *The Civic Culture,* Princeton, Princeton Uni-versity Press, 1963; cf. especially Chap. 10.

10. Robert Lane, *Political Ideology,* New York, The Free Press of Glencoe, 1962, Chap. 26.

those political attitudes which political scientists consider important—about attitudes toward political issues or toward partisan affiliation. When the individual does not respond in ways that fit the researcher's view as to what a consistent political ideology is (for instance, he does not take consistent and well-reasoned liberal or conservative positions), he is considered to have no political ideology. But by focusing on basic value orientations— often implicit assumptions about the nature of man and the nature of physical reality—we may find a set of political attitudes that, though not structured as the political philosopher might structure them, nevertheless have a definite and significant structure. Since an individual's involvement in society is likely to be only peripherally political—since he is likely to invest more concern and affect in his personal relations or economic relations than in his political ones—it is quite likely that he will structure his political attitudes in ways that derive from his structuring of attitudes toward these more salient areas of activity rather than in terms of the ways in which political scientists or political theorists structure the political world.[11]

Though political culture is closely connected with other aspects of the cultural system, the analytical separation from general culture of those values, cognitions, and expressive states with political objects is useful. It is useful because it allows us to concentrate on those areas of attitudes that are most relevant for politics. It is useful also because the connection between general culture and political culture is not one of complete identity. Under some circumstances, for instance, there may be discontinuities between the values associated with political interactions and those associated with interactions of other sorts—personal or economic interactions, for instance. By separating political beliefs from other beliefs one can explore the nature of their interrelationship.

The relationship among the various beliefs that individuals have—both

11. On this general point see Almond and Verba, *op. cit.*, Chaps. 6 and 10. The mode of structuring political beliefs by the students of the subject suggests in turn that much of what, in the absence of direct evidence on political attitudes, we have assumed to be the political culture of a society may in fact be the political ideology of political elites or the political theory of political scientists. The attitudes of the ordinary man may not be structured around those aspects of politics that concern political elites or political scientists. Some recent work by Philip Converse and Georges Dupeux ("Politicization of the Electorate in France and the United States," *Public Opinion Quarterly*, Vol. 26, 1962, pp. 1–23) suggests that the familiar characterization of French political culture as involving a number of highly ideological and principled political subcultures may be more a characterization of political elites than of the political mass. The French electorate appears to be quite a bit less ideologically oriented than one would expect from a consideration of the nature of political debates in the National Assembly of the Fourth Republic.

Of course the political culture of the elites may be more important than that of the mass, but the example suggests that one might have to be careful in describing the elite culture also. The categories of belief of the analyst may be different from those of the elites studied.

political and non-political—represents one of the most important topics of discussion for the student of political culture. Though in dealing with culture we tend to think of patterned relationships among beliefs, this ought not to imply that all sets of beliefs are perfectly integrated. It may be that political beliefs are sharply discontinuous from or in some way inconsistent with other beliefs. One can conceive of a society in which cynicism is reserved for politics but does not pervade other social interactions. A more usual situation would be one in which the formal values stressed in the political realm were not consistent with those stressed in other areas of social life. One of the predominant features of the cultural patterns in most of the transitional nations discussed in this volume is that belief systems stressing modernity in politics are sharply different from the more traditional beliefs associated with other aspects of life, and this may cause severe strain for those who are forced to act within the political culture and the more general culture at the same time.[12] Similarly, the relationship between basic political beliefs and political behavior is not unambiguous. The same belief can be converted into action in a number of ways, just as the same action can have its roots in many alternate beliefs. But though the relationship between political beliefs and general beliefs on the one hand and political behavior on the other may vary, it is clear that they are never irrelevant to each other. Inconsistencies between belief and belief or between belief and action have significant implications for a political system.[13]

Furthermore, when a relationship is found between political beliefs and general social beliefs, one cannot assume that general social beliefs affect political beliefs with no reciprocal effects. Though it is probably true that individuals are more likely to generalize from basic social values to political values, political values may very well have effects on values in other spheres of life. In democratic political systems the belief that one ought to participate in political decisions is often used as a justification for participation in

12. In this connection see Almond and Verba, *op. cit.*, Chaps. 10 and 15. We argue there that the extent to which the political value system interpenetrates with the system of general social values is a major dimension of political culture with significant implications for the operation of the political system. See also the discussion below of discontinuities in the socialization process when the values in one sphere of life are not congruent with those in some other.

Harry Eckstein's discussion of Weimar Germany, where authority patterns in non-political relationships were sharply different from those formally institutionalized in politics, is relevant here. The attendant strains from such discontinuity resemble those in new nations where new political norms are laid upon a traditional base (see Eckstein's *A Theory of Stable Democracy,* Princeton, Center of International Studies, 1961).

13. Not all such inconsistencies are destabilizing. See the discussion of the role of inconsistencies between behavior and belief within democratic political systems in Almond and Verba, *op. cit.*, Chap. 15, which gives examples of the way in which inconsistencies play a positive role in democratic stability.

non-political decisions. In Germany and the United States, for instance, "democracy" in the home or in the school has been justified in terms of its appropriateness for a democratic political system.

THE HOMOGENEITY OF CULTURE

Lastly a word must be said about the problem of cultural homogeneity in a political system. The focus on political *culture* rather than political *attitudes* implies a concentration upon the attitudes held by all the members of a political system rather than upon the attitudes held by individuals or particular categories of individuals. As anthropologists have used the term "culture," it has frequently referred to those aspects of belief systems that are shared by members of a society and that are distinctive to that group.[14] Our approach is somewhat different. To concentrate only on shared beliefs might lead one to overlook situations where significant political beliefs were held only by certain groups, and where the very fact that these attitudes were not shared by most members of the system was of crucial importance. This is particularly a problem as one begins to deal with societies as large and complicated as the nation-state. Our approach is to begin with a set of belief dimensions that seem particularly crucial for the understanding of the operation—in particular the development and adaptability—of a political system, and then ask whether or not members of a political system share attitudes on these dimensions.

The degree to which basic political attitudes are shared within a political system becomes thus a crucial but open question. A major pole of differentiation among political cultures is the number of basic political attitudes that are widely shared and the patterning of the differences in political belief among the various groups in society. To a greater or lesser extent, all the essays in this volume deal with important differences between the political culture of various elite groups and mass political culture; and, as the essays on Italy and Ethiopia remind us, differences among regions or among ethnic communities may be as large as differences among nations. Of course for the purposes of predicting the political future of a nation the beliefs of certain groups are more crucial than others—those in actual political power, members of organized groups, those living near the centers of communicat'ons, and the like. But in an era of rapid political change when the mobilization of mass support is so eagerly pursued, few political sub-cultures can be ignored.

The degree to which political beliefs are shared may be a good indicator

14. "By 'culture' we mean that historically created definition of the situation which individuals acquire by virtue of participation in or contact with groups that tend to share ways of life that are in particular respects and in their total configuration distinctive." (Clyde Kluckhohn, "The Concept of Culture," in *Culture and Behavior*, Richard Kluckhohn ed., New York, The Free Press of Glencoe, 1962.)

of the cohesiveness of a society. But this is probably more true of certain types of beliefs than of others, as discussed below. Some basic political values may indeed lead to conflict if shared on the level of generality we are discussing. Thus all members of a system—to use an example discussed more fully later—may share a belief that output of the political system ought to benefit a fairly parochially defined group—their own family or perhaps their local region. But though this implies a sharing of political values on one level—a shared set of criteria for evaluating governmental output—the fact that on a different level the specific group used as a criterion differs among the members of the system could lead to conflict. Similarly, the existence of an "ideological" political style through a shared cultural norm may institutionalize divisiveness. Though the commitment to ideology is shared throughout the system, the ideologies to which individuals are committed vary from group to group.

Further Suggested Readings

Almond, Gabriel A., and Verba, Sidney. *The Civic Culture*. Princeton: Princeton University Press, 1963.

Balandier, George. "Le contexte sociologique de la vie politique en Afrique noire," *Revue Française de Science Politique,* 9 (September 1959), 598–609.

Binder, Leonard. "Egypt: The Integrative Revolution." In *Political Culture and Political Development*. L. Pye and S. Verba, eds. Princeton: Princeton University Press, 1965, pp. 396–449.

Dennis, Jack. "The Major Problems of Political Socialization Research," *Midwest Journal of Political Science,* 12 (February 1968), 85–114. Bibliography.

Easton, David, and Dennis, Jack. *Children In The Political System*. New York: McGraw-Hill, 1968.

——— and Robert Hess. "The Child's Political World," *Midwest Journal of Political Science,* 6 (1962), 229–46.

Geiger, Kent. "Changing Political Attitudes in Totalitarian Society: A Case Study of the Role of Family," *World Politics,* 8 (1956), 189–205.

Greenstein, Fred. *Children and Politics*. New Haven: Yale University Press, 1965.

————. "Personality and Political Socialization: The Theories of Authoritarian and Democratic Character," *Annals,* 361 (1965), 81–95.

Hyman, Herbert. *Political Socialization.* Glencoe, Ill.: Free Press, 1959.

Jennings, M.K., and Niemi, R.G. "Family Structure and the Transmission of Political Values," *American Political Science Review,* 62 (1968), 169–84.

LeVine, Robert. "Political Socialization and Cultural Change." In *Old Societies and New States,* edited by C. Geertz, pp. 280–303, New York: Free Press, 1963.

————. "The Role of the Family in Authority Systems," *Behavioral Science,* 5 (1960), 291–96.

Pinner, F.A. "Student Trade-Unionism in France, Belgium and Holland: Anticipatory Socialization and Role Seeking," *Sociology of Education,* 37 (1964), 177–99.

Pye, Lucian W., and Verba, Sidney, eds. *Political Culture and Political Development.* Princeton: Princeton University Press, 1965. Bibliography.

Torney, Judith. *The Development of Political Attitudes In Children.* Chicago: Aldine, 1967.

4

Comparative Electoral Systems

Introduction

There are two broad categories of electoral systems in terms of the purposes they are designed to serve. First, there are competitive participatory systems which have as their ultimate objective the expression of individual judgments regarding policy alternatives. This is accomplished by providing the individual with choices to be selected in a competitive manner. In this sense, by making choices the individual "participates" in setting the overall direction of the society. This point may not appear evident except in the specific case of referenda because of the fact that elections perhaps seem always to be concerned with personalities rather than policies and issues. The point is that behind these personalities lies the political party and its known position on the issues of the day. Such competitive systems are usually associated with democratic systems of government.

The second category of electoral system is mobilizational, that is, involving individuals in electoral activities in order to increase their general commitment to the political regime. The emphasis here is more upon the ritualistic aspect of elections and their legitimizing functions than upon the choice of one policy versus another. The individual is in the position of being either directed in his choices or in having his range of choices narrowly restricted. This mobilizational category is the one customarily associated with authoritarian forms of government. This kind of election is thought, perhaps erroneously, to be relatively well understood among scholars. At least, it is the case that most of the scholarly literature is concerned with the pros and cons of various modes of the competitive variety.

Electoral systems are located at the point of intersection of the ideals and realities of any political system. Every political system determines by the nature of its constitution who is to be considered politically relevant or irrelevant. Electoral systems are then designed and enacted to carry out the constitutional provisions of age, literacy, property, class, etc., which govern political participation. It is the specific nature of the electoral system and how well it approximates these ideal prescriptions which forms the bulk of the academic electoral system literature. For example, it is in this perspective of ideals and realities that the large debate of the proponents of proportional representation (P.R.) versus the proponents of plurality systems takes place and is to be understood (the pros and cons of the debate and their political implications are summarized in the reading by Milnor). Given a general democratic commitment, the P.R. spokesmen argue that the principle of "one man, one vote" is meaningless in an electoral system (a plurality one) where a losing 49 percent of those voting have their vote in effect thrown away. Instead they argue that proportional representation is the most mathematically accurate way of giving the individual the full effect of his vote.

All systems of proportional representation involve calculating a quota: the number of seats plus one divided into the total number of votes cast. Each individual receiving the stipulated quota is then considered elected. Two main systems of P.R. have utilized these quotas with differing effects. The first of these systems is that of the single transferable vote in which the voter ranks the candidates of his choice and each reaching the quota is declared elected. The candidate receiving the smallest number of votes is declared defeated and his votes are distributed among the remaining candidates until the requisite number are elected. This puts a premium upon the role of personality over party.

The list system advocated by Hare, on the other hand, permits the party, not the voter, to rank the candidates on a given list. The quotas are then applied and the party in effect determines who is to be elected.[1] Contrary to many critics, the P.R. systems of transferable votes and lists do not appear to create a multi-party system.[2] What they seem to do is reduce the importance of single parties and equalize the importance of other parties in the system. Thus, one of Hermens' concerns as well as those of other critics is the responsibility that they feel must be assigned to proportional representation for fragmenting the party system of Weimar Germany and thereby contributing to the advent of the Nazi movement. In fact, the party system was not fragmented in any greater degree than in pre-World War I Germany, and if P.R. had any direct effect it may have been its contribution to the greater diffusion of power by not allowing one of the democratic parties to become dominant. Thus perhaps the greatest indictment of P.R. is that it tends to perpetuate pre-existing cleavages in the society. This is something, however, that plurality systems might do as well, as will be noted below, or might at best paper over and in doing so contribute to the explosive character of the political system. If proportional representation

1. Thomas Hare, *A Treatise on the Election of Representatives* (London: Longman, Brown, Green, Longmans and Roberts, 1859). For a modern argument in support of P.R. see Enid Lakeman, *How Democracies Vote*, 2nd ed. (London: Faber and Faber, 1970), pp. 160–67.

2. This point of view is represented by F. A. Hermens, *Democracy or Anarchy?* (Notre Dame, Ind.: Review of Politics, 1938), pp. 16ff.

systems have a kind of fluidity about them and can be characterized as being highly intellectualized in both their rationalization and formulation, plurality systems are more simple.

Plurality systems are predicated upon the reality and/or the desirability of polarized cleavages existing in a society. Much of the element of the adversary "trial by strength" relationships, found in Anglo-Saxon law, is implicit in the operation of plurality systems. Therefore it is not surprising that plurality systems are most common in Anglo-Saxon countries and that the plurality system is predicated upon the principle that the winner takes all. It is felt that the winner can take all because underlying the plurality system is the enormous assumption that sufficient consensus exists in the society that the winner will not seek to persecute or eradicate the loser. This assumption is at best a tenuous one in Third World nations and goes a long way toward understanding why the so-called Westminster parliamentary model initially adopted by so many emerging nations has succumbed to authoritarian single-party or military rule. The reasons why plurality electoral systems have experienced so much difficulty in Third World areas can perhaps be seen more clearly if we consider some of the further assumptions and preconditions seemingly inherent in the successful working of such a system.

First, it can be observed that a culturally pervasive and reinforcing practice of elections is likely to exist at all levels and aspects of the society. No organizational undertaking can begin until officers are elected (e.g., boards of directors of business firms, voluntary organizations, etc.) and policies voted upon. Second, there is an assumption of a profusion of secondary interest groups with overlapping memberships possessing the element of compromise essential to the diminution of sharp conflict. Finally, there is present the element of adversary justice, already referred to, which assumes simultaneously that political justice is best arrived at competitively and by test of strength and that an underlying value system exists that is basically supportive of the system.

We can note in conclusion that this discussion of the respective merits of P.R. and plurality systems is further related to a central concern of this volume, namely the normative aspects of the pluralistic bias inherent in contemporary political analysis. Both P.R. and plurality systems are based on a pluralist assumption of heterogeneous and competing social groupings but they differ on how these groups operate. The plurality system assumes that the interaction of a multitude of these groups in the society as a whole and the electoral process itself will produce consensus at the legislative level. In short, the sharpest social and political conflicts will be blunted and compromised even before the legislature meets. The P.R. system, on the other hand, fosters the legislature rather than the society as a whole as the arena of conflict and compromise. It might be suggested that in Third World areas, lacking as a consequence of their economic underdevelopment an interest group infrastructure, the legislature arena might be a better place for conflict resolution than inter-tribal, inter-religious and inter-sectional polarizations. Our reading by Milnor well summarizes the implications of both types of electoral systems for political stability in general and their impact upon particular political structures. Among these structures covered in succeeding chapters are interest groups, political parties, and bureaucracies.

Contemporary Perspectives on Electoral Systems

Elections and Political Stability

A. J. Milnor

In this [. . .] chapter some tentative conclusions are drawn about the relationship between electoral systems and their environment and about the problems of representation through techniques of election. Perhaps in this manner the volume may be summarized while at the same time some of the questions proposed in the text will be clarified.

1. Two propositions immediately come to mind about the impact of proportional representation and plurality upon government stability and popular representation. Because proportional representation, particularly the list system, tends to emphasize representation more than stability of the governing coalition, other things being equal, there will be a larger number of parties represented in the legislature than would be the case under plurality and the governmental coalition will therefore be more difficult to maintain. Under proportionality it is obviously more difficult to mold a policy coalition that will persist over time with sufficient strength to hold a steady and constant line of policy. If the electoral system tends to build into the processes of government patterns of instability, particularly if the electoral system cannot prevent the emergence of potentially destructive issues in the upper levels of the government, such as linguistic or religious conflicts in legislature or cabinet, elections come to have very clear implications for the complex processes of economic and political development. Less clear is the implication of short-term instability in the face of powerful internal change, perhaps exemplified by the emergence of social homogeneity in Western Europe since the Second World War. It is precisely in this area, where the forging of a coalition for long-term governing is important, that proportionality, with its emphasis upon the immediate representation of differences in the society, is so likely to cause major difficulties. In relatively stable societies it is of less consequence, but in periods of significant social

change proportional representation may fail the social system by not providing a stable political coalition powerful enough to weather the social challenge.

2. If the effect of proportional representation is to place obstacles in the path of stable governing coalitions, it is of course even more effective in dispersing the party structure of opposition. Since proportionality creates a number of parties with little inclination to reduce their numbers down to two, there is an inevitable tendency for the larger parties to form together a government coalition at least temporarily in power. Since it is obviously a simpler process to build a governing majority out of larger parties rather than smaller, the opposition is often reduced to a cluster of smaller parties unable to cooperate during elections and now left to cooperate in the legislature, united by little more than their dislike of the government in power. And even then the opposition is not cemented by a realistic hope that it is an alternative to the government in power, for at best a given minor party might hope to be an ally of some larger party asked to form a new coalition, but the more likely prospect is for the large parties in the defeated coalition to widen the spectrum just enough to create a new coalition. Opposition fueled on such hopes is not likely to be united, useful, or important. In turn, the failure of opposition to coalesce throws the full weight of opposition upon components of the governmental coalition itself. Whether a government without an organized opposition, facing the only significant challenges from within its own ranks, can husband its energies sufficiently to pursue policy lines and maintain its own stability is a difficult question.

3. A major distinguishing factor between the advocates of proportional electoral systems and those of plurality electoral systems is their almost diametrically opposite assumptions about the character of the legislative process. For the proportionality advocate, the legislature approximates a mirror reflection of the society at the time of election, and by the first meeting of the legislature few if any of the societal cleavages will have been settled. As a natural consequence, the proportionally elected legislature is best described as an arena for the formation of coalitions behind policy rather than as an arena in which a partially preforged coalition is activated for policy making. Therefore, the proportional legislature will have a wider range of issues before it than will the plurality legislature, since in the plurality legislature the prescreening process of electoral coalition will reduce the number of legitimate questions at the same time that it produces greater policy stability in the assembly. Underlying these observations is the nature of the relationship between elections and legislative activity. The act of legislating for the proportionality advocate is separate from the act of electing: the election reproduces the society in the legislature while the act of legislating raises issues for this society writ small to consider. In a very real sense these become conceptually different processes. On the other hand, the plurality advocate sees the act of legislating as an extension of the act of

electing, since the nomination, campaign, and election phase of electioneering have all been based around the formation of a coalition sufficiently strong to ensure local victory. Precisely because plurality election systems force the contenders to seek out like-minded partners in order to assure victory, the nature of the questions and in part the nature of the legislative answers are consciously forged before the legislature itself ever convenes. In that sense, it is conceptually much more difficult to separate the legislative aspect from the electoral aspect in plurality systems, perhaps accounting for the vast amount of research that has been done on the legislative process and constituency behavior in plurality systems.

3a. There are a number of corollary observations that flow from this initial distinction. In the first place, if the proportional systems tend to duplicate the fissures in the society in the legislature, as a conceptually separate process from the act of policy making, the legislature itself is faced with two choices. It may, first, merely apply those fissures and cleavages to the legislative proposals at hand; and the legislators, upon discovering that such cleavages make legislative life intolerable, may do nothing. Or secondly, they may attempt to bridge over these disputes and create a coalition for policy making although the elements of the coalition may be rather unstable. In any case, the most important question is whether the legislature will be able to forge a coalition that was not possible in the electoral campaign. In short, with proportional representation it is assumed that legislatures are the proper arena for the creation of policy coalitions and that there should be little, if any, prelegislative effort at coalition formation. With plurality systems the opposite is assumed, since the dynamics of the plurality system will by and large force an early coalition arrangement, either in the form of large, heterogeneous parties or at least working coalitions, such as the French Federation of the Left. Whether these arrangements are any more stable than those executed under proportionality may be questioned, but at least there is the possibility for some prelegislative policy negotiation, an important phase conspicuously absent from the proportional systems.

3b. This general observation can also create problems for the plurality advocate. Insofar as a society is deeply divided, particularly along geographic lines, plurality systems may create many more problems than they can solve. The assumption that large fissures in the society have been papered over in a prelegislative stage may be totally unwarranted; and if the legislature meets either with an understanding to ignore certain questions—for example, the questions of communal relations in Malaya—or with a policy coalition that has excluded certain volatile and important components of the society—for example, the American urban Negro—plurality has done a severe disservice to the policy process. On the other hand, if the legislature—and in a broader sense the whole government—is viewed as the agent through which basic cleavages in the society will be negotiated out of existence at the governmental level, and if that government is elected through a prescreening device such as plurality, the legislature and the whole governmental structure may fall apart, asked to do that which it cannot. It is perhaps useful to cite the Nigerian experience here, although the existence of federalism in that unhappy country was an additional complicating device. In such a case perhaps the only effective alternative is a system that combines a modified federalism, guaranteed representation for minorities, and pressures toward coalition building through a partial application of the plurality principle.

4. The legislative functions under plurality and proportionality are distinctly different processes, and the impact of this distinction is an important determinant of other institutional behavior. It follows that if the form of the electoral system has important implications for the workings of the legislature, it must also have implications for the working of the majority coalition, particularly in parliamentary regimes.

4a. Obviously, party discipline and ministerial stability are far greater under plurality because of the partial integration during the election phase. To a greater extent than under proportionality the legislative and governmental leadership will be known, as in the case of the parliamentary system, where the leadership of the major pretenders to power and the obvious coalition lines are observable in advance. With proportionality, given the difficulty of keeping electoral coalitions together (should any form), given the tendency for larger numbers of parties to find representation, and finally given the relatively more difficult task of maintenance, elite prediction is more difficult and more alternatives exist for the elite to expand and shift with whims in the legislature.

4b. By the same token, however, a breakdown in the linkage between the coalition in the legislature and the popular ideological distribution will have a far more severe impact on the plurality legislature than upon the proportional legislature, particularly if the latter has a larger number of parties. The elite in the plurality legislature will have been chosen by a prescreening process that may have substantially filtered out the very elements that now form the center of the societal distribution. Proportionality is far more likely to give representation to such a fledgling movement, and its greater range of alternatives in the legislature itself make the construction of a timely elite a more viable possibility. In this case the coalition pressures of plurality election systems may have obscured the growth of popular cleavages and contributed to the isolation of the legislature from the general policy requirements of the society.

4c. The character of the plurality coalition and its proportional counterpart has internal implications as well. Given the prescreened nature of the ideal plurality majority, party discipline and ministerial stability should be higher than in the comparable proportional legislature. But by the same token, since the stability of the legislative majority is expected to be higher than in a more heterogeneous legislature elected under proportionality, the impact of government fall will be considerably greater than under proportionality. To argue the same thing another way, the possibility of preresolution of societal tensions leads to assumptions about the stability of the legislature itself, and the cracking of this electoral coalition, sufficient to bring down a government in parliamentary regimes, is far more serious under plurality than under proportional systems. In the proportional system fissures of the society are expected in the legislature. In plurality systems, where the organizational stability made possible by the electoral coalition creates an image of permanence, the breaking of the coalition implies the inadequacy of the whole electoral-legislative coalition. Consequently, while governmental falls in parliamentary plurality regimes will be infrequent, they will also be far more serious than in the proportional systems.

5. The general character of the voter-party-legislature relationship is substantially different under the two broad types of electoral systems. Because the plurality model forces coalition building, there are more likely to be broad political (although unorganized) challenges that do not achieve representation. These unrepresented numbers will be added to those excluded by other parties and their followers who have gathered their forces in coalition. As a result the voter in a plurality system may be faced more frequently with a demand that he cast his ballot as an affirmation of his faith in the political system rather than for policy preferences. As the number of voters participating for sheer system maintenance increases, the validity of the prelegislative coalition as a policy device in plurality legislatures is challenged and rendered less important. A plurality coalition is an effective policy device only so long as citizen commitments are largely instrumental and only secondarily systemic.

The general argument may be seen more clearly in terms of the exchange concept. In normal elections voters will cast their ballots for the party that comes closest to their own policy preferences, and in doing so, they will not support other parties and candidates who are further from their own perceived positions. For a gratifying party policy the voter exchanges his freedom to support other alternatives. In proportional systems, most clearly the list system, the voter is able to approximate closely his own policy positions because of the larger number of contenders and the relatively easier task of gaining representation. As in the French Fifth Republic, the problem becomes one of a higher order when the voter in majority systems is asked to support a coalition in an electoral district on the single ground that it will prevent the success of another group that is perceived as a threat to the entire political system. The voter is asked to make a qualitatively different kind of exchange in this process, for he is asked to support a coalition for reasons other than policy and only in the name of system maintenance. Insofar as the exchange process is one of system maintenance and not of policy exchanges, the prelegislative coalition can only claim to be one that is predisposed to hold the political system together, one in which there is little prior agreement on policy. An inadequate policy coalition in a legislature whose design and assumptions assume the existence of some sort of prescreening of social cleavage creates problems discussed in 3b above.

The distinction between policy exchanges and system maintaining ones, clear from an examination of the French majority election system, applies to the pure plurality form of election. It too forces interests to aggregate in order to prevent a victory by a large plurality, asking voters to accept a narrower range of policy alternatives than proportional representation might afford. The dynamic at work is the same though less obvious in extent. If, for example, a third-party candidate in the Canadian West appears likely to gather 35 percent of the vote based in a residential (and generally leftist) university community, it behooves the two major parties either to come to some sort of agreement or at least to suppress the possibility that the major party vote will be further divided by the emergence of a new party on the right. The same general argument can be made in another context, the perceived threat of parties of the German right against the established political order of the Bonn Republic. In each of these cases the normal fractionalization of the electorate would provide a strong opportunity for a candidate whose inclinations favor a restructuring of the social or political system. Supporters of that order are now asked to accept a limited set of political alternatives in order that their forces be concentrated behind candidates whose credentials make them more acceptable to the political establishment. In the process of electing such candidates, however, the notion of policy coalition is discarded in favor of system maintenance, quite a different order of political temper.

6. It is not only the legislature that is substantially affected by the exclusive character of plurality and the representative character of proportionality. The pressures within a society that are denied access in their proportional influence may yet have an opportunity to evade the legislative coalition and obtain a hearing elsewhere in the political system. In particular, the channels of the bureaucracy may be open to specific losers in the policy debate. In short, the concept of representative bureaucracy may be more consistent with plurality election than it is with the open representation characteristic of proportional elections, and it may well be the bureaucracy that establishes itself as the channel through which policy positions outside the general policy coalition dominating the legislature are able to be heard. By the same token the strength of the executive, particularly a separate presidential form, may make it an agent of involvement with groups selected out by the coalition process during the elections, especially if a head of state is willing to use his office as a teaching lectern for the whole society.

Care must be exercised to separate the phenomenon of representative bureaucracy under plurality from a heightened executive under proportionality. Groups able to appeal to the bureaucracy as losers in the electoral coalition are able to do so only as advocates of positions whose rationality is forceful. They have little influence in the legislature and as a consequence are not able to bring extraordinary pressure to bear on any part of the executive that is not cooperative. They are in a true sense pleaders at the table, and whether the bureaucracy becomes an advocate of their cause is for that body alone to decide. Proportionality presents quite a different picture, since the general role of the executive may be vastly heightened by quarreling ineffectiveness on the part of the legislature attempting to pursue policy goals. At the end point, if the legislature is completely unable to agree on policy lines or, worse, on a set of ministers to govern, the tasks of administering the state become the tasks of policy formulation coincident with execution. The heightening of executive power in the presence of a legislature dominated by a negative majority is a political phenomenon of a totally different magnitude from representative bureaucracy under plurality regimes. In the latter case, the bureaucracy becomes advocate of a minority position, although admittedly the creation of effective clientele relationships has been known to be of use to agencies in the past.

7. It is in the area of ecology that the most important of the questions [. . .] can be found. Casually suggested in such discussions as those of Weimar Germany and the West German Republic, and found also in cases as widely diverse as Japan and Illinois, the general hypothesis might be pursued that it is the character of political forces extant at the time of constitution writing that will determine the distance a polity can move toward the exclusiveness of plurality or toward the representation implicit in proportionality. Simply enough, were the memories of Weimar so fresh that West Germany could not adopt a scheme of proportional representation? Were the divisions in the German society so real that plurality would have left too many interests unrepresented? This explanation has barely been touched, and yet the interaction between election system and the environment which created it is perhaps the most important of all.

In simplest terms, [. . .] election systems have been treated neither as completely dependent upon some other set of forces nor as completely independent variables. Rather, the election system is an intermediate variable able to influence the nature and behavior of institutions of government while itself being the target of other influences. The impact of the electoral system is in two linked stages. In the first place, and often unrecognized as an influence on the political system itself, the selection of the form of the electoral system is a dependent variable affected by a host of factors, not the least of which is the character of the society itself. A society in which large segments are strongly alienated from the general population, at the same time that they are not geographically isolated, probably will not be able to employ simple plurality as an electoral device. On the other hand, if a population is relatively homogeneous—has no deep internal conflicts— then the society probably will be able to employ with considerable success the plurality technique. It is certainly true that the history of socialist parties in Europe is a history of flirtation with proportional representation, while the history of those states in which ideological movements have had difficult going is one of plurality election. In these cases it is certainly a first hypothesis that the election system may not be an independent variable, but may be partially dependent upon the general character of the social system.

The second effect of the electoral system is in the development of the society itself. While social systems are dynamic, electoral systems are not, and to boot they are often creators of entrenched interests willing and able to defend the election device. Thus, while the society may evolve considerably beyond its initial phase, of either discord or unity, the electoral system that was initially the dependent variable may continue to reflect the initial state. In this form the electoral system in fact impedes the development of the society, when proportional systems act as a brake on the growth of unity and plurality systems act as a goad toward consensus. Additional recalcitrance is a product of policy makers whose political fortunes are in part linked with the form of election system to which they owe their political rise. It is these policy makers in turn who must support or at least tacitly not oppose the new election system changed social conditions might require. By means of this two-step, linked process the electoral system has its impact on the entire legislative system and to some degree on the entire political system.

It is from this last perspective that we see the tremendous potential of the electoral system as a generator of power for the legislature and, beyond its confines, for the whole governmental system. An electoral system which produces a legislative coalition attuned to the demands and needs of the population while providing a policy coalition that can produce results for the entire political system is capable of generating policy of enormous authority. In that sense policy capacity is generated for the legislature and for the government as a whole, since the policy process is able to extend and expand toward objectives perhaps otherwise proscribed. If, on the other hand, the electoral system creates a fundamentally ill-attuned legislative coalition, the capacity for performance is substantially reduced, and governmental power is lessened because governmental authority has been lessened. Authority means more than popularity. An unpopular coalition is lessened in its capacity by its inability to mobilize popular organizational support as well as popular acceptance. Insofar as the government has fewer active supporters in the population, force is required to gain its way, and there are fewer willing in the population to identify actively with the state. The end result is an approach to the politics of system survival and a movement away from the politics of system maintenance and of course systemic innovation. The effort expended in forced acceptability is further reductive of the available capacity of government. In these terms it can be argued that a well aligned electoral system and society produce a government able to expand its power and influence, an improperly aligned system reduces that capacity.

Further Suggested Readings

Duverger, Maurice. "The Influence of Electoral Systems on Political Life," *International Social Science Bulletin,* 3 (Summer 1951), 342–70.

Institute of Electoral Research. *A Review of Elections.* London Annual.

LaPonce, J.A. "The Protection of Minorities by the Electoral System," *Western Political Quarterly,* 10 (June 1957), 338–49.

Mackenzie, W.J.M. *Free Elections.* New York: Rinehart, 1958.

————. "Representation in Plural Societies," *Political Studies,* 12 (February 1964), 54–69.

McDonald, Ronald. "Electoral Systems, Party Representation and Political Change in Latin America," *Western Political Quarterly,* 20 (1967), 694–708.

Merkl, Peter. "Political Cleavages and Party Systems," *World Politics,* 21 (April 1969), 469–85.

Rae, Douglas. *The Political Consequences of Electoral Laws.* New Haven: Yale University Press, 1967.

Rokkan, Stein. "Electoral Mobilization, Party Competition and National Integration." In *Political Parties and Political Development,* edited by J. LaPalombara and M. Weiner, pp. 241–66. Princeton: Princeton University Press, 1966.

Rustow, Dankwart. "Some Observations of Proportional Representation," *Journal of Politics,* 12 (February 1950), 107–27.

5

Comparative Interest Groups

Introduction

The political science literature on political groups is as enormous as it is limited in its application to comparative politics. Its greatest pretension is any claim that it constitutes a theory of politics. That is to say, all politics are to be understood in terms of the interaction and competition of existing political groups or so-called potential groups.[1] As noted in our introductory chapter, the so-called group approach to politics was a direct consequence of the normative concern with political pluralism. As such it is especially ethnocentric, so American in its inspiration that there are even doubts of its appropriateness to the study of European politics.[2] It is useful, therefore, to make a distinction between a group theory of politics on the one hand and the more limited empirical study of interest groups on the other.

The concept of interest groups has about it some of the pluralistic biases of the more general approach but it is at least more specific and empirical in its orientation. The idea of interest group is tied closely to the modernization process. As the economic division of labor develops, various secondary groups (as opposed to such primary ones as family and clan) grow up around new economic processes and political institutions such as labor, industry, bureaucracy, and the military. Much of the concern with interest groups first arose in the American political system because of the abuses of these groups in the political process, among them, the Anti-Saloon League, Standard Oil, and the American Medical Association. As a result, until fairly recently this literature had devoted little attention to interest groups in non-American research situations. The promise that this approach seemed to hold for comparative politics is well evidenced in the Social Science Research Council report included among our readings. An amendment to the sanguineness of the report appeared shortly by one of its authors.

1. For the main exponents of groups as a theory of politics, see the works by Bentley, the pioneer of this approach, and Truman, cited in the Suggestions for Further Reading at the end of this chapter.

2. Joseph LaPalombara, "The Utility and Limitations of Interest Groups Theory in Non-American Field Situations," *Journal of Politics*, 23 (February 1960), 34.

LaPalombara indicated (1) the inappropriateness of the general group ap-proach for non-American field research, and (2) the qualifications one must introduce even when the approach is narrowed to a concern with interest groups *per se*. In his estimation, the political significance of interest groups must go beyond their simple presence to the larger consideration of the context within which they occur. It is only then that the determination can be made as to whether or not a given political outcome is the result of interest group activity or some other factor like family or class or, in Italy, sub-cultural groupings such as Catholic, and Northern or Southern regions.[3]

The important evidence that interest groups are not merely the product of liberal democratic systems is found in the article by Schwartz and Keech detailing the operation of interest groups within the Soviet Union and its authoritarian (sometimes termed totalitarian) form of rule. Schwartz and Keech's analysis suggests the conclusion that interest groups are a corollary of industrialization. Thus the less industrialized states, especially of Africa and Asia, are not likely to give much evidence either of the existence of such groups or their importance. In short, the concept of interest group is perhaps like many in political science, namely it should compel us to notice its presence but not expect its presence to be self-explanatory. Explanation remains something to be done in a more total and configurative fashion. One part of this effort at determining the context within which such groups operate is that we will want to determine whether there are linkages of interest groups to political parties and, if so, their nature and strength. The answer to this question is full of implications for the overall integration of the political system, especially, for example, in the case of single-party systems where weak linkage to the party sometimes provides organizational opportunities for independent political influence or even opposition.

3. *Ibid., passim.*

The Comparative Study of Interest Groups

A Comparative Study of Interest Groups and the Political Process

Gabriel A. Almond

The first research planning session of the Committee on Comparative Poli-tics of the Social Science Research Council was held on April 5–10, 1957 at the Center for Advanced Study of the Behavior Sciences at Stanford,

Reprinted from American Political Science Review, *LII (March 1958), 270–282, by special permission of the author and the publisher.*

California. The participants included some of the recipients of SSRC grants for field studies of political groups, as well as a number of other scholars planning field research on these problems.[1] The purpose of the Committee in sponsoring planning sessions among its grantees and other interested scholars is to enhance the cumulative value of research efforts now under way or planned for the near future. As a result of the SSRC program, as well as of a number of other organized and individual efforts, we can anticipate in a few years an extensive monographic literature dealing with political groups and processes in a great many foreign countries and a variety of different culture areas. Systematic information on this scale may not only fill in "areas of ignorance," but offer an opportunity for significant advances in the general theory of politics. Our present theories of interest groups, political parties, and public opinion are based on American and to a lesser extent European experience. We can now look forward to a situation in the near future in which theories of interest groups, parties, and public opinion can be built up on the basis of a rich collection of intensive studies.

The likelihood of a significant theoretical product resulting from this fairly large group of individual efforts may be enhanced by the discussion of hypotheses and research approaches prior to field work, as well as by the pooling and exchanging of information and hypotheses during the course of research and the subsequent analysis. The purpose of the five-day planning session at Palo Alto was to explore the possibilities of agreement about research objectives and methods, and to codify the conclusions of the participants in the form of a research program statement. The planning session proceeded by plenary discussions and the presentation of specific reports by work groups concerned with special problems. The conclusions reached in the general discussions and the reports of the work groups are summarized in the present statement. The topics discussed during the session were as follows: (1) the general objectives of the comparative study of interest groups; (2) general description of the interest group system; (3) the selection of specific interest groups; (4) interest groups and public opinion; (5) interest groups and political parties; (6) interest groups and the legislature; (7) interest groups and the bureaucracy; and (8) the inclusion of non-Western countries in the comparative study.

1. The personnel of the session and the areas represented were as follows: France, Henry Ehrmann, University of Colorado; United Kingdom, Leon Epstein, University of Wisconsin; Germany, Sigmund Neumann, Wesleyan University and Gabriel A. Almond, Princeton University; Italy, Joseph LaPalombara, Michigan State University; Belgium, Val Lorwin, University of Oregon; Spain, Juan Linz, University of California (Berkeley); Burma, Lucian W. Pye, Massachusetts Institute of Technology; India, Myron Weiner, University of Chicago; Latin America, George Blanksten, Northwestern University and Bryce Wood, Social Science Research Council.

I. THE GENERAL OBJECTIVES

Comparative analyses of political institutions have thus far been confined to formal governmental institutions, and to political party and electoral systems. Dissatisfaction with these formal comparisons is widespread in view of the generally appreciated fact that formally similar governmental and party systems often function in radically different ways. And the search for explanation of the formally similar but differently functioning political systems has turned to vague residual categories such as "social structure," "national character," "consensus" or its absence, and "public opinion." In Duverger's study of political parties he concluded:

> The development of parties has burst the bonds of the old political categories inspired by Aristotle and Montesquieu. The classic contrast between parliamentary, presidential, and National Convention regimes can henceforth no longer serve as the pivot for modern constitutional law. Kemalist Turkey, Soviet Russia, and Hitler Germany were profoundly similar because each was a single-party state, although the first practised the National Convention regime, the second a semi-parliamentary regime, and the third a semi-presidential regime. In spite of their common attachment to the parliamentary regime, Great Britain and the Dominions, under a two-party system, are profoundly dissimilar from Continental countries under a multi-partist system, and in certain respects are much closer to the United States in spite of its presidential regime. In fact the distinction between single-party, two-party, and multi-party systems tends to become the fundamental mode of classifying contemporary regimes.[2]

In Duverger's subsequent remarks it becomes clear that even his distinctions between single-party, two-party and multi-party systems are inadequate as principles of explanation of the functioning of political systems. He and other scholars have noted the fact that the multi-party systems of France and Italy differ from those of the Scandinavian and Low Countries, and that the one-party system of Spain is rather different from those of Russia and Nazi Germany. To understand the differences between the multi-party systems of France and Italy and those of the Scandinavian countries we would have to look "below" the levels of the party systems into the "interest group" systems of these countries and into basic popular attitudes toward political authority, partisanship, and interest—their "political cultures" in other words. The differences between the one-party regimes of countries such as the Soviet Union and Nazi Germany on the one hand and Spain on the other are to be accounted for largely by the different goals and practices of the groups controlling the authoritative governmental institutions.

In our search for types of polities and the principles governing their

2. Maurice Duverger, *Political Parties* (New York, 1954), pp. 392–93.

behavior it would be a mistake simply to go one or two steps beyond Duverger, and say not the party system, but the interest groups and political culture ". . . become the fundamental mode of classifying contemporary regimes." The mistake arises out of the search for some single "crucial institution" or principle of explanation. In other words we turn to the comparative study of interest groups not with the hope that these rather than parties or governmental institutions will yield *the principles* of discrimination between types of political systems, but rather with the expectation that the systematic examination of interest groups in their complex interrelations with public opinion, political parties and formal governmental institutions will enable us to differentiate more accurately between political systems as *wholes*. In other words, the growing concern among scholars with interest groups and public opinion is the consequence of a search for a more complete and systematic conception of the political process as a whole, rather than a search for an approach which is an *alternative* to the present emphasis on formal governmental institutions.

As Truman[3] and other scholars have pointed out, interest groups may be articulate or inarticulate, manifest or latent, formally organized, or simply a condition of like-mindedness and informal communication about issues. A comparison of Western and non-Western political systems brings out sharply the "latency" of the typical non-Western political system in contrast to the overtness of Western politics.[4] How different are the problems of public policy-making in a society where there are no effective mechanisms for the articulation of political demands, from one in which there is an elaborate set of structures for the formulation of demands, and the transmission of these demands into the party and governmental systems? The kinds of interest groups which are present in a society, the specificity or diffuseness of their demands, their conceptions of the political arena and of the "rules of the game," the ethos which they bring with them into the political process—these are the "raw materials" of politics—the unaggregated demands—which some set of mechanisms must transform into political personnel and public policy.

These general observations about interest groups not only suggest their importance as a subject of study, but set certain specifications in research design if the maximum value of a comparative study is to be attained. A good research job on interest groups in a particular country which may make possible meaningful comparisons with other countries, must examine the interest group system in its relations with the social structure and culture on the one hand and the other parts of the political structure on the other. In identifying the interest group system in any particular country this broad functional approach will prevent us from identifying interest groups with

3. David B. Truman, *The Governmental Process* (New York, 1951), pp. 14ff.

4. Lucian W. Pye, *Guerrilla Communism in Malaya* (Princeton, N.J., 1956), pp. 346ff.

any particular kind of structure. The function of articulating and transmitting group interests may be performed in one system typically by the well organized and bureaucratized "pressure groups" familiar in the West, or it may be performed in another system typically through an informal and intermittent process of communication between and among class and status groups such as large landholders or businessmen, and cliques of bureaucrats and/or army officers. If it is possible to state the theme of the comparative study in the form of a single question it might be: What form does the articulation of political interests take in various societies, and how are these interests transmitted to other parts of the political and governmental structure, and translated into choices of political personnel and public policy?

II. THE GENERAL DESCRIPTION OF THE INTEREST GROUP SYSTEM

It was the general conclusion of the planning session that each of the participants in the comparative study would attempt a general survey of the system of interest groups in his country, describing the kinds of interest groups which are present, their membership size in relation to potential, their financial resources, activities, patterns of coalition and interaction among them, and internal patterns of organization and decision-making. The usefulness of such a descriptive census was defended on the ground that many of the most significant differences among interest group systems will come out sharply through such description. Thus, three of the distinguishing characteristics of American interest groups—the large number of civic and ethnic interest groups, and the relatively high degree of membership participation in decision-making within interest groups—would come out clearly in such a comparative description. A comparison of the structure, the membership and the financial resources of the trade unions on the European continent will tell us a great deal about the differences between the political systems of France and Italy as compared with Germany, the United Kingdom, the Low Countries, and the Scandinavian countries. The predominance of functionally specific, bureaucratized, associational types of interest groups in the West, and of kinship groups, status groups, and of informal cliques in the non-Western areas is one of the most crucial distinctions between these types of political systems. Again the clearer distinction between the functions of parties and interest groups in the United States, the United Kingdom and the Commonwealth, than obtains on the European continent and the non-Western areas, is a major clue to the special properties of Anglo-American politics.

The planning session was in full agreement on the desirability of such a general survey and appraisal of the interest group system as a whole. At the same time the discussion pointed up clearly the radically different conditions of research in the areas represented which might make such a general survey a full-time problem in one area, and an easier task in another.

For example, in a country such as Germany, the high degree of formal organization of interest groups, the availability of directories, of interest group publications, and of monographic studies by German scholars, would make such a survey a relatively simple problem and quite consistent with a major allocation of research time to the characteristics and functioning of a limited number of selected groups. In India on the other hand even an attempt at an accurate survey of the kinds and characteristics of interest groups might very well constitute a full-time research operation. Even on the European continent the search for comprehensiveness of coverage and accuracy of detail in some countries might seriously conflict with other research purposes.

A review of the range of problems which might confront the participants in the comparative study in making such general surveys and appraisals led the group to the conclusion that these would in every case be ranked as a research goal, secondary to the more intensive analyses of the characteristics of specific, selected interest groups. They would be carried on primarily as a by-product of the documentary research and interviewing programs of the participants. It was recognized that this would make some of these general appraisals less well documented and more speculative than others. It was also agreed that the general descriptive material gained from such surveys, and the general hypotheses about the characteristics of interest group systems as wholes, would be reported by each participant in the form of a general introductory chapter or chapters in his monographic report. It was also agreed that these general appraisal chapters would be exchanged by the participants as early as possible in order to have included in the individual country studies propositions about similarities and differences between the interest groups of the particular country studied and those of the other countries.

III. The Selection of Specific Interest Groups

While all the participants in the planning session had expressed the intention of studying interest groups in their particular countries, considerable variation emerged in the kind of group or groups which had been selected for emphasis. The original preferences were based on prior research interests and the salience of particular kinds of groups in the countries studied. The planning session brought out the point that while the choice of group or groups differed from one country to the next, all the studies had in common a concern with the political function of articulating and transmitting demands into the political process. The different choices of types of groups was largely due to the fact that different kinds of interest groups performed these functions in the various countries. Thus in the Western European countries, the job of translating the interests of different segments of the society into political demands, and bringing these demands to bear in the policy-making process was largely performed by the trade union movements, the agricultural federations, business groups and trade associations, and church groups of one kind or another. On the other hand, in Asia, the Middle East and Latin America two major classes of interest groups were in operation, one typical of the more modern, industrialized and westernized sectors of these societies, and the other typical of that part of the society less affected by change. Hence, a study of interest groups in the non-Western countries would have to sample both the older and the newer types of structures. It would have to look into the activities of the emerging trade union, business, and student movements in the modernized, primarily urban parts of these societies, and the status groups, kinship and lineage, religious and ethnic groups of the village and the countryside. The problem of interest group research in these areas is not only that of describing the characteristics and functioning of these two types of interest group systems, but also examining their relations with one another.

In the course of the discussions it was agreed that, while each participant might give greater emphasis to research on a particular class of groups, some attention would be given to the activities of the other significant groups. The argument here was that a study which, for example, concentrated on the political activities of trade unions would be incomplete without some attention to business groups and trade associations, agricultural organizations, and religious groups. Hence, those concerned with the European countries agreed that some attention would be paid to each of the major classes of interests. Specific decisions about the allocation of emphasis and methods would have to be made by the researcher in the field, in the light of the availability of information, the relative importance of these groups, and his special interests. Those concerned with the non-Western areas agreed on the desirability of sampling the "modern, urban" type of interest groups, the interests operating within governmental agencies including the army, and the traditional groupings. Here again the specific selections would have to take into account the special characteristics of the political system in the area, as well as the conditions of research.

The general conclusion was that by being concerned with the "function" of interest in the political process, rather than certain kinds of structures, and by being concerned with sampling the interest group universe, a significant step toward comparability and cumulativeness of theory would be accomplished.

IV. INTEREST GROUPS AND PUBLIC OPINION[5]

One of the most challenging opportunities presented by the comparative study was that of systematically introducing public opinion data into the study of political interests. One of the central problems in interest

5. This discussion was led by Seymour M. Lipset of the University of California and Gabriel A. Almond, Princeton University.

group theory is the relation between manifest and latent interest. To what extent can organized, overt interests be taken as reflecting the interest tendencies of the general population? The phenomena of the mob in non-Western countries, of riots in totalitarian countries, of "Caesarism," "Poujadism," and "incivisme," in the European area suggest that popular attitudes and tendencies are a separable factor in the political process, the properties of which cannot be inferred from the existing organized tendencies and from electoral behavior. Any characterization of a political system would be incomplete if it was confined solely to a description of current organizational patterns and processes. Latent interest may not only result in future changes in organization and process, it establishes an atmosphere which affects the contemporary operations of the political process.

It was agreed that the relations between interest groups and public opinion would be an important dimension of the comparative study. One of the main, but by no means the only, source of information about public opinion, would be the accumulations of public opinion data available in many of the European countries. In the course of the discussions of the kinds of polling material which were available it became clear that while there was much that might be useful there was relatively little that dealt directly with the problems of legitimacy and consensus, that is, popular attitudes toward governmental authority, and the attitudes of groups in the population toward one another. Thus, certain basic hypotheses about the relations between the condition of political opinion and the functioning of political systems in the European area had never been directly investigated, but were now in the form of inferences from the behavior of groups and institutions. The question put before the session was: Would it be possible through a survey of comparative political opinion to establish (1) that the British political process with its moderate interest groups, and its effectively functioning two-party system, is related to a homogeneous, secular, and loyal public opinion; (2) that the French and Italian political processes with their fragmented party and interest group systems, are related to fragmented, only partly secularized, and largely alienated political cultures; and (3) that the political systems of the Scandinavian and Low Countries with their "working multi-party systems," and their relatively moderate interest group systems were related to political communities in which the "consensual bond" was stronger than in France and Italy, and in which the great majority of the population viewed governmental authority as having a useful and constructive function in relation to their interests?

All the participants agreed to examine the accumulations of public opinion data in their countries and to use whatever information they could get from these sources on attitudes toward interest, party, and state. In addition they agreed to consult and advise in the planning and execution of a comparative opinion survey which might deal more directly with these phenomena, if such a survey should be undertaken as a part of the program.

A second aspect of the relations between interest groups and public opinion was discussed, the propaganda and information activities of interest groups. The ways in which interest groups conceive of their audiences, and the ways in which they represent their interests to the public should throw light on the functioning of the political system as a whole. For example, French business associations are different from the American in that they do not engage openly and on a large scale in public "informational" activities. This may reflect a general condition of fragmentation in political communication in France, a condition of distrust and alienation among interests. The general proposition was advanced that certain patterns of interest communications activity are associated with certain basic conditions of the political community.

It was agreed that the "public relations" of interest groups would be examined with the following questions in mind: (1) How does the interest group conceive of its audience? (2) How is the public relations function organized and what is the magnitude of the public relations effort? (3) How are interest groups related to the specialized communications system of the society (*e.g.*, press, radio, educational system and the like)?

V. INTEREST GROUPS AND POLITICAL PARTIES[6]

In the discussions and conferences of the Committee on Comparative Politics over the last three years, and in papers prepared by Committee members and other participants in the Committee's work, the broad outlines of a theory of comparative political systems have slowly developed.[7] In part, this theory has been concerned with the development of models of the various forms of the political process in existence today. During the planning sessions in Palo Alto these models were again discussed; they influenced much of the research design which is reported below. It may be useful to summarize these characterizations of the Anglo-American systems, the

6. The report on this topic was presented by Sigmund Neumann of Wesleyan University and Val Lorwin of the University of Oregon.

7. Kahin, Pauker, Pye, "Comparative Politics of Non-Western Countries," this *Review* [*American Political Science Review*] (Dec., 1955), pp. 1022ff.; Almond, Cole, Macridis, "A Suggested Research Strategy in Western European Government and Politics," *ibid.*, pp. 1042ff.; Almond, "Comparative Political Systems," *Journal of Politics* (August, 1956), pp. 391ff.; Francis X. Sutton, "Social Theory and Comparative Politics," (unpublished paper); Samuel H. Beer, "Pressure Groups and Parties in Britain," this *Review* (March, 1956), pp. 1ff.; Dankwart Rustow, *Politics and Westernization in the Near East,* Center of International Studies, Princeton University, March, 1956; Rustow, "New Horizons for Comparative Politics," *World Politics* (July, 1957); Sigmund Neumann, "Comparative Politics, A Half Century Appraisal," *Journal of Politics* (August, 1957); Gabriel Almond and Myron Weiner, "A Comparative Approach to the Study of Political Groups," Agenda Paper for the Dobbs Ferry Seminar of the Committee on Comparative Politics, June, 1956.

varieties of non-Western political systems, the French-Italian "crisis" system, and the "working multi-party" systems of the Scandinavian and the Low Countries.

In the Anglo-American type of political system the functions of political parties and interest groups are sharply differentiated. Interest groups articulate political demands in the society, seek support for these demands among other groups by advocacy and bargaining, and attempt to transform these demands into authoritative public policy by influencing the choice of political personnel, and the various processes of public policy-making and enforcement. Political parties tend to be free of ideological rigidity, and are aggregative, *i.e.*, seek to form the largest possible interest group coalitions by offering acceptable choices of political personnel and public policy. Both the interest group systems and the party systems are differentiated, bureaucratized, and autonomous. Each unit in the party and interest group systems comes into the "market," so to speak, with an adjustive bargaining ethos. Furthermore, the party system stands between the interest group system and the authoritative policy-making agencies and screens them from the particularistic and disintegrative impact of special interests. The party system aggregates interests and transforms them into a relatively small number of alternative general policies. Thus this set of relationships between the party system and the interest group system enables choice among general policies to take place in the legislature, and assures that the bureaucracy will tend to function as a neutral instrument of the political agencies.

We might take as our second type a model summarizing the properties of the political systems which are to be found in Asia, the Middle East and Latin America in which neither parties nor interest groups are fully differentiated. Associational interest groups such as trade unions and business associations may exist in the urban Westernized parts of the society, but in the village and the countryside interest organization takes the form of lineage, caste, status, class and religious groups, which transmit political demands to the other parts of the political structure by means of informal communication. In one version of this class of systems parties tend to be *ad hoc* coalitions without permanent bureaucracies, and without grass roots organization. They exist primarily in election periods and in effect cease to exist in the intervals between. Given such weak and non-aggregative party systems the capacity of the legislatures to formulate alternative policy choices may be seriously impaired, as is their capacity to control the bureaucracies. In many of these political systems the significant political groups are neither the parties, nor the associational interest groups, but elements or cliques within the bureaucracy, and the army; and cliques, informal groupings and powerful families formed within such non-associational interests as religious communities, the large landowners, the business community, and the like. The political process consists of the informal communication and flow of influence between these informally organized interests, and groups within the bureaucracy and the army.

The instabilities of this type of political system arise out of the fact that the agencies for the articulation, communication, and aggregation of interests are incomplete and unrepresentative, as well as out of the fact that the demands transmitted into the political system from interest groups are vague, diffuse, and of radically unlike content and intensity. Latent interests, lacking overt and organized channels of expression may suddenly break into the political arena. The information available to influential groups and individuals about the expectations and attitudes of the various interests in the society cannot be complete or accurate. Hence, calculation is impossible, and the flow of political interaction involves under-reaction and over-reaction, violence and apathy, alternations of periods of political latency, with sudden and violent shifts in power.

Given the basic instability of this general class of political systems, authoritarian stabilizations are a frequent event. Indeed, in many of them the developmental pattern is one of a shift from an unstable pluralism to authoritarianism, and then back again, or a shift from the authoritarianism of one clique to that of another. Authoritarianism may be based on control of the army either by a clique of army officers, or a clique of bureaucrats controlling the army, or by a coalition of both. Still another pattern is one in which the desire on the part of a controlling group to secure its own power and destroy opposition, or to mobilize the society for industrialization and national expansion, leads to the formation of an authoritarian party which actually penetrates the countryside. In some cases as in Turkey and in India the objectives of the ruling groups and of the dominant party are tutelary. That is, the function of the party is not only control and mobilization, but also political acculturation, the preparation of the ground for the emergence of a Western-type associational system and of a Western-type party system with a coherent, responsible, and loyal opposition.

Thus, it should be quite clear that there are many kinds of non-Western political systems. They all appear to have in common (1) a fragmented political culture as a consequence of Westernization, in many cases added on to an indigenous cultural heterogeneity, (2) poor political communications and a high degree of interest latency which renders political calculation difficult if not impossible, and (3) a party system which is incapable of aggregating and synthesizing interest demands into a small number of political alternatives either of personnel or of public policy. On a scale of political differentiation one would have to say that certain kinds of structures such as associational interest groups, the mass media of communication, and the kind of party system common in the West and essential for the functioning of a modern mass-suffrage parliamentary system, are present at best in only a limited degree. On a scale of functional specialization one would have to say that in the absence of fully developed associational interest groups, party systems, and modern media of communication, the functions of interest articulation, aggregation, communication and transmission are largely performed by bureaucratic or army cliques, traditional structures such as lineage or status groupings, and by mobs, street demonstrations and the like, which serve as one of the agencies by means of which latent interests are articulated and transmitted.

A third type of political system is exemplified by France and Italy and by the Germany of the Weimar Republic. Contemporary Germany appears to be moving in the direction of an autonomous interest group system and an aggregative two-party system; toward the Anglo-American model, in other words. In the French and Italian political systems parties and interest groups are organized and bureaucratized, but they are not autonomous systems. They interpenetrate one another and consequently fail to realize the two-stage pattern of the political process characteristic of the English and American systems. There are some parties which more or less control interest groups (e.g., the Communist party and the Communist-dominated trade unions, and to a lesser extent the Socialist parties and the Socialist trade unions). There are some interest groups which more or less control other interest groups and parties (e.g., the Church, the Catholic trade unions, and the Catholic parties, business interest groups, and the center and right wing parties, and the like).

When parties control interest groups they inhibit the capacity of interest groups to formulate pragmatic specific demands; they impart a political-ideological content to interest group activity. When interest groups control parties they inhibit the capacity of the party to combine specific interests into programs with wider appeal. What reaches the legislative process from the interest groups and through the political parties thus are the "raw," un-aggregated demands of specific interests or the diffuse, uncompromising, or revolutionary tendencies of the Church and the movements of the extreme right or left. Since no interest group is large enough to have a majority, and the party system cannot aggregate different interests into a stable majority and a coherent opposition, the electoral and legislative processes fail to provide alternative, effective choices. The result is a legislature penetrated by relatively narrow interests and uncompromising ideological tendencies, a legislature which can be used as an arena for propaganda, or for the protection of special interests, by veto or otherwise, but not for the effective and timely formulation and support of large policy decisions. And without a strong legislature, special interests and ideological tendencies penetrate the bureaucracy, and undermine its neutral, instrumental character.

A fourth type of political system is exemplified by the Scandinavian and Low Countries. These systems appear to differ from the French and Italian in two respects. First, the party systems tend to be aggregative (e.g., the Scandinavian Socialist parties, the Belgian Socialist and Catholic parties). Second, the relations between parties and interests appear to be more consensual, which makes stable majority and opposition coalitions possible. Thus, though the party systems fail to aggregate interests as thoroughly as in the British case, the public policy-making function of the legislature is not undermined to the same extent as in the French and Italian cases. What appears to happen in the Scandinavian and the Low Countries is that the function of interest aggregation and general policy formulation occurs at both the party and parliamentary levels. The parties are partly aggregative of interests, but "majority-minority" aggregation takes place finally in the coalition-making process in the legislature. This coalition-making process may be organized by parties in the formation of cabinets and the enactment of legislation or it may take the form of interest coalitions organized around issues of public policy. The capacity for stable majority-minority party coalitions and for relatively flexible issue-oriented interest coalitions is dependent upon the existence of a basic political consensus which affects both parties and interest groups. These appear to be the properties of the so-called "working multi-party systems."[8]

These simplified models of political systems represent some of the general theory of political groups shared by the participants in the planning session. It represents a set of hypotheses about the characteristics and consequences of the main types of interest group systems to be found in the countries in which field research is planned. The problem of research tactics, of how to test, elaborate, and develop our theories further remains to be specified.

The discussion stressed that the relation between political parties and interest groups could be viewed as a continuum with substantial autonomy at one limit and sub- and super-ordination at the other. The relationship patterns which exist in historical political systems always involve two-way flows of influence, which differ from one another in the dominant direction of the flow and the different patterns which are occasioned by different kinds of issues. Thus the extreme case of the Communist Party-Communist trade union dominance still involves a flow of information and influence from trade union to party, but the dominant direction of the flow is from party to trade union. In the case of the church and Catholic parties the flow of influence varies from country to country, and even among regions within countries. In addition, in certain areas of policy Catholic parties may be relatively free of church influence, or may even influence the church to take a position consistent with or supportive of that of the party. In Germany, for example, the fact that the CDU has both Protestant and Catholic support seriously limits the power of the Catholic church to intervene in party policy-making. In other legislative fields, the freedom of Catholic parties may be sharply circumscribed by a rigid church position, as in the field of educational subsidies and the like. In other policy areas, *e.g.,* social-economic, there may be more give and take in the relations between church and Catholic party.

These considerations suggested that analysis of the flow of influence be-

8. See Dankwart Rustow, "Scandinavia: Working Multi-party Systems," in Sigmund Neumann (Ed.), *Modern Political Parties* (Chicago, 1956), pp. 169ff.

tween parties and interest groups would require not only an examination of the interconnections through financing, interlocking memberships and directorates, sharing of ideological beliefs and the like, but would also require a judicious use of case study methods to discover the way in which different kinds of legislative issues affected the flow and pattern of influence between interest groups and parties.

It was generally agreed that a first task in analyzing parties and interest group relationships would involve a study of the history of these organizations and of their interrelations. In some cases parties formed or were influential in the forming of interest groups (*e.g.*, the Communists and the "Red Unions," the Socialists and the *Force Ouvrière*); in many others interest groups formed or influenced the formation of parties (*e.g.*, some labor parties by trade unions, Catholic parties by the church and/or elements of Catholic Action, and agrarian parties by agrarian interest groups). Whatever the history of the relationship may be, it will provide an important body of evidence on the relationship between the two and changes in the relationship through time.

A second major research task would involve a careful analysis of the structure, internal politics, activities, and ideologies of specific interest groups and parties as they relate to the flow of influence. (1) What is the relative financial strength of interest group and party? To what extent does the interest group finance the party, or *vice versa?* What is the special pattern of election financing? (2) What is their relative manpower potential? *E.g.*, does the party depend on the interest group for personnel during elections as is the case for Catholic and labor parties, or does it have a manpower reserve of its own? (3) What is the relative effectiveness of the grass roots organizations of parties and interest groups? *E.g.*, is the party organized primarily at the center and dependent on interest groups for the penetration of local areas, or does the party have an autonomous local organization of its own? (4) To what extent is there overlapping in membership and officers as between interest group and party? (5) What are the factional and ideological characteristics of interest groups and parties, and how do they affect the pattern of influence?

VI. INTEREST GROUPS AND THE LEGISLATIVE PROCESS[9]

Interest groups tend to seek out the important points of access in the legislative process; the points where legislative policy is initiated, and where revision, vetoing, and favorable action are possible. Hence, the constitutional separation and distribution of powers, legislative organization and procedure, the characteristics of the electoral system and the parliamentary

9. The report to the planning session on this topic was presented by Leon Epstein and Henry Ehrmann.

party organization, set the problem of interest group access in the legislative process. Thus, the American system of federalism, and separation of powers, creates a different interest group "target structure" than does the British parliamentary-cabinet system. The American federal system produces a party structure with its center of gravity at the state level. This kind of decentralized party organization limits the possibilities of congressional party discipline and hence opens the legislative process to interest group penetration. The susceptibility of the legislature to interest group penetration is enhanced by the American single-member district electoral system which frequently exposes the legislator to the effective pressure of interests which may be especially concentrated in his constituency. In addition, the American separation of powers system grants a powerful and independent role in legislation to both the House and Senate. And since relatively large collegial bodies are, other things being equal, less able to aggregate interests and protect themselves against interest penetration than Cabinet-dominated parliaments, this aspect of American constitutional structure contributes significantly to interest group action in the legislative process. If we consider this constitutional and statutory structure on the one hand, and the economic, regional, ethnic, and religious composition of the American population on the other, it is hardly surprising that the penetration of the legislative process by interest groups in the United States is greater than in the United Kingdom. There, a unitary constitution, and a Cabinet-dominated parliament make possible a disciplined parliamentary party system which protects the legislative process from effective interest group penetration. The main targets of interest groups are the upper levels of the parliamentary and extra-parliamentary party structure where power is concentrated, and the bureaucracy. And because of the cohesion of the party system and the concentration of legislative power in the Cabinet, the impact of any single interest group—with the exception of the trade unions—is quite limited.

France presents yet another problem of interest group access. In the United States aggregation and synthesis of interests is performed by the party system and a powerful presidency responsible to a national constituency. France has neither a powerful executive nor an aggregative party system. A culturally and politically fragmented society choosing its legislators by means of proportional representation produces a legislature capable of producing only weak and unstable coalitions. The standing committees of the *Assemblée* are in many cases colonized by powerful interests.[10] The net effect of this situation is a legislative process which can only rarely enact significant "national-interest" legislation, but which regularly and characteristically protects and subsidizes special interests. Still a fourth type of legislative interest group pattern is to be found in the Scandinavian

10. Henry W. Ehrmann, *Organized Business in France* (Princeton, Princeton University Press, 1957), ch. V.

countries where a stronger executive and a more aggregative party system limits the impact of interest groups in the legislative process.

These characteristics of constitutional, legislative, and party structures affect not only the tactics of interest groups, but the very goals and objectives which they can reasonably attain. A disciplined party system and a powerful executive force interest groups to direct their energies to the upper levels of the executive and the bureaucracy where only moderate claims, well supported with technical information, become possible. A non-aggregative and undisciplined party system as in France opens up the legislative process to covert interest group domination of legislative committees and agencies, or to propagandistic interest group maneuvers of which "Poujadism" is only an extreme instance.

These hypotheses about patterns of interest-group-legislative relations in the European area suggest the importance of a careful analysis of the functioning of the constitutional, legislative, electoral, and party systems as they relate to interest group access. In other words, the aim of research in interest-group-legislative relations will be to determine the extent to which the parliamentary parties, or extra-parliamentary legislative institutions such as the American Presidency, are able to maintain independence of interest groups and relative freedom to legislate or influence legislation (a) by combining several interest groups in their support, and (b) by establishing and maintaining the discipline of the parliamentary party as a means of withstanding interest group pressures.

The discussions in the planning session turned on the question of how to test these hypotheses economically and effectively. It was agreed that research here would concentrate on four problems.

1. The first of these is the analysis of the "target structure" itself. This would involve an examination of the distribution and location of legislative power as between the parliament, the executive, and the bureaucracy; the internal organization and procedure of the parliament; the organization and operations of the party system in the parliament; and the effect of the electoral system on the party system and on the position of the individual parliamentarian. This phase of research would also include an examination of the various devices for formal interest group representation such as "economic councils" and advisory committees and groups of one kind or another.

2. Closely related to this first task is a study of how interest groups perceive and appraise the "target structure" of the legislative process. Such analysis would bring out significant differences between the interest groups in particular countries as well as between countries. If our general impressions are correct we would expect to find that British interest groups would share the same picture of legislative reality, and that it would tend to be a relatively accurate picture. In France, we would expect to find quite different conceptions of constitutional and legislative reality among interest groups. Thus, the different pictures of constitutional reality characteristic

of the church and the Communist trade unions would be the consequence of basically different ideological presuppositions and political experience. The C.G.T. would view the French legislative process as incapable of realizing working class objectives. Consequently, their primary objective *vis-à-vis* the French Constitution would be to immobilize it, and to destroy it. The Church, on the other hand, would view the French legislative process as more amenable to pressure through access to the M.R.P. and right-wing parties, and through sympathetic elements in the bureaucracy. In many non-Western countries we would expect to find relatively new and inexperienced interest groups with highly inaccurate or vague pictures of political reality.

3. A third task involves study of the objectives of interest groups in the legislative process. Thus, in the United Kingdom we would expect to find interest groups entertaining moderate, secular objectives in the legislative process, in France we would expect to find interest groups seeking extreme, incompatible, and rigid objectives; in non-Western countries we would expect to find many interest groups seeking "expressive" rather than "instrumental" objectives.

4. A fourth area of study is of the means or techniques employed by interest groups to attain their objectives—what we might call the interest group style. Here, we would be concerned with whether or not the techniques are overt or covert, whether propaganda, negotiation, bribery, or demonstration and riot are the preferred means. In the United Kingdom we would expect to find an overt style, with propaganda, negotiation, and bargaining the favored means of interest groups. In France, we should find that much interest group activity is covert, and that demonstration and bribery occur with some frequency. In many non-Western countries the style of interest groups may be largely covert, and the techniques heavily on the riot, demonstration, and bribery side.

VII. Interest Groups and the Bureaucracy[11]

The ideal of a neutral, instrumental bureaucracy, responsible to the political arm, comes closest to being realized in political systems where the political culture tends to be secular and rational, and where the functions of political choice—that is, the articulation and aggregation of interests and the making of public policy—are performed by specialized agencies. If the interest group system fails to articulate and communicate the demands of significant sectors of the population, or if the political demands which it transmits are irreconcilable, then the capacity of the party system to aggregate and to compromise demands and facilitate political choice in the legislative process is undermined. If the parliament and the "political executive" fail to perform the functions of interest articulation and aggregation,

11. The report on this topic was presented by Juan Linz and Joseph LaPalombara.

then the problem gravitates to the bureaucracy, and its capacity for neutral, responsible administration is weakened. Under these circumstances the bureaucracy tends to be multi-functional. It articulates and aggregates interests, makes public policy and administers it. To be sure the so-called neutral bureaucracies in the West do these same things, but only to a limited extent and under control, and in situations where there are effective political agencies outside the bureaucracy.

For purposes of the planning session four types of interest-group-bureaucracy relationships were discussed. The first of these is illustrated by the situation in the United Kingdom where moderate interest groups, representative of the significant interest tendencies in the population, are aggregated by disciplined parties. Both of these conditions make possible an effective organization of the legislative process, and an effective political control over the bureaucracy. The second is illustrated by the Scandinavian countries where aggregation of interest is less thoroughgoing than in the United Kingdom. In the Scandinavian countries aggregation occurs both in the party system and in the coalition-making process in the parliaments. Nevertheless an effective parliamentary process makes possible a neutral, instrumental bureaucracy. The third type is illustrated by the situation in France where effective aggregation of interests and policy making does not occur in the party system, the parliament or the bureaucracy. The net result is a political system in which the agencies of political choice fail to function, and in which basic policy decisions cannot be made. It tends to be a government of "protection and maintenance" in which the effective agencies are the interest groups and the bureaucracy. The bureaucracy cannot be a neutral, responsible instrument under these circumstances. It is "colonized" by interest groups, and penetrated by incompatible ideological tendencies.

The non-Western areas present a variety of interest-group-bureaucracy relationships. In one quite common pattern parties and associational interest groups are only in their beginnings, and the political process operates primarily within the bureaucracy itself. The bureaucracy is a congeries of interests—family, religious, status, class, professional, ideological, and the like. A bureaucratic or army clique makes informal coalitions of these interests and maintains contact through them with their counterparts outside the bureaucracy. The political process may take the form of an unstable pluralism, or in a second variety, a particular clique or individual may establish authoritarian control and operate with the backing of the army. Another non-Western pattern is one in which an authoritarian party is formed, one of its main functions being to mobilize groups in the society, articulate their interests and bring them to the support of the ruling groups. If the tendency of the authoritarian leadership is conservative, then traditional interests—status, economic, religious—will have favored access to the bureaucracy. If the tendency is toward modernization then urban, professional, industrial and labor interests may have favored access to the bureaucracy, and the traditional interests may be in a disadvantaged position.

The planning sessions agreed on the following specifications for research on interest-group-bureaucracy relationships: (1) Each study would have to appraise the substantive areas of economic and social life affected by the bureaucracy. This would indicate the kinds of interests which were being affected by bureaucratic activity, and the ways in which they are being affected. (2) Each study would have to examine the organizational and influence pattern of the bureaucracy. To what extent and by what means is the bureaucracy controlled by extra-bureaucratic agencies such as the cabinet and/or the parliament? To what extent is the bureaucracy internally cohesive and subject to central control? Or put the other way around, to what extent are specific agencies and sub-agencies independent? Needless to say both the external political and internal control patterns would set some of the problems of access of interest groups to the bureaucracy. (3) What are the characteristics of the members of the bureaucracy—particularly its higher echelons? From what social groups are they recruited? What are the training patterns, and what kinds of skills do they possess? What are their ideological and partisan characteristics? All of these attributes would affect their susceptibility to interest group pressures. (4) What are the goals and tactics of the various interest groups *vis-à-vis* the bureaucracy? Are they primarily concerned with gaining specific family, status group, class, or professional advantages, or do they advocate diffuse ideological objectives, or both? What methods of influence do interest groups employ in relation to the bureaucracy? Is bribery or violence a common pattern? Or is propaganda, negotiation, and the provision of information about the consequences of bureaucratic action for specific interests the typical pattern? (5) To what extent do interest groups actually penetrate the bureaucracy? Here we are not only concerned with formal provision for interest group representation in specific agencies in advisory capacities, or with the special relations between administrative agencies and their particular constituencies (*e.g.,* labor ministries, economic ministries, agriculture ministries, and the like), but also with the direct control over specific bureaucratic functions, in other words the "colonization" of the bureaucracy by interest groups.

VIII. COMPARISON OF WESTERN AND NON-WESTERN INTEREST GROUPS[12]

One of the most challenging questions confronting the planning sessions was the problem of comparing Western and non-Western political systems.

12. Reports on this problem were presented by Myron Weiner, Lucian Pye, George Blanksten and Bryce Wood.

Are they so different in culture and practice as to constitute basically different political species? Was the approach of political science scholarship in the study of Western and non-Western politics so different as to rule out effective collaboration? Did the group participating in the discussions and planning field studies share a common theory of politics which would make collaboration possible? The discussions led to the conclusion that Western and non-Western political systems have much in common, and that the particular group of scholars present shared a common approach and theory of politics.

The basis of this common outlook might be called the "functional" approach. The participants in the comparative study agreed that they were concerned with the functions of political choice, and with the ways in which these functions were performed in different societies. Every independent society makes political choices, *i.e.,* broad policy decisions which are backed up by severe sanctions. In making and enforcing these political decisions all societies have some way of articulating and communicating political demands, aggregating these demands, translating them into choices of political personnel and public policy, executing these decisions in specific cases, and testing the appropriateness of these specific actions. In studying interest groups comparatively the participants in the study are primarily concerned with the structures, institutions and processes by means of which these functions are accomplished. Research conclusions as to which structures and processes perform which functions in different societies, and how they perform them, will provide the basic materials for comparative analysis.

Not only are these functions performed in all independent political systems—Western and non-Western—but the structures and processes which perform them in both areas overlap to a considerable extent. The West is more like the non-West than we sometimes think. Even in the most differentiated and specialized political systems in the West, such interest groups as families, status groups, and religious communities affect the political process. And in most of the non-Western countries—however "underdeveloped"—the beginnings of functionally specialized political parties, and associational interest groups such as trade unions and trade associations, may be found. Even in the field of political communication the highly elaborated mass communication systems of Western societies should not obscure the fact that informal and face-to-face communication is still a political factor of enormous importance.

In still another respect Western and non-Western systems are alike. While it is true in general that Western political structures are more specialized than the non-Western, there is much "multi-functionalism" in the West. Thus in a country such as France political parties and interest groups are not sharply differentiated from one another. And in all countries the structural specialization of policy-making and administration is by no means complete, nor can it ever be complete. If it is peculiar to non-Western countries that bureaucracies are penetrated by interest groups and ideological tendencies, this situation differs only in degree from the Western pattern where rationality, responsibility, and neutrality are only partially realized at best.

The comparative study of interest groups will include a number of cases in Asia and Latin America. In particular it is anticipated that there will be studies of Malaya, Burma, India, and Indonesia in Asia; and of Brazil, Mexico, Cuba, and Peru in Latin America. The non-Western specialists at the planning session agreed to follow much the same pattern as the European specialists. This would include a general appraisal of the kinds of interest groups to be found in these countries, their composition, size, goals, methods of influence, and the like. It would also include more detailed investigations of selected interest groups. These intensive studies are likely to include trade unions, peasant groups, student groups, religious and tribal or ethnic groups. Some attention would be paid to the "mob" as an "anomic" interest group phenomenon, resulting from lack of effective access of some social groupings to politics, and generally poor political communications.

The planning session at Palo Alto was followed by another held in June, 1957 at Michigan State University for a number of scholars about to undertake research on political groups in Latin America. A third is planned for the late Spring in 1958 for recipients of grants for field research on political groups during the present year. By setting common questions and discussing common approaches the Committee on Comparative Politics hopes to introduce greater coherence in the research efforts under way. More recently it has begun to plan a series of comparative analyses which will draw the findings of these and other research efforts together.

Interest Groups and Authoritarian Politics

Group Influence and the Policy
Process in the Soviet Union*

Joel J. Schwartz and William R. Keech

It has become widely recognized that Soviet officials do not formulate public policy in a vacuum, and that, indeed, their deliberations take into account in some fashion the needs and demands of various elements of the society.

The authors wish to express their appreciation to the University of North Carolina Research Council for supporting the research on this subject.

Reprinted from American Political Science Review, *LXII (September 1968), 840–851,* by special permission of the authors and the publisher.

Further, it has been observed that social groups of various types play a noticeable, if only rudimentary role in articulating interests to the top of the hierarchy. In fact one author has gone so far as to assert that communist policy-making results from a "parallelogram of conflicting forces and interests."[1] While such viewpoints are now far more widely accepted than in the early fifties, relatively little effort has been devoted to illustrating or illuminating how Soviet public policy in general or even a given Soviet policy can be importantly affected by group activity.

We propose here to make a contribution in that direction. Using the Educational Reform Act of 1958 as an exemplary case, we intend to show how and through what process groups can affect policy outcomes, and by identifying circumstances under which this takes place to generate some hypotheses about when such influence is most likely to recur. In their excellent analysis of Soviet policy formation, Professors Brzezinski and Huntington identify what they call "policy groups," which come closest of any nongovernmental groups to participating in policy formation. These groups, such as the military, industrial managers, agricultural experts and state bureaucrats

> whose scope of activity is directly dependent on the allocation of national resources and which are directly affected by any shift in the institutional distribution of power, . . . advocate to the political leadership certain courses of action; they have their own professional or specialized newspapers which, at times and subject to overall Party control, can become important vehicles for expressing specific points of view.[2]

In this article we will investigate an instance wherein such groups seemed to influence policy with the result of virtually scuttling one of Khrushchev's own major proposals.

We do not mean to challenge the view that ultimate power in the U.S.S.R. resides at the top of the Communist Party hierarchy. Neither do we mean to infer that the top party leadership was forced by a "policy group" to act against its will. We do not suggest that the instance we cite is modal. Indeed it is the best example we are aware of. We hope that the major payoff in this paper will be in showing why things happened as they did. This is the first step in finding out whether and how often to expect them again.

The first major section of the paper will describe the situation we use as a basis for our speculative analysis about the Soviet decision making process. The second will attempt to explain why things happened as they

1. H. Gordon Skilling, "Interest Groups and Communist Politics," *World Politics*, 18 (April, 1966), p. 449.

2. Zbigniew Brzezinski and Samuel P. Huntington, *Political Power: U.S.A./U.S.S.R.* (New York, 1963), p. 196.

did, and the third will report some hypotheses about when such phenomena are likely to recur.

I. Debate Over the 1958 Act

A prominent feature of post-Stalin Russia has been the nationwide discussion of certain legislative proposals. This does not constitute a totally new innovation in the Soviet Union. During the preceding period such important laws as the constitution of 1936 received nationwide discussion before enactment. A few differences, however, deserve mention. First, the frequency of these discussions has substantially increased. Second and more important, the impact of these discussions on the proposed legislation has in some instances been far more than peripheral. This especially applies to the debate which surrounded the Educational Reform Act of 1958. A closer look at this debate will afford us an opportunity to consider how the opinion of various "publics" can influence the policy process.

There can be little doubt about whose initiative lay behind the proposed reform. At the thirteenth Komsomol Congress in April of 1958, First Party Secretary Khrushchev severely criticized the existing school system and demanded fundamental changes.[3] This attack seems to have been motivated by three problems facing Soviet society in the mid-fifties, the cause of which Khrushchev linked to the existing school system.

First, the Soviet press had unceasingly criticized the denigrative attitudes of the younger generation toward physical labor.[4] In the opinion of the First Secretary, the undue emphasis upon classical academic training and the neglect of the polytechnical side of education were largely responsible for this attitude.

Second, competition for admission to higher education had reached an excessive degree and this likewise had caused great concern among political leaders.[5] The competition itself has largely been a by-product of changes in the economic and educational systems.

Prior to 1950 the rapid growth of the economy and the underdeveloped secondary educational facilities maintained the demand for skilled technical cadres at a higher level than the supply. Throughout this period the number of available places in higher education exceeded the number of secondary

3. Khrushchev's statement can be found in XIII *S"ezd vsesoiuznogo leninskogo kommunisticheskogo souiza molodezhi: stenograficheskii otchet* (Moscow, 1959), pp. 278–282.

4. See, for example, L. Bueva, "Tvorcheskii trud- osnova kommunisticheskogo vospitaniia molodezhi," *Kommunist*, Vol. 37, No. 3 (Feb., 1961), p. 53; and also *Komsomol' skaia pravda*, March 2, 1956; February 10, 1957.

5. See XIII *S'ezd, op. cit.*, p. 280. See also S. Pavlov, "Sovetskaia molodezh' v bor'be za kommunizm," *Kommunist*, Vol. 36, No. 4 (March, 1960), p. 63.

school graduates. The post war years, however, witnessed a remarkable acceleration of secondary school facilities and enrollment. In 1949, out of a total enrollment of thirty-three million pupils only about one million were in grades eight to ten. Four years later the number of pupils in secondary education had risen to four and one half million.[6] Now the annual supply of secondary school graduates greatly exceeded the number of vacancies in higher education. Since the Soviet regime, for reasons of its own, was unwilling to widen the availability of higher education, the gates of universities were closed to millions of youth regardless of their educational attainment.

An inevitable consequence has been the intensification of competition for the available number of places.[7] The pressures for admission became abnormally high because of the widespread notion that a college degree represents the key to individual advancement and entrance into the new class of Soviet intelligentsia. Consequently, those high school graduates initially denied admission refused to accept their fate. Instead of entering the labor force, many of them became perennial college candidates. Very often they applied to schools whose area of specialization was of no genuine interest to them. But in the absence of alternatives they would often enter an agricultural institute just to be able "to study somewhere."[8] Here again Khrushchev charged that the educational system had bred such attitudes. By allowing students to continue their education uninterruptedly and by stressing almost exclusively academic material, the schools naturally generated the expectation that the path to life lay solely through higher education.

The third problem involved the increasing stratification of Soviet society. The notion that higher education was the key to membership in the "new class" had a firm basis in fact. Yet these educational channels for upward social and political mobility were being drastically constricted as a consequence of their preemption by the incumbent political and bureaucratic elites. Khrushchev himself admitted that in the competition for admission to college the influence of parents often proved more important than the merit of the candidates. He further stated that only thirty to forty per cent of the enrolled students in higher education institutions came from worker and peasant backgrounds.[9] The differential access to a prime source of mobility gravely concerned the First Secretary. Both the content and tenor

6. Nicholas DeWitt, *Education and Professional Employment in the USSR* (Washington, 1961), p. 140.

7. In his speech to the XIII Komsomol Congress, Khrushchev noted that "last year higher educational institutions were able to accept 400,000 new students, half of them for full time study. . . . However, at least 700,000 secondary school graduates failed to gain admission last year to higher or technical schools and between 1953–1956 about 2,200,000 failed to gain admission" *XIII S"ezd, op. cit.*, p. 278.

8. *Ibid.*, p. 282.

9. *Pravda,* September 21, 1958.

of his statements clearly indicate that Khrushchev sought to eliminate privilege and inequality from the Soviet educational system.[10]

Finally we should mention an additional factor which *may* have influenced the reform movement. At the time of the debate some western scholars argued that the specifics of Khrushchev's proposals owed much to the serious labor shortage the Soviet economy was about to experience.[11] The argument may be briefly summarized as follows. Because of severe war losses and a declining birth rate in the post war period the Soviet Union would have one-third fewer people entering the labor force during the late fifties and early sixties than normally would have been the case. Consequently the ambitious economic growth program could be achieved only if the vast majority of young people were channelled into the active labor force instead of higher education. It is important to note, however, that the Soviet press never cited a labor deficit as cause for the reform. Other evidence also casts doubt upon the validity of this thesis.[12]

While there is room for disagreement as to what problems motivated the reform, there is no ambiguity regarding Khrushchev's proposals for dealing with them. In September of 1958, the party secretary published his "thesis" on school reorganization.[13] He suggested that continuous academic education be abolished and that all students be required to combine work with study. In effect this meant phasing out the ten year school which at that time constituted a completed secondary education. After finishing a seven or eight year primary school, said Khrushchev, every young person should enter the labor force. Those who wished to prepare themselves for higher education could continue their studies in evening and correspondence schools. Successful students would receive two or three days released time from work to facilitate studying.

The substitution of part time work and study for full time education in secondary day schools had, from Khrushchev's point of view, two advantages. First, it would instill in the younger generation a respectful attitude toward physical labor. Second, it would equalize access to higher education. The secondary day schools had become the province of children from the urban intelligentsia. Evening and correspondence schools, on the other hand, recruited most of their students from worker and peasant families. The difference in the quality of education offered by these two divisions gave the day school graduate an obvious advantage. By fusing the two channels into one undifferentiated system, Khrushchev hoped to eliminate

10. *XIII S"ezd, op. cit.,* p. 280.

11. See, for example, DeWitt, *op. cit.,* p. 15.

12. For a refutation of the labor deficit thesis see "Facts and Figures," *Bulletin of Radio Free Europe,* September 22, 1958.

13. See *Pravda,* September 21, 1958.

the class bias in Soviet education. The road to a higher education would be the same for all irrespective of the positions or jobs which the parents held in society.

Study in higher educational institutions was also to be put on a part time basis. The student would acquire the first two or three years of his college education through evening or correspondence courses. Thereafter he could complete his training on a full time schedule. Moreover, no individual was to be granted admission to higher education unless he had already worked full time after completing secondary school. Once again we see Khrushchev's determination to deemphasize the purely academic side of education and to enhance the importance of work experience.

If we compare Khrushchev's September Memorandum with the actual law adopted in December 1958 we find that the two differ not only in detail but in basic principle.[14] To begin with, the old secondary day school was preserved more or less intact both in form and content. Khrushchev's demand that work be combined with study had received token satisfaction by increasing the number of hours devoted to polytechnical training *within* the schools. But the quantity and quality of academic subjects had in no way been sacrificed. The law established an eleven year day school to replace the old ten year day school system. The addition of another year permitted greater emphasis upon labor training without simultaneously diluting the quality of academic education. Indeed, the number of hours devoted to purely academic subjects proved to be *exactly the same* under the new system as it had been under the old.[15]

The maintenance of continuous secondary full time education must be seen as a rebuff to Khrushchev's demands. When the new law went into effect, it became apparent that nearly all the former ten year schools would continue to operate as part of the new eleven year system. Some figures also suggest that the number of students enrolled in the new system was comparable in size to the two senior grades of the old ten year school.[16] It is true that Khrushchev recognized in his memorandum the need for *some* full time day schools. But he envisaged that they would operate only during a transitional period and he expected their number to be sharply reduced right from the beginning of the reform.

While the eleven year system might have satisfied the demand that work

14. For a text of the law see *Spravochnik partiinogo rabotnika* (Moscow, 1959), pp. 517–533.

15. For an analysis of this point see an article by Klaus Mehnert in *Die Welt,* July 18, 1959.

16. The actual law left this point unclear but later developments indicated that just as many children—about a third of the total—would attend full time high schools as had been the case before the reform. See Thomas Bernstein, "Soviet Educational Reform," (M. A. Thesis, Columbia University, 1962), p. 111, and articles in *The New York Times,* September 2, 1959; *Wall Street Journal,* June 29, 1960.

be combined with study, it could not possibly have achieved Khrushchev's other expressed purpose—the elimination of privilege and inequality. The perpetuation of a bifurcated full time and part time school system insured that inequality would persist. Nevertheless the disadvantages faced by the evening and correspondence student might have significantly diminished had the law incorporated Khrushchev's suggestion regarding released time for study. Yet in this area as well important modifications were made. The reorganization decree left this question open and subsequent legislation resulted in a far less liberal policy.[17] Under these circumstances the vast majority of college students would continue to come from the full time secondary schools and an inevitable by-product would be the continuation of class bias in higher education.

The provision for admission to and study in higher educational institutions likewise markedly deviated from Khrushchev's suggestions. Instead of *absolutely* requiring full time work before admission, the law merely stipulated that *priority* would be granted those with the record of employment or military service. But precedence for people with production experience already existed before the reorganization of the school system. Thus the wording of the law gave only formal recognition to an on-going practice. It cannot be interpreted as a "concession" to the demands made by Khrushchev in his memorandum.

His insistence upon part time study during the first few college years appears to have been more successfully realized. At least the law accepted it in principle. However, even here some important alterations occurred. The law explicitly exempted from this requirement all students in difficult theoretical disciplines. Similarly, the requirement would be inoperative in both non-technical higher educational institutions and in arts faculties at universities since "factory work for students cannot in these cases be connected with their future job."[18]

Generally speaking, the education reform failed to implement the most important goals and purposes which Khrushchev had articulated in his memorandum. What factors can account for the observable disparity between the September proposal and the December law? To answer that question we must look briefly at the discussion which ensued during this period of time. The content of that debate clearly revealed that different societal groups, or at least some members of them, opposed Khrushchev's reform.

17. Instead of the two to three days released time from work as suggested by Khrushchev, students in evening schools received only one additional free day for study. See A. I. Shebanova, "O l'gotakh dlia lits sovmeshchaiushchikh rabotu s obucheniem," *Sovetskoe gosudarstvo i pravo*, Vol. 30 (November, 1960), pp. 99–102.

18. This point was made by the Soviet Minister of higher education and was reflected in the final law. See V. P. Eliutin, "Soveshchanie rabotnikov vysshei shkoly," *Vestnik vysshei shkoly*, Vol. 16, No. 10 (October, 1958), p. 9.

Teachers and administrators identified with the ten year school obviously wished to preserve and protect their institutional bailiwicks. But a frontal assault on the First Secretary's ideas would not have been good politics. Instead they opposed the reform more deviously. Essentially they argued that to prepare youth for manual labor it was not necessary to send them after the eighth grade to factories or farms. A much better way would be to bring the factories and farms into the schools by setting up first class workshops. Under these conditions it would be possible to teach pupils the same skills they could learn by entering the labor force. To substantiate their case the proponents of this approach assumed the initiative even *before* the appearance of Khrushchev's September memorandum. Prior to the opening of the school year in 1958, Y. I. Afanasenko, Minister of Education for the Russian Republic, announced that the number of schools giving training in industrial and agricultural skills would double. He further announced that the Russian Republic had begun to experiment with extending secondary schools from ten to eleven years. Under the extended program students would spend half of their time at school and the other half at jobs on farms, in factories, or at construction sites. He mentioned that fifty schools with this program had operated the last year and this number would increase to two hundred this year. Here, in embryonic form, was the eleven year school system that became law in December of 1958. Thus, through word and deed, those occupational groups associated with full time secondary education sought to protect the organization they had built with effort and care.[19]

Other groups opposed to the reform included higher educational and scientific personnel. Their arguments were perhaps more telling. They warned that it would be impossible under the new system to ensure the supply of highly qualified cadres for economic and societal growth. How can we, they asked, perfect and advance scientific knowledge when new entrants to higher educational schools would have only eight years of regular schooling behind them and who, in the following years, would have forgotten the little they had once learned. Several prominent educators and scientists went so far as to assert that a hiatus between incomplete and complete secondary school as well as between complete secondary school and higher education would result in irreparable damage to the state. For creative work in scientific research often manifests itself when the individual has reached his mid-twenties and the acquisition of theoretical knowledge on a large scale demands uninterrupted study.[20]

19. *Literaturnaia gazeta*, August 30, 1958.

20. For examples of such arguments see *Literaturnaia gazeta*, June 26, 1958; December 20, 1958; *Pravda*, September 24, 1958; October 17, 1958; November 19, 1958. K Ia Kondrat'ev and P.A. Shi'lov, "O nekotorykh voprosakh universitetskogo obrazovaniia," *Vestnik vysshei shkoly*, Vol. 16, No. 10 (October, 1958), pp. 17–23.

The warning of experts reinforced grave doubts raised by many parents. The basic argument of the latter was that a shortened basic school program would adversely affect the physical and intellectual maturation of adolescents. Furthermore, it was said that channeling young people into production at an early age does not give them a chance to adequately choose a skill which best suits them.[21] While both of these points had merit, parental views were somewhat suspect because other motives could be readily discerned. As Khrushchev himself pointed out, many parents were determined that their children receive opportunities for maximum education. They saw his plans as a threat to that opportunity and responded by attacking it. To the extent that pedagogical experts echoed parental concerns, as some did, they served as a linkage between public opinion and political decision makers. By articulating the interests of an amorphous group in technical terms, the experts transformed their claims into a politically relevant issue.

A few words must also be said about the attitudes of factory managers. Although their opposition did not find explicit expression in the debate, their behavior left few doubts as to where they stood on the issue. Long before the question of reform had arisen, managers had displayed a reluctance to hire and train juvenile workers. Under the new arrangements they would become responsible for all sorts of educational functions for which the factory was ill-prepared. Moreover, the large influx of school children and the necessity to train them would inevitably divert managers from their own duties of production and plan fulfillment. In light of this fact it is not surprising that the reform act failed to implement Khrushchev's suggestions regarding released time from work. That would have greatly complicated the managers' tasks and we can assume that their views were transmitted to the proper authorities.[22]

At this point, our task is to account for the role of groups in forming educational policy in this instance by interpreting a number of facts. The objective facts we must work from are, in summary, that Khrushchev made a far-reaching proposal to deal with a number of educational problems facing the regime, and that the substance of the proposal was radically modified. The major proponent of the reform was obviously Khrushchev himself. The most important—indeed the only—opponents of the changes we can identify are the social groups cited above.

Here we should note that if one quantifies the number of articles which appeared during the debate, the oppositional point of view is clearly a minority. It is quite possible that a "war of memoranda" may have been

21. See *Pravda*, November 30, 1958; December 2, 1958; *Literaturnaia gazeta*, December 20, 1958.

22. For a scathing criticism of managerial attitudes toward juvenile workers see the lead editorial in *Pravda*, September 25, 1957.

raging behind the scenes and that during this exchange the minority position was in fact the majority point of view.[23] Whatever may have been the case, it is undeniable that the oppositional arguments were closer to the form of the finally enacted law.

There are several possible interpretations which would explain the outcome of the educational reform debate. One might argue, for example, that the disparity between the September memorandum and the December law resulted from Khrushchev changing his mind. Once the technocratic elites had pointed out the potentially dangerous consequences inherent in Khrushchev's proposals, the First Secretary simply revised his original position. There is no way, of course, to verify or falsify this interpretation. Since we have no knowledge of Khrushchev's preference schedule or to whom he would most likely listen, we must allow for the possibility that anyone who had a position and stated it prior to the outcome might have influenced Khrushchev. If we accept this interpretation, however, we must resolve certain questions which detract from its credibility.

When Khrushchev spoke to the Komosomol Congress in April, 1958, he stated that the Party Central Committee had *for some time,* been discussing the improvement of public education. Presumably, experts had been consulted during the course of such discussions. We might also presume that Khrushchev sounded out experts between April and September when he was preparing a detailed proposal for educational reform In light of this, it seems unlikely that Khrushchev changed his mind because he heard convincing arguments which had not been made in the far longer period which preceded publication of his memorandum.

It is also important to recall that Khrushchev clearly identified himself personally with the issue of educational reform. He placed his public prestige squarely upon the line. As Richard Neustadt has pointed out, chief executives cannot afford to make indiscriminate public pronouncements. If they are sensitive to the prerequisites of power and influence, they must carefully weigh the consequences which flow from what, when and how they say things.[24] All the evidence we have on Khrushchev's career suggests that he was highly sensitive to the requisites of power and influence. Thus

23. There is some evidence that the opposition was far greater than one would gather from simply reading the official press. For example, relatively few parental criticisms found their way into print. But during 1963–64 when the first author of this paper was conducting interviews in the Soviet Union, it was learned that a very large number of urban middle class parents had strongly criticized Khrushchev's proposals at "PTA" meetings held during the reform debate period. Similarly, Professor William Johnson of the University of Pittsburgh told the same author that opposition among educational officials was far more widespread than the official press revealed. Professor Johnson was in the Soviet Union at the time of the debate and is known to have extensive contacts with Soviet educators.

24. Richard Neustadt, *Presidential Power* (New York, 1964).

not only did the First Secretary have ample opportunity to consult expert opinion on the educational question, but he also had a vested political interest in doing so before publicly stating his position.

Our own inclination then is to discount, though not categorically reject, the possibility that Khrushchev simply changed his mind between September and December. An alternative interpretation is that bureaucratic groups prevailed over the First Secretary and forced him to act against his will.[25] To accept this, however, would demand a rewriting of the literature on political power and resources in the Soviet Union that we think is neither necessary nor appropriate. It is quite easy on the other hand to imagine more important actors prevailing over Khrushchev with the social groups associating themselves spuriously, so to speak, with the stronger actors. In suggesting this interpretation we must argue inferentially because the only direct evidence we have about opposition to the proposal relates to the groups. In the section below we will attempt to account for what happened and to assess the role of the social groups in it.

II. THE ROLE OF SOCIAL GROUPS IN SHAPING THE ACT

Brzezinski and Huntington express the orthodox interpretation in arguing that the key political resource in the Soviet Union is control of the party organization, and that such control can be shared only at the top.

> Thus, insofar as there are limits on the power of the top leader in the Soviet Union, they stem from his sharing control of the *apparat* with a small number of colleagues . . . the principal limits on the power of the Soviet leader are inside the Kremlin.[26]

We agree, and we feel that those colleagues were crucially important in defeating Khrushchev's proposal. But the opposition of the groups identified above was not coincidental. We submit that the groups were mobilized after the dispute was left unresolved at the top.

Such an argument forces us to take sides in a dispute among Soviet scholars about whether or not there is conflict within the Soviet leadership at times other than succession crises. It is the position of the "conflict" school that policy issues such as those on agriculture, heavy industry, consumer goods, foreign affairs, Stalinism, economic reorganization and education are continuous sources of dispute among the top leadership. When one issue is resolved, another is likely to take its place. We think there is strong

25. For an analysis of the reform with this type of implication see David Burg, "Some thoughts on the Soviet educational reform," *Bulletin,* 6 (March, 1959), 32–36.

26. Brzezinski and Huntington, *op. cit.,* p. 145.

evidence for this viewpoint, which became more compelling than ever with Khrushchev's political demise in October, 1964.[27]

In this specific case, Khrushchev stated in April, 1958, that the Party Central Committee was presently engaged in preparing a resolution on the improvement of public education.[28] But the September "theses" proved to be simply a note by Khrushchev with the "approval" of the Central Committee, instead of a formal resolution by that august body. This suggests that Khrushchev's educational reform was a highly personal document which lacked support among a substantial element of the top political leadership. Esoteric evidence to support this thesis is provided by the unusual silence of the top political leadership during the educational reform debate. Khrushchev appears to have been the only Praesidium member to have played a significant role in the reform discussions and to have clearly and publicly expressed his attitudes. Sidney Ploss has argued that in the context of Soviet politics the silence of leaders on a topical issue must be construed as disagreement with the expressed viewpoint of their colleagues.[29] It is also significant that major amendments to Khrushchev's plan were reflected in the Central Committee resolution on education reform which was finally issued on November 16, 1958.[30]

If, as we have argued, the important conflict was on the top leadership level, and if the persons on that level have the power to determine policy outcomes, what role did the social groups play? The answer hangs on the nature of conflict among the leaders. It is well known that such conflict involves elements of power struggle and elements of dispute over policy alternatives.[31] Sometimes these elements operate independently of one another; more often they intertwine. Since Khrushchev had decisively defeated his rivals for power in 1957, we can assume that in the case of the education reforms of 1958 the elements of power struggle were less important than at almost any time since Stalin's death, and that the elements of unadulterated policy dispute were correspondingly more important. Indeed, it is unlikely that Khrushchev would have survived such a defeat as this had this policy dispute involved much power struggle.

Insofar as this was really a policy dispute, it involved numerous problem-solving considerations, as we emphasized above. The problems and policy positions associated with them involved a number of questions of judgment about what courses of action would solve the problem, and what the con-

27. See for example, Carl A. Linden, *Khrushchev and the Soviet Leadership 1957–1964* (Baltimore, 1966).

28. See *XIII S"ezd, op. cit.,* p. 282.

29. See *Conflict and Decision-Making in Soviet Russia* (Princeton, 1965), pp. 17–18.

30. For an analysis of these amendments see Rudolph Schlesinger, "The Educational Reform," *Soviet Studies,* 10 (April, 1959), 432–444.

31. See Brzezinski and Huntington, *op. cit.,* pp. 267, 269–283, 295–300.

sequences of such action would have for other goals of the regime. It is here that the groups play an important role. Numerous groups have recognized expertise about what problems are in their own area. The ten year school personnel had an authoritative position for a judgment that students could get work experience without radically changing the school organization and curriculum. The scientific community had good claim to special insight into the needs of training scientists. Parents may be viewed as having some legitimate judgment about the needs of adolescents, although this is less apparently expertise. One student of the reform debate has argued that

> The most important factors responsible for the change in Khrushchev's original proposals probably were the arguments of experts—the function of expert opinion was to point out to the leadership the possibly harmful consequences to Soviet society of the literal adoption of Khrushchev's original plans.[32]

It is hard to identify any concrete resource other than their own recognized expertise which the groups might have used in the dispute. Neither money, votes nor popularity were relevant to its resolution. Only the expert judgment was clearly relevant. The only reasonable alternative would seem to be that the regime may have accorded the positions of these groups a certain legitimacy just because they were group preferences, much as an American public official might yield to a constituent's demand simply because he views it as legitimate and because he may view his job as one of servicing such demands when they are legitimate and do not conflict with other goals. We have no reason to believe that Soviet officials view their jobs this way. Communist ideology, unlike democratic ideology, supplies its own policy goals, rather than depending on public expressions of preference to define them. Besides, we have already seen that the goals of these groups conflicted with the goals of none other than the First Secretary of the Communist Party. It does seem apparent that insofar as groups influenced the outcome of this issue it was through the communication of their expert judgments to people at the top of the hierarchy who *were* in a position to influence outcomes. The expertise became a resource to be used in making a case that more harm than good would result from the proposed reform.[33] We contend that in the Soviet Union policy issues are often de-

32. Bernstein, *op. cit.*, p. 119. See also Brzezinski and Huntington, p. 214.

33. In this instance, many political leaders may have been especially inclined to "believe" these arguments. As primary members of the new class, Communist Party cadres had good reason to support the educational *status quo*. They were among the chief beneficiaries of the existing system. Their children enjoyed advantageous access to full-time secondary and higher education. There is no question that such cadres hoped to perpetuate the provision of such education for their children. Khrushchev's proposals surely must have caused consternation among party cadres which other top

cided on the basis of such debates. If such is the case the arguments of persons who are recognized as being knowledgeable can be an important resource for the proponent or opponent of a policy proposal.[34]

One can see elements of ambiguity in this interpretation of the role of these groups as articulators of expert judgment. It may appear, for example, that the ten year school personnel are looking out for themselves when they oppose changes in their institution. The position of the parents seems even more transparent. There may even have been some self-interest involved in the position of the scientists. The point is that there is no objective way for either Soviet leaders or American scholars to clearly separate the elements of self-interest from those of expert predictions of dire consequences. We would argue that in western democracies as well there is often an almost indecipherable mixture of preference and prediction in policy debate. For example, social welfare policies in the United States are commonly defended in terms of the prospects of contraction and recession if welfare funds are not fed into the economy. The very ambiguity between preference and prediction may serve to enhance the prospects of group influence through the pressing of interests with the support of expert judgments. The congruence of one's interests with one's predictions is probably less important than the persuasiveness of the predictions and the acknowledged expertness of predictors, no matter whose interests they seem to support.

This almost inevitable mixture of self-interest and expertise provides a channel through which groups in the Soviet Union *may* influence policy when higher powers seek their judgment. We do not know how common this occurrence is, but we are confident that expertise is not used in this way to resolve all policy disputes. We will devote the remainder of this paper to an assessment of conditions leading to such a state, and to hypotheses about when to expect it. Our first set of hypotheses deal with what conditions within the current post-Stalin regime will be associated with such group influence. The second set will attempt to identify what it is about post-Stalinist Russia that makes this possible in contrast with the Stalin era.

III. SOME HYPOTHESES

Leadership conflict has already been cited as an important factor in leading top officials to look to group expertise. It is more than conceivable that

---

party leaders would readily have been conscious of. In this respect the party itself was probably an important constituent pressure group which reinforced the doubts Khrushchev's colleagues had about the wisdom of his proposals.

34. For a view of government as problem solving and adapting to environments in which communications play a crucial role, see Karl W. Deutsch, *The Nerves of Government* (New York, 1963).

monolithic leadership would itself seek expert advice, but we expect that it would do so more surreptitiously than through semi-public debate. More importantly, it could ignore the advice when it chose to rather than in effect being reversed by it. Under conditions of leadership conflict, unresolved disputes may lead some of the participants to broaden the scope of conflict by involving policy groups who might shift the balance. The dynamic involved may be something like the following. There is a split, for example, among the Politboro, wherein the First Secretary is about to prevail. Holders of the minority position may react to their imminent defeat by contacting their sympathizers among the "policy groups" and urging them to state their position on the issue in their specialized publications, in hopes that the balance of power will shift in their favor when more actors are involved. Broadening the scope of conflict may change the outcome.[35]

> We hypothesize that the more and greater the disputes on the top policy making level, the more likely it is that policy groups will be involved and listened to.

Brzezinski and Huntington point out that policy-makers are "more responsive to the demands or aspirations of groups" during a struggle for power, which would seem to bear out our point.[36] They use Khrushchev's struggle as an example but they themselves point out elsewhere that victors in power struggles often reverse themselves and adopt the policies advocated by their opponent.[37] This pattern would seem to reduce the long term impact of group influence in a power struggle. Our own example is of an unreversed policy decided in a period when the heat of the struggle for power had diminished, whether it had completely died or not. Indeed the absence of a threat to his power may well have made Khrushchev more willing to yield. Brzezinski and Huntington say that while policy is the means to power in succession struggles,

> In stable dictatorial conditions, however, the leader may sometimes exercise power in matters that do not affect the security of his position. Then, as with the education reform of 1958, he can tolerate substantial amendments to his original proposal.[38]

35. See Ploss, *op. cit.*, pp. 61, 84, 286, for other examples and a discussion of changes in the scope of conflict in the Soviet Union. See also E. E. Schattschneider, *The Semisovereign People* (New York, 1960), for a discussion of the impact of other kinds of changes in patterns of conflict in the United States.

36. *Op. cit.*, p. 198.

37. *Ibid.*, pp. 193, 240–252.

38. *Ibid.*, p. 270.

It may be, then, that conditions of tranquility lend themselves more effectively to more or less permanent and far-reaching group influence than do power struggles. Leaders are probably more eager to solicit the support of groups when they are trying to secure power or ward off threats to their position, but group influence may be more permanent and real outside of power struggles. We are not prepared to predict that group influence over policy will be greater under power struggles or more ordinary policy conflicts, but we are prepared to argue that under either of these conditions of leadership conflict group influence will be greater than when leadership is relatively monolithic. Such an hypothesis is at the core of our whole argument.

Bauer, Inkeles and Kluckhohn observe that the failure of a policy may lead the Politboro to adopt an approach that they recently opposed.[39] Our example does not directly support this observation, although of course it does not conflict with it, but the important point suggested by it is that the nature of the issue may be an important variable. Pursuing the rationale for our argument of group influence in the educational reforms it is apparent that the problematic character of the issue and the fact that the consequences of a shift were not known with certainty made the judgment of policy groups more important than they would have been otherwise. The obvious implication of this is that the more problematic the consequences of a given course of action the more likely it is that groups would be involved.

A related point that is derived from interest groups politics in western democracies is that groups are likely to be more influential in policy outcomes when the issue is narrow and technical than when the issue is broad and general.[40] In democratic polities, this is partly because other publics are less likely to be paying any attention or to care when the issue is technical. Thus the field is left relatively open for the interested group. A further rationale would be pertinent in the Soviet Union. It is not so much that other actors are or are not concerned; it is rather that technical advice and opinions are at a premium on technical issues.

> We hypothesize that the more problematic and technical the issue, the more dependent on expert judgment elites will be. Consequently they will be more likely to consult policy groups, who will thereby be more influential on such issues.

While we hope that the above hypotheses help account for conditions varying *within* the current post-Stalinist regime which we associated with such group influence as we have illustrated, we do not argue that such influence ever occurred in the Stalin era. We know of no such prominent

39. Raymond A. Bauer, Alex Inkeles and Clyde Kluckhohn, *How the Soviet System Works* (New York, 1956), p. 98.

40. See Harry Eckstein, *Pressure Group Politics* (Stanford, 1960).

examples. In this final section we will identify several underlying conditions which in part distinguish the two eras and make groups more important in policy formation, or at least potentially so, in the present.

One important change is that the rigid dictatorial one-man rule of the Stalin period has given way to collective leadership. While there may be one dominant leader, his power is shared among several key figures at the apex of the political structure. Under conditions of a diffused power structure, group influence is far more likely.[41] When power is exercised in an autocratic manner, groups must gain the ear of the all-powerful leader if they are to influence the policy process. During a period of collective leadership the access routes to points of decision making become more numerous. Indeed, the very nature of collective leadership may make political leaders more responsive to group demands.

Carl Linden has argued that the transition from autocracy to oligarchy brings with it a constant struggle for political primacy at the very. top. Since no individual is automatically assured of predominant power he must secure that position by winning and holding the support of a combination of societal groupings. His actual or potential rivals, on the other hand, can build their own constituency coalitions by identifying with those elements discontented with an incumbent leader's policy. The politics of leadership struggle then intertwines with the politics of group conflict. It is this interdependence which facilitates group influence on the policy process.[42]

> We hypothesize that the larger and more collective the top leadership, the greater the prospects for the sort of disputes that can lead to the involvement of social groups in policy formation.

The attitudes of those leaders and their methods of social control will also have an important bearing on the prospects for group influence. Under a system of terror individuals are frightened into silent submissiveness and live in an atomized state. Unaware that others share common attitudes, grievances and interests, the terrorized citizen accepts his lot and does not attempt to influence the behavior of decision makers.[43] Only when terror subsides does this condition of "pluralistic ignorance" end and the opportunity for interest articulation emerge. For now communication, both through the formal mass media and through informal personal interaction,

41. Dispersion of decision making can assume a "personalized" as well as an institutional form. Instead of separation of powers between executive, legislative, and judicial groups one may find a separation of powers between leaders at the top of an outwardly monolithic political structure. See Ploss, *op. cit.*, p. 286. On the relationship between group influence and a diffusion of power see Harry Eckstein, "Group Theory and the Comparative Study of Pressure Groups," *Comparative Politics* edited by Harry Eckstein and David Apter (New York, 1963), p. 396.

42. *Op. cit.*, pp. 20–21.

43. This condition of "pluralistic ignorance" is discussed in Bauer and others, *op. cit.*, p. 263.

assumes a more candid and realistic nature. Under these new conditions the communication process itself facilitates group influence. It serves to generate widespread awareness of commonly shared attitudes which in turn becomes a powerful factor inducing groups to influence policy outcomes in their favor.

The leashing of terror enhances the prospect for group influence in other ways as well. David Easton points out that not all societal claims and demands are converted into policy outputs. Only those which become public issues have this possibility.[44] In any polity this requires the patronage and support of some political authority figure. In a system where terror is no longer all-pervasive individuals may be far more likely to risk identification with unresolved issues since the consequences of poor choices are far less serious. At best it may mean that one's power position remains static. At worst it may mean a diminution in political power and perhaps even demotion. But it does not mean internment or execution as it so often did during the Stalinist period. The individual has lost a political battle but not necessarily the war. He remains on the scene with the possibility of recouping his losses and rising once again to top political positions.

> We hypothesize that groups will be influential as technocratic spokesmen only when terror subsides and the regime accords them legitimacy of expression of their point of view.

The kind of expert judgment involved in the interest articulation we have described is a function of the nature of the society. Harry Eckstein has noted that modernization increases the significance of groups in the political process.[45] We suggest that the modernization of Russia positively relates to potential group influence in several ways. First, it introduces a functional specialization and differentiation into the society which in turn generates a diffusion of interests competing with one another to write the laws of society to their advantage. During the early stages of Soviet rule the party preempts interest articulation not only because it wants to but also, to some degree, because it has to. The society which the Bolsheviks inherited was largely composed of an undifferentiated mass of peasants who had traditionally played a politically passive role. Thus the task of identifying and articulating interests fell to the party by default.

This is not to say that at the time of Bolshevik ascendancy there were no functionally specialized groups with political experience in the protection of their interests. They existed but they were far fewer and far less significant than in the present period. Furthermore, those groups tended to be

44. David Easton, "The Analysis of Political Systems," *Comparative Politics: Notes and Readings,* edited by Roy C. Macridis and Bernard E. Brown (Homewood, 1964), pp. 94–95.

45. "Group Theory and the Comparative Study of Pressure Groups," *Comparative Politics, op. cit.,* p. 395.

stigmatized by their identification with the old regime. Thus any demands put forth by them lacked an essential ingredient for success—the presumption of legitimacy. The *a priori* belief of the party that such individuals were disloyal deprived them of any political currency which could be used in the process of trading support for recognition of their demands.

The modernization of Russia has fundamentally altered this situation. Not only has it generated a complex economic and social pluralism but it also has provided new cadres to staff these skilled groups.[46] Those who possess scarce technical capabilities are far more likely to exert influence today than in the past. Such technocrats are products of the new system (the new Soviet man) and their loyalty is not impugned. Consequently, their attempts to influence the political process are perceived in legitimized rather than counterrevolutionary terms. The arguments of scientific, educational, and managerial experts may have been motivated by selfish concerns. But, as we noted earlier these arguments were made in the context of what would best serve the interests of the Soviet Union. Given the fact that these experts are the products of the Soviet period, their counsel cannot be ignored on the grounds that the purveyors of such ideas are politically suspect. The handicap which afflicted old specialists simply does not operate in the contemporary period.

Stalin's transformation of Russia insured the increased importance of groups in the policy process in yet another way, although the full impact of this development had to await the dictator's death. It was during the thirties and forties that the politicization of society reached totalitarian dimensions. As politics came to predominate in all areas of life individuals realized that the protection of their interests could be achieved only by gaining access to and influencing the political structure. Unlike western political systems where many issues are resolved in the private sector of the society, the struggle over who gets what when and how in the Soviet Union takes place entirely within the public domain.[47] Thus individuals and groups are perforce compelled to focus their attention and pressure on the decision-making process if they hope to maintain or improve their status.

46. For an interesting, suggestive article on the growth of pluralism in Russian society, see Henry L. Roberts, "The Succession to Khrushchev in Perspective," *Proceedings of the Academy of Political Science*, 28 (April, 1965), 2–12.

47. We are identifying here a difference of degree. As Eckstein notes, pressure groups have become very active and significant in the postwar political systems of Britain, France, etc., for similar reasons. "One rather obvious reason for this development is the growth of the social service state—of positive government regulating, planning, directing, or entirely drawing into itself all sorts of social activities. This trend has given social groups a greater stake in politics and therefore mobilized them to a much greater extent while making government increasingly dependent on the collaboration and advice, technical or otherwise, of the groups," *Comparative Politics, op. cit.*, p. 395.

The fourth contribution of modernization stems from the fact that a complex technological society requires stable occupational group membership. As we have already suggested the behavior of managers, teachers, educators and scientists was motivated in part by their desire to protect interests derived from their occupational roles. Such a phenomenon occurs, however, only when individuals have an opportunity to firmly anchor themselves in one occupational role so that it becomes for them an important reference group. This connotes, in turn, an absence of the recurring purge so characteristic of the Stalinist period. Stalin purposefully removed leading strata of important groups lest they become too closely identified with the interests of those groups and more specifically lest they use the economic, social and political resources inherent in those groups for the purpose of delimiting the decision making power of the leader.

Now this is a very costly procedure and one that a developed society cannot afford to engage in for very long. Managers, teachers, scientists and other specialists are not created overnight and their summary purge means not only a loss of experienced and skilled personnel but also the forfeiture of scarce economic resources invested in their education and training. As Soviet society has become more complex and sophisticated this type of gross economic waste proved intolerable. We do not imply, of course, that high ranking Soviet personnel are no longer removed from their positions. The official press is full of accounts concerning the removal of such personnel. We do argue, however, that "the purge" today significantly differs from its Stalinist predecessor. At present leading occupational strata are not removed in the wholesale manner reminiscent of the thirties and forties. More importantly their removal is seldom if ever accompanied by internment or execution. Most often they seem to be demoted to a less prestigious and influential job but within the same area of expertise.

> We hypothesize that the more modern the society, the more dependent it is on technical expertise, which in turn improves the prospects that groups may influence policy when higher powers seek their judgment.[48]

We have attempted in this article to illustrate that under some circumstances social groups can influence policy formation in the Soviet Union. We have specified those circumstances as clearly as we could, providing hypotheses according to which we expect group influence to vary. If our analysis is sound and valid, we hope that it may provide some guidelines for further research on group influence in the comparative study of Communist political systems.[49] Indeed, we hope that some parts of our analysis

48. See S. N. Eisenstadt, *The Political Systems of Empires* (New York, 1963), for a suggestive analysis of the role of skill groups in historical bureaucratic empires.

49. See Robert C. Tucker, "On the Study of Comparative Communism," *World Politics,* 19 (January, 1967), 242–257.

may be relevant to the study of the role of groups in policy formation in non-communist political systems as well.

Further Suggested Readings

Beer, S. H. "Pressure Groups and Parties in Great Britain," *American Political Science Review,* 50 (March 1956), 1–23.

Bentley, Arthur. *The Process of Government.* Bloomington, Ind.: Principia Press, 1949 (1908).

Ehrmann, Henry. *Interest Groups on Four Continents.* Pittsburgh: University of Pittsburgh Press, 1958.

Garceau, Oliver. "Interest Group Theory in Political Research," *Annals* (September 1958), 104–12.

LaPalombara, Joseph. *Interest Groups in Italian Politics.* Princeton: Princeton University Press, 1964.

Latham, Earl. *The Group Basis of Politics.* Ithaca, N.Y.: Cornell University Press, 1952.

Loveday, Peter, and Campbell, Ian, eds. *Groups in Theory and Practice.* Melbourne: Cheshire, 1962.

Macridis, Roy. "Interest Groups in Comparative Analysis," *Journal of Politics,* 23 (February 1961), 25–45.

Schmitter, Philippe. *Interest Conflict and Political Change in Brazil.* Stanford, Calif.: Stanford University Press, 1971.

Skilling, H. Gordon. "Interest Groups and Communist Politics," *World Politics,* 18 (April 1966), 435–51.

Truman, David. *The Governmental Process.* New York: Alfred Knopf, 1950.

Weiner, Myron. *The Politics of Scarcity: Public Pressure and Political Response in India.* Princeton: Princeton University Press, 1962.

Zeigler, Harmon. *Interest Groups in American Society.* Englewood Cliffs, N.J.: Prentice-Hall, 1964.

6

Comparative Political Parties

Introduction

The study of political parties is complex; this should become apparent in what follows. The study of political parties has also at least a formal importance in that parties are so obviously present—it is difficult to think of a political system with a grouping that does not lay claim to being called one. Political scientists' preoccupation with them makes it seem at times as if their study can be equated with the discipline of political science itself. Whether this assumption is justified is open to debate, as our reading by King indicates. Regarding the issue of complexity there is no controversy. The literature on political parties abounds in case studies, theoretical propositions, typologies, and definitions, many of which seem contradictory. A likely factor contributing to our confusion about political parties is that for a long time they have been extra-constitutional in character. Until 1945 almost without exception parties were not even mentioned in constitutional documents. Unlike bureaucracies, legislatures, and executives, they have thus escaped the legal definition which gives us the illusion at least of knowing what it is we are dealing with. This has undoubtedly contributed in a major way to the vagueness and lack of precision surrounding discussion of them.

There has been a multitude of definitions of political parties, but for our purposes a political party can be defined as an association formed with the intention of implementing broad policy objectives through the control of or influence upon government. A party seeks to do so by acquiring the support of the politically relevant members of the political system. The key elements of the definition which tend to distinguish the political party from, for example, interest groups are those of "broad policy objectives" and "control" of government. Characteristically, whether by reason of commitment to an all-encompassing ideology or simply as the assemblage of diversified interests, the party tends to set policy objectives broader than those of special interest groups. Also characteristically, almost in every case the party seeks at the outset to control government. If it ends up merely influencing government, perhaps as an opposition party or a member of a

292

ruling coalition, this exercise of influence falls short of its goal to control rather than influence. This definition further sets the political party apart from the military junta, for example, in that it seeks to expand its support among the politically relevant members of the political system rather than being content to restrict itself to a narrower basis of political support.

Well, if parties are indeed complex and if they might indeed be important and if we can accept the preceding definition, what is it that parties do? What parties supposedly do is carry out their functions, and as King points out in his article, perhaps we know very little about these functions. Whatever the extent of our understanding, it is commonly agreed that party functions can be said, again after King, to consist of:

1. structuring the vote
2. integrating and mobilizing the mass public
3. recruiting political leaders
4. organizing government
5. forming public policy
6. aggregating interests

The manner in which these functions of the political party are related to the broad structures of society can be perhaps appreciated if we view the manner in which the political party is related in its intermediate role to social structure on the one hand and government on the other. This can be depicted diagrammatically along with the primary orientations of the preceding party functions as follows:

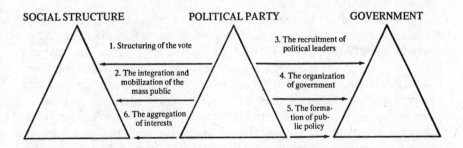

SOCIAL STRUCTURE POLITICAL PARTY GOVERNMENT

1. Structuring of the vote
2. The integration and mobilization of the mass public
3. The recruitment of political leaders
4. The organization of government
5. The formation of public policy
6. The aggregation of interests

So far we have accepted the term "function" in reference to political party, yet as Scarrow and King have indicated, the term "function" used in political party literature really has to mean "the consequences of the party for the political system."[1]

Unlike Scarrow, however, we should not rest content to simply make this observation. He does note the striking fact that scholar after scholar

1. The reference to Scarrow is to the article listed in the suggested readings found at the end of this chapter. King's article is reprinted in this chapter.

refers to political parties and party systems interchangeably. In short, so preoccupied are scholars with the functions or consequences of the political party for the political system as a whole that they have often failed to deal either with the political party as an entity unto itself or with the specifics of the manner in which the party is linked in organizational terms to society and government.

Our readings have been chosen to call attention to the importance of the latter consideration. Three large questions (the linkage of party to social forces, the internal power relationships, the linkage of party to government) are suggested by our diagrammatic rendering of the linkage role of the political party and how the customarily attributed functions of the political party extend its appeal into the society as a whole. The familiar answer in terms of our own democratic experience is that it does so by the persuasiveness of its programs. Leaving aside for the moment its questionableness (demonstrated by the political machine in American cities, for example), it is manifestly less true in the less democratic and non-democratic nations which form a majority of the world's political systems. Because many of these systems are less modernized, we need to know how political party structure within them is related to more traditional kinds of authority like chiefs, village headmen, and landowners. It is for this reason that the concept of patron-client (notable-peasant) relations is so important.[2]

While the patron-client concept does not account for all neo-traditional authority relations, it is helpful for understanding much of the rural politics of the world. The patron acts as the intermediary, particularly in an agricultural setting, between the individual and the political party and, beyond that, the political system as a whole.

If the nature of the patron-client relationship begins to explain much of the nature of individual allegiances to parties, particularly but not exclusively in Third World areas, what about the characteristics of the internal makeup of the party? Although a great deal could be said regarding these in specific reference to policy formulation, leadership characteristics, and so forth, the classic question of the political party literature is Michels' "iron law of oligarchy," which posits that organization (specifically, political party organization) is basically incompatible with the principles of direct democracy due to the inevitable growth of internal ruling elites within the party. This proposition has been challenged because it is too simplistic, overlooking the complexities of the decision-making process.[3]

2. For an elaboration upon the significance of this concept, see John Powell, "Peasant Society and Clientelist Politics," *American Political Science Review*, 64 (June 1970), 411–25; and Rene Lemarchand and Keith Legg, "Political Clientelism and Development," *Comparative Politics*, 5 (January 1972), 149–78.

3. Peter Y. Medding, "Framework for the Analysis of Power in Political Parties," *Political Studies*, 17 (March 1970), 1–17.

Unbelievable as it may seem, the third major question of the consequences of the political party for government has seldom been systematically researched despite the assumptions about the importance of the political party, a number of which are posited precisely upon its impact upon government. One scholar who has explored this question has suggested that, for the English example at any rate, the political party both in leadership recruitment and policy formulation may not be as important as often supposed.[4]

A final major consideration in the study of political parties is that of the single party. At the outset, it should be noted that there is a certain persuasive argument to the effect that single parties cannot be considered parties in the literal sense inasmuch as they either lay claims to being the single legitimate spokesman for a political system or, in fact, are. This skepticism often has a linguistic basis; namely, since *party* is derived from the Latin word *pars,* meaning *part,* how can something that represents the whole be a part? More seriously, scholars have argued that a definition of political parties must include a notion of competition, asserting the true political party can exist only within a competitive and democratic framework.

We have deliberately used a definition of political parties whose key terms of "implementing" policy and "control" of government have been chosen to include the single party among the universe of political parties. We have done so because, even for those who reject the "party" character of the single party, single parties always owe their inception if not their perpetuation to having set themselves apart from some segment of the political order, whether it be termed colonial regime, traditional leadership or traditional values, capitalism or imperialism. In a penetrating statement included among our readings, Huntington terms this struggle for supremacy a precondition of the single party's existence.

Furthermore, when the six functions of the political party (listed in the preceding chapter) are considered, these seem to apply to single parties as well. If we examine the function, for example, that the party structures the vote, it is evident that single parties do this as well as competitive parties. Where the difference lies is in the purpose of the election in the single party (often authoritarian) system contrasted with the competitive party (usually democratic) system. In the former case, elections are used primarily to legitimize the political order whereas in the latter they are intended primarily to provide the opportunity for selecting new political leaders or representatives and expressing opinion regarding policies.

4. Richard Rose, "The Variability of Party Government: A Theoretical and Critical Critique," *Political Studies,* 17 (December 1969), 413–45.

The Comparative Study of Political Parties

Political Parties in Western Democracies

Some Skeptical Reflections—Anthony King

A glance at the bookshelves of most political scientists or at the index of almost any professional journal would satisfy most of us that one of the major concerns of political science is the political party.* Parties, having once been neglected by scholars, are now the subject almost of a sub-discipline within the profession. To take one simple measure, parties have featured more prominently in the pages of the *American Political Science Review* over the past decade than any other single process or institution.[1] Moreover, the claims made on behalf of the political party are often extreme. It is said not merely that parties, like executives and legislatures and electoral systems, are essential prerequisites of modern democracy but that parties perform an extraordinarily wide range of political functions, sometimes to the virtual exclusion of other political structures. The party, like some vast commercial enterprise, is seen as operating in a wide variety of political markets and as wielding something approaching monopoly power in a considerable number of them.

This paper sets out to do two things. The first is to provide a critical commentary on the varying ways in which the concept of "party" is construed in the literature, and also on the meanings of the various functional concepts that are conventionally associated with party. The second is to question whether the role actually played by parties in Western democracies is as large as is usually assumed. The paper is thus concerned with parties both in the scholarly literature and in the real world. In the absence of the

*This is a revised version of a paper delivered at the annual meeting of the American Political Science Association, Washington–Hilton Hotel, Washington, D.C., September 1968. For their comments on drafts of this paper the writer is especially grateful to Jack Dennis, Lewis Edinger, Fred Greenstein, Austin Ranney, and Alan Ryan. Needless to say, the writer remains solely responsible for the blemishes that remain.

1. For more detail on this point see the original version of this paper. In the 1968 *Biographical Directory* of the American Political Science Association more political scientists list Parties and Elections as their first-choice field of specialization than any other single field except International Politics; see *P.S.*, II (Winter 1969), p. 13.

Reprinted from Polity, *Vol. II, no. 2 (Winter 1969), 111–141, by special permission of the author and the publisher.*

kind of comparative research that would make fuller conclusions possible about parties in the real world the paper in this connection simply sets out a number of reflections. Before even this limited task is undertaken, however, we must begin by considering the concept of party. It turns out that we have to come to terms with, not one concept of a party, but at least three.

THREE CONCEPTS OF PARTY

Consider the following assertions, chosen pretty much at random from writings in the field:

1. Party is organized opinion.[2]

2. A party is a community with a particular structure.[3]

3. Political parties are autonomous groups that make nominations and contest elections in the hope of eventually gaining and exercising control of the personnel and policies of government. . . . [They] are a special case under the general heading "human groups."[4]

4. The major problem posed for the student of political parties is not, however, one of selecting among these or other definitions. Students of political parties have increasingly ignored these types of definitions and have begun to study patterned sets of behavior of the participants in party systems. These studies of recurrent, patterned sets of actions have given rise to a new meaning of political parties . . .[5]

5. . . . the party, an association that activates and mobilizes the people, represents interests, provides for compromise among competing points of view, and becomes the proving ground for leadership, appears to be the rule today.[6]

In the first three of these statements, party is conceived of as a cluster of human beings, a group, an association, a community, an organization. In

2. Disraeli, quoted by D. W. Brogan in his Foreword to Maurice Duverger, *Political Parties: Their Organization and Activity in the Modern State* (London: Methuen, 1954), p. v.

3. Duverger, *Political Parties*, p. xv.

4. Austin Ranney and Willmoore Kendall, *Democracy and the American Party System* (New York: Harcourt, Brace, 1956), pp. 85, 198.

5. Beryl L. Crowe and Charles G. Mayo, "The Structural-Functional Concept of a Political Party," in Mayo and Crowe, eds., *American Political Parties: A Systematic Perspective* (New York: Harper & Row, 1967), p. 2.

6. Roy C. Macridis in his Introduction to Macridis, ed., *Political Parties: Contemporary Trends and Ideas* (New York: Harper Torchbooks, 1967), p. 9.

the fourth, the conception is one of a set of patterned actions or behaviors (not necessarily the actions or behaviors of any particular group or organization). In the fifth, party is conceived of partly as an association but partly also as a producer of consequences (*e.g.,* the mobilization of the people, the compromise of competing points of view).

Although any given writer may use two or more of these concepts interchangeably, even simultaneously, the three are clearly analytically distinct. Each concept of party presents certain difficulties. Each has certain advantages (or at least two of the three do). Each predisposes the user to undertake certain types of analysis or to avoid them.[7] It is important to see what the operational characteristics of the three concepts are.

Much the most commonly used is, of course, the conception of party as group or association or organization. This usage coincides with the commonsense notion of a party as a collection of individuals. The chief advantage of this conception is that the party or parties in question can be established as distinct entities for purposes of analysis; in other words, it is possible to establish the boundaries of the party or parties. Individuals are either in or they are out. The criteria for inclusion or exclusion will vary considerably depending on the purposes of the analyst. For instance, an American party may variously be construed as consisting of the party's office holders, and/or the men and women who participate in its extra-governmental activities, and/or the citizens who vote for it at elections.[8] No confusion need arise as long as the analyst is clear himself, and makes it clear to others, to whom he is referring when he refers to a party or parties in a particular context. When conceived of in this way, political parties, like other social formations, may be said to have goals, to take decisions, to exercise power, and even to govern. Writers who conceive of parties in this way are typically interested in such matters as party organization, the distribution of power within parties, the strength of particular parties, and their attitudes and ideologies.

But the concept of party as group can be restricting. A writer may wish to refer not merely to the individuals who compose a particular party, either in their individual or corporate capacity, but to their relationships and activities. Eldersveld, for example, begins with a group definition but then adds something when he writes, "The political party is a social group, a

7. And vice versa: students of parties typically (and perfectly properly) decide which aspects of political parties they wish to study and then, consciously or unconsciously, choose whichever concept of party seems most appropriate.

8. It is common in the United States for writers on parties to refer to "the party in the electorate," sometimes as if it were on a par with the party in Congress or the party organization. The notion of party-in-the-electorate seems a strange one on the face of it. It is rather as though one were to refer not to the buyers of Campbell's soup but to the Campbell-Soup-Company-in-the-market.

system of meaningful and patterned activity within the larger society."[9] More important, political scientists have good reasons for wanting to analyze, not particular parties merely, but the interaction of parties in party systems. They also have good reasons for wanting to consider the consequences of parties and party systems—their existence, structure and behavior—for political systems as a whole. For this type of analysis what is required are conceptions of party more abstract than the concept of party as group. As Scarrow has shown, the scholarly literature contains numerous sentences which have "party" or "parties" as their grammatical subject but which make sense only if they are construed as statements not about party or parties as such but about the presence of parties, their nature, or their patterned actions.[10]

The danger in abstract conceptions of party is the same danger that lurks in all efforts to employ abstract concepts operationally: the concept is likely not to be defined at all precisely, with the result that it may be impossible to know how one would go about determining whether statements containing it were true or false. If party is conceived of as a set of patterned actions or behaviors, it is crucial that criteria be set out by which one could decide, for example, which of a particular set of phenomena that one was interested in could correctly be attributed to "party" and which could not. The failure to set out such criteria may lead to all political phenomena being interpreted as in some way party phenomena. McDonald some years ago complained of an approach to the study of parties "which loses party by indistinguishably fusing it, except for mere name, with all of politics" and a recent reader on political parties contains nineteen papers of which at least ten have nothing to do with parties by any normal definition of the term.[11] Sorauf was clearly expressing a preference for conceiving of party as group or association when he wrote: "There is a strong case . . . that the major theoretical contributions to the study of political parties have come from that sector of the literature in which the party as an empirically observable organization dominates the work."[12]

9. Samuel J. Eldersveld, *Political Parties: A Behavioral Analysis* (Chicago: Rand McNally, 1964), p. 1.

10. Howard A. Scarrow, "The Function of Political Parties: A Critique of the Literature and the Approach," *Journal of Politics*, 29 (November 1967), pp. 772–74. Scarrow's paper, to which I am greatly indebted, and the present one touch on many of the same questions.

11. Neil A. McDonald, *The Study of Political Parties* (New York: Random House, 1955), p. 5. The reader referred to is Mayo and Crowe, *American Political Parties*. It does not follow from what is said in the text, of course, that the reader is not a good one.

12. Frank J. Sorauf, "Political Parties and Political Analysis" in William Nisbet Chambers and Walter Dean Burnham, eds., *The American Party Systems: Stages of*

Finally, if the first two conceptions of party, as group and as set of patterned actions, each has advantages as well as disadvantages, the third party, conceived of as producer of consequences, has only disadvantages. If any entity is defined in terms of its consequences, it becomes analytically impossible to ask of the entity whether it in fact produces those consequences. Moreover, the user of such a definition may (depending on the exact terms of the definition) be disposed to infer from the fact that the postulated consequences are not present that the entity is not present (indeed in strict logic he is bound to do so), or even to infer the presence of the entity from the presence of the consequences. If, for example, parties exist, and if political leaders are recruited, and if one of the presumed functions of party is to recruit political leadership, it is easy to assume that parties are performing the political recruitment function without bothering to analyze the process of recruitment further. Indeed, claims that parties perform particular functions in Western democracies are often so framed as to be exceedingly hard to refute (or confirm). Definitions of party in terms of consequences are almost never used explicitly; the literature nevertheless abounds in what Hempel calls "covert tautologies."[13]

The importance of this discussion of concepts of party will emerge as the argument proceeds, but we must turn now to a consideration of party functions and of parties in the real world. Do parties play as large a role in Western democracies as is usually assumed? How crucial are parties to the performance of certain important political functions?

PARTIES IN ACTION AND PARTY FUNCTIONS

Two ways of dealing with these questions suggest themselves, one highly impressionistic but perhaps suggestive, the other more systematic. The first is to select a number of important episodes in the recent history of Western democracies and to ask what role political parties played in them. If parties are as important as political scientists are inclined to suppose, then they ought, either as groups or as sets of patterned actions, to have featured prominently in the cases chosen—and in most of the other cases that might

---

Political Development (New York: Oxford University Press, 1967), p. 36; cf. pp. 38–39. One of the chief difficulties about studying parties arises from the simple fact that in the West parties are nearly ubiquitous: it is almost impossible to find jurisdictions in which parties are absent to compare with jurisdictions in which they are present. It thus becomes very hard to gauge the impact of parties in any systematic way. Even nonpartisan jurisdictions in the United States are located in a highly partisan environment. See the brief comments in Fred I. Greenstein, *The American Party System and the American People* (Englewood Cliffs, N.J.: Prentice-Hall, 1963), pp. 54–55.

13. Carl G. Hempel, "The Logic of Functional Analysis" in Llewellyn Gross, ed., *Symposium on Sociological Theory* (New York: Harper & Row, 1959), p. 295.

have been chosen. Three examples come to mind, one chosen from each of three major Western countries: the Negro revolution in the United States; the efforts of two British governments to gain entry to the European Economic Community; and the upheaval in France in the summer of 1968. Each of these developments was at least potentially critical for the country concerned. Two of the three—the Negro revolution and the May riots in France—directly involved large numbers of people. All three raised questions, central to the putative functions of political parties, concerning the relationship in a democracy between governors and governed. The main facts concerning the three are reasonably well known, and there is no need to go into detail here.

What seems fairly obvious is that neither the political parties of the three countries nor (except very indirectly) their party systems played a central role in any of these developments. Historical accounts of them could be produced, and indeed have been, in which political parties figure hardly at all.[14] Moreover, few political scientists analyzing these events as case studies in the workings of particular political systems would single out parties as having been critical actors. If parties were made the focus of scholarly attention, it would probably be with a view to showing that the parties and party systems of all three countries had in one way or another failed to perform the functions that are conventionally attributed to them.[15] Any amount of evidence can be drawn on to reinforce these points. Many of the leading figures in all three episodes—Martin Luther King, Sir Eric Roll, Daniel Cohn-Bendit, not least General de Gaulle himself—were recruited outside the party system. To the extent that political integration and mobilization took place, they occurred in structures largely set apart from the parties: civil rights organizations in America, the Campaign for Europe and other less formal groupings in Britain, trade unions and student organizations in France. In no case did a political party, as a party, formulate policy in any strict sense; nor, except briefly in Britain (1963–65), did the political parties structure the choices available to either the mass publics or the governments concerned. The aggregation of interests proceeded to a greater or less degree in all three countries, but political parties were seldom the chief agencies involved.

But, it may be objected, to proceed in this way, episode by episode, is to miss a large part of the point. Individual parties may or may not be critical actors in particular situations; but parties and party systems play a large part in creating and maintaining the political culture and political structures which characterize political systems as a whole and in the context of which

14. See, *e.g.*, Miriam Camps, *Britain and the European Community 1955–1963* (London: Oxford University Press, 1963), and Anthony Lewis *et al.*, *Portrait of a Decade* (New York: Random House, 1966).

15. Cf. Scarrow's comments in "The Function of Political Parties," p. 790, n. 56.

particular situations develop. To take the British case, the Conservative and Labour Parties as such may not have had much to do with the efforts to enter Europe; but the British party system produced the governments which took the decisions; recruited the chief political decision-makers, and (at least in 1964) created the circumstances in which the electorate could choose between a party committed to entering Europe and one not so committed. In other words, even though parties and party systems may in large part be the products of their political environment, nonetheless they perform, it is claimed, certain critical functions in all Western democratic systems.

This line of reasoning has to be treated with respect, and it brings us to the second, more systematic way of assessing the importance of parties. This is to analyze in turn each of the alleged functions of party. Fortunately, lists of such functions are ready to hand; at least one list is to be found in almost every book on political parties, usually toward the beginning. No definitive compilation exists, and the functions generally cited are often interrelated and overlapping. Even so, there is a broad consensus about what the main functions are, and some of the differences between the lists are largely verbal. The aim in what follows is not to produce a new, more coherent catalog of functions but to examine the catalog already in general use.

Two further points should be made before proceeding. The first is that the term "function" is used both here and in most of the literature in a fairly loose way. A few writers, adopting a self-consciously functionalist approach, wish to assert that the performance of certain functions is critical to the maintenance of some particular system or class of systems, the relevant characteristics of which are specified. But most writers, at least most writers on parties, although they may allude to the fact that the performance of this or that function helps to maintain this or that political system, are really using "function" to mean "productive of consequences." As Nagel puts it, "the word 'function' is frequently employed . . . to designate a more or less inclusive set of consequences that a given thing or activity has either for 'the system as a whole' to which the thing or activity supposedly belongs, or for various other things belonging to the system."[16] Thus, the phrase "parties perform the leadership recruitment function" can be translated to read "the activities of parties have as one of their consequences [intended or unintended] the recruitment of leaders." It does not matter much which language is used so long as the principles of translation are borne in mind. The language of functions perhaps has the advantage of drawing attention to the fact that, if there are needs that for one reason or another have to be met and if one entity or process is not meeting them, then some other entity or process must be.

16. Ernest Nagel, *The Structure of Science* (New York: Harcourt, Brace, 1961), p. 525.

The second point concerns the infrequency with which the standard catalog of party functions is examined empirically. As Lowi has remarked, "The more traditional students of politics . . . tend so strongly to assume the importance of their institutions that they move directly into descriptions of how they are organized and what they do."[17] Thus, most writers on parties note what they take the functions of party to be, but they do not go on to ask whether parties actually perform these functions and, if so, to what extent and under what conditions.[18]

To quote Lowi again:

> . . . textbooks and studies of political parties usually present an inventory of "the functions of party" as though these were as regularly a part of the political process as stages in the passage of a bill or what the judicial system does . . . At the present time, political scientists cannot state with any degree of confidence the conditions under which any political structure will function in a particular way, and yet we continue to talk about [party] functions as though the whole issue was settled.[19]

Lowi is surely right in urging in the same passage that the alleged functions of party "should be guides for inquiry rather than items in an inventory."

What, then, are the alleged functions of party, and what can be said about them? It probably does relatively little violence to the complexity of the subject to discuss six, and only six, of the most general functions: (1) the structuring of the vote; (2) the integration and mobilization of the mass public; (3) the recruitment of political leaders; (4) the organization of government; (5) the formation of public policy; and (6) the aggregation of interests. Other functions will be touched on in passing, but these seem to be the main ones referred to in the literature.

STRUCTURING THE VOTE

"Structuring the vote," in Epstein's words, "is the minimum function of a political party in a modern democracy."[20] A group or organization that did

17. Theodore J. Lowi, "Toward Functionalism in Political Science: The Case of Innovation in Party Systems," *American Political Science Review*, LVII (September 1963), p. 582. Traditional political scientists in Lowi's sense may use the most up-to-date methods.

18. A notable exception is Sorauf; see *Political Parties in the American System* (Boston: Little, Brown, 1964) and *Party Politics in America* (Boston: Little, Brown, 1968) both *passim*. Sorauf does not produce a theory of party functioning, but is consistently sceptical about whether parties in fact monopolize the functions claimed for them. See also Leon D. Epstein, *Political Parties in Western Democracies* (New York: Praeger, 1968), esp. pp. 7–8.

19. Lowi, "Toward Functionalism," p. 571.

20. Epstein, *Political Parties*, p. 77.

not attempt to structure the vote in its own favor would not normally be called a party; a group that did would generally be regarded as a party even if, like the typical French rally, it tried to claim it was not one. Efforts to structure the vote can range from the simple allocation of party labels to candidates to the conduct of large-scale educational and propaganda campaigns. Indeed, vote-structuring is often bound up with the educational, persuasive, and representational functions to which many writers refer.[21] Whether in a particular political system the parties are in fact performing a vote-structuring function depends ultimately on whether the voters respond (at a single election or over a longer period) to the labels the parties present. On the one hand, parties might make heroic efforts, yet find that the voters responded much more to considerations of class or race or personality. On the other hand, the parties might (say, in a particular election) make few efforts to appeal to voters, yet discover when the behavior of voters was analyzed that party had been the main structuring factor. In the latter case one would probably want to say, not simply that party had structured the vote, but rather that the vote had been structured along party lines as a consequence of past or present party activity, or as a consequence of the past or present workings of the party system.

The political scientist is thus presented with two broad questions: What entities seek to structure the vote? What entities, as the result of their activities or even of their mere existence, have the effect of structuring the vote? And of course political scientists are right in asserting that the best single answer to both questions is "political parties." Formally-organized political parties in all Western democracies attempt to structure the vote more assiduously, more continuously, and more single-mindedly than any other kind of agency. As regards how the vote is actually structured, it is clear from an abundance of studies that in most countries at most times the major electoral alignments are in large part party alignments.[22] The scholar who wishes to study vote-structuring will inevitably find himself studying parties—although not only parties, since parties in all Western systems share this function with a wide variety of other agencies: candidates, who may not wish (especially in the United States) to associate themselves too closely with the party label, elements in the media of communications, interest groups and broader social movements, and other kinds of citizen groups. And in exceptional circumstances vote-structuring may take

21. See, *e.g.*, Sorauf, *Parties in the American System,* pp. 2–3; Macridis, *Political Parties,* p. 18; Sigmund Neumann, ed., *Modern Political Parties: Approaches to Comparative Politics* (Chicago: University of Chicago Press, 1956), p. 396.

22. Although true, this point may on occasion be fairly jejune. If, for example, the party division within a particular country is in some way a consequence of a preexisting class division, it will not be adding very much to say that the resulting alignment is a "party" alignment. Scarrow makes a similar point in a different context; see "The Function of Political Parties," pp. 783–85.

place without parties at all, as in the numerous American jurisdictions with nonpartisan elections.[23]

But there is another point to which attention ought to be drawn. The term "structuring" and others like it—Bryce referred to parties' "bring[ing] order out of chaos"[24]—may be used in rather different senses. They may refer simply to parties' efforts to persuade voters to respond to particular party labels, and to voters' responses to those labels. Or they may refer to parties' efforts to persuade citizens to adopt particular opinions, and to the consequences of party activity and the configuration of the party system for the structure of political opinion in a community. Epstein is clearly using the term in its minimal sense when he writes:

> All that is meant by the awkward word "structuring" is the imposition of an order or pattern enabling voters to choose candidates according to their labels. . . . The structure may be little more than that provided by the label itself and the voters' acquaintance with it. . . .[25]

But Neumann, although using similar terminology, evidently had something more elaborate in mind when he said of parties:

> They are brokers of ideas, constantly clarifying, systematizing, and expounding the party's doctrine. . . . They maximize the voters' education in the competitive scheme of at least a two-party system and sharpen his free choice.[26]

Vote-structuring, in short, is related to opinion-structuring.

To some extent the point is obvious. Political scientists have long been aware, for instance, that political parties are programmatic in widely varying degrees, the communist and social democratic parties of Western Europe contrasting with the mainly nondoctrinal parties of the United States and Canada. They have long been aware, too, that even doctrinal parties often fail to communicate their doctrines to the mass of voters or even to their own supporters. But there is another more profound point at issue. Irrespective of whether the parties in a system seek to structure opinion in any elaborate way, there may come to exist, for one reason or another, a radical discontinuity between the structure of alternatives presented to the electorate by the parties and the attitudes and demands of the electorate or of important sections of it. There may, in other words, cease to be a high

23. See Epstein, *Political Parties*, pp. 93–97.

24. Quoted in Neumann, *Modern Political Parties*, p. 396.

25. Epstein, *Political Parties*, p. 77.

26. Neumann, *Modern Political Parties*, p. 396.

degree of "fit" between the pattern of party opinion and the pattern of mass opinion.[27]

That this is not a remote possibility is suggested by the recent history of a number of Western countries. The last half-decade has witnessed the increasing violence of the Negro revolution in the United States and the mounting evidence of Negro alienation from conventional political life, the rapid growth in Britain of Scottish and Welsh nationalist movements intent on breaking up the United Kingdom, the momentary descent of France into chaos in 1968, the student unrest in West Germany following on the creation of the grand coalition, and the growth in Canada of French Canadian separatism. The list could be extended further.[28]

It is not yet possible to explain these phenomena fully. In particular, it is not clear to what extent the explanation for them lies in the "malfunctioning" (however that term is used) of the party system in the countries in question; indeed it may be that the nature and workings of the various party systems have been such as to reduce levels of conflict that might have been higher under other circumstances. Even so, the altered temper of a good deal of Western politics in the late 1960s raises serious questions: To what extent are parties performing an opinion-structuring function? Is it necessary that this function be performed? If so, is it necessary that it be performed by parties? If not by parties, then by what other agencies? If by other agencies, then what are the consequences for parties and party systems and for the other functions of party? Whatever the answers to such questions, it is evident that when political scientists speak of the representational or linkage or communication functions of parties they are speaking of functions that parties may perform completely, incompletely, or not at all. And the extent to which they are performing such functions is to be determined by empirical inquiry, not by fiat.

At this point discussion has shifted from the structuring of the vote to another alleged function of party: the integration and mobilization of the political community.

INTEGRATION AND MOBILIZATION

This function, like most of the others, has been described in a variety of ways. LaPalombara and Weiner note that somehow "the party must articulate to its followers the concept and meaning of the broader

27. Needless to say, one should not take it for granted that mass opinion is highly structured, as regards either individuals or aggregations of individuals; see Philip E. Converse, "The Nature of Belief Systems in Mass Publics," in David E. Apter, ed., *Ideology and Discontent* (New York: Free Press, 1964).

28. See the brief discussion in the editors' Introduction to Seymour M. Lipset and Stein Rokkan, eds., *Party Systems and Voter Alignments* (New York: Free Press, 1967), pp. 54–56.

community. . . ."[29] Kirchheimer similarly observes that parties have functioned "as channels for integrating individuals and groups into the existing political order. . . ."[30] Neumann went rather further and maintained that parties transformed the private citizen himself:

> They make him a *zoon politikon;* they integrate him into the group. Every party has to present to the individual voter and to his powerful special-interest groups a picture of the community as an entity.[31]

Such ideas are clearly part of what is normally understood by the concept of political socialization. However the ideas are phrased, those who use them are referring to the processes whereby individuals acquire psychological and social attachments to political parties and, through them, to the wider political order. (It goes without saying that some parties seek to do the reverse, to engender hostility to the established order; but in a discussion as brief as this such parties will have to be ignored even though they raise serious conceptual problems in connection with almost any kind of functional analysis.)

The problems that confront the political scientist are to ascertain whether political integration and mobilization are taking place at all and, if so, to what extent and with respect to whom; and also, if integration is taking place, to discover which agencies or processes are responsible for it. In this connection it is worth noting that students of politics, especially students of Western politics, have tended to assume, sometimes in a rather Panglossian way, that a satisfactory degree of integration is in fact taking place. They have assumed, in other words, that the mass publics of Western democracies (at any rate the assertive elements in them) accept the existing political order or at least accept the existing rules for changing it. Events in the past two decades in the United States, France, Canada and elsewhere should give one pause before this assumption is made too readily—quite apart from the political turmoil that has characterized the history of many European countries since at least the beginning of this century.

But, insofar as integration is taking place, is it taking place as a consequence of the presence and activities of parties? A full answer to this question would have to be very complex, since parties could in principle perform an integrative function in various ways. Individuals and groups in mass publics could be integrated into the political system by party because they developed favorable attitudes toward parties and party systems as such; or

29. Joseph LaPalombara and Myron Weiner, eds., *Political Parties and Political Development* (Princeton, N.J.: Princeton University Press, 1966), p. 3.

30. Otto Kirchheimer, "The Transformation of the Western European Party Systems," in LaPalombara and Weiner, pp. 188–189.

31. Neumann, *Modern Political Parties,* p. 397.

because they came to have favorable attitudes toward particular parties (which were not themselves hostile to the system); or because, in addition to developing favorable attitudes, they came into personal contact with parties either as citizens whose votes were being solicited or as party members or activists.

Comparatively little empirical work has been done on any of these processes; some of them, indeed, would be extraordinarily hard to study, certainly within the confines of any one country. But what few findings are available cast doubt on the centrality of party's role. Dennis investigated support for the American Party system amongst a section of the American public and found "mixed and not highly supportive feelings about the institution of party." He concluded:

> In our system, as no doubt in many others—where leaders from Mobutu to de Gaulle have been calling for an end to partisan politics—anti-party norms and images are present as a living part of the political culture.[32]

Parties can hardly be said to be performing a positive integrative function if there exists widespread antipathy or even indifference toward them; rather the reverse. As Dennis points out, lack of enthusiasm for parties could at a time of great environmental stress deprive a political system of an important potential source of support.[33]

Equally problematical is the strength of the psychological bond connecting citizens to individual parties and thence to political systems as a whole. Most American research testifies to the widespread incidence and strength of partisan identifications in the United States, and it seems reasonable to suppose that in America favorable dispositions toward a particular party as one main element in the citizen's political universe are associated with, and even reinforce, favorable views of much else in his universe. Certainly the stronger the individual's sense of attachment to one of the parties, the greater his psychological involvement in politics generally, although the nature of the causal nexus here is far from clear.[34] Moreover, when the pattern of party identification is fairly stable, as it is in the United States, an important stabilizing factor is thereby introduced into the political system as a whole.

It seems, however, that what is true for America—and probably most of the other Anglo-Saxon democracies—is not true for some of the continental countries in Europe, notably France. Kirchheimer noted that, "In the single-load job of integrating the *couches populaires* into the French polity

32. Jack Dennis, "Support for the Party System by the Mass Public," *American Political Science Review*, LX (September 1966), pp. 613, 615.

33. Dennis, p. 614. The whole passage is of great interest.

34. Angus Campbell *et al.*, *The American Voter* (New York: Wiley, 1960), p. 143.

the performance of the political party remained unimpressive."[35] He was referring to the Third Republic, but recent French history suggests that French parties and the French party system have not performed an integrative function any more effectively since the war than before. This conclusion is buttressed by the well-known finding of Converse and Dupeux that the incidence of party identification is much lower in France than in the United States.[36] If parties are playing a part in integrating successfully the political communities of West Germany and Italy, it would seem that they have been doing so only fairly recently, given the frequent changes of both regime and party system in both those countries.[37]

Political integration may take a purely psychological form; it may in addition involve the mobilization of men and women into active political work. Political activists may, as a by-product of their activities, more fully integrate their less active fellows into the political system; persons not active in politics may become more completely members of the political community as the result of having their votes solicited on the doorstep or of attending a party picnic or bazaar. At the same time, the political activists may themselves become more fully integrated into the system as a consequence of their efforts.

Leaving aside the question of how important political mobilization is for the achievement of political integration (assuming that the two are not defined as the same thing), we can question the effectiveness of the activities of those active in political parties as distinct from other agencies. We can also ask how important parties are generally in promoting political activity.

There exist several studies dealing with the impact of party activity on the mass public. Their findings are broadly similar, and it is probably fair to take Eldersveld's study of Wayne County as representative (although how far the data gathered in one American city are useful for comparative purposes is of course open to question).[38] Exposure to party activity,

35. Kirchheimer in LaPalombara and Weiner, p. 180.

36. Philip E. Converse and Georges Dupeux, "Politicization of the Electorate in France and the United States" reprinted in Angus Campbell *et al.*, *Elections and the Political Order* (New York, Wiley, 1966), pp. 269–91.

37. On the role of German parties, see Lewis J. Edinger, *Politics in Germany* (Boston: Little, Brown, 1968), pp. 276–90.

38. In addition to Eldersveld, *Political Parties,* see, *e.g.*, Daniel Katz and Samuel J. Eldersveld, "The Impact of Local Party Activity upon the Electorate," *Public Opinion Quarterly,* 25 (Spring 1961), pp. 1–24; and Phillips Cutright and Peter Rossi, "Grassroots Politicians and the Vote," *American Sociological Review,* 23 (1958), pp. 171–179. A brief summary of the available findings is provided by Greenstein in *American Party System,* pp. 46–47. Detroit's usefulness for comparative purposes is limited by the fact that its municipal elections are conducted on a nonpartisan basis. However, Greenstein reports (p. 46) that even in non-southern cities of over 100,000 population the proportion of voters reached by the parties in the presidential campaign of 1956 was only about 20 per cent.

Eldersveld found in Detroit, did have an impact on individuals' political dispositions. For example, an analysis of the relationship between exposure to party activity and indices of political optimism and pessimism led Eldersveld to conclude: "Party contact appears . . . to fortify and accentuate public confidence by making the citizen feel that he has some importance in our complex political system."[39] Yet at the same time, even though the Wayne County study was conducted in a densely-populated urban area with a highly-articulated party system, fully 44 per cent of the sample had not been exposed to party activity at all. The writer notes that as a result "party impact is severely restricted."[40] Moreover, when Eldersveld tried to assess the relative roles of television and party in fostering support for the political system, television seemed at least as powerful an agency as party.[41] And there are many other agencies at work: family, friends, work associates, formal associations, the press, contact with government officials. Some of these agencies mediate the influence of party, but others do not, at least not in any direct way.

It remains to consider, not the impact of political activity, but the activists themselves, whether their participation takes place via party or through other channels. Active political participation often leads to consensus and integration. The acts of participation—voting, soliciting votes, collecting campaign contributions, speaking at meetings, leading delegations, and so on—may themselves contribute to the functioning of political systems; and active paritcipants in politics usually have, if anything, a more favorable attitude toward existing political procedures than do mass publics. One may recall the famous dictum that two deputies, one of whom is a revolutionary, have more in common than two revolutionaries, one of whom is a deputy. But of course participation may on occasion be linked to profound disagreements and may lead to dissensus and even disintegration.

Whatever its impact on integration, to what extent in modern democracies does political activity take the form of party activity?[42] Although hard data are not easy to come by, the incidence of specifically partisan activity has almost certainly declined in most Western countries, perhaps partly as a result of the growing professionalization of party politics. Other kinds of politically-engaged groupings, however, appear to flourish. In the United States in recent years an increasing proportion of political activity has been channelled through civil rights and student organizations, citizens' political

39. Eldersveld, *Political Parties*, p. 500.

40. Eldersveld, *Political Parties*, pp. 442, 526.

41. Eldersveld, *Political Parties*, pp. 519–22.

42. What is being discussed here is, in effect, the ratio of party activity to all political activity. The suggestion being made is that party activity has declined in amount. But of course we cannot be sure whether the ratio has declined unless we know, which we do not, whether the total level of political activity has changed over time.

clubs, protest movements (of right as well as left), and the followings of individual candidates for office. All seek to influence party structures; but many combine outside the existing party system, some against it. As Sorauf has noted:

> . . . men and women continue to participate in the political process and perform the traditional political services. But they no longer work exclusively or largely within the political party. . . . the political party in the United States finds it progressively harder to monopolize its traditional political activities.[43]

And of course a significant proportion of current political activity in America (as elsewhere) is not "traditional" in any usual sense.

In most European countries political parties still play a more dominant role. A larger proportion of political participation has long been organized via the party, and the more militant parties continue to perform an expressive function not undertaken by the parties of the United States.[44] Even so, there have been manifestations of anti-party activism in France, Germany, the Netherlands and Denmark, and Britain is frequently reported, possibly accurately, to be going through a phase of disillusionment with traditional party politics. More to the point, Epstein has thoroughly documented the secular decline in the mass-membership basis of many of Europe's major parties. In France, to take the extreme case, the membership of the Communist Party declined from more than 900,000 just after the war to about 500,000 in the late 1950's; the Socialists' membership fell from a peak of 354,000 to about 50,000, the MRP's from 400,000 to roughly 40,000.[45] In Europe as in America, party is likely to remain one important factor in political integration and mobilization: in Europe as in America it has never been the only one and it seems possible that its importance is declining.

So far we have considered two functions having to do with mass politics. The next has to do with political leadership and with the relationship between political leaders and led.

LEADERSHIP RECRUITMENT

The recruitment function can be dealt with somewhat more straightforwardly, partly because the concept of recruitment is itself tolerably precise, and partly because the role of party in recruitment is relatively—though only relatively—easy to delimit. All those who have catalogued

43. Sorauf, *Parties in the American System*, p. 55; cf. p. 56.

44. See Giovanni Sartori, "European Political Parties: The Case of Polarized Pluralism" in LaPalombara and Weiner.

45. Epstein, *Political Parties*, pp. 253–54; see generally pp. 164–65, 251–55.

party functions refer to leadership recruitment. It is seldom defined in detail as a function, but presumably it has to do with the processes by which men and women are selected out of the broader society to fill political positions or to play more or less full-time political roles.[46] A full discussion of recruitment would have to deal with, among other things, the motives which lead individuals to seek or accept political roles or inhibit them from doing so; the "catchment pools" from which the political classes are drawn, whether social strata, parties or other groupings; the criteria by which they are selected; and the characteristics and aims of those selecting them.

That recruitment does take place in Western democracies—that the recruitment function is being performed—is beyond question. Whether it is performed well or badly in particular systems is not immediately relevant; what we are interested in is how important a part political parties play in the recruitment process. Certainly the claims made on behalf of party in this connection are sometimes extreme. Seligman, while not sharing this view fully himself, notes that, "for some, the functions of nominating and electing candidates for political elective office are attributed exclusively to political parties."[47] He observes at another point that "in selection of leadership, political parties play a special and sometimes exclusive function."[48]

There is one sense in which the central role of parties cannot be doubted. Insofar as political leaders are popularly elected, and insofar as parties play a large part in elections, parties are undoubtedly deeply implicated in the performance of the recruitment function. To assess the overall role of parties, however, requires asking, among other things, the extent to which political leaders are in fact popularly elected. Much depends on how broadly or narrowly the notion of political position or role is defined. It is often defined—by Seligman in his work and Schlesinger in his—in such a way that parties are bound to loom large.[49] Schlesinger, for example, confines himself (perfectly appropriately, given his interests) to senators and governors, and notes that others have analyzed the backgrounds and careers

46. This is a narrower definition than the one suggested by Almond; see Gabriel A. Almond and James S. Coleman, eds., *The Politics of the Developing Areas* (Princeton, N.J.: Princeton University Press, 1960), p. 31.

47. Lester G. Seligman, "Political Parties and the Recruitment of Political Leadership" in Lewis J. Edinger, ed., *Political Leadership in Industrialized Societies* (New York: Wiley, 1967), p. 295.

48. Seligman, "Political Parties," p. 315.

49. Seligman, on p. 307 of "Political Parties," writes: "The full leadership recruitment tasks of parties include the following: (1) the nomination of candidates for public office . . . ; (2) the selection of officials for executive positions; and (3) the selection of party organization officials. Throughout this chapter, we shall refer only to the selection of parliamentary candidates." See Joseph A. Schlesinger, *Ambition and Politics: Political Careers in the United States* (Chicago: Rand McNally, 1966).

of presidents, cabinet members, Supreme Court justices, congressmen, and state legislators.[50] Epstein (again appropriately, given his concerns) deals exclusively with the selection of candidates for elective office.[51]

Yet to narrow the definition of political position in this way is to introduce distortion, since by any of the usual criteria the chief political decision-makers in developed political systems include not only elective officeholders but also appointed executive officials, senior civil servants, military officers, judges appointed rather than elected, and the leading figures in interest groups and social movements. Occupants of some of these positions may be appointed by elected officials who have themselves been recruited via the party system, but the role that party plays is no more than indirect. It may be that Europeans are more sensitive than Americans to this fact, given Europe's long history of a strong, nonpartisan civil service and the relatively recent appearance in some countries of party government. Daalder has suggested that:

> Perhaps the best measure to distinguish the relative hold of party elites on a political system as against that of other elites is to ask how far positions of political influence can be obtained through, as compared to outside, party channels.[52]

By this measure, Daalder implies, European countries would vary considerably. And even in the United States it would seem that the hold of party on political recruitment is weaker than some writers suggest. American cabinet officers, not to mention senior career bureaucrats, military officers and interest group leaders, are often selected irrespective of party affiliation and by procedures which have little or nothing to do with party.

Even in connection with recruitment to elective offices, the role of party is at least problematical. Seligman and Sorauf have testified to the importance of "self-recruitment" in leading individuals to seek candidatures in the United States, and there is reason to believe that in all countries the motives that lead men to seek elective office may arise independently of party.[53] In most jurisdictions in the United States it is hard for candidates to be elected who do not bear a party label; they are thus recruited by party in the sense that the law provides mechanisms for attaching labels to candidates and voters respond almost exclusively to label-bearing candi-

50. Schlesinger, *Ambition and Politics*, p. 12.

51. Epstein, *Political Parties*, pp. 167, 201.

52. Hans Daalder, "Parties, Elites and Political Developments in Western Europe" in LaPalombara and Weiner, p. 75.

53. See, *e.g.*, Lester G. Seligman, "Political Recruitment and Party Structure: A Case Study," *American Political Science Review*, LV (March 1961), pp. 77–86; Frank J. Sorauf, *Party and Representation* (New York: Atherton, 1963), pp. 107–20.

dates. In this sense the successful candidates are recruited to political office via the party system. At the same time, however, the role of party conceived of as group or organization, may be quite limited. The institution of the direct primary makes it possible for men to seek nominations (especially at state and substate level) who have little or no connection with organized party; the primary electorate in turn is likely to consist of voters few of whom are party "members" in any more than a psychological sense (and perhaps not even in that); primary electors may consciously cast their ballots for candidates they believe to be independent of organized party. "The fact is," in the words of Epstein, "that there are large areas of American politics in which candidate selection is not controlled by any regular party process."[54] Parties, indeed, monopolize the candidate-selection aspect of recruitment more successfully in Europe than in America.

Thus, although parties are everywhere deeply implicated in the leadership recruitment process, the importance of the role they play varies and it may on occasion be little more than tautologous to say that parties perform the recruitment function. The same point can be made in connection with the next alleged function of party, which has to do with one of the roles of party in government.

ORGANIZATION OF GOVERNMENT

In dealing with recruitment, we touched on what might be called the "reach" of political parties; i.e., the range of decision-making positions— legislative, executive, judicial, etc.—which are filled by men chosen by or from the parties or somehow via the party system.[55] The reach of party may extend into the judiciary and the upper echelons of the administration as in the United States, or it may be restricted to legislature and cabinet as in Britain. When we come to deal with the organization function, we are concerned with the "grasp" of parties: how far they are able as organized entities to extend their authority over the various elements of government, or alternatively how far the conduct of government bears the imprint of the presence of parties, their nature and their activities. It is apparent that parties in one system may recruit for a wide range of decision-making offices yet have little subsequent impact on the decision-makers. Equally, in another system the parties may recruit to few offices but have an impact on many. The Anglo-American contrast comes to mind once again.

The organization function is referred to in almost all writings on parties but, like the recruitment function, is seldom defined precisely. In some contexts words like "control" and "integration" are as appropriate as

54. Epstein, *Political Parties,* p. 205; cf. Sorauf, *Parties in the American System,* pp. 113–15.

55. The term "reach" is being used in a more precise sense here than in Daalder: cf. Daalder in LaPalombara and Weiner, pp. 58–67.

"organization." What is meant is the arrangements under which, or the processes whereby, persons in government or the various elements of government come to act in concert. Unlike the recruitment function, the organization function is one that need be performed not at all, or at least only to a limited degree. Men in government and the various elements of government may not act in concert; on the contrary, governments are at least as likely to be at the mercy of centrifugal as of centripetal forces, with colleague divided from colleague, department from department, judiciary from executive, executive from legislative.

To the extent that organization in this sense takes place, it may be achieved constitutionally, extra-constitutionally, formally or informally. There is likely to be not one organizing agency but many: administrators and their allies in the legislature, friendship networks, groups that come together *ad hoc* on the basis of shared interests. But such agencies are unlikely to have the effect of organizing more than fragments of government. If more general integration is to occur, it will almost certainly have to be as the result of the presence and activities of more highly articulated, probably more formal structures. Governments have from time to time been organized by military juntas, religious sects, powerful industrial combines, and even (if certain nineteenth-century writers are to be believed) by the Freemasons. But in modern democracies it seems fairly clear that the only entity through which governments can be organized—if they can be organized at all—is the political party.

How far is party an organizing agency in governments in the West? The question is not a simple one, partly because this is clearly a point at which it is essential to make overt the distinction between party conceived of as a cluster of individual human beings and party conceived of as a patterned set of actions or behaviors. If party is thought of as a group of human beings, then the question "Did party have influence?" will usually refer to a party or coalition of parties and will be resolvable into questions of the form, "Did the party leader, or the legislative party, or the party activists, have influence?" Similarly, questions about party policy resolve themselves into questions about the authoritative procedures for making policy within the party (if any) and about the decisions taken by particular individuals or groups in the context of those procedures. If, however, party is conceived of not as an actor or actors but as a set of patterned activities, then the question "Did party have influence?" resolves into a number of questions, possibly quite a large number, about men's recruitment and socialization into parties, their psychological ties to them, their associations within them, their ambitions, the place of party in their attitude structures, and so on. Conceived of in this way, party may have influence without any party leader or group attempting to wield influence and possibly without any individual's being aware that his attitudes or behavior are in fact party-influenced. Greenstein and Jackson have shown that the answer to the question "Did party have influence?" may be very different indeed depending on which concept of party is being used.[56] The disadvantage of the group concept, as we have already remarked, is that it may be unnecessarily restrictive. The disadvantage of the patterned-behaviors concept is that it may be extremely difficult to use operationally: it may be very hard to separate "party" influence from other kinds of influence.[57]

Whichever concept is used, it remains to be determined empirically how firm the grasp of party is in a particular government and into how many elements of government it extends. This is a point on which a certain amount of evidence exists, at least as regards the United States, because of course the whole question of party-in-government got caught up some twenty years ago in the (by now rather tiresome) debate over whether or not the American parties should become more "responsible." The proponents of the idea of responsible party government agreed on using a group concept of party—as they were bound to do given their reformist aims— and both they and their critics agreed that party grasp of government in the United States was in fact quite limited. Grodzins went so far as to describe American parties as "anti-parties," since they dispersed segments of power instead of gathering them together and wielding them as one.[58] Looking abroad, both sides in the debate also agreed on the existence of a sharp contrast between the United States and most countries in Europe. In America political parties, for good or ill, did not govern; in Europe, for good or ill, they did. The matter is too complex to be gone into in detail here, but this contrast almost certainly was—and is—overdrawn. Britain provided the model to which most advocates of responsible party government looked, yet in a recent paper Rose concludes that Britain was "a political system in which administrative government is much more nearly the case than party government."[59] Daalder has similarly noted that:

> Partly as a consequence of historical factors European parties have differed greatly in the extent to which they have permeated and enveloped other political elites. In some countries the role of parties has become all-pervasive; in others the parties have penetrated far less successfully to the mainspring of political power.[60]

56. Fred I. Greenstein and Elton F. Jackson, "A Second Look at the Validity of Roll-Call Analysis," *Midwest Journal of Political Science*, VII (May 1963), pp. 160–64.

57. See Scarrow, "The Function of Political Parties," pp. 783–85.

58. Morton Grodzins, "Party and Government in the United States" in Robert A. Goldwin, ed., *Political Parties, U.S.A.* (Chicago: Rand McNally, 1964), pp. 132–33.

59. Richard Rose, "Party Government vs. Administrative Government: A Theoretical and Empirical Critique," paper delivered to the Political Studies Association of the United Kingdom, York, April 1969, p. 13.

60. Daalder in LaPalombara and Weiner, p. 58; this essay as a whole is full of interest.

Certainly party cohesion is greater in the parliaments of Europe than in American legislatures, but of course it does not follow from this that European parties have also been able to extend their grasp over the executive and administration and, for example, publicly-owned industries.

Moreover, a party's or coalition's grasp of government, even if it were firm and extensive, and even if it achieved concerted action, might not serve ends which were distinctively its own. The policies of the authoritative decision-makers, although acquiesced in or even enforced by the party or coalition, might not have emanated from party sources and indeed might run counter to the declared aims of the party or parties in government. We must turn therefore to a consideration of the fifth alleged function of party: the formation of public policy.

POLICY FORMATION

When scholars maintain that parties perform a policy-making function, they are clearly using party in its group or association sense. The activities of parties and the operations of the party system might, of course, have an impact on public policy formation in a particular system without any particular party's policy becoming public policy and even without the parties in the system deliberately seeking to make policy. But in these circumstances one would not normally say that parties had formed policy; and most of those who have discussed parties as policy-formers have been concerned with the policy stances of particular parties, the content and quality of the debate amongst particular parties, and the power of parties to impose their policies upon governments. Like the organization-of-government function, the policy function conceived of in these terms has lain for a long time at the heart of the controversy over party government and, because of the controversy, American students of parties refer to the policy function less consistently than to the others. When they do refer to it, it is in a somewhat diffident manner.

The policy-making role of party can be discussed from two different points of view: in terms of the relationship between party and electorate (Schattschneider and the party reformers, for instance, wanted parties to formulate policy so that they could perform their representational function more effectively); and in terms of the relationship between party and government. Parties in government may implement party policy for electoral reasons; they may implement it for all sorts of other reasons ranging from conscientious ideological belief to pressure from (say) the party militants; or they may not implement it at all. The electoral aspect of the policy function has been discussed fully elsewhere, notably by Epstein.[61] It is worth saying a word here about the governmental aspect.

The question is: How far in Western democracies are parties as associa-

61. See Epstein, *Political Parties,* chapter X.

tions or organizations influential in the making of public policy? Of course, if a particular government is organized by party, there is a wholly trivial sense in which it can always be said that the government's policies are *ipso facto* party policies.[62] But there are probably only three strict ways in which political parties can influence public policy apart from the role they play in the selection of political leaders: by influencing the content of political thought and discussion; by adopting specific policies or programs which the party's leaders, once elected, feel constrained (for whatever reason) to implement; or by successfully bringing pressure to bear on government, as when a governing party's followers in the legislature or in the country use the processes of the party to force the government to adopt particular policies.

Simply to list these three possibilities is to be reminded that organized parties in the United States do not play a central role in forming public policy and probably never have. American parties are not major forums for policy discussion; party platforms in the United States are more significant as indices of the strength of party factions than as statements of what future administrations are likely to do; American party organizations seldom wield much influence in government, certainly not at the federal level and in most of the larger states. So much is generally agreed. What is less widely recognized is that the policy role of party is also sharply restricted outside the United States. With the general decline of parties as bearers of ideology has gone a reduction in the role that parties play as vehicles for policy innovation, and also in the importance that even socialist parties attach to detailed programs and platforms. To take a simple example, the British Labour party manifesto of 1945 consisted of a detailed catalog of pledges which both electors and party members could regard as authoritative; the same party's manifesto in 1966 had about the same uncertain status as an American presidential platform. The same tendencies have been manifested widely in Europe and the white Commonwealth although perhaps rather less in Italy than elsewhere. Epstein has concluded:

> The plain fact of the matter is that a cohesive party, assuming an organizational responsibility for governing in the style of a British parliamentary party, is only somewhat more of a policy-maker than a loose American party. It may enact policies as a party in a way that an American party cannot regularly manage, but the policies may be the product of particularized interest groups rather than of any programmatic commitments backed by majority support.[63]

62. Labour prime ministers in Britain are sometimes sophistical in this way, when they reply to the criticism that they are deviating from party policy by claiming that whatever is the policy of a Labour government is automatically also the policy of the Labour Party. See the pertinent remarks of Scarrow, "The Function of Political Parties," pp. 783–85.

63. Epstein, *Political Parties*, p. 282; see in general pp. 272–88.

The policies may, as Epstein says, be the product of interest groups. They may also be the product of individual politicians, civil servants, departments and interdepartmental committees, academics, television and the newspapers. They may also, as often as not, be the product largely of force of circumstances.

Nor have party organizations outside the United States been particularly successful in imposing their will when their own leaders have either formed the government or participated in a governing coalition. The past decade or so in Europe provides several examples of new governments, mainly radical ones, pursuing much the same policies as the governments they replaced, and of existing governments executing abrupt policy shifts without prior warrant from the party organizations of their supporters and sometimes in the face of strong party opposition. To refer to Britain again, the Labour administration elected in 1964 has applied to join the Common Market despite the Labour Party's hostility to joining, expressed both before and after the 1964 and 1966 elections; and the government persisted in supporting United States policy in Vietnam despite the passage at successive Labour Party conferences of resolutions calling on the Labour government to dissociate itself from America.[64] Similarly, when the socialist parties of Germany and Italy joined coalition governments in those countries, the policy changes that followed were at the margin only. The role of party in policy-making in France has been negligible at least since 1958. Organized party generally remains one of the forces with which Western governments must contend in the formation of public policy; but it has never been the only one, and there is reason to suppose that in many countries in the late 1960's it is not even a major one.

It may be contended, however, that although the policy role of parties is circumscribed they nevertheless perform a related, perhaps more important function, one that may indeed subsume the policy-making function: the function of interest aggregation. This is the sixth and last of the functions in our catalog.

INTEREST AGGREGATION

The aggregation of interests is the newest functional concept to be associated with party (at least the phrase is new), and it deserves separate treatment even though it overlaps all of the functions discussed already. As it happens, however, the concept is not an easy one to work with. Etymologically the verb "to aggregate" means simply to gather together, to unite; the noun "aggregation" has two distinct meanings, referring either to the act of aggregating, or to the whole or mass formed as the result of acts of

---

64. For a more general discussion see Richard Rose, "Party Government vs. Administrative Government."

aggregation. In political analysis, by contrast, the concept has not been defined precisely. Almond in one of the original formulations wrote:

> Every political system has some way of aggregating the interests, claims, and demands which have been articulated by the interest groups of the polity. Aggregation may be accomplished by means of the formulation of general policies in which interests are combined, accommodated, or otherwise taken account of, or by means of the recruitment of political personnel, more or less committed to a particular pattern of policy.[65]

Almond and Powell say simply that, "The function of converting demands into general policy alternatives is called interest aggregation."[66]

It is fairly clear from these definitions that their authors do not wish to assert that the interest-aggregation function is being performed simply by virtue of the existence of certain aggregations of interest (broadly-based political parties or peak interest associations). Nor (somewhat surprisingly) do the authors seem to want to refer to the bringing into being of such aggregations of interests (as in the formation by a number of interest groups of a peak association). Rather, the definitions clearly refer to the actions of groups or associations that are already in existence. The actions referred to cover a wide range, from simply "taking account" of interests through "accommodating" them to "converting them into general policy alternatives." It is evident that these may be very different actions; a group or association could take account of various demands placed before it without accommodating them, just as it could accommodate them without necessarily converting them into a general policy alternative. It is equally evident that the results of an empirical assessment of whether the interest-aggregation function were being performed and, if it were, of whether it were being performed by political parties, would depend on whether the concept of interest aggregation was being used in (say) its accommodation-of-interests sense or in its general-policy-alternatives sense. Moreover, as those who use the concept recognize, it is exceedingly difficult to separate acts of interest aggregation conceptually from acts of interest articulation and rule-making, and also to distinguish between acts of aggregation that are more and less inclusive.[67]

In a diffuse way interest aggregation of one sort or another undoubtedly takes place in all political systems just as it takes place in all societies, associations, interest groups, trade unions, bowling clubs, and families. It is a matter of contingent fact whether interest aggregation in the sense of accommodation takes place in any given system in such a way as to con-

65. Almond and Coleman, *Politics of Developing Areas*, p. 39.

66. Gabriel A. Almond and G. Bingham Powell Jr., *Comparative Politics: A Developmental Approach* (Boston: Little, Brown, 1966), p. 98; cf. p. 29.

67. Almond and Powell, *Comparative Politics*, p. 99.

tribute to the system's capacity to maintain and adapt itself. Almond and Powell suggest that the "political party may be considered the specialized aggregation structure of modern societies," yet they also note that "party may or may not be a major interest aggregator in a given system."[68] Given that interest aggregation occurs everywhere to some extent, whether or not successfully in the system-maintenance sense, the question arises: Are parties in fact the major interest aggregators in the West?

The answer, irrespective of whether aggregation is used in its accommodation-of-interests sense or in its general-policy-alternatives sense, would seem to be "no"—that the interest aggregation function, like most of the others discussed here, is performed by a variety of structures of which the political party is only one and not necessarily the most important. As regards the reaching of accommodations and compromises, the workings of party systems in some countries do appear to contribute to the creation of a political climate conducive to accommodation and compromise (although of course it is usually hard to say whether a particular kind of party system engenders a particular kind of political culture, or vice versa). But the role of the parties themselves is often rather peripheral.[69] One can think of trade union demands in France, which are increasingly dealt with at the centre by face-to-face confrontations between unions and government; or of the claims of the North and the Mezzogiorno in Italy, which are accommodated, if at all, by the civil service, semi-autonomous public bodies, and loose alliances of individual politicians, hardly at all by the parties; or of the claims of different sections of the farming community in the United States, which are typically adjusted by the Department of Agriculture and by Congress and its committees; or of the competing demands of rival linguistic and religious groups in Belgium and the Netherlands, which tend to be compromised, if at all, as much in the national legislatures and bureaucracies as by political parties; or of the competing claims of European cooperation and an independent aircraft industry in Britain, which have hardly ever been discussed, much less compromised, in any party arena.[70]

As regards the conversion of demands into broad policy alternatives, here too the role of organized parties is often not central. Instead alternatives are typically formulated by individual political leaders, as when de Gaulle offered the French people the choice between regional devolution and continuing centralization; by cabinets, as with the British government's 1969 proposals for the reform of trade union law; by civil servants, as witness the determining part played by the Department of Health, Educa-

---

68. Almond and Powell, *Comparative Politics,* p. 102.

69. It is fairly clear that when Almond and Powell and others discuss parties in this connection they are thinking of parties as groups or organizations; see, *e.g.,* the examples in *Comparative Politics,* pp. 98, 104.

70. See the brief discussion in Scarrow, "The Function of Political Parties," p. 782.

tion and Welfare in structuring the medicare debate in the United States; by individual politicians, publicists and intellectuals, as in the American debate over Vietnam. The most that parties seem generally able to do is to present electorates with highly generalized platforms and with alternative candidates committed to very general policy standpoints. Probably on major issues, given their desire to mobilize the maximum number of votes, most parties in the West could do little else. But they thereby leave the function of interest aggregation largely to others.

CONCLUSIONS

This brings us to the end of our discussion of the six major functions which, it is claimed, political parties perform in Western systems. In the opening part of the paper we examined briefly a number of different concepts of party and considered the implications of the various usages. Throughout the subsequent discussion a good deal of attention was paid to the importance, whether in analyzing parties or party functions or both, of conceptual clarity. The discussion has been brief, and almost every point that has been made is open to some sort of qualification and elaboration. Nevertheless, on the basis of the discussion it would seem that we are entitled, at the very least, to a certain scepticism concerning the standard catalog of party functions, and also concerning the great importance attached to parties in large segments of the political science literature. What conclusions should we draw?

There is one conclusion that we should not draw: namely, that parties are unimportant and therefore undeserving of study. It has been suggested that political parties are, after all, "organizations whose purpose it is to affect a process which would continue with or without them."[71] This is undoubtedly true as stated, and indeed there exist in most countries small jurisdictions in which parties are scarcely active and have hardly any impact. But the experience of all Western societies suggests that, where there is any degree of freedom and where power is both worth having and hard to get, men and women will combine to form political parties. The parties they form are certain to play a large part in almost every process of democratic politics, the electoral, the legislative, the administrative, even the judicial. If the study of political parties did not exist, it would clearly have to be invented.

The conclusions suggested by the argument of this paper have to do, not at all with abandoning the study of parties, but rather with the way in which parties should be studied. In the first place, if the role played by party in the performance of this or that political function is to be assessed, it is crucial that the function in question be defined precisely and in detail.

71. Joseph A. Schlesinger, "Political Party Organization" in James G. March, ed., *Handbook of Organizations* (Chicago: Rand McNally, 1965), p. 774.

Too many discussions of party function are bogged down by conceptual muddle, although the authors of them often seem unaware of it (indeed this paper may well not have escaped entirely). In the second place, if a party function is to be studied, the focus should almost certainly be on the function and not on the party, since otherwise the importance attached to party is likely to be exaggerated simply as the result of the approach employed. It may be that in future the most significant findings about political parties will emerge from studies that, in conception at least, have not focused on party at all. In the third place, as Lowi has pointed out, what is needed above all else are attempts to specify the conditions under which political parties and other political structures will or will not perform the various political functions.[72] Many of the statements in this paper may well be shown to be false by future research. Even if they all turn out to be true, they will not constitute in themselves the kind of comparative empirical theory required.

Once the theory exists—and constructing it, although a difficult task, ought not to be an impossible one—what will be its general import? My hunch is that it will show, in the words of Kirchheimer, that "the political party's role in Western industrial society today is more limited than would appear from its position of formal preeminence."[73] But that is only a hunch, and hunches are no substitute for disciplined inquiry.

72. Lowi, "Toward Functionalism," p. 571.

73. Kirchheimer in LaPalombara and Weiner, p. 200.

The Single Party

Social and Institutional Dynamics of One-Party Systems
Samuel P. Huntington

AUTHORITARIAN POLITICS AND MODERN SOCIETY

The events of the 1930s led many people to question the future of democratic government. In somewhat similar fashion, the events of the 1960s led many people to question the viability of authoritarian governments. The communist dictatorship governing the world's largest country collapsed into chaos. In East Europe the Yugoslav and Czech regimes moved significantly toward greater liberalization and democratization. Throughout the

Pp. 3–47, Chapter I, Part I, "One-Party Systems: Theories and Approaches—Social and Institutional Dynamics of One-Party Systems," by Samuel P. Huntington in Authoritarian Politics in Modern Society: The Dynamics of Established One-Party Systems, *edited by Samuel P. Huntington and Clement H. Moore;* © 1970 *by Basic Books, Inc., Publishers, New York. By permission of the publisher.*

communist world there seemed to be a conflict between the forces of the future reflecting economic rationality and political liberty and those of a disowned but still real Stalinist past. The Soviet system, one scholar argued, faced a choice between degeneration and fundamental transformation. In a similar vein, a Yugoslav observer held that the communist systems "will either have to relinquish power voluntarily as the result of free elections or try to retain their power by imposing open police dictatorships. . . ."[1] At the other end of Europe, the dictatorships in Spain and Portugal faced increasing opposition and dissent which heightened the prospect that they would not long survive their aging leaders. The fate of the revolutionary Cuban regime without Castro seemed as uncertain as that of the militaristic Taiwan regime without Chiang. While democratic systems of government clearly faced many problems, the very survivability of many authoritarian systems seemed to be in doubt.

Beneath these more immediate and specific premonitions of collapse was the more general feeling that authoritarian government could well be incompatible with a complex, highly developed, industrialized, modern society. Most rich countries are democratic countries. It is not probable, even inevitable, as societies become economically well off and socially complex, that their political systems will also have to become more open, participant, responsive? A few years earlier, as Raymond Aron pointed out, social scientists had pondered the question: How monopolistic can a monopolistic party be? More recently they were asking: How non-monopolistic can such a party become? At times the pessimistic view of the future of authoritarianism became a simple optimistic view of the inevitability of democracy.[2] "All versions of Communism are becoming decadent. They must inevitably change into a democratic society."[3] The theory of "convergence" popular among pundits and scholars in the early 1960s posited that: (1) societies with similar economic and social systems have similar political systems; and (2) complex, modern, industrialized societies have democratic political systems. Authoritarian politics, in short, is incompatible with modern society.

The primary purpose of this chapter [. . .] is to examine these assumptions and propositions more concretely and systematically. Authoritarian

1. Mihajlo Hihajlov, *A Historic Proposal* (New York: Freedom House, 1966), p. 7; Zbigniew K. Brzezinski, "The Soviet Political System: Transformation or Degeneration," *Problems of Communism*, XV (January–February 1966), 1–14.

2. To keep things simple, an authoritarian government is defined as a non-democratic one. A democratic government is one whose principal leaders are chosen at regular intervals through competitive elections in which the bulk of the adult population has the opportunity to participate.

3. Raymond Aron, "Can the Party Alone Run a One-Party State?" *Government and Opposition*, II (February 1967), 165; Milovan Djilas in C. L. Sulzberger, "A Conversation with Yugoslavia's Djilas—'We Are Going Toward the Death of All Isms,' " *New York Times Magazine*, June 9, 1968, p. 112.

systems obviously have existed throughout history and have assumed a variety of forms. Clearly also the political institutions of a society have some relationship to the level of development of that society. It seems reasonable to assume that the more traditional and simple forms of authoritarian rule (like the more simple and traditional forms of democratic rule) are impossible in a highly complex, modern society. Such societies are not likely to be governed effectively—or even governed at all—by absolute monarchs, personalistic dictatorships, or military juntas. These traditional and relatively simple types of political systems have recurred again and again throughout history. Substantial evidence plus common sense suggests that such political systems cannot indefinitely survive the modernization of their societies. The more important and interesting question concerns not the fate of these political systems but rather that of the principal modern form of authoritarianism: the one-party system.

One-party systems exist in great number and variety. Whatever their form, however, they are themselves the product of modernization. Their roots, as Clement Moore shows, can be traced to the Puritans and Jacobins. While they first emerged in the nineteenth century, they are preeminently a twentieth century political phenomenon, products of the convulsive processes of social, economic, and political change of that century: social revolution, world war, nationalist struggle. The one-party system is the principal modern form of authoritarian government. Quite clearly, however, a one-party system can cease to be a one-party system without ceasing to be authoritarian (by "reverting" to a more traditional, militaristic, or personalistic form of authoritarianism), and conceivably a one-party system can cease to be authoritarian without ceasing to be a one-party system (a possibility which is examined more closely in the last section of this chapter). But in general the fate of authoritarianism in modern society depends upon the viability of the one-party system in modern society. If increasing complexity, affluence, differentiation, and industrialization disintegrate one-party systems, they also shatter the future of authoritarianism—unless political innovators should develop new and more adaptable forms of authoritarian rule.

The issue is thus the viability in modern societies of the most modern form of authoritarianism. What are the dynamics of one-party systems? Under what conditions do they arise? Under what conditions do they survive? To what extent is it possible to distinguish among different types of systems and to discover different patterns of evolution in these systems? What can their evolution in the past tell us about their prospects for the future?

POLITICAL AUTHORITY: STRONG AND WEAK ONE-PARTY SYSTEMS

Party systems are commonly classified by the number of parties in them. In these terms, a one-party system can presumably be distinguished from a no-party system and a pluralistic party system. A no-party system is typically a tradition system. Parties are the products of modern politics and, more particularly, the extension of social mobilization, the expansion of political consciousness, and the growth of mass political participation. Parties structure mass participation in politics. They did not exist anywhere before the democratic revolution of the last half of the eighteenth century, and they do not exist today in many places where political modernization is still in its early phases. At some point in this process factions and cliques become more stable, regularized organizations which engage in a continuous struggle for control over government. In the classic pattern, parties emerge out of legislative factions whose members find that they have to establish organizations in the constituencies in order to stay in office. The politics of factions and legislative cliques is, in a sense, multi-party politics in embryo. Different types of social structures and cleavages give rise to different types of pluralistic party systems. These systems may be dominant-party, two-party, or multi-party systems, and their parties may be cohesive, ideological parties of integration or loose, pragmatic parties of representation.[4]

In a one-party system, in contrast, other parties may exist—as, indeed, they do in Poland, China, and Mexico—but they have little effect on the course of events. They are like the minor parties in a two-party system. A one-party system thus differs from a dominant party system, where there is one major party capable of governing and several smaller parties which the major party cannot ignore in its political calculations. The line between the two systems cannot be precisely defined, but in the 1950s it presumably lay somewhere between Mexico and India. The Congress Party was the dominant party in India, but it could not govern in total disregard of what went on outside its ranks. The smaller parties served, in Rajni Kothari's phrase, as "parties of pressure" and, like pressure groups in a two-party system, they at times exercised significant influence on decisions on policy and leadership within the Congress Party.[5] In Mexico, on the other hand, the *Partido Revolucionario Institucional* (PRI) could and did virtually ignore the other parties. Someone who wished to protest in Mexico might join a minor party, but someone who wished to exert pressure would operate within the PRI. In a single-party system, interests are articulated within the party; in a dominant-party system they are articulated both within the dominant party and through the smaller parties. The difference between the two systems was well reflected in the distribution of votes. In Mexico the PRI almost never

4. See Seymour Martin Lipset and Stein Rokkan, eds., *Party Systems and Voter Alignments* (New York: Free Press, 1967), esp. pp. 1–64; and Sigmund Neumann, ed., *Modern Political Parties* (Chicago: University of Chicago Press, 1955).

5. Rajni Kothari, "The Congress 'System' in India," *Asian Survey,* IV (December 1964), 1161–1173.

got less than 80 per cent of the vote in a national election; in India the Congress never got more than 50 per cent of the vote in a national election.

One-party systems can thus be distinguished from no-party and pluralistice party systems. To call a polity a one-party system, however, does not really tell us very much apart from that. The differences between any two one-party systems could conceivably be just as great as those between early eighteenth century England and the late twentieth century United States, both of which, it has been alleged, were two-party systems. One-party systems, like other types of party systems, have to be distinguished in terms of the role of the parties in the total political system. Every political system consists not only of parties but also of other institutions and groups. Each numerical type of party system can itself be subdivided according to the relative importance of the parties in the political system as a whole. What is the role, power, authority of the party or parties compared to legislatures, executives, bureaucracies, interest groups, and other political actors? Strong party systems can be distinguished from weak party systems by, among other things, the extent to which the party or parties monopolize: (1) the legitimation of the political system; (2) the recruitment of political leadership; and (3) interest aggregation and policy-making. Judged by these criteria, the American two-party system for instance, is weaker than the British two-party system. More generally, it is possible to make a rough classification of party systems along numerical and power dimensions as in Table 1.[6]

TABLE 1   TYPES OF PARTY SYSTEMS

STRENGTH OF PARTIES	NUMBER OF PARTIES				
	NONE	ONE	DOMINANT	TWO	MULTI
Strong					
Moderate					
Weak					

The relative strength of the party vis-à-vis other institutions and groups is particularly crucial in a one-party system. In pluralistic party systems, change is in large part mediated through the party system itself. The evolution of the society is mirrored in the fortunes of the parties in the system: their origin and demise and the changing balance of power among them. In a one-party system, however, change is in part reflected in the shifting role of groups within the party, but it is even more reflected in the changing balance between the party and other institutions and groups. Reflecting theories of totalitarianism, writers often assume that in one-party systems

6. Cf. my *Political Order in Changing Societies* (New Haven: Yale University Press, 1968), pp. 420ff.

the party is the only significant actor. They assume, in effect, that the scope of the political system is limited to that of the party system. This is far from the case. In strong one-party systems the party may to a large extent perform all three functions mentioned above, but it never monopolizes them completely. In weak one-party systems, there may well be only one party but that party may also play only a minor role in the political system as a whole. Most significantly, the importance of the party itself may change as the system evolves, and the relative importance of the other sources of power and authority which can challenge it may also change.

The other principal actors who may play roles in single-party political systems can be loosely grouped into five categories: personalistic actors, such as the charismatic political leader; traditional actors, such as the church or the monarchy; bureaucratic actors, like the state administration, the police, and the military; parliamentary actors, such as national assemblies, local government bodies, and associations; and functional social-economic groups, such as peasants, workers, managers, technical specialists, and intellectuals. In some systems the key non-party groups will be traditional; in others bureaucratic; in others parliamentary. In some one-party systems one or more of these groups may play dominant roles, eclipsing that of the party. In others three may be an uneasy balance of power between party and non-party groups. In still others the party may be the dominant institution on the political scene.

The evolution of a one-party system can, in some measure, be traced in the shifting roles of these other actors and forces that contest with the party for supremacy in the system. At any one time, a mixture of traditional, personalistic, bureaucratic, and parliamentary actors and associated social-economic groups may coexist with the party. In general, however, modernization in societies with one-party systems produces changes in the most significant non-party actors. The power of the traditional actors, if they are not completely overthrown by the revolutionary effort which brings the system into existence, tends to decrease. Personalistic leadership, particularly of the charismatic type, often plays a major role in the inauguration of one-party systems, but then declines as the operations of the system become formalized and institutionalized. Bureaucratic groups similarly pose challenges in the initial phases and either displace the party as the dominant force or arrive at an accommodation which usually means accepting a secondary role. Finally, while modernization in its first phase promotes the centralization of power and then the expansion of power, it often eventually leads to the dispersion of power. The problem then becomes reconciling parliamentary bodies with the continued primacy of the single party and providing for the representation of functional social-economic groupings within the party framework.

Clearly there is no easy or precise way by which to answer the question: How important is the party in a single-party system? Experts on the Mexican political system differ drastically on the role which they assign to the PRI, on the one hand, and to the presidency and the "Revolutionary Family," on the other.[7] Keeping in mind the three criteria suggested above, however, it is possible to make rough comparisons and judgments between different systems and between different phases in the evolution of the same system. In the totalitarian systems of the 1930s, as Franz Neumann suggests, the party was more important than the state in the Soviet Union, the state was more important than the party in Italy, and the balance in Germany lay somewhere in between.[8] Clearly also in the Soviet Union the party was more important vis-à-vis the top leadership in the 1960s than it was in the 1940s during the heyday of Stalin's personal rule.

The differences between a strong one-party system and an extremely weak one are highlighted by the contrast between the post-Stalin Soviet Union and Franco Spain. In the former the party and its *apparat* was the preeminent group. The church and the traditional elite had all but been eliminated. Parliamentary and representative bodies had purely dignified roles. The social and economic elites were products of the system. The police had been subordinated to the party immediately following the death of Stalin. The army, after a brief excursion into politics in the mid-1950s, had resumed its more normal subordinated role. The state bureaucracy or managers, whom many observers had seen as the nucleus of a new ruling class, had displayed neither the unity nor the desire nor the talents to act as an independent political force. Finally, the seeming efforts by Khrushchev to expand his personal power had been brought to a sharp halt by his removal from power by the collective action of the Presidium backed by the Central Committee. In the Soviet Union, perhaps more than in any other state, the party did come close to monopolizing legitimacy, political recruitment, and the determination of policy. The Soviet Union, clearly, was a strong one-party system.

Franco Spain, on the other hand, was a weak one-party system, if, indeed, it even deserved to be called that. Insofar as it was a party system at all, it was a one-party system, but the party was a not very important part of the system, and the continued existence of many traditional and bureaucratic groups and institutions significantly weakened the party. In this "Mediterranean" syndicalist pattern of politics, as Kalman Silvert calls it,[9] the aggregation of power under any auspices, much less that of a single

7. Contrast Robert E. Scott, *Mexican Government in Transition* (Urbana: The University of Illinois Press, 1959), chap. 5, and Frank Brandenburg, *The Making of Modern Mexico* (Englewood Cliffs, N.J.: Prentice-Hall, 1964), pp. 142–145.

8. Franz Neumann, *Behemoth: The Structure and Practice of National Socialism, 1933–1944* (New York: Oxford University Press, 1944), p. 67. [. . . .]

9. Kalman, Silvert, ed., *Expectant Peoples* (New York: Random House, 1963), pp. 358–361.

party, becomes very difficult. In Spain, the regime rested to varying degrees on support from the army, the church, the monarchists, the Carlists, the financial oligarchy, Opus Dei, and the Falange. The latter was only one pillar among many. During the Civil War the Falange had been an important force. Once the war was over, the level of political mobilization declined drastically and with it the influence and role of the regime's political party. For a generation old Falange types dreamed of the day when they would come into their own and the movement would become the system, but Franco was careful to insure that this would never happen. Temporary increases in Falange power were the products of Franco's manipulation and were designed to balance off increases in the power of other groups in order to enhance Franco's own. "Franco conceived of the FET," as Stanley Payne observed, "as the party of the state, but he never thought of his regime as a real party-state. The Falange, far from controlling the state, was no more than an instrument for holding the state together. Whenever its political pretensions threatened to disturb the internal equilibrium worked out by the Caudillo, he quickly cut the party down to size."[10] The party in Spain was a feeble rival to the army, the church, and even the monarchists, not to mention, of course, the Caudillo himself. As a result, when political consciousness and activity begin to rise significantly in the late 1960s, the Franco regime was caught in a dilemma. If such political participation were channeled into the Falange it would disrupt the balance within the regime. But if it were not absorbed into some element of the regime, it would eventually threaten the system itself.

In the short run a reasonably stable and effective authoritarian system may exist with only a weak party. In the longer run, however, it would appear that the strength of an authoritarian regime will, in large measure, depend on the strength of its party. Significantly, when authoritarian regimes with weak parties confront crises, the party tends to reemerge as a more important actor. Nasser responded to three major crises—the need to consolidate power in 1954 after his victory over Naguib, the need to unify the Egyptian people behind him in 1957 after the Suez crisis, and the shift to a socialist policy in 1962—by attempting to create a mass political organization.[11] Somewhat similarly, crises in the evolution of the Franco regime were not infrequently followed by a new burst of life in the Falange. In both Egypt and Spain a crisis may generate new political interest and activity, and the authoritarian regime, which normally survives through popular indifference, suddenly discovers the need to have some organized

10. Stanley G. Payne, *Falange: A History of Spanish Fascism* (Stanford: Stanford University Press, 1961), p. 200.

11. See Leonard Binder, "Political Recruitment and Participation in Egypt," in Joseph LaPalombara and Myron Weiner, eds., *Political Parties and Political Development* (Princeton: Princeton University Press, 1966), pp. 218–219.

and controlled structure through which otherwise potentially threatening political action may be channeled. Unless it can guarantee indefinitely a relatively low level of political mobilization, an authoritarian regime may have little choice but to organize and develop a political party as an essential structural support.

SOCIAL BIFURCATION: EXCLUSIONARY AND REVOLUTIONARY ONE-PARTY SYSTEMS

Party systems originate in the patterns of cleavage and alignment among social forces. Different relationships among social forces and different sequences in the development of cleavages among them give rise to different types of party systems. Once the systems take root, however, they develop a life of their own. The events and choices of one decade may thus have consequences for a century to come. The question here is: What type of social structure, what configuration of social forces furnishes fertile soil for the emergence of one-party systems? At one point in time, the southern United States, Nationalist China, and Soviet Russia were all one-party systems. Are there any social conditions that may serve to link together such otherwise disparate political forms?

Two theories are commonly made relating one-party systems to social structure. First, it has been argued, particularly by Africans, that party systems reflect the class structure of societies, and in a society where there are no pronounced differences among social and economic classes, there is no social basis for more than one party. Anglo-Saxon two-party systems, Julius Nyerere says, are "a reflection of the society" in which they developed and in which "there was a struggle between the 'haves' and the 'have-nots,' each of whom organized themselves into political parties—one party associated with wealth and the status quo, and the other with the masses of the people and change." The "idea of class," however, "is something entirely foreign to Africa," and a homogeneous society requires only one party. Or, as Madeira Keita put it, "there is no fundamental opposition among us" and hence why is "there any reason to remain divided and split into parties that fought one another?"[12]

A second rationale for one-party systems argues along just the opposite lines. Instead of the single party reflecting a homogeneous society, its justification is found in the need to counterbalance the fissiparous tendencies of a heterogeneous society. The source of the single-party system is in need rather than nature. It is, indeed, seen as an artificially created mechanism or institution to hold together a society which would otherwise fly apart. With some, if not wanton, disregard for logic, many African leaders have held this view simultaneously with the homogeneous society view, reconcil-

12. Paul E. Sigmund, ed., *The Ideologies of the Developing Nations* (New York: Frederick A. Praeger, 1963), pp. 175, 198.

ing the two by the differences between class and tribe as social forces. Competitive elections, in Keita's words, oblige political leaders "to play on regionalism and what we have called internal racism." In this view, the political elite plays an innovative and autonomous role, using the party to correct the deficiencies in social structure and to impose unity on a divided society. "One-man one-party regimes," in Rupert Emerson's words, "are necessary in Africa precisely because the nations rest on such shaky foundations and are confronted by such urgent and monumental tasks of integration and development."[13]

Neither the homogeneous thesis nor the heterogeneous thesis is an adequate explanation of the emergence of viable one-party systems. The homogeneous argument is based on the Marxist premise of the direct correspondence between social class and political organization. It rationalizes the emergence of one-party systems in Africa with independence, but it hardly explains their collapse shortly thereafter. Nor does it explain the emergence of one-party systems in other societies that by no stretch of the imagination could be described as either homogeneous or consensual. Nor does it explain, assuming any validity to de Tocqueville and Louis Hartz, why the United States has two parties instead of one. The heterogeneous thesis, on the other hand, is more of a prescription than an explanation: it states why one-party systems should exist rather than why they do exist. It deals more with what are alleged to be the effects of one-party systems than with their causes. If the conditions that are otherwise required for the creation of strong one-party systems exist in Africa, the consequences of those systems for national integration may well be beneficial.

The social origins of one-party systems are to be found in neither homogeneity nor heterogeneity but in bifurcation. Societies in which the impact of modernization on traditional structures produces a complex pattern of cross-cutting cleavages typically evolve into pluralistic party systems. The democratic party systems of Western Europe, for instance, "reflect differences in the national histories of conflict and compromise" across the cleavage lines between center and periphery, state and church, land and industry. These multiple lines of cleavage gave rise to a variety of party systems, but in no case was there a sharp bifurcation of the society with all lines of social and political cleavage reinforcing each other. None of the countries of Western Europe, as Robert Dahl has observed, "closely approaches the pattern described . . . as full-scale political polarization, where sharp political, socioeconomic, and psychological dualisms all coincide."[14]

One-party systems, in contrast, tend to be the product of either the

13. *Ibid.*, p. 172; Rupert Emerson, "Parties and National Integration in Africa," in LaPalombara and Weiner, *op. cit.*, p. 296.

14. Robert A. Dahl, ed., *Political Oppositions in Western Democracies* (New Haven: Yale University Press, 1966), p. 385.

cumulation of cleavages leading to sharply differentiated groups within society or of the ascendancy in importance of one line of cleavage over all others. A one-party system is, in effect, the product of the efforts of a political elite to organize and to legitimate rule by one social force over another in a bifurcated society. The bifurcation may be between social-economic groups or between racial, religious, or ethnic ones. In the past in Europe, for instance, in those cases where intense religious, linguistic, and ethnic polarizations did develop, the result was either "a separation into different countries so that the cleavages became international rather than national, as with the separation of Ireland from Britain or Norway from Sweden" or "the creation of a one-party authoritarian or totalitarian states, as in the case of Fascist Italy, Nazi Germany, and Franco Spain."[15] One-party systems, in short, arise from pronounced bifurcations that cannot be resolved by secession and territorial separation. The breakdown of a traditional social order and the escalation of political participation in a revolutionary situation naturally lead to the polarization of social forces, to intense struggle and violence between revolutionary and counter-revolutionary groups, and so to the establishment of a one-party system. Such, at least, has been the outcome of twentieth century revolutions in Russia, Mexico, China, Turkey, Yugoslavia, Bolivia, Cuba, Albania, and Vietnam. On the other hand, one-party systems also tend to arise in situations of intense ethnic or religious division and conflict. Revolutionary societies and plural societies are the natural habitats of one-party systems. Each has a bifurcated social structure.

One-party systems have appeared in societies at almost all levels of social, economic, and cultural modernization. Yet the great bulk of one-party systems, and particularly those with the greatest staying power, come into existence in societies in the early and early-to-middle phases of modernization. There are good reasons for this. The sharp bifurcation of society, which is the prerequisite to the establishment of a viable one-party system, is most likely at that stage of change. The largest number of one-party systems are produced by social revolutions, and revolutions, in the grand sense, occur only at particular times in the process of modernization and development. The tendency to polarization comes with the breakdown of traditional society structures and the mobilization of new groups into politics. The single-party system is created by leaders of a more modern social force confronting a more backward social force. The constituency of the party becomes more highly mobilized, socially and politically, than the target of the party. That target, indeed, is usually either a traditional elite to be exterminated, a traditional mass to be modernized and assimilated into the party's constituency, or a less modernized, "inferior" race to be held in subjection.

15. *Ibid.*, p. 386.

TABLE 2 RELATIVE CAPACITIES OF POLITICAL SYSTEMS

TO CONCENTRATE POWER	TO EXPAND POWER	
	LOW	HIGH
Low	Praetorian system	Two-party system Multi-party system
High	Absolute monarchy Bureaucratic empire Military dictator "Modernizing autocracy"	One-party system Dominant-party system

One-party systems created in societies that have not reached the necessary level of development—and cleavage—are, as in tropical Africa, likely to be weak and fragile. Efforts to introduce a one-party system in a complex and differentiated society are also likely to fail. A strong one-party system cannot be created in a backward society because *all* organizations are weak and it cannot be created in a highly developed society because *other* organizations are strong. In the latter society, power is already so dispersed that its reconcentration into a strong single-party system requires a "permanent revolution" of accelerating mass mobilization against the existing complex social, economic, and political structures. The tensions created by such efforts are likely to drive the regime into expansionist foreign policies which, as with Nazi Germany, may undo it even if it is able temporarily to surmount the domestic problems. Dahomey in the 1960s was too backward to establish a stable one-party system; Germany in the 1930s was too advanced to do so.

A strong one-party system appears to meet certain functional needs for a society in the early to middle phases of modernization. In an era when modernization involves the expansion of political participation, the single party is the functional equivalent of the absolute monarchy of seventeenth century Europe. The absolute monarchy centralized power to promote modernizing reform, but it then proved incapable of expanding power to assimilate new groups into the political system. The one-party system, however, is unusual among political institutions in providing significant capacities for both the concentration and the expansion of power. It is thus peculiarly relevant in the later modernizing societies which, unlike the early modernizers, confront a highly telescoped modernizing process and hence face simultaneous needs to concentrate and to expand power.[16] Whether the one-party system also provides an effective means for dispersing power in the third phase of political modernization will be discussed in the latter part of this chapter.

16. See Frederick W. Frey, *The Turkish Political Elite* (Cambridge: MIT Press, 1965), chap. 13, and Samuel P. Huntington, "The Political Modernization of Traditional Monarchies," *Daedalus*, XCV (Summer 1966), 766–772.

Ideology plays a major role in the emergence of a one-party system, and ideology along with political mobilization and organizational discipline is a product of struggle and violence. The ideology of a one-party system identifies a chosen people or constituency, targets an enemy, proclaims the necessity for a struggle against the enemy, and holds forth the assurance of ultimate victory. Strong one-party systems come into being only when there is an explicit recognition of the difference between "we" and "they" and of the necessity for conflict between the two. The leaders of the party mobilize supporters from one social group for war against another group and its institutions. In its origins the one-party system must be intensely anti-capitalist, anti-traditionalist, anti-imperialist, anti-Semitic, or anti-something.

The creation of a one-party system redefines the scope of the political community. The basis of that community is the "chosen" social force, and other social groupings must either be assimilated to it or permanently excluded from the scope of politics. Legitimate political participation is limited to the members of the constituency social force, and the party which speaks for that social force monopolizes, at least in theory, legitimate political activity. Every one-party system comes into existence with a concept of the community of the chosen and of the party as the political expression of that community. The community may be in part a social fact pre-existing the creation of the one-party system, and it may also in part be the product of political action by the leaders of the party. If that community does not pre-exist the establishment of the party, the first task of the party is to bring it into existence.

The most appropriate theory of the one-party system is the Leninist theory. But it applies not just to the proletariat but to any dominant social force in a bifurcated society. "The dictatorship of the proletariat," in Lenin's words, "is the class struggle of the proletariat which has achieved victory and seized political power," and the dictatorship of the proletariat is "in essence, the dictatorship of its organized and class conscious minority," that is, the party.[17] The single-party system, moreover, is the product of struggle as well as cleavage. "The dictatorship of the proletariat is the fiercest, sharpest and most merciless war of the new class against its *more powerful* enemy, the bourgeoisie, whose resistance is increased *ten-fold* by its overthrow. . . . The dictatorship of the proletariat is a stubborn struggle —sanguinary and bloodless, violent and peaceful, military and economic, educational and administrative—against the forces and traditions of the old society."[18]

Experience suggests that the strength of a one-party system depends upon the duration and intensity of the struggle to acquire power or to consolidate

17. Lenin, quoted in Joseph Stalin, *Problems of Leninism* (New York: International Publishers, 1934), pp. 36–37.

18. Lenin, *'Left' Communism: An Infantile Disorder,* quoted in Joseph Stalin, *Foundations of Leninism,* rev. trans. (New York: International Publishers, 1932), p. 47.

power after taking over the government. "One party systems which emerge out of revolutions, consequently, are more stable than those produced by nationalist movements, and those produced by prolonged nationalist movements are more stable than those produced by movements whose struggle was brief and easy."[19] If a party that desires to establish a single-party system comes to power without a struggle, it must exacerbate social cleavages in order to consolidate its rule. The contrast between the communist regimes which took over government in the wake of the advancing Red Army and the African regimes which came to power in the wake of the retreating imperial powers is very marked. The communist regimes consciously and explicitly fired up social conflict in East Europe. During the late 1940s and early 1950s they were, in their terminology, in the phase of "people's democracy," which meant intensification of class struggle. Between 1948 and 1953, "the emphasis on class struggle made organized violence an integral characteristic of the people's democracy as a social system."[20] If the society was not polarized before the communists came to power, it certainly was afterward. The people's democracy phase, as another scholar has described it, was

> characterized as a process of highly intensified class struggle. Usually the fight was initiated shortly after the seizure of power. A newly installed Stalinist elite, unwilling to share authority or power with other political and economic factions, began to draw sharp distinctions between class friends and class enemies in the social structure of the people's democracy.[21]

This process of bifurcation gave the East European communist regimes a relatively secure hold on power.[22]

In the absence of pronounced bifurcation and struggle between social forces, efforts to establish one-party systems usually prove abortive. In

19. Huntington, *Political Order in Changing Societies,* p. 425.

20. Zbigniew K. Brzezinski, *The Soviet Bloc: Unity and Conflict,* rev. ed. (Cambridge: Harvard University Press, 1967), p. 90.

21. Andrew Gyorgy, "The Internal Political Order," in Stephen Fischer-Galati, ed., *Eastern Europe in the Sixties* (New York: Frederick A. Praeger, 1963), p. 162.

22. A similar policy of deliberately firing up social conflict was adapted by Càrdenas in Mexico and had similar results in strengthening the single-party system and redefining the political community. "Càrdenas accomplished the feat of bringing off a class war, while at the same time subordinating it to the overriding theme of Mexican nationalism. Major surgery was performed upon economic and social insitutions of long standing. Social realignments and change in stratification arrangements took place, and national sentiment and unity triumphed in these changes. Modern evolutionary Mexico was ready to emerge based upon the twin assumptions of nationalism and modernization as the overriding values of the future." L. Vincent Padgett, *The Mexican Political System* (Boston: Houghton Mifflin, 1966), pp. 39–40.

many African states, the party came to power easily, without a major struggle, and consequently had no legacy of struggle upon which to live and no incentive to struggle by which to develop. Hence it withered in power. Political leaders only mobilize and organize masses when they have a real need—ideological or political—to do so. If they are already in power and have no ideological drive to split and to remake their societies, they have no reason to make the effort to develop and maintain a strong party. Indeed, after independence, African party leaders attempted to minimize social conflict, to emphasize national unity, and obscure or ignore the differences between the modernized elite and the traditional masses. The political elites became the victims of their own theories, all of which postulated, in one form or another, that "the CPP is Ghana, and Ghana is the CPP." In the event, their parties turned out to be as weak as their theories. They had no real function to perform. The one-party state, in Immanuel Wallerstein's phrase, became the no-party state, and its leaders were easily overthrown whenever military leaders had the inclination to do so.

In similar fashion an abortive one-party system may derive from the efforts of a regime in power to organize a party without dividing its society. As with Nasser and Ne Win, the effort is made to include everyone in the party. One indication of the strength of a one-party system, however, is the premium put on membership in the party. The more important the party is in the system, the more difficult it is to become a member and the more frequent are the purges expelling members. If party membership becomes universal, it becomes meaningless. Paradoxically, a competitive party system can be organized from the top down since the political elite has to create a strong party in order to stay in power. But a one-party system cannot be created this way because those in power lack the competitive impetus to develop and to maintain a strong party organization.

Successful one-party systems have their origins in bifurcation; the party is the means by which the leaders of one social force dominate the other social force. The party monopolizes or tries to monopolize all political activity. With respect to the cleavage and the subordinate social force, however, the political leaders can follow one or a combination of two policies. On the one hand, they can accept the bifurcation of the society and use the party as a means of mobilizing support from their constituency while at the same time suppressing or restricting political activity by the subordinate social force. In effect, the party maintains its monopoly over political participation by limiting the scope of political participation. Systems in which this policy is followed are *exclusionary one-party systems.* Alternatively, the party leadership can attempt to eradicate the bifurcation of society by shrinking society to correspond to its constituency through liquidation of the subordinate social force or by expanding its constituency to correspond to society by the assimilation of the subordinate social force. These systems are *revolutionary one-party systems.*

In one-party systems based on ethnic or racial bifurcation, the party usually follows an exclusionary policy. Exclusionary systems emerge out of competitive systems when a new ethnic or racial group appears to threaten a previously homogeneous society. In the oldest one-party system in the world, in Liberia, party competition prevailed until the 1880s. At that time, however, the settlers began to expand into the interior and to have more direct contacts with the indigenous Africans. As a result,

> Americo-Liberians found themselves captives of the very situation they had created through expansion of the republic into the hostile tribal hinterland beyond the five coastal counties and the subsequent conflicts with the British and the French, who were coveting the same areas. It was the need for solidarity in meeting the twin threats to their supremacy, posed by tribal rebellion and foreign occupation, which convinced Americo-Liberians of the value of the single-party system.[23]

At about the same time the cousins of the Americo-Liberians in the New World were furnishing an impetus to the development of a one-party system in the American South roughly comparable to that which the tribal Africans were furnishing to the Americo-Liberians. In similar fashion, as South Africa increasingly became a bifurcated society between white and non-white, it also became more of a one-party system. With increasing emphasis on the need for common action by whites against the domestic and foreign foe, the support for the United Party dwindled away, and the Nationalists acquired an overwhelming predominance in the national and provincial legislatures. In 1965 the Minister of Justice, B. J. Vorster, suggested that the country would become a one-party state, and a cautious scholar the same year observed that South Africa was "a two-party system, tending towards a one-party system, within an ethnic oligarchy or pigmentocracy."[24] Tribal and religious dualities similarly provide a basis for some single party systems in West Africa. In Northern Ireland religion is the source of bifurcation; the Ulster Unionists, the overwhelmingly dominant party, "unite Protestants, including many industrial workers who might otherwise be drawn to the Labour party, in opposition to the minority of Catholics favoring ties to Eire rather than Britain."[25]

Exclusionary systems do not necessarily, however, rest on a racial or religious base. In effect, the Republican People's Party in Turkey was such a

23. J. Gus Liebenow. "Liberia," in James S. Coleman and Carl G. Rosberg, eds., *Political Parties and National Integration in Tropical Africa* (Berkeley: University of California Press, 1964), p. 451.

24. Leonard M. Thompson, *Politics in the Republic of South Africa* (Boston: Little, Brown, 1966), p. 151.

25. Leon D. Epstein, *Political Parties in Western Democracies* (New York: Frederick A. Praeger, 1967), p. 54; B. J. O. Dudley, "Traditionalism and Politics: A Case Study of Northern Nigeria," *Government and Opposition,* II (July–October 1967), 509ff.

system during the 1920s and 1930s: political participation was effectively limited to the westernized urban classes and the mass of the traditional peasantry were excluded from power. "It is the essence of the Ataturk Revolution," Frederick Frey has observed, "that it *exploited* the communications bifurcation existing in Turkish society rather than lamenting it or immediately attacking it, as a number of other nationalist movements have done." During the same years, the Kuomintang followed a somewhat similar policy with respect to the Chinese peasantry, and after its removal to Taiwan a somewhat looser exclusionary policy was followed with respect to the bifurcation between mainlanders and islanders. In Colombia the bi-party agreement to alternate the presidency and to divide parliamentary seats was a less highly developed mechanism designed to achieve, however, basically the same purpose of excluding the lower classes from political power.[26]

The leadership of an exclusionary single party is thus dedicated to the indefinite maintenance of a bifurcated society and the indefinite exclusion of the subordinate group from politics. The leadership of a revolutionary single party, in contrast, is dedicated to the rapid end of the bifurcation of society through the elimination of conversion of the opposing social force. In most cases the constituency social force of a revolutionary one-party system is defined in class, occupational, or other economic terms. One notable case of a revolutionary one-party system which attempted to define an ethnic base is Nazi Germany. Indeed, it was precisely this combination of racial constituency plus revolutionary goals which was responsible for its uniquely frightening characteristics and which led straight to its genocidal policies.

TABLE 3   BIFURCATION AND ONE-PARTY SYSTEMS

| | POLICIES TOWARD BIFURCATION | |
BASIS OF BIFURCATION	EXCLUSIONARY	REVOLUTIONARY
Ethnic-Religious	Ulster Liberia	Nazi Germany
Economic	Kemalist Turkey Nationalist China	Communist regimes Mexico

More usually, the constituency social force in a revolutionary one-party system is defined in economic terms, and its political leadership attempts to induce, persuade, or coerce "nationalist bourgeoisie" or "peasantry" to

26. Frederick W. Frey, "Political Development, Power, and Communications in Turkey," in Lucian Pye, ed., *Communications and Political Development* (Princeton: Princeton University Press, 1963), p. 313. For comparison of the Colombian Front to one-party systems, see Robert H. Dix, *Colombia: The Political Dimensions of Change* (New Haven: Yale University Press, 1967), pp. 392–399.

adopt the proper "proletarian" code of behavior. It is a mobilizing, prosely-tizing movement dedicated to the creation of a society of equals—or a classless society—which will forever end social cleavage. Obviously it never achieves its goal completely, but obviously also revolutionary single-party systems do bring into existence societies in which the ideal is equality and in which the fact is far greater homogeneity and equality than ever existed in the pre-one-party society.

FROM MONOPOLY TO COMPETITION: THE DEMOCRATIZATION OF EXCLUSIONARY ONE-PARTY SYSTEMS

In an exclusionary system a single significant political organization repre-senting the interests of the dominant social force monopolizes power and the subordinate social force is indefinitely excluded from political roles. The system is a modern version of a two-class or two-caste society. The aristocracy of birth or wealth, however, is formalized and organized through a party structure. Modern forms of political organization are used to main-tain a non-modern pattern of society. Societies with more modern social structures, in contrast, typically have either revolutionary one-party systems or competitive party systems. The maintenance of an exclusionary one-party system depends on: (1) a sympathetic or indifferent international environment that does not challenge the legitimacy of the system; (2) a significant difference in political consciousness and political mobilization between the constituency and excluded social forces; and (3) a relatively high degree of unity within the political elite of the constituency social force.

Social and economic modernization, in the long run, undermines these conditions. To the extent that the society is open to influence from the world community, the two-class system will gradually lose its legitimacy. A mod-ern society implies at least formal equality among citizens. The maintenance of a bifurcated social system increasingly loses support among the elite of the system and the system itself becomes open to sanctions and pressures from the more modern societies with which it becomes involved. At this point the society may withdraw from the international community and, like South Africa, attempt to return to a modern version of the "splendid isola-tion" by which Sparta maintained its two-class system. Or, if isolation is impossible, the system may have to adapt to the political, moral, and ideo-logical pressures brought to bear on it from outside. In 1945 the Turks felt the need to progress toward a more democratic politics in order to conform to the model of the victorious western powers in World War II and to be accepted into the United Nations. Two years later the need for U.S. military and economic assistance reinforced these tendencies. As Adnan Menderes, the future leader of the Democratic Party, remarked in 1946:

> The difficulties encountered during the war years uncovered and showed the weak points created by the one-party system in the structure of the

country. The hope in the miracles of one-party system vanished, as the one-party system countries were defeated everywhere. Thus, the one-party mentality was destroyed in the turmoil and fire of the second World War. No country can remain unaffected by the great international events and the contemporary dominating international currents. This influence was felt in our country too.[27]

In similar fashion, the independence of other African countries impelled President Tubman to remove the formal distinctions between Americo-Liberians and natives, and the economic and social incorporation of the South into the American national community brought increasing pressures against its racial bifurcation and single-party systems.

Modernization of the society also tends to produce changes in the excluded social force, such as increasing literacy, urbanization, and education, which lead to increased political consciousness and mobilization. Economic and social change also tends to diversify the social and political elite, to introduce potentially disruptive antagonisms within the single party and the constituency social force, and eventually to produce new, more complex lines of cleavage cutting across the previously dominant bifurcation.

The political leadership of an exclusionary system can react to these challenges in one or a combination of three ways. It can attempt to slow down social and economic change and to channel it in ways that will minimize conflict within the existing elite and hamper the development of political consciousness by the excluded social force. In Liberia, for instance, government policy encouraging foreign investment tended and in part was designed to prevent the emergence of a Liberian entrepreneurial elite controlling relatively autonomous sources of economic power. For many years, in the American South, educational policies tended to slow down the development of higher economic and political aspirations on the part of Negroes. Secondly, the political leaders can resort to repression to contain elite disunity and mass dissatisfaction on the part of the excluded social force. Increasing use of police, population control measures, internal passports, and informer systems among the excluded social force mark the gradual evolution of the one-party system into a full-scale garrison-police state. More repression of the excluded social force may also require more participation by the constituency social force in the control functions. The constituency population is armed and organized into militia and self-defense units. As the system becomes increasingly authoritarian with respect to one social force, it becomes increasingly populistic with respect to the other. Through these means the political elite may well be able to postpone—perhaps indefinitely—the breakdown of the political system that guarantees its authority. It will, however, always remain vulnerable to the potential

27. Quoted in Kemal H. Karpat, *Turkey's Politics: The Transition to a Multi-Party System* (Princeton: Princeton University Press, 1959), p. 140n.

mobilization of the excluded social force by an effective counterelite, and if this social force is equal in size to or larger than the constituency social force, such mobilization can well destroy the system through either secession or revolution. The Chinese Communists, capitalizing on long-standing peasant grievances and the politicizing impact of the Japanese occupation, successfully mobilized the peasants and overthrew the exclusionary Nationalist regime in mainland China.

A third course for the political leadership of an exclusionary one-party system is to accept both modernization and its political consequences (elite disunity and excluded social force mobilization) and to attempt to adapt their political system to these developments. One segment of the political elite, for instance, may downgrade the importance of the existing bifurcation and appeal to the previously excluded social force for support in its struggle with the other segments of the political elite. Conceivably, this mobilization could take place within the established single-party and both constituency social force and previously excluded social force could articulate their interests through the same political framework. In fact, however, this does not happen. The party system presupposes bifurcation. The dissident segment of the political elite that appeals to the excluded social force usually forms a new political vehicle for that purpose. Alternatively and less frequently, the dominant leadership group in the established party takes the lead in appealing to the excluded force and the dissident segment of the political elite forms a new political organization based on the previously dominant social force. Or, conceivably, two or more parties come into existence that appeal along new lines of cleavage to elements of both the previous constituency and excluded social forces. A portion of the previously dominant political elite may thus preserve its authority at the expense of the political institutions with which it was once identified. But the shift is still made from a single-party system to a competitive-party system.

The elite within an exclusionary system is often preeminently a political elite. Its power derives from its control over the governmental and party apparatus; its members see politics as the preferable and natural career for themselves. In Turkey during the 1920s and 1930s the political system was dominated by military officers, bureaucrats, and others who generally disdained private careers and carried over into republican Turkey many of the identifications characteristic of the Ottoman bureaucracy. In Liberia the decline of commercial enterprise on the part of the Americo-Liberians in the latter part of the nineteenth century coincided with the emergence of the single-party system; "government, politics and law became the only respectable ways of getting a living, and so they have remained until very recently."[28] In the American South traditionally there was a similar pref-

28. Merran Fraenkel, *Tribe and Class in Monrovia* (New York: Oxford University Press, 1964), p. 18.

erence for legal and governmental skills compared to commercial and industrial ones. On Taiwan the mainlanders who dominated the higher echelons of the Kuomintang played little role in the tremendous expansion of the private economic sector in the 1950s and 1960s.

In all these cases not only did the elite of the constituency social force monopolize political leadership positions, but, like Spartans, they also tended to eschew other career opportunities. To the extent that members of this elite did go into business enterprises, they were typically enterprises closely associated with the government and the capital for them typically came, legally or illegally, from the public treasury. The principal threat to the maintenance of this type of system comes from the diversification of the elite resulting from the rise of new groups controlling autonomous sources of economic power, that is, from the development of an independently wealthy business and industrial middle class. In the Ottoman Empire, for instance, commercial activities had been the preserve of Greeks, Armenians, and other minorities. The republic eliminated these groups by migration or massacre, and it was almost a generation before their places were taken by new Turkish entrepreneurs. These years "saw the rise for the first time in history of a Turkish business class."[29] Many members of this class emerged out of politics, using political connections as stepping stones to economic independence. Others made their way purely through the economic realm and only entered politics after achieving economic success. In any event, businessmen of both types played leading roles in the events of the mid-1940s, which transformed Turkey from a single- to a multi-party system.

The shift to a competitive party system in Turkey in 1945 and 1946 was led by members of the existing political elite, representing the interests of middle-class business and entrepreneurial groups who were unhappy with the economic policies of the Republican Peoples Party (RPP) government. "These new Turkish business men and managers," as one scholar has noted, "were self-confident, self-reliant, and ambitious; they were becoming very resentful of the controls and restrictions imposed upon them by what they had begun to regard as the dead hand of officialdom. The civil servant was falling from the dizzy eminence that he once occupied in the Turkish social hierarchy. . . . The appearance of a new and flourishing commercial class was radically changing the political balance of forces in the country, and affecting even her traditional social ethos."[30] The first opposition party was founded in July, 1945 by an extremely wealthy Istanbul industrialist. In January, 1946 it was displaced as the leading opposition by the Democratic

29. Dankwart A. Rustow, "Politics and Development Policy," in Frederick C. Shorter, ed., *Four Studies on the Economic Development of Turkey* (London: Frank Cass, 1967), p. 12.

30. Bernard Lewis, *The Emergence of Modern Turkey* (New York: Oxford University Press, 1961), p. 467.

Party founded by four leading political figures of the Republican Peoples Party. Significantly, the principal leader in the formation of the Democratic Party in 1945 was Celal Bayar, a bureaucrat turned banker; the dominant figure in its successor party, the Justice Party, in the 1960s was Suleyman Demirel, a bureaucrat turned businessman. The Democratic Party endorsed five of the six principles of Kemalism, but attacked the policy of etatism and advocated a shift toward a more liberal reliance on private enterprise.[31]

The emergence in Turkey of an entrepreneurial middle class and of a segment of the political elite which identified with that class confronted the leadership of the RPP with three possible choices. They could, conceivably, adopt a policy of repression, using the power of the state to confiscate or reduce the autonomous centers of economic wealth and to purge and imprison the dissident political leaders. Such a course, however, would have had harmful effects on economic development and also would clearly have injured Turkey's somewhat probationary standing in the post-war Allied-dominated international community. Alternatively, the RPP leaders could have attempted to contain this emerging social force and the dissident political leadership within the framework of the dominant party. This, however, would have required some major changes in the thrust of government policy and, more importantly, a sharing of power and office with the dissident leadership (one of whom, Bayar, was a former premier and a potential replacement of Inonu as President). From the viewpoint of the RPP leadership, a third course was clearly preferable: respond to international pressure and domestic development by permitting the dissident elements to organize one or more opposition parties. Such a course would involve some costs in terms of political criticism and opposition, but the position of the RPP was so overwhelmingly dominant it was hard to conceive of it being dislodged from power.

If this was the calculation, it was wrong. The events of 1946–1950 demonstrated the extent to which the dynamics of competition can transform a political system. The Democratic Party attracted almost all those elements who for two decades had accumulated grievances against the RPP. The gradual penetration of communications media into the countryside in the 1930s and 1940s made it possible for the new party to break down the previously existing bifurcation between urban elite and rural peasantry. Combining appeals to the traditional religious values and to the concrete economic interests of the farmer, the Democratic Party was able to mobilize the peasantry into politics as a massive voting bloc on its side.

Turkey is the most clear-cut instance of the shift from an exclusionary one-party system to a competitive system. In somewhat more complex fashion, however, the same processes of external pressure, elite diversification, and social mobilization have been responsible for the gradual break-

31. Karpat, *op. cit.*, pp. 148ff.; Rustow, *op. cit.*, p. 24.

down of the one-party systems in the American South. In these cases, too, a crucial role has been played by the emergence of an indigenous business and industrial elite, which is more concerned with promoting economic growth than with preserving the racial status quo and which consequently does not hesitate to follow its economic predilections and identify itself with the Republican Party. In Taiwan in the 1960s the development of a prosperous islander middle class posed problems of adaptation for the Kuomintang (KMT) leadership comparable to those which confronted Turkey in the 1940s. The KMT faced a rising opposition vote in the urban areas; in 1964 it elected mayors in only two of the five major cities on the island. Like the RPP leadership, that of the KMT had the choice of suppressing this opposition, assimilating it into the KMT, or permitting it to continue to develop. In the 1960s in some measure it did a little of all three. Perhaps most significantly, unlike the RPP, it made some efforts to incorporate the new groups into the party. In the fall of 1968 the KMT leadership announced a policy of achieving greater separation between party and government and appointed prominent businessmen to head the party in the two main cities on the island.[32]

In Liberia, in contrast, the political leadership adopted policies designed to maintain the existing system. After his first election to the presidency in 1944, Tubman announced a "unification" policy that would abolish the previous distinctions between Americo-Liberians and natives. Some changes were, indeed, made in the representation of the natives in the legislature, in reducing compulsory labor and the confiscation of tribal lands, and in providing better educational and welfare facilities. These measures were, in large part, required by the growth of African nationalism in the rest of West Africa and, as a result, it no longer became acceptable "in Liberia publicly to make distinctions between civilized and uncivilized elements of the population or, indeed, to use the traditional designations of Americo-Liberians and Natives." The changes, however, did not affect fundamentals. "The fiction of equality receives official sanction; but in matters of structure and substance, it remains fiction."[33] While acquiescing in the rhetoric of equality between constituency and excluded social groups, the government also pursued economic policies designed to minimize diversification among the elite. Tubman's so-called open door policy with respect to foreign investment maintained a distinction between economic and political power. Foreigners were allowed to invest but were not allowed to become citizens or to own land. Foreign investment, in turn, precluded Liberians themselves from amassing fortunes except through government channels. Economic neocolonialism, in a sense, thus underwrote the exclusionary political sys-

32. *The New York Times,* October 13, 1958, p. 16.

33. George Dalton, "History, Politics, and Economic Development in Liberia," *Journal of Economic History,* XXV (December 1965), 585.

tem. The political elite remained united and secure in its monopoly of power. For the Americo-Liberians, "it is the ethic of Mississippi that most nearly characterizes their outlook: to retain power in traditional fashion and to keep the Natives in their place."[34]

FROM REVOLUTION TO INSTITUTION: THE EMERGENCE OF ESTABLISHED ONE-PARTY SYSTEMS

In the exclusionary one-party system the breakdown of the bifurcation of society means the breakdown of the system. Conversely, if the party system changes, the bifurcation is also undermined. One is the corollary of the other. It would be wrong, however, to generalize this pattern of evolution to revolutionary systems. Exclusionary one-party systems change when they fail; revolutionary one-party systems change when they succeed. In both cases, the end of the bifurcation undermines the basis of the system, but in the revolutionary system the end of bifurcation is the goal of the system. The result is change but a different pattern of change from that which characterizes the exclusionary systems. The end of the bifurcation leads not to the emergence of a pluralistic party system but instead to what may be termed an established one-party system. The system is adapted to changed circumstances, much as ruling monarchies eventually became constitutional ones or the aristocratic two-party system of late eighteenth century England eventually evolved into the mass-party system of the twentieth century. The established one-party system is the descendant of the revolutionary one-party system, but it is also a new type of system with different characteristics and must be judged by different criteria. It reflects the needs of a relatively consensual society rather than those of a sharply divided one.

The revolutionary one-party system is a familiar phenomenon to social scientists. Its social dynamism, autocratic and charismatic leadership, disciplined party, highly developed ideology, stress on propaganda and mass mobilization combined with coercion and terror, and its commitment to the destruction of existing institutions have been fully delineated in, among others, the Friedrich-Brzezinski model of totalitarianism and the Tucker model of the movement-regime.[35] Both models offer appropriate standards by which to analyze revolutionary one-party systems. They are inappropriate to the analysis of exclusionary one-party systems, a limitation which Friedrich-Brzezinski recognize but Tucker does not. More significantly, both

34. *Ibid.*, p. 584.

35. Carl J. Friedrich and Zbigniew K. Brzezinski, *Totalitarian Dictatorship and Autocracy*, 2nd ed., rev. by Friedrich (New York: Frederick A. Praeger, 1966), esp. pp. 375–378; Robert C. Tucker, "Towards a Comparative Politics of Movement-Regimes," *American Political Science Review*, LV (June 1961), 281–289. See also Brzezinski's later critique of Soviet adaptation, "The Soviet Political System," pp. 1–14.

models are inappropriate for the analysis of one-party systems that have evolved from the revolutionary phase reflecting the bifurcation of society to the post-revolutionary phase based on a high degree of homogeneity in society. Friedrich-Brzezinski argue that the future of totalitarian regimes is "unclear," although some "internal transformation" is possible and "an increasing recognition of law and legal restraints" could provide the way to greater stability. Tucker says that movement-regimes may lose their "revolutionary momentum eventually" and become what he terms " 'extinct' movement-regimes,"—surely a classic case of semantically ducking the issue, since his phrase implies that the movement-regime is dead, but gives no indication of what may have taken its place.

Lack of a model of a post-revolutionary one-party system encourages the tendency to judge such systems by the standards of their predecessors. One-party systems are evaluated by their deviations from the revolutionary, totalitarian, or movement-regime model, and when they do deviate, as they must, are judged to be verging on "degeneration" or "extinction." In effect, the achievements of the child are judged by the standards of the parent. This may be appropriate if the child attempts to duplicate the achievements of the parents. But if the child responds to different needs and has different goals—as in the Buddenbrooks-Rostow dynamics, he is almost certain to have—then his performance must be analyzed and evaluated in terms of a different model. Such a model of an "established one-party system" may differ from the revolutionary one-party system as much as the latter differed from the traditional Tsarist, Porfirian, Manchu, or colonial autocracy which it succeeded.

The evolution of a revolutionary one-party system into an established one-party system goes through three phases, which may be usefully labeled *transformation, consolidation,* and *adaptation.* These phases are analytically distinct. They may overlap in practice, but a minimum sequence is maintained in that a revolutionary one-party system enters the transformation phase before it enters the other two, and it enters the consolidation phase before it begins the process of adaptation. In each phase the party and its political leadership confront the consequences of their successes in the earlier phase. They may not deal successfully with those consequences; they may, indeed, like the leadership of China in the 1960s, attempt to stop the transition from one phase to another. But, in general, there are no inherent reasons why a revolutionary one-party system cannot evolve into an established one-party system.

Revolutionary one-party systems usually achieve in their early phases a fairly high level of organizational and institutional development, combining mass participation and a strong party organization, which creates the possibility of adapting the system to changing requirements of its environment. In this respect, a striking difference exists between a strong, revolutionary one-party system and a weak, abortive one-party system. In Franco Spain, for instance, even those most active in the political system had little hope for the adaptation of the system from within. Consequently, those who wished to change the system withdrew from the system. "I no longer saw hope of democratic evolution," said one former cabinet minister explaining why he left the government.[36] The expectations in Spain during the last years of the Franco regime were that change would be brought about after the death of Franco by the emergence of new political leaders and forces who had not been identified with the system. In East Europe, in contrast, in the 1960s it became clear that modifications of the system could take place and were taking place as a result of the initiative of key participants within the system. Significant economic reforms were introduced in many East European communist states; important adaptations of political institutions took place in Yugoslavia and, briefly in Czechoslovakia; the displacement of Novotny by Dubcek demonstrated that an important change in leadership could be mediated through the institutional processes of a one-party regime. In East Europe, apparently, change of the political system could come from within the system; in Spain, it would come from outside the system.

Transformation The conquest of formal authority by the revolutionary party inaugurates a phase in which the principal aim is the transformation of society: the destruction of the old order and its replacement by new political institutions and social patterns appropriate for a homogeneous rather than a bifurcated society. The nature and success of these efforts, in large part, depend on the level of social and political development achieved in the pre-revolutionary society. In a highly complex society like the Germany of the 1930s, "Gleichschaltung" will necessarily be violent and extreme and even then not entirely successful. In a less developed society, the revolutionary transformation may be much more all-encompassing.

The familiar revolutionary, movement-regime, and totalitarian models of one-party systems stress the monistic tendencies toward the atomization of society and the subordination of all groups to party control. In the transformation phase of a revolutionary one-party system these tendencies dominate. The survival of the system may well depend upon the ability of the party to assert itself against fissiparous tendencies of autonomous interest groups. In Bolivia, for instance, the worker and peasant organizations were created independent of the party and maintained substantial autonomy through the period of MNR rule. They were often able to defy the government, and the independence of the miners was, indeed, one factor leading to the overthrow of the MNR regime in 1964. This experience may be contrasted with that of the Neo-Destour. In Tunisia the business and farmer organizations were created by the party and in large part led by

36. Quoted in J. H. Huizinga, "Franco and the Spanish Furies," *Interplay,* I (April 1968), 17.

party workers whose loyalties were first to the party and then to their organized group. The labor federation, on the other hand, had developed with a high degree of autonomy from the party but was effectively brought within the party after the struggle between Bourguiba and Ben Salah in 1956. Similar assertions of the control of the party over interest associations have taken place in most of the one-party states of tropical Africa.[37] The strongest resistance against the process usually comes from the most entrenched conservative institutions, of which the church is most important. Where the Catholic church has existed for an extended period of time, as in Poland and Mexico, the revolutionary party may well have to settle for accommodation with it rather than elimination of it.

In the transformation phase the party organization is the leading force for innovation and change. In its efforts to destroy and to reconstruct, it inevitably clashes with the state bureaucracy inherited from the previous regime. In Russia, for instance, the bifurcation of the society was, in some measure, reflected in a bifurcation between party and bureaucracy. The bureaucracy was essentially a part of the old order, and the party had to develop an elaborate system of political commissars and other forms of control to guard against its potentially anti-Soviet actions. Subsequently the party brought into existence new schools and other institutions to create Soviet military officers, manager, experts, and bureaucrats. The bifurcation between party and bureaucracy was eased, and in due course the extreme forms of party control over the bureaucracy could be moderated or abandoned. Throughout these phases, however, the party was the generator of change and the bureaucracy the defender of continuity.

The struggle with the old order and the effective destruction of its institutions typically require the concentration of revolutionary authority in a single autocratic leader. Some political orders are the work of many men, but one-party systems seem to be more the work of one man than other types of systems. Lenin, Mao, Hitler, Mussolini, Tito, Paz Estenssoro, Castro, Bourguiba, Nkrumah, Toure, Nyerere, created their parties, and for a while, system, party, and man tended to be identified one with another. The party is the organizational instrument of the leader; the leader is the charismatic embodiment of the party. The core of the party is the lieutenants of the leader, and the identity of interest between party and leader in the conquest of power and the destruction of the old order is virtu-

---

37. See Immanuel Wallerstein, "Voluntary Associations," in Coleman and Rosberg, *op. cit.,* pp. 337–339, and Elliot J. Berg and Jeffrey Butler, "Trade Unions," *ibid.,* pp. 341, 366; Clement H. Moore, in Charles A. Micaud, *et al., Tunisia: The Politics of Modernization* (New York: Frederick A. Praeger, 1964), pp. 86, 104; Clement H. Moore, "Mass Party Regimes in Africa," in Herbert J. Spiro, ed., *Africa: The Primacy of Politics* (New York: Random House, 1966), p. 105; Douglas E. Ashford, *The Elusiveness of Power: The African Single Party State* (Ithaca: Cornell University Center for International Studies, 1965), pp. 11–14.

ally complete. The disappearance of the traditional sources of authority creates the opportunity and the need for charismatic leadership to fill the vacuum.

For similar reasons ideology also plays a legitimating role during the revolutionary phase. It defines the goal, identifies the enemy, and justifies the struggle. It furnishes a plan to guide the intellectual leadership of the party and a means of mobilizing popular support and participation in the efforts to destroy the old political institutions and old social structure.

Consolidation   The reconstitution of society is thus guided by and legitimated by an ideology and a leader. Initially, both of these serve the ends of the party. Once the old order, however, has been substantially destroyed and the social basis laid for a new one, both ideological commitment and charismatic leadership tend to become dysfunctional to the maintenance of the new system. The consolidation of that system requires the establishment of the supremacy of the party as the source of legitimacy and the source of power against the leader and the ideology which earlier played indispensable roles in the liquidation of the old order.

Ideology is often identified as necessarily playing a major role in one-party systems. In actuality, of course, ideology is linked not to any particular form of organization but rather to the process of change. In periods of intense, rapid, and violent change and conflict, ideology naturally plays an important role. Once the society settles down, the need for ideology declines, and the ideology itself begins to "erode." In a bifurcated society, ideology is essential; in a consensual society, it is superfluous. It is no longer required to legitimate the system, and, indeed, a stress on ideology and its role may threaten the existence of the system.

Unless the party leadership makes strenuous efforts to prevent it, ideology tends to become less important and less relevant in revolutionary one-party systems. In East Europe, as H. Gordon Skilling observes, there has been "a diminution of faith in the official theory despite persistent efforts to impose it on the minds of men." Ideology, as another scholar has put it, is "gradually being replaced by pragmatism." In the Soviet Union, similar trends were observed in the 1950s and 1960s. "Marxist-Leninist doctrine for some time," it was argued in 1966, "has had little effect on the attitudes and feelings of the people of the U.S.S.R. . . . Most party members are mere careerists who use Marxist doctrine only as a shield to defend their own actions and as a sword against their rivals."[38] Party leaders often respond to the decline in ideology by promoting greater efforts by their propaganda and agitation departments to inculcate new generations in the old faith. The result is self-defeating, as the concepts and slogans that play

38. H. Gordon Skilling, *The Government of Communist East Europe* (New York: Thomas Y. Crowell, 1966), pp. 210–211; Joseph R. Strayer, "Problems of Dictatorship: The Russian Experience," *Foreign Affairs*, XLIV (January 1966), 272–273.

useful roles in the transformation of society are found to have little relevance to the consolidation of that society. "What do these phrases mean?" as one young activist at Moscow State University asked the head of the CPSU's ideological commission. "If they mean something, please tell us; if they don't mean anything, why do you keep on saying them?"[39]

The key question concerns the effects of ideological erosion on the system. The argument here is that the decline of ideology in one-party systems is a sign not of decay but of stability—an indicator not of the weakness but of the strength of the regime. Historically ideology is clearly linked to conflict and cleavage. In modern societies, indeed, any serious cleavage takes on ideological overtones. The decline of ideology consequently would be impossible if the one-party were threatened by serious social tensions. It may, indeed, become increasingly in the interests of the regime to promote this decline. The erosion of ideology, in short, goes hand in hand with the acceptance, stability, and long-term vitality of the system.

The relation between ideological emphasis and institutional weakness is clearly visible in non-communist one-party systems. In the mid-1960s the weaker, the more tentative, the more fragile the system, the greater the emphasis the leaders of the system placed on ideology. The efforts to formulate and propagate an ideology on the part of people like Nkrumah, Sukarno, Toure, Nyerere, and others varied more or less directly with the instability of their systems. In contrast, in the two most firmly established non-communist one-party systems, those of Mexico and Tunisia, ideology received much less attention. In Mexico the myths and symbols of the Revolution were regularly invoked by all political groupings to justify their actions, but no one seriously claimed that the Revolution had an ideology or tried to develop one. In Tunisia, Bourguibism was the local label for pragmatism and a synonym for gradualism. The more stable communist one-party systems may also be those in which ideology receives the shortest shrift. In the 1960s Yugoslavia was probably the least ideological of the communist states. Yet was it not also probably the most stable? Renewed stress on ideology, as in China, in contrast, is usually a portent of social tension and political conflict.

Except in the special, limited sense in which Karl Mannheim used the term, ideology almost always implies a critique of the existing situation and of existing institutions. A new system of political institutions may well be legitimated in ideological terms. In due course, however, this becomes increasingly difficult. Existing institutions may be rationalized and defended in terms of a conservative ideology, but they cannot be effectively justified by an "ideational" ideology, whether socialist, Marxist, or liberal. The justi-

39. Quoted in Peter Grose, "The Communist Party Is the Rear Guard of Russia," *New York Times Magazine*, March 27, 1966, p. 131.

fication of the political system comes increasingly to rest on its institutional rather than its ideological characteristics. Indeed, as Carl Beck suggests, as with the American system, sheer "historical givenness" may well become the most persuasive legitimation of the system.[40]

At some point in the consolidation of a one-party system, ideology ceases to be a way of achieving consensus and instead becomes a threat to consensus. In Poland in the late 1960s, for instance, various ideological groups played significant roles. These included orthodox Marxist-Leninist-Gomulkaists, Stalinists, Maoists, "liberal" Marxists, non-Marxist socialists, and the non-Marxist Catholics of the Znak group. On the ideological level, these groups divided sharply and even profoundly. None of them, however, challenged the legitimacy of existing Polish political and economic institutions. The Catholic intellectuals of Znak, for instance, "accept the existing political and social system and the foreign and domestic policies of the regime," and they played active roles in the Sejm and the State Council. Yet they also "reject Marxism, proclaim openly their adherence to a Catholic world view, and defend their religious interests in legislative matters." In the words of one of their leaders, "Despite differences in world outlook between Catholics and Marxists, we desire within the framework of the socialist system to cooperate in everything which is good, moral and creative for the individual and the community, in all which can lift the social masses to a higher level of economic, cultural and moral life."[41] In such a situation, the interests of the regime are to minimize its ideological rationale, which would clearly alienate erstwhile supporters on both left and right, and instead to stress its justification in the realities of the situation and in the operating effectiveness of its institutions. The regime gains by down-playing its own ideology as well as everyone else's. Similarly, in Mexico, the leaders of the PRI have little interest in maintaining ideological purity if this means antagonizing foreign and domestic business interests with which they must do business. Support for the regime—or at least acceptance of the regime— is broader than acceptance of the theoretical rationale behind it. Just as in the United States or other western societies, many individuals and groups with varying ideological beliefs—explicit and unarticulated—may accept the existing system. In this sense, Kolakowski was undoubtedly right when he argued that in Poland "the word 'Marxist' no longer means a person who recognizes a definite, meaningful view of the world, but a person of a definite intellectual make-up who is distinguished by his readiness to recognize the views established institutionally."[42]

40. See my "Conservatism as an Ideology," *American Political Science Review*, LI (June 1957), 454–473, and Carl Beck, "Bureaucracy and Political Development in Eastern Europe," in Joseph LaPalombara, ed., *Bureaucracy and Political Development* (Princeton: Princeton University Press, 1963), pp. 299–300.

41. Skilling, *op. cit.*, p. 129; Jerzy Zawieyski, quoted in Richard Hiscocks, *Poland: Bridge for the Abyss?* (New York: Oxford University Press, 1963), p. 326.

42. Quoted in Brzezinski, *Soviet Bloc*, p. 310.

The relationship between leader and party changes in a similar way. In the initial struggle for power, the interests of the party and leader are virtually identical. The movement or party is an extension of the leader. This identity of interest continues at least for a while after the leader and party have acquired the formal attributes of power. The party is then the means by which the leader extends his control over existing social and governmental institutions or attacks and destroys those institutions. A parallel identity of interest between party organization and aspiring leader may also occur during succession struggles within the one-party system. In the Soviet case Stalin and Khrushchev identified their interests with those of the party *apparat* and their conquest of power also represented a victory for the party organization against its personal and institutional rivals.

Once the leader and party are securely in power, however, their interests begin to diverge. The leader wishes to maximize his own power, which means that he must avoid becoming the prisoner of any particular institution or group. Unlike the president or premier in a constitutional system, he does not have any institutional basis of authority. He may hold many offices or none at all, but his power clearly is personal, not institutional. He thus necessarily opposes the development of institutions that could restrain his power. He tries to reduce the authority of the party and to balance it off against the army, the bureaucracy, the police, mass organizations, and other groups. The leader comes to see the party as more and more of a challenge to his personal authority as leader.

Eventually, the leader goes beyond his efforts to subordinate the party by balancing it with external checks and attempts to weaken and perhaps even to destroy the party internally. At this point, the leader explicitly articulates the contrast between his personal, charismatic authority, and the routinized, bureaucratic authority embodied in the party. The leader typically attempts to revive the enthusiasm, the dynamism, the egalitarianism, and primitive austerity that characterized the movement in its earliest phases. Literally and symbolically, Mao returns to Yenan, Castro to the Sierra Maestra, Ben Gurion to the Negev, and Nyerere to the bush. In Tanganyika alone, however, was this effort to restore revolutionary dynamism linked to efforts to strengthen the party. Elsewhere, the drive to "keep the revolution going" was a drive to expand popular mobilization and to reduce party institutionalization, in short, to undermine the stability of the one-party system. In Cuba, Castro continuously resisted Soviet urgings that he strengthen and institutionalize the party organization; he wanted to keep it at a low level of institutionalization. In China, the relatively high level of institutionalization achieved by the Chinese Communist Party required Mao to resort to the frenzied activities of the Cultural Revolution to reduce the authority of party from both within and without.

The extent to which the party consolidates its authority vis-à-vis the leader can be measured in terms of three criteria. One is the extent to which the party monopolizes access to the top leadership position. Where the authority of the party is strong the top leader will be a product of the party and will be a party careerist, having worked his way up through the ranks of the party organization. This is the situation in both Mexico and the Soviet Union. Where party authority was weak, the top leader may be a party member, but he may, more importantly, be a product of the military or civil bureaucracies or of a populist mass movement not dominated by the party. A second criterion of party strength vis-à-vis the leader is the extent to which the party monopolizes the process by which the top leader is chosen. If military, religious, labor, or other groups or leaders play a key role in the selection of the top leader for the political system, clearly the authority of the party is weak vis-à-vis that leader (and those other groups). In this sense, as Merle Fainsod has suggested, the extent to which the removal of Khrushchev and the emergence of his successors was handled entirely within the CPSU structure was an indication of the strength of the party in the 1960s as compared to its weaker position in the 1950s when the secret police, managers, and army played roles in the post-Stalin succession struggle.[43] Finally, the authority of the party is enhanced to the extent that the formal office which the leader occupies is a party office. If the top leader is President of the Republic, the Osagyefo, Der Fuehrer, or Il Duce, he has claims to authority transcending those which he derives from the party.

Perhaps the gravest threat to stability in a one-party system is the problem of succession. In a non-party, traditional monarchy, succession was institutionalized through heredity. In competitive party systems, succession is institutionalized within the system by the alternation of parties in office and within the parties by their own rules and procedures for selecting officers and candidates. In a one-party system succession has to take place within the party and the way in which succession is arranged goes directly to the heart of the problem of the relationship between the leader and the party. With one exception all one-party systems are the product of the twentieth century and most the product of the mid-twentieth century. In almost all systems—communist and non-communist—the founding leader remains in office until he dies. The only clear-cut exceptions to this rule are the two Latin American one-party systems in Mexico and Bolivia and two of the East European systems, Poland and Hungary, where, however, the founding leader was less important than in other systems because of the foreign influences responsible for bringing it into being. In all other one-party systems the founding leader either died in office or was in office in 1968. The creation of a succession system, consequently, normally has to wait until the death of the leader, and normally, of course, the leader has little interest in attempting to develop a means of providing a successor.

43. Merle Fainsod, "The Dynamics of One-Party Systems," in Oliver Garceau, ed., *Political Research and Political Theory* (Cambridge: Harvard University Press, 1968), pp. 221–246.

In most political systems, unlike the American system, the death of the top leader produces a succession struggle. A political system, however, which allows the tenure of its top leaders to be determined by health and accident is not a particularly highly developed one. Presumably more adaptable and complex systems have ways of changing leaders under other circumstances and through other means. The development of such techniques is a major turning point in the consolidation of one-party systems. The means of regularizing and providing for NDIO (non-death-in-office) successions differ significantly for those one-party systems where electoral competition retains some reality and for the communist systems where it does not. In Mexico and Bolivia (as in Liberia) the presidential term was set at four to six years, and in all three countries constitution or custom limited tenure to one or two terms. This pattern was broken in Liberia after 1943 when Tubman was regularly reelected to office; Paz Estenssoro also broke it in Bolivia in 1964, thereby contributing to the events which led to the overthrow of him and his party. In Mexico, on the other hand, six NDIO successions occurred on schedule between 1934 and 1968. In all three countries the choice of a successor for the incumbent president was made through the party machinery. In Liberia generally and in Bolivia open struggles for the sucession were resolved in the party's convention. In Mexico the process of *auscultación* was more closed and oligarchical with the incumbent president in effect playing the major role in the selection of his successor in consultation with former presidents and the other principal leaders of the party.

In communist one-party systems the NDIO problem is more difficult to resolve since the position of first secretary or general secretary carries no fixed term of office. As of 1968 communist one-party systems had undergone fourteen successions, eight of which were NDIO successions. One was the removal of Khrushchev. The other seven communist NDIO successions occurred in the East European communist states. Intervention by the Soviet Union, however, played a decisive role in four of these successions (Poland, 1948; Czechoslovakia, 1951; Hungary, July and October 1956); and a partial role in one of them (Bulgaria, 1954). Only the voluntary replacement of Ochab by Gomulka in Poland in 1956 and the involuntary replacement of Novotny by Dubcek in Czechoslovakia in 1968 were NDIO successions determined almost entirely by in-system influences. In 1968 communist systems were thus still evolving procedures for the peaceful removal of first secretaries. The ousters of Khrushchev and Novotny, however, provided possible models for the way in which this could occur.

In general the institutionalization of leadership in a one-party system requires that it be limited in tenure, limited in power, collectivized, or subjected to some combination of these changes. If tenure is limited the leader may exercise extensive power during his term of office and, as in Mexico, have the dominant say in the choice of his successor. If the power of the leader is limited, the penalties for losing power will also be limited, and the way will be opened for irregular but frequent changes in the top leadership without disrupting the system and with the possibility that people will be able to move in and out and back again into leadership positions. The struggle will, in effect, be regulated by rules of the game.[44] Finally, if the leadership is collectivized in a council or bureau, changes can take place in its membership gradually, again without disrupting the system. The authority of the council may be absolute, but the authority of each of its members is limited and a majority of the council can renew itself by co-opting new members and purging old ones.

The inherent conflict between personal leadership and party institutionalization produces a tendency toward bureaucratic and oligarchical leadership in one-party systems. In both Mexico and the Soviet Union, certainly, the top leaders have tended increasingly to be products of the party bureaucracy: "mediocre *apparatchiki*," Zbigniew Brzezinski calls them in the Soviet Union; "managerial specialists" Robert Scott calls them in Mexico.[45] In Mexico the office of the president has become increasingly institutionalized at the same time that the tenure of its occupants has remained strictly limited. In the Soviet Union the tendency is toward oligarchy and to bring into existence "an institutional collective leadership, designed to prevent any one leader from using a particular institution as a vehicle for obtaining political supremacy."[46] The institutionalization of power in a one-party system would appear to lead either toward the division of power among several men for an indefinite period of time or the concentration of power in one man for a limited period of time.

Adaptation The change from a revolutionary to an established one-party system involves struggles between the party organization and a Weberian sequence of opponents. In the initial transformation phase, the party destroys the traditional sources of authority. In the second phases, it consolidates its authority as an organization against the charismatic appeals of the founding leader. In the third, adaptive phase, the party deals with legal-rational challenges to its authority which are, in large part, the product of its earlier successes. The creation of a relatively homogeneous society and the emergence of new social forces require the party to redefine its roles within that society. Four developments which the party must come to terms with are: (1) the emergence of a new, innovative, technical-managerial class; (2) the development of a complex group structure, typical of a more industrial society, whose interests have to be related to the political sphere;

44. See Jerome M. Gilison, "New Factors of Stability in Soviet Collective Leadership," *World Politics*, XIX (July 1967), 571–572.

45. Brzezinski, "The Soviet Political System," p. 5; Robert E. Scott, *op. cit.*, p. 216.

46. Brzezinski, "The Soviet Political System," p. 4.

(3) the reemergence of a critical intelligentsia apart from and, indeed, increasingly alienated from the institutionalized structures of power; and (4) the demands by local and popular groups for participation in and influence over the political system.

Innovative Technocrats In a revolutionary one-party system the party is clearly the principal source of social, economic, and institutional innovation. In an established one-party system, the party plays a very different role. As a result of modernization and economic development, the society and the economy are more complex; organizational and functional units are more numerous. What is required is no longer a general staff directing the fundamental change from one type of society and economy to another but rather a coordinating staff relating to each other the various initiatives taking place within the society. Once a new technical bureaucracy develops identified with the one-party system, it becomes the source of innovations designed not to destroy the system but to improve it. The innovators are not the reds but the experts. The party apparatus, on the other hand, becomes a gyroscope rather than a motor.

Many social scientists see the managerial and technical bureaucracy as a second New Class on the verge of preempting the position and power of the party *apparatchiki*. Such theories represent the application to the one-party state of Veblen's concept of a soviet of engineers, Burnham's theory of the managerial revolution, and Lasswell's projection of a garrison state ruled by military or police specialists. These theories are all, in a sense, the latter day counterpart of Engels' view that the "governing of men" would be replaced by "the administration of things." They all posit the resolution of the conflict between the political generalist and the technical specialist by the displacement and disappearance of the former. Such theories are unhistorical and apolitical. The conflict between political generalist and managerial specialist is built into modern society just as the conflict between church and state was built into medieval society. This conflict is inherent but limited. A complex society requires both increased functional autonomy for managerial specialists *and* increased political authority for the central political leadership. Meeting this latter need is the principle function of the party *apparat*. It is as essential to the system as the expert bureaucracy.

In such a system the conflict between the political generalists and the managerial specialists continues, but it is a conflict between complements, the existence of each of which is necessary for the existence of the other. The erosion of ideology tends to reduce the differences between political needs as seen by the party elite and technical-administrative needs endorsed by the managerial specialists. The conflict becomes unbearable only when the top political leadership, as in China, refuses to adapt to the increasing complexity of society and instead attempts to maintain the original social dynamism of the revolutionary movement. In such a situation, to be revolutionary is to be reactionary. In one-party systems like those in Mexico, East Europe, and the Soviet Union, on the other hand, the managers have been able to exercise increasing initiative in their specialized areas because the principal function of the party organization is now not to change the system but to integrate it. The reversal of roles between party and bureaucracy was explicitly recognized by the Czech party newspaper, which declared: "We are now at the threshold of the scientific-technical revolution. The main initiative and responsibility for its realization is in the hands of the intelligentsia, which has thus become the guarantor of social progress. In this sense, it has become the most revolutionary factor in society.[47]

In an established one-party system party membership, consequently, becomes more and more heterogeneous as more specialized and diverse elite groups join; in due course these groups also play more important roles in the middle and upper echelons of the party bureaucracy. In 1945, for instance, intellectuals made up less than 10 per cent of the 210,000 members of the Polish Communist Party. In 1960, intellectuals comprised 43.5 per cent of a total membership of 1,550,000. Within the "intellectual" category about 25 per cent of the total membership consisted of technical and managerial specialists.[48] At the same time, however, the functions of the party activists become even more distinctive and specialized. In this respect, the middle ranks of the party apparatus tend to become increasingly conservative and resistant to change. The pattern tends to develop in which the technical and managerial specialists become the proponents of change, the middle-level *apparatchiki* the opponents of change, and the top-level party leaders the arbiters and mediators of change.

Interest Groups In established one-party states professional, industrial, commercial, labor, and other socioeconomic groups play a more and more important role in society and increasingly require some definition of their relationships to the political system. In the East European communist states theorists like Dordjevic and Lakatos have stressed the natural role of interest groups in a complex socialist society, and official dogma has also been altered to recognize the legitimacy of specialized interest groups articulating their own needs. In 1966, for instance, the Hungarian Communist Party Congress explicitly stated that within the "broad national unity" that prevailed "with regard to the most important political issues, the building of socialism, and the defense of peace . . . there may appear, for objective and subjective reasons, in some cases temporary but with respect to certain issues even more lasting differences between certain social strata, groups,

47. *Rude Pravo,* quoted in Morton Schwartz, "Czechoslovakia: Toward One-Party Pluralism?" *Problems of Communism,* XVI (January–February 1967), 24.

48. Richard F. Starr, *Poland, 1944–1962: The Sovietization of a Captive People* (Baton Rouge: Louisiana State University Press, 1962), pp. 174–179.

or between local and public interests generally." These "contradictory interests and differences of opinion" are appropriately expressed in debates and are to be taken into consideration by the party in the formulation of policy.[49] In East Europe generally it is likely that representative bodies "may indeed seek increasingly to embody, not the 'public will,' but the specialized and expert views of various segments of society."[50] This willingness to permit interest groups to articulate their needs presumably goes hand in hand with the assumption that the party apparatus will remain the arbiter among these interests.

The theory and analysis of interest groups in politics originally developed in the United States and has had its primary applicability there. In varying degrees, efforts have been made to extend interest group analysis to Western Europe and to the modernizing countries of Asia, Africa, and Latin America. In fact, however, it would appear that the interest group approach is more relevant to established one-party systems—communist and non-communist—than it is to multi-party systems or to the transitional political systems of modernizing societies. A focus on interest groups implicitly assumes a high degree of consensus on fundamental issues in the society and hence the greater importance in political affairs of the conflicts among specific groups over particular interests. The appeal of interest group analysis to East European theorists is an accurate reflection of the nature of politics in those societies.[51]

People associate interest groups with pluralism, and pluralism with liberal democracy. But pluralism can take a corporate form as well as a liberal one, and it would seem to be precisely this pattern that is characteristic of the established one-party in both Mexico and East Europe. Old theories of functional representation, guild socialism, syndicalism, and even Beer's Old Tory and Old Whig theories of the representation of the fixed, corporate interests of the Kingdom seem to find new relevance in the established one-party systems.

Group interests may be related to the political system in one or more of three ways. In Mexico the sectoral organization of the party provides for the representation of interests directly within the party structure. In communist systems the tendency is to maintain the purity of the party and to provide for group representation in either the legislature or through a front coalition. Formal legislative representation is most highly developed in Yugoslavia with its five-chambered National Assembly including, in addition to a territorial Federal Chamber, chambers of Economy, Education,

49. Quoted in Paul Lendvai, "Hungary: Charge vs. Immobilism," *Problems of Communism*, XVI (March–April 1967), 14.

50. Skilling, *op. cit.*, p. 231.

51. See, generally, H. Gordon Skilling, "Interest Groups and Communist Politics," *World Politics*, XVIII (April 1966), 435–451.

Social Welfare and Health, and a Political-Administrative Chamber. Legislation is passed either by the Federal Chamber alone or by the Federal Chamber and one of the functional chambers. The whole structure suggests the late medieval systems of estates, such as prevailed in Sweden until 1865, with its parliament composed of four chambers representing nobles, clergy, bourgeois, and peasants. Czechs have suggested the possible desirability of adapting the Yugoslav system to their country. Lakatos recommended that interest groups nominate candidates for the representative assemblies and that the people be able to choose among them in competitive elections. A third channel for the articulation of group interests may be furnished by a front organization dominated by the Communist Party but including spokesmen for other parties and groups. In Czechoslovakia in the spring of 1968, for instance, the National Front included the Communist and four other parties, plus thirty-four other organizations including labor, youth, student, professional, literary, women's, consumers' cooperative, producers' cooperative, and nationality groups. There was, as one observer commented, "something of the representation-by-guild idea about it all—curious kin to the nonparty formations proposed by the French, Italian, Spanish and Latin American syndicalists in 1900–1914 to serve as law-giving trade-union councils in lieu of corrupt parliamentary parties, an idea seized upon and prostituted by Benito Mussolini when he came to power and tried to fake a corporate state."[52]

The advocacy of somewhat similar ideas of group representation in Hungary in the late 1960s produced a counter-tendency, in which influential party members were "worried about the erosion of the party's power and about the crystallization of social and economic interest groups which will eventually demand decision-making power."[53] There were, as one aide of the Czech Central Committee expressed it, "possible contradictions between specific group interests and the general, predefined aim of society." Groups must be allowed to express their conflicting views in the appropriate arenas in the state structure. At the same time the articulation of group interests does not reduce the need for guidance from the central political institutions. The "overall governmental political leadership," as Mlynar continued, "must not be allowed to be influenced by tendencies to place local or group interest above the needs of society as a whole." The party, of course, remains the exclusive guardian of the interests of society as a whole.[54] "Corporate centralism," Scott's phrase for the Mexican system, would seem to be equally relevant to Eastern Europe.

52. Albert Parry, "Why Moscow Couldn't Stand Prague's Deviation," *New York Times Magazine,* September 1, 1968, p. 47.

53. Lendvai, *op. cit.,* p. 16; Schwartz, *op. cit.,* p. 22; Skilling, *Communist East Europe,* pp. 133, 231.

54. Schwartz, *op. cit.,* p. 25.

Critical Intelligentsia   A revolution is a dramatic and violent expansion of political participation, involving the mobilization of peasant and worker masses by an ideologically motivated intellectual elite. At the close of the revolutionary struggle, popular involvement in politics subsides, but the involvement of the intellectual elite continues, since it is this group that furnishes the cadres to staff the new government. The subsequent history of the one-party system, however, involves marked changes in this pattern. The second generation of leadership comes out of the party apparatus and is largely composed of bureaucrats, not intellectuals. The result is a widening gap between a regime responding to political and institutional needs and intellectuals who in a relatively stable society have lost all their functions except that of criticism. Criticism from intellectuals is the hallmark of any established political system including a one-party system. The stability of the system, in turn, depends upon the capacity of the political elite to mobilize the support of the masses against the intellectual elite.

The separation of the political elite from the intellectuals is signaled by the criticisms of the former by the latter. The concern of the intellectuals with ideology and with the reformulation of the original revolutionary ideology to give it new "meaning" intensifies in the same ratio in which the political elite becomes indifferent to ideology. Every revolutionary one-party state eventually produces both its New Class and its Milovan Djilas to lambaste the New Class. In Mexico, for instance, the typical political leader, in the words of Jesus Silva Herzog, became "the profiteer of the Revolution, concerned exclusively with personal profit." In Poland Kuron and Modzelewski made similar criticisms of the "central party bureaucracy" exploiting the workers.[55] In part, the conflict between the intellectuals and political bureaucracy reflects the differences in functional role; in part, also, it normally reflects differences in social origins. The intellectual critics are likely to come from middle-class, educated backgrounds; they may well, indeed, be children of the political elite. The political leaders, on the other hand, are likely to come from more humble backgrounds and to have made their way to the top through the new avenues of social mobility opened by the revolution. In part, it is precisely their earthiness, vulgarity, and populism that antagonizes the intellectuals. Alienation of the intellectuals, it has been said, is the precursor of revolution. But it is also the consequence of revolution.

The reaction of the political elite to the challenge by the intellectuals usually takes three forms. The direct response is, of course, the coercive one. Most prominent among the intellectuals' demands is that for intellectual freedom. The political elite typically responds to this by carefully circumscribing the permissible area of activity by the intellectuals and jailing

55. See Michael Gamarnikow, "Poland: Political Pluralism in a One-Party State," *Problems of Communism*, XVI (July–August 1967), 4–6; Stanley R. Ross, ed., *Is The Mexican Revolution Dead?* (New York: Alfred A. Knopf, 1966), pp. 17, 22–23.

the most notable dissidents. At the same time the political leaders attempt to divide the intellectual elite from the managerial elite. The managers' demands are usually concrete and limited; those of the intellectuals more diffuse and general. To grant the demands of the intellectuals would be to jeopardize the authority of the political elite and perhaps even the stability of the entire system. To grant the demands of the managerial elites for functional autonomy is to improve the efficiency and performance of the system without posing any real threat to the position of the political leadership. Hence, the political leaders frequently acquiesce in the various demands of the managerial elites and thus provide economic reform and decentralization as substitutes for political liberalization.

Finally, the political elite counters the challenge from the intellectuals by mobilizing against them segments of the masses. In contrast to the middle and upper strata, the lower classes tend to be less tolerant, less liberal, more ethnically and religiously prejudiced, and more favorably disposed to authoritarian solutions. In established one-party states, mass participation in politics thus serves the interest of the political elite. "By mobilizing the masses into social control organizations," as one study has suggested, "the regime attempts to limit and to suppress deviant behavior among other groups in the population."[56] Reliance on such organizations appears to depend on the extent of the challenges to the regime. "The more unstable the regime," as Gyorgy has pointed out with respect to East Europe, "the more extensive the proliferation of these organizations; the smaller the 'core' or 'cadre' of the Party, the larger their size and the broader their professional base." In Albania, Bulgaria, and Czechoslovakia during the 1950s, where there was little effective opposition, mass organizations played a little role. In Hungary and Rumania, they were more important, while in the German Democratic Republic they "displayed a truly phenomenal range and variety in their scope and activities."[57] To support their position, the political elite also often has recourse to populistic appeals of a chauvinist character, such as anti-Semitism, for use against the intellectuals.

Popular Participation   In the first phase of a revolutionary one-party system, the party leadership attempts to mobilize its constituency to play a major role in the destruction and reconstruction of economic, social, and political institutions. In the consolidation phase, mass participation declines sharply as the ideological and charismatic factors connected with it tend to disappear or to become routinized. With the weakening of the bifurcation in society and the effective reconstitution of society, the original need for substantial popular participation in political affairs disappears. Most importantly, the party elite loses its interest in stimulating such participation.

56. Zbigniew Brzezinski and Samuel P. Huntington, *Political Power: USA/USSR* (New York: Viking, 1964), p. 99.

57. Gyorgy, *op. cit.*, pp. 185–187.

The evolution of the system from the consolidation to the adaptation phase produces the social basis for new forms of political participation. In contrast to participation in the reconstitution phase, the legitimation of this new participation derives not from the extreme conflict of interest between two social forces but rather from the absence of major conflicts of interests within the society. It is premised on basic harmony in society rather than fundamental bifurcation.

During the transformation phase popular participation is generally expressed through the social-mobilization organization in which people are enlisted to achieve goals prescribed by the party leadership. In the adaptation phase, in contrast, participation may also assume a more spontaneous form and electoral participation tends to play a more meaningful role. In the transformation phase elections enable the party to legitimate its activities and to identify the populace with its goals. In the adaptation phase, the fundamental identity between the populace and the system tends to be assumed, and the elections enable the populace to make choices between individuals for party and governmental posts. The rationale is simple—and almost unavoidable: If the domestic enemies of the system have been eliminated, why then should not the populace have the opportunity to choose among competing individual candidates all of whom share the same fundamental commitment to the party and the system? If some enemies appear to still exist, electoral competition may also be one way of mobilizing mass sentiment in support of the party against the criticisms of the intellectuals about its "undemocratic" character.

Electoral competition, however, also poses at least a potential threat to the existing party *apparat* whose members have achieved their positions through bureaucratic rather than electoral processes. Consequently, electoral competition is more likely initially to develop for governmental than for party positions. Its inauguration also may be aided by the extent to which the initially dominant founder-leader has been able to survive and see it in his interest, as well as the party's, to introduce electoral competition. The way in which Tito and Nyerere have been able to shake up their party cadres through the mechanism of elections may, in some measure, reduce incentives to accomplish similar results outside the party through either a Stalinist terror or a Maoist Cultural Revolution.

A fairly significant amount of electoral competition among individuals has already developed in several one-party systems. In Yugoslavia in 1965 there were twice as many candidate as seats in the elections for the commune assemblies, and a total of 1,653 candidates ran for the 1,196 seats in the federal parliament. In the 1967 elections, 25 per cent of the seats in the federal assembly were contested by more than one candidate. In 1965 in Poland 617 candidates contested 460 seats in the national assembly. In Hungary in February, 1965 Janos Kadar spoke of the desirability of multiple candidates for elected bodies, and in November, 1966, the Hungarian parliament passed a law permitting voters to have a choice between two candidates.[58] In Tanzania intraparty elections produced substantial turnover not only in candidates for the legislature but also in party regional chairmen and members of the National Executive Council.

In Mexico a system of party primaries, inaugurated in 1946, was abandoned in 1950 largely because of opposition from labor groups and from the "dangerous public demonstrations of internal party conflict" it encouraged.[59] Fifteen years later the problem of popular participation in the nominating process was still with the PRI. Carlos Madrazo, elected party president in 1964, made major efforts to democratize the internal functioning of the party. A year later he resigned in protest due to the opposition from the party bureaucrats. The issue came to a head in Sonora in December, 1966 when the party organization authorized five candidates to campaign freely for the nomination for governor of the state. In February, 1967, however, the party leadership shut off this competition and announced its choice of the candidate. The result was riots and disorder as students and other urban groups protested this action. While the PRI pioneered in the development of mechanisms for group representation within the party, it was much slower in developing the mechanisms for popular electoral participation through the party.

Intraparty electoral competition among individual candidates furnishes an effective means of identifying local groups with the party and of promoting turnover in low-level and middle-level party and governmental posts. It also, however, poses two potential threats to the single-party system. Electoral competition has consequences for group identification and intergroup relations. In Tanzania, Yugoslavia, and elsewhere, it added incentives for candidates to make tribal and nationality appeals that the one-party system without competition had tended to suppress. Where electoral competition does take place, consequently, such appeals are usually formally prohibited, although obviously not prevented. In addition to activating communal identifications and rivalries, individual electoral competition could lead to the formation of blocs and continuing political organizations or subparties within the single party. Conceivably such a system could become multiparty in all but name, as individuals with similar interests and policies in different parts of the country coalesced together for the mutual promotion of their political futures. It might well be argued, indeed, that a system of individual electoral competition is inherently unstable and must eventually give way to competition between organized factions, blocs, and political machines.

Such a development is possible but not inevitable in an established one-

58. Lendvai, *op. cit.*, p. 14; Skilling, *Communist East Europe*, pp. 131–132; M. George Zaninovich, *The Development of Socialist Yugoslavia* (Baltimore: Johns Hopkins Press, 1968), pp. 152–155.

59. Scott, *op. cit.*, p. 142. [. . . .]

party system. The experience of other societies demonstrates quite conclusively that electoral competition can exist for indefinite periods of time with little or no continuing political organization. There is no law that personal politics and loose factional politics must give way to more organized forms of political competition. The widespread failure of electoral competition to generate enduring coalitions and broad-based organizations in noncommunist modernizing societies is a sign of the potential success of such competition in communist and other established one-party systems.

THE STABILITY OF ESTABLISHED ONE-PARTY SYSTEMS

The established one-party system that emerges from the process of transformation, consolidation, and adaptation differs from a revolutionary one-party system in six ways.

1. Ideology is less important in shaping its goals and the decisions of its leaders; pragmatic considerations are more important.

2. The political leadership tends to be oligarchical, bureaucratic, and institutionalized rather than personalistic, charismatic, and autocratic.

3. The sources of initiative are dispersed among technocratic and managerial elites instead of concentrated in the party elite; the party *apparat* becomes the mediator between change and stability.

4. A plurality of important interest groups exist, giving rise to a corporate social structure, with the party *apparat* becoming the aggregator and regulator of competing special interests.

5. The intellectuals criticize the system instead of ruling it.

6. Popular participation in the system is less the product of mobilization by the party and more the result of competition through elections within the party.

In addition, the most significant difference between established and revolutionary one-party systems concerns the scope of politics. In a revolutionary system the ideology of the leadership encourages it to assign political meanings to almost all types of social behavior and to attempt to subject this behavior to political control. Politics is monopolized by the party and society is dominated by politics. The transformation of society requires the politicization of society. In due course, however, the increasing complexity of society compels changes in the relations among these three elements. The effective functioning of an established one-party system requires relaxation of the political controls on the increasingly complex and diversified activities in society. Economics, technical, social units require greater degrees of autonomy in order to accomplish effectively the ends of the system. As in Yugoslavia in the 1960s, "depoliticization" becomes the order of the day.

The extent to which the party continues to monopolize politics in an established one-party system depends upon the extent to which politics plays less of a role in society. The continued subjection of all major sectors of social life to political controls is beyond the capacity of the party in a way which was not true of the transformation and consolidation phases. Consequently, the failure to restrict the scope of the political system can leave other elements—interest groups, bureaucratic groups, the military— with no choice but to play political roles because the decisions of primary concern to them are made on political rather than technical or functional grounds. If school curricula, factory organization, and tactical doctrines are determined primarily by political criteria, then pedagogues, managers, and colonels will want a role in shaping those criteria. If, on the other hand, such issues are defined as essentially "non-political" and are decided primarily on "functional" grounds, then by restricting the scope of politics, the party is better able to maintain its authority over politics.

That authority, in turn, depends upon the extent to which the party monopolizes the legitimation of the political system, the recruitment of political leadership, and the formulation and implementation of policy. In a revolutionary one-party system, the party comes close to exercising exclusive control over all these functions. In an established one-party system, its control over them varies from one to the other. The emergence of interest groups and the restriction of the scope of political decision-making gives the party a less monopolistic although still important role in the aggregation of interests and the formulation of policy. Policy initiatives may come from many different sources, but only the party *apparat* is in a position to mediate the conflict of interests that the diversification of society produces. In a welter of special interests, it alone can lay some claim to represent the interests of the whole.

In an established one-party system the party maintains firmer control over political recruitment than over policy formulation. The crucial question here concerns the extent to which individuals may rise to high positions of political leadership through bureaucratic or popular channels outside the party organization. Conceivably, for instance, top-ranking military officers or industrial managers could come to the top of their respective hierarchies and then either be coopted into or force their way into the top positions of political leadership. The extent to which such lateral entry into politics does not take place depends on: (1) the degree to which the various functional bureaucracies are isolated from politics, that is, the effectiveness of "depoliticization" in the society; and (2) the relative status and skill of those political bureaucrats who come up through the party hierarchy. For the party the latter involves the problem of how to maintain the status of the political career in a diversified society and how to attract to that career both the children of nonpolitical elite groups and the upwardly mobile children of non-elite groups.

The other potential source of challenge to the party monopoly of political leadership recruitment might come from individuals alienated from or never a part of the party *apparat* who are able to win wide popular support in the society. The likelihood of such a populist challenge, however, is relatively remote. Party control over the media of mass communication and the maintenance of guidelines, if not outright censorship, over the bounds of legitimate political discourse make it difficult for a dissident figure to develop a popular appeal outside the party without being treated as a traitor to the entire society. Even in as relatively an open one-party system as Mexico, a dissident like Carlos Madrazo, for instance, affirmed his intention of working through the party rather than against it. In addition, to the extent that the party internalizes a system of electoral competition, it provides openings for potential dissident leaders to rise up through the party structure and presumably be assimilated into that structure.

Of most significance to the continued stability of an established single party is the maintenance by the party of its monopoly of the legitimation of the system. In a revolutionary one-party system, the party reconstructs society by reducing the existing bifurcation and expanding its constituency social force to encompass, at least in theory, all elements of the society. In an established one-party system the legitimacy of the system continues to depend upon the identity of interest between party and society. The party can countenance all sorts of groups representing and expressing special interests, but it cannot permit another group to promote a competing general interest, a competing image of the good society, or a competing view of the moral basis of political authority. It is precisely for this reason that the party elite cannot tolerate the existence of "real" opposition parties.

In the development of an established one-party system, the party may play a declining role in the day-to-day workings of society, through the reduction of the scope of politics, and a declining role in the day-to-day workings of government, through the increased initiatives assumed by interest groups and functional bureaucracies. The immediate power of the party can be limited in this way, however, only because its ulitmate authority is unchallenged. The party has no alternative but to reserve to itself the right to speak for the society as a whole: it was, indeed, this right which it established for itself in the revolutionary process. In the mid-1960s the Yugoslav League of Communists seemed to be moving in this direction. The party, it was said, would give up its "commanding role in Yugoslav life" and instead devote itself to the ideological and moral guidance of the society. The communists, as Zaninovich interprets it, would become "a sort of overriding Brahmanic caste, in that they immunize themselves from the 'dirty business' of politics and become the exclusive (and priestly) guardians of socialist morality." Another analogy might be the Supreme Court of the United States, with the party, like the Court, being the final arbiter of what is and is not permissible within the constitutional principles and institutional framework of the political system. "We talk of the withering away of the state," Tito said, "but the withering away of the League (party) is not to be considered."[60]

The need for the party to maintain its position as the source of political legitimacy sets the limits of permissible dissent. A Mihajlo Mihajlov who bases his argument for an opposition journal on the provisions of the Yugoslav constitution is either naive or disingenuous. The source of legitimacy in Yugoslavia is not the constitution but the party, and any effort to invoke the constitution as a source of legitimation against the party is clearly not tolerable. The limits of dissent are set by the fundamentals of the system, of which the party's monopoly of ultimate authority is the most sacrosanct. As one journalist commented with respect to Yugoslavia: "The press is nominally free but does not exercise the liberty to criticize the party, its top leaders or its program. Churches are free to hold religious services, but not to run schools or participate in politics. People are free to associate in non-party groupings as long as they are not politically oriented. Speech is free except that statements against the party from a public platform are punishable."[61] Similarly, the parliaments in communist one-party systems may assume a more significant role in shaping policy and even in forming governments. Yet such efforts are tolerable only so long as they do not threaten the ultimate supremacy of the party. If parliamentary deputies were to claim to be sovereign representatives of the will of the people, the established one-party system would confront a constitutional crisis.

Many efforts have been made to identify the types of dissent and opposition that may exist in political systems, including one-party systems. In most instances, opposition is categorized on substantive grounds. Distinctions are made between opposition to the personnel of government, to specific policies, to the political structure, and to the social-economic system. In a somewhat similar vein, Skilling distinguishes integral opposition to the system itself, fundamental opposition within the system to basic policies, and specific opposition to aspects of the system.[62] In an established one-party system, however, the more important consideration is not what is opposed but where it is opposed. Opposition articulated through the one-party system can be much more sweeping in its criticism than opposition

60. Zaninovich, *op. cit.*, p. 145; Ghita Ionescu, *The Politics of the European Communist States* (New York: Frederick A. Praeger, 1967), pp. 244–248.

61. David Binder, *The New York Times*, May 29, 1966.

62. Dahl, *op. cit.*, p. 342; H. Gordon Skilling, "Background to the Study of Opposition in Communist Eastern Europe," *Government and Opposition*, III (Summer 1968), 297–301.

expressed outside the system. As in any relatively stable political order, procedural regularity furnishes the dissenter with his opportunity and his opiate. In an established single-party system, as in a democratic, competitive party system, political stability is measured by the degree to which the system possesses the institutional channels for transforming dissenters into participants.

Further Suggested Readings

Allardt, Eric, and Littunger, Y., eds. *Cleavages, Ideologies and Party Systems.* Helsinki: Academic Bookstore, 1967.

Coleman, James, and Rosberg, Carl, eds. *Political Parties and National Integration in Tropical Africa.* Berkeley: University of California Press, 1966.

Duverger, Maurice. *Political Parties.* New York: John Wiley & Sons, 1954.

Eldersveld, Samuel. *Political Parties: A Behavioral Analysis.* Chicago: Rand McNally, 1964.

Hodgkin, Thomas. *African Political Parties.* Harmondsworth, U.K.: Penguin, 1961.

Huntington, Samuel, and Moore, C.H., eds. *Authoritarian Politics in Modern Society.* New York: Basic Books, 1970.

Kilson, Martin L. "Authoritarian and Single-Party Tendencies in African Politics." *World Politics,* 15 (January 1963), 262–94.

LaPalombara, J., and Weiner, M., eds. *Political Parties and Political Development.* Princeton: Princeton University Press, 1966. Bibliography.

Michels, Robert. *Political Parties.* New York: Collier, 1962.

Morgenthau, Ruth Schacter. "Single Party Systems in West Africa." *American Political Science Review,* 55 (June 1961), 244–57.

Neumann, Sigmund, ed. *Modern Political Parties: Approaches to Comparative Politics.* Chicago: University of Chicago Press, 1956.

Ostrogorski, M.I. *Democracy and the Organization of Political Parties in the United States and Great Britain.* Garden City, New York: Doubleday, 1964 (abridged).

Rose, Richard, and Urwin, D. "Social Cohesion, Political Parties and Strains in Regimes." *Comparative Political Studies,* 2 (April 1969), 7–67.

Scarrow, Howard. "The Function of Political Parties: A Critique of the Literature and the Approach." *Journal of Politics,* 29 (November 1967), 770–90.

Schlesinger, Joseph. "Political Party Organization." In *Handbook of Organizations,* edited by James March, pp. 764–801. Chicago: Rand McNally, 1965.

Zolberg, Aristide. *Creating Political Order: The Party States of West Africa.* Chicago: Rand McNally, 1966.

7

Comparative Bureaucracy

Introduction

The study of bureaucracy is the study of the administrative apparatus of the state. Why, you might ask, study bureaucracy? What is political about the faceless faithful carrying out executive orders? The answer is that the holders of bureaucratic office may be neither faceless nor faithful. They may be either self-recruited into the political process or drawn in upon the initiative of others as what have come to be called "technocrats." Also, depending on the vantage point chosen, a bureaucratic structure can be seen as a political group which in the context of the overall political system makes self-seeking political demands different from those of simply carrying out instructions and in turn has demands made upon it which likewise are different from the mere issuance of directives.

In short, the bureaucracy can be viewed in this fashion and, in addition, in terms of its inner dynamic properties that contribute to its adaptation to differing environmental contexts whether these be characterized as developed societies, developing ones, or transitional ones. To the extent it is possible to speak of political development, and more will be said of this in the final chapter, part of this adaptation is involved in the role of the bureaucracy in the development process.

Political scientists concentrate their attentions on two political institutions. The first of these is the political party and, as we noted in the preceding chapter, its corollary, the question of the relevance of the political party—the possibility being that a political party might well be nearly politically irrelevant. Whatever the validity of this statement, it would be far more difficult to make a similar statement regarding a bureaucracy, the other focal point of political scientists' attentions. The mere existence of a modern state predicates the existence of a bureaucracy. So intrinsic is it to that state that the greatest social science theorist of the twentieth century, Max Weber, has even defined moderniy in terms of its existence.

What led Weber to this formulation is perhaps evident in the label he attached to it. He termed it a legal-rational system. "Legal" suggests the universality of the characteristics of the system; its organizational features are so uniform that it is possible to express them in a codified form that makes them universally applicable. "Rational" completes the characterization by suggesting the essential, instrumental, means-end mentality underlying the system in order to make it operable. Rationality is understood to be synonymous with the modern mentality.[1]

The problem with this elaboration of Weber's concept is that we find ourselves nodding in agreement with what seem to be some obvious points. Therein lies the danger, for what Weber has characterized as the modern order of society might only be the modern order of the European (and American) society from the observation of which Weber derived his formulation. In fairness to Weber, it should be noted that he was not attempting to characterize only the bureaucracy *per se* but rather was constructing an ideal type of total society in a more subtle and comprehensive manner than it has been possible to restate here. Nevertheless, Weber himself and Eisenstadt, whose article is included in this chapter, have identified different kinds of bureaucracies appropriate to the type of societies within which they are found; for example, Eisenstadt's primitive, feudal and centralized types.

Eisenstadt's formulations enhance our understanding of the political relevancy of a bureaucracy by insisting upon typologies that are appropriate to a given political context, whether these be the centralizing monarchies of seventeenth and eighteenth century Europe as so-called earlier modernizers or the centralizing late modernizers of the Third World in the post-World War II era of decolonization. As Eisenstadt has noted especially clearly as the case of the early European modernizers, central administration was usually established as a counter-force to some social element such as the aristocracy. Perhaps less obviously but in the same manner, bureaucracies established in the process of nation-building in former colonial areas are likewise aimed at challenging the authority of local authorities, whether they be termed landowners, rajas, village headman, or chiefs. But therein lies a dilemma: in order to challenge local authority some degree of coercion is necessary. The instruments of that coercion are modern, whether modern in organizational terms such as an European-inspired model of a ministry of the interior, or in the para-military tactics and instruments of riot control, water cannon or automatic weapons. Individuals trained in the operation of these organizations, tactics, and instruments typically have acquired the life-styles, attitudes, and values of the colonial administrators they replaced after achieving independence. This process of what Frantz Fanon has called embourgeoisement alienates the administrator from the masses of the population, and therein lies the other side of the dilemma.[2]

1. For a translation of Weber's works, see list of suggested readings at the end of this chapter.

2. Frantz Fanon, *The Wretched of the Earth*, trans. C. Farrington (Harmondsworth, U.K.: Penguin, 1967).

Trained and experienced in the modern techniques necessary to defeat a colonial power in a national liberation struggle and then having supplanted the colonial administrator, the new bureaucrat and the regime he represents adopt an ideology often tinged with Marxist contempt for feudal elements, thereby making these traditional authority structures targets of state authority. While usually incapable of marshaling coercive power sufficient to destroy these feudal elements, the regime is also unable to coopt them and ends up by alienating them. Thus the bureaucrat's lack of empathy for traditional local culture is compounded by active opposition led by local authorities, be they landowners, village headmen, or notables. If the regime is fortunate, the result of all this is a stalemate and a situation of relative stability. This situation has been called a "no-party state" in which a single political party is supposed to supplement and buttress the central administration as in Algeria, Senegal, Egypt, or Tanzania, but in fact, both administration and, especially, party end up having only a tenuous relation to the local population. If the regime is less fortunate, outright rebellion by local elements might take place as has happened in Morocco, Tunisia, and parts of India. On occasion the regime is able to come to terms with such elements and incorporate them into the overall administrative process; in the Ivory Coast, for example.

Just as in the preceding chapter we noted the crucial aspect in the study of political parties is to view them in their total societal context, so also must we do the same in the case of the administrative system. If this is done, then we can begin to assess the political effectiveness of the administrative structure as it functions in the process of political change.

Bureaucracy and Political Development

Bureaucracy and Political Development [1]

S. N. Eisenstadt

I

The term "political development" has recently evoked much discussion and is often used in conjunction with the term "economic development." To some extent, the latter's criteria are "objectively" or quantitatively deter-

---

1. This chapter is based on a series of comparative studies of political systems and bureaucracy by the author. Some of these studies which contain full bibliographical references on source material are quoted in the footnotes.

From Bureaucracy and Political Development, *ed. by J. LaPalombara (copyright ©* *1963 by Princeton University Press), No. 2, Studies in Political Development, pp.* *96–119. Reprinted by permission of Princeton University Press.*

mined, but the meaning of political development has not yet been precisely or clearly established. In this chapter political development will be used in a specific way. It will be used, if with less precision, as the economist uses "self-sustained" growth to mean a continuous process of growth which is produced by forces within the system and which is absorbed by the system.

Within the political sphere, the equivalent of such self-sustained growth is the ability to absorb varieties and changing types of political demands and organization. It also includes the skill to deal with new and changing types of problems which the system produces or which it must absorb from outside sources. The concept complies with two views. It is closely related to a view of a political system which emphasizes authoritative decisions by rulers over subjects who pressure for such decisions, as well as to an approach which stresses the articulation of many interests, as it is to one which is concerned with the aggregation of political functions in the ruling institutions.[2]

Neither the different analytical implications of such approaches nor the actual differences between them will be discussed. Suffice it to indicate that according to this view every political system, by its nature, deals with demands and issues of political struggle. The demands and struggles are a very part of the definition of any such system. They may be classified according to the extent to which they seek either to determine broad policy or simply to accrue particular benefits to individuals and groups. Those which seek to influence or determine policy are usually articulated as specific political issues, while those which seek to accrue personal benefit are usually much less articulated in political terms.

Political organizations may also be classified according to whether they are concerned with political activities alone or whether they also deal with other social activities and kinds of groupings. Accordingly we may distinguish between different types of political organization and activities. There is the simple petitioning which may range from that of an individual to that of a group. There may be attempts to obtain group representation or to usurp power positions. There is also the structural accumulation of different kinds of cliques and the formation of political groups and parties which participate in and attempt to influence central political decisions.[3]

2. D. Easton, *The Political System, An Inquiry into the State of Political Science,* New York, Knopf, 1953. G. Almond, "A Functional Approach to Comparative Politics," G. Almond and J. Coleman, eds., *The Politics of the Developing Areas,* Princeton, Princeton University Press, 1960, pp. 3–65.

3. In concrete cases an overlapping of these criteria always exists, but they have been found useful for analytical distinction in comparative studies. For a fuller exposition of these criteria see S. N. Eisenstadt, "The Comparative Analysis of Historical Political Systems," a mimeographed paper prepared for the Committee on Comparative Politics, Social Science Research Council, 1958. Also S. N. Eisenstadt, *The Political Systems of Empires,* Glencoe, Ill., The Free Press, 1963.

II

Different types of political systems are able to deal with specific types of political demands and organization which have different levels of articulation. The capacity to deal with these is actually built into the structure of a political system. The more a political system is differentiated or organized into specific roles and structures, the more it can develop autonomous orientations and goals. It enlarges the scope of policies as well as the administrative services which are provided to the various groups in the society. The variety of political demands and organization which the system can absorb increases, especially those demands and organizations which are specifically political.

It seems that the more the political system is differentiated, the more sensitivity is has also to "objective" problems like international relations, population movements, or economic fluctuations. External events may obviously impinge upon any given polity. But the more differentiated the system, the greater is its ability to cope or to attempt to cope with such problems as well as to manipulate and influence such external conditions. If we make a general comparison of historically different political systems, such as primitive with feudal, or feudal with centralized empires, differences in the elements already discussed will be readily apparent.[4]

Related to, though not identical with, the ability of a political system to absorb varied types of demands is a political system's capacity to deal with orientations which were not anticipated in its basic framework or ideology, even if they were actually generated by the system's own internal forces.

Various political systems may exhibit different degrees of flexibility when it comes to their ability to absorb such "unexpected" changes. Despite the variety which different historical political systems exhibit when compared with one another, most of them evince relatively little of such capacity. Some partial institutionalization of the capacity did, however, develop in some of them—especially in those of the centralized empires. This ability is probably connected both with the extent to which the political system is differentiated and with the major goals upheld by the rulers and the major value orientations prevalent among different strata in the society.[5]

4. S. N. Eisenstadt, "Primitive Political Systems: A Preliminary Comparative Analysis," *American Anthropologist,* Vol. 61, No. 2, April 1959, pp. 200–220. S. N. Eisenstadt, "The Political Struggle in Bureaucratic Societies," *World Politics,* IX, 1, October 1957, pp. 15–36. S. N. Eisenstadt, "Internal Contradictions in Bureaucratic Polities," *Comparative Studies in Society and History,* VI, October 1958, pp. 58–75. S. N. Eisenstadt, "Les Causes de la Désintegration et de la Chute des Empires, Analyses Sociologiques et Analyses Historiques," *Diogene,* Vol. 34, Avril–Juin 1961, pp. 87–112.

5. These problems as related to the political systems of the centralized empires are dealt with in S. N. Eisenstadt, "Internal Contradictions . . . ," *op. cit.* S. N. Eisenstadt, "Les Causes . . . ," *op. cit.* S. N. Eisenstadt, *The Political Systems . . . , op. cit.*

III

Generally, this potential capacity to sustain continuously changing, new types of political demands and organizations develops only within those processes which can be denoted as political modernization or initial "pre-modernization." Historically, political modernization can be equated with those types of political systems which developed in Western Europe from the seventeenth century and which spread to other parts of Europe, to the American continent, and, in the nineteenth and twentieth century, to Asian and African countries.

Typologically, political modernization is characterized by the development of a series of basic features. Some of these features also existed in the pre-modern systems and often served as precursors and prerequisites of modernization.

The first characteristic of political modernization is a high degree of differentiation in political roles and institutions and the development of a centralized and unified polity with specific goals and orientations. The second characteristic is the extension of the activities of the "central" administrative and political organizations and their gradual permeation into all spheres and regions of the society. The third is the tendency of potential power to spread to wider and wider groups in the society—ultimately to all adult citizens. Fourth, it is further characterized by the weakening of traditional elites and tradition legitimation of rulers and by the increase in ideological and institutional accountability of the rulers to the ruled who hold potential power.

These transformations are all connected with the continuous development of great fluidity in political support while political allegiance based on ascriptive commitment to a given ruler or groups of rulers diminishes. This diminution of ascriptive commitment forces rulers continuously to seek the political support of the ruled in order to maintain themselves in effective power. This support is also needed for specific goals and policies which rulers propagate and want to implement. The culmination of the process, as it has gradually developed in the outright modern systems, is the citizen's participation in the selection of rulers in setting up major political goals. To a smaller extent they further take part in the formulation of policies. In most modern political systems elections have evolved in different ways to allow for the formal expression of this participation. Even the rulers of the totalitarian regimes, unlike the rulers of traditional regimes, cannot take political passivity and traditional identification for granted. They are even afraid of such passivity, for it has the potential of becoming a focus around which the citizens' political power may crystallize. The difference between modern democratic, semi-democratic, and totalitarian political systems does not lie in the spread of power, for this is common to all of them. The difference lies in the ways in which the rulers react to this power. The spread of potential political power is a characteristic of all modern political systems, including the totalitarian as distinct from premodern or traditional.

Though the citizens of totalitarian regimes are not allowed to exercise their potential power, it is formally recognized in their right to "vote." Most of the very restrictive measures of the rulers of these regimes, unlike those of the rulers of traditional ones, are based on the recognition of this potential power. The rulers also fear the potential dangers to themselves of its spontaneous organization—hence their attempts to organize, to manipulate, and to direct its expression.

Charismatic and traditional (feudal) relations between rulers and ruled still prevail in modern political systems. This is particularly the case with charismatic relations. Legitimation or "accountancy" of the rulers to the ruled may be based upon charisma, rational legality, or the "social" when the latter term is used to mean devotion to secular social values (this category may be akin to Weber's "Wertrational," though he did not use it in his classification of types of legitimation). But in no modern political system can traditional legitimation or criteria of accountancy of the rulers to the ruled be the predominant ones.

The analysis of political modernization presented here does not postulate any overall evolutionary trend. The dominance of the traditional ceded to some non-traditional elements through the strong possibility of reversal remains. But this is not related to whether the orientation will be charismatic, legal-rational, or "value" based.

IV

It is necessary to distinguish between the scope of the demands which a given political system can absorb in general and the general propensity of a political system to change and the ability to absorb such changes continuously within its institutions. These continually changing demands and issues are specific to modern political systems, where they derive from the broader conditions of modernization which will be analyzed shortly.

Political leaders and institutions, in the modern systems as in all others, have to deal with both "objective" problems like international relations, economic conditions, economic resources, and the mobilization of political support. The connection between these two in modern political systems is much closer than in other types of political systems. The growing participation of wider strata of the population in the political struggle increases sensitivity to and interest in, if not always understanding of, the objective problems.

Similarly, the ways in which political demands and activities are articulated in modern political systems is closely related to the provision of resources for the political elite. Continuous use of these resources by the polity requires that the ruled be effectively organized politically. This prerequisite, which enables the political elite to mobilize support and to articulate political demands, is of crucial importance to the working of modern systems. Different patterns of articulation of political demands and of mobilization of political support developed at various stages of the modernization process. But it is possible to discern some general institutional devices in almost all modern political systems.

Interest groups, social movements, public opinion, and political parties are the specific types or organizations through which political demands are articulated. The first three may to some extent be seen as components of the last—the parties—which are the most articulate forms of modern political organization. They also, however, have autonomous existence and orientations of their own.

The interest or pressure group is usually directed to gaining concrete and specific ends—whether economic, religious, cultural, or political. It is concerned primarily to promote this interest or at least to assure its optimal promotion in a given situation. Interest groups are, of course, diverse. They may be economic, professional, religious, ethnic, or tribal, and their specific interests may vary greatly from situation to situation.

Social movements are a second type of organization through which political adaptations and demands are articulated. Social movements usually aim at the development of some new total society or polity. They attempt to interject certain values or goals into a given institutional structure or to transform such a structure according to these aims and values. These aims are usually inclusive and diffuse. A social movement usually has a strong future orientation. It tends to depict the future as greatly different from the present and to fight for the realization of this change. It very often contains some apocalyptical semi-messianic elements, and it usually makes demands of total obedience or loyalty on its members while making extreme distinctions between friends and foes.

The third element through which either the membership or leadership articulate demands in a modern political system can be called "general, diffuse, and intelligent interests in public issues." This refers to people or groups who have a more flexible attitude to both specific issue and to "total" ideas and claims. They are not firmly attached to any given interest group, movement, or organization but are mainly interested in the "sober" evaluation of a political program, in values, and in concrete possibilities.

Each of these ways of articulating interests also existed in pre-modern political systems—but with differences. One of the differences was the lack of firm legitimate recognition within the central political institutions of processes for representation. Petitions or entreaties by interest groups or cliques were a partial exception. But social or social-religious movements were either entirely apolitical or non-legitimate in the view of the existing institutions. A second difference was that these groups were mostly concerned with petitioning the rulers for various concrete benefits, and not with the determination of major political goals or the selection of rulers. A third factor is that only in modern political systems do these different interest groups and movements tend to become integrated into the framework of a common continuous political activity and organizations. A continuous orientation develops to the central political institutions, namely in political parties.

Political parties tend to integrate the different types of political organizations. They attain this integration within their own organization through the development of specific party organs, leadership, and programs. The integration is effected through the subsumption of various concrete interests under some more general rules or aims which have some appeal to a wider public. It also occurs through the translation of the inclusive, diffuse aims of the social movements into more realistic terms of concrete goals, issues, and dilemmas.

Different parties may evince different degrees of predominance of each of these elements. But whatever such relative predominance, the integration of each of these elements into the parties is never complete. Interest groups, social movements, and public opinion may retain autonomous orientations and activities which often tend to burst the frameworks imposed on them by the parties. Their autonomy is maintained by presenting demands directly to the central political institutions of the executive, the legislature, or the bureaucracy without the mediation of any given party. They attempt to mobilize support and resources for themselves directly and not through a party.

V

The tendency was for these various characteristics of modern political systems to develop gradually. Not all of them developed in any given regime, and the tempo or temporal sequence differed in different countries. But their development and crystallization may be seen as the focus of the process of political modernization. They developed within the wider framework of social, economic, and cultural modernization. The combined impact of these conditions gave rise to the continuous production of new types of political demands and organization which the central political institutions had to absorb. Within any modern political system there is a continuous interplay between changing political demands and forms of political organization. There is also an interplay between attempts by the political elites to direct and channelize these demands and the possibilities of absorption and of non-absorption.

Hence the central problem of modernization in any modern political system is the ability to deal with such changing demands. They must be absorbed in policy making while assuring continuity to the system. Sustained political growth thus becomes a central problem of political systems.

At different stages of modern development different problems and different types of political organization appeared. Suffrage and the definition of the new political community were of the greatest central importance at one stage. At other stages problems of religious toleration and secularization of culture predominated. Economic and social problems, and problems of organization, have been dominant at various times. The appearance of each of these problems was connected with the entrance of different groups and strata into the political arena, and has sharply posed the question of the ability of the political institutions to cope with them.

VI

In principle any modern political system could deal with this problem in several distinct ways. One is to attempt to minimize the development of any changes which would generate new political demands and patterns of development. The second is to control and manipulate such changes and their political expressions. The third is to absorb, within certain limits, such new demands and organization.

Obviously, in any concrete regime there exists some mixture of these three orientations. It is the nature of the mixture which varies among different regimes, and the relative predominance of any of them which also differs. But not even those regimes which prefer to minimize changes can entirely neglect the problem of absorption of change which is inherent in any modern system.

Although the propensity to generate changes and to deal with them is built into the institutional structure of modern political systems, the capacity to deal with them effectively varies greatly.

The history of modern political systems is full of cases of unsuccessful adaptation or lack of adaptation or existing political structures to new types of demands and organization. Or, in terms of this discussion, the capacity for continuous growth and continuous sustenance of such growth can be blocked or impaired. This impairment is manifested in the inability of various groups to articulate demands clearly, or in not providing resources for political elites and institutions, or by presenting demands more intensively or extensively than existing institutions can absorb them.

Political eruptions, or more or less violent outbreaks of political activities with symbols which are directed against the existing system and its symbols, are external manifestations of blocking. Such eruptions are usually very closely related to and manifested in the lack of integration of interest groups into any wider common framework. They result when social movements are not institutionalized within the framework of parties and policy making.

The more "primitive" eruptions or mob activities are evident in the simple lack of ability of elites to organize and articulate the potential political demands of various groups. When the eruptions are articulated they are manifested as organized political activities with discordant premises from those of prevailing parties and political institutions. It signifies a failure on the part of the erupting leaders to integrate their demands within the existing framework. If such eruptions are not merely transitory, they may cause either the destruction of a given political system or the successful suppression of the new demands by the rulers to a level at which they and the institutions are capable of dealing with them.

VII

Modern political systems, like other political systems, are, then, faced with the problem not only of balancing demands and policies but of balancing through absorption. Sustained political growth is thus the central problem of modernization, and ability to deal with continuous change is the crucial test of this growth.

A modern system may itself retard further political modernization, but this does not make it non-modern. There is a basic difference between Nepal prior to the 1950's, Franco's Spain, or even Salazar's Portugal. The difference lies in the suppression and manipulation by Spain and Portugal of demands which are partially rooted in the system but which are denied free political expression. There is no provision for making demands on the central political authorities in either formulations or decision making. In a traditional system, on the other hand, this problem does not exist because various groups and strata do not evince such needs.

The only way in which a modern system can entirely obliterate, rather than simply limit or retard, modernization is if it can succeed in changing the basic social conditions which cause such demands to develop. Obliteration may temporarily succeed in systems which are just on the threshold of modernization, but it does not succeed in the more autocratic modern systems.

VIII

The ability of modern political systems to absorb changing political demands is closely related to the development of several basic institutional frameworks. First in importance are the various executive and legislative bodies. Political parties through which the political demands of different interest groups and social movements are articulated are second, and, third, there are the centralized bureaucratic administrations. Though the tempo of development differs from place to place, all three are to some extent basic corollaries of any process of modernization. Their role in the institutionalization of the capability to absorb changing political demands and organization is crucial.

It is with the place of the bureaucracies in this process that this chapter is concerned. An attempt will be made to analyze the bureaucratic administration's role in both early and late modernization. Early and late modernization constitute the two main types of political systems which can be classified as precursors, or as initial stages, of modern political systems as they developed in centralized empires—especially in the centralized European states during the Age of Absolutism and in the middle nineteenth century post-colonial regimes in Asia and Africa.

In both of these cases bureaucracies were of crucial importance in shaping the framework of differentiated systems as well as in serving as important instruments of political unification and modernization. They also proved capable, however, of becoming important impediments to further modernization. A brief comparative analysis of the bureaucracies in historically early and late cases of initial modernization may provide some important clues for the conditions under which these bureaucracies may facilitate or impede the establishment of unified centralized polities. It may also indicate how systematic capacity for change and the absorption of change develop.

The creation of a "historical centralized" polity was very often aimed against various groups—aristocratic groups and strata, traditional urban groups, and religious elites. It was either through the invention of a bureaucratic administration or the reorganization of an existing administration on a centralized pattern that the strength of these traditional strata was undermined. Their privileges and monopolies in political and administrative positions were also withdrawn.

Whether the rulers succeeded in establishing these polities usually depended upon either the existence or the creation of specific conditions within those societies. The most important of these conditions were a relatively differentiated social structure, elements of a market economy, some degree of flexibility in the status system, and the growth of some universalistic cultural orientations. All of these were connected with the development of free-floating resources and with the emerging predominance of non-ascriptive rural and urban groups.

The expansion of bureaucratic organizations and their activities in turn contributed to the establishment and continuation of conditions and premises upon which the polity was based. The relatively differentiated and non-traditional strata were the backbone of these polities. They provided the free resources needed by the rulers and maintained dependable relations for them.[6]

---

6. For a fuller exposition see S. N. Eisenstadt, *The Political Systems* . . . , *op. cit.*

IX

Bureaucratic administrations played a similarly crucial part in cases of late initial modernization in the post-colonial empires.[7] Most of these countries usually had two or three bureaucracies or layers of bureaucratic organization and structure. What remained in the post-colonial new states was the personnel, organizational structure, and tradition of the old colonial civil service. After the attainment of independence, it provided the basic framework for further extension and development of bureaucratic administration.

Within these societies, this initial extension of administration was rooted in the need of the colonial powers for resources and for the maintenance of law and order. It was based on political control by the metropolitan powers who participated only minimally in the indigenous life of the community. This way of functioning greatly affected the scope of the colonial powers' activities. They were necessarily limited to basic administrative services. It also determined the administrations' structural characteristics and resulted in a high degree of centralization, of adherence to legal precepts and rules, and a small amount of internal differentiation.

Thus, on the one hand, these colonial bureaucracies help to establish the framework of modern legal and administrative practices. On the other hand, they were highly apolitical since they did not meddle in politics, maintained the ideal of a politically neutral civil service, and refrained from participating in the political life of the country in which they served. Their very limited goals were set by the colonial powers who were neither responsible to the political groups nor to the opinions of the country in which they ruled. They performed only secondary functions in the regulation of internal political interests and activities among the colonial population. Whatever internal political activities were undertaken by them were preceived mostly in terms of administrative injunctions and enforcement of law.

The second layer of the bureaucracies in the new states consists of those departments and echelons which were developed after attainment of independence. Here a new civil service was developed. It was new in personnel, goals, and even departments and activities. This new bureaucracy had to be

7. A more complete discussion can be found in S. N. Eisenstadt, "Problems of Emerging Bureaucracies in Developing Areas and New States," a mimeographed article prepared for the North American Conference on the Social Implications of Industrialization and Technological Change, Chicago, 1960. R. Braibanti, "The Relevance of Political Science to the Study of Underdeveloped Areas," R. Braibanti and J. J. Spengler, eds., *Traditions, Values and Socio-Economic Development,* Durham, University of North Carolina Press, 1961, pp. 139–181. R. Braibanti, "The Civil Service of Pakistan: A Theoretical Analysis," *South Atlantic Quarterly,* Vol. 58, Spring 1959, pp. 258–304. W. J. Siffin, ed., *Toward the Comparative Study of Public Administration,* Bloomington, University of Indiana Press, 1957.

staffed with new recruits, often inadequately trained, whose main qualification for office was former participation in the nationalistic political movements. These new bureaucracies were the bearers of new types of goals such as economic advancement, social betterment, educational advancement, or other types of community development.

Most of these new recruits usually had a much clearer, more articulate political orientation and a sense of political responsibility than did the former colonial civil service. They very often saw themselves as representatives of their respective movements, parties, or sectors. They saw their function as mainly political, and sought to fulfill it by either implementing political goals or representing, articulating, and regulating the political interests and activities of different groups and social strata.

The relations between the older bureaucracy and the newer echelons were not always easy, especially in the first period after independence when an attitude of distrust on the part of the nationalist leaders toward the remnants of the older colonial services usually prevailed. In some cases this may have led to an almost complete destruction of the older structure. In most cases some sort of *modus vivendi* developed between the older and newer echelons in which one or the other tended to predominate. The implementation of new social, political, and economic goals were strongly emphasized and involvement in the political process was much greater than before.

X

The bureaucracies in developing countries which have not been under colonial rule exhibit a somewhat different although not entirely dissimilar pattern. Within them there first existed a traditional bureaucracy whether "royal," as in the Middle Eastern countries, or "oligarchical-republican" as in most Latin American countries. These bureaucracies usually dominated the political scene until the end of the Second World War. Some traditional elements were mixed with more modern ones which were very often copied from some European country. The strong influence of the French pattern in most Latin American countries is an example.

These administrations tended usually to uphold the interests of the ruling oligarchies and to implement rather limited social and economic objectives. Whatever tendency to modernization they may have exhibited, as in the fields of military affairs or education, their major political aim was to limit those minimal spheres which were necessary to maintain the viability of the then existing system.

With growing modernization came an increased impact of internal democratization and the development of new social, political, and economic goals which caused the bureaucracies to extend the scope of their activities and to recruit new personnel. The older pattern continued to leave its imprint on the new echelons and departments through administrative training and organizational methods. Social and political orientations also reinforced these to some extent. Only in a few of these countries like Mexico did widespread, well-organized, semi-revolutionary parties succeed in upsetting the oligarchy and in establishing a stable and viable modern political framework. A somewhat new pattern of bureaucratic organization was established which was not dissimilar from those of new states, although much more efficient and stable.[8]

XI

In all these societies, whether historical or new states, the bureaucracies were posed between the rulers and some of the major groups and strata. There was a conflict between the rulers' desire to use the bureaucracies for their own needs and purposes, and the rulers' and administrators' need to mobilize economic resources and political support. A further factor was the development of expectations of service and some standard rules from the bureaucracies by the non-ruling power groups.

In conjunction with these varied pressures, the bureaucratic administration, and especially their higher echelons, tended to develop some specific organizational characteristics and political orientations of their own. The most important of these was the tendency to emphasize internal organization and professional autonomy.

This tendency was manifest in two major aspects of their activities. Some autonomy developed toward both the rulers and the various strata as a result of attempting to meet the demands and interests of both. Certain general usages, or rules and standards of service, developed. General interests of the population were considered, and ability grew to resist the pressures of those seeking continuous and intermittent change for their own benefit. Secondly, most of these administrations tended to develop some conception of themselves as servants of the state or the community. They conceived of themselves as having a responsibility to the polity and developed criteria of service and professional performance.

These tendencies could combine with different types of organizational structure. Needless to say, many of these administrations did not necessarily develop all the characteristics of pure Weberian bureaucracies. The extent to which such characteristics were developed differed greatly from case to case and should constitute a subject of separate study. But even the preceding analysis tends to show that these organizational characteristics of the administration did not appear in a void but were to a large extent a product

8. See, for instance, R. E. Scott, *Mexican Government in Transition*, Urbana, University of Illinois Press, 1959.

of the broader social conditions. Because of this, whatever their exact organizational characteristics, the bureaucracies performed broader social and political functions and participated in the political process from their beginning.

XII

It was these characteristics that facilitated the bureaucratic administrations' performance of several important functions in the polity. They helped to maintain the framework of a unified polity as well as the capacity to absorb varied demands and to regulate them effectively. Not only were they important instruments for unification and centralization, but they enabled the rulers to implement continuous policy. In addition, they also served as important instruments for mobilization of resources—taxes, manpower, and political support.

Beyond these, the bureaucracies performed crucial functions of the bureaucratic administrations in regulating the political struggle. When continuous administrative organizations were staffed by professional personnel whose activities were regulated by mechanisms independent of other groups, technical services and facilities became assured for the wide strata of the population. These administrations also facilitated the regulation of several aspects of the interrelations and potential conflicts between the main groups of the society, assured them of continuous service and upheld their rights, irrespective of momentary changes in their power relations.

In a similar way, the bureaucratic administrations also helped to regulate the relations between the political sphere, the rulers, and other groups in the society. To some extent they regulated the demands of the rulers for various resources from the main social groups, assured some regularity and continuity in the mobilization of these resources, and provided the major social groups with some continuous services on behalf of the rulers. In this way they could segregate the provision of services from the daily political struggle. The latter centered in other institutional frameworks such as court-cliques, royal councils, parliaments, and parties. By providing different services, they gave the rulers a framework through which the satisfaction of some of the interests and demands of various groups could be assured.

Once these bureaucracies were established and used, they could perform very important duties in political socialization. They could function in accommodating various groups to the framework of the centralized polity and to its basic institutions and norms. They could also facilitate identification with the goals of the rulers of these polities. In this way they could not only enhance the ability of these political systems to absorb different types of political demands; they could also enhance their own ability to deal with the varying types of demands.

XIII

The very performance of these functions has necessarily involved the bureaucratic administrations in the political process within these societies. But the ways in which they become involved in this process of modernization differed in historical empires, in colonial and in post-colonial countries. The main difference lay in the extent to which wider groups in the society participated actively in politics and in the nature of the basic legitimation of the rulers.

In historical empires the bureaucratic administrations provided the rulers with the basic resources which they needed and participated in the formulation as well as the implementation of policies. To some extent, they also participated with other active groups, such as the aristocracy and the religious elites, in the more central political struggle. This struggle was not yet fully articulated and what interests it did articulate were relatively simple. There were large parts of the population which did not participate and many interests were neither articulated nor organized into specific political forms. By providing services and through its general framework, the bureaucracy was able to keep these demands at a relatively low level. The functions it performed in political socialization were to accustom the various groups to the framework of a centralized polity, to uphold the traditional legitimation of the rulers, and to maintain the basic social framework for these groups.

In post-colonial societies which are cases of initial late modernization, the bureaucracies became much more involved in the political process. They became geared to having wider groups participate in the central political process at a higher level of activity. They also helped to confer legitimation on rulers who did not enjoy any traditional base.[9] This greater extent of the bureaucracy's involvement in the political process can be seen in several ways.

In many of these countries it constitutes itself as an effective executive or part of it, in addition to being the administrative arm of the empowered execuitve. It plays a part in setting up, determining, and implementing political goals as well as in establishing major policy directives. Apart from the head of the executive, it is the only body, in many countries, which is capable of formulating clear objectives which may be either political or administrative.

9. For a wider discussion of the problems of new states see G. Almond and J. Coleman, eds., *The Politics* . . . , *op. cit.* E. A. Shils, "Political Development in the New States," *Comparative Studies in Society and History,* II, 3, April 1960, pp. 266–292, 379–410. S. N. Eisenstadt, *Essays on Sociological Aspects of Political and Economic Development,* The Hague, Mouton, 1961. J. J. Spengler, "Economic Development: Political Preconditions and Political Consequences," *The Journal of Politics,* Vol. 22, August 1960, pp. 387–416.

The second major aspect of the bureaucracy's involvement in the political process in these countries is its tendency to develop as one of the main instruments of political regulation. It is one of the main channels of political struggle in which and through which different interests are regulated and aggregated. Its role in this aspect of the political process may be not only important but predominant. In some cases the bureaucracy may become a very important pressure and interest group in its own right with strong alliances with other oligarchical groups, as in some Latin American countries.

Thus in all these countries the bureaucracy may tend to fulfill different types of political functions and, like parties, legislatures, and executives, become a center of different types of political activity. Through these activities it may establish some of the basic frameworks of modern politics, but it may also minimize the extent of differentiation of various types of political roles and activities. It thus impedes the development of autonomous and differentiated political activities, organizations, and orientations.

The emerging bureaucracies are also the major instruments of social change and of political socialization in their respective countries. They are initially, at least, based on universalistic and functionally specific definitions of the role of the official and the role of the client. But the majorities of the populations of these countries have a different orientation. In their social life their traditional orientations and structures, such as the extended family, are predominant. The major part of a person's role-relations in these societies are set within traditional groups. Rights and duties are defined in terms of personal relationships. Previous experience with bureaucratic organizations is restricted and rarely of great importance.

Thus the contacts of the public with governmental organizations may provide a framework for a wider and more intensive process of political socialization. The public's accommodation to the new political structure becomes dependent, to a considerable extent, upon its successful learning in these situations of contact. This has very often forced the bureaucracies to go beyond their specialized roles and to assume various roles of social and political leadership and tutelage. This is what enabled them to effect changes in the behavior of the population at large. It was this need to foster change which often extended the scope of the activities of bureaucrats beyond those of specific goals and made them reach out into the realm of family, kinship, and community life of wide strata of the population.

XIV

Whatever the differences between these cases of initial early and late modernization, the bureaucracy performed some crucial functions of political socialization and regulation in both. But the continuous performance of these functions by the bureaucracies was neither given nor assured by the continuity of their existence. In many cases they could develop into stumbling-blocks on the road to political unification, to continuous modernization and development. These possibilities were rooted in the inherent tendency to bureaucratization which is the extension of a bureaucracy's sphere of power and influence beyond what is deemed to be its legitimate concern.[10]

In the cases just discussed this tendency toward bureaucratization could occur because the bureaucracies became involved in the political processes in these societies. In conjunction with this involvement they tended to develop several distinct types of political orientations, and some of these were closely related to the potential tendency to bureaucratization which could undermine the very premises of the unified polities within which they developed. They could also act to minimize the bureaucracy's ability to deal with changing problems.

Despite many differences in detail, some crucial similarities can be found in the political orientations of the bureaucracies in cases of both early and late modernization.

There were three important political orientations developed by the bureaucracies in the historical empires. They could maintain service orientations to both the rulers and the major strata with greater emphasis on the services to the rulers in the societies in early stages of modernization. It was possible for them to develop into a merely passive tool of the ruler with but little internal autonomy or performance of services to the different strata of the population. They might displace service goals to the various strata and to the polity in favor of goals of self-aggrandizement, usurpation of power exclusively in their own favor, and the favoring of a group with which they became closely identified.

In the last case, the bureaucracy tended usually to weaken and to de-emphasize the distinctiveness of its occupational and career patterns as well as of its professional ideology and self-image as servants of the country. It tried to lend to its positions the basic attributes of aristocratic status and to make the offices into some sort of private hereditary possessions or fiefs. It sought also to limit recruitment into the bureaucracy to members of the bureaucratic families and to minimize its accountability to various strata and, in extreme cases, even to the rulers.

Needless to say, all the bureaucratic administrations in the historical bureaucratic polities usually evinced some mixture or overlapping of these tendencies or orientations. However, a particular tendency usually could become predominant in any of them.

10. On this tendency of bureaucracies see S. N. Eisenstadt, "Bureaucracy and Bureaucratization: A Trend Report," *Current Sociology*, VII (1959). S. N. Eisenstadt, "Bureaucracy, Bureaucratization and Debureaucratization," *Administrative Science Quarterly*, Vol. 4, December 1959, pp. 302–321.

Similar but not identical social and political orientations of the bureaucracy can be discerned in the later stages of modernization in post-colonial
regimes. In these cases some of the orientations become somewhat more
crystallized and sharpened.

The first such orientation is similar to the first, and to a smaller extent
to the second, political orientation of bureaucracies in the centralized
empires. It is manifest in the development of a relatively efficient framework of modern administration. Legal norms and rules are upheld and basic
services maintained even if this is effected through the monopolization by
the bureaucracy of many political functions. Thus it extends the scope of its
activities and its officials assume many social and political leadership roles.
In such cases the bureaucracy may generate, through the establishment of
new political frameworks and through the development of such activities,
many new social organizations and activities on both the central and local
level. It may also contribute to the establishment of viable political frameworks and conditions conducive to economic and political development.

The second major type of possible orientation of the bureaucracies in the
new states is characterized by its development in a direction similar to that
of the last two, and especially of the third, orientation in the centralized
empires. In such cases, the bureaucracy tends not only to monopolize some
central political functions but also to become a major interest group. As
such it is usually closely allied with some institutional groups and with
various oligarchical strata. Because of this alliance the bureaucracy tends
to become a center of attraction for various white-collar aspirants and over-
staffed. It may also easily become a narrow interest group which tends to
stifle any development of independent political action.

XV

These different types of political orientations were similar in the initial
phases of both early and late modernization, and may similarly influence
the ability of these systems to maintain their basic frameworks as well as
to foster and absorb further modernization.

In the historical empires when the bureaucracy maintained its basic
service orientations to both the rulers and the major strata it was able to
contribute to the continuity and stability of the regime. It was able to maintain the basic conditions of the centralized bureaucratic regimes even when
it more strongly favored the rulers. In those societies, in periods in which
the bureaucracy maintained service orientations, their help enabled rulers
to maintain both their own and supporting strata's positions. This was partially achieved by keeping in check those strata which were opposed to the
prerequisite of the centralized political systems as to the development of the
more flexible political orientations. This was the way in which the bureau-

cracy could contribute to the maintenance of the unified, relatively differentiated political systems, and to their ability to absorb relatively articulated political demands and organizations.

The total subservience of the bureaucracy to the ruler as found in the cases of Prussia and the Ottoman Empire was usually connected with a very high degree of the use of force. The rulers implemented their goals by force against a very strong opposition. They received relatively little direct support from groups such as urban classes or free peasantry which could provide the requisite types of resources which the rulers needed to implement their goals and to develop centralized bureaucratic polities. When the bureaucracy had this kind of orientation, usually rigid political systems were involved which did not suffer any high degree of articulated political demands and organizations. Such orientations contributed to the weakening or alienation of the more flexible groups and strata, and to the freezing or undermining of the centralized political systems.

When service goals were displaced by the bureaucracy with illegitimate, usurpatory goals of self-aggrandizement, the flexible non-traditional strata tended to be gravely weakened. Self-aggrandizement was usually connected with at least the partial aristocratization of the bureaucracy. Economic resources and political support were withheld by the non-traditional strata from the aristocratized bureaucracy, thus leaving it without the support it required to continue functioning. This process became a contributory cause to the gradual disintegration of these policies into a more differentiated type of political structure.

Similar potential effects of the different orientations of the bureaucracy on the stability of political systems may be discerned in the new states. When these bureaucracies maintain some basic loyalty to the overall goals of the polity, in combination with a service orientation to the ruling elites and the major social groups, they are able to contribute to the establishment of the frameworks of unified centralized polities. They can also further the development of the capacity to absorb changing new political demands and to solve changing political problems.

The structure and patterns of activities of the bureaucracies which develop under these conditions may differ greatly from those of classical bureaucratic organizations. The relatively wide scope of their activities, especially when combined with a firm political orientation and a high measure of political consensus may facilitate the maintenance of relative stability and continuity. It may induce and generate various new types of economic entrepreneurship, professional activities, and political leadership on the local and even on the central level. The bureaucracy may further give rise to a gradual diversification of functionally specific groups as well as to independent public opinion and leadership. It is interesting to note that in these cases there usually also exist rather strong party-bureaucracies. Conflicts may develop initially between them and the civil service. But the existence of some initial diversification of functions within a relatively unified political framework may help to produce change and economic development.

The second major type of political orientation of bureaucracies in the new states may easily contribute to what Riggs has called "negative development."[11] As it becomes a relatively narrow and yet very strong pressure group, it may easily obstruct schemes of economic development which threaten its own level of income, power, and influence. Such a bureaucracy may often attempt, through suppressive policies, to lower the level of political demands and organization. It may undermine the framework of a unified polity and facilitate the outbreak of various types of eruptions.

XVI

Thus we see that in the initial stage of either early or late modernization a bureaucracy's similar political orientations may produce similar results. These orientations influence the extent of institutionalization of a centralized polity and facilitate or block further political development and modernization. These varied types of political orientations of the bureaucracy tend to persist, if somewhat transformed, in later stages of modernization. They are rooted in the internal structure of the bureaucracy and in the wider framework of the political process in these societies. Truly enough, in these later stages of modernization the bureaucratic administrations tend to become somewhat more specialized, professionalized, and fully organized bodies. Even here, however, it is only in the fully constitutional-democratic regimes that the ideal of the politically neutral civil service develops, though it may never become a full-fledged reality.

Even this type of neutral civil service constitutes only a specific subtype of what has been called service bureaucracy in this chapter. It necessarily denotes a certain type of engagement in the political process. As with all other types of political orientations which the bureaucracy may hold, this one too develops under certain specific structural conditions. It is important for this discussion to analyze what these varied conditions are.

The extent to which the bureaucracy maintains some basic service orientations while restraining both its inherent tendency to displace goals and its tendency to obtain autonomous power depends upon the interplay between several basic components of the political process in the pre-modern and modern societies.[12]

11. F. W. Riggs, "Economic Development and Local Administration: A Study in Circular Causation," *Philippine Journal of Public Administration,* Vol. 3, January 1959, pp. 56–147.

12. S. N. Eisenstadt, "Bureaucracy . . . ," *op. cit.* S. N. Eisenstadt, "Primitive Political . . . ," *op. cit.* S. N. Eisenstadt, "The Political Struggle . . . ," *op. cit.*

The first such condition is the existence of strong political elites. They must be able to articulate political goals. They must also establish and maintain frameworks of both political and legal institutions as well as direct communication with the major social and political groups. The second is the continuous development and vitality of groups and strata which are politically and socially articulate. They must be able to implement various social and political goals through their own activity. And they must concurrently provide the bureaucracy with a broader social setting from which to recruit its manpower.

Thus the existence of strong elites in the initial stages of political unification and modernization is to some extent more important than the existence of political groups which are strongly articulate. Such groups which tend to develop very intensive political demands and pressures may undermine the stability and viability of the political framework, and may also inhibit the rulers' ability to implement realistic policies. They are highly necessary, however, to provide resources to rulers and to restrain their autocratic tendencies.

The weakness of rulers and of such various strata may facilitate, in the initial stages of modernization, the developments of the bureaucracies into an omniverous consumer of resources. It may give them a monopoly on the articulation of political demands which acts to undermine the incapacity to provide services and the rulers' capacity to absorb demands coming from wider strata.

As has been indicated above, the concrete manifestations of these tendencies varied in different historical settings. In the centralized empires the bureaucracy's maintenance of a service orientation to the rulers and the major strata was very closely related to its partial incorporation in various flexible and "free" strata. When it was not incorporated, it was at least not alienated from such strata. At the same time it accepted and expanded the duty of service to the rulers, and of power as an autonomous criterion of social status.

On the other hand, the development of tendencies in the upper echelons of the bureaucracies to displace service-goals was closely connected with the development of the bureaucracy into some sort of ascriptive stratum. It either grew into an independent, semi-aristocratic, or gentry stratum, or it became part of the already existing aristocratic stratum. This alienated it from the rulers, to some extent at least. When there was a similar tendency on the part of the rulers to ally themselves with aristocratic elements the structural positions and the frameworks of the centralized polities were weakened.[13]

In the new states one of the main problems facing the elites and the bureaucracy is the extent to which they may be able to overcome the

13. This is more fully analyzed in S. N. Eisenstadt, *The Political . . .* , *op. cit.*

pressure for a higher level of consumption. They must foster wider educational schemes which can provide adequate training for personnel in technical fields while regulating the pressures on the white-collar jobs.

Here the maintenance by the bureaucracy of a basic service orientation and of activities which can facilitate the solution of these problems depends upon the existence of some basic unitary political framework. There must also be a relatively unified political elite and some degree of political consensus. Institutional interest groups such as the army or the churches which can easily monopolize power and economic positions must be relatively weak. Their position must be subordinate to the ecological strata and the more modern functional groups which are able to provide resources to the ruling elites while also tending to identify with the new centralized framework.

These bureaucracies may develop a negative orientation when a unified political framework and consensus does not exist. This is likely to occur when there is either a rift between the traditional and modern elites, or when a lack of consensus within the modern elite is very great. It also occurs when institutional interest groups like the church, the army, and other narrow oligarchical groups predominate in the social and economic structure.[14]

In later stages of modernization, when more specialized types of bureaucracy develop, the stage shifts to the stability of the genreal framework of political struggle. Emphasis is also upon the continuity of political symbols, the extent of political articulation, and the cohesion within and between major social groups. At this stage the very availability of ruling elites with their political and organizational ability depends on the stability of such framework as well as on the availability of cohesive articulated strata. The interaction between these frameworks and the different strata influences the development of the bureaucracy's different political orientations. But the analysis of these historical manifestations is already beyond the scope of this chapter.

14. S. N. Eisenstadt, "The Problems . . . ," *op. cit.* S. N. Eisenstadt, *Essays on Sociological* . . . , *op. cit.*

Further Suggested Readings

Berger, Morroe. "Bureaucratic Theory and Comparative Administration," *Administrative Science Quarterly,* 1 (March 1957), 518–29.

Diamant, Alfred. "The Relevance of Comparative Politics to the Study of Comparative Administration," *Administrative Science Quarterly,* 5 (June 1960), 87–112.

Eisenstadt, S.N. "Political Struggle in Bureaucratic Societies," *World Politics,* 9 (October 1956), 15–36.

————. *The Political Systems of Empires: The Rise and Fall of the Historical Bureaucratic Societies.* New York: Free Press, 1963.

Golembiewski, Robert, *et al,* eds. *Public Administration: Readings.* Chicago: Rand McNally, 1972.

Heady, Ferrel. *Public Administration: A Comparative Perspective.* Englewood Cliffs, N.J.: Prentice-Hall, 1966.

Jordan, Robert, ed. *International Administration.* London: Oxford University Press, 1972.

LaPalombara, Joseph, ed. *Bureaucracy and Political Development.* Princeton: Princeton University Press, 1963–1967. Bibliography.

Litwak, Eugene. "Models of Bureaucracy Which Permit Conflict." *American Journal of Sociology,* 67 (September 1961), 177–84.

Montgomery, John, and Siffin, W.J., eds. *Approaches to Development: Politics, Administration and Change.* New York: McGraw-Hill, 1966.

Riggs, Fred W. *Administration in Developing Countries: The Theory of Prismatic Society.* Boston: Houghton Mifflin, 1964.

Siffin, William J., ed. *Toward the Comparative Study of Public Administration.* Bloomington, Ind.: Dept. of Government, Indiana University, 1957.

Thompson, James D., *et al. Comparative Studies in Administration.* Pittsburgh: University of Pittsburgh Press, 1959.

Weber, Max. *The Theory of Social and Economic Organization.* Translated with an introduction by T. Parsons. New York: Free Press, 1964.

Wittfogel, Karl. *Oriental Despotism—A Comparative Study of Total Power.* New Haven: Yale University Press, 1957.

8

Political Change

Introduction

The subject of political change has been reserved until last because it is perhaps the most important one not only in the study of comparative politics but of politics in general. Whether speaking of the modernization process in a Third-World developing nation of Asia or Africa or in such disparate economically developed nations such as Northern Ireland, Belgium, or the United States in the late 1960s we sense and experience political change and struggle to understand it. In the effort to understand it we come face to face with its very complexity. It is this complexity which has led us to deal with it last in the conviction that the parade of institutions and concepts covered thus far in this volume has been necessary to detail the process of political change. The observant reader will have noted that already there has been frequent reference in article after article to political development, political modernization, and less frequent reference to political integration and change. In the case of development and modernization, these must be recognized in their various guises as political change and call for comment and clarification. Change as a subject of political analysis is like most things in political science—as old as Aristotle. Nevertheless, again as is often the case in political science, we have now reached a point of stressing the subject anew.

First there must be a clarification of terminology. As our article by Huntington points out in making the case for the label political change rather than political modernization or development, the latter terms are borrowed ones. Instead of being terms generic to political science and political science problems, political modernization has been borrowed from sociology and political development from the discipline of economics. The reasons for this borrowing of concepts are varied, but a key one may simply be timing—sociology and economics began to deal with problems of change earlier than political science did. Political science simply took over these concepts from other disciplines and in the process created some conceptual problems of what happens when one discipline borrows concepts appropriate to one discipline with one set of assumptions and attempts to apply them in a discipline with a differing set of assumptions.[1]

One of the consequences of this disciplinary borrowing in political science has been the tendency of political scientists to deny the primacy of political decisions in determining the policy direction of the groups, institutions, and political systems that they have been studying.[2] To state it succinctly, there has been a practice in taking over, for example, economic development theory to make the economic factor (the independent variable) the one that explains the political one (the dependent variable). The point is that this flies in the face of commonsense because a policy of economic development had to be a political decision in the first place. It is now argued that political science must recover its sense of identity by beginning with the assumption of the primary independent variable status of the discipline's subject matter.

There is a further problem with the use of the terms political development and modernization; this problem is related to the one set out in the beginning of this volume. We mentioned that normative considerations in the post-behavioral phase of political science have regained an important place in our thinking. These terms return us once again to this concern by their teleological implications; that is, the kind of political society which, it is implied, is the outcome of the development of modernization process. Scholars judged the processes of modernization and development in other countries by what they understood to be the same processes which Europe and America had undergone to reach their state of modernization and development in the 1960s. In short, political modernization and development meant a political approximation of the pluralistic democratic character of America and Western Europe contemporaneous with the scholars. Other areas of the world, however, might not choose these paths in political change. Furthermore, it is increasingly evident in view of the plethora of military and other coups d'etat that such change is unlikely to have democratic outcomes. The normative predilections of the scholar studying comparative politics are probably inevitably intertwined with his efforts to be objective. By referring to political change rather than development or modernization, the attributed end result is left at least definitionally open.

Directly related to this point, however, is a further one. In leaving the end result of political change definitionally open we incur an obligation as scholars. Namely, we must make maximum effort to empathize with the

1. For a discussion of this problem of inter-disciplinary borrowing, see especially Giovanni Sartori, "From the Sociology of Politics to Political Sociology" in S. M. Lipset, ed., *Politics and the Social Sciences* (London: Oxford University Press, 1969), pp. 65–100. This entire volume is devoted to the examination of the problem.

2. Dankwart Rustow, "Modernization and Comparative Politics," *Comparative Politics*, 1 (October 1968), 766.

political system under study to understand as accurately as possible the
political ends it has established for itself. These "ends" are of course closely
tied in with the question of political legitimacy discussed in earlier chapters.
In this fashion, at least at the empirical if not the conceptual level, we can
approach accurate description and analysis. Huntington shows his awareness of these problems in the reading included here.

A further aspect of this question is the unilinear assumption of the
process, namely that such modernization was inevitable. Huntington notes
that a suitable theory of political change must allow for political decay as
well as growth. In this sense, the concept of political integration although
not as susceptible to criticism on normative grounds as those of modernization does share the inevitable integrated outcome. Again, political change
is a more open-ended concept.

The preceding point regarding the teleological problem is related to a
further issue in the whole question of the study of political change—the
dichotomous nature of the categories used. The literature of comparative
politics and social science is full of references to the polar typologies of
traditional and modernity. These dichotomous categories are subject to
oversimplification when we deal with political change, specifying how a
political system gets from one state to the other. A prior problem however
has been that of defining the typologies themselves. As Huntington notes
in his selection in this chapter, the usual practice has been to define rather
carefully what is meant by political modernity (albeit the ethnocentric one
of the point just made about teleology), perhaps because it has been the
most familiar. Tradition in this view is thus defined negatively, that is,
everything that is not modern is traditional. This reflects the fact that
modernity has been receiving the greatest amount of scholarly attention to
the detriment of better understanding the nature of political change. In
other words, in order to better understand the process of change, we need
to know something about the point at which it begins. Realization of this is
what Huntington refers to as "modernization revisionism." A key element
of this revisionism is the realization that traditional society itself can be
adaptive and possess resources of its own in the process of change. This
adaptive quality was touched upon in Chapter 6 in reference to traditional
patron-client relations.

There has been a tendency of social scientists to emphasize the typology
of modernity and to assume that the process of modernization is necessarily
a socially and psychologically dislocating one. That is to say that modernization is necessarily a destructive process in which family structure and
psychological identity are destroyed with deleterious "anomic" consequences for the individual. This train of thought is traceable to the nineteenth century French social scientist Durkheim but is also present in other
social theorists such as Marx, Comte and Tönnies. These theorists based
their thought on observations of and reflections upon the European Indus-

trial Revolution. Our own conceptions of that industrializing process have been influenced largely by these thinkers. If their theorizing stands in need of major emendation as a result of the fact that the revisionists see social and political change in continuous rather than discontinuous terms, then our own received notions of ourselves as Americans and Europeans likewise may be in need of reinterpretation. It may be that the Industrial Revolution was not so rending an experience as has been thought and this might call into question to what extent it was indeed a "revolution."

Lest we conclude on a note that seems too abstract let us bring the point home more concretely. The implication of the foregoing might be that rather than being able to brashly identify ourselves as moderns who have somehow heroically severed ourselves behaviorally from our traditional past, regarding ourselves as more secular and egalitarian than our ancestors, in fact we may act more nearly like them than we think. If this is indeed the case, it should not surprise us too much, for historians of intellectual history and especially of American political thought have emphasized the continuities of this thought. It should not be surprising, though nonetheless self-illuminating, to discover that the continuities of thought should find their counterparts in behavior. This emphasis upon the continuous instead of the discontinuous in our own cultural experience has a number of implications, but a major one is in terms of cultural identity. To stress continuities is to state positively the relationship of present identity to past identity. The ability to do this can act as a counter-force to what has been called the "identity crisis" or "alienation," assumed to be intrinsic to contemporary culture.[3]

It should be clear that the study of the sub-field of comparative politics that can prompt speculation on such ultimate, and dare one say relevant, questions, is a rich one indeed.

3. The factors of identity crisis and alienation are common topics in modern social science discourse. For a discussion of alienation in the context of comparative politics, see Leonard Binder, "Crises of Political Development" in L. Binder *et al.*, eds., *Crisis and Sequences in Political Development* (Princeton, N.J.: Princeton University Press, 1971), pp. 36–37.

The Problem of the Study of Political Change

The Change to Change

*Modernization, Development, and Politics**—Samuel P. Huntington

I. POLITICAL SCIENCE AND POLITICAL CHANGE

Change is a problem for social science. Sociologists, for instance, have regularly bemoaned their lack of knowledge concerning social change. In 1951 Talcott Parsons flatly stated, in italics, that *a general theory of the processes of change in social systems is not possible in the present state of knowledge.* Thirteen years later Don Martindale could see little improvement. Sociology, he argued, could account for structure but not for change: *"its theory of social change,"* said he, also in italics (!), *"is the weakest branch of sociological theory."* Other sociologists have expressed similar views.[1] Yet, as opposed to political scientists, the sociologists are relatively well off. Compared with past neglect of the theory of political change in political science, sociology is rich with works on the theory of social change. These more generalized treatments are supplemented by the extensive literature on group dynamics, planned change, organizational change, and the nature of innovation. Until very recently, in contrast, political theory in general has not attempted to deal directly with the problems of change. "Over the last seventy-five years," David Easton wrote in 1953, "political research

---

*This essay was written while I was a Fellow of the Center for Advanced Study in the Behavioral Sciences in Palo Alto. It will subsequently appear in a volume edited by Daniel Bell, Theories of Social Change, copyright by The Russell Sage Foundation. I am indebted to Ronald D. Brunner and Raymond F. Hopkins for helpful comments.

---

1. Talcott Parsons, *The Social System* (Glencoe, 1951), p. 486; Don Martindale, "Introduction," in George K. Zollschan and Walter Hirsch, eds., *Explorations in Social Change* (Boston, 1964), p. xii; Alvin Boskoff, "Functional Analysis as a Source of a Theoretical Repertory and Research Tasks in the Study of Social Change," *ibid.,* p. 213; Robin Williams, *American Society* (New York, 1960), p. 568. By 1969, however, Williams felt a little more optimistic about the prospects for a breakthrough in the sociological study of change. See Robin Williams, *Sociology and Social Change in the United States* (St. Louis, Washington University Social Science Institute, Studies in Comparative International Development, vol. 4, no. 7, 1968–69).

Reprinted from Comparative Politics, *III:3 (April 1971), 283–322, by special permission of the author and the publisher.*

has confined itself largely to the study of given conditions to the neglect of political change."[2]

Why did this happen? Several factors would seem to play a role. While the roots of political science go back to Aristotle (whose central concern was "to consider things in the process of their growth"), modern political science is a product of the late nineteenth and early twentieth centuries. It came into being in the stable political systems of Western Europe and North America, where radical change could be viewed as a temporary deviation in, or extraordinary malfunctioning of, the political system. In Parson's terminology, political scientists might study change *in* a system (such as the fluctuations in power of political parties or of Congress and president), but they did not concern themselves with change *of* the system.[3] Political scientists neglected change because they focused their primary attention on states where change did not seem to be much of a problem.

Reinforcing this tendency was the antihistorical temper of the more avant garde movements in political science. Born of history out of law, political science could establish itself as a discipline only by establishing its independence from its parents. Consequently, political scientists deemphasized their ties with history and emphasized the similarities between their discipline and other social sciences. Political science evolved with the aid of periodic infusions of ideas, concepts, and methods from psychology (Harold Lasswell in the 1930s), social psychology (David Truman and the group approach of the late 1940s), sociology (structural-functionalism of the 1950s), and economics (equilibrium, input-output game theory, in the 1960s). The behavioral stress on survey data, interviewing, and participant-observation reinforced the rejection of history.

Political scientists attempt to explain political phenomena. They view politics as a dependent variable, and they naturally look for the explanations of politics in other social processes and institutions. This tendency was reinforced by the Marxian and Freudian intellectual atmosphere of the 1930s and 1940s. Political scientists were themselves concerned with the social, psychological, and economic roots of political behavior. Consequently, social change, personality change, and economic change were, in their view, more fundamental than political change. If one could understand and explain the former, one could easily account for the latter.

Finally, political change tended to be ignored because comparative politics tended to be ignored. With rare exceptions, such as the work of Carl Friedrich and a few others, political scientists did not attempt systematic comparative analyses of similar processes or functions in different political systems or general comparisons of political systems as systems. In book titles and course titles, comparative government meant foreign government.

2. David Easton, *The Political System* (New York, 1953), p. 42.

3. Talcott Parsons, *The Social System* (Glencoe, 1951), pp. 480ff.

The study of political change is, however, intimately linked to the study of comparative politics. The study of change involves the comparison of similarities and differences through time; comparative politics involves the analysis of similarities and differences through space. In addition, the comparison of two political systems which exist simultaneously but which differ significantly in their major characteristics inevitably raises the questions: Is one system likely to evolve into a pattern similar to that of the other? Are the two systems related to each other in an evolutionary sense? Thus, the analysis of political change is not likely to progress unless the study of comparative politics is also booming.

Not until the mid-1950s did a renaissance in the study of comparative politics get under way. That renaissance began with a concern with modernization and the comparison of modern and traditional political systems. It evolved in the early 1960s into a preoccupation with the concept of political development, approached by way of systems theory, statistical analysis, and comparative history. In the late 1960s, the focus on political development in turn yielded to broader efforts to generate more general theories of political change.

II. THE CONTEXT OF MODERNIZATION

General theory of modernization   The new developments in comparative politics in the 1950s involved extension of the geographical scope of concern from Western Europe and related areas to the non-Western "developing" countries. It was no longer true that political scientists ignored change. Indeed, they seemed almost overwhelmed with the immensity of the changes taking place in the modernizing societies of Asia, Africa, and Latin America. The theory of modernization was embraced by political scientists, and comparative politics was looked at in the context of modernization. The concepts of modernity and tradition bid fair to replace many of the other typologies which had been dear to the hearts of political analysts: democracy, oligarchy, and dictatorship; liberalism and conservatism; totalitarianism and constitutionalism; socialism, communism, and capitalism; nationalism and internationalism. Obviously, these categories were still used. But by the late 1960s, for every discussion among political scientists in which the categories "constitutional" and "totalitarian" were employed, there must have been ten others in which the categories "modern" and "traditional" were used.

These categories were, of course, the latest manifestation of a Great Dichotomy between more primitive and more advanced societies which has been a common feature of Western social thought for the past one hundred years. Their post-World War II incarnation dates from the elaboration by Parsons and Edward Shils of their pattern variables in the early 1950s and the subsequent extension of these from "choices" confronting an "actor" to characteristics of social systems undertaken by Frank Sutton in his 1955 paper on "Social Theory and Comparative Politics."[4] Sutton's summary of modern and traditional societies (or, in his terms, "industrial" and "agricultural" societies) encompasses most of the generally accepted distinguishing characteristics of these two types:

Agricultural Society	Modern Industrial Society
1. Predominance of ascriptive, particularistic, diffuse patterns	1. Predominance of universalistic, specific, and achievement norms
2. Stable local groups and limited spatial mobility	2. High degree of social mobility (in a general—not necessarily "vertical"—sense)
3. Relatively simple and stable "occupational" differentiation	3. Well-developed occupational system, insulated from other social structures
4. A "deferential" stratification system of diffuse impact	4. "Egalitarian" class system based on generalized patterns of occupational achievement
	5. Prevalence of "associations," i.e., functionally specific, non-ascriptive structures

The essential difference between modern and traditional society, most theorists of modernization contend, lies in the greater control which modern man has over his natural and social environment. This control, in turn, is based on the expansion of scientific and technological knowledge. To a sociologist such as Marion Levy, for instance, a society is "more or less modernized to the extent that its members use inanimate sources of power and/or use tools to multiply the effects of their efforts."[5] Cyril Black, an historian, argues that modern society results from adaptation of "historically evolved institutions . . . to the rapidly changing functions that reflect the unprecedented increase in man's knowledge, permitting control over his environment, that accompanied the scientific revolution."[6] Among political scientists, Dankwart A. Rustow holds that modernization involves a "rapidly widening control over nature through closer cooperation among men."[7] To virtually all theorists, these differences in the extent of man's control

---

4. Frank X. Sutton, "Social Theory and Comparative Politics," in Harry Eckstein and David Apter, eds., *Comparative Politics: A Reader* (New York, 1963), pp. 67ff.

5. Marion Levy, *Modernization and the Structure of Societies* (Princeton, 1966), I:11.

6. Cyril E. Black, *The Dynamics of Modernization* (New York, 1966), p. 7.

7. Dankwart A. Rustow, *A World of Nations* (Washington, 1967), p. 3.

over his environment reflect differences in his fundamental attitudes toward and expectations from his environment. The contrast between modern man and traditional man is the source of the contrast between modern society and traditional society. Traditional man is passive and acquiescent; he expects continuity in nature and society and does not believe in the capacity of man to change or to control either. Modern man, in contrast, believes in both the possibility and the desirability of change, and has confidence in the ability of man to control change so as to accomplish his purposes.

At the intellectual level, modern society is characterized by the tremendous accumulation of knowledge about man's environment and by the diffusion of this knowledge through society by means of literacy, mass communications, and education. In contrast to traditional society, modern society also involves much better health, longer life expectancy, and higher rates of occupational and geographical mobility. It is predominantly urban rather than rural. Socially, the family and other primary groups having diffuse roles are supplanted or supplemented in modern society by consciously organized secondary associations having more specific functions. Economically, there is a diversification of activity as a few simple occupations give way to many complex ones; the level of occupational skill and the ratio of capital to labor are much higher than in traditional society. Agriculture declines in importance compared to commercial, industrial, and other nonagricultural activities, and commercial agriculture replaces subsistence agriculture. The geographical scope of economic activity is far greater in modern society than in traditional society, and there is a centralization of such activity at the national level, with the emergence of a national market, national sources of capital, and other national economic institutions.

The differences between a modern polity and a traditional one flow from these more general characteristics of modern and traditional societies. Political scientists have attempted various formulations of these differences. Perhaps the most succinct yet complete checklist is that furnished by Robert E. Ward and Rustow.[8] A modern polity, they argue, has the following characteristics which a traditional polity presumably lacks:

  1. A highly differentiated and functionally specific system of governmental organization;

  2. A high degree of integration within this governmental structure;

  3. The prevalence of rational and secular procedures for the making of political decisions;

  4. The large volume, wide range, and high efficacy of its political and administrative decisions;

8. Dankwart A. Rustow and Robert E. Ward, "Introduction," in Ward and Rustow, eds., *Political Modernization in Japan and Turkey* (Princeton, 1964), pp. 6–7.

5. A widespread and effective sense of popular identification with the history, territory, and national identity of the state;

6. Widespread popular interest and involvement in the political system, though not necessarily in the decision-making aspects thereof;

7. The allocation of political roles by achievement rather than ascription; and

8. Judicial and regulatory techniques based upon a predominantly secular and impersonal system of law.

More generally, a modern polity, in contrast to a traditional polity, is characterized by rationalized authority, differentiated structure, mass participation, and a consequent capability to accomplish a broad range of goals.[9]

The bridge across the Great Dichotomy between modern and traditional societies is the Grand Process of Modernization. The broad outlines and characteristics of this process are also generally agreed upon by scholars. Most writers on modernization implicitly or explicitly assign nine characteristics to the modernization process.

1. Modernization is a *revolutionary* process. This follows directly from the contrasts between modern and traditional society. The one differs fundamentally from the other, and the change from tradition to modernity consequently involves a radical and total change in patterns of human life. The shift from tradition to modernity, as Cyril Black says, is comparable to the changes from prehuman to human existence and from primitive to civilized societies. The changes in the eighteenth century, Reinhard Bendix echoes, were "comparable in magnitude only to the transformation of nomadic peoples into settled agriculturalists some 10,000 years earlier."[10]

2. Modernization is a *complex* process. It cannot be easily reduced to a single factor or to a single dimension. It involves changes in virtually all areas of human thought and behavior. At a minimum, its components include: industrialization, urbanization, social mobilization, differentiation, secularization, media expansion, increasing literacy and education, expansion of political participation.

3. Modernization is a *systemic* process. Changes in one factor are related to and affect changes in the other factors. Modernization, as

9. See Samuel P. Huntington, *Political Order in Changing Societies* (New Haven, 1968), pp. 32–37.

10. Black, *Modernization*, pp. 1–5; Reinhard Bendix, "Tradition and Modernity Reconsidered," *Comparative Studies in Society and History*, IX (April 1967), 292–93.

Daniel Lerner has expressed it in an oft-quoted phrase, is "a process with some distinctive *quality* of its own, which would explain why modernity is felt as a *consistent whole* among people who live by its rules." The various elements of modernization have been highly associated together "because, in some historic sense, they *had* to go together."[11]

4. Modernization is a *global* process. Modernization originated in fifteenth and sixteenth century Europe, but it has now become a worldwide phenomenon. This is brought about primarily through the diffusion of modern ideas and techniques from the European center, but also in part through the endogeneous development of non-Western societies. In any event, all societies were at one time traditional; all societies are now either modern or in the process of becoming modern.

5. Modernization is a *lengthy* process. The totality of the changes which modernization involves can only be worked out through time. Consequently, while modernization is revolutionary in the extent of the changes it brings about in traditional society, it is evolutionary in the amount of time required to bring about those changes. Western societies required several centuries to modernize. The contemporary modernizing societies will do it in less time. Rates of modernization are, in this sense, accelerating, but the time required to move from tradition to modernity will still be measured in generations.

6. Modernization is a *phased* process. It is possible to distinguish different levels or phases of modernization through which all societies will move. Societies obviously begin in the traditional stage and end in the modern stage. The intervening transitional phase, however, can also be broken down into subphases. Societies consequently can be compared and ranked in terms of the extent to which they have moved down the road from tradition to modernity. While the leadership in the process and the more detailed patterns of modernization will differ from one society to another, all societies will move through essentially the same stages.

7. Modernization is a *homogenizing* process. Many different types of traditional societies exist; indeed, traditional societies, some argue, have little in common except their lack of modernity. Modern societies, on the other hand, share basic similarities. Modernization produces tendencies toward convergence among societies. Modernization involves movement "toward an interdependence among politically organized societies and toward an ultimate integration of societies."

11. Daniel Lerner, *The Passing of Traditional Society* (Glencoe, 1958), p. 438.

The "universal imperatives of modern ideas and institutions" may lead to a stage "at which the various societies are so homogeneous as to be capable of forming a world state. . . ."[12]

8. Modernization is an *irreversible* process. While there may be temporary breakdowns and occasional reversals in elements of the modernizing process, modernization as a whole is an essentially secular trend. A society which has reached certain levels of urbanization, literacy, industrialization in one decade will not decline to substantially lower levels in the next decade. The rates of change will vary significantly from one society to another, but the direction of change will not.

9. Modernization is a *progressive* process. The traumas of modernization are many and profound, but in the long run modernization is not only inevitable, it is also desirable. The costs and the pains of the period of transition, particularly its early phases, are great, but the achievement of a modern social, political, and economic order is worth them. Modernization in the long run enhances human well-being, culturally and materially.

Modernization in intellectual history This theory of modernization, as it emerged in the 1950s, contrasted sharply with the theories of historical evolution and social change which prevailed in Western thought during the 1920s and 1930s. The social theory of these decades was overwhelmingly pessimistic in its view of the future of man and society. Two schools of pessimism can be distinguished. One, typified by writers such as Oswald Spengler, Vilfredo Pareto, Pitirim Sorokin, and Arnold Toynbee, focused on the patterns of evolution of particular civilizations or cultures. They attempted to generalize sequences of the origins, growth, maturity, and decline of these great human societies. Theirs were, in essence, cyclical theories of history. The lesson applied to contemporary Western civilization was that it was at, or had passed, its zenith and that it was beginning the process of degeneration. The other strand of pessimism focused more exclusively on Western society. Its proponents tended to argue that Western society had earlier been integrated and conducive to human self-fulfillment. At some point in the past, however, a fundamental change had set in and Western history had begun a downward course. The breakup of human community, the attenuation of religious values, the drift into alienation and anomie, the terrifying emergence of a mass society: these were the products of secularization, industrialization, urbanization, and democratization. The processes which the 1950s viewed benevolently as modernization, the 1930s viewed with alarm as disintegration. Some authors dated the fall from grace

12. Black, *Dynamics of Modernization,* pp. 155, 174.

with the Reformation; others, with the Renaissance, the industrial revolution, or the French Revolution. At some point, however, Western history went off the track, and a special process started. It began with the rejection of religion and the breakup of community and led consistently and irreversibly down the steep hill to mass politics, world wars, the purge trials, and Dachau. In some versions of this essentially conservative *Weltanschauung,* modern liberalism became only a "soft" version of the fundamental misconceptions which underlay communism and fascism. "In almost every instance," as Reinhold Niebuhr said, "the communist evil is rooted in miscalculations which are shared by modern liberal culture. . . ." "If you will not have God (and He is a jealous God)," agreed T. S. Eliot, "you should pay your respects to Hitler or Stalin."[13]

Other thinkers stressed the decline of religion less and the disintegrative effects of industrialization and democratization more. Some, like Karl Mannheim and Hannah Arendt, warned of the totalitarian tendencies toward mass society.[14] Those who were reluctant to trace the downward turn of the West back to the sixteenth or even the eighteenth century saw World War I as the turning point. At about that time, Lasswell argued, the trend of history was reversed "*from* progress toward a world commonwealth of free men, *toward* a world order in which the garrison-prison state reintroduces caste-bound social systems." In similar vein, Walter Lippmann started in 1938 to develop his argument that 1917 was the truly revolutionary year in which governments began to crack under the strains of war and upheaval and Western society began moving toward paralysis, chaos, and totalitarianism.[15] The secular pessimism of the interwar years reflected the perceived catastrophes and chaos of Western society brought about by the processes of industrialization, urbanization, and the like. The modernizing optimism of the 1950s and 1960s reflected the perceived social, economic, and political successes of Western society brought on by those same processes.

The modernization theory of the 1950s and 1960s thus contrasts starkly with the secular pessimism of the 1920s and 1930s. Its most striking resemblance is, instead, to the evolutionary optimism of a half century earlier. The social theory of the late twentieth century more closely resembles that of the late nineteenth century than it does that of the early twenti-

13. Reinhold Niebuhr, *Christian Realism and Political Problems* (New York, 1953), p. 5; T. S. Eliot, *The Idea of a Christian Society* (New York, 1940), p. 64.

14. Karl Mannheim, *Man and Society in the Age of Reconstruction* (London, 1940); Hannah Arendt, *The Origins of Totalitarianism* (New York, 1951).

15. Harold D. Lasswell, "The Universal Peril: Perpetual Crisis and the Garrison-Prison State," in Lyman Bryson, Louis Finkelstein, and R. M. MacIver, eds., *Perspectives on a Troubled Decade: Science, Philosophy, and Religion, 1939–1949* (New York, 1950), p. 323; and Walter Lippmann, *The Public Philosophy* (Boston, 1955), pp. 3–8.

eth century. Victorian styles of thought, like Victorian styles in furniture, suddenly acquired a new respectability in the late 1950s. The Great Dichotomy of tradition and modernity had itself, of course, received its most influential original formulations in Sir Henry Maine's 1861 distinctions between status and contract, in Ferdinand Tonnies' contrast between *gemeinschaft* and *gesellschaft* in 1887, and in Max Weber's discussion of traditional and rational sources of authority.[16] Similarly, many of the characteristics and consequences which the post-World War II theorists ascribed to the Grand Process of Modernization will be found in the writings of nineteenth-century writers such as Herbert Spencer and Karl Marx. In both cases, human society is seen as moving in response to essentially economic causes through an identifiable sequence of ever more beneficent phases.

The nineteenth-century theories of progress were discredited by world wars, economic collapse, political chaos, and totalitarianism in the first part of the twentieth century. Neither Social Darwinism nor Marxism provided an accurate key to the future. The question remains whether twentieth century theories of progress will be any more successful. Twentieth century social scientists have been as confident of modernization in the Third World as nineteenth century Marxists were of revolution in the First World. The latter were predicting the future by the extension of the past; the former are predicting the future by the transfer of the past. The failure of the one suggests caution as to the possibilities for success of the other.

The optimism of the Social Darwinists and Marxists of the late nineteenth century was rooted in the contemplation of the progress which Western society was making at that time and consequently looked forward to the future bliss of Spencer's industrial society or Marx's socialist commonwealth. It was an optimism of future progress. The optimism of the twentieth century theorists of modernization, on the other hand, is essentially an optimism of retroactive progress. Satisfaction about the present leads to an optimism about the past and about its relevance to other societies. The modernization theory of the 1950s and 1960s had little or nothing to say about the future of modern societies; the advanced countries of the West, it was assumed, had "arrived"; their past was of interest not for what it would show about their future but for what it showed about the future of those other societies which still struggled through the transition between tradition and modernity. The extraordinary acceptance of modernization theory in both Western and non-Western societies in the 1950s derived in part from the fact that it justified complacency in one and hope in the other. The theory of modernization thus rationalized change abroad and the status quo at home. It left blank the future of modernity. Modernization

16. Sir Henry Maine, *Ancient Law: Its Connection with the Early History of Society and Its Relation to Modern Ideas* (London, 1861); Ferdinand Tonnies, *Gemeinschaft und Gesellschaft* (Leipzig, 1887); Max Weber, *Wirtschaft und Gesellschaft*, Part I (Tübingen, 1922).

theory combined an extraordinary faith in the efficacy of modernity's past with no image of the potentialities of modernity's future.[17]

Modernization revisionism   Modernization theory, like any social theory, thus suffered from a limited perspective deriving from its particular temporal and social origins. In addition, however, there were some logical and inherent weaknesses in the theory itself. In the later 1960s a small-scale corrective reaction set in which tended to pinpoint some of the difficulties of mainstream modernization theory. Among the theorists associated with modernization revisionism were Joseph Gusfield, Milton Singer, Reinhard Bendix, Lloyd and Suzanne Rudolph, S. N. Eisenstadt, and F. C. Heesterman.[18] Perhaps significantly, the empirical work of many of these scholars focused on India, the twentieth century's most complex traditional society. The criticisms which these analysts made of the traditional theory of modernization focused on: (a) the meaning and usefulness of the concepts of modernity and tradition; (b) the relationship between modernity and tradition; and (c) the ambiguities in the concept of modernization itself.

In the first place, as many modernization theorists themselves pointed out, modernity and tradition are essentially asymmetrical concepts. The modern ideal is set forth, and then everything which is not modern is

17. The late 1960s saw the emergence of "postmodern" theorizing, the leading scholars of which, however, had not been primarily involved in the analysis of the transition from tradition to modernity. These theories arose out of concern with the impact of technology on modern rather than traditional society. See Daniel Bell, "Notes on the Post-Industrial Society," *The Public Interest,* VI (Winter 1967), 24–35, and VII (Spring 1967), 102–18, and Zbigniew Brzezinski, *Between Two Ages: America's Role in the Technetronic Era* (New York, 1970). Both Brzezinski and Bell would probably assign many of the nine characteristics of modernization mentioned above to the transition from modernity to what follows. Both stand generally in the optimistic stream and in that sense share more with the modernization theorists than they do with the early twentieth century pessimists. More than the modernization theorists, however, both have been criticized by other writers who view with alarm the prospect of a postindustrial or technetronic society. Political scientists have yet to probe very deeply the political implications of this new historical transition.

18. See Joseph R. Gusfield, "Tradition and Modernity: Misplaced Polarities in the Study of Social Change," *American Journal of Sociology,* LXXII (January 1966), 351–62; Reinhard Bendix, "Tradition and Modernity Reconsidered," *Comparative Studies in Society and History,* IX (April 1967), 293–346; Lloyd and Suzanne Rudolph, *The Modernity of Tradition* (Chicago, 1967); S. N. Eisenstadt, "Breakdowns of Modernization," *Economic Development and Cultural Change,* XII (July 1964), 345–67, and "Tradition, Change, and Modernity," Eliezer Kaplan School of Economic and Social Sciences, Hebrew University: J. C. Heesterman, "Tradition in Modern India," *Bijdragen Tot de Taal-, Land- en Volkenkunde,* Deel 119 (1963), 237–53; Milton Singer, ed., *Traditional India: Structure and Change* (Philadelphia, 1959); Rajni Kothari, "Tradition and Modernity Revisited," *Government and Opposition,* III (Summer 1968), 273–93; C. S. Whitaker, Jr., *The Politics of Tradition: Continuity and Change in Northern Nigeria, 1946–1966* (Princeton, 1970).

labeled traditional. Modernity, as Rustow said, "can be affirmatively defined," while "tradition remains largely a residual concept."[19] Dichotomies which combine "positive" concepts and residual ones, however, are highly dangerous analytically. In point of fact, they are not properly dichotomies at all. They encourage the tendency to assume that the residual concept has all the coherence and precision of the positively defined concept. They obfuscate the diversity which may exist in the residual phenomenon and the fact that the differences between one manifestation of the residual concept and another manifestation of the same concept may be as great as or greater than the differences between either of the residual manifestations and the more precisely defined other pole of the polarity. This is a problem common to many dichotomies; the concept "civil-military relations," for instance, suffers from a similar disability and one which has had a serious impact upon the understanding of the relationship between the military and the multifarious nonmilitary groups in society, whose differences among themselves often exceed their differences from the military.[20] Tradition is likewise simply too heterogeneous to be of much use as an analytical concept. The characteristics which are ascribed to traditional societies are the opposites of those ascribed to modern societies. Given the variety among nonmodern societies, however, obviously the "fit" of any particular society to the traditional ideal type will be haphazard and inexact at best. Pigmy tribes, Tokugawa Japan, medieval Europe, the Hindu village are all traditional. Aside from that label, however, it is difficult to see what else they have in common. Traditional societies are diverse in values and heterogeneous in structures.[21] In addition, the concept of a tradition as essentially changeless came under attack. Traditional societies, it was argued, are not static. "The view that tradition and innovation are necessarily in conflict has begun to seem overly abstract and unreal."[22]

The concept of modernity also suffers some abiguities. These stem from the tendency to identify modernity with virtue. All good things are modern, and modernity consequently becomes a mélange of incompatible virtues. In particular, there is a failure to distinguish between what is modern and what is Western. The one thing which modernization theory has not produced is a model of Western society—meaning late twentieth century West-

19. Rustow, *World of Nations*, p. 12.

20. See Samuel P. Huntington, "Civilian Control of the Military: A Theoretical Statement," in Heinz Eulau, Samuel J. Eldersveld, and Morris Janowitz, eds., *Political Behavior: A Reader in Theory and Research* (Glencoe, 1956), 380–85 and "Civil-Military Relations," *International Encyclopedia of the Social Sciences* (New York, 1968), II: 487.

21. See, especially, Singer, ed., *Traditional India*, pp. x–xvii and Heesterman, "Tradition in Modern India," pp. 242–43.

22. Gusfield, "Misplaced Polarities," p. 352.

ern European and North American society—which could be compared with, or even contrasted with, the model of modern society. Implicitly, the two are assumed to be virtually identical. Modern society has been Western society writ abstractly and polysyllabically. But to a nonmodern, non-Western society, the processes of modernization and Westernization may appear to be very different indeed. This difficulty has been glossed over because the modern, non-Western box in the four-way breakdown of modern-nonmodern and Western-non-Western societies has, at least until the present, been empty. Presumably, however, Japan is either in or about to enter that box, and it is consequently surprising that a Japanese scholar should take the lead in raising squarely the issue of how much of modernity is Western and how much of Western society is modern.[23] How do two modern societies, one of which is non-Western, resemble each other as compared to two Western societies, one of which is nonmodern? (It should also be noted that non-Western is, like nonmodern, a residual concept: the differences between two non-Western societies may well be greater than the differences between any one non-Western society and a Western society.)

Other questions have developed about the relations between tradition and modernity. The simpler theories of modernization implied a zero-sum relation between the two: the rise of modernity in society was accompanied by the fading of tradition. In many ways, however, modernity supplements but does not supplant tradition. Modern practices, beliefs, institutions are simply added to traditional ones. It is false to believe that tradition and modernity "are mutually exclusive."[24] Modern society is not simply modern; it is modern *and* traditional. The attitudes and behavior patterns may in some cases be fused; in others, they may comfortably coexist, one alongside the other, despite the apparent incongruity of it all. In addition, one can go further and argue not only that coexistence is possible but that modernization itself may strenghten tradition. It may give new life to important elements of the preexisting culture, such as religion. "Modern developments," as Heesterman has said, "more often than not go to strengthen tradition and give it a new dimension. To take a well-known example: modern means of mass communications, such as radio and film, give an unprecedented spread to traditional culture (broadcasting of Sanskrit mantras or of classical Indian music, films on mythological and devotional themes)." Tribal and other ascriptive "traditional" identities may be invigorated in a way which would never have happened in "traditional" society. Conversely, traditional attitudes and behavior may also help modernization: the ex-

---

23. See Hideo Kishimoto, "Modernization versus Westernization in the East," *Cahiers d'Histoire Mondiale*, VII (1963), 871–74, and also Heesterman, "Tradition in Modern India," 238.

24. Bendix, "Tradition and Modernity," p. 326, and also Whitaker, *Politics of Tradition*, pp. 3–15.

tended family may become the entrepreneurial unit responsible for economic growth; the caste may be the group facilitating the operation of political democracy. "Traditional symbols and leadership forms can be vital parts of the value bases supporting modernizing frameworks."[25]

For all the ambiguities involved in the concepts of modernity and tradition, their rough outlines nonetheless appear possessed of comparative conceptual clarity when compared with the fuzziness which goes with the concept of modernization. In general, the writings on modernization were much more successful in delineating the characteristics of modern and traditional societies than they were in depicting the process by which movement occurs from one state to the other. They focused more on the direction of change, from "this" to "that," than on the scope, timing, methods, and rate of change. For this reason, they were more theories of "comparative statics" than they were theories of change.[26] The dichotomic developmental theories, moreover, were often ambiguous as to whether the phases which they posited were actual stages in historical evolution or whether they were Weberian ideal-types. As ideal-types, they were abstract models which could be used to analyze societies at any point in time. As historical concepts, however, the traditional category was presumably losing relevance and the modern category was gaining it. Inevitably, also, the dual character of the concepts undermined the conceptual dichotomy. Obviously all actual societies combine elements of both the traditional and modern ideal-types. Consequently, all actual societies are transitional or mixed. Viewed in terms of static ideal-types, this analysis presented no problems. One could still use the traditional and modern models to identify and relate the traditional and modern characteristics of any particular society. Viewed as a theory of history or change, however, the addition of a transitional category tended to exclude the traditional and modern stages from the historical process. Traditional society (like the state of nature) could only have existed as a hypothetical starting point in the distant past. A truly modern society would only exist if and when traditional remnants disappear in the distant future. Traditionalism and modernity thus cease to be stages in the historical process and become the beginning and ending points of history. But if all real societies are transitional societies, a theory is needed which will explain the forms and processes of change at work in transitional societies. This is just what the dichotomic theory failed to provide.

Beyond this, each of the assumptions which underlay the original, simple image of modernization could also be called into question. Contrary to the

25. Gusfield, "Misplaced Polarities," p. 352; Heesterman, "Tradition in Modern India," p. 243; Lloyd I. and Suzanne Hoeber Rudolph, "The Political Role of India's Caste Associations," *Pacific Affairs*, XXXIII (March 1960), 5–22.

26. See Wilbert Moore, "Social Change and Comparative Studies," *International Social Science Journal*, XV (1963), 523; J. A. Ponsioen, *The Analysis of Social Change Reconsidered* (The Hague, 1962), pp. 23–25.

view that modernization is revolutionary, it could be argued that the differences between traditional and modern societies are really not that great. Not only do modern societies incorporate many traditional elements, but traditional societies often have many universalistic, achievement oriented, bureaucratic characteristics which are normally thought of as modern.[27] The cultural, psychological, and behavioral continuities existing within a society through both its traditional and modern phases may be significantly greater than the dissimilarities between these phases. Similarly, the claim that modernization is a complex process could be challenged by the argument that modernization involves fundamental changes in only one dimension and that changes in other dimensions are only consequences of changes in that fundamental dimension. This was, of course, Marx's argument.

Contrary to Lerner's view of the systemic qualities of modernization, it can be argued that the various elements of the modernization process are historically discrete and that, while they have their roots in common causes, progress along one dimension has no necessary relationship to progress along another. Such a view is, indeed, implied by rejection of the mutually exclusive nature of modernity and tradition. If these concepts, moreover, are thought of simply as ideal types, and "If we are to avoid mistaking ideal types for accurate descriptions, we must take care to treat the clusters of attributes as *hypothetically,* not as actually, correlated." In addition, as Bendix went on to argue, a distinction ought to be maintained between modernization and modernity. "Many attributes of modernization, like widespread literacy or modern medicine, have appeared, or have been adopted, in isolation from other attributes of a modern society. Hence, modernization in some sphere of life *may* occur without resulting in 'modernity.' "[28] By extension, this argument also challenges the assumption that modernization is a global process. Modernization may be simply a peculiarity of Western culture; whatever changes are taking place in African and Asian cultures could be of a fundamentally different character and have very different results from those changes which occurred in Western societies.

The early assumptions about the timing and duration of modernization were also brought under criticism. The latecomers, it could be argued, can modernize rapidly through revolutionary means and by borrowing the experience and technology of the early modernizers. The entire process can thus be telescoped, and the assumption that there is a well-defined progression of phases—preconditions, takeoff, drive to maturity, and the like—through which all societies must move is likely to be invalid. Contrary to the common idea that modernization produces homogenization or con-

27. Bendix, "Tradition and Modernity," pp. 313–14; Gusfield, "Misplaced Polarities," pp. 352–53.

28. Bendix, pp. 315, 329; Eisenstadt, "Tradition, Change, and Modernity," pp. 27–28.

vergence, it could be said that it may reinforce the distinctive characteristics of each society and thus broaden the differences between societies rather than narrow them. To the contrary of the idea that modernization is irreversible, it could be argued that it is a cyclical process with major ups and downs over time or that a turning point in the process will eventually be reached where the "upward" secular trend of modernization will be replaced by a sustained "downward" trend of disintegration or primitivization. Finally, contrary to the view that modernization is a progressive process, it may be argued, as earlier twentieth century thinkers asserted, that modernization destroys the more intimate communities in which alone man can realize his full personality; it sacrifices human, personal, and spiritual values to achieve mass production and mass society. This type of argument against change was very popular at times in the past. The relative absence of such a traditional, romantic opposition to modernization among theorists in modern societies and politicians in modernizing societies was some evidence of the extent to which the fever of modernization gripped the intellectually and politically conscious world of the 1950s. Nonetheless, by the late 1960s some opposition to and criticism of modernization along these lines were beginning to appear among intellectuals in many developing societies.

III. THE CONCEPT OF POLITICAL DEVELOPMENT

Definitions of the concept Sharing the concern of other social scientists with the Great Dichotomy of modernity and tradition and the Grand Process of Modernization, political scientists in the 1960s began to pursue more actively their interests in what was variously called political modernization or political development. Their starting point was the concepts of tradition and modernity; eventually this essentially comparative and static focus gave way to a more dynamic and developmentally oriented set of concerns. This shift can be clearly seen in the work of the Social Science Research Council (SSRC) Committee on Comparative Politics and particularly of Gabriel Almond, its chairman and intellectual leader during the 1950s and early 1960s.

The volume which undoubtedly played the major role in first focusing the attention of political scientists on development problems was *The Politics of the Developing Areas,* edited by Almond and James S. Coleman and published in 1960 under the sponsorship of the Comparative Politics Committee and the Princeton Center for International Studies. The bulk of the book consisted of descriptions and analyses in terms of a common format of politics in five developing areas. The principal intellectual impact of the book, however, came from the introduction by Almond and, to a lesser degree, the conclusion by Coleman. This impact was very largely the result of their application to the politics of non-Western countries of a general concept of the political system. Almond used this framework to distinguish

between "developed" and "underdeveloped" or "developing" political sys-
terms. Developed political systems are characteristic of modern societies
and underdeveloped ones of traditional societies. Almond's concepts of "tra-
ditionality" and of "modernity" or, as he seemed to prefer, "rationality," are
described in Parsonian terms derived from the central stream of sociological
analysis. Almond's distinctive contribution in this respect, however, was the
insistence that all political systems are culturally mixed, combining elements
of modernity and tradition. "All political systems—the developed Western
ones as well as the less-developed non-Western ones—are transitional systems. . . ." He was appropriately critical of some sociological theorists for
promoting "an unfortunate theoretical polarization" in not recognizing this
"dualistic" quality of political systems.[29]

  The Politics of the Developing Areas is a work in comparative politics,
not one in political development. This volume presents a behavioral and
systems approach for the analysis of comparative politics; it does not
present a concept or theory of political development. The phrase "political
development" is, indeed, notably absent from its vocabulary. It is concerned with the analysis of the political systems of societies which are presumed to be developing (or modernizing) and the comparison of those
systems with the political systems presumed to exist in modern societies.
Its key categories are system, role, culture, structure, function, socialization.
With the possible exception of socialization, no one of these refers to a
dynamic process. They are categories essential to the comparative analysis
of political systems; they are not oriented to the change and development
of political systems. Almond posited a number of functions which must be
performed in any political system and then compared systems in terms of
the structures which perform those functions. "What we have done," he
said, "is to separate political function from political structure." Almond also
argued that, "We need dualistic models *rather than* monistic ones, and
developmental *as well as* equilibrium models if we are to understand differences precisely and grapple effectively with the processes of political
change."[30] In this book, Almond and his associates presented the elements
of a dualistic model of the political system, but they did not attempt to
present a "developmental model" which would contribute to the understanding of "the processes of political change."

  For Almond that task came six years later with another major theoretical
work coauthored with C. Bingham Powell, Jr. Unlike the earlier volume,
this book was concerned with political dynamics and focused explicitly on
political development as a subject and as a concept. Almond recognized

29. Gabriel Almond, "Introduction: A Functional Approach to Comparative Politics,"
in Almond and James S. Coleman, eds., *The Politics of the Developing Areas* (Princeton, 1960), pp. 23–24.

30. Ibid., p. 25.

the limitations of his earlier work in relation to the problems of political change. That earlier framework, he said, "was suitable mainly for the analysis of political systems in a given cross section of time. It did not permit us to explore developmental patterns, to explain how political systems change and why they change."[31] The earlier set of political functions (now called "conversion functions") was now supplemented by categories which described more fully the demands and supports which operate on the "input" side of the political system and by categories which described the "output" capabilities of the political system in relation to its environments (extractive, regulative, distributive, symbolic, and responsive).

Political development, Almond and Powell argued, is the response of the political system to changes in its societal or international environments and, in particular, the response of the system to the challenges of state building, nation building, participation, and distribution. Political development itself was thought of primarily in terms of political modernization. The three criteria of political development were held to be: structural differentiation, subsystem autonomy, and cultural secularization. Almond thus came face to face with the problem which was gripping many other political scientists at that time. What is political development?

The answers to this question were more numerous than the answerers. Almost every scholar or group of scholars concerned with the politics of the developing areas had to come up with at least one formulation. Even to attempt to itemize them all here would be a tiresome and not particularly useful task. Fortunately, however, in 1965 Lucian W. Pye compiled a fairly comprehensive listing of ten meanings which had been attributed to the concept of political development:

1. the political prerequisite of economic development;
2. the politics typical of industrial societies;
3. political modernization;
4. the operation of a nation-state;
5. administrative and legal development;
6. mass mobilization and participation;
7. the building of democracy;
8. stability and orderly change;
9. mobilization and power;
10. one aspect of a multidimensional process of social change.

In a noble effort at synthesis, Pye attempted to summarize the most prevalent common themes on political development as involving movement toward: increasing *equality* among individuals in relation to the political system; increasing *capacity* of the political system in relation to its environ-

31. Gabriel A. Almond and G. Bingham Powell, Jr., *Comparative Politics: A Developmental Approach* (Boston, 1966), p. 13.

ments; and increasing *differentiation* of institutions and structures within the political system. These three dimensions, he argued, are to be found "lying at the heart of the development process."[32] In a similar vein, another effort to generalize about definitions of political development found four oft-recurring concepts: rationalization, national integration, democratization, and mobilization or participation.[33]

This "quest for political development," in John Montgomery's phrase,[34] necessarily led political scientists to grapple with three more general issues. First, what was the relationship between political development and political modernization? The tendency was to think of political development as virtually identical with political modernization. Political development was one element of the modernization syndrome. Political scientists might disagree as to what types of change constituted political development, but whatever they did choose was almost invariably thought of as a part of the more general process of modernization. The principal dissent from this point of view came in 1965 from Samuel P. Huntington, who argued that it was highly desirable to distinguish between political development and modernization. The identification of the two, he said, limited too drastically the applicability of the concept of political development "in both time and space." It became restricted to a particular phase of historical evolution, and hence it was impossible to talk about the "political development" of the Greek city-state or of the Roman Empire. In addition, political development as political modernization made the former a rather confusing complex concept, tended to reduce its empirical relevance, and made it difficult if not impossible to conceive of its reversibility, i.e., to talk about political decay.[35]

A second issue which political scientists had to deal with in their definitional efforts was whether political development was a unitary or a complex concept. Since so many people had so many ideas as to what constituted political development, the prevalent tendency was to think of it as a complex concept. This tendency was explained or, perhaps, rationalized by Pye on the grounds that the "multi-function character of politics . . . means that no single scale can be used for measuring the degree of political development."[36] Hence, most scholars used several dimensions: Pye himself, as indicated above, suggested three; Almond also had three; Ward and Rustow,

32. Lucian W. Pye, *Aspects of Political Development* (Boston, 1966), pp. 31–48.

33. Samuel P. Huntington, "Political Development and Political Decay," *World Politics*, XVII (April 1965), 387–88.

34. John D. Montgomery, "The Quest for Political Development," *Comparative Politics*, I (January 1969), 285–95.

35. Huntington, "Political Development and Political Decay," pp. 389–93.

36. Lucian W. Pye, "Introduction," in Pye, ed., *Communications and Political Development* (Princeton, 1963), p. 16.

eight; Emerson, five; Eisenstadt, four.[37] This all seems very reasonable, since political development clearly would appear to be a complex process. Yet, obviously also, this approach can lead to difficulties. What are the relationships among the component elements of political development? Thus, although Pye argued that equality, capacity, and differentiation constitute the development syndrome, he also had to admit that these do not "necessarily fit easily together." On the contrary, "historically the tendency has usually been that there are acute tensions between the demands for equality, the requirements for capacity, and the processes of greater differentiation." In a similar vein, Almond argued that "there is a tendency" for role differentiation, subsystem autonomy, and secularization "to vary together," but that the relation between each pair of these three variables "is not a necessary and invariant one."[38] Almond, indeed, presented a two-way matrix with secularization and differentiation on one axis and subsystem autonomy on the other. He found some type of political system to occupy each of the nine boxes in his matrix. The question thus necessarily arises: What does political development mean if it can mean everything? On the other hand, if political development is defined as a unitary concept, the tendency is either to define it narrowly—as Huntington, for instance, did in identifying it exclusively with institutionalization—and thus to rob it of many of the connotations and the richness usually associated with it, or to define it very generally, as for instance Alfred Diamant did, which in effect masks a complex concept under a unitary label.[39]

A third problem in the definitional quest concerned the extent to which political development was a descriptive concept or a teleological one. If it was the former, it presumably referred either to a single process or to a group of processes which could be defined, in terms of their inherent characteristics, as processes. If it was a teleological concept, on the other hand, it was conceived as movement toward a particular goal. It was defined not in terms of its content but in terms of its direction. As in the more general case of modernization, the goals of political development were, of course, valued positively. The definition of political development in terms of goals would not have created difficulties if there were clear-cut criteria and

37. See Pye, *Aspects*, pp. 45–48; Almond and Powell, *Comparative Politics*, pp. 299ff.; Ward and Rustow, *Japan and Turkey*, pp. 6–7; Rupert Emerson, *Political Modernization: The Single-Party System* (Denver, 1963), pp. 7–8; S. N. Eisenstadt, "Bureaucracy and Political Development," in Joseph LaPalombara, ed., *Bureaucracy and Political Development* (Princeton, 1963), p. 99.

38. Pye, *Aspects*, p. 47; Almond and Powell, *Comparative Politics*, p. 306. For an intriguing analysis of some of these problems, see Fred W. Riggs, "The Dialectics of Developmental Conflict," *Comparative Political Studies*, I (July 1968), 197ff.

39. Alfred Diamant, "The Nature of Political Development," in Jason L. Finkle and Richard W. Gable, eds., *Political Development and Social Change* (New York, 1966), p. 92.

reasonably accurate indices (e.g., the political equivalent of per capita Gross National Product) to measure progress toward those goals. In the absence of these, however, there was a strong tendency to assume that, because both scholarly analyst and, presumably, the political actors he was analyzing, wanted political development, it was therefore occurring. The result was that "Almost anything that happens in the "developing" countries—coups, ethnic struggles, revolutionary wars—becomes part of the process development, however contradictory or retrogressive this may appear on the surface."[40]

These definitional problems raised very real questions about the usefulness of political development as a concept. Referring to Pye's list of ten definitions, Rustow argued that this "is obviously at least nine too many."[41] In truth, however, one should go one step further. If there are ten definitions of political development, there are ten too many, and the concept is, in all likelihood, superfluous and dysfunctional. In the social sciences, concepts are useful if they perform an aggregating function, that is, if they provide an umbrella for a number of subconcepts which do share something in common. Modernization is, in this sense, an umbrella concept. Or, concepts are useful because they perform a distinguishing function, that is, because they help to separate out two or more forms of something which would otherwise be thought of as undifferentiated. In this sense, manifest functions and latent functions are distinguishing concepts.

Political development in general is of dubious usefulness in either of these ways. To the extent that political development is thought of as an umbrella concept encompassing a multiplicity of different processes, as in the Almond and Pye cases discussed earlier, these processes often turn out to have little in common except the label which is attached to them. No one has yet been able to say of the various elements subsumed under the label political development what Lerner, at a different level, was able to say about the broader processes subsumed under the label modernization: that they went together because "in some historical sense, they *had* to go together." Instead, it is clear that the elements included in most complex definitions of political development do not have to go together and, in fact, often do not. In addition, if political development involves differentiation, subsystem autonomy, and secularization, as Almond suggests, do not the really interesting and important questions concern the relations among these three, as Almond himself implies in his conclusion? The use of the term political development may thus foster a misleading sense of coherence and compatibility among other processes and obscure crucial questions from discussion. To the extent, on the other hand, that political development is identified with a

40. Huntington, "Political Development and Political Decay," p. 390.

41. Dankwart A. Rustow, "Change as the Theme of Political Science" (Paper delivered at International Political Science Association Round Table, Torino, September 1969), pp. 1–2.

single, specific process, e.g., political institutionalization, its redundancy is all the more obvious. What is to be gained analytically by calling something which has a good name by a second name? As either an aggregating concept or a distinguishing concept, in short, political development is superfluous.

The principal function that political development has in fact performed for political scientists is neither to aggregate nor to distinguish, but rather to legitimate. It has served as a way for political scientists to say, in effect: "Hey, here are some things I consider valuable and desirable goals and important subjects to study." Such would indeed appear to be the principal function for the discipline served by the debates over the meaning of political development. This aspect of the use of the concept has perhaps been particularly marked in the arguments over the relation of democratization to political development and the perennial uneasiness faced by political scientists when they consider the issue: Is the Soviet Union politically developed? The concept of political development thus serves in effect as a signal of scholarly preferences rather than as a tool for analytical purposes.[42]

The popularity of the concept of political development among political scientists stems perhaps from the feeling that they should have a political equivalent to economic development. In this respect, political science finds itself in a familiar ambiguous methodological position between its two neighboring disciplines. In terms of the scope of its subject matter, political science is narrower than sociology but broader than economics. In terms of the agreement within the discipline on goals, political scientists have more shared values than sociologists, but fewer than economists. Sociology is comprehensive in scope; economics is focused in its goals; political science is not quite one or the other. The eclecticism and diffuseness of sociological theory are excused by the extent of its subject. The narrowness and parochialism of economics are excused by the precision and elegance of its theory.

In this situation, it is quite natural for political scientists to borrow concepts from sociologists and to imitate concepts of economists. The sociological concept of modernization is, quite properly, extended and applied to political analysis. The concept of political development is created in the image of economic development. In terms of choosing its models, one might generalize, a discipline will usually tend to copy the more structured and

42. Some people may say that people in glass houses should not throw stones on the grounds that I did, after all, argue that political development should be defined as political institutionalization in my 1965 article on "Political Development and Political Decay." My answer would be: true enough. But I do not mind performing a useful function by throwing stones and thus encouraging others to move out of their glass houses, once I have moved out of mine. In my 1968 book, *Political Order in Changing Societies,* which otherwise builds extensively on the 1965 article, the concept of political development was quietly dropped. I focus instead on what I conceive to be the critical relationship between political participation and political institutionalization without worrying about the issue of which should be labeled "political development."

"scientific" of its neighboring disciplines. This leads to difficulties comparable to those normally associated with the phrase "misplaced concreteness."
Economists, it will be said, do differ over what they mean by economic
development and how one measures it. These differences, however, shrink
to insignificance in comparison with the difficulties which political scientists
have with the term political development. If, on the other hand, political
scientists had modeled themselves on the sociologists and talked about
political change in imitation of social change rather than political development in imitation of economic development, they might have avoided many
of the definitional and teleological problems in which they found themselves.

Approaches to political development   Many of the things that are often
labeled studies in political development are not such in any strict sense. The
study of political development is not the study of politics in societies at
some given level of development. If this were the case, there would be few
if any studies of politics which were not studies in political development,
since those polities which are usually assumed to be developed are also
presumably still developing. Yet not infrequently studies in the politics of
less developed societies are treated as if they were studies in political
development. Tunisia, it is said, is a developing society; therefore, its polity
is developing polity; therefore a study in Tunisian politics is a study in
political development. The fallacy here is to look at the subject of the study
rather than at the concepts with which that subject is studied. Depending on
the concepts which were used and hence the questions which were asked, for
instance, a study of John F. Kennedy's presidency might be a study in the
uses of power, the institutionalization of an office, legislative-executive relations, consensus-building, the psychology of leadership, the role of intellectuals in politics. Or it could, conceivably, be a study in political development or political change. Exactly the same possibilities would exist for a
study of Habib Bourguiba's presidency. There is nothing in the latter which
makes it inherently more "developmental" than the former. Precisely the
same is true for the innumerable studies of the role of the military, bureaucracy, and political parties in developing societies. More likely than not,
these are simply studies of particular institutions in particular types of societies rather than studies in change or development. Depending upon the
conceptual framework with which these subjects were approached, they
could just as easily be studies in civil-military relations, organizational
behavior, and political behavior, as studies in political development. They
are the latter only if the categories employed are formulated in terms of
change.

It could, of course, be argued that change is so pervasive that it is virtually synonymous with politics itself and that hence it cannot be studied as a
separate subject. The rejoinder is that, to be sure, politics is change, but
politics is also ideas, values, institutions, groups, power, structures, conflict,

communication, influence, interaction, law, and organization. Politics can be studied, and has been studied, in terms of each of these concepts. Each sheds a different light on the subject, illuminates different areas, suggests different relationships and generalizations. Why not also analyze politics in terms of change or development?

In fact during the 1950s and 1960s a variety of scholars did just that. Many different approaches were employed. Without making any claim to inclusiveness or to systematic rigor, it is perhaps useful to focus on three of these approaches: system-function, social process, and comparative history.

System-function   In the analysis of political development, a close relation existed between systems theory, in the strict sense, and structural-functional theory. It is, indeed, impossible to apply a functional approach without employing some concept of the political system. The varieties of theory encompassed in this general category are reflected in the names: Talcott Parsons, Marion Levy, David Easton, Gabriel Almond, David Apter, Leonard Binder, Fred Riggs. The principal contribution of these scholars has been to develop a set of concepts and categories, central to which are those of "system" and "function," for the analysis and comparison of types of political systems. Among their other key concepts are: structure, legitimacy, input and output, feedback, environment, equilibrium. These concepts and the theories associated with them provide an overall model of the political system and the basis for distinguishing types of political systems in terms of the structures which perform the functions which must be performed in all political systems.

The advantages of the system-function approach clearly rest in the generality of the concepts which it deploys on the plains of analysis. One problem of the approach for the study of political change is the defect of this great virtue. It is primarily a conceptual framework. This framework does not necessarily in and of itself generate testable hypotheses or what are often referred to as "middle level generalizations." Scholars using the framework may come up with such hypotheses or generalizations, but it is an open question whether the conceptual framework is not more of a hindrance than a help in this respect. The approach itself provides little incentive for scholars to dig into empirical data. Indeed, the tendency is in just the opposite direction. The theory becomes an end in itself. It is striking how few facts there are not only in general works, such as Levy's two volumes, but even in case studies attempting to apply the system-function approach to a specific society, such as Binder's study of Iran.[43]

A more fundamental problem is that this approach does not inherently focus on the problem of change. It is possible to employ the concept of

43. See Levy, *Modernization and the Structure of Societies,* and Leonard Binder, *Iran: Political Development in a Changing Society* (Berkeley and Los Angeles, 1962).

"system" in a dynamic context, focusing on lags, leads, and feedback. In actuality, however, much of the theorizing on political development which started from a systems approach did not primarily employ these dynamic elements in that approach. The stress was on the elaboration of models of different types of political systems, not different types of change from one system to another. In his two-volume opus, *Modernization and the Structure of Societies,* Levy, for instance, is overwhelmingly concerned with the second element in his two-component title. The bulk of his work is devoted to discussing the characteristics of societies in general and then distinguishing between those of "relatively modernized societies" and of "relatively non-modernized societies." The question of modernization and its political components gets short shrift in the first and last chapters of this 800-page work. As we noted earlier, Almond himself saw somewhat comparable limitations in the framework which he used in *The Politics of Developing Areas.* The much more elaborate and change-oriented scheme which he and Powell present in *Comparative Politics: A Developmental Approach* does not entirely escape from this difficulty. Among those works in the system-function tradition directly concerned with political development, David Apter's *The Politics of Modernization* has probably been most successful in bringing to the fore dynamic concerns with the rate, forms, and sources of change. Yet to the extent that he has done this, it has in large part flowed from his independent concerns with normative questions and ideologies, which are derived from sources other than the system-function framework which he also employs. The structural-functional approach, as Kalman Silvert has pointed out, was initially employed by social scientists interested in studying either very primitive societies (the anthropologists) or very complex societies (Parsons). It is an approach peculiarly limited in what it can contribute to the understanding of societies undergoing fundamental change. It is, moreover, rather ironic that political scientists should have seized upon this approach in order to study political change at the same time that the approach was coming under serious criticism within sociology because of its insensitivity to, and limited usefulness in, the study of change.

As has often been pointed out, a related difficulty in attempting to deal with change in this intellectual context is the extent to which the concept "equilibrium" also tends to be implicitly or explicitly linked to the system-function approach. The equilibrium concept presupposes the existence of a system composed of two or more functionally related variables. Changes in one variable produce changes in others. The concept, as Easton has pointed out, is closely linked with the ideas of multiple causation and pluralism. In addition, however, equilibrium also means that the variables in the system tend to maintain "a particular pattern of interaction."[44] In its pure form the theory conceives of equilibrium as a state of rest. In all forms

---

44. Easton, *Political System,* pp. 266–67, 272ff.; Harold Lasswell and Abraham Kaplan, *Power and Society* (New Haven, 1950), p. xiv.

it presupposes tendencies toward the restoration of an original condition or a theoretically defined condition of equilibrium.

Equilibrium theory has obvious limitations as a framework for exploring political change. As one sociologist observed, the theory, "does not attend to intrinsic sources of change, does not predict changes that have persistent directionality (but only those that restore balance if that is disturbed), and thus does not readily handle past changes that clearly affect the current state of the system."[45] In effect, change is viewed as an extraneous abnormality. It is held to be the result of strain or tension, which gives rise to compensating movements that tend to reduce the strain or tension and thus restore the original state. Change is "unnatural"; stability or rest is "natural." Some thinkers have attempted to reconcile equilibrium and change through the concept of moving equilibrium. By itself, however, this concept is inadequate to account for change. If the equilibrium remains the same but is itself moving as a whole, the concept does not explain the cause or direction of its movement. If the equilibrium is itself changing, then moving equilibrium really means multiple equilibria, and again some theory is necessary to explain the succession of one equilibrium by another.

Social process   The social-process approach to political development starts not with concepts of the social system and the political system but rather with a focus on social processes—such as industrialization, urbanization, commercialization, literacy expansion, occupational mobility—which are presumed to be part of modernization and to have implications for political change. The emphasis is on the process, not the system. The approach is more behaviorally and empirically oriented than the system-function approach, and it typically leads to the accumulation of substantial amounts of data, often quantitative in nature (surveys or aggregate ecological data), about these social processes which it then tries to relate to political changes. While the scholar working with the system-function approach typically attempts to impute functions, the scholar employing the social-process approach attempts to correlate processes. He may attempt to move beyond correlation to causation and to shed light on the latter through various techniques of causal or path analysis.

The scholars most prominently associated with this type of approach to political development and related questions in the 1950s and 1960s included Daniel Lerner, Karl Deutsch, Raymond Tanter, Hayward Alker, Phillips Cutright, and Michael Hudson. The two most important early works, which stimulated much of what followed, were Lerner's *The Passing of Traditional Society* (1958) and Deutsch's 1961 article, "Social Mobilization and Political Development."[46] The system-function scholar begins with

45. Moore, "Social Change and Comparative Studies," pp. 524–25.

46. Karl W. Deutsch, "Social Mobilization and Political Development," *American Political Science Review*, LV (September 1961), 493–514. For a suggestive effort to

a concept of the political system, then differentiates different types or models of political systems, and finally attempts to spell out the consequences and implications of these distinctions. His approach typically is concerned with linking a pattern of action to the system as a whole, i.e., idenitfying its function within the system, while the social-process scholar is concerned with relating one pattern of action to another pattern of action.

The great virtue of the social-process approach is its effort to establish relationships between variables and particularly between changes in one set of variables and changes in another. In this respect, it does focus directly on change. Its limitations in dealing with change are threefold. First, more often than not, the variables which have been used concern levels of development rather than rates of development. Since it is empirically oriented, the variables employed are shaped by the availability of data. Data on levels of literacy in different societies at the same time (i.e., now) are easier to come by than data on levels of literacy in the same society over time. The latter, however, are necessary for longitudinal analysis and the use of rates of change in literacy. While cross-sectional analyses may be useful and appropriate in studying some types of relationships, they are also frequently inferior to longitudinal analyses in studying other types of relationships. The difficulty of getting data on the changes in variables over time in most modernizing societies in Asia, Africa, and even Latin America has consequently led many social-process analysts back to the study of Western European and North American societies. Here is a clear case where knowledge of political change or political development is advanced by studying developed rather than developing societies. A related difficulty is the extent to which the social-process approach has been applied primarily to the comparison of national societies, which are often units too large and complex to be useful for comparative generalization for many purposes.

A second problem in the social-process approach concerns the links between the usually social, economic, and demographic independent variable and the political dependent ones. The problem here is the general methodological one of the causal relationship between an economic or social change (which is in some sense "objective") to political changes which are normally the result of conscious human effort and will. If the problem is, for instance, to explain voting participation in elections or the frequency of coups, how meaningful is it to correlate these phenomena with rates of economic growth, fluctuations in price levels, or literacy levels? The relation between the "macro" socioeconomic changes and "macro" political changes has to be mediated through "micro" changes in the attitudes,

---

relate Almond, Huntington, and SSRC Comparative Politics Committee theories of political development to the available quantitative data, see Raymond F. Hopkins, "Aggregate Data and the Study of Political Development," *Journal of Politics*, XXXI (February 1969), 71–94.

values, and behavior of individuals. The explanation of the latter is the weak link in the causal chain which is assumed to exist in most social-process analysis. To date, the most prevalent and effective means of dealing with this problem has been the various form of the "relative deprivation" and "frustration-aggression" hypotheses utilized to relate socioeconomic changes to political instability.[47] Finally, at the dependent end of the causal chain, social process analysts often have trouble in defining political variables, identifying indices for measuring those variables, and securing the data required for the index.

One more general criticism which can be raised about the social-process approach concerns the extent to which it makes politics dependent upon economic and social forces. That the latter are a major influence on politics is obvious, and this influence is perhaps particularly important in societies at middle levels of social-economic modernization. In its pure form, which, to be fair, most of its practitioners rarely use, the social-process approach would leave little room for social structure and even less for political culture, political institutions, and political leadership. One of the great culture problems of the social-process approach to political change has been to overcome this initial deficiency and to find ways for assigning independent roles to cultural, institutional, and leadership factors.

Comparative history A third approach to political development is somewhat more diverse and eclectic than the two just considered. Its practitioners share enough in common, however, to be loosely grouped together. They start neither with a theoretical model nor with a focus on the relationship between two or more variables, but rather with a comparison of the evolution of two or more societies. What "the system" is to the system-functions man and "process" is to the social-process man, "society" is to the comparative-history man. He is, however, interested not just in the history of one society but rather in the comparison of two or more societies. The system functions man conceptualizes, the social-process man correlates; the comparative history man, naturally, compares. Among social scientists concerned with political development who would fit primarily into this school are Cyril Black, S. N. Eisenstadt, Dankwart Rustow, Seymour Martin Lipset, Barrington Moore, Jr., Reinhard Bendix, and, in some measure, Lucian W. Pye and the members of the SSRC Committee on Comparative Politics.

The work of these people tends to be highly empirical but not highly quantitative. They are, indeed, concerned with precisely those factors with

47. Ibid.; James C. Davies, "Toward a Theory of Revolution," *American Sociological Review*, XXVII (February 1962), 5ff.; Ivo K. and Rosalind L. Feierabend, "Aggressive Behaviors within Politics, 1948–1962: A Cross-National Study," *Journal of Conflict Resolution*, X (September 1966), 253–54; Ted Gurr, *Why Men Rebel* (Princeton, 1970).

which the social-process analysts have difficulty; institutions, culture, and leadership. Their approach is to categorize patterns of political development either by general stages or phases through which all societies must pass or by distinctive channels through which different societies may pass, or by some combination of these "vertical" and "horizontal" types of categories. Moore, for instance, distinguishes three patterns of modernization, under bourgeois (England, United States), aristocratic (Germany, Japan), and peasant (Russia, China) auspices. While he admits there may conceivably be a fourth way (India?), he is very dubious that this possibility will materialize. Consequenlty, every modernizing society will presumably have to find its way to modernity by way of liberal capitalism, reactionary fascism, or revolutionary communism. Cyril Black, on the other hand, starts by identifying four phases of modernization through which all societies pass: the initial challenge to modernity; the consolidation of modernizing leadership; economic and social transformation from a rural, agrarian to an urban, industrial society; and the integration of society, involving the fundamental reordering of social structure. He then specifies five criteria for distinguishing among societies in terms of how they have evolved through these phases and proceeds to classify all contemporary societies into "seven patterns of political modernization" on the basis of these criteria. He thus combines vertical and horizontal categories into a truly all-encompassing scheme of comparative history, and he very appropriately subtitles his book, "A Study in Comparative History."[48]

In a slightly different vein, Dankwart Rustow and the SSRC Committee on Comparative Politics have attempted to identify the types of problems which confront modernizing societies and to compare the evolution of these societies in terms of the sequences with which they have dealt with these problems. Rustow argues that there are three key requirements of political modernization: "identity is essential to the nation, authority to the state, equality to modernity; the three together form the political basis of the modern nation-state."[49] The critical differences among societies concern the extent to which they had to deal with these problems simultaneously or sequentially, and, if the latter, the order in which these problems were dealt with. On the basis of comparative analysis, Rustow suggests that the identity-authority-equality sequence leads to the most successful and least traumatic modernization. In a somewhat similar spirit and parallel endeavor, the SSRC Committee identified five crises which societies would have to

---

48. Barrington Moore, Jr., *Social Origins of Dictatorship and Democracy* (Boston, 1966); Cyril E. Black, *The Dynamics of Modernization: A Study in Comparative History* (New York, 1966).

49. Rustow, *World of Nations*, p. 36. For a thoughtful discussion of sequences in political development, see Eric A. Nordlinger, "Political Development: Time Sequences and Rates of Change," *World Politics*, XX (April 1968), 494–520.

deal with in the process of political modernization: identity, legitimacy, penetration, participation, and distribution. A rough equivalence presumably exists between these two efforts as well as that of Almond:

Almond—*Challenges*	Rustow—*Requirements*	CCP—*Crises*
nation-building	identity	identity
state-building	authority	legitimacy, penetration
participation, distribution	equality	participation, distribution

Interestingly, the SSRC Committee originally had a sixth crisis, integration, which concerned the "problems of relating popular politics to governmental performance. . . ."[50] This, however, turned out to be a rather nebulous and slippery crisis to handle; eventually it was dropped from the scheme.

The great virtue of the comparative-history approach is that it starts by looking at the actual evolutions of societies, attempts to classify those evolutions into patterns, and then attempts to generate hypotheses about what factors are responsible for the differences in patterns. It starts, in short, with the "real" stuff of history, at the opposite end of the methodological scale from the system-function approach with its abstract model of the system. Nor does it, like the social-process approach, assume that certain variables, such as urbanization and instability, can be lifted out and generalized about independently of their context. This approach thus clearly lacks generality. In effect, it comes back to a focus on the historically discrete phenomenon of modernization, and it deals with particular phases in the evolution of particular societies. Like most "developmental" analyses, its concepts are "less generalized than those of equilibrium analysis."[51] In comparison to the system-function man with his conceptual complexity and the social-process man with his high-powered quantitative analyses, the comparative-history fellow often seems like a rather pedestrian, traditional plodder, whose findings lack theoretical and scientific precision. On the other hand, he is, unlike his competitors, usually able to communicate those findings to readers who will not read jargon and cannot read numbers.

Each of these three approaches has obviously contributed much to the study of political development. At the same time each has the defect of its virtues. From the viewpoint of a theory of political change, the system-function approach is weak in change, the social-process approach is weak in politics, and the comparative history approach is weak in theory. By

50. See Pye, *Aspects*, pp. 62–67.

51. Lasswell and Kaplan, *Power and Society*, p. xv.

building upon and combining the strengths of all three approaches, however, it may be possible to overcome the deficiencies of each.

IV. THEORIES OF POLITICAL CHANGE

The study of modernization and political development thus generated concern for the formulation of more general theories of political change. In the late 1960s the analysis of political change became in itself a direct focus of political science work, quite apart from any relations it might have had with the social-economic-cultural processes of modernization or the teleological preoccupations which underlay much of the work on political development. In the course of a decade the work of political scientists moved from a generalized focus on the political system to the comparative analysis of modern and traditional political systems, to a more concrete concern with the discrete historical process of modernization, to an elaboration of related concepts of political development, and then back to a higher level of abstraction oriented toward general theories of political change. The transition from the static theory to dynamic theory, in short, was made by way of the historical phenomenon of modernization.

These new theories of political change were distinguishable from earlier approaches because of several characteristics. First, the theoretical frameworks could be utilized for the study of political changes in societies at any level of development. Second, these frameworks were either unrelated to the process of modernization or, at best, indirectly related to that process. Third, the variables and relationships which were central to the theories were primarily political in character. Fourth, the frameworks were sufficiently flexible to encompass sources of change and patterns of change in both the domestic and the international environments of the political system. Fifth, in general the theories were relatively more complex than earlier theories of political modernization and political development: they encompassed more variables and looked at the more extensive relationships among those variables.

One transitional approach was presented by Huntington in his 1968 volume on *Political Order in Changing Societies*. In this volume, the central focus of political change is held to be the relationship between political participation and political institutionalization. The relationship between these determines the stability of the political system. The fundamental source of expansion of political participation is the nonpolitical socioeconomic processes identified with modernization. The impact of modernization on political stability is mediated through the interaction between social mobilization and economic development, social frustration and nonpolitical mobility opportunities, and political participation and political institutionalization. Huntington expresses these relationships in a series of equations:[52]

52. Huntington, *Political Order*, p. 55.

$$(1) \quad \frac{Social\ mobilization}{Economic\ development} = Social\ frustration$$

$$(2) \quad \frac{Social\ frustration}{Mobility\ opportunities} = Political\ participation$$

$$(3) \quad \frac{Political\ participation}{Political\ institutionalization} = Political\ instability$$

Starting with a central concern of the social-process approach to modernization, i.e., the relationship between socioeconomic changes (urbanization, industrialization), on the one hand, and the political participation, political instability, and violence, on the other, this approach thus attempts to introduce into the analysis elements of social (mobility opportunities) and political (political institutionalization) structure.

Huntington is concerned with the relationship between political participation and political institutionalization. The source of the former is ultimately in the processes of modernization. What about the sources of the latter? Here he is less explicit. Implicitly, however, he suggests that there are two principal sources. One is the political structure of the traditional society. Some traditional political systems are more highly institutionalized than others (i.e., more adaptable, complex, coherent, and autonomous); these presumably will be better able to survive modernization and accommodate broadened patterns of participation. In addition, Huntington suggests that at particular phases in the process of modernization certain types of political leadership (aristocratic, military, revolutionary) and certain types of conflict may also produce institutionalization.

The relationship between political institutionalization and political participation, however, is clearly one that can be abstracted from a concern with modernization. The latter may be one major historical source of changes in participation, but it need not be the only one. The problem of balancing participation and institutionalization, moreover, is one which occurs in societies at all levels of development. The disruptions involving Negroes and students in the United States during the late 1960s could be profitably analyzed from this framework. In central cities and in universities, existing structures were challenged to provide new channels through which these groups, in the cliché of the times, could "participate in the decisions which affect them."

This theoretical approach, originally focused on the relationship between two political variables, could be extended to include more or different ones. One of the striking characteristics of much of the work on political development was the predominance of concern with the *direction* of change over the concern with the *objects* of change. This, of course, reflected the origins of political development research in the study of the transition from tradi-

tional to modern society. The first step in analyzing political change, however, is simply, as William Mitchell put it, to identify "the objects that are
susceptible to changes."[53] It is to identify what are or may be the components of a political system and then to establish what, if any, relations exist
in the changes among them. Such an approach focuses on *componential
change*.

A political system can be thought of as an aggregate of components, all
changing, some at rapid rates, some at slower ones. The questions to be
investigated then become: What types of change in one component tend to
be related to similar changes or the absence of change in other components?
What are the consequences of different combinations of componential
changes for the system as a whole? The study of political change can be
said to involve: (1) focusing on what seem to be the major components of
the political system; (2) determining the rate, scope, and direction of
change in these components; and (3) analyzing the relations between
changes in one component and changes in other components. The political
system can be defined in a variety of ways and conceived of as having
various components, as, for instance, the following five:

(a) culture, that is, the values, attitudes, orientations, myths, and
beliefs relevant to politics and dominant in the society;

(b) structure, that is, the formal organizations through which the
society makes authoritative decisions, such as political parties, legislatures, executives, and bureaucracies;

(c) groups, that is, the social and economic formations, formal and
informal, which participate in politics and make demands on the
political structures;

(d) leadership, that is, the individuals in political institutions and
groups who exercise more influence than others on the allocation of
values;

(e) policies, that is, the patterns of governmental activity which are
consciously designed to affect the distribution of benefits and penalties
within the society.

The study of political change can fruitfully start with the analysis of
changes in these five components and the relations between change in one
component and change in another. How is change in the dominant values
in a system related to change in its structures? What is the relation between
mobilization of new groups into politics and institutional evolution? How is
turnover in leadership related to changes in policy? The starting assumption

53. William C. Mitchell, *The American Polity* (New York, 1962), pp. 369–70.

would be that, in any political system, all five components are always changing, but that the rate, scope, and direction of change in the components vary greatly within a system and between systems. In some instances, the rate of change of a component may approach zero. The absence of change is simply one extreme rate of change, a rate rarely if ever approximated in practice. Each component, moreover, is itself an aggregate of various elements. The political culture, for instance, may include many subcultures; the political structures may represent a variety of institutions and procedures. Political change may be analyzed both in terms of changes among components and in terms of changes among the elements of each component.

Components and elements are the objects of change. But it is still necessary to indicate what types of changes in these are significant to the study of *political* change. One type of change which is obviously relevant is change in the power of a component or element. Indeed, some might argue that changes in power are the only changes with which political analysis should be concerned. But to focus on power alone is to take the meaning out of politics. Political analysis is concerned with the power of ideologies, institutions, groups, leaders, and policies. But it is also concerned with the content of these components and with the interrelation between changes in content and changes in power. "Power" here may have the usual meaning assigned to it in political analysis.[54] The "content," on the other hand, has to be defined somewhat differently for each component. The content of a political culture is the substance of the ideas, values, attitudes, and expectations dominant in the society. The content of the political institutions of the society, on the other hand, consists of the patterns of interaction which characterize them and the interests and values associated with them. The content of political groups refers to their interests and purposes and the substance of the claims which they make on the political system. The content of the leadership refers to the social-economic-psychological characteristics of the leaders and the goals which they attempt to realize. And the content of policies, of course, involves the substance of the policies, their prescriptions of benefits and penalties.

The analysis of political change may in the first instance be directed to simple changes in the power of components and elements of the political system. More important, however, is the relation between changes in the

54. Major contributions to the analysis of power by contemporary social scientists include: Lasswell and Kaplan, *Power and Society,* pp. 74ff.; Herbert Simon, "Notes on the Observation and Measurement of Political Power," *Journal of Politics,* XV (November 1953), 500–16; James G. March, "An Introduction to the Theory and Measurement of Influence," *American Political Science Review,* XLIX (June 1955), 431–14; Robert A. Dahl, "The Concept of Power," *Behavioral Science,* II (July 1957), 201–15; Carl J. Friedrich, *Man and His Government* (New York, 1963), pp. 159–79; Talcott Parsons, "On the Concept of Influence," *Public Opinion Quarterly,* XXVI (Spring 1963).

power of individual components and elements and changes in their content. If political analysis were limited to changes in power, it could never come to grips with their causes and consequences. The recurring problems of politics involve the trade offs of power and content. To what extent do changes in the power of a political ideology (measured by the number of people who adhere to it and the intensity of their adherence) involve changes in the substance of the ideology? Under what circumstances do rapid changes in the power of political leaders require changes in their purposes and goals (the "moderating" effects of power) and under what circumstances may the power of leaders be enhanced without significant changes in their purposes? History suggests, for instance, that professional military officers can acquire political power in liberal, socialist, or totalitarian societies only at the expense of abandoning or modifying the conservative military values.[55] In most systems, the enhancement of the power of an ideology, institution, group, leader, or policy is bought at the price of some modification of its content. But this is by no means an invariable rule, and a variety of propositions will be necessary to specify the trade-offs between power and content for different components in different situations. One important distinction among political systems may indeed be the prices which must be paid in content for significant increases in the power of elements. Presumably the more highly institutionalized a political system is, the higher the price it exacts for power.

Political change may thus be analyzed at three levels. The rate, scope, and direction of change in one component may be compared with the rate, scope, and direction of change in other components. Such comparisons can shed light on the patterns of stability and instability in a political system and on the extent to which change in one component depends upon or is related to change or the absence of change in other components. The culture and institutions of a political system, for instance, may be thought of as more fundamental to the system than its groups, leaders, and policies. Consequently, stability might be defined as a particular set of relationships in which all components are changing gradually, but with the rates of change in culture and institutions slower than those in other components. Political stagnation, in turn, could be defined as a situation in which there is little or no change in the political culture and institutions but rapid changes in leadership and policies. Political instability may be a situation in which culture and institutions change more rapidly than leaders and policies, while political revolution involves simultaneous rapid change in all five components of the system.

As a second level of analysis, changes in the power and content of one element of one component of the system may be compared with changes in

55. See Samuel P. Huntington, *The Soldier and the State* (Cambridge, 1957), pp. 80–97 and *passim*.

the power and content of other elements of the same component. This would involve, for instance, analysis of the rise and fall of ideologies and beliefs, of institutions and groups, and leaders and policies, and the changes in the content of these elements associated with their changing power relationships. Finally, at the most specific level of analysis, attention might be focused upon the relation between changes in power and changes in content for any one element, in an effort to identify the equations defining the price of power in terms of purposes, interests, and values.

A relatively simple set of assumptions and categories like this could be a starting point either for the comparative analysis of the more general problems of change found in many societies or for the analysis in depth of the change patterns of one particular society. It could furnish a way of bringing together the contributions which studies of attitudes, institutions, participation, groups, elites, and policies could make to the understanding of political change.

A somewhat different approach, suggested separately by both Gabriel Almond and Dankwart Rustow, focused on *crisis change* and also provided a general framework for analyzing political dynamics. Earlier theories of comparative politics and development, Almond argued, could be classified in terms of two dimensions.[56] To what extent did they involve an equilibrium or developmental models? To what extent were they predicated upon determinacy or choice? Reviewing many of the writers on these problems, Almond came up with the following classification:

Approaches to Comparative Politics

	Equilibrium	Developmental
Determinacy	I Parsons Easton	III Deutsch Moore Lipset
Choice	II Downs Dahl Riker	IV Harsanyi Leiserson

He then went on to argue that each of these approaches has its appropriate place in the analysis of political change. Change from one state to another can be thought of as going through five phases. In the first phase, an antecedent equilibrium can be assumed to exist, and for the analysis of this phase Type I and Type II theories are most appropriate. Change can be assumed to begin with the impact on the equilibrium of exogenous variables from the nonpolitical domestic environment or from the international

56. Gabriel A. Almond, "Determinacy-Choice, Stability-Change: Some Thoughts on a Contemporany Polemic in Political Theory" (Center for Advanced Study in the Behavioral Sciences, Stanford University, August 1969).

environment of the political system. These Phase 2 developments produce changes in the structure of political demand and in the distribution of political resources, and can be most appropriately analyzed by Type III theories. In the next phase, political factors—the changing structure of political demand and distribution of political resources—become the independent variables. Political leadership manipulates these variables so as to produce new political coalitions and policy outcomes. For this purpose, Type IV "coalition theory and leadership skill and personality theory" are most useful. In the next or fourth phase, these policy outcomes and political coalitions produce cultural and structural changes. The relations in this phase require analysis by all four types of theories. Finally, a new "consequent equilibrium" emerges in Phase 5, which again can be studied in terms of Type I and Type II theories.

In formulating this theoretical framework, Almond once again played a leading and a representative role in changing thinking on comparative politics. Unlike his earlier formulations, this framework was precisely designed to deal with the problem of change and it was also clearly independent of any particular historical context. It was not tied in with modernization. It was instead a general framework for the analysis of political change which could be applied to a primitive stateless tribe, a classical Greek city-state, or to a modern nation-state. It encompassed both political and nonpolitical variables and recognized that each could play both dependent and independent roles. Perhaps most significantly, it effectively incorporated leadership and choice into a model of political change. All in all, it neatly synthesized several conflicting approaches to development and change in such a way as to capitalize on the particular strengths of each. The model was especially relevant to the analysis of intense changes of limited duration. Hence, it is not surprising that Almond and his associates applied it to the study of clearly delimitable historical crises, such as the Reform Act of 1832, the creation of the Third Republic, the Meiji Restoration, the Bolshevik Revolution, and the Càrdenas reforms of the 1930s.[57]

In a parallel endeavor, Rustow came up with a somewhat similiar model.[58] Political change, he suggested, is the product of dissatisfaction with the existing situation. This dissatisfaction produces political action; political action, indeed, is *always* the result of dissatisfaction. This action either suc-

57. For an initial application of the Almond modes, see Wayne A. Cornelius, Jr., "Crisis, Coalition-Building, and Political Enterpreneurship in the Mexican Revolution: The Politics of Social Reform onder Làzaro Càrdenas" (Project on Historical Crises and Political Development, Department of Political Science, Stanford University, July 1969).

58. Dankwart A. Rustow, "Change as the Theme of Political Science," pp. 6–8. See also his "Communism and Change," in Chalmers Johnson, ed., *Change in Communist Systems* (Stanford, 1970), pp. 343–58, and "Transitions to Democracy: Toward a Dynamic Model," *Comparative Politics*, II (April 1970), 337–63.

ceeds or fails. If it succeeds, the organization, movement, or other group responsible for the success either develops new goals or it withers and dies. If its effort for change fails, either the group responsible for the effort dissolves or it continues to pursue its old objective with decreasing expectation of ever achieving it. In addition, Rustow argues, the forces involved in the creation of a government or the conquest of power by a group or individual are very different from those which sustain the government or keep the individual or group in power over the long haul. A theory of political change has to account for and to systematize these differences. Thus Rustow, like Almond, puts a primary emphasis on the choices which have to be made by political leadership.

A third approach to the analysis of political change was developed by Ronald D. Brunner and Garry D. Brewer.[59] In their study of the political aspects of modernization, they developed a model of a *complex change* involving twenty-two variables and twenty parameters. Ten of the variables and eight of the parameters were disaggregated in terms of rural and urban sectors; three variables and three parameters constituted the demographic subsystem, nine variables and six parameters the economic subsystem, and ten variables and eleven parameters the political subsystem. The relations among these variables and parameters were expressed in twelve equations derived from general theories of modernization and from analysis of the evolution of Turkey and the Philippines from the 1940s to the 1960s. Their model included variables which could be directly influenced by governmental action and others not subject to such influence. Using the model it is possible to calculate the probable effects on support for the governments (measured by the proportion of the population voting for the government party) and on the standard of living (measured by per capita consumption) of governmental policy changes—such as birth control programs producing a 5 percent decrease in the rate of natural increase of population, increases or decreases of 5 percent in urban tax rates, and changes in the relative preference accorded the urban and rural sectors in governmental expenditures. Alternatively, one policy parameter—such as governmental preference for urban and rural sectors—can be intensively analyzed to demonstrate how various degrees of change within it might affect dependent variables such as government support and standard of living.

The Brunner-Brewer approach opened up new horizons in political analysis. Theoretically, it provided a highly simplified but highly precise model of a political system encompassing a significant number of demographic, economic, and political variables, the relations among which could be expressed by equations. Practically, it pointed scientific inquiry in a direction which could ultimately provide policymakers with a means of

---

59. Ronald D. Brunner and Garry D. Brewer, *Organized Complexity: Empirical Theories of Political Development* (New York, 1971).

analyzing the probable consequences of policy choices for outcomes directly relevant to their purposes. In effect, this model building introduced into political science the type of complex analysis of relations among variables which has long prevailed in economics. On the other hand, the Brunner-Brewer approach was limited by its initial theoretical assumptions and the relevance of those assumptions to the actual political systems to which the model was oriented. The twelve-equation model furnished a reasonably good guide to the interaction of the variables and parameters in Turkey and the Philippines during the 1950s and 1960s. Its relevance to the future was based on the assumption that the structure of the model and the magnitude of the parameters did not vary over time. The model provided ways of test-ing the consequences of major changes in governmental policy or major changes in other variables brought about by other means. It did not provide means for predicting major changes of the system unless or until these changes were reflected in significant changes in some variables in the model. Thus, the model could not predict a military coup bringing to power a radical, nationalist junta of officers. Once such a junta came to power the model might be able to predict some of the consequences of new policies they introduced. Its ability to do this would depend upon the continued existence of the relationships among variables which had existed in the past. The first goals of the revolutionary junta might be to change those relation-ships. Thus, the usefulness of the Brunner-Brewer approach was limited by the degree of discontinuity in the political system.

These various theories of componential change, crisis change, and com-plex change all tended, in one way or another, to liberate political analysis from the static assumptions which had limited it in one earlier phase and from the teleological concerns with modernization and development which had preoccupied it in a later phase. They indicated increasing parallelism between the study of political change and the study of social change. Most important, they were the very modest and first steps toward the formulation of general theories of political dynamics, the initial response to Rustow's challenge: "Aside from the refinement of evolutionary models and the more sophisticated use of historical data, is it not time to introduce some notion of change into our very conception of politics itself?"[60]

60. Dankwart A. Rustow, "Modernization and Comparative Politics: Prospects in Research and Theory," *Comparative Politics,* I (October 1968), 51.

Further Suggested Readings

Ake, Claude. *A Theory of Political Integration.* Homewood, Ill.: Dorsey Press, 1967.

Apter, D.E. *The Politics of Modernization.* Chicago: University of Chicago Press, 1965.

————. *Some Conceptual Approaches to the Study of Modernization.* Englewood Cliffs, N.J.: Prentice-Hall, 1968.

Binder, Leonard, *et al. Crises in Political Development.* Princeton, N.J.: Princeton University Press, 1972.

Black, Cyril. *The Dynamics of Modernization: Essays in Comparative History.* New York: Harper, 1966.

Coleman, James S., ed. *Education and Political Development.* Princeton, N.J.: Princeton University Press, 1965. Bibliography.

Debray, Regis. *Revolution in the Revolution.* New York: Monthly Review Press, 1967.

Deutsch, Karl W. *Nationalism and Social Communication.* 2nd ed. Cambridge, Mass.: M.I.T. Press, 1966.

————. "Social Mobilization and Political Development." *American Political Science Review,* 55 (1961), 493–514.

Eckstein, Harry, ed. *Internal War.* New York: Free Press, 1964.

Eisenstadt, S.N. *Modernization: Protest and Change.* Englewood Cliffs, N.J.: Prentice-Hall, 1966.

Fanon, Frantz. *The Wretched of the Earth.* Trans. C. Farrington. Harmondsworth, U.K.: Penguin, 1967.

Finkle, J.L., and Gable, R.W., eds. *Political Development and Social Change.* New York: John Wiley & Sons, 1966.

Geertz, Clifford, ed. *Old Societies and New States: The Quest for Modernity in Asia and Africa.* New York: Free Press, 1963.

Huntington, S.P. *Political Order in Changing Societies.* New Haven: Yale University Press, 1968.

Kautsky, John. *The Political Consequences of Modernization.* New York: John Wiley, 1972.

Lerner, Daniel. *The Passing of Traditional Society.* New York: Free Press, 1958.

Lipset, S.M. "Some Social Requisites of Democracy: Economic Development and Political Legitimacy." *American Political Science Review,* 53 (March 1959), 69–105.

Nettl, J.P. *Political Mobilization. A Sociological Analysis of Methods and Concepts.* New York: Basic Books, 1967.

Organski, A.F.K. *The Stages of Political Development.* New York: Knopf, 1965.

Pye, Lucian W. *Aspects of Political Development.* Boston: Little, Brown, 1966.

Pye, Lucian W., ed. *Communications and Political Development.* Princeton, N.J.: Princeton University Press, 1963. Bibliography.

Rustow, Dankwart. *A World of Nations: Problems of Political Modernization.* Washington, D.C.: Brookings Institution, 1967.

Rustow, Dankwart, and Ward, Robert E., eds. *Political Modernization in Japan and Turkey.* Princeton, N.J.: Princeton University Press, 1964.

Shils, Edward. *Political Development in the New States.* New York: Humanities Press, 1962.

Weiner, Myron, ed. *Modernization: The Dynamics of Growth.* New York: Basic Books, 1966.

———. "Political Integration and Political Development." *Annals,* 358 (1965), 52–64.

General Works on Foreign Political Systems

Each of the preceding chapters has been followed by bibliographies which have been analytical and theoretical in character. In this section, a partial listing of empirically based studies is offered, organized by major world regions and including the most recent studies. A useful general bibliography is American University Field Staff, *A Selected Bibliography: Asia, Africa, Eastern Europe, Latin America*. New York, 1960–69. For additional and more recent writings on these areas see the *Public Affairs Information Service* which indexes books and articles. For articles only, see the *Social Sciences and Humanities Index*.

MAJOR EUROPEAN POLITICAL SYSTEMS

A. BRITAIN

Baker, Richard John Stenson. *Administrative Theory and Public Administration*. London: Hutchinson and Co., 1972.

Berry, David R. *The Sociology of Grass Roots Politics: A Study of Party Membership*. London: Macmillan, 1970.

Brown, R. *The Administrative Process in Britain*. London: Methuen, 1970.

Hindess, Harry. *The Decline of Working Class Politics*. London: Mac-Gibbon & Kee, 1971.

James, Robert Rhodes. *Ambitions and Realities: British Politics 1964–70*. London: Weidenfeld & Nicolson, 1972.

Lieber, Robert J. *British Politics and European Unity: Parties, Elites, and Pressure Groups*. Berkeley: University of California Press, 1970.

Mackintosh, John Pitcairn. *The Government and Politics of Britain*. London: Hutchinson, 1970.

Robertson, James Hugh. *Reform of British Central Government*. London: Chatto & Windus, 1971.

Walker, Patrick Gordon. *The Cabinet: Political Authority in Britain*. New York: Basic Books, 1970.

B. FRANCE

Campbell, Peter. *French Electoral Systems and Elections, 1789–1957*. New York: Praeger, 1958.

Chapman, Brian. *The Prefects and Provincial France*. London: Allen & Unwin, 1955.

Charlot, Jean. *The Gaullist Phenomenon: The Gaullist Movement in the Fifth Republic*. Translated from the French by Monica Charlot and Marianne Neighbour. London: Allen & Unwin, 1971.

Gregoire, Roger. *The French Civil Service*. Brussels: International Institute of Administrative Science, 1964.

Hartley, Anthony. *Gaullism: The Rise and Fall of a Political Movement*. New York: Outerbridge & Dienstfrey, 1971.

Noonan, Lowell G. *France: The Politics of Continuity in Change*. New York: Holt, Rinehart & Winston, 1970.

Pickles, Dorothy. *The Fifth French Republic*. New York: Praeger, 1962.

Ridley, F., and Blondel, J. *Public Administration in France*. New York: Barnes & Noble, 1965.

Touraine, Alain. *The May Movement: Revolt and Reform: May 1968— The Student Rebellion and Workers' Strikes—The Birth of a Social Movement*. Translated by Leonard F. X. Mayhew. New York: Random House, 1971.

Williams, Philip Maynard. *French Politicians and Elections, 1951–1969*. London: Cambridge University Press, 1970.

———. *Politics and Society in de Gaulle's Republic*. London: Longman, 1971.

Wilson, Frank Lee. *The French Democratic Left, 1963–1969: Toward a Modern Party System*. Stanford, Calif.: Stanford University Press, 1971.

C. GERMANY

Arndt, Hans-Joachim. *West Germany: The Politics of Non-Planning.* Syracuse, N.Y.: Syracuse University Press, 1966.

Chalmers, Douglas A. *The Social Democratic Party of Germany.* New Haven: Yale University Press, 1964.

Grosser, Alfred. *Germany in Our Time: A Political History of the Postwar Years.* Translated by Paul Stephenson. New York: Praeger, 1971.

Jacob, Herbert. *German Administration Since Bismarck: Central Authority versus Local Autonomy.* New Haven: Yale University Press, 1963.

Krieger, Leonard. *The German Idea of Freedom.* Boston: Beacon Press, 1957.

Loewenberg, Gerhard. *Parliament in the German Political System.* Ithaca, N.Y.: Cornell University Press, 1966.

Plischke, Elmer. *Contemporary Government of Germany.* Boston: Houghton Mifflin, 1961.

Rothfels, Hans. *The German Opposition to Hitler.* Chicago: Regnery, 1948.

Sontheimer, Kurt. *The Government and Politics of West Germany.* Translated from the German by Fleur Donecker. London: Hutchinson, 1972.

Verba, Sidney. "Germany: The Remaking of Political Culture." In *Political Culture and Political Development,* edited by Lucian W. Pye and Sidney Verba. Princeton, N.J.: Princeton University Press, 1965.

D. SOVIET UNION AND EASTERN EUROPE

Arendt, H. *The Origins of Totalitarianism.* New York: Harcourt, Brace, 1951.

Armstrong, John A. *The Soviet Bureaucratic Elite.* New York: Praeger, 1959.

Barghoorn, Frederick Charles. *Politics in the U.S.S.R., A Country Study.* 2nd edition. Boston: Little, Brown, 1972.

Black, C.E., ed. *The Transformation of Russian Society: Aspects of Social Change Since 1861.* Cambridge: Harvard University Press, 1960.

Brzezinski, Zbigniew, and Huntington, Samuel. *Political Power: U.S.A./ U.S.S.R.* New York: Viking Press, 1964.

Cornell, Richard, ed. *The Soviet Political System: A Book of Readings.* Englewood Cliffs, N.J.: Prentice-Hall, 1970.

Dornberg, John. *The New Tsars; Russia Under Stalin's Heirs.* Garden City, N.Y.: Doubleday, 1972.

Fainsod, M. *How Russia Is Ruled.* 2nd ed., Cambridge: Harvard University Press, 1963.

Laird, Roy D. *The Soviet Paradigm: An Experiment in Creating a Mono-hierarchical Polity.* New York: Free Press, 1970.

Leites, N. *A Study of Bolshevism.* Glencoe, Ill.: Free Press, 1953.

————, and Bernaut, E. *The Ritual of Liquidation.* Glencoe, Ill.: Free Press, 1954.

Marcuse, H. *Soviet Marxism.* New York: Columbia University Press, 1958.

Moore, Barrington. *Terror and Progress: U.S.S.R.* Cambridge: Harvard University Press, 1954.

————. *Soviet Politics—The Dilemma of Power.* Cambridge: Harvard University Press, 1948.

Rothberg, Abraham. *The Heirs of Stalin Dissidence and the Soviet Regime, 1953–1970.* Ithaca, N.Y.: Cornell University Press, 1972.

Swearer, Howard. *The Politics of Succession in the U.S.S.R.* Boston: Little, Brown, 1964.

E. OTHER EUROPEAN STATES

Board, Joseph B. *The Government and Politics of Sweden.* Boston: Houghton Mifflin, 1970.

Legg, Keith R. *Politics in Modern Greece.* Stanford, Calif.: Stanford University Press, 1969.

Papandreou, Andreas George. *Democracy at Gunpoint: The Greek Front.* Garden City, N.Y.: Doubleday, 1970.

Rustow, Dankwart A. *The Politics of Compromise: A Study of Parties and Cabinet Government in Sweden.* New York: Greenwood Press, 1969.

Willis, Frank Roy. *Italy Chooses Europe.* New York: Oxford University Press, 1971.

F. LATIN AMERICA

Fitzgibbon, Russell Humke. *Latin America: A Panorama of Contemporary Politics.* New York: Appleton-Century-Crofts, 1971.

Johnson, Kenneth. *Mexican Democracy: A Critical View.* Boston: Allyn and Bacon, 1971.

Moreno, Francisco José. *Legitimacy and Stability in Latin America: A Study of Chilean Political Culture.* New York: New York University Press, 1969.

Ranis, Peter. *Five Latin American Nations: A Comparative Political Study.* New York: Macmillan, 1971.

Snow, Peter G. *Political Forces in Argentina.* Boston: Allyn and Bacon, 1971.

Tomasek, Robert Dennis, ed. *Latin American Politics: Studies of the Contemporary Scene.* 2nd ed., rev. and updated. Garden City, N.Y.: Anchor Books, 1970.

Von Lazar, Arpad J. *Latin American Politics: A Primer.* Boston: Allyn and Bacon, 1971.

G. MIDDLE EAST AND NORTH AFRICA

Antoun, Richard, and Iliya, Harik, eds. *Rural Politics and Social Change in the Middle East.* Bloomington, Ind.: Indiana University Press, 1972.

Binder, Leonard. *The Ideological Revolution in the Middle East.* New York: John Wiley, 1964.

Fein, Leonard. *Politics in Israel.* Boston: Little, Brown, 1967.

Hudson, Michael. *The Precarious Republic: Political Modernization in Lebanon.* New York: Random House, 1968.

Ismael, Tareq. *Governments and politics of the Middle East.* Homewood, Ill.: Dorsey, 1970.

Khadduri, Majid. *Republican Iraq*. London: Oxford University Press, 1969.

Mayfield, Paul. *Rural Politics in Nasser's Egypt*. Austin: University of Texas Press, 1971.

Moore, Clement H. *Politics in North Africa*. Boston: Little, Brown, 1970.

Quandt, William. *Palestinian Nationalism: Its Political and Military Dimensions*. Santa Monica, Calif.: Rand Corporation, 1971.

————. *Revolution and Political Leadership: Algeria, 1954–68*. Cambridge, Mass.: M.I.T. Press, 1969.

Rudebeck, Lars. *Party and People: A Study of Political Change in Tunisia*. New York: Praeger, 1970.

Rustow, Dankwart. *Middle Eastern Political Systems*. Englewood Cliffs, N.J.: Prentice-Hall, 1971.

Seale, Patrick. *The Struggle for Syria*. London: Oxford University Press, 1965.

Vatikiotis, P.J., ed. *Revolution in the Middle East*. London: Allen and Unwin, 1972.

Waterbury, John. *The Commander of the Faithful: The Moroccan Political Elite*. New York: Columbia University Press, 1970.

Zonis, Marvin. *The Political Elite of Iran*. Cambridge, Mass.: M.I.T. Press, 1971.

H. SOUTH ASIA

Ali, Tariq. *Pakistan: Military Rule or People's Power*. New York: W. Morrow, 1970.

Chopra, Pran. *Uncertain India: A Political Profile of Two Decades of Freedom*. Cambridge, Mass.: M.I.T. Press, 1969.

Das, Durga. *India from Curzon to Nehru & After*. London: Collins, 1969.

Fox, Richard Gabriel. *Kin, Clan, Raja, and Rule; State-Hinterland Relations in Preindustrial India*. Berkeley: University of California Press, 1971.

Hanson, Albert Henry. *India's Democracy*. New York: W.W. Norton, 1972.

Hardgrave, Robert L. *India: Government and Politics in a Developing Nation*. New York: Harcourt, Brace & World, 1970.

Kothari, Rajni. *Politics in India*. Boston: Little, Brown, 1970.

Loshak, David. *Pakistan Crisis*. New York: McGraw-Hill, 1971.

Morris-Jones, Wyndraeth H. *The Government and Politics of India*. 3rd rev. ed. London: Hutchinson, 1971.

I. SOUTHEAST ASIA

Allen, Sir Richard Hugh Sedley. *A Short Introduction to the History and Politics of Southeast Asia*. New York: Oxford University Press, 1970.

Butwell, Richard A. *Southeast Asia Today—and Tomorrow; Problems of Political Development*. 2nd rev. ed. New York: Praeger, 1969.

Pye, Lucien W. *Southeast Asia's Political Systems*. Englewood Cliffs, N.J.: Prentice-Hall, 1967.

Tilman, Robert O., ed. *Man, State, and Society in Contemporary Southeast Asia*. New York: Praeger, 1969.

J. FAR EAST

Barnett, A. Doak. *Cadres, Bureaucracy, and Political Power in Communist China*. New York: Columbia University Press, 1967.

————, ed. *Chinese Communist Politics in Action*. Seattle: University of Washington Press, 1969.

Chung, Kyung Cho. *Korea: The Third Republic*. New York: Macmillan, 1971.

Cole, David Chamberlin. *Korean Development: The Interplay of Politics and Economics*. Cambridge: Harvard University Press, 1971.

Han, Sujin. *Asia Today: Two Outlooks*. Montreal: McGill-Queen's University Press, 1969.

Ike, Nobutaku. *Japanese Politics: Patron-Client Democracy.* 2nd ed. New York: Knopf, 1972.

Kim, Se-Jin. *The Politics of Military Revolution in Korea.* Chapel Hill: University of North Carolina Press, 1971.

Langdon, Frank. *Politics in Japan.* Boston: Little, Brown, 1967.

Lindbeck, John M.H., ed. *China: Management of a Revolutionary Society.* Seattle: University of Washington Press, 1971.

Thayer, Nathaniel Brown. *How the Conservatives Rule Japan.* Princeton, N.J.: Princeton University Press, 1969.

Waller, D.J. *The Government and Politics of Communist China.* London: Hutchinson, 1970.

Ward, Robert Edward. *Japan's Political System.* Englewood Cliffs, N.J.: Prentice-Hall, 1967.

K. SUB-SAHARAN AFRICA

Arkhurst, Frederick S., ed. *Africa in the Seventies and Eighties.* New York: Praeger, 1970.

Carter, Gwendolen, ed. *National Unity and Regionalism in Eight African States.* Ithaca, N.Y.: Cornell University Press, 1966.

First, Ruth. *The Barrel of a Gun: Political Power in Africa and the Coup d'Etat.* London: Allen Lane, 1970.

Hatch, John Charles. *A History of Post-War Africa.* New York: Praeger, 1968.

Jordan, Robert. *Government and Power in West Africa.* New York: Africana Publishing Corp., 1969.

Keesing's Research Report. *Africa Independent.* New York: Scribner, 1972.

Lloyd, Peter. *Africa in Social Change.* Baltimore: Penguin, 1967.

Lofchie, Michael, ed. *The State of the Nations: Constraints on Development in Independent Africa.* Berkeley: University of California Press, 1971.

Mazrui, Ali. *Cultural Engineering and Nation Building in East Africa.* Evanston, Ill.: Northwestern University Press, 1972.

McGowan, Patrick J. *African Politics: A Guide to Research Resources, Methods and Literature.* Syracuse, N.Y.: Syracuse University Press, 1970.

Richards, Audrey. *The Multicultural States of East Africa.* Montreal: McGill University Press, 1969.

Spiro, Herbert, ed. *Patterns of African Development; Five Comparisons.* Englewood Cliffs, N.J.: Prentice-Hall, 1967.